U.S. NOMINAL GDP AND ITS COMPONENTS

Year	GDP	Personal Consumption Expenditures	Gross Private Domestic Investment	Government Purchases	Net Exports
	(billions of dollars)				
1959	494.2	318.1	78.8	99.0	-1.7
1960	513.3	332.4	78.7	99.8	2.4
1961	531.8	343.5	77.9	107.0	3.4
1962	571.6	364.4	87.9	116.8	2.4
1963	603.1	384.2	93.4	122.3	3.3
1964	648.0	412.5	101.7	128.3	5.5
1965	702.7	444.6	118.0	136.3	3.9
1966	769.8	481.6	130.4	155.9	1.9
1967	814.3	509.3	128.0	175.6	1.4
1968	889.3	559.1	139.9	191.5	-1.3
1969	959.5	603.7	155.2	201.8	-1.2
1970	1010.7	646.5	150.3	212.7	1.2
1971	1097.2	700.3	175.5	224.3	-3.0
1972	1207.0	767.8	205.6	241.5	-8.0
1973	1349.6	848.1	243.1	257.7	0.6
1974	1458.6	927.7	245.8	288.3	-3.1
1975	1585.9	1024.9	226.0	321.4	13.6
1976	1768.4	1143.1	286.4	341.3	-2.3
1977	1974.1	1271.5	358.3	368.0	-23.7
1978	2232.7	1421.2	434.0	403.6	-26.1
1979	2488.6	1583.7	480.2	448.5	-23.8
1980	2708.0	1748.1	467.6	507.1	-14.7
1981	3030.6	1926.2	558.0	561.1	-14.7
1982	3149.6	2059.2	503.4	607.6	-20.6
1983	3405.0	2257.5	546.7	652.3	-51.4
1984	3777.2	2460.3	718.9	700.8	-102.7
1985	4038.7	2667.4	714.5	772.3	-115.6
1986	4268.6	2850.6	717.6	833.0	-132.5
1987	4539.9	3052.2	749.3	881.5	-143.1
1988	4900.4	3296.1	793.6	918.7	-108.0
1989	5250.8	3523.1	832.2	975.2	-79.7
1990	5546.1	3761.2	808.9	1047.4	-71.4
1991	5722.9	3906.4	736.9	1099.3	-19.6
1992	6038.5	4139.9	796.5	1131.8	-29.6
1993	6374.0	4390.6	892.0	1157.1	-65.7

MACROECONOMICS

An Integrated Approach

Alan J. Auerbach
University of Pennsylvania

Laurence J. Kotlikoff
Boston University

SOUTH-WESTERN College Publishing

An International Thomson Publishing Company

Acquisitions Editor: Jack C. Calhoun
Developmental Editor: Dennis Hanseman
Production Editors: Sharon Smith, Rebecca Roby
Production House: Lifland et al., Bookmakers
Cover and Internal Design: Craig LaGesse Ramsdell
Cover and Part Opener Illustration: © 1994 Alan Brown, Photonics Graphics
Cartoons: Naples Cartoon Research
Marketing Manager: Denise Carlson

HD62AA

FOR ALEX, ANDY, AND ETHAN

Library of Congress Cataloging-in-Publication Data

Auerbach, Alan J.
Macroeconomics: an integrated approach / Alan J. Auerbach, Laurence J. Kotlikoff.
p. cm.
Includes bibliographical references and index.
ISBN 0-538-82474-3 (alk. paper)
1. Macroeconomics. I. Kotlikoff, Laurence J. II. Title.
HB172.5.A85 1995
339—dc20 94-27136
CIP

ISBN: 0-538-82474-3
1 2 3 4 5 6 7 8 9 0 Ki 3 2 1 0 9 8 7 6 5 4
Printed in the United States of America

This book is printed on acid-free paper that meets Environmental Protection Agency standards for recycled paper.

I(T)P
International Thomson Publishing

South-Western College Publishing is an ITP Company. The ITP trademark is used under license.

Alan Auerbach

Alan J. Auerbach is Professor of Economics at the University of Pennsylvania and a Research Associate of the National Bureau of Economic Research. He received his B.A. *summa cum laude* from Yale University and his Ph.D. from Harvard University, where his dissertation won the Wells Prize. His teaching career includes stints at Harvard University and the University of California, Berkeley.

Auerbach has served as Deputy Chief of Staff (Chief Economist) for the Joint Committee on Taxation of the U.S. Congress. He has testified frequently before Congressional committees on a variety of topics, including tax reform, national saving and investment, international competitiveness, and mergers and acquisitions. He is a Fellow of the Econometric Society and a member of the American Economic Association's Executive Committee.

Professor Auerbach's numerous papers on investment, taxation, finance, social security, savings, and fiscal policy have appeared in a wide variety of top journals. He is author, coauthor, or editor of six books including *The Taxation of Capital Income, Handbook of Public Economics,* and *Dynamic Fiscal Policy.* He also finds time to serve on the editorial boards of the *American Economic Review*, the *Journal of Economic Literature,* and several other journals.

Laurence Kotlikoff

Laurence J. Kotlikoff is Professor of Economics at Boston University and a Research Associate of the National Bureau of Economic Research. He received his undergraduate degree *summa cum laude* from the University of Pennsylvania and his Ph.D. from Harvard University. Besides his current position, he has also taught at UCLA and Yale.

Kotlikoff has served as Senior Economist with the President's Council of Economic Advisers, as Associate Editor of the *American Economic Review,* and as consultant to the IMF, the World Bank, the OECD, and several U.S. government agencies. He has testified on numerous occasions before Congressional committees. He is a Fellow of the Econometric Society.

Professor Kotlikoff has published extensively in professional journals, newspapers, and magazines on such issues as deficits, generational accounting, the tax structure, social security, pensions, saving, and insurance. He is author or coauthor of six books, including *Generational Accounting, Dynamic Fiscal Policy,* and *What Determines Savings?*

PREFACE

Toward an Integrated Approach

This text was great fun to write. How could it be otherwise? Macroeconomics is a fascinating subject that few economists can resist. But part of the fun was meeting a challenge—the challenge of providing an integrated analysis of macroeconomics. Like many other instructors of undergraduate macro, we've been frustrated by texts that treat macroeconomics as a set of distinct topics, rather than as a connected body of theory and empirical findings. These texts typically confront students with a plethora of quite different and very partial models: one for the long run and one for the short, one with flexible prices and one with sticky prices, one for the closed economy and one for the open, and so forth. The books spend so much space developing their different models that they have little space left over either to link the models to one another or to confront them with the macroeconomic facts.

Our text has the same breadth as existing texts and requires no more mathematical sophistication. But it uses a single analytical framework—the simple two-period life-cycle model—to examine each of the major issues in contemporary macroeconomics. Our use of the life-cycle model does not restrict our ability to convey fairly and fully all schools of macroeconomic thought. Quite the contrary. The life-cycle framework is so versatile that it can encompass the whole range of macroeconomic views simply by altering key assumptions. Assume price and wage flexibility, and the life-cycle model is neoclassical with real business cycles. Assume price or wage rigidity, and the model is Keynesian, of the traditional IS-LM form. Assume an extra country, and the model is open. Assume that parents care about their children's welfare, and the model is Ricardian. And so on.

Besides being versatile, the life-cycle model has two other important advantages. First, it links macro outcomes to micro foundations, showing students how the collective economic decisions of individual households and firms influence aggregate economic activity. Second, the model is dynamic. It teaches students that the long and short runs are inextricably connected—that current economic decisions, both public and private, have longer-term consequences.

Because students need to learn only one basic model, we have space to explore important topics that other texts either skim or ignore completely. These include credit constraints, real business cycles, coordination failures, monetary history, precautionary saving, bequests, generational accounting, monetary control, and financial markets.

In discussing these and the traditional topics of saving, investment, growth, recessions, unemployment, and fiscal and monetary policy, we continually compare theory with fact. We use over 70 case studies and a much larger number of graphs, charts, and tables to assess the strengths and weaknesses of alternative macroeconomic points of view. Many of the case studies deal with foreign economies, giving the book a very special international dimension. The case studies are also meant to teach students how to apply the analytical tools they've learned. An example is the detailed case study of the Great Depression in Chapter 12, which challenges the student to explain this episode.

ORGANIZATION

Our text is divided into four sections. Part One, consisting of Chapters 1 through 6, develops the basic dynamic life-cycle model and uses it to study long-run growth, economic transitions, and international trade and investment. This section also provides an introduction to economic fluctuations and presents national income accounting. Part Two, containing Chapters 7 and 8, introduces and illustrates the practice of fiscal and monetary policy, the two main tools of government macroeconomic policy intervention. Part Three, comprising Chapters 9 through 12, considers alternative theories of economic fluctuations, unemployment, and stabilization policy. Finally, Part Four includes Chapters 13 through 16, which focus on specific institutions, markets, and behavior, with important macroeconomic implications. This section considers exchange rates and international finance, the banking system, precautionary saving, bequests, credit markets, and business investment and finance.

DESIGNING YOUR OWN COURSE

Our book is designed to permit considerable flexibility with respect to course length and choice of topics. The first half of the book, Chapters 1 through 8, provides an introduction to most of the key issues of macroeconomics: saving, investment, growth, economic fluctuations, unemployment, national income accounting, inflation, international trade and investment, and monetary and fiscal policy. After covering this material, the instructor of a course emphasizing economic fluctuations and government policy would go directly to Part Three. Instructors of courses with a primary emphasis on financial markets might skip Part Three and focus more on the enrichments to the basic analysis provided by Chapters 13 through 16. Instructors seeking to limit the discussion of international issues might omit Chapters 6 and 13. Each of these sample courses provides an organized and complete presentation of the chosen topics.

Whichever chapters a course omits, the book's integrated nature will make it possible for the interested student to read such chapters on his or her own at a later time. Because we do not have to develop a new model for each situation, we have space to cover more of what students really want to learn: macroeconomics.

LEARNING TOOLS

CHAPTER ORGANIZATION. Each chapter begins with a short overview and a list of questions to be addressed. In the body of the chapter we present the key analytical ideas. To connect these ideas to real-world economies, we provide a wide range of data graphs, tables, and case studies. Each chapter ends with a summary of main results.

KEY TERMS. Important terms are boldfaced in the text and defined in the margins.

QUESTIONS FOR REVIEW. A variety of questions and exercises appear at the end of each chapter. Review Questions focus on key concepts. Numerical Questions and Analytical Questions provide opportunities to work with the theoretical machinery developed in the chapter.

APPENDICES. We have employed appendices to indicate how the model may be extended to study variable labor supply, population growth, and technological progress. Other appendices cover the transition path of the world economy, the effects of distortionary taxation, and the liquidity trap.

SUPPLEMENTS

Student Study Guide

Professor Charlie Turner of Old Dominion University has developed a Study Guide for our text. Each chapter in the Study Guide contains a variety of problems and exercises that enable the student to check his or her progress. Full answers to all questions are provided.

Student Software

Professor Eugene Kroch of Villanova University has designed some exciting computer software to accompany the text. This software enables users to employ the two-period life-cycle model to study a variety of economic situations. It also contains a data analysis module that may be used to study actual economic data.

Instructor's Manual

Professors Martin Asher and Robert DeFina of Villanova University have written an excellent manual for instructors. Each chapter in the Manual includes an overview of the corresponding chapter in the text as well as a chapter outline. Also included are a variety of pedagogical tips as well as answers to all the end-of-chapter questions in the text. The Manual also features a Test Bank with 800 multiple-choice and true/false questions.

Computerized Test Bank

The Test Bank is also available in computerized form in South-Western's easy-to-use MicroExam 4.0 format. It allows the instructor to create new questions as well as edit or delete existing questions. MicroExam 4.0 runs on all MS-DOS personal computers.

Transparencies

A complete set of transparency masters of all the figures and tables in the text is available from the publisher.

ACKNOWLEDGMENTS

This book was truly a collective enterprise involving an outstanding team at South-Western College Publishing and a terrific group of reviewers. Dennis Hanseman served as our developmental editor and was extraordinarily helpful in all stages of the writing of the book. Craig Ramsdell is South-Western's gifted artist responsible for the book's unique cover and pleasing interior design. Rebecca Roby and Quica Ostrander shepherded the manuscript through production with efficiency and grace. Finally, Scott Person and Denise Carlson have proven to be an excellent marketing team.

Thanks also go to Denis Lamb of the Organization for Economic Cooperation and Development for making available the cross-national data set we have employed throughout the book.

As with any text that breaks new ground, external reviewers are extremely important. We are very grateful to the following economists for their invaluable comments and suggestions:

Sumru Altug
University of Minnesota

David Aschauer
Bates College

Richard Baillie
Michigan State University

James Barth
Auburn University

Mark Bils
University of Rochester

John Boschen
College of William & Mary

John Bryant
Rice University

Betty Daniel
SUNY/Albany

Allen Drazen
University of Maryland

Timothy Fuerst
Bowling Green State University

James Gapinski
Florida State University

Jagadeesh Gokhale
Federal Reserve Bank of Cleveland

David Hakes
University of Northern Iowa

Gary Hansen
University of California, Los Angeles

Beth Ingram
University of Iowa

Yannis Ioannides
Virginia Polytechnic Institute

Nancy Jianakoplos
Colorado State University

Frederick Joutz
George Washington University

Kent Kimbrough
Duke University

Finn Kydland
University of Texas, Austin

S. Paul Lau
Australian National University

Stephen Miller
University of Connecticut

Carol Rogers
Georgetown University

David Romer
University of California, Berkeley

Benjamin Russo
University of North Carolina, Charlotte

Robert Rossana
Wayne State University

Julio Rotemberg
Massachusetts Institute of Technology

Don Schlagenhauf
Arizona State University

Laurence Seidman
University of Delaware

Harinder Singh
San Diego State University

Bruce Smith
Cornell University

Charles Swanson
Temple University

Bart Taub
University of Illinois

Anne Villamil
University of Illinois

Douglas Waldo
University of Florida

Ping Wang
Pennsylvania State University

We are particularly grateful for the extensive suggestions we received from Ben Russo and Bruce Smith.

Our research assistant, Bhashkernand Hardeo, was extremely helpful in constructing charts and checking calculations. We also wish to thank our secretaries, Debbi Trejos and Norma Hardeo, for helping us with all the details, large and small, arising in the production of this book. Finally, we wish to thank our wives, Gay and Dayle, for putting up with our many late-night conversations and for their constant encouragement.

Alan Auerbach
Laurence Kotlikoff

Brief Contents

Contents

Chapter 1
Output, Inputs, and Growth 10

Chapter 2
The Dynamic Supply of Inputs 42

Chapter 4
Economic Fluctuations 120

Chapter 5
The Measurement of Output 154

Chapter 8
Money and Prices in the Closed Economy 266

Chapter 10
Understanding Recessions 347

Chapter 11
The Nature and Costs of Unemployment 391

Chapter 12
Countercyclical Policy 431

Chapter 15
Saving Behavior and Credit Markets 538

Chapter 16
Financial Markets and the Investment Decision 576

P R O L O G U E

The Questions of Macroeconomics

Macroeconomics is the study of the economy's overall performance—why and how the economy grows, why it fluctuates, what causes inflation and unemployment. Macroeconomics is also the study of how government policy influences the economy's performance. It departs from microeconomics in focusing on the whole economy rather than its constituent parts. In looking at the big picture, macroeconomics asks the following kinds of questions.

Macroeconomics *The study of the economy's overall performance*

Why do economies grow at different rates? The answer is important. During past decades some developing countries have grown rapidly enough to join the developed world. Other developing countries have stagnated, and their populations have languished in extreme poverty. Certain developed countries, such as Japan, have been growing so fast that their living standards may eventually eclipse that of the United States.

Why do certain economies save and invest more than others? Knowing why matters. People who don't save end up poor. The same is true for countries. In recent years, the U.S. has saved very little of its national income, whereas other developed countries have saved at extraordinarily high rates.

How do foreign trade and investment affect the domestic economy? This question has never been more important. International economies have become increasingly linked through the expansion of foreign trade and investment. Take the U.S. in the second half of the 1980s. During these years foreigners were responsible for almost as much net investment in the United States as were U.S. citizens.

What causes recessions and their attendant high unemployment? This is the most intriguing and controversial issue in macroeconomics. It's also extremely important. Learning the cause of recessions could offer the key to their prevention and save jobs. During the Great Depression of the 1930s, one-quarter of all U.S. workers were unemployed. Although nothing quite as extreme has occurred since, the U.S. unemployment rate did exceed 10 percent as recently as the early 1980s.

What is money and its economic function? At one level, the answer to this question is trivial. Money is, simply, a means of payment—the cash or checks we use to make purchases. But money plays a special role in influencing the level and growth of prices and output, leading governments to try to control its supply.

How do monetary and fiscal policies affect the economy in the short and long run? Governments use their ability to control the money supply and to tax, borrow, and spend as a means of influencing economic growth and fluctuations. Understanding these policy tools and how well they operate is critical to reaching an informed judgment about macroeconomic policy.

What causes inflation? How does it relate to unemployment? Inflation—the rate at which prices change over time—varies tremendously across countries. Some countries have nearly stable prices. Others have inflation rates of several hundred percent per month. Even in the U.S., the inflation rate has varied over time, frequently rising at the same time unemployment is falling. Since macroeconomic policy is often targeted to achieve particular inflation and unemployment rates, it's important to know what causes inflation and unemployment and how they are related.

What role do banks play in the economy? Anyone wishing to understand monetary aspects of the macroeconomy must consider the role of the banking system. As one of many financial institutions that intermediate between suppliers and demanders of funds, banks take deposits and make loans. But banks also play a special role in determining the size of the money supply, which places them in a position to either facilitate or impede the conduct of monetary policy.

What is the exchange rate and how is it determined? An exchange rate determines the amount of foreign money that can be acquired in exchange for one unit of domestic money. Exchange rates are generally set in foreign exchange markets. Governments often intervene in these markets, buying or selling money in order to change the exchange rate. Since this intervention changes the money supply, exchange rate and monetary policies are interdependent. Learning about one necessitates learning about the other.

How do credit and insurance markets operate and alter macroeconomic outcomes? The public's ability to borrow through credit markets and to hedge risks by buying insurance influences a range of microeconomic decisions with potentially major macroeconomic implications. Understanding these markets is essential to grasping fully the way economies grow and fluctuate.

AN INTEGRATED APPROACH TO MACROECONOMICS

The questions listed above may seem unrelated, but they are actually closely connected. For example, the ability to borrow through credit markets influences how much the entire society saves, how much it invests, and how fast it grows. Economic growth, in turn, influences the public's demand for money and the rate of price inflation. And the inflation rate influences the choice of monetary and fiscal policies, which have their own independent effects on the economy's saving, investment, and growth.

Because these questions *are* connected, studying them requires a theoretical framework, or model, capable of linking the answers to each question to those of the others. Such an integrative approach is the hallmark of this text. It uses a single model—the life-cycle model—to explore and connect all of the central issues of macroeconomics.

The life-cycle model provides a set of building blocks that can be used to form a great variety of structures. These building blocks are the microeconomic behavior of households and firms. In building its macroeconomic structures on microeconomic foundations, the life-cycle model recognizes a fundamental fact of macroeconomic life: the macroeconomy must reflect the sum of its parts—the collective microeconomic behavior of households and firms.

The life-cycle model's integration of macro- and microeconomics is one reason we say that this text adopts an integrated approach. But the text is integrated along other dimensions as well. As we proceed, we'll show how short-run decisions and policies affect the economy's long-run growth path. We'll see how that long-run growth path, in turn, constrains what short-run decisions are possible. We'll explore the links between foreign trade and domestic investment, between fiscal and monetary policies, and between goods and financial markets. We'll learn about the economy's potential to sustain full employment as well as experience unemployment. Finally, we'll constantly compare theoretical predictions with actual outcomes in order to test macroeconomic theory against macroeconomic fact.

Let's briefly consider what economists mean by an **economic model**, discuss the historical practice of modeling the macroeconomy, describe the life-cycle model in general terms, and indicate how economists test their theories.

THE ROLE OF ECONOMIC MODELS

Economists simplify reality in order to understand it. This simplification is particularly important in macroeconomics, a subject concerned with hundreds of national economies, thousands of markets, millions of firms, and hundreds of millions of workers. Anyone trying to understand all this complexity at once is likely to end up missing the forest for the trees. Accordingly, economists try to

Economic model
A simplified description that captures key aspects of a real economic issue

focus on the most important factors influencing economic outcomes while ignoring what they believe to be minor details. Economists' **models** are thus simplified descriptions of reality. Good models are those that capture the key relationships.

Consider, for example, how an economist would model the demand for ice cream. That demand undoubtedly depends on many factors, but an economist might focus on two: the price of ice cream and the level of household income. In ignoring other factors and specifying precisely how ice cream demand depends on price and income, the economist is constructing an economic model. If price and income turn out to be the major determinants of ice cream demand, then the economist has constructed a good model. But if she has ignored another important determinant of demand, say, the temperature outside, then her inferences may be invalid—she may attribute some changes in ice cream sales to changes in price when they are really due to changes in temperature. As a result, her forecasts of future ice cream sales may be quite inaccurate. Thus, an economic model can be a valuable tool as long as the economist knows how much simplification is appropriate.[1]

The life-cycle model adopted here has proven to be a very good economic model. Though simple, it still captures a great range of very important economic relationships in a clear-cut manner. Mastering the life-cycle model—its basic graphs and equations—is straightforward, requiring only a modicum of high school algebra. And once you learn this basic model you can apply it to a wide variety of macroeconomic issues.

MODELING MACROECONOMIC BEHAVIOR

The macroeconomy, with its many interacting markets, presents a much more formidable challenge for the economic modeler than the market for ice cream does. In the past, the complexity of the macroeconomy often led economists to simplify their analysis by using a variety of unrelated models to explain different macroeconomic phenomena. They would use one model to analyze economic growth, another to study international trade, and yet another to consider saving and investment. These disparate models often bore little relation to one another and were poorly connected to the underlying microeconomic behavior of households and businesses.

Recent economic events have made economists aware of the severe problems caused by this approach to macroeconomics. For example, they've learned that it's impossible to understand the large U.S. international trade deficit of the 1980s without looking at U.S. saving behavior during the same era. They've also learned that changes in U.S. saving behavior can be understood only by considering the determinants of household saving.

---

1. Economists' tendency to make overly simplifying assumptions is captured by a familiar fable. A physicist, an engineer, and an economist are stranded on a desert island with lots of canned food, but no can opener. First the physicist tries to open a can by heating it, but it explodes. Next the engineer climbs a tree and drops a rock on a can, but it splatters far and wide. Finally the economist offers the solution: "Assume we have a can opener."

Our simple life-cycle model provides a unified framework for studying all the key issues of macroeconomics. The framework is very flexible; it can be used to describe the controversies among different macroeconomic schools of thought. Indeed, most viewpoints can be illustrated in the life-cycle model simply by altering particular assumptions. For example, in studying what determines economic fluctuations, we can illustrate different explanations by assuming that some prices adjust slowly, as we do in Chapter 9, or that technology changes over time, as we do in Chapter 10. It's the same model, implemented with different assumptions.

THE LIFE-CYCLE MODEL

The life-cycle model is dynamic. It describes the evolution of the economy over time in terms of the behavior of overlapping generations of individuals, each of whom lives for two periods: youth and old age. Each individual's economic decisions, such as how much to save, affect his behavior both when young and when old. We analyze macroeconomic behavior by aggregating the behavior of all the young people into one group and the behavior of all the old into another and then considering the impact of the combined behaviors of the two groups.

This aggregation is one aspect of the model's simplification. As with any economic model, we shouldn't take the life-cycle model's simplifying assumptions too literally. Remember that we're trying to capture essential relationships without too much confusing detail. We don't really think there are only two types of individuals in society (the young and the old), or that individuals differ only with respect to their age. But studying these two types of individuals is the simplest way to recognize the important differences between those who work and those who are retired, and between those who save and those who don't. If it helps, you might think of our analysis as applying to a typical old or young person, not to every such person. And, as we will point out, some of our results involving the behavior of the young and the old may be reinterpreted in terms of other group distinctions (such as rich versus poor).

Another simplification is that we look at each individual only twice, once when young and once when old. As with any good modeling strategy, the point here is to eliminate unnecessary complexity in order to highlight what's important. We don't really think individuals make economic decisions only twice in their lifetimes, but the qualitative conclusions reached by assuming that they do carry over to more detailed, and much more complicated, models.

EVALUATING ECONOMIC THEORIES

Macroeconomics is a very controversial discipline. Partly, this is because the stakes are so high. The choice of a particular economic policy, or no policy at all, can influence the incomes, employment, and general well-being of millions of citizens. Partly, the controversy arises because economists, for lack of definitive empirical evidence, differ quite sharply about the causes, severity, and cure

"SURE, WE'RE DEALING WITH TINY PARTICLES, BUT YOUR FORMULA IS JUST A SYMBOLIC REPRESENTATION."
S. Harris

for economic downturns. In terms of economic models, these differences can be cast as conflicting hypotheses about which simplifying assumptions are appropriate. In this book, we will use our life-cycle model to explore many theories about macroeconomic behavior.

Which theory is right? The obvious way to answer this question involves seeing which theory best explains the facts. Unfortunately, the scientific method of testing hypotheses, which consists of comparing predictions with experimental outcomes, is complicated by the fact that economists usually can't conduct controlled experiments. Microeconomists can't vary the outside temperature to determine if it has any impact on ice cream demand, nor can macroeconomists construct experimental economies to evaluate different theories of the effectiveness of government policy. Instead, they must rely on **natural experiments**—variations in actual economic conditions or policies—that help them judge alternative macroeconomic points of view.

Natural experiment *A naturally occurring variation in actual economic conditions or policies*

Our text is full of U.S. and international case studies based on natural experiments. These case studies illustrate macroeconomic concepts and test alternative hypotheses. For example, Chapter 10 evaluates different theories about the macroeconomic importance of the price of oil by considering what happened to the U.S. economy in periods when oil prices rose or fell sharply. Chapter 12 evaluates the effectiveness of monetary and fiscal policy in reducing economic fluctuations by comparing the relative stability of the economy during periods when the degree of government activism differed. And Chapter 16 evaluates how the banking system influences investment by comparing investment in Japan and the United States, whose banking institutions are quite different.

SUMMARY

Macroeconomics is a fascinating but challenging subject. As you read this book, you will learn a systematic way to interpret macroeconomic outcomes, to understand various policy proposals, and to appreciate how individuals and firms fit into the big picture. The text is your guide. Although we have taken great pains to make the story as clear as possible, macroeconomics is not a subject that can be mastered by a cursory skimming of the assigned chapters. Your instructor's lectures, this textbook, and your own hard work will combine to make learning macroeconomics a satisfying and enjoyable experience.

Key Concepts

Macroeconomics
Economic model
Natural experiment

P A R T 1

From Micro to Macro: Modeling Income Determination and Growth

C H A P T E R 1

Output, Inputs, and Growth

INTRODUCTION

Advanced economies produce a multitude of goods and services ranging from pencils and haircuts to supercomputers and organ transplants. The means used to produce these commodities are as varied as the commodities themselves, but certain features are common to all production processes. All production involves the use of basic *inputs*, such as workers, managers, machines, and factories, to generate final products—the *outputs*. Each production process involves a method—a **technology**—for combining inputs to make outputs.

Technology *Methods of combining inputs to produce output*

Gross domestic product (GDP) *The total value of all final goods and services produced in an economy during a given year*

Macroeconomists are concerned with a country's total production of final goods and services—its **gross domestic product**, or **GDP**.[1] When a nation's output grows faster than its population, its standard of living rises. There is more output and, on average, more output per person. But why does output grow?

1. Another, closely related measure of a nation's output or income is its *gross national product* (GNP). GNP equals a country's domestic output—its GDP—plus its net foreign income—the income the country earns on its foreign investments less the income earned by foreigners on their investment in the country itself. For the U.S. the two measures are quite close in magnitude.

What determines how fast it grows? Answering these questions is a key goal of macroeconomics and one we'll begin to address in this chapter. The answers depend, in part, on the availability and quality of inputs, on how efficiently those inputs are combined to produce output, and on scientific and engineering advances that make it possible to produce more output from given amounts of inputs.

The answers also depend on the state of the economy. As the Great Depression of the 1930s made painfully clear, there is no guarantee that available inputs will be utilized, let alone utilized efficiently, or that very much production will actually take place. Between August 1929, the month the Great Depression began in the U.S., and March 1933, when it reached its depth, U.S. GDP declined in *real terms* (after adjusting for changes in the prices of the various commodities included in GDP) by 30 percent. Since there was very little change in available inputs and technology over this period, the decline in *real GDP* represented a failure of the economy to produce with the resources it had on hand. Understanding why slowdowns in production occur and how to prevent them is another important goal of macroeconomics. So too is understanding how real output evolves during more normal economic times.

Figure 1-1 graphs U.S. real GDP in the years since 1929. The values of real GDP are expressed in "1987 dollars." As we'll make precise in Chapter 5, this means the various goods and services entering the calculation of real GDP in particular years are valued using the prices for those commodities that prevailed in 1987.[2] Hence, a "1987 dollar" refers to the amount of goods and services a dollar could purchase at 1987 prices.

The figure shows that real GDP has risen steadily since the Great Depression, with the exception of a number of short-lived declines, the sharpest of which occurred in the aftermath of World War II. Periods of declining output, which are shaded in the figure, are called *recessions*. Notwithstanding the Great Depression and subsequent recessions, U.S. real GDP was six times larger in 1993 than in 1929. This remarkable increase in output was certainly not due to changes in the utilization of a fixed amount of inputs with a given technology, but rather to an increased availability of inputs and improvements in technology.

Economists refer to increases over time in real GDP as *economic growth*. Our principal task in this chapter is to describe how more inputs and improvements in their productivity produce economic growth. Although we'll discuss the determinants of productivity, we leave for future chapters a full explanation of how input availability changes through time and how recessions and *expansions*—periods of positive growth—affect the utilization of available inputs.

Spelling out how more inputs and better technology translate into more output requires describing the production process. After we do so, we'll explore the implications of economic growth for countries' living standards and ask whether economic growth is leading to more or less equality in living standards

2. As described in Chapter 5, real GDP may be contrasted with *nominal GDP*, which measures the value of output during a particular period of time at *current prices*—at the prices that actually prevailed during that period of time. Unlike real GDP, nominal GDP may increase over time simply because of increases in prices, or *inflation*. Such changes in nominal GDP do not represent any change in the quantity of goods and services produced in the economy.

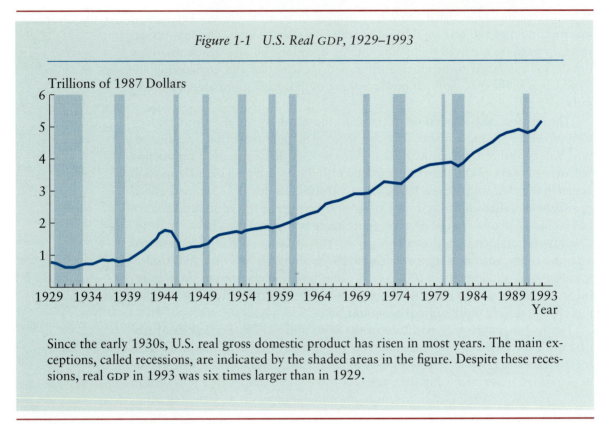

Figure 1-1 U.S. Real GDP, 1929–1993

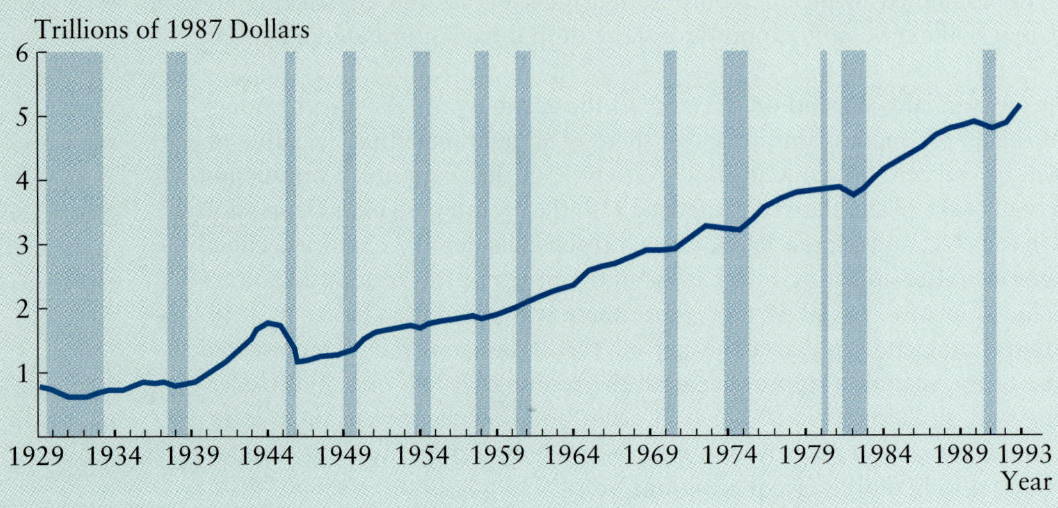

Since the early 1930s, U.S. real gross domestic product has risen in most years. The main exceptions, called recessions, are indicated by the shaded areas in the figure. Despite these recessions, real GDP in 1993 was six times larger than in 1929.

Source: *Economic Report of the President,* 1994

between developed and developing countries. We'll also present a case study on the sources of U.S. economic growth and consider why the productivity of U.S. workers has grown so slowly in recent years. Finally, we'll consider whether the U.S. standard of living is falling behind those of other industrialized countries.

The following are some specific questions we'll raise and try to answer in this chapter:

- How do economists conceptualize the production process?
- What are the key inputs in production?
- Why do small differences in growth rates make such a large difference over time in living standards?
- What is growth accounting, and what does it tell us about the sources of postwar U.S. economic growth?
- How do economists measure workers' productivity?
- What explains the recent slow growth in the productivity of U.S. workers?
- Is economic growth widening the gap between developed and developing nations?

Figure 1-2 U.S. Real GDP per Capita, 1929–1993

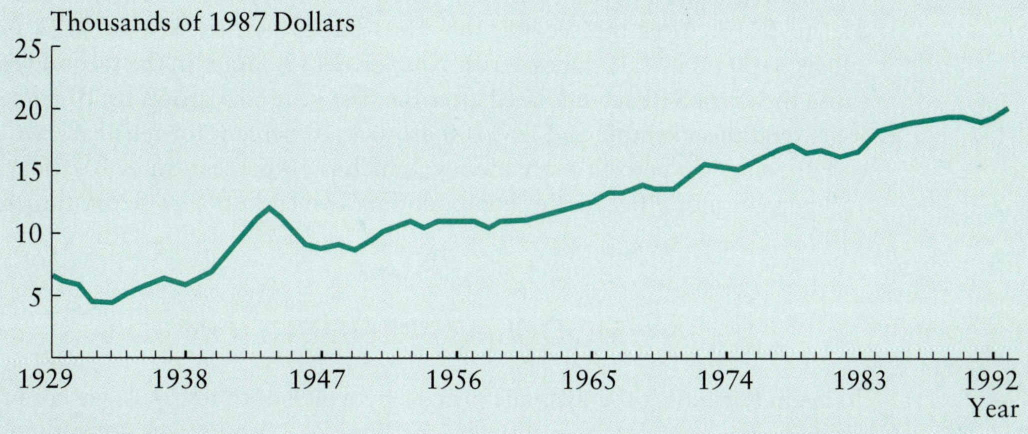

Measured on a per person basis, the U.S. standard of living has tripled since 1929.

Source: *Economic Report of the President*, various issues

THE IMPORTANCE OF ECONOMIC GROWTH TO A COUNTRY'S STANDARD OF LIVING

To set the stage, let's consider the importance of economic growth to a country's living standard as measured by *per capita GDP*—output per person. As shown in Figure 1-2, U.S. per capita GDP rose from $6,749 in 1929 to $19,874 in 1993. To adjust for inflation, each of these dollar amounts is expressed in terms of the amount of real goods and services they could have purchased in 1987. Thus, on a per person basis, America's standard of living has almost tripled since 1929.

On the average, per capita GDP grew 1.70 percent per year between 1929 and 1993. Had this growth rate been twice as large, U.S. per capita output would have risen a whopping eight times over since 1929 and the typical citizen's standard of living would be almost triple what it is now![3] This example illustrates how small differences in growth rates, if they continue over long periods, can make very substantial differences in a country's living standard. The reason is that growth differences *compound*; an extra bit of output this period

3. A growth rate of 3.40 percent is well within the range of historical experience. In the years between 1950 and 1973, real per capita GDP grew at even faster rates in Austria, Belgium, Finland, France, Germany, Italy, Japan, and the Netherlands. The Japanese standard of living increased eightfold over just these 23 years. See Angus Maddison, *Phases of Capitalist Development* (New York: Oxford University Press, 1982), Table 3.1, A8.

means more than just this extra bit of output in future years because this extra bit will itself grow.

To better understand compounding, consider what happens if $100 grows for two years at 10 percent per year. After the first year, the $100 has grown by $10 to $110. After the second, the $110 has grown by $11 to $121 (which equals $100 times 1.10 times 1.10). Now growth is larger in the second year because the extra $10 accumulated after the first year also grows by 10 percent. If we extend this example and let $100 grow at 10 percent for ten years, we don't end up with 100 percent more money (which is 10 percent times 10), but rather 159 percent more. Because of compounding, we end up with $259, rather than $200.[4]

MODELING PRODUCTION

Cobb-Douglas production function
A mathematical relationship indicating how much output can be obtained from particular amounts of capital and labor, given a particular level of technology

Labor
The effort supplied by workers, managers, and owners of business enterprises

Capital
Buildings, equipment, inventories, residential structures, consumer durables, and other non-human inputs used to produce goods and services

To begin explaining the dynamic process by which output grows, we need to describe how economists conceptualize, or "model," production. Accordingly, we present a simple relationship known as the **Cobb-Douglas production function,** in which output depends on the amounts of two inputs employed, capital and labor, and on the efficiency with which they are used. **Labor** refers to the efforts supplied by workers, managers, and owners of business enterprises. Over time, population growth ensures that the amount of available labor will grow. At the same time, better training and education make the available labor more productive. **Capital** refers to the non-human inputs employed in production, and includes buildings, machinery, business *inventories* of raw materials, parts, and finished goods, residential structures such as houses and apartment buildings, and *consumer durables* such as refrigerators, televisions, and furniture. Another category of capital is land, which is an important input to agricultural production.

Our Cobb-Douglas function describes the production of *final* goods, those that will not undergo further processing. It doesn't describe the production of intermediate inputs (such as wing assemblies for jet aircraft or integrated circuits for computers). As their name suggests, such inputs represent an intermediate stage of production that can safely be skipped for purposes of understanding growth in GDP which, again, only measures the output of *final* goods and services.

The Cobb-Douglas Production Function

The Cobb-Douglas production function was named after Paul Douglas and Charles Cobb. Douglas was an economics professor who eventually gave up academics to become U.S. Senator from Illinois. In 1927, before running for office, he became intrigued by an empirical regularity he observed in U.S. macroeconomic data—namely, that the shares of output paid out as income to capital

4. To reach $259, multiply 1.10 by itself ten times and then multiply the resulting amount, 2.59, by $100.

and labor appeared to be stable through time. He realized that not all production functions, in the presence of competitive labor markets, would produce this result. So he asked his friend Charles Cobb, a mathematician, to help him derive a production function that did.

The result was a simple algebraic expression relating the amount of output produced during a particular time period to the contemporaneous inputs of capital and labor as well as the prevailing level of technology. The function can be used to explain production over any time period we wish to consider. For example, in the two-period life cycle model we will develop beginning in the next chapter, a period represents roughly 30 years, corresponding to the division of an adult's life into two 30-year periods of youth and old age.

What does the Cobb-Douglas function look like? Let Y_t stand for the amount of output produced at time t, and let K_t and L_t be the amounts of capital and labor used in production at time t. Finally, let A_t stand for the level of **multifactor productivity**, or simply productivity. As we will see, A_t measures how efficiently capital and labor are used together to produce output.

Multifactor productivity
A measure of the ability of capital and labor to produce output

With these definitions, we can write the Cobb-Douglas function as

$$Y_t = A_t K_t^{\beta} L_t^{1-\beta}$$

The exponent β (beta) is called a *parameter* of the production function. It is a fixed value that helps determine the function's characteristics. We'll show in Chapter 3 that in a competitive economy operating with a Cobb-Douglas production function, the share of output paid by firms to the suppliers of capital turns out to equal β. It follows that 1 – β is the share of output paid to suppliers of labor (workers and managers). If β remains constant through time, the output shares of capital and labor will also remain constant, which is exactly the situation Cobb and Douglas were trying to explain.

Figure 1-3 graphs, for each year from 1960 through 1993, capital's share of U.S. GDP. Note that capital's share has been remarkably close to 30 percent throughout the entire period. Consequently, in using the Cobb-Douglas function throughout this book we'll assume that β equals .30.

Getting Acquainted with the Cobb-Douglas Production Function

To get a feeling for the Cobb-Douglas function, let's try a few values for A_t, K_t, and L_t. First, set A_t equal to 10, K_t equal to 300, and L_t equal to 100.[5] Then

$$Y_t = 10 \times 300^{.30} \times 100^{.70} = 1390$$

5. We can measure inputs and outputs in whatever units we'd like. For example, we can measure labor in terms of the number of workers or in terms of the number of hours worked by the workers or in terms of the number of minutes worked by the workers, etc. Changing the units in which we measure either output, capital, or labor will change the units in which we measure the technology coefficient, A. The adjustment of the units of A explains why we can relate output measured in units of, say, 1987 dollars to the inputs of capital and labor, measured in units of, say, 1987 dollars and hours worked, respectively.

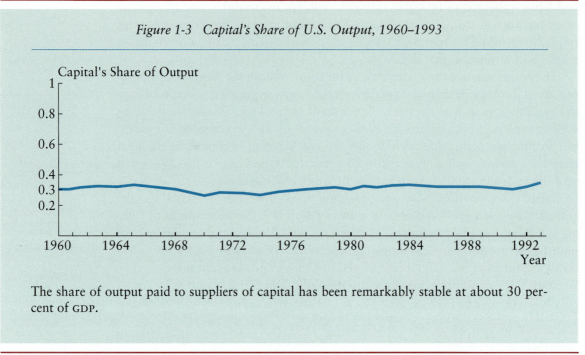

Figure 1-3 Capital's Share of U.S. Output, 1960–1993

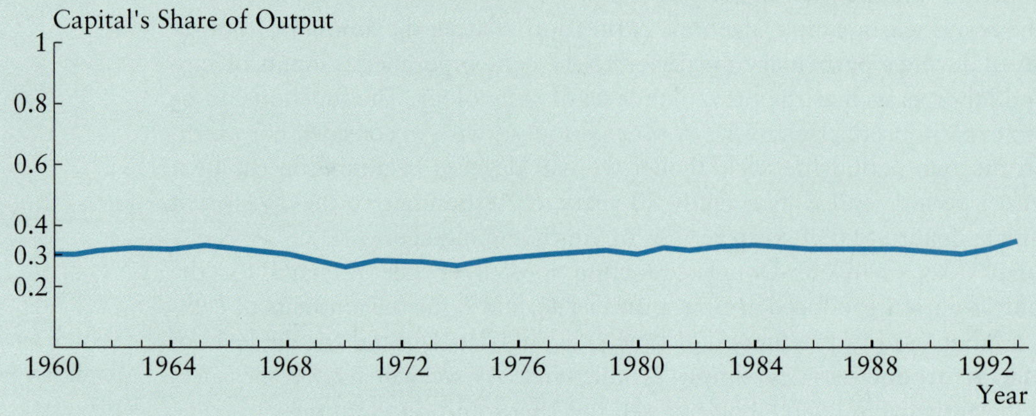

The share of output paid to suppliers of capital has been remarkably stable at about 30 percent of GDP.

Source: *Economic Report of the President*, 1994

Next, let's double the capital and labor inputs, leaving the level of productivity unchanged. We see that output doubles, since

$$Y_t = 10 \times (2 \times 300)^{.30} \times (2 \times 100)^{.70}$$
$$= 2 \times 10 \times 300^{.30} \times 100^{.70} = 2 \times 1390$$

This property of the Cobb-Douglas function—that a doubling of inputs leads to a doubling of outputs—is called *constant returns to scale*. In everyday language, constant returns means that increasing both inputs by a given percentage (we just considered an increase of 100 percent) leads to an equal percentage increase in output.

The Cobb-Douglas function also exhibits *diminishing returns* to each of the inputs, holding the other input fixed. For example, suppose we increase the capital input from 300 to 400, holding labor input constant at 100. Output will increase by 126 units, to a total of 1516. If we increase capital by another 100 units, output will increase again, but this time by only 105 units. Add yet another 100 units of capital and output will rise by 91 units. The fact that successive increments to output (126 followed by 105 followed by 91) diminish in size in response to equal 100-unit increments to capital is due to diminishing returns.

As we add more capital to a given amount of labor, output increases by smaller amounts. The same holds true for adding more labor to a fixed amount of capital. In either case, the input becomes less productive (produces smaller increases in output) the more of it we use. Note that we avoid diminishing returns and have constant returns if we increase both capital and labor by the same percentage.

Now that you've gained some familiarity with the Cobb-Douglas production function, let's take a closer look at the meaning and measurement of capital, labor, and productivity. Then we'll show how output growth can be traced to changes in these three elements.

MEASURING CAPITAL

In any modern economy, a wide variety of capital goods are used to help produce output. One category, called equipment, includes the metal-forming tools used in producing jet engines, the vans used to deliver pizza, and the printing presses that produced this text. Another category is business structures, which includes primarily office buildings, factories, and retail spaces. Land, inventories, and residential structures are also considered types of capital.[6]

How can such an assortment of goods be combined into a single measure of capital? The usual approach is to convert them to constant dollar terms. As with real GDP, we measure the real capital stock in 1987 dollars. Each different type of capital good in use in a particular year—each United Van Lines truck, each Chrysler Corporation paint sprayer, each Holiday Inn hotel—is valued using its price in 1987.[7] The idea is that changes in the constant dollar value of the capital stock fully reflect changes in the physical quantity of capital available.

Figure 1-4 shows how the U.S. business capital stock grew and changed in composition between 1950 and 1990. Measured in 1987 dollars, it almost tripled, rising from \$3.3 trillion to \$9.1 trillion. This growth in the overall capital stock was far from uniform across different types of capital. For example, equipment's share of capital grew significantly over the four decades.

The data presented in Figure 1-4 take account of the fact that capital depreciates (wears out) over time. Each year, business firms undertake **investment**, the acquisition of new capital goods. Some of this investment goes to replace older, worn-out capital; the rest represents net additions to the capital stock. The capital stock data we use are *net of accumulated depreciation*; they reflect the productive capital actually available to firms.

Investment
The acquisition of new capital goods

The formula relating the capital stock at time $t + 1$, K_{t+1}, to the capital stock at time t, K_t, is given by

$$K_{t+1} = K_t + I_t - D_t$$

In this formula I_t stands for new purchases of capital between time t and time $t + 1$, which we call *gross investment*. The term D_t stands for the depreciation of

6. The majority of residential structures are owned by households, not businesses, and are not included in the calculations that follow.

7. Hence, a "1987 dollar" of capital refers to the amount of capital goods a dollar could purchase based on 1987 prices of capital goods.

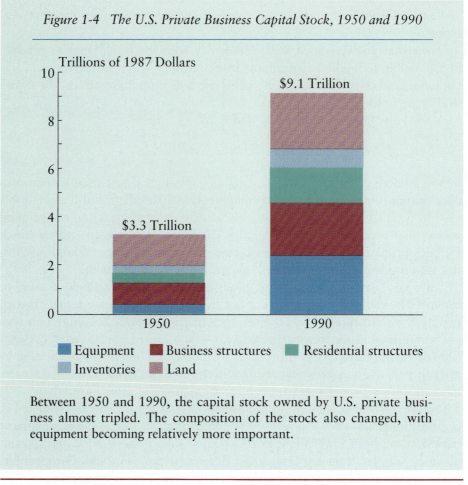

Figure 1-4 The U.S. Private Business Capital Stock, 1950 and 1990

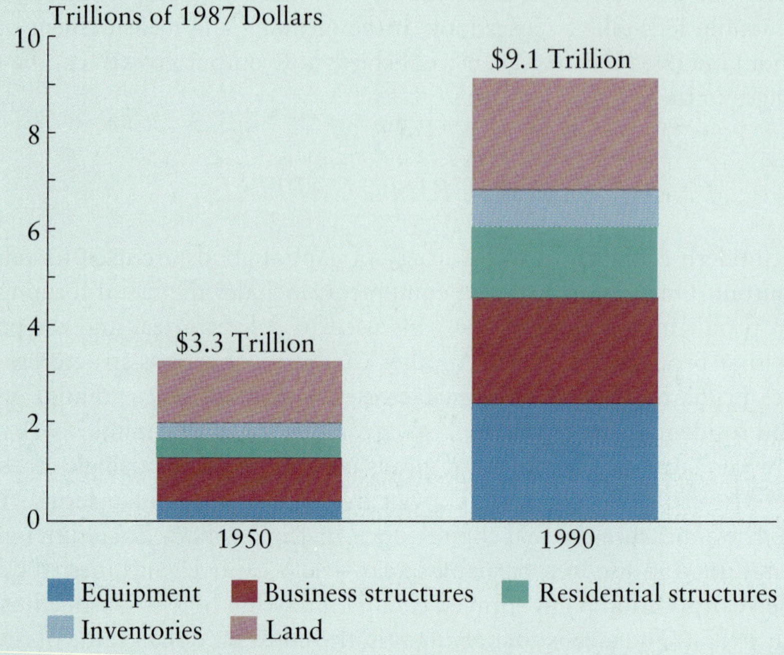

Between 1950 and 1990, the capital stock owned by U.S. private business almost tripled. The composition of the stock also changed, with equipment becoming relatively more important.

Source: Bureau of Labor Statistics

the capital stock that occurs between time t and time $t + 1$. The difference between I_t and D_t represents the increase in the economy's productive capital, which we call *net investment*. So, the capital stock next period will be this period's stock plus net investment.

The rate at which capital depreciates depends on the type of capital in question. Some equipment loses as much as one-third of its value each year, whereas business structures lose only 2–3 percent of their value annually. Given the current mix of U.S. capital, the depreciation rate of the entire capital stock is about 4 percent per year.

An Aside: The Relationship of Stocks to Flows

Our equation relating the capital stock to investment and depreciation highlights an important distinction among macroeconomic variables. Quantities, such as investment, depreciation, and GDP, that arise between two points in time are called **flow variables.** Flows are distinguished from **stock variables,** such as the stock of capital, whose values are defined at a single point in time. We talk of investment *during* 1994, but of the capital stock *on* December 31.

Flow variable
A variable defined over an interval of time

Stock variable
A variable defined at a particular point in time

Flow variables relate to *changes* in stock variables between periods. For example, the flows of gross investment and depreciation account for the change in the stock of capital between any two periods. Consider the analogy between the capital stock and a pot of water. Suppose that over a period of 10 minutes you add 5 quarts of water to a pot that initially holds 3 quarts. We can say the initial stock of water was 3 quarts, the flow of water over the 10 minutes was 5 quarts, and the final stock is 8 quarts.

MEASURING LABOR

Economists typically measure labor input by the number of hours worked. Hours worked is the product of three terms: the number of potential workers, given by the size of the adult population; the fraction of the adult population that is employed, known as the employment-population ratio; and the number of hours worked by those employed. In words,

$$\text{Hours Worked} = \text{Population} \times \text{Employment/Population} \times \text{Hours/Employment}$$

Each factor on the right side of this equation can have an important impact on total hours worked. To illustrate, let's examine changes in these factors in the U.S. since 1950. Figure 1-5 considers the first two factors: the size of the adult population and the fraction of the adult population that is employed. The numbers shown are, in many ways, quite remarkable. In just 43 years the U.S. adult population increased by 89 million individuals to the 1993 total of 194 million. To put this in perspective, the increase exceeds the current population of Germany. It also exceeds the combined populations of Austria, Belgium, the Netherlands, Sweden, Finland, Denmark, Norway, Ireland, Portugal, and Switzerland. Over the same period, the number of employed adults increased by 61 million.

Absorbing 61 million additional workers was no small feat, but the economy managed to do so without a long-term decline in the fraction of U.S. adults who were employed. In fact, because of changes in female employment, this fraction actually rose over the period from 56 percent to 62 percent. In 1950 only one in three adult women was employed, compared with one in every two in 1993. Consequently, women represented less than a third of total U.S. employment in 1950, whereas they represented almost half in 1993. Over the same interval, the employed fraction of adult males declined. In 1993, 70 percent of adult males were employed, compared with 82 percent in 1950.

Although total U.S. civilian employment doubled between 1950 and 1993 (reflecting both population growth and an increase in the employment-population ratio), total hours worked by all persons in the U.S. business sector rose by only 52 percent. Part of the reason was a decline in average hours

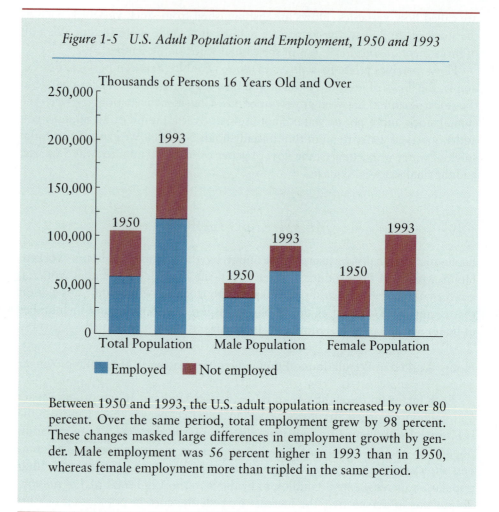

Figure 1-5 U.S. Adult Population and Employment, 1950 and 1993

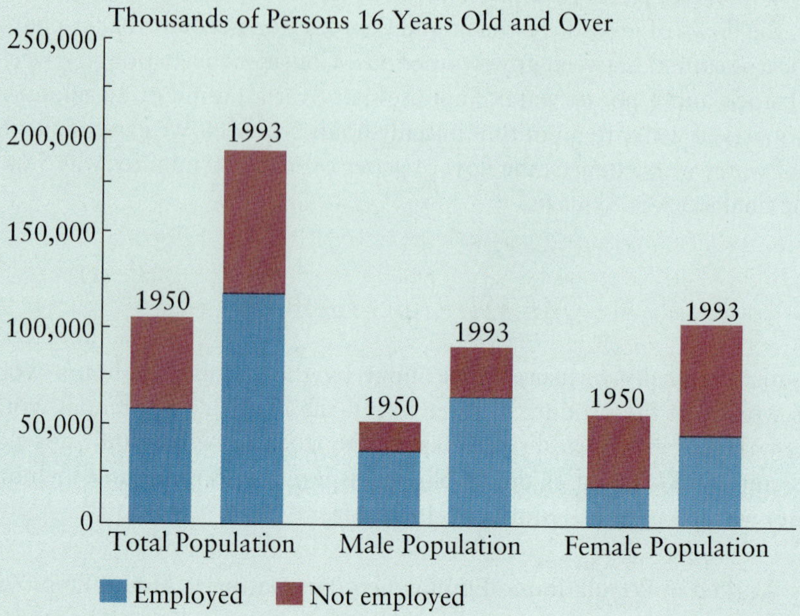

Between 1950 and 1993, the U.S. adult population increased by over 80 percent. Over the same period, total employment grew by 98 percent. These changes masked large differences in employment growth by gender. Male employment was 56 percent higher in 1993 than in 1950, whereas female employment more than tripled in the same period.

Source: *Economic Report of the President*, 1994

worked per week (from 40 hours in 1950 to 34 hours in 1993). The rest of the discrepancy reflects the trend toward working fewer weeks per year.

THE ROLE OF MULTIFACTOR PRODUCTIVITY

The term A_t in the Cobb-Douglas production function plays a special role in determining the economy's capacity to produce. It measures productivity, or the efficiency with which capital and labor are used to generate output. Over time, improvements in productivity make it possible to produce more output without additional inputs. Since 1950, the level of productivity has increased by over 70 percent. With only the inputs available in 1950, America can now produce 70 percent more output!

What causes productivity to change? A variety of factors are important, and we can classify them as either improvements *embodied* in the capital and labor inputs or *disembodied* changes that boost productivity in a more general way.

Embodied productivity improvements increase the *quality* of labor and capital. Better education, increased training, and improved health all mean that a labor hour in 1994 is more productive than an hour in, say, 1950. Since labor is generally measured in terms of hours worked, and the measurement is not adjusted for changes in the quality of labor, such changes in *effective* labor input will be captured in A_t. In a similar way, a unit of capital is better—more productive—today than in the past. Computers today are faster and more powerful; automobiles are more fuel efficient; lasers make surgery safer, quicker, and less painful.[8] Better design helps speed the flow of work through factories. All of these changes help to squeeze more production from a given number of labor hours, machines, and buildings.

Disembodied productivity changes are a little harder to grasp, though no less important. They include better production processes, substitution of cheaper materials for more expensive ones, quicker transfers of knowledge from the laboratory to the production line, and reorganizations of production and distribution. Many of these disembodied productivity changes typify the idea of "working smarter, not harder." Disembodied productivity also reflects the presence of any productive factors not measured as capital or labor inputs. For example, if the measured input of capital includes only capital in the private sector, disembodied productivity growth will reflect the presence of government capital, or infrastructure, which makes production more efficient. Examples of infrastructure are interstate highways, bridges, dams, and airports, all of which help reduce the transportation and communication costs facing business.

Case Study: How Does Productivity Grow?

Over the long term, productivity improvements have permitted astounding changes in incomes and the quality of life. Some of the most obvious examples come from the transportation sector. Since the 1920s, the automobile has radically transformed life in the United States and elsewhere. People no longer need to cluster in urban centers, living and shopping within walking distance of their workplaces. Refrigerator cars on trains, and later refrigerated trucks, permitted shipment of perishable food items across the country and around the world. And the jet airplane has saved billions of hours of time for business and recreational travelers.

Many other examples are less obvious. Just in the last decade, the introduction of quality circles has provided a forum for workers to suggest productivity-enhancing improvements to their supervisors. The Japanese-inspired "just in time" method of production reduces the amounts of resources firms have tied

8. For example, an IBM 4381-2 mainframe computer sold in 1984 for the same price an IBM 7070 mainframe sold for in 1960, but had a calculating power 1452 times greater. This example is taken from Robert J. Gordon, "The Postwar Evolution of Computer Prices," in *Technology and Capital Formation*, eds. Dale W. Jorgenson and Ralph Landau (Cambridge, MA: MIT Press, 1989).

up in inventory. Once retailers and producers were able to settle on a standard system, bar coding was introduced very rapidly and has helped speed up checkout lines at supermarkets.

Students of technology, such as Stanford University's Nathan Rosenberg, claim that small but continuous incremental changes probably do more to boost the economy's level of productivity than bigger, discrete changes do.[9] A good example is the phenomenon called "learning by doing." The phenomenon was first identified before World War II when aircraft manufacturers noticed how the cost of assembling a plane decreased steadily and predictably over time. The cost reductions were closely tied to the total number of aircraft assembled at a plant or by a company. Since then, the same effects have been found in a variety of production environments. As the cumulative number of units produced increases, the average cost of production falls, probably because workers learn from their mistakes and find better ways of doing things.

Another example of the importance of small changes comes from Boston University economist Andrew Weiss. Weiss studied the electronics industry by visiting production plants in the United States and Japan. His conclusions were quite surprising. For example, he found no differences in absenteeism, no differences in labor turnover, and no evidence that the Japanese work harder than Americans. In fact, the pace of production in Japanese electronics plants was slower than in comparable plants located in the United States. In spite of these similarities, the Japanese plants were more productive. Why? One reason is that the Japanese support their workers with a high ratio of engineers to production workers. By investing heavily in engineering and by locating engineers on the shop floor, Mitsubishi Electric, Hitachi, and NEC were able to achieve almost continuous improvement in their production processes. In the United States, by contrast, there is much more emphasis on marketing than on manufacturing. Engineers tend to be segregated in design facilities far from the production line.

ACCOUNTING FOR GROWTH

According to the Cobb-Douglas function, increases in output over time reflect either growth in inputs (K_t and L_t) or improvements in productivity (through A_t). With a little manipulation we can use the Cobb-Douglas function to write the percentage change in output between any two time periods in terms of the growth rates of capital, labor, and productivity. Let's denote the change in any variable X between two points in time as ΔX. Then the growth *rate* of X over that period is the change in X divided by the original level of X: $\Delta X/X$. For example, the growth rate of productivity is $\Delta A/A$. The relationship among our four growth rates is[10]

9. Rosenberg's *Inside the Black Box* (New York: Cambridge University Press, 1982) is a fascinating collection of his work on technology.

10. This relationship is derived by taking natural logarithms of both sides of the Cobb-Douglas relationship: $\ln Y_t = \ln A_t + \beta \ln K_t + (1 - \beta)\ln L_t$. If we measure this relationship in two successive periods and take the difference between them, we have $\ln Y_{t+1} - \ln Y_t = \ln A_{t+1} - \ln A_t + \beta(\ln K_{t+1} - \ln K_t) + (1 - \beta)(\ln L_{t+1} - \ln L_t)$. Since the difference of logarithms is approximately equal to the percentage change in a variable, we obtain the approximation given in the text.

$$\frac{\Delta Y}{Y} = \frac{\Delta A}{A} + \beta\frac{\Delta K}{K} + (1 - \beta)\frac{\Delta L}{L}$$

In words, the formula says the growth rate of output is approximately equal to the sum of (1) the rate of productivity improvement, (2) capital's share of output (β) multiplied by the growth rate of capital, and (3) labor's share of output ($1 - \beta$) multiplied by the growth rate of labor.

We have relatively good data on output and hours worked and fairly good data on capital. What about multifactor productivity, A_t? Because it reflects the influence of a variety of factors, including improvements in the quality of the capital and labor inputs and advances in technology, productivity is hard to measure directly. Therefore it is usually estimated by finding the value of A_t that makes the Cobb-Douglas production function "fit" the available data on output, labor, and capital. Robert Solow, who won a Nobel Prize for his work on economic growth, devised this "residual" method of determining the growth rate of productivity.[11] Solow plugged known values of $\Delta Y/Y$, $\Delta L/L$, $\Delta K/K$, and β into the above equation and estimated $\Delta A/A$ as the value that made the two sides of the equation equal. This so-called Solow residual reflects the amount of output growth that cannot be explained by (or, that's left over after) growth in the quantities of capital and labor. The residual is also sometimes known as the *rate of technological progress.*

As an example, suppose we know that the growth rates of output, capital, and labor between periods t and $t + 1$ are 3.0 percent, 2.0 percent, and 1.0 percent, respectively. Then the estimated rate of technological progress at time t is 1.70 percent (3.0 percent – .30 × 2.0 percent – .70 × 1.0 percent). We can use these estimated growth rates to do **growth accounting** by decomposing the overall growth rate of output into components that reflect the contributions of labor, capital, and productivity. In our example, the increase in the capital stock accounted for 0.60 percentage points of the total 3.00 percent growth in output. Growth in the labor input accounted for another 0.70 percentage point. We then attribute the remainder of the total growth rate—1.70 points—to improvements in productivity.

Growth accounting *The tracing of output growth to growth in inputs and multifactor productivity*

Case Study: Sources of U.S. Growth Since 1950

Growth accounting is a very handy tool for understanding why economies grow. It tells us what's important and what is not. Let's apply our growth accounting framework to understand the sources of the 3.4 percent annual growth rate of real output in the U.S. private business sector between 1950 and 1990. Figure 1-6 shows the shares of this average growth rate due to growth in productivity, capital, and labor. About two-fifths of the economic growth over the period is explained by productivity improvements. One-third is explained by growth in the capital stock, and the rest is due to growth in labor hours.

The sources of economic growth have changed over time. Annual growth in U.S. private business real GDP averaged 4.0 percent from 1950 to 1973, but

11. Robert M. Solow, "A Contribution to the Theory of Economic Growth," *Quarterly Journal of Economics*, February 1956, pp. 65–94.

Figure 1-6 Sources of U.S. Private Business Sector GDP Growth, 1950–1990

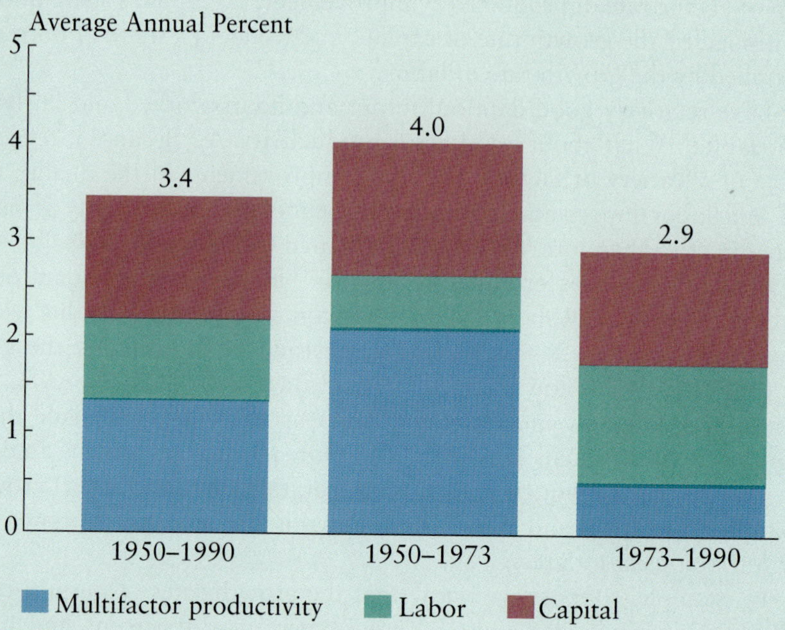

Between 1950 and 1990, U.S. real output increased at an average annual rate of 3.4 percent. About two-fifths of that growth was attributable to productivity improvements. One-third was explained by increases in the capital stock, and the rest was due to growth in labor hours.

The sources of growth have changed over time. Between 1950 and 1973, real output increased at an average annual rate of 4.0 percent. During that period, the major source of growth was multifactor productivity improvements. Since 1973, growth has slowed dramatically, to about 2.9 percent per year. In these years, growth in hours was the most important source of growth.

Source: Bureau of Labor Statistics

only 2.9 percent from 1973 to 1990. Labor's contribution to growth was more important in the latter period than in the former. In the latter period, growth in hours accounted for about two-fifths of total growth, compared with about one-eighth in the former period. Whereas capital's contribution was roughly constant, productivity's contribution declined from more than half in the earlier period to less than one-fifth in the latter.

Growth accounting is only as good as the raw data employed. Because productivity is computed as a residual, it's hard to say exactly what fraction of productivity growth is attributable to improvements in input quality (and, therefore, should be added to capital's and labor's contribution to growth), what fraction represents disembodied technological change, and what fraction is just measurement error.

Independent studies by Harvard University economist Dale Jorgenson and University of Groningen economist Angus Maddison suggest that most of measured productivity change takes the form of embodied quality improvements, particularly in capital.[12] Maddison estimates that embodied and disembodied changes in capital input explain over half the growth in U.S. output between 1973 and 1984.[13] In the period 1950–1973, disembodied changes played a more important role, but capital was still the most important source of growth. The theoretical model we will develop in later chapters highlights the importance of capital accumulation in generating economic growth.

LABOR PRODUCTIVITY

So far we've used the Cobb-Douglas function to discuss the level and growth rate of total output. Now let's use it to consider the amount of output per unit of labor input, which is called **labor productivity**.[14] Labor productivity is a key indicator of welfare, for reasons we'll explore shortly. To define labor productivity, we simply divide our Cobb-Douglas formula for output by the amount of labor input, L_t. What results is a formula for output per unit of labor input, also referred to as the Cobb-Douglas function in *intensive form*:

Labor productivity *The amount of output produced per unit of labor input*

$$\frac{Y_t}{L_t} = \frac{A_t K_t^{\beta} L_t^{1-\beta}}{L_t} = A_t \left(\frac{K_t}{L_t}\right)^{\beta}$$

In this text, lowercase letters are often used to denote variables measured on a per capita basis. So, if we let y_t stand for output per unit of labor input (labor productivity) and k_t stand for the ratio of capital to labor, we can write this equation compactly as

$$y_t = A_t k_t^{\beta}$$

Thus, we see that labor productivity depends on two factors, the level of multifactor productivity and the ratio of capital to labor. Not surprisingly, the more efficiently inputs are used (the larger the value of A_t), the more productive labor will be. Labor will also be more productive if it has more capital to work with—

12. See Dale W. Jorgenson, "Investing in Productivity Growth," in *Technology and Economics* (Washington, DC: National Academy Press, 1991), pp. 57–63, and Angus Maddison, "Growth and Slowdown in Advanced Capitalist Economies," *Journal of Economic Literature*, June 1987, pp. 649–698.

13. A recent study of Jeremy Greenwood, Zvi Hercowitz, and Per Krusell ("Macroeconomic Implications of Investment-Specific Technological Change," Federal Reserve Bank of Minneapolis, Discussion paper no. 76, Oct. 1992) suggests an even larger role for capital accumulation in U.S. growth.

14. We can define capital's productivity symmetrically as output per unit of capital.

that is, if the capital-labor ratio is larger. This is just another implication of diminishing returns. As we increase the amount of capital relative to labor, capital becomes more abundant and less productive. Labor, on the other hand, becomes relatively scarce and more productive.

Our formula for labor productivity holds for any period, t. If we are studying period 0, then $t = 0$ and the formula becomes $y_0 = A_0 k_0^\beta$. It tells us how labor productivity in period 0 relates to the level of technology and the capital-labor ratio in period 0. If we are interested in period 1, the formula becomes $y_1 = A_1 k_1^\beta$, which tells us how labor productivity relates to the level of technology and the capital-labor ratio in that period. We can now use our formula to think about how labor productivity changes over time.

Figure 1-7 shows how. Consider first the lower curve, which graphs our formula for labor productivity assuming the value of A_t equals 10 in all time periods. Suppose that at time 0 the capital-labor ratio equals 3. To find labor productivity at time 0, we can set t equal to 0 in the formula, read up to the lower curve, and record $y_0 = 13.9$. Next suppose that between period 0 and period 1 the capital-labor ratio increases from 3 to 5. This corresponds to a movement along the lower curve. To find labor productivity in period 1, we locate $k_1 = 5$ on the horizontal axis, set t equal to 1, and read up to the curve to find that y_1 equals 16.2. Thus, we can explain the increase in labor productivity between time 0 and time 1 in terms of an increase in the capital-labor ratio from 3 to 5.

Now suppose that technology improves so that the value of A_t jumps to 15. This improvement shifts the entire production function upward. With the capital-labor ratio still at $k_1 = 5$, labor productivity, found by reading up to the now higher curve, jumps to $y_1' = 24.3$.

In most years, both technology and the capital-labor ratio will be increasing. Our example shows how an overall change in labor productivity, $y'_1 - y_0$, can be explained in terms of an increase in the capital-labor ratio (a movement along the production function) coupled with a technological improvement (a shift upward in the curve itself).

Does Labor Productivity Influence Workers' Pay?

Labor productivity is closely related to labor's *marginal product*—the additional output that can be produced by holding technology and capital fixed and increasing labor by one unit. In the case of the Cobb-Douglas function, labor's marginal product is simply $(1 - \beta)y_t$, the quantity $(1 - \beta)$ multiplied by labor productivity. As we'll describe in Chapter 3, competitive firms pay workers a wage equal to their marginal product. Hence, if the Cobb-Douglas function provides a good description of production and firms hire workers competitively, workers' compensation should be closely related to labor productivity. This is

Figure 1-7 The Relationship of Output per Worker to the Capital-Labor Ratio and Technology

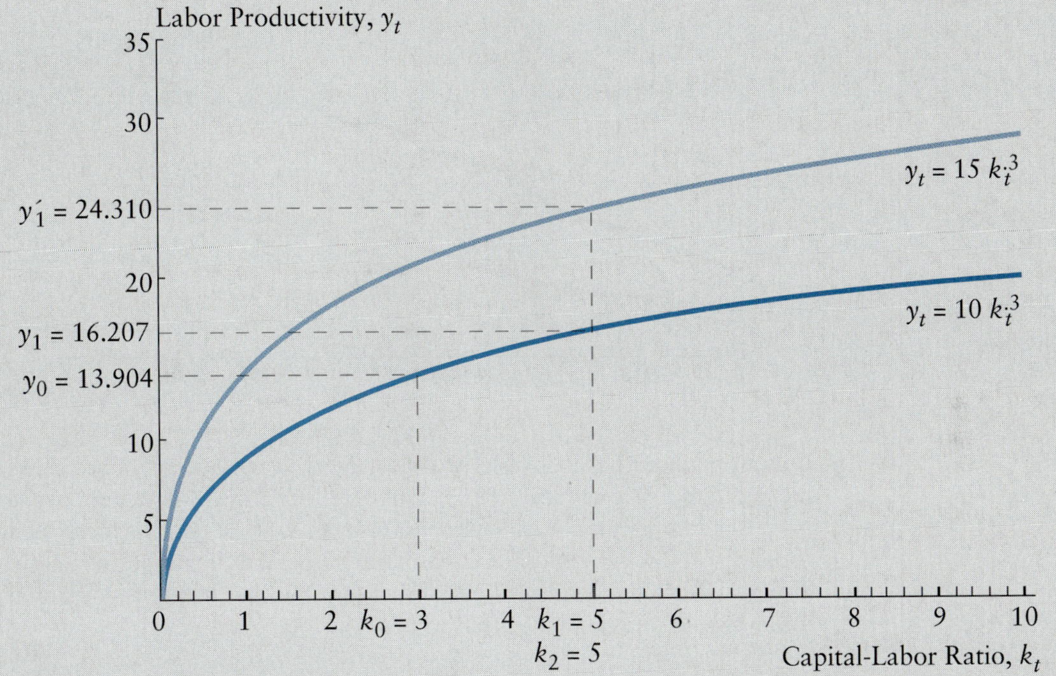

According to the Cobb-Douglas production function, output per worker—labor productivity—increases as the ratio of capital to labor increases. This is shown in the positive slopes of the two curves in this figure. As the amount of capital per worker increases (as we move to the right on the graph), capital becomes more abundant and less productive. This effect of diminishing returns to capital explains why the curves become flatter as the capital-labor ratio increases.

Labor productivity also depends on the level of technology. The lower curve is drawn for a particular value of the technology coefficient, A = 10. If technology improves, say to A = 15, the entire curve shifts upward.

indeed the case. Figure 1-8 shows that real compensation per hour in the United States closely tracks output per hour.

The tie to workers' compensation is one of the main reasons we are interested in studying labor productivity. Another is that, other things equal, a higher level of labor productivity means more output per person, which is economists' measure of an economy's standard of living.

Figure 1-8 U.S. Real Output and Real Labor Compensation per Hour, 1950–1992

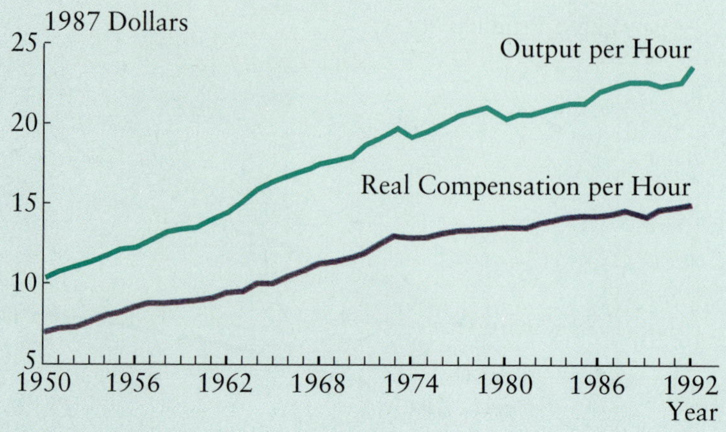

Output per hour has increased in almost every year since 1950, but it has increased more slowly since 1973. This is reflected in the flattening of the output per hour curve. Real compensation per worker hour is closely tied to labor productivity; in fact, it is about 70 percent of output per hour. The slowdown in productivity growth after 1973 has meant a slowdown in the growth of real compensation per hour.

Source: Bureau of Labor Statistics

WHY HAS THE U.S. EXPERIENCED A LABOR PRODUCTIVITY SLOWDOWN?

We've seen that the United States has been experiencing a slowdown in the rate of growth of GDP. What is the connection, if any, between labor productivity growth and output growth? It is certainly possible for labor productivity to speed up even as output growth slows.[15] Unfortunately, the slowdown in U.S. output growth *has* been associated with a slowdown in labor productivity growth. Figure 1-9 shows that since 1973 labor productivity has been growing at roughly a third the rate observed between 1950 and 1973. The labor productivity slowdown has contributed to the slow growth since 1973 in real compensation per hour. Had labor productivity grown as fast between 1973 and 1990 as it did between 1950 and 1973, real compensation per hour would have been almost two-fifths larger in 1990!

15. Leaving aside technology, total output depends on the absolute amounts of capital and labor employed. In contrast, labor productivity depends on the *ratio* of capital to labor. The capital-labor ratio can rise at the same time total output growth slows down. How? If the absolute amounts of both capital and labor grow more slowly than in the past, output will rise more slowly. If, in addition, labor grows more slowly than capital, the capital-labor ratio will rise and labor productivity will increase.

Figure 1-9 Growth in Labor Productivity, Multifactor Productivity, and the Capital-Labor Ratio, U.S. Private Business Sector, 1950–1990

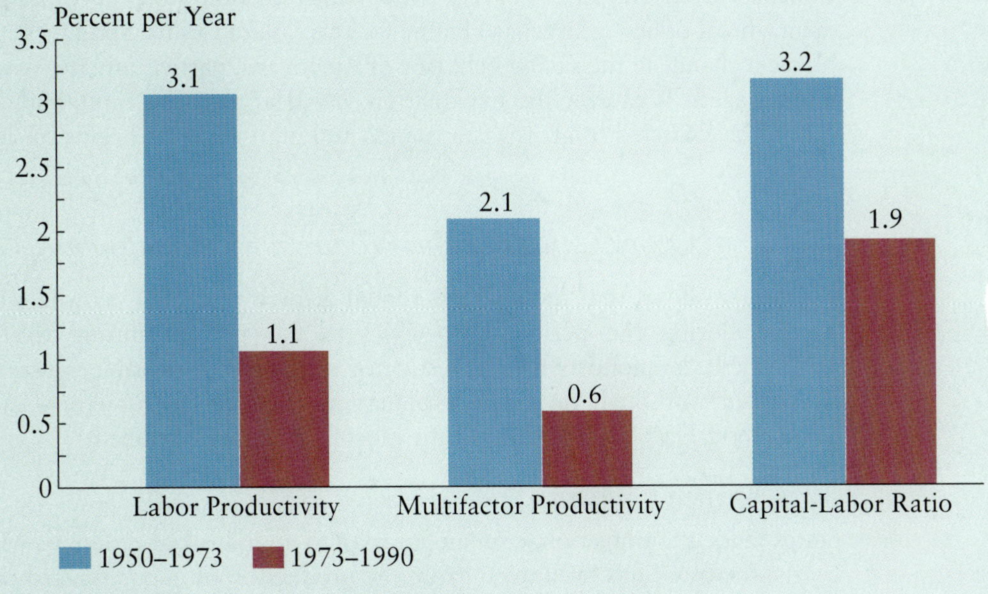

Labor productivity grew much more slowly in the period 1973–1990 than between 1950 and 1973. Much of this change can be traced to slower improvement in multifactor productivity, especially improvement embodied in capital and labor inputs. However, a slowdown in the rate of capital deepening also contributed to the slower labor productivity growth.

Source: Bureau of Labor Statistics

About a quarter of the decline in labor productivity growth can be traced to slower *capital deepening*—growth in the amount of capital per worker. The rest of the decline results from slower growth in multifactor productivity. Let's consider each in turn.

The Role of Capital Deepening

Since 1973, labor force growth has accelerated. Changes in labor force participation, which we've already documented, have combined with the large number of births during the postwar baby boom to produce sizable increases in the working age population. Over the same period, the rate of investment has slowed down. The capital stock is still growing, but its growth has slowed relative to that of employment. If the capital-labor ratio of the U.S. private business sector had grown as fast between 1973 and 1990 as it did between 1950 and 1973, the capital-labor ratio would now be a fourth larger.

Why has net investment—the growth in the capital stock net of depreciation—lagged? As we'll discuss in the next chapter, investment is financed by saving—output not consumed. A decline in the rate of investment must ultimately be explained by a decline in the rate of saving. Over the last two decades the U.S. has saved and invested very little. Many economists believe the government's fiscal policy is largely to blame for this failure to save and invest. Others blame a change in the saving behavior of Americans, particularly the young and middle aged. Whatever the explanation, it's clear that the capital-labor ratio cannot be expected to grow faster unless and until America begins to save at a higher rate.[16]

Other Causes of the Productivity Slowdown

Figure 1-9 shows that the average annual growth rate of A_t slowed from 2.1 percent during the period 1950–1973 to 0.6 percent during the period 1973–1990. Economists have investigated a number of possible causes of this slowdown. Although no single explanation is entirely satisfactory, each has some merit. Let's consider four of the most frequently mentioned.

A CHANGING PRODUCTION MIX. Early in the twentieth century, the United States made the transition from an agrarian to an industrial economy. More recently, the trend has been away from the production of *goods* toward the production of *services*. Manufacturing's share of GDP fell from 29 percent in 1950 to only 19 percent in 1988. By contrast, the share of GDP produced in finance, insurance, real estate, and other services rose from 20 percent in 1950 to 35 percent by 1988. This shift of production to sectors where the scope for productivity improvement is limited can help explain the overall slowdown in labor productivity growth.

Many people think productivity growth occurs mainly in the industrialized sectors of the economy, as new production methods and inventions are applied to make goods more efficiently and cheaply. In fact, primarily thanks to advances in the computer industry, labor productivity growth in manufacturing *has* outpaced that in services. For the period 1973–1987, growth in output per worker-hour in manufacturing was 2.6 percent annually. Over this period the same measure of labor productivity grew at an annual 0.4 percent rate for the service sector in general and fell at an annual 0.5 percent rate in the finance, insurance, and real estate component of the service sector. The shift in production away from manufacturing to services certainly lowered overall U.S. labor productivity growth, but other changes in the production mix had the opposite effect. Specifically, the shift away from mining and construction raised overall productivity growth because labor productivity growth in these industries was quite weak.[17]

---

16. As we'll see in the next chapter, some of the saving done by foreign countries has been used to finance investment in the U.S., but has not been enough to offset the effect on U.S. investment of a decline in U.S. saving.

17. See Martin N. Baily and Robert J. Gordon, "The Productivity Slowdown, Measurement Issues, and the Explosion of Computer Power," *Brookings Papers on Economic Activity* (1988):2, Table 4.

Reprinted with special permission of Gary Brookins and North America Syndicate, Inc.

CHANGES IN THE QUALITY OF CAPITAL AND LABOR. The slower growth in the U.S. capital stock has meant a slower rate of improvement in the quality of the capital stock. Jorgenson's and Maddison's research suggests that as much as one-third of the decline in multifactor productivity growth might be due to this factor. Slower growth in the quality of labor is another potential culprit. As mentioned, the U.S. **labor force**—those employed or seeking employment—has been changing in recent years as a greater percentage of women have entered the labor force. The labor force also swelled, beginning around 1970, as the large post-war "baby boom" generation began seeking employment.

Labor force
All noninstitutionalized individuals, 16 years of age and older, who are either working or actively looking for work

This increase in the proportion of relatively inexperienced workers is often cited as a cause of the labor productivity slowdown. So is the slower rate of improvement in the education of the U.S. workforce. Indeed, average scores on the college entrance exam—the SAT—suggest that the level of education may actually be declining. Average verbal test scores on the SAT are 21 points lower than averages in 1972, and average math scores are 10 points lower. Other measures are even more troubling. A 1993 study by the U.S. Department of Education found that nearly half of all adult Americans read and write so poorly that they can't hold a decent job and that almost four-fifths have math skills that are insufficient to perform simple calculations such as determining the correct change from a restaurant meal.

In terms of our formula for labor productivity, the argument here is that labor input is being incorrectly measured, having suffered a reduction in quality during the period. However, adjusting the measured labor input for changes in the age-sex mix and educational attainment can, it appears, explain only a small fraction of the post-1970 decline in labor productivity.

DECLINING RESEARCH AND DEVELOPMENT. Economists who study the question have found that research and development (R&D) spending contributes to technological progress, providing new, more efficient production methods. The lack of adequate R&D has often been cited as a cause of the recent slowdown in labor productivity growth. Indeed, U.S. research and development spending did slow beginning in the mid-1960s, from just over 4 percent of industry sales to just under 3 percent in the late 1970s. However, the evidence indicates that this shift had only a small effect on technological change, accounting for perhaps 10–15 percent of the overall slowdown in labor productivity growth.[18]

GOVERNMENT REGULATION. Since the mid-1960s, governmental health, safety, and environmental regulations have proliferated. These regulations have had many beneficial effects in improving the quality of life in the United States, but they have also contributed to the slowdown in productivity growth. The effects of regulation have been felt in a variety of ways. For example, more resources are now dedicated to simply complying with regulations—undergoing more inspections, completing paperwork, and planning. Edward Denison, a leading productivity researcher, estimated that about 1 percent of resources have been diverted to pollution abatement, where they do not contribute to measured GDP. The same sort of phenomenon results from health and safety regulations: measured output falls as resources are shifted from producing GDP to improving the quality of life. Pollution control devices themselves may render capital less efficient in producing output. Finally, regulations create uncertainty and, as a result, make businesses think twice about the wisdom of installing new, expensive capital. These effects are all quite difficult to measure, but a reasonable estimate is that they explain about 15 percent of the productivity problem.

Summary: Why Has Growth in U.S. Labor Productivity Slowed?

About one-quarter of the post-1973 slowdown in labor productivity growth is due to slower growth of capital relative to labor, arising from a relatively low rate of investment coupled with rapid growth in the labor force. The remainder of the labor productivity slowdown is due to a decline in multifactor productivity growth. Slower growth in the quality of capital may explain as much as one-third of this decline. Another third or so of the decline appears to be due to the changing production mix, a decline in labor quality, and a reduction in R&D spending. Explaining the rest of the decline in multifactor productivity is not easy. Part appears due to a somewhat greater frequency of recessions in the past two decades (technological progress appears to be less rapid during recessions). Part may be due to a slower growth rate in government infrastructure, which

18. See Zvi Griliches, "Productivity Puzzles and R&D: Another Nonexplanation," *Journal of Economic Perspectives*, Fall 1988, pp. 9–21. Economists estimate the productivity of R&D spending using a production function approach like the one we have outlined in this chapter, adding the stock of research knowledge to capital and labor as inputs in the production process.

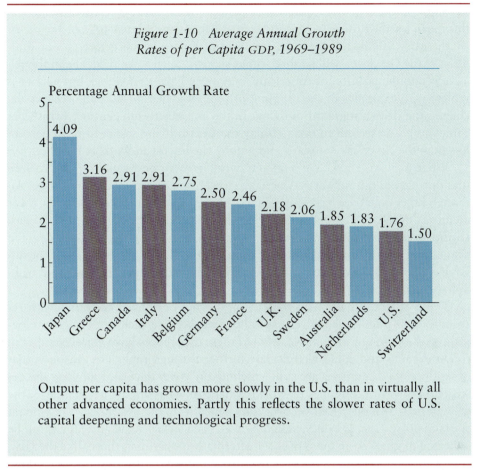

Figure 1-10 Average Annual Growth Rates of per Capita GDP, 1969–1989

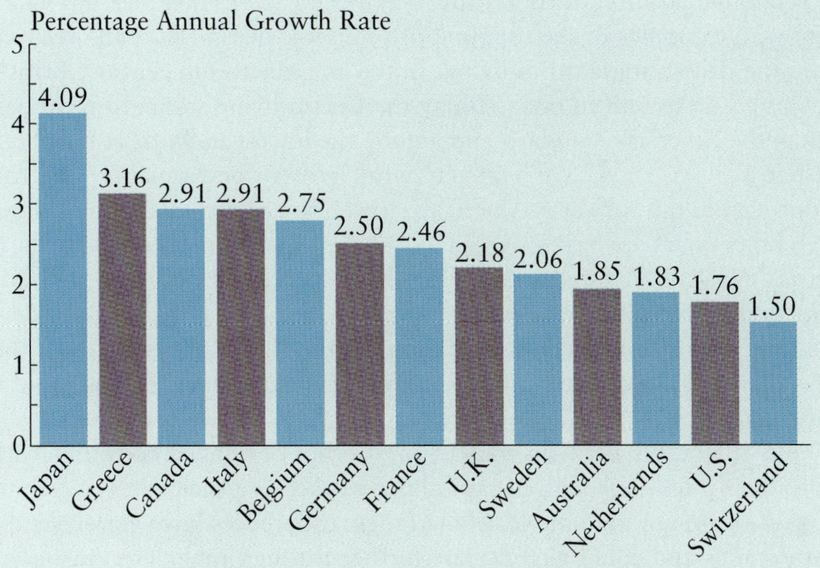

Output per capita has grown more slowly in the U.S. than in virtually all other advanced economies. Partly this reflects the slower rates of U.S. capital deepening and technological progress.

Source: U.S. Joint Committee on Taxation, *Factors Affecting the International Competitiveness of the United States, May 30, 1991*

we'll document in Chapter 7. Part may be due to measurement errors. And part may be due to other factors not yet fully understood.

IS THE U.S. STANDARD OF LIVING GROWING MORE SLOWLY THAN THOSE OF OTHER ADVANCED ECONOMIES?

Like the United States, other advanced countries have experienced slower growth in recent years. Nevertheless, per capita output is growing at a higher rate in almost all these countries than it is in the United States. Figure 1-10 displays average annual growth rates of real GDP per capita for the U.S. and twelve other developed countries over the period 1969–1989. With the exception of Switzerland, the U.S. per capita growth rate of 1.76 percent ranks lowest. Japan's rate was over twice the U.S. rate, and Germany's rate was almost one and one-half times the U.S. rate.

Suppose these growth differences persist for the next 50 years. What will this mean for the future living standards of Americans relative to, say, Japanese? By the early 2040s, the Japanese standard of living, which is now about four-fifths of the U.S. level, will be three times as high! Such a rapid decline in the relative economic position of Americans may seem hard to imagine, but history is replete with examples of the toppling of economic giants. Take the relative decline in the British standard of living. In the late nineteenth century, British per capita GDP was second to none. Today the British living standard is 30 percent less than the American standard and among the lowest in Western Europe.

What explains the U.S.'s relatively weak growth performance? We've seen that one part of the answer is America's slower rate of capital accumulation. Although other countries have invested less of their output in recent decades, these countries have still invested a far larger share of their output than the U.S. has. During each of the last three decades, no country shown in Figure 1-10 devoted a smaller share of GDP to investment than did the U.S. The other part of the answer is that other developed countries have been experiencing more rapid technological progress.

These differences between the U.S. and other developed countries with respect to their rates of growth in capital per worker and their rates of technological progress are not immutable. In fact, these differences have gotten smaller in recent decades and could well decline further through time. The reason is that other developed countries are still "catching up" with the U.S. following the destruction of their economies in World War II. As we'll discuss in Chapter 3, the growth path a country follows over time depends on the position it is in when it starts to grow. Countries devastated by war, such as Germany and Japan, can be expected to grow more quickly in the aftermath of war than those, like the U.S., that were not hit so hard. Part of this process involves the restoration of these countries' capital stocks. And part involves the acquisition by these countries of technology already being used in countries with higher per capita incomes.

IS ECONOMIC GROWTH WIDENING THE GAP BETWEEN DEVELOPED AND LESS DEVELOPED NATIONS?

The problems of developing countries are in some ways quite different from those of developed countries. The issue of growth and its determinants is probably more important for countries that have yet to achieve the relatively high living standards enjoyed in the developed world. The central questions concerning growth and development are: Why do living standards vary so much across countries, and why are some countries more successful than others at making the jump from "developing" to "developed"?

After World War II, the devastated economies of Germany and Japan were essentially in the "developing" category in terms of living standards. Yet both countries grew rapidly during the postwar years, closing the gap with the developed world. The experience of other, truly developing countries has been more

Figure 1-11 Real GDP per Capita in Four Developing Countries, 1960–1988

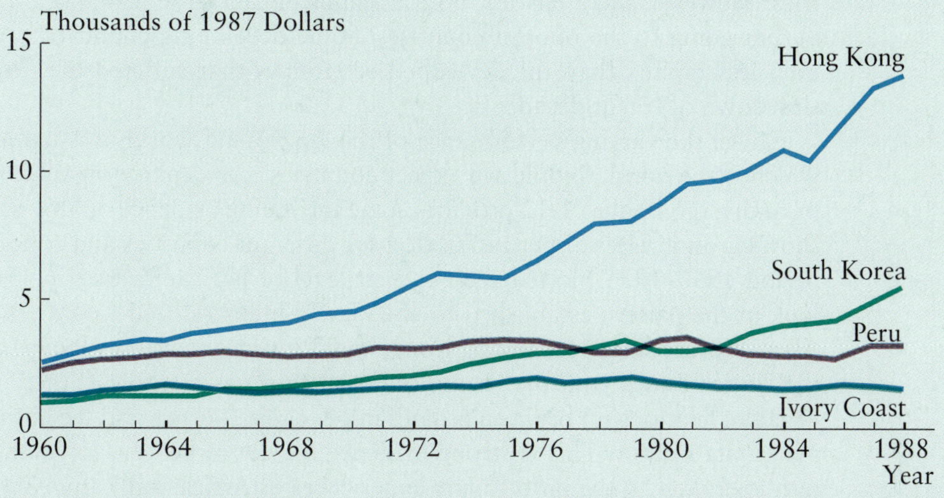

Since 1960, some developing economies have experienced dramatic growth while others have stagnated. In 1960, South Korea and the Ivory Coast each had real per capita GDP of about \$1,000. Likewise, Peru and Hong Kong each had real per capita GDP of about \$2,000. By 1988, Hong Kong had four times Peru's standard of living and South Korea's living standard was over twice that of the Ivory Coast. Some countries have caught up with the developed world, but growth is clearly not inevitable.

mixed. Some, like South Korea and Hong Kong, have rapidly approached the living standards of the developed world; others have fallen further behind.

Figure 1-11 shows real GDP per capita for South Korea, Hong Kong, the Ivory Coast, and Peru.[19] In 1960, the Ivory Coast and South Korea each had real per capita GDP of about \$1,000. Hong Kong and Peru each had per capita GDP of just over \$2,000 (compared to the U.S. figure of about \$10,000). Over the period 1960–1988, per capita real GDP in South Korea and Hong Kong grew at average annual rates of 6.3 percent and 6.4 percent, respectively, far outstripping the corresponding U.S. rate of 2.2 percent and even surpassing Japan's rate of 5.5 percent. But Peru's per capita GDP grew at an annual rate of just 1.0 percent over this period, and the Ivory Coast's growth rate was only 0.9 percent. These different growth records had dramatic effects on the countries' relative living standards. Hong Kong, which started in 1960 with the same level as Peru, had four times Peru's per capita real GDP by 1988. And South Korea,

19. These figures come from an unpublished appendix to Robert Summers and Alan Heston, "The Penn World Table (Mark V): An Expanded Set of International Comparisons, 1950–88," *Quarterly Journal of Economics*, May 1991.

which started 1960 at half of Peru's living standard, had double the Peruvian standard by 1988. Thus, the evidence shows the clear possibility for developing countries to approach the high standards of living enjoyed in developed countries. However, there has not been a significant increase in the share of world output going to the poorest countries. Some developing countries have grown even less rapidly than the developed economies that suffered the productivity slowdown of recent decades.

Given the varying performance of the developing world, it is natural to ask which is the norm. Should we expect countries' per capita outputs to converge or to diverge? Figure 1-12 provides some intriguing evidence on this question. It shows growth rates of per capita GDP for different countries and regions for the period 1960–1985 plotted against their level of per capita GDP in 1960. If we look at the pattern established by the Newly Industrialized Countries (NICs) of Asia—Korea, Singapore, Hong Kong, and Taiwan—as well as Japan, Germany, the United States, and the Group of Seven (G-7) as a whole,[20] there is a clear negative relationship between growth in per capita output and the initial level of per capita output. This is strong evidence for convergence. However, this pattern is broken by the unfortunate experiences of Africa and Latin America over the period.

The basic economic model we will develop in the chapters to come does predict the type of convergence observed among the Asian NICs, Japan, Germany, and the United States. But there is more to the world than the basic model captures, including certain aspects of government performance or nonperformance. Many countries of Africa and Latin America have not been blessed with stable, efficient governments.

Furthermore, with some modifications of our basic model, we can generate a process of self-propelled technological change. In this modified model there is no necessary requirement that growth rates and living standards of different countries converge. Models exhibiting self-propelled growth are called *endogenous growth* models and are at the forefront of modern research on the economics of growth. We'll discuss endogenous growth briefly in Chapter 3.[21]

Chapter Summary

1. Measured in 1987 dollars, the U.S. economy in 1993 produced over $5 trillion of output (gross domestic product)—six times the output produced in 1929. Economic growth is highly dependent on the state of the economy, with recessions marked by negative growth and expansions by positive growth. The most severe recession on record—the Great Depression—is a case in point. During its first four years, U.S. output fell by 30 percent.

20. The G-7 are the developed economies of Japan, Germany, Canada, France, Italy, the United Kingdom, and the United States.

21. See Robert E. Lucas, Jr., "On the Mechanics of Economic Development," *Journal of Monetary Economics*, vol. 22, 1988, pp. 3–42, and Paul M. Romer, "Capital Accumulation in the Theory of Long Run Growth," in *Modern Business Cycle Theory*, ed. Robert J. Barro (Cambridge, MA: Harvard University Press, 1989).

Figure 1-12 Per Capita GDP: Growth versus Level, 1960–1985

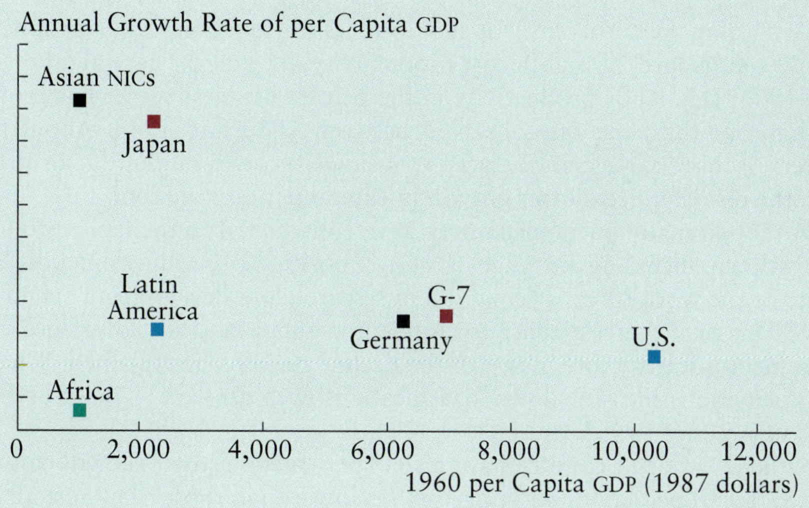

If poorer economies grow faster than richer economies, we should expect per capita outputs of different nations to converge in the long run. Japan and the Newly Industrialized Countries of Asia had small per capita GDPs in 1960, which grew at high rates over the following quarter-century. The U.S., Germany, and the G-7 industrialized nations already had large per capita GDPs in 1960; their growth since then has been more modest. These data support the idea of convergence. On the other hand, the experience of Africa and Latin America provides evidence against convergence. Economies there started poor and grew slowly.

2. Economists measure a country's standard of living in terms of per capita real GDP. The U.S. level of real per capita GDP has grown at an average rate of 1.70 percent per year since 1929. Consequently, the U.S. standard of living is now almost three times its 1929 level.

3. Growth rates compound, meaning that small differences in growth rates translate into large differences over time in living standards. Had the post-1929 U.S. growth rate of per capita output been twice as high, America's standard of living would be almost three times larger than its current value.

4. The Cobb-Douglas production function is a simple and empirically sensible way to model output. It relates output to inputs of capital and labor and the level of multifactor productivity and provides a basis for growth accounting.

5. Capital is measured as the value of business and residential structures, equipment, land, and inventories, expressed in prices from a particular year (e.g., 1987). Labor is typically measured as total hours worked, which is the product of three factors: the adult population, the fraction of that population employed, and hours worked per employed person.

6. Growth of real output in the U.S. private business sector has slowed in recent decades. The relative contributions of technological progress and capital accumulation declined, while the relative contribution of labor input growth increased.

7. According to the Cobb-Douglas production function, labor productivity depends on the level of multifactor productivity, A_t, and the capital-labor ratio. Since 1973, U.S. labor productivity in the private business sector has grown at less than one-third the rate observed between 1950 and 1973. About three-quarters of this decline can be traced to a slower growth in multifactor productivity; the rest is due to slower growth in capital per unit of labor.

8. Although many phenomena may have contributed to the labor productivity slowdown, including a change in the composition of production, a decline in quality of the work force, a reduction in research and development spending, a slower rate of net investment, government regulation, and slower growth of government infrastructure, much of the decline remains unexplained. Whatever the explanation, the slowdown has meant slower growth in the real hourly wages of American workers.

9. Other developed countries are also experiencing growth slowdowns. Still, the U.S. rate of per capita output growth is lower than those of almost all other developed countries. Among developing countries—those with a substantially lower standard of living than countries like the U.S., Japan, and Germany—there has been a divergence of growth rates. Some developing economies, notably the Newly Industrialized Countries of Asia, have grown quite rapidly—indeed, even more rapidly than countries in the developed world. Other countries, many of which are in Africa and Latin America, have grown at very slow rates. This suggests that rapid development is possible, but by no means assured.

Key Concepts

Technology
Gross domestic product (GDP)
Cobb-Douglas production function
Capital
Labor
Multifactor productivity
Investment
Flow variable
Stock variable
Growth accounting
Labor productivity
Labor force

Review Questions

1. What is *real* GDP? How is real GDP calculated? What term is used to describe an increase in real GDP? a decrease?

2. What is the difference between a *stock* and a *flow*? How are the two related? Classify the following as either a stock or a flow: the size of the labor force; investment; depreciation; real GDP; an office building; the current state of technology.

3. What is a *production function*? How is the *Cobb-Douglas* production function written? To what does each of the variables refer? Provide an economic interpretation of the exponents.

4. What do economists mean when they refer to *labor* and *capital*? How is each typically measured?
5. Define *gross investment*, *net investment*, and *depreciation*. How are the three concepts related? How do the three help determine the size of the capital stock?
6. What is *multifactor productivity* and how is it measured in the Cobb-Douglas production function? What is the difference between *embodied* and *disembodied* productivity change? Give some examples of each.
7. To what extent have changes in the amounts of labor and capital and in multifactor productivity contributed to U.S. real GDP growth during the past 40 years?
8. Define *labor productivity*. How does labor productivity differ from the *marginal product of labor*? How is the marginal product of labor affected by an increase in the amount of labor? in the amount of capital?
9. What is the recent record of labor productivity growth in the United States? What are some potential explanations of the recent trend?
10. How do economists measure the *standard of living*? How has the U.S. standard of living changed over the past few decades? How has this performance compared to the changes observed in other countries?

Numerical Questions

1. Suppose that U.S real GDP is expected to grow by 2.5 percent per year.
- **a.** If real GDP is currently \$5 trillion, what will real GDP equal in ten years?
- **b.** 2.5 percent of \$5 trillion is \$0.125 trillion. If real GDP grows by \$0.125 trillion per year, it will equal \$6.25 trillion after ten years. Is your answer to part a greater than or less than \$6.25 trillion? Why?

2. Suppose that a company currently owns two types of capital: two copy machines and eight personal computers. All the capital is new. Expressed in 1987 dollars, copiers cost \$1,000 each and personal computers cost \$800 each.
- **a.** What is the total amount of capital owned by the company?
- **b.** Suppose that copy machines depreciate at the rate of 20 percent per year and computers at the rate of 40 percent per year. (Helpful hint: The annual amount of depreciation, D_t, for a particular type of capital equals the capital's depreciation rate in decimal form times the existing amount of that capital, K_t.) What will the company's capital stock be in two years?
- **c.** Assume the same initial values of capital calculated in part a and the same depreciation rates as in part b. If the company buys another computer at the end of year 1, what will its total capital stock be at the end of year 2?

3. Output of the Chip Off the Old Block granite company is given by a Cobb-Douglas production function in which, for 1992, capital is 400, labor is 100, multifactor productivity is 5, and the exponents on capital and labor are 0.3 and 0.7, respectively.
- **a.** What is the initial level of output?
- **b.** What is the total compensation paid to the employees of the firm?
- **c.** Does Chip Off the Old Block's production function exhibit constant

returns to scale? (Helpful hint: Increase both capital and labor by 50 percent and observe the resulting change in output.)

d. Suppose that between 1992 and 1993 output grows by 2.5 percent, capital grows by 1 percent, and labor grows by 2 percent. What must have been the growth rate of multifactor productivity over the year?

4. Annual output of the Every Day Is Sundae ice cream company is given by a Cobb-Douglas production function in which capital is 200, labor is 100, multifactor productivity is 2, and the exponents on capital and labor are 0.4 and 0.6, respectively.

a. Calculate the ice cream company's labor productivity using the *intensive* form of the production function.

b. Suppose that Every Day Is Sundae doubles its ratio of capital to labor. Compute the impact on labor productivity.

c. Does your answer to part b depend on *how* the ratio is doubled? That is, does it matter whether the capital stock doubles or the labor force is cut in half?

d. Suppose the company's multifactor productivity rises to 3 from 2, while capital and labor remain at their initial values of 200 and 100, respectively. Calculate the impact of the multifactor productivity change on labor productivity.

5. Suppose that an economy's production is described by a Cobb-Douglas production function in which the exponents on capital and labor are 0.3 and 0.7, respectively. Answer the questions in parts a and b, given the following data.

Year	Multifactor Productivity	Capital	Labor
1983	10	1000	500
1993	11	1100	600

a. Calculate output in each year and its percentage change during 1993.

b. What proportion of total output growth is accounted for by growth in multifactor productivity? by growth in capital? by growth in labor? (Recall that the formula for growth accounting is an approximation, so the percent change in output may slightly exceed the sum of the contributions of the three components.)

Analytical Questions

1. Using the growth accounting framework, explain how the following economic policies would affect the economy's ability to produce output and why.

a. Congress votes to increase spending on public infrastructure.

b. Congress passes a law that limits the amount of immigration.

c. The president succeeds in convincing Congress to pass an investment tax credit that reduces the price of plant and equipment by 10 percent.

d. Congress relaxes antitrust laws to permit greater cooperation between firms in research and development endeavors.

e. The Occupational Safety and Health Administration imposes new restrictions on the layout of factory floors.

2. The text identified certain developing countries whose living standards were approaching those of developed countries, and others whose living standards were not. Some analysts have argued that countries that have not seen their living standards converge have suffered because their economies are based on centralized decision making and state ownership rather than free markets and private ownership. Evaluate this idea within the context of the growth accounting model. (Helpful hint: How might greater reliance on free markets and private ownership affect the factors underlying growth?)

3. The following is a tabular representation of a Cobb-Douglas production function. The numbers along the top indicate varying amounts of labor; the numbers down the side indicate varying amounts of capital. The number in each cell in the table gives the amount of output produced for given amounts of capital and labor. For instance, if labor is 400 and capital is 10, then 264.53 units of output are produced. Answer the questions in parts a through c using the data in the table.

	Labor		
Capital	400	800	1200
10	264.53	429.73	570.76
20	325.67	529.06	702.69
30	367.80	597.49	793.58

a. Using the data, give examples of diminishing returns to labor and of diminishing returns to capital.

b. Suppose the development of a revolutionary and powerful computer chip raises multifactor productivity by 5 percent. How would such a development affect the data in the table?

c. Does the production function represented in the table exhibit constant returns to scale? Answer by referring to specific numbers.

C H A P T E R 2

The Dynamic Supply of Inputs

INTRODUCTION

Life-cycle model
A framework that explains an individual's decision about how much to consume and save in each period of his or her life

As we've seen, the forces driving economic growth are improvements in technology and accumulation of inputs. We've discussed a number of sources of technological progress, but we now need to explain or, as economists say, "model" changes over time in the capital and labor inputs used to produce output. To do so, we will develop a very simple version of the **life-cycle model** of economic growth. In subsequent chapters we'll use this model, or variants of it, to understand business cycles, international capital flows, macroeconomic policy, short-run Keynesian macroeconomics, foreign exchange markets, credit markets, and a host of other issues.

The life-cycle model was developed in the early 1950s by Nobel Laureate Franco Modigliani and University of Pennsylvania economist Albert Ando.[1] It traces the supplies of capital and labor to household decisions about how much

1. Albert Ando and Franco Modigliani, "The 'Life Cycle Hypothesis' of Saving: Aggregate Implications and Tests," *American Economic Review* 53: (1963).

to save for retirement and how much and how long to work prior to retirement. The model also shows how household supplies of capital and labor, at any point in time, match up with firms' demands for these inputs. As we'll see, this dynamic (through time) equalization of the supplies of capital and labor to their respective demands is accomplished through adjustments in wages and interest rates.

This chapter describes the dynamic supply of inputs. We'll leave to Chapter 3 the task of describing the dynamic demand for inputs as well as the equalization of input supplies and demands. We begin by pointing out that households, rather than firms, are the ultimate owners and suppliers of inputs. We underscore this point by laying out the supply side of our model, which connects the economy's aggregate supplies of capital and labor to the saving and work decisions of individual households.

After discussing and illustrating the supply side of our model in aggregate terms, we turn to explaining precisely how individual households make their saving and work decisions. This microeconomic underpinning to our macro model is valuable. It reminds us that the aggregate variables of a typical macro economy, such as that of the United States, ultimately reflect the collective behavior of millions of individual households and firms. It also gives us a means of tracing out the macroeconomic consequences of government policies that operate by altering individual households' saving and work decisions.

An added benefit of studying household saving and work decisions is that we learn how to do **present value discounting**. Present value discounting tells us how to compare funds to be received in the future with funds received today. It also enables us to compare future payments with current payments. For instance, it shows whether paying $100 today is more or less expensive than paying $150 eight years from now. Present value discounting is extremely important to anyone trying to buy a house, select a career, or make any of an array of financial decisions that involve the receipt or payment of money over time.

Present value discounting
Determining the present value of a sum of money to be received or paid in the future

Once we understand individual saving, we'll be in a position to understand a country's aggregate saving, or **national saving**, and to derive a fundamental macroeconomic identity—namely, that national saving equals **national investment**. National investment is the additional amount of capital accumulated either at home or abroad in a given period of time. In a case study we'll describe the critically low rate of national saving that has prevailed in the U.S. since the early 1980s. Given the saving-equals-investment identity, reduced U.S. national saving has meant less national investment. In the case study we'll learn that the reduction in U.S. national investment has come from reduced *domestic investment* (investment done in the U.S.) as well as lower *net foreign investment* (U.S. investment abroad minus the amount invested in the U.S. by foreigners).

National saving
Gross national product minus consumer spending by households minus government spending on goods and services

National investment
The amount of capital accumulated by a nation, either at home or abroad, during a given period of time

The low rate of U.S. national saving threatens to persist. Consequently, that part of the slowdown in economic growth resulting from slow growth in the U.S. capital stock is also likely to continue. Another reason to expect slow growth in the future is that demographic factors will be reducing growth in the U.S. labor supply. Recall that labor supply growth in the past two decades was due primarily to the dramatic increase in female labor force participation coupled with the entrance of the large baby boom generation into the labor market. By now, these factors have largely run their course.

If supply-side factors will be slowing U.S. growth in capital and labor inputs, what will they do to the ratio of capital to labor, on which labor productivity depends? As we'll describe in another case study, the capital-labor ratio will gradually rise. Furthermore, since Japan and most Western European countries are experiencing similar demographic changes, *capital deepening* (a rise in the capital-labor ratio) will occur in these countries as well, albeit at different paces.

Before plunging ahead, it may help to list some of the questions we'll consider in this chapter:

- How does *saving*, the acquisition of additional assets, relate to investment, the acquisition of additional capital?
- How do people decide how much to save and how hard to work?
- In deciding how much to save, how do people value income they'll receive and expenditures they'll make in the future?
- Why do capital and labor supplies change through time?
- Has the U.S. saving rate declined in recent years?
- How will the rapid aging of the U.S., European, and Japanese populations alter their supplies of capital and labor over the next 50 years?
- Why are American males retiring at younger ages at the same time American females are retiring at older ages?

WHO OWNS AND SUPPLIES INPUTS?

Understanding the supply side of the economy requires thinking about who owns inputs and how much of their inputs the owners bring to market. Owners of labor services are individuals with a capacity to work in some productive enterprise. The amount of labor supplied depends on the number of such persons, but also on how many hours per year they choose to work. In addition, there is a quality dimension to labor supply. The supply of **human capital**—the total quantity of labor adjusted for quality—will reflect the training and education workers have accumulated as well as their raw talents. Finally, households decide how many future workers to supply to the economy when they decide how many children to bring into the world.

Human capital *Labor input adjusted for skills, training, and on-the-job experience*

Real assets *Capital goods, such as plants and machinery, used in conjunction with labor to produce output*

Financial asset *A legal claim to the income generated by real assets (rather than a claim to the real assets themselves)*

The ultimate owners of physical capital are households, although their ownership is often indirect. Consider, for example, the plants and machinery that General Motors uses to produce automobiles. General Motors Corporation, as a legal entity, holds the physical titles (bills of purchase) to these **real assets**. But General Motors is itself owned by the million or so households that hold shares of GM stock.

Financial assets and liabilities arise as a way of recognizing indirect ownership. For General Motors' shareholders, GM stock represents a **financial asset** rather than a real asset. The stock gives them legal claim to the income generated by GM's real assets, rather than a direct legal claim to the assets themselves. Other examples of financial assets are bonds, saving and checking accounts, cer-

Table 2-1 U.S. Private Domestic Net Worth 1993 (trillions of dollars)

	Sector with Direct Ownership		
Real Assets	**Household[a]**	**Business**	**Total**
Residential structures	4.226	1.273	5.499
Plant and equipment	.476	5.068	5.544
Inventories	0	1.133	1.133
Consumer durables	2.338	0	2.338
Land	2.865	1.365	4.230
Total Real Assets	9.905	8.839	18.744

[a]Includes nonprofit institutions.

Source: Board of Governors of the Federal Reserve System

tificates of deposit, money market funds, accounts receivable, stock options—each of which gives its owner a claim to income in the future.

For each financial asset, there is an offsetting *financial liability* of equal value. In the case of GM stock, the shares represent a financial asset of the shareholders but a financial liability of the corporation. The owner of an AT&T bond has a financial asset. But AT&T, as issuer of the bond, has a financial liability—namely, to make the principal and interest payments specified on the bond. From an economy-wide perspective, the financial assets and liabilities cancel each other out. If we add up the values of all a country's real and financial assets and then subtract the values of all its financial liabilities, we are left with just the value of its real assets, which is called its *domestic net worth*. This makes sense; ultimately a country's domestic net worth equals the value of the physical capital within its borders.

Case Study: Who "Owns" the U.S. Private Capital Stock?

In 1993 the U.S. private sector capital stock totaled $19 trillion, which was a bit less than three times 1993 GDP. Table 2-1 indicates that about half this capital was directly owned by households. The rest was directly owned by businesses and, consequently, indirectly owned by households. Unincorporated businesses directly owned about a quarter of so-called business capital, but this capital really belonged to the proprietors and partners who ran these firms. The remaining business capital was directly owned by corporations. As we've seen, that means it was really owned by the individual stockholders of these companies.[2]

2. We'll have much more to say about the ownership of corporations in Chapter 16 where we discuss corporate finance.

Table 2-1 also shows the different types of real assets "owned" by each sector. Household real assets consist primarily of owner-occupied homes, the land beneath them, and consumer durables. Business real assets include plant and equipment, inventories, and land. They also include some residential structures, primarily apartment buildings and other rental units owned by private and corporate landlords.

In addition to the $19 trillion of U.S. private capital in 1993, about $3 trillion in land, buildings, equipment, bridges, roads, and other capital was "owned" by the government. Like private capital, government capital is fundamentally owned by people, since the government is ultimately under society's control.

THE TWO-PERIOD LIFE-CYCLE MODEL

Saving means refraining from consuming all of current output now in order to facilitate greater consumption and production in the future. But there is another meaning attached to the word saving—namely, the acquisition of additional real assets. These two meanings are consistent. Whether the newly produced capital good is a Boeing 777 or inventoried rice, it is output not consumed at the time it is produced. It is also output whose titles of ownership are acquired, directly or indirectly, by savers. Understanding the process of capital accumulation thus requires a link between acquisition of claims to new capital and the forgoing of current consumption in order to produce more output in the future. Our life-cycle model provides that link. It clarifies how individuals' asset accumulation is connected to their sacrifice of immediate consumption.

As we'll see, the model is very simple and for that reason may seem unrealistic. Be assured that much more elaborate and realistic versions of this simple model have been constructed.[3] We develop this simple model not because it provides highly accurate quantitative predictions (it doesn't) but because it provides the same qualitative predictions and economic insights as more detailed models. The version of our model presented in this chapter is stripped down. Among other things it leaves out international trade, macroeconomic fluctuations, government taxation and expenditures, money and monetary policy, wage and price rigidities, saving for reasons other than retirement, and credit markets. These and many other issues will be addressed in later chapters.

The Model's Basic Structure

Our model considers a single country which, for the moment, has no government. The inhabitants live for just two time periods. In their first period of life, people are young. In the second, they are old. At any given time there are young people who have just been born and old people who have one more period to go. All individuals born at the same time are identical. If it helps, think of repro-

3. See, for example, Alan J. Auerbach and Laurence J. Kotlikoff, *Dynamic Fiscal Policy* (New York: Cambridge University Press, 1987).

duction occurring by test tube so that all members of a generation (all those born at the same time) are clones.

Although we'll refer simply to "periods of time" in presenting the model, each period can be thought of as consisting of roughly 30 years of adulthood. The 30 years between ages 20 and 50 can be termed "youth," and the 30 years between ages 50 and 80 can be termed "old age." Admittedly, it would be more realistic to consider not just people's youth and old age, but every year of their lives. But this is an example of the general point made above; adding more time periods would make the model much more complex without altering the basic insights.

There is only one commodity in this country's economy: corn. This commodity is the model's consumption good as well as its capital good. It can either be consumed (literally eaten) or be invested (planted) to produce additional output (corn). This may sound like a description only of agricultural production (and one that's perhaps a bit corny), but the ideas carry over to the more general context of a modern industrial economy.

When they are young, people work, and when they're old, they are retired. At the end of their first period of life, young people are paid in units of the commodity (in kernels of corn) for their work effort. They consume some of these labor earnings and put aside, or save, the rest. Since there are no inheritances (at least until Chapter 15), this saving by the young out of their labor earnings constitutes the assets they bring into their old age.

At the beginning of their old age, people invest their assets. For simplicity, we'll assume that old people invest their accumulated corn in their own firms (farms). The assets of the old thus represent their stock of capital. To obtain labor to work with their capital, the elderly hire the new batch of young people. At the end of their old age, the output of the firms emerges (the new crop of corn is harvested).

The old people give part of the output to their young workers as wage payments. They keep the rest as a return on the capital they invested (planted). We refer to this income as capital income. The elderly consume this capital income plus the amount they originally invested (their principal). In effect, we assume that the capital the elderly invest at the beginning of their old age does not depreciate and can be fully recovered (dug up) and consumed. Since the assets of the old are positive at the beginning of their last period but zero at the end, the old eat up all their assets (they dissave) during their second period of life. The time line in Figure 2-1 describes the ordering of events in our model for periods of time before, during, and after time period t.

DYNAMIC INPUT SUPPLIES WHEN THE LABOR SUPPLY IS FIXED

Let's now use some very simple equations to describe the supplies of capital and labor under the assumption that the young always work full time. We'll focus first on generation t, which is born at the beginning of time period t and which earns wages, consumes, and saves at the end of period t. It invests its assets at

Figure 2-1 The Two-Period Model's Time-Line

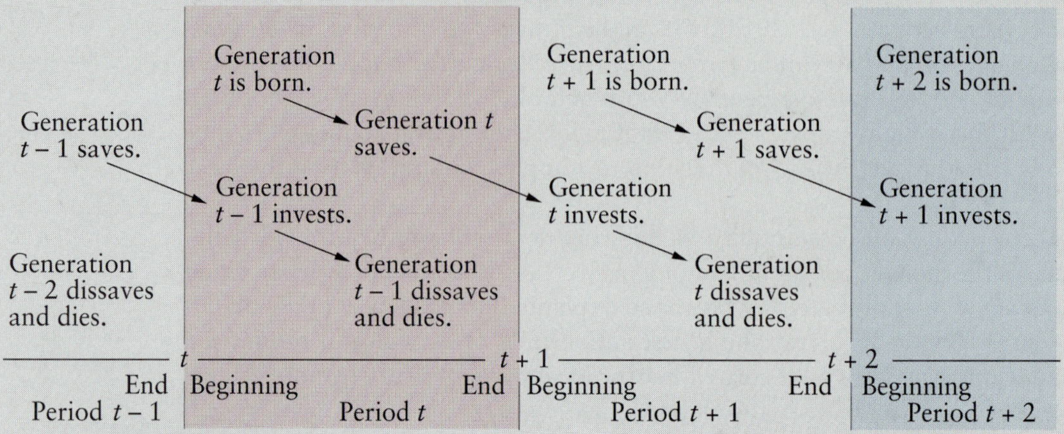

In the life-cycle model, each generation lives for two periods. Generation t is born at the beginning of time period t. It earns wages, consumes, and saves at the end of period t. It invests its assets at the beginning of period $t + 1$, consumes the principal plus interest at the end of period $t + 1$, and then dies. The same life-cycle pattern is experienced by every other generation: $t + 1$, $t + 2$, and so on. Each earns wages and saves when young. Each invests and consumes principal and interest when old.

the beginning of period $t + 1$, consumes the principal plus interest on its assets at the end of that period, and then immediately dies.

Let c_{yt} denote consumption when young (hence the subscript y) by a member of generation t (hence the subscript t). In addition, we'll use w_t to denote the wage earnings of each young person in generation t. Then $w_t - c_{yt}$ equals the amount each member of generation t saves. This is also the amount of assets, denoted by a_{t+1}, each member of generation t brings into period $t + 1$. In symbols,

$$a_{t+1} = w_t - c_{yt}$$

If each member of generation t brings a_{t+1} units of corn, or capital, into old age, how large is the economy's total capital stock at the beginning of time $t + 1$? The answer depends on the size of generation t. To keep things simple, we'll assume that there are N members of generation t, and of every other generation as well. In other words, there is no population growth; at any given time there are N young people and N old people alive, making the total population equal to $2N$. If we let K_{t+1} stand for the economy's total capital stock at the beginning of time $t + 1$, we have

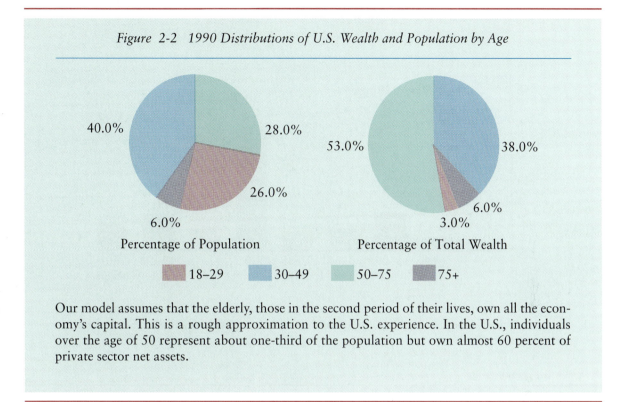

Figure 2-2 1990 Distributions of U.S. Wealth and Population by Age

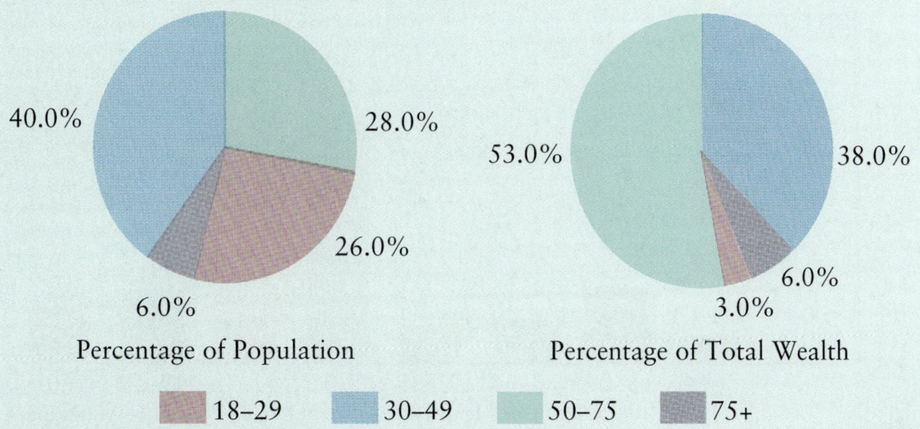

Our model assumes that the elderly, those in the second period of their lives, own all the economy's capital. This is a rough approximation to the U.S. experience. In the U.S., individuals over the age of 50 represent about one-third of the population but own almost 60 percent of private sector net assets.

Source: Board of Governors of the Federal Reserve System

$$K_{t+1} = Na_{t+1} = N(w_t - c_{yt})$$

Thus, the total capital stock at $t + 1$ is simply the number of old people around at time $t + 1$ times the amount each saved when young, $w_t - c_{yt}$. Intuitively, we see that the supply of capital at any time equals the total assets held by all generations alive at that point. In our model, only the old have assets, so total assets held by members of all generations are just the total held by the elderly.

The notion that the elderly hold claims to all the economy's capital is actually not far from the truth, especially if we are willing to stretch the definition of elderly a bit. In the U.S., individuals over age 50 own 59 percent of total private-sector net assets despite making up only 34 percent of the population.[4] Figure 2-2 shows the shares of the 1990 private U.S. wealth owned by different adult age groups. It also shows the percentages of the population represented by those groups.

Since we've assumed, for the moment, that young people work full time, the total labor supply during period t (L_t) can be measured simply by the number of young workers at time t, which is N; thus,

4. By the way, the American Association of Retired Persons—the powerful lobby for America's elderly—counts those over age 50 as among the aged since it sets age 50 as the minimum age required for membership.

Figure 2-3 Distribution of Hours Worked per Week, March, 1993

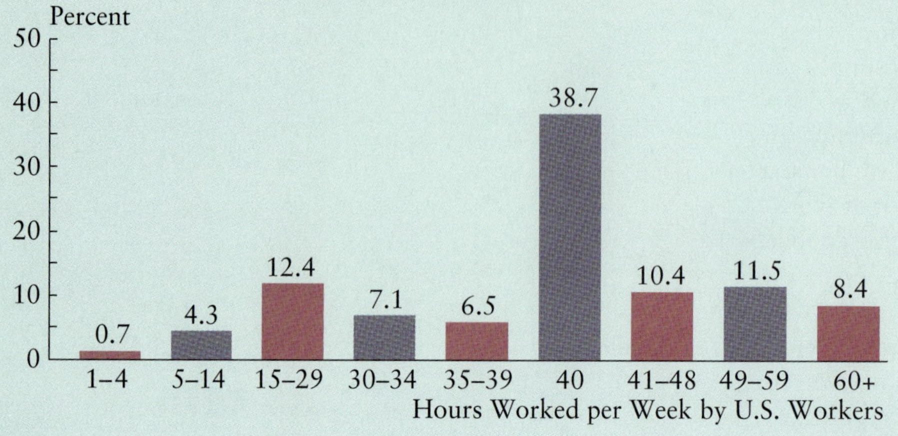

Our model assumes that when people work, they work full time. This is a reasonable approximation to the U.S. situation. Over three-quarters of U.S. workers spend more than 35 hours per week on the job.

Source: U.S. Bureau of Labor Statistics

$$L_t = N$$

In Chapter 1 we measured labor in number of hours. Here we are measuring as one unit of labor the amount of work that one person does in one period (rather than one hour). Since each young person works one period and there are N young people, total labor supply is N. The assumption that when people work they work full time is fairly close to the mark, at least in the U.S. Figure 2-3 shows the distribution of weekly hours worked in March of 1993 by U.S. workers. In that month over three-quarters of all workers spent more than 35 hours per week on the job.

Returning to our two formulas for the supplies of capital and labor, note that there is nothing special about time period t. We could just as well have written the formulas for some other time period; the only difference would have been the time subscript. The formulas for the supplies of capital and labor hold for all time periods. For example, the supply of capital at time t, K_t, is simply N times $(w_{t-1} - c_{yt-1})$, and the supply of labor at time $t - 1$, L_{t-1}, is just N. In period $t + 10$ the supply of capital, K_{t+10}, is N times $(w_{t+9} - c_{yt+9})$, and the supply of labor, L_{t+10}, is N.

So far, the formula for the labor supply is not very interesting.[5] It says that the amount supplied is the same every period. The formula for the supply of

5. A more interesting formula is developed in the Appendix to this chapter.

capital, on the other hand, says that the capital supplied by each member of generation t depends on the wages the person earns and the amount the person consumes when young. Recall that the wage, w_t, is the price paid to labor at the end of period t—the amount that must be paid for the services of a young worker for that period. The size of the wage is the outcome of a market equilibrium in which input supply equals input demand. The wage, then, is determined by market forces and is outside the control of any particular individual. The same is true of the interest rate, r_t, the amount paid to use a unit of capital for one period, which we'll discuss momentarily.

The point at which a typical member of generation t, let's call her Joan, can really exercise control over her saving is in deciding how much to consume when young. At the beginning of period t, Joan must decide how much to consume. With the wage fixed at w_t, this consumption decision also determines how much she saves, $w_t - c_{yt}$, and therefore the amount of assets she carries into old age, a_{t+1}. Given the interest rate, it also determines old-age consumption, which is $a_{t+1}(1 + r_{t+1})$. So a decision about how much to consume when young is simultaneously a decision about how much to save when young and how much to consume when old.

To understand this consumption decision and its implications, consider how much Joan can afford to consume in both periods of her life. We begin by examining her lifetime budget constraint.

THE LIFETIME BUDGET CONSTRAINT

If Joan earns w_t when young, consumes c_{yt}, and saves a_{t+1}, how much will she be able to consume when old? Since she is retired in period $t + 1$, she must rely on the assets she accumulated when young. The maximum amount she can, and will, consume is the principal amount she saved when young, a_{t+1}, plus her total capital (or interest) income earned on that investment, $a_{t+1}r_{t+1}$. Putting this all together, we can determine her consumption when old, c_{ot+1}. (The subscript o denotes old age, and the subscript $t + 1$ reminds us that individuals born at time t are old in period $t + 1$.) In symbols,

$$c_{ot+1} = a_{t+1}(1 + r_{t+1})$$

Let's combine this formula with the one relating assets when old to the amount of saving when young. Specifically, let's substitute $w_t - c_{yt}$ for a_{t+1} in the above equation, and rearrange it:

$$c_{yt} + \frac{c_{ot+1}}{1 + r_{t+1}} = w_t$$

This expression is called the **lifetime budget constraint**, and it connects consumption when young, consumption when old, and the wage and interest rates. It determines all the different combinations of consumption when young and old that a member of generation t can purchase based on her wages and the rate

Lifetime budget constraint
An algebraic description of all combinations of consumption when young and old an individual can purchase, given the wage rate and the rate of return on saving

of return she can earn on her saving. One affordable combination is to consume as much as possible when young and nothing when old. This amounts to setting c_{yt} equal to w_t so that c_{ot+1} equals zero. At the opposite extreme, Joan could save all her wages when young (set c_{yt} equal to zero) and consume $w_t(1 + r_{t+1})$ when old. Of course, there are many intermediate possibilities. We'll see later which possibility is chosen.

Figure 2-4 plots Joan's lifetime budget constraint. To graph the constraint, we use the familiar idea that two points determine a straight line. That is, if we can find two points that satisfy the budget constraint, we can connect them to form a line showing all other points that satisfy it. As we've seen, one combination is $c_{yt} = w_t$ and $c_{ot+1} = 0$. This is shown as point A on the horizontal axis. Another point is $c_{yt} = 0$ and $c_{ot+1} = w_t(1 + r_{t+1})$. This determines point B on the vertical axis. Connecting A and B gives us the lifetime budget constraint shown in Figure 2-4. Notice that all points lying on or southwest of the budget constraint are affordable.

The slope of this budget line is the "rise" divided by the "run." As consumption when young increases from 0 to w_t, consumption when old falls from $w_t(1 + r_{t+1})$ to 0. So, the slope is $-w_t(1 + r_{t+1})/w_t$, which equals $-(1 + r_{t+1})$. It indicates the rate at which a young individual can trade consumption when old for consumption when young. A slope of -1.5, for instance, means that each extra unit of consumption when young requires giving up 1.5 units of consumption when old.

A higher interest rate will shift the vertical axis intercept upward, causing the budget line to rotate in a northeasterly direction around w_t and expanding the affordable combinations of consumption when young and when old. A higher wage rate will also expand consumption opportunities; it will produce an equal percentage increase in both intercepts and shift the budget constraint outward to a position parallel to its original position. Consequently, the lifetime budget constraints for members of other generations will differ if either the wage they earn when young or the rate of return they earn on their assets when old differs from those available to members of generation t.

Although it may seem a bit strange at first, the lifetime budget constraint is exactly analogous to a budget constraint in a static setting faced by a consumer who spends his income Y on, say, apples and bananas. If A and B stand for the amounts of apples and bananas purchased and P_A and P_B are their respective prices, the static budget constraint is

$$P_A A + P_B B = Y$$

In the lifetime budget constraint, lifetime income, w_t, takes the place of current income, and the quantities of consumption when young and old, c_{yt} and c_{ot+1}, take the place of the quantities of apples and bananas consumed. But what are the analogues of the prices P_A and P_B?

From the perspective of a young person, the price of anything is the amount (of corn) he must give up today, at time t, to get it. The price of one unit of con-

Figure 2-4 The Lifetime Budget Constraint

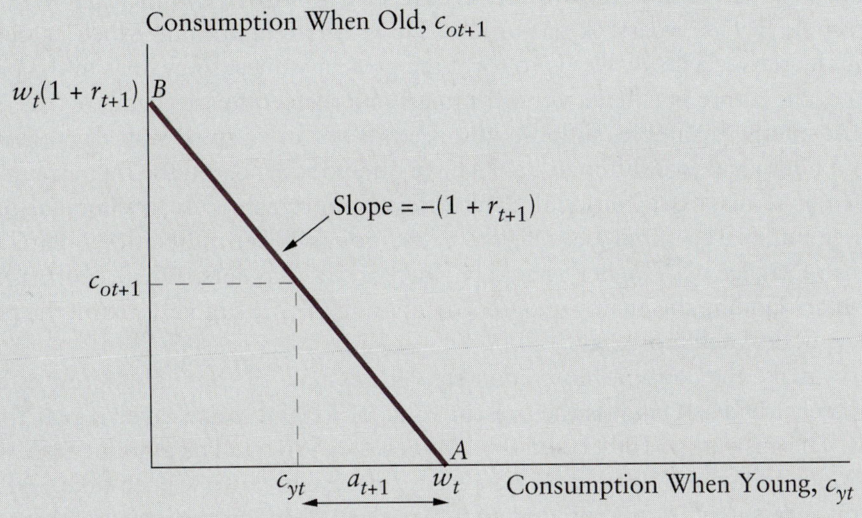

The lifetime budget constraint depicts all combinations of consumption when young and when old that an individual can afford over a lifetime. It is drawn for given values of the wage and interest rate. The constraint slopes downward, indicating that increased consumption when young comes at the cost of reduced consumption when old. The slope of the constraint reflects the amount of consumption when old a person must sacrifice in order to consume one more unit when young.

sumption when old is $1/(1 + r_{t+1})$. Why? To consume one kernel of corn when old at time $t + 1$, a young person needs to put aside $1/(1 + r_{t+1})$ kernels of wage earnings at time t. When invested, this amount will yield, in principal and interest, $1/(1 + r_{t+1})$ kernels times $(1 + r_{t+1})$, or one kernel in the future. So the price, evaluated at time t, of consuming one unit of corn in the future equals (involves giving up) $1/(1 + r_{t+1})$ units at time t.

From the perspective of a young person at time t, the price of a unit of consumption when young is just 1. Why? Because consuming one kernel of corn at time t just costs one kernel of the total kernels earned at time t.

PRESENT VALUES—A DIGRESSION

For a member of generation t, the price $1/(1 + r_{t+1})$ converts quantities of corn tomorrow into their value in the present (which is time t). A shorter way to say "value in the present" is "present value." Learning how to compute present values is extremely important in everyday economic life. Take the case of choosing between two careers. One career, call it A, pays very little early in life, but a lot later on; the other—career B—pays a constant amount each year. Suppose the constant amount paid by career B exceeds the payments in the early years in career A. In later years, A pays more. How do we figure out which career is more lucrative? The answer is to form the present values (the values in the present) of the future payments in both careers and then compare them.

As another example, suppose you need to borrow a fixed sum of money to buy a house and two different banks have offered to lend you the money, but on different terms. First National Bank offers a mortgage with low annual payments, but a large initial fee (referred to as "points"). Second National Bank offers a mortgage with higher annual payments, but no points. Which mortgage is cheaper? Finding the answer requires comparing the present value of all the payments under each mortgage.

To make the concept more concrete, let's assume the annual interest rate is 10 percent and ask what is the present value of \$100 to be received a year from now. The answer is $\$100/(1 + .10) = \$100/(1.1) = \$90.91$. The amount \$90.91 is the value today of \$100 received a year from now because we can take \$90.91 today, invest it at 10 percent, and end up with \$100 in one year. Therefore, having \$90.91 today has the same value as having \$100 a year from now.

Dividing \$100 by one plus the interest rate is known as "discounting." To find its present value, we discount (reduce in size) the \$100 because it will not be received for a year. Indeed, if we had \$100 in the present, we could invest it at 10 percent and end up with \$110 a year from now. Thus, the present value of having \$100 a year from now is not the same as the value of having \$100 today (i.e., it's not \$100).

If the present value of \$100 received a year from now is \$90.91, how much is the present value of \$100 received, say, in three years? To make the problem a bit more interesting, suppose the annual interest rate will be 10 percent for the next two years and 8 percent in the third year. We can compute this present value using a little algebra. Denote the present value of \$100 to be received three years from now as the amount D. Then we know that investing D, as well as accrued interest earned on the investment, for two years at 10 percent and then one year at 8 percent will yield a total amount of \$100 in three years. After one year, the original amount D invested will have grown to $D \times 1.10$; after two years, the amount will be $(D \times 1.10) \times 1.10$; after three years, the amount will be $(D \times 1.10 \times 1.10) \times 1.08 = \$100$. We can use this simple equation to solve for D, the present value of \$100 received in three years: $D = \$100/(1.10 \times 1.10 \times 1.08)$. This value is \$76.52.

Compound interest *Interest earned on interest*

Note that the investment of \$76.52 grows by 30.68 percent to equal \$100 in three years. The 30.68 percent increase is larger than 28.00 percent, the sum of the three annual interest rates. This reflects **compound interest**—the fact that interest is earned on previously accrued interest. Algebraically speaking, compounding refers to the fact that the three interest rates (.10, .10, and .08) are not summed to form a total discount factor of 3.28. Instead, the three discount factors (1.10, 1.10, and 1.08) are multiplied together to form a total discount factor of 1.3068.

THE SAVING DECISION

We have seen that the lifetime budget constraint indicates all the affordable combinations of consumption when young and old. But which combination will a member of generation t choose? The answer depends on the consumer's desires or preferences. We can describe preference about consumption when young versus consumption when old in terms of a *utility function*. A utility function is a happiness meter; the larger a person's utility, the happier she or he is.

Economists sometimes speak of utility being measured in abstract units called utils. They might just as well measure it in number of smiles. Why smiles? Why not? Utility can be measured in any units we choose—in utils, smiles, good vibes, or warm glows. Happiness is a relative concept. It's hard—apparently impossible—for anyone to know precisely how happy anyone else really is. Fortunately, what matters for economic choice is not the absolute level of happiness, but the relative happiness provided by different economic alternatives. Thus, we can think of a utility function as ranking different combinations of consumption when young and old, with a combination producing more smiles ranked above a combination producing fewer smiles.

The utility function we'll use to consider the saving decision has the same Cobb-Douglas form as the production function introduced in Chapter 1:

$$u_t = c_{yt}^{\alpha}\, c_{ot+1}^{1-\alpha}$$

In this equation u_t stands for the utility of a typical member of generation t like Joan. (Recall that all members of a generation are identical and so all have the same utility function.) Joan's utility level (her happiness) depends on the amounts she consumes when young and old and the preference parameter, α. The more Joan consumes when young and old, the happier she is. The parameter α determines how Joan feels about consuming when young versus consuming when old. The larger α is, the more important consumption when young is to Joan's utility and the less important consumption when old. Thus, α determines Joan's *time preference*—how much she prefers consuming when young to consuming when old. For the utility function to make sense, more consumption in either her youth or her old age must make Joan better off. Accordingly, α must lie between zero and one. Otherwise, the exponent on either c_{yt} or c_{ot+1} would be negative, meaning that either more consumption when young or more consumption when old would result in lower utility. In this and future chapters we generally consider a value of α equal to .5.

Given her utility function, Joan's saving decision amounts to determining her consumption combination, which is a particular amount of consumption when young and a particular amount when old. She considers consumption combinations that satisfy her lifetime budget constraint until she finds the combination that gives her the most utility. As we'll show very shortly in general terms and in precise terms in footnote 7, Joan's search for the best affordable combination always leads to choices of consumption when young and old that satisfy the following two formulas:

$$c_{yt} = \alpha w_t$$
$$c_{ot+1} = (1 - \alpha) w_t (1 + r_{t+1})$$

According to these formulas, Joan chooses to consume when young the fraction α of her lifetime labor income (w_t in this case). Since she earns w_t when young and consumes αw_t, Joan saves $w_t - \alpha w_t = (1 - \alpha)w_t$. This saving is the amount of assets she brings into her old age—i.e., $a_{t+1} = (1 - \alpha)w_t$. When Joan is old at time $t + 1$, she consumes her assets plus the interest earned on them, just as the formula for c_{ot+1} says. Note that although Joan's old-age consumption depends on the interest rate she receives when old, her consumption when young does not. As the Appendix shows, with some modifications to the model, consumption when young may also depend on the interest rate.

Since a_{t+1} equals $(1 - \alpha)w_t$, and the total supply of capital at time $t + 1$ equals Na_{t+1}, we have

$$K_{t+1} = N(1 - \alpha) w_t$$

According to this equation, the economy's total supply of capital available at time $t + 1$ equals the number of old people at time $t + 1$, N, multiplied by the amount of assets, $(1 - \alpha)w_t$, brought into old age by each of these old people who were young at time t. The equation connects the wage in period t to the capital stock in the following period. Hence, we see how the dynamic supply of capital depends on the dynamic evolution of the wage rate.

A Closer Look at the Consumption and Saving Decision

One way Joan could choose the affordable consumption combination that makes her most happy is by mental trial and error. But this is quite tedious and ultimately unnecessary. Joan can simply use the two formulas for consumption when young and old to tell her exactly how much to consume in those two periods, given specific values of the wage and interest rate.

Indifference curve *A curve that shows all combinations of two commodities that yield the same level of utility*

Marginal rate of substitution (MRS) *The rate at which an individual is willing to substitute one good for another while maintaining utility at a constant level; the slope of an indifference curve at a particular point*

To understand these two formulas, consider Figure 2-5, which shows Joan's **indifference curves**. The curves are based on her utility function. Each curve refers to a particular level of utility and shows all consumption combinations that produce that level.

Although we don't show them, there is an indifference curve running through every combination of c_{yt} and c_{ot+1}. Indifference curves lying farther to the northeast correspond to higher levels of utility. The reason is that Joan prefers more consumption to less, and as we move from one indifference curve to another in a northeasterly direction, we are increasing the amounts of both consumption when young and consumption when old, thus raising utility.

The slope of Joan's indifference curve is called the **marginal rate of substitution (MRS)**, because it tells us the rate at which Joan is willing to substitute consumption when young for consumption when old. To see this, consider point A, where the slope of the indifference curve equals –1.5. Starting from point A, the

Figure 2-5 Indifference Curves

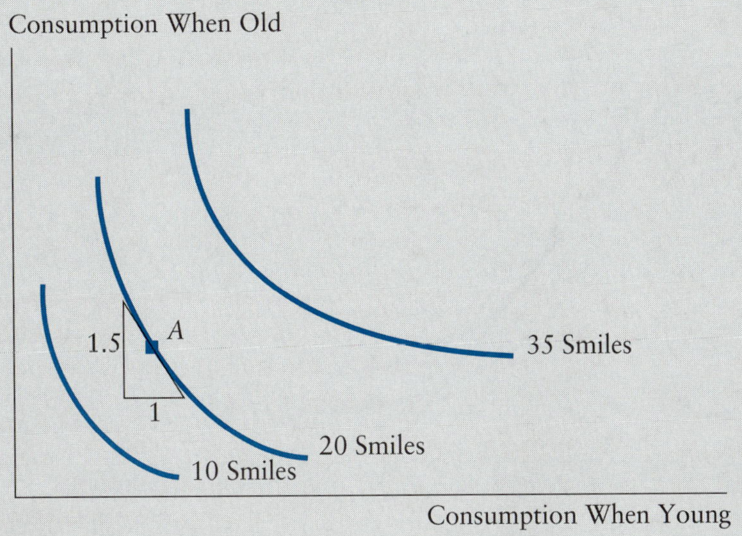

An indifference curve shows all combinations of consumption when young and when old that give a person a particular amount of utility. There is an indifference curve running though each possible consumption combination; three typical examples are shown here. Curves farther to the northeast indicate higher levels of utility.

The slope, or steepness, of an indifference curve at a particular point is called the marginal rate of substitution (MRS). It indicates the rate at which the individual is willing to substitute consumption when young for consumption when old while maintaining the same level of happiness. At point *A*, the MRS of −1.5 indicates that the individual can give up 1.5 units of consumption when old in return for 1 unit when young and remain equally happy.

MRS of −1.5 means that Joan is willing to give up 1.5 units of consumption when old in order to get an additional unit when young, as she will remain equally happy. Stated differently, the rate at which Joan is willing to exchange consumption when old for consumption when young is 1.5 to 1.[6]

6. For the Cobb-Douglas utility function, the marginal rate of substitution is $-\alpha c_{ot+1}/(1-\alpha)c_{yt}$. If you know calculus, you can check this by totally differentiating the utility function, setting the total differential equal to zero (since utility does not change along an indifference curve), and solving the resulting equation for dc_{ot+1}/dc_{yt}, which is the MRS.

Figure 2-6 Utility Maximization

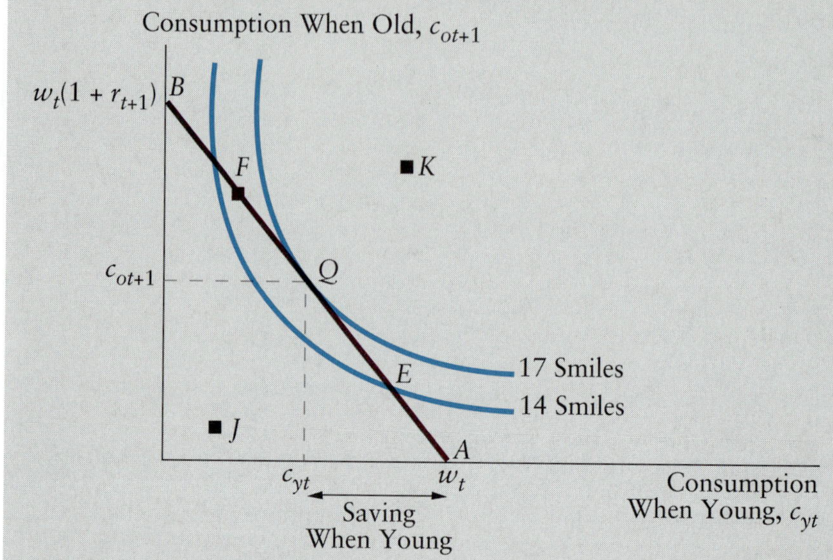

An individual maximizes utility by choosing the consumption combination on the budget constraint yielding the highest level of utility (i.e., on the highest attainable indifference curve). In this figure, the utility-maximizing combination is c_{yt} and c_{ot+1}, as shown at point *Q*. At *Q*, the indifference curve for 17 smiles is tangent to (just touches) the budget constraint. The choice of point *Q* also determines saving when young, the difference between the wage earned when young, w_t, and first-period consumption, c_{yt}.

A Graphical Depiction of Joan's Consumption and Saving Decision

Let's now combine Joan's indifference curves and her lifetime budget constraint in Figure 2-6 to consider her life-cycle consumption and saving decision. In looking at this diagram, Joan first realizes that she wants to choose a combination of c_{yt} and c_{ot+1} that is on her budget constraint, *AB*. A combination such as point *K*, which lies above the constraint, is not affordable. An affordable combination such as *J*, which lies below the constraint, will not be chosen either. Even though *J* is affordable, there are other affordable points *on* the constraint, such as *E* or *F*, that include more consumption when young *and* more when old. If she prefers more consumption to less, Joan will always select a point *on* her lifetime budget constraint.

Joan will choose a point on her budget line, but which point will it be? We assume that her goal is to maximize her happiness, so it will be a point on her highest attainable indifference curve. The optimal point is Q, where the indifference curve of 17 smiles is tangent to (just touches and has the same slope as) the budget constraint. Note that all other points on the lifetime budget constraint, such as E and F, lie on lower indifference curves and reflect lower levels of happiness. The values of c_{yt} and c_{ot+1} corresponding to point Q determine the optimal consumption combination for Joan and other members of generation t.[7] These values are the ones dictated by our two equations. They also determine each individual's first-period saving—the difference between wage income and consumption when young. This saving is shown as the distance $w_t - c_{yt}$, measured along the horizontal axis. In choosing to consume when young and old at point Q rather than point A (which indicates Joan's wage earnings when young), Joan smooths her consumption over her lifetime. She consumes less than her income when young; she consumes more than her income when old.

THE DEPENDENCE OF SAVING ON INTEREST AND WAGE RATES

Our next task is to consider how Joan's saving decision depends on the wage she earns when young and the interest she earns on her assets when old. We'll focus first on the effects of a higher wage, holding the interest rate fixed. Figure 2-7 shows how a higher wage (w_t' rather than w_t) would affect Joan's consumption combination. The higher wage causes an outward shift of Joan's original budget constraint to a parallel position. Intuitively, the higher her lifetime earnings, the more Joan can afford to consume when young and when old. The new budget constraint is parallel to the original constraint because the same interest rate determines the slopes of both.

As our formulas for Joan's consumption and saving decision indicate, Joan now consumes $\alpha w_t'$ when young and $(1 - \alpha)w_t'(1 + r_{t+1})$ when old; she saves $(1 - \alpha)w_t'$ when young. Since w_t' exceeds w_t, the higher wage leads Joan to consume more both when young and when old and to save more when young. The increases in Joan's consumption when young and old are referred to as **income effects**—the effects of having more income (more precisely, a larger present value of lifetime income) on consumption decisions.

Income effect
The effect of an increase in income on the quantity demanded of a commodity, holding relative prices constant

Next, let's examine the effect of a higher interest rate. Note that the relative price of consuming when young in terms of consuming when old is $1 + r_{t+1}$. Intuitively, we see that the higher the interest rate, the more expensive it is to consume when young because each unit consumed when young requires forgoing

7. The slope of the budget line is $-(1 + r_{t+1})$, and the slope of the indifference curve is the marginal rate of substitution, $-\alpha c_{ot+1}/(1 - \alpha)c_{yt}$. At optimal point Q, the two are equal, so $1 + r_{t+1} = \alpha c_{ot+1}/(1 - \alpha)c_{yt}$. This equation (the tangency condition) is one condition Joan needs to satisfy in choosing her best combination, c_{yt} and c_{ot+1}. The other is the lifetime budget constraint. If we solve for consumption when young from one of these two relationships and substitute in the other, we end up with the formula for consumption when young: $c_{yt} = \alpha w_t$. Plugging this formula into the budget constraint gives us the demand relationship for consumption when old: $c_{ot+1} = (1 - \alpha)w_t(1 + r_{t+1})$. These relationships have the property that the shares of lifetime income spent on consumption when young and when old equal the corresponding exponents in the utility function.

Figure 2-7 Income Effects

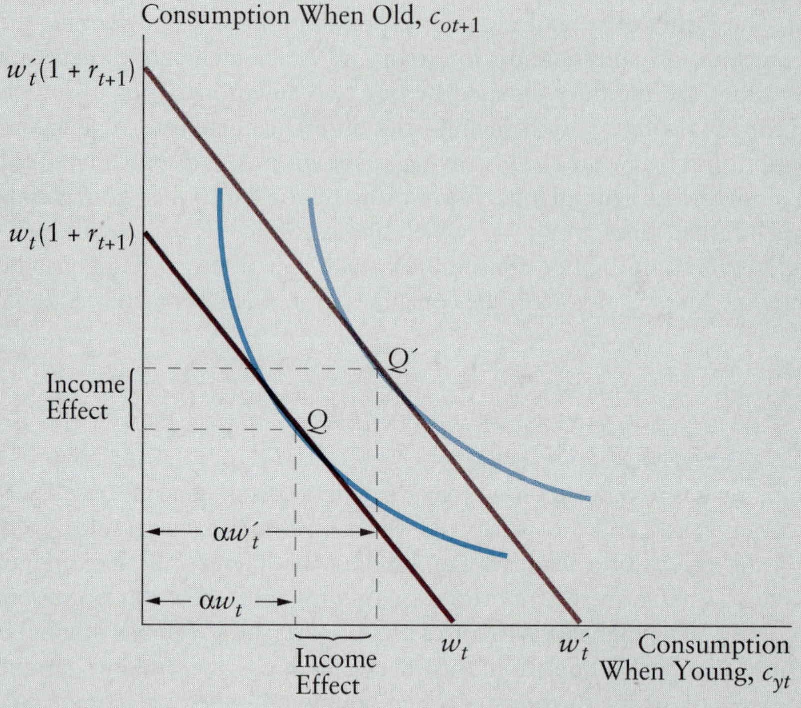

As the wage rate rises, the budget constraint shifts outward to a parallel position. Following an increase in the wage rate from w_t to w'_t, point Q is no longer the utility-maximizing consumption point. Point Q' is the new best combination, as the individual attains a higher indifference curve. The income effects measure how much consumption when young and consumption when old rise as a result of the higher lifetime income. Consumption when young increases from w_t to w'_t. Consumption when old also rises.

Substitution effect *The effect of an increase in the relative price of a commodity on the quantity demanded, holding utility constant*

more consumption when old. To be precise, each unit consumed when young can otherwise be saved, producing an additional $1 + r_{t+1}$ units of consumption when old.

Substitution effects are changes in consumption due purely to a change in the relative price (the ratio of prices) of different commodities.[8] When the relative price of a commodity rises, the substitution effect leads the individual to

8. As we'll see, income and substitution effects are important to our discussion in Chapter 7 of distortionary fiscal policy—government policy that alters saving or work incentives.

Figure 2-8 The Impact of a Rise in the Interest Rate: Income and Substitution Effects

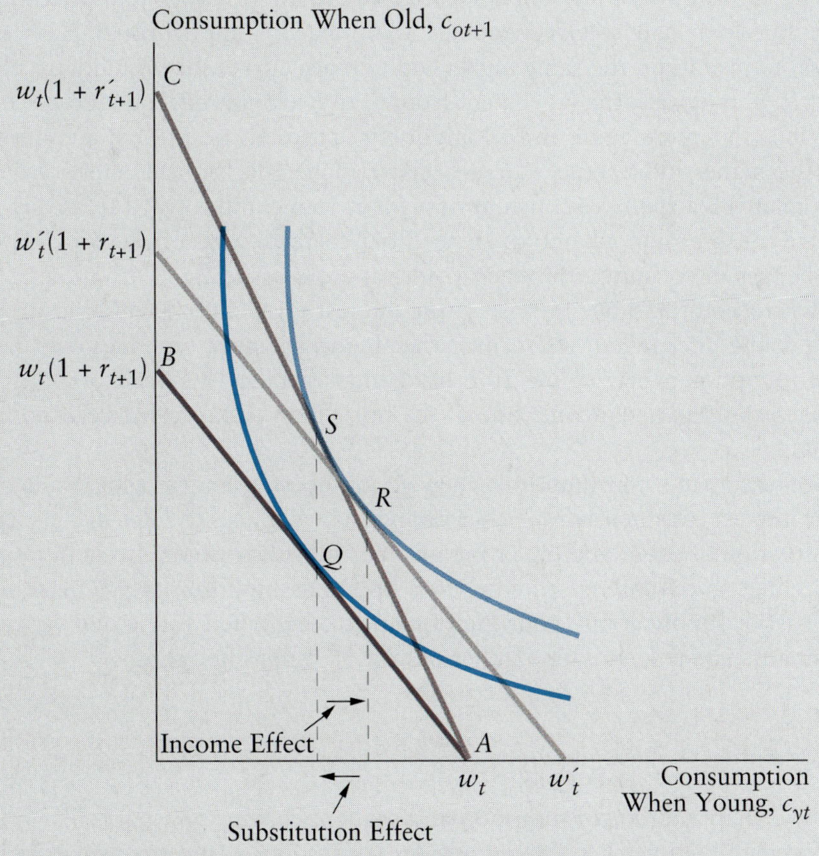

An increase in the interest rate rotates the budget constraint, permitting the individual to consume more when young and when old. However, the higher interest rate makes consumption when young relatively more expensive and leads the individual to substitute consumption when old for consumption when young.

In this figure, the optimal consumption point changes from *Q* to *S*; the individual consumes more when old, but no more when young. The movement from *Q* to *S* may be decomposed into an income effect (*Q* to *R*) and a substitution effect (*R* to *S*).

purchase less of that good and more of other goods—i.e., to substitute away from the relatively more expensive good. Figure 2-8 shows Joan's reaction to a higher interest rate (relative price of consumption when young). The higher interest rate increases Joan's consumption opportunities by rotating her budget constraint outward about its horizontal axis intercept. Joan can now afford to consume more both when young and when old. However, she chooses point *S* on her new constraint, which involves the same amount of consumption when young (namely, αw_t), that she chose at point *Q* on her initial constraint.

The substitution effect explains why. If the interest rate Joan faces hadn't risen, but Joan had received enough additional income (through, let's say, a bonus) to just attain the same higher indifference curve, she would have chosen point *R*. In that case, the movement from *Q* to *R* would reflect an income effect. But when the interest rate rises, Joan doesn't need any additional income to attain the higher indifference curve because of her decision to substitute away from relatively expensive consumption when young and toward relatively inexpensive consumption when old. Hence, Joan's substitution effects are defined as the changes in consumption when young and old associated with moving from point *R* to point *S*. Since the rise in the interest rate leaves Joan's consumption when young unchanged, we surmise that Joan's substitution effect with respect to consumption when young (the horizontal distance between points *R* and *S*) exactly offsets her income effect (the horizontal distance between points *Q* and *R*).

Because Joan's consumption when young doesn't change as a result of the lower interest rate, neither does her saving. As we'll discuss later in the chapter, this situation of equal and offsetting income and substitution effects in response to a change in the interest rate depends on the assumptions we've made about Joan's labor supply. Joan's consumption and saving when young *will* depend on the interest rate if Joan works in her old age as well as her youth.

NATIONAL SAVING EQUALS NATIONAL INVESTMENT

We have analyzed the consumption and saving behavior of a particular generation over its lifetime. Let's now consider consumption and saving by both the young and the old at the same point in time and show that their combined saving equals the economy's total investment. In other words, we will show that the economy's national saving equals its national investment. This equality simply reflects the fact that the real assets saved by individuals in our model are made available to firms in the form of additional capital. Additions to the capital stock, as we've seen, are called investment.

We can always determine a country's national saving by subtracting its total consumption from its total output, Y_t. In our model total consumption during a period of time is just the sum of consumption expenditures by the young and the old. Since there are *N* young people who each consume c_{yt} and *N* old people who each consume c_{ot}, total consumption expenditures at time *t* equals *N* times c_{yt} plus *N* times c_{ot}.

Let's use S_t to indicate total national saving. Then the formula for national saving is just

$$S_t = Y_t - Nc_{yt} - Nc_{ot}$$

Our goal is to show that S_t equals national investment at time t, I_t. By definition, investment equals the change in the capital stock, $K_{t+1} - K_t$,[9] so we really need to show that $S_t = K_{t+1} - K_t$. This is easy. First, as we'll explain in the next chapter, total output is fully paid out to the young in the form of wage payments and to the old in the form of capital (or interest) income:

$$Y_t = Nw_t + r_tK_t$$

In words, output equals the total number of workers, N, times the wage payment to each worker plus the total amount of capital times the interest payment to each unit of capital. Substituting this expression for output into our previous formula for national saving and rearranging leads to

$$S_t = N(w_t - c_{yt}) + (r_tK_t - Nc_{ot})$$

This equation says that total national saving is the sum of the saving by the young plus the saving by the old. Next, recall that $w_t - c_{yt}$ equals a_{t+1}, the assets the young at time t bring into their old age, and c_{ot} equals $a_t(1 + r_t)$, the principal plus interest earned by the old at time t on their assets, a_t. Because $K_t = Na_t$, we can see that the saving by the old, $r_tK_t - Nc_{ot}$, equals $Na_tr_t - Na_t(1 + r_t)$, which simplifies to $-Na_t$, a negative number. The old *dis*save because they consume more than their (interest) income.

Returning to the expression for national saving and recalling that $K_{t+1} = Na_{t+1}$, we end up with

$$S_t = Na_{t+1} - Na_t = K_{t+1} - K_t = I_t$$

So we've shown that national saving does indeed equal national investment. We've also shown that national saving equals the economy's net asset accumulation between times t and $t + 1$; specifically, national saving equals the accumulation of assets (the saving) by the young, Na_{t+1}, less the decumulation of assets (the dissaving) by the old, Na_t. The young start at time t with zero assets and end up at time $t + 1$ with total assets of Na_{t+1}. The old start at time t with total assets of Na_t and end up at time $t + 1$ with zero assets.

Case Study: The Decline in U.S. Saving and Its Impact on Domestic Investment

A country's rate of saving—its national saving as a fraction of its gross domestic product (GDP)—provides a comprehensive measure of its saving behavior. Since assets are held in the form of capital and since saving is the change in assets, understanding saving is central to understanding changes over time in the supply of capital. In the U.S. the national saving rate has declined considerably since

9. Recall that we've assumed that capital does not depreciate. Otherwise, as we learned in Chapter 1, $I_t = K_{t+1} - K_t + D_t$. The equality of saving and investment also holds if D_t is positive.

1980. Between 1950 and 1980 the rate averaged 17 percent per year. After 1980 it averaged 15 percent per year, and since 1985 it has averaged only 13 percent per year.

What explains this almost one-quarter decline in the rate of saving? Part of the explanation may involve the slowdown in the rate of productivity growth discussed in the previous chapter. When productivity grows at a slower rate so do wages, leaving younger workers with less income out of which to save. In our model it is the young workers whose positive saving counterbalances the dissaving by the elderly. But young Americans are not the only ones saving less. Recent studies suggest that old and young Americans alike have reduced their saving.[10] Research now underway should help clarify how much of the precipitous drop in U.S. saving can be explained by factors such as the slowdown in technological progress, changes in demographics, changes in the government's fiscal and monetary policies, and changes in basic preferences about consuming today versus tomorrow (which we capture in our model with the parameter α).

What are the implications of lower saving for investment? As we've seen, national saving equals national investment. In a closed economy (one not open to international trade and investment), all of a country's saving is invested at home. So national investment equals domestic investment—the increase in the domestic capital stock. As we'll clarify in Chapters 5 and 6, in an open economy some of the country's saving may be invested abroad. In this case national investment still refers to the increase in capital, but now it refers to the increase in the domestic capital stock plus the increase in a country's net ownership of foreign capital. Thus, in the case of an open economy, national investment is the sum of domestic investment (e.g. investment in the U.S.) plus net foreign investment (U.S. investment abroad minus foreign investment in the U.S.). Since national saving equals national investment, which, in turn, equals the sum of domestic investment plus net foreign investment, lower national saving doesn't necessarily mean lower domestic investment. It could simply mean lower net foreign investment.

Figure 2-9 graphs U.S. national saving and U.S. domestic investment, each expressed as a percentage of U.S. GDP, for the years from 1950 through 1993. Note that although U.S. national saving and domestic investment have moved roughly in tandem over time, they have rarely been equal. The difference between the two is the net foreign investment just mentioned.

Since the early 1980s U.S. net foreign investment has been negative—meaning that foreigners have been investing more in the U.S. than Americans have been investing abroad.[11] Indeed, in the years 1986–1988 foreigners were responsible for financing almost one-fifth of all the new capital acquired by U.S. firms. Since then net foreign investment has declined, with the result that U.S.

10. See, for example, Barry Bosworth, Gary Burtless, and John Sabelhaus, "The Decline in Saving: Some Microeconomic Evidence," *Brookings Papers on Economic Activity* (1991).

11. We'll discuss the determinants of net foreign investment in Chapter 6.

Figure 2-9 U.S. Rates of National Saving and Domestic Investment, 1950–1993

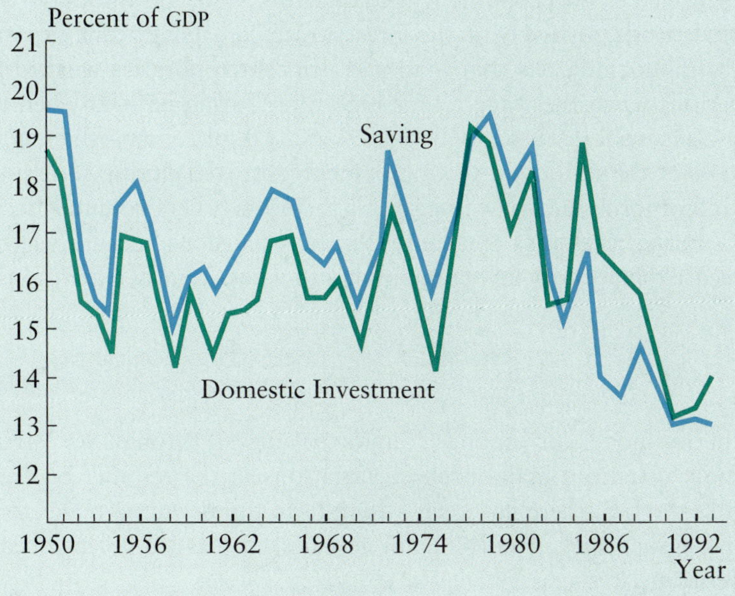

The text demonstrates that national saving must equal national investment. Since the early 1980s, there has been a significant decline in national saving and, thus, in national investment. National investment is the sum of domestic investment and net foreign investment. U.S. net foreign investment, the vertical distance between national saving and domestic investment, has been negative in recent years; foreigners have been investing more in the U.S. than Americans have been investing abroad.

Source: *Economic Report of the President*, 1994

domestic investment is being financed primarily by U.S. national saving. Since this saving is fairly low, so too is U.S. domestic investment.

EXPANDING THE MODEL TO INCLUDE VARIABLE LABOR SUPPLY

Up to this point our model has not incorporated any explanation for changes in labor supply. Although we will use this simple model, with labor supply fixed, throughout most of the book, we show in the Appendix how to incorporate variable labor supply into the model. We do this, first, by letting individuals work in old age as well as in their youth and, second, by letting them choose how much to work in both periods.

The expanded version of our model tells us a number of things. First, the amounts of leisure enjoyed when young and old, and, therefore, the amounts of labor supplied, depend on the wage rate when young, the wage rate when old, and the interest rate. If wage and interest rates change through time, the amount of labor supplied to the economy will change too. Also, the amount of saving by the young depends positively on the interest rate, r_{t+1}. Finally, the expanded version of the model indicates that Joan and her contemporaries will work harder during periods when the wage rate is high than during periods when the wage rate is low. As we'll discuss in Chapters 4 and 10, one view—the *real business cycle* view—of the reduction in employment observed during recessions relies on this kind of formula. According to this theory, workers voluntarily choose to work less during recessions and more during expansions because wages during recessions are temporarily low compared with wages during expansions.

Case Study: The Trend Toward Early Retirement in the United States

Old age in our model corresponds roughly to ages 50 through 80. Variations in labor supply when old mainly reflect variations in the number of years spent working. In the U.S. there has been a long-term trend among males to retire at earlier and earlier ages. The trend for females, at least in recent decades, has been to retire at later ages.

Figure 2-10 shows how male and female *labor force participation rates* have changed since 1950 for the age groups 55 to 64 and 65 and over. A labor force participation rate is defined as the fraction of a specified population that is either employed or seeking employment. Figure 2-10 indicates that changes in postwar labor force participation have been truly remarkable. Take, for example, the participation rate of males age 65 and over. In 1950 this rate was 46 percent, but by 1990 it was only 16 percent. Or consider females aged 55 to 64. Their rate almost doubled from 27 percent in 1950 to 49 percent in 1990.

Why are males retiring earlier and females later? The answer may lie in income and substitution effects analogous to those mentioned earlier. In the past 40 years government transfer programs, particularly Social Security, have raised the incomes of older Americans and may, through the income effect, have induced them to "purchase" more leisure. This income effect explanation for earlier retirement of American males should also hold for American females. But we know females have generally been working more, not less, in their older ages.

If the income effect from Social Security has been inducing earlier retirement of both males and females, is there something else that has been inducing females to work more in their old age? The answer may be the substitution effect arising from recent increases in the wages of females. As we describe in the Appendix, where we add variable labor supply to our model, the wage not only tells us what people earn from working; it also tells us the opportunity cost of not working—i.e., of enjoying leisure. So when the wage rises, the cost (or price) of enjoying leisure rises as well, and workers have an incentive to substitute

Figure 2-10 Labor Force Participation Rates for Older Males and Females, 1950–1992

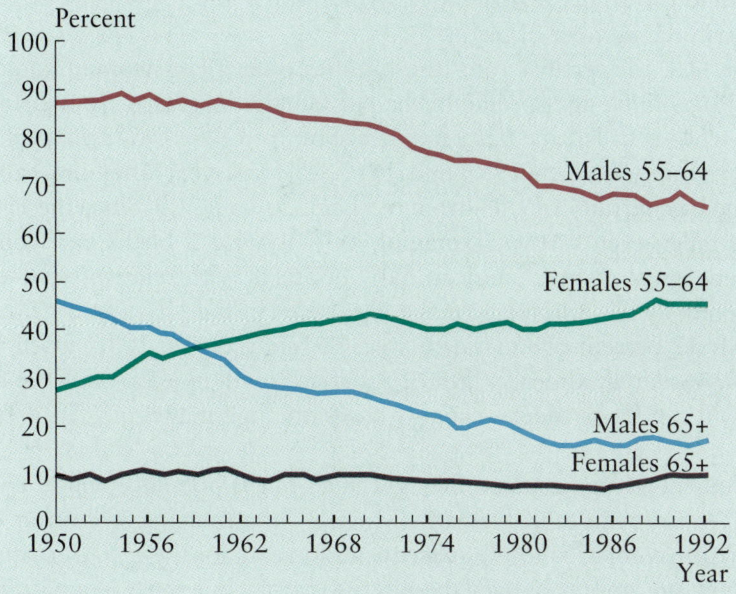

Since 1950 there has been a long-term trend in which males have retired at earlier ages and females have retired at later ages. These trends are reflected in the declining labor force participation rates for men aged 55–64 and aged 65 and over. The rates for females aged 55–64 have increased over the period. These changes may reflect a common income effect but different substitution effects.

away from enjoying leisure toward working more and, therefore, consuming more goods and services.

Since 1980 the ratio of the median weekly wages of females employed full time to those of males employed full time has risen from .63 to .73. So the propensity of males to retire earlier may reflect an income effect for males that exceeds their substitution effect, whereas for females the opposite may be the case.

Case Study: The Worldwide Demographic Transition and the Relative Supplies of Capital and Labor

Another way of expanding our model to encompass variation in labor supply is to allow the population sizes of generations to differ. In the real world neither the relative sizes of different generations nor the absolute sizes of countries' populations remain constant. Indeed, there is a remarkable demographic transition currently underway in which the average ages of the populations in the leading industrialized countries are slowly, but steadily, rising. This reflects the very large increase in the number of children born in the U.S., Western Europe, and Japan in the 20 or so years after World War II and the equally large decline thereafter in the number of births.

In the U.S. the fertility rate (the number of births a woman could expect based on prevailing age-specific births per female) increased from 2.9 in 1946, the year what is called the *baby boom* began, to 3.8 in 1957, the peak year of the baby boom. Between 1957 and 1965, the first year after the baby boom ended, the U.S. fertility rate fell from 3.8 back down to 2.9. Since the 1960s, fertility has fallen even further, averaging only about 1.8 births per woman. Because there are so many American baby boomers with relatively few children, baby boomers will continue to make big waves in the U.S. age distribution. In 1990, only 12 percent of Americans were 65 and older. In 2030, when the baby boomers are retired, almost a fifth of Americans will be 65 or older and almost a third will be 55 or older—roughly the same age makeup as in present-day Florida!

As Figure 2-11 makes clear, the "graying" of the populace will be even more pronounced in Japan and Germany. Most of Japan's aging will occur over the next 20 years, compared to the subsequent 20 years for the U.S. Germany's population will age smoothly over the next 40 years, but more dramatically than that of either the U.S. or Japan. By 2030, almost one-quarter of the German population is projected to exceed age 65.

The low fertility rates of recent decades will also greatly affect population growth in the industrialized nations. Between 1990 and 2030 the total U.S. population is expected to grow by 51.8 million—only a 21 percent total increase. This compares with a 64 percent increase between 1950 and 1990. Although U.S. population growth over the next 40 years is projected to be small, it will nonetheless be positive. Japan's population, in contrast, is expected to remain essentially fixed in size over the next 40 years. And Germany's population is actually projected to fall by 11 percent by 2030!

Projections are projections, and a lot can change in 40 years. Still, it is worth asking how these demographic changes may change the relative supplies of capital and labor in the future. Recall that labor productivity depends on the capital-labor ratio. Demographic change that raises this ratio will raise labor productivity and improve living standards. In our model the capital-labor ratio at any given time equals the assets per old person multiplied by the number of old people, divided by the number of young people (who are also the workers). That is, the capital-labor ratio equals the amount of assets per old person times the ratio of the old to the young. So far we've assumed that the ratio of the old to the young is one. But if this ratio rises, it will raise the economy's capital-labor ratio, ignoring any associated changes that might arise in assets per old person.[12]

12. As we'll see in Chapter 3, the aging of society is likely to be associated with higher wages and, thus, higher assets per old person, which equal $(1 - \alpha)$ times wages.

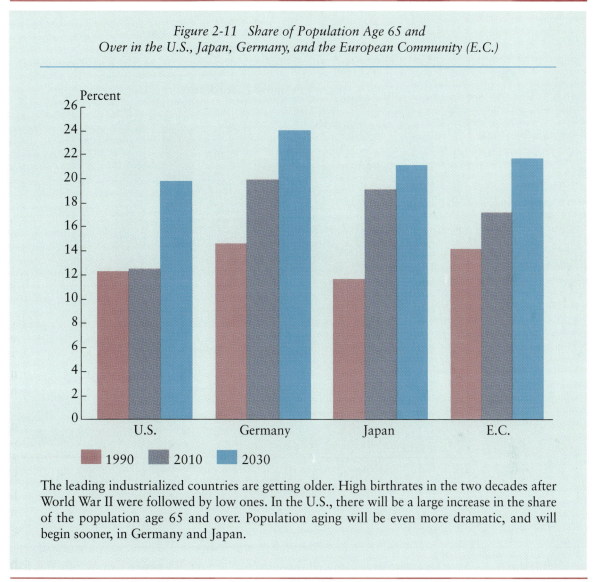

Figure 2-11 Share of Population Age 65 and Over in the U.S., Japan, Germany, and the European Community (E.C.)

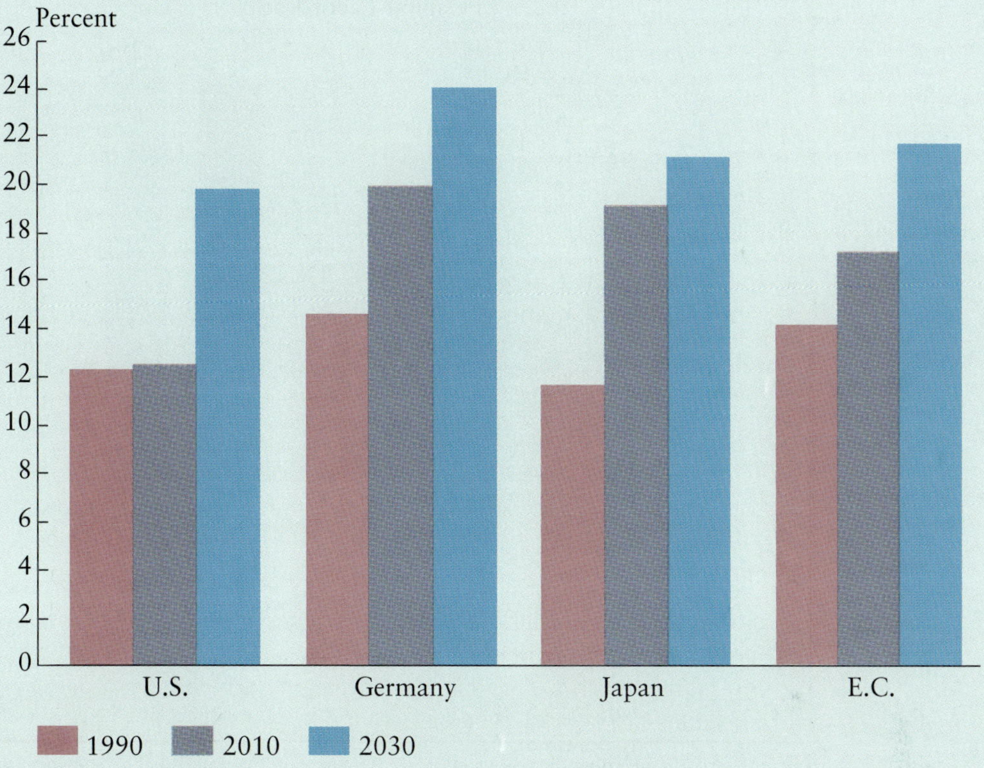

The leading industrialized countries are getting older. High birthrates in the two decades after World War II were followed by low ones. In the U.S., there will be a large increase in the share of the population age 65 and over. Population aging will be even more dramatic, and will begin sooner, in Germany and Japan.

Source: R. Bulato, E. Bos, P. W. Stephens, and M. T. Vu, *World Population Projections* 1989–1990 ed.

Figure 2-12 shows how the impending changes in the U.S. age distribution will alter the ratio of U.S. household wealth relative to labor over the next 40 years, ignoring any changes over time in net asset holdings by age. According to the figure, the U.S. capital-labor ratio will increase by almost 30 percent by the year 2030 simply as a result of demographic change.

Figure 2-12 Projected Growth in the U.S. Capital-Labor Ratio Due to Population Aging

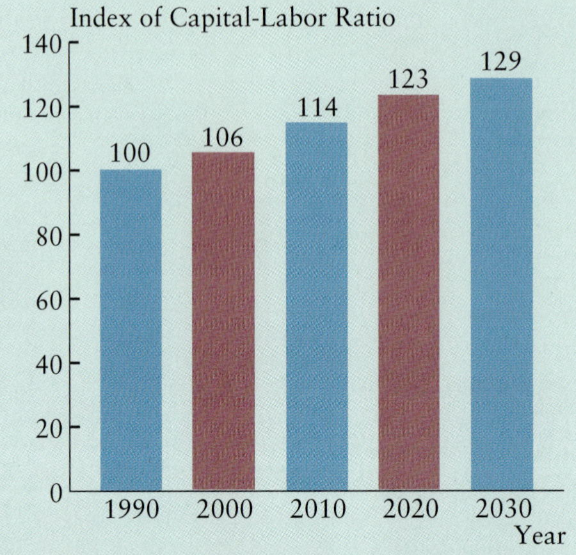

The capital-labor ratio will rise as the U.S. population ages. The reason is that there will be more old people (who own capital) relative to young people (who supply labor).

Source: Board of Governors of the Federal Reserve System and Bureau of Labor Statistics

Chapter Summary

1. This chapter examined the supply of inputs. We began by pointing out that the ultimate owners and suppliers of labor and capital are households. Households control the quantity and quality of labor they supply to the marketplace. They also decide how much of their income to save—i.e., how much of their income to spend acquiring assets.

2. For the economy as a whole, the capital stock is simply the total of its real assets. These real assets are directly owned either by households or by businesses. Households own business capital indirectly through their roles as proprietors and partners in unincorporated businesses and as stockholders of incorporated businesses. In the U.S. about half of the capital stock is directly owned by households.

3. In our simple two-period life-cycle model, individuals work full time when young and are retired when old. Hence, the supply of labor depends on the number of young workers at a point in time. The supply of capital is determined

by the amount of assets the elderly accumulated in the previous period when they were young.

4. The lifetime budget constraint indicates all the different combinations of consumption when young and old that are affordable given the individual's earnings when young and old. Derivation of the lifetime budget constraint leads to the introduction of the concepts of present value and discounting.

5. Individuals in our model decide how much to consume when young and old by determining the indifference curve that is just tangent to their lifetime budget constraint. The resulting decision about how much to consume when young implies a decision about how much to save when young. That, in turn, determines the assets accumulated for old age.

6. Labor supply is fixed in the simple version of our model, but the model can easily be expanded to include the choice of how much to work when young and old. As shown in the Appendix, these choices depend on the prevailing and prospective wage rates and interest rates.

7. In our simple model with fixed first-period labor supply, the young consume a fraction α of their wages. Higher interest rates do not affect consumption when young because of offsetting income and substitution effects. As shown in the Appendix, the interest rate will influence consumption and saving when young if we expand the model to permit second-period labor supply. Thus, the supplies of capital and labor will, in general, depend on the values of both the wage and interest rate.

8. We used our model to consider not only the saving done by individuals but also aggregate, or national, saving. Specifically, we derived the fundamental identity that national saving equals national investment. In recent years the U.S. saving rate has been about three-quarters of the average annual rate observed between 1950 and 1979. The decline in U.S. national saving has not only meant less national investment. It has also meant less domestic investment.

9. Understanding why Americans are choosing to save less and, therefore, to supply less capital is an important challenge for economic research. So too is understanding precisely why American males are supplying less labor at the same time American females are supplying more labor.

10. Demographics also play an important role in determining an economy's supply of capital and the ratio of its capital stock to its labor force. In our model, extended to consider changes through time in generation sizes, a decline in the number of young people relative to the number of old people raises the capital-labor ratio. Because of postwar baby booms, a decline in the working share of the population is underway in the U.S., Japan, and Western Europe. This demographic transition should raise capital-labor ratios in these countries in the decades ahead. Absent the demographic transition that is slowing the growth in the U.S. labor force, the U.S. capital-labor ratio would likely decline as a result of the low U.S. rate of saving.

Key Concepts

Life-cycle model
Present value discounting
National saving
National investment

Human capital
Real assets
Financial assets
Lifetime budget constraint
Compound interest
Indifference curve
Marginal rate of substitution (MRS)
Substitution effect
Income effect

Review Questions

1. What is *human capital*? Who owns human capital? What factors determine the amount of available human capital?
2. Who owns *physical capital*? What is the difference between direct ownership and indirect ownership of physical capital? Give an example of each.
3. What is the difference between *real assets* and *financial assets*? How can the income generated by a real asset represent both a financial *asset* and a financial *liability*? How is a country's *domestic net worth* calculated?
4. Give two definitions of the term "saving."
5. In the two-period life-cycle model, what activities do *young people* undertake? What activities do *old people* undertake?
6. Write the life-cycle model variables representing consumption, the wage, the interest rate (return on capital), and the number of young people and of old people. Use those variables to define a young person's saving; an old person's assets; the total labor force; the total capital stock; an old person's consumption. Be careful to use appropriate and consistent time subscripts in each case.
7. In what sense is a young person's decision about how much to spend when young also a decision about how much to save when young and how much to consume when old?
8. Use the symbols of the model to write an individual's *lifetime budget constraint*. Which variables in the constraint are outside an individual's control? Over which variables can an individual exercise choice? Describe in words the information provided by the lifetime budget constraint. What does a graph of the budget constraint look like?
9. What is the *present value* of a future payment? To what does the term *discounting* refer?
10. What information does a *utility function* provide? How is the *Cobb-Douglas* utility function written for present and future consumption? What aspect of the Cobb-Douglas utility function describes a person's *time preference*?
11. What are *indifference curves*? What is the *marginal rate of substitution* and how is it calculated?
12. What is the *substitution* effect? What is the *income* effect?
13. Explain why, in the life-cycle model, total saving in the economy equals total investment.
14. What is *net foreign investment*? How has U.S. net foreign investment behaved over the past several decades?
15. What is the *labor force participation rate*? What have trends in the U.S. rates for older men and women looked like over the past several decades? What are possible reasons for observed differences?

16. What changes in the age distribution of the U.S. population can be expected over the next 40 years? What implications might these have for future capital-labor ratios?

Numerical Questions

1. Suppose that you can reasonably expect a return of 5 percent on any investment that you make.

a. If someone gives you \$100 today, what will that \$100 be worth in six years?

b. If someone promises to pay you \$100 three years from now, what is that promised payment worth to you today?

c. Suppose that you are promised three payments: \$10 in one year; \$40 in two years; and \$20 in three years. What is the *year 2* value of the promised payments?

d. What is the present value of \$200 paid three years from now if the interest rates over the three years are 5 percent, 7 percent, and 9 percent, respectively?

Use the following information to answer questions 2 through 5: $A = 4$, $K_0 = 300$, $N = 200$, $\alpha = .5$, and $\beta = .30$.

2. **a.** What is the value of output in period 0?

b. How much income is paid to labor (i.e., to all workers combined)?

c. How much income is received by an individual worker?

d. What is the total income earned by capital?

e. What is the interest rate? (Helpful hint: Remember that the total income earned by capital equals $r_t K_t$.)

f. What are the values of consumption and saving by the young generation, given the amount of income computed in the previous question?

3. Answer the following questions about economic activity in period 1.

a. What is the value of the *aggregate* capital stock in period 1?

b. Compute *aggregate* investment in period 1.

c. What is the value of production in period 1?

d. What is the value of each individual's lifetime income for those who are young in period 1?

e. What is the value of the interest rate in period 1?

4. Answer the following questions regarding consumer utility.

a. What is the value of consumption by the old in period 1?

b. What is the value of utility of the generation born in period 0?

c. What is the marginal rate of substitution at the combination of period 0 and period 1 consumption calculated above?

5. Answer the following questions regarding the lifetime budget constraint.

a. Give the formula for the lifetime budget constraint.

b. What are the values of the vertical and horizontal intercepts of the budget constraint? Interpret these values.

c. What is the value of the slope? Interpret this value.

d. Verify that the combination of period 0 and period 1 consumption calculated above satisfies the lifetime budget constraint.

Analytical Questions

1. What would be the effect on capital accumulation of a rise in the interest rate (r) offset by a reduction in lifetime income (w) that leaves an individual at the same level of utility?

2. Disenchantment with the spending binge of the 1980s, sometimes called "the Decade of Greed," has led people to place greater weight on future consumption and well-being. How would such a development be reflected in the life-cycle model? What implications does this development have for the current level of investment and future levels of the capital stock and output?

3. "The dynamic supply of capital depends on the dynamic evolution of the wage rate." Without using numbers, explain this statement.

4. Consider a feasible consumption combination yielding a marginal rate of substitution of −1.05. If the rate of interest is 10 percent, should the individual raise or lower current consumption to achieve the optimal consumption combination?

5. How would an advance in robotics be reflected in the life-cycle model? Without using numbers, describe the effect such a change might have on current period output, on total labor and capital income, and on the wage rate and interest rate.

APPENDIX

The Labor Supply Decision

Let's expand Joan's Cobb-Douglas utility function so that she cares not only about how much she consumes when young and old, but also about how much leisure she enjoys in her two periods of life. In choosing how much leisure time to enjoy, Joan simultaneously decides how much to work. Let's denote Joan's leisure when young by l_{yt} and her leisure when old by l_{ot+1}. Her expanded utility function is

$$u_t = c_{yt}^{\alpha} \, c_{ot+1}^{\eta} \, l_{yt}^{\theta} \, l_{ot+1}^{1-\eta-\theta-\alpha}$$

This utility function features two more exponents, which, like α, have values between zero and one. The terms for leisure when young and leisure when old refer, respectively, to the portion of Joan's youth and old age that she spends enjoying leisure (i.e., not working). Hence, l_{yt} and l_{ot+1} are fractions whose values lie between zero and one. For example, if l_{yt} equals .3, this means that Joan spends 30 percent of her youth relaxing and 70 percent $(1 - l_{yt})$ working. So $(1 - l_{yt})$ indicates the supply of labor when young, and $(1 - l_{ot+1})$ indicates the supply of labor when old.

Joan's lifetime budget constraint needs modification to take account of the fact that she works less than full time when young and more than zero time when old. The modified budget constraint is

$$c_{yt} + \frac{c_{ot+1}}{1 + r_{t+1}} = w_t(1-l_{yt}) + \frac{w_{t+1}\,(1 - l_{ot+1})}{1 + r_{t+1}}$$

The left-hand side of the budget constraint is unchanged. The right-hand side indicates the present value of Joan's lifetime earnings. Note that we are multiplying the wages when young and old (w_t and w_{t+1}) that Joan would earn if she worked full time by the respective fractions of her youth and old age that she spends working.

Leisure when young and old, like consumption when young and old, can be thought of as commodities that Joan purchases. Joan purchases the corn she consumes when young and old from producers of corn. But she purchases her leisure time from herself. The more leisure Joan purchases from herself—the more of her time she spends relaxing—the less money she earns and the less she is able to consume. The price to Joan of purchasing leisure involves her forgone earnings.

To clarify the prices of leisure when young and old, let's move the terms involving leisure from the right-hand side of the budget constraint to the left-hand side.

$$c_{yt} + \frac{c_{ot+1}}{1 + r_{t+1}} + w_t l_{yt} + \frac{w_{t+1} l_{ot+1}}{1 + r_{t+1}} = w_t + \frac{w_{t+1}}{1 + r_{t+1}}$$

The right-hand side of this rewritten budget constraint is Joan's full lifetime income. Here the word "full" refers to the fact that this is the present value of Joan's lifetime income if she were to work full time both when young and when old. On the left-hand side, the terms w_t and $w_{t+1}/(1 + r_{t+1})$ are the prices of purchasing leisure when young and old. Intuitively, we see that the price of each unit of leisure when young is the wages Joan could otherwise be earning during the time she is relaxing. The same holds for leisure when old, except that we need to discount the wage rate by the interest factor $1 + r_{t+1}$ because we are considering all prices at the time that Joan is young.

We can now use the previously mentioned property of the Cobb-Douglas utility function—the share of expenditure on each commodity equals that commodity's exponent in the utility function—to write down the rules for how much Joan decides to consume when young and old and how much leisure she decides to enjoy when young and old:

$$c_{yt} = \alpha \left[w_t + \frac{w_{t+1}}{1 + r_{t+1}} \right]$$

$$c_{ot+1} = \eta \left[w_t + \frac{w_{t+1}}{1 + r_{t+1}} \right] (1 + r_{t+1})$$

$$l_{yt} = \theta \left[w_t + \frac{w_{t+1}}{1 + r_{t+1}} \right] \frac{1}{w_t}$$

$$l_{ot+1} = (1 - \alpha - \eta - \theta) \left[w_t + \frac{w_{t+1}}{1 + r_{t+1}} \right] \frac{1 + r_{t+1}}{w_{t+1}}$$

To see that the property of the Cobb-Douglas utility function holds, consider the formula for l_{ot+1}. If we multiply both sides of this formula by the price of leisure when old, $w_{t+1}/(1 + r_{t+1})$, we see that the total expenditure on leisure when old—the amount of leisure multiplied by its price—equals the exponent of leisure when old, $1 - \alpha - \eta - \theta$, multiplied by the amount of full lifetime income.

According to these formulas, Joan's consumption when young and old as well as the labor she supplies when young and old ($1 - l_{yt}$ and $1 - l_{ot+1}$, respectively) all depend on the wage rates she faces when young and old and the interest rate she can earn on her assets. In this expanded model, Joan and her contemporaries will work harder during periods when the wage rate is high than when the wage is low. To see this, consider the ratio of leisure when young to leisure when old:

$$\frac{l_{yt}}{l_{ot+1}} = \frac{\theta}{(1-\alpha-\eta-\theta)(1+r_{t+1})}\,\frac{w_{t+1}}{w_t}$$

According to this formula, the higher wages are at time $t + 1$ compared to time t, the greater leisure when young will be compared to leisure when old—i.e., the greater labor supply at time $t + 1$ will be compared to labor supply at time t.

For the entire economy, the labor supply at time t is given by $N(1 - l_{yt}) + N(1 - l_{ot})$. Plugging in the formulas for l_{yt} and l_{ot} shows that the aggregate supply of labor at time t depends on the wages and interest rates prevailing at times t and $t + 1$ and the wage that prevailed at time $t - 1$.

CHAPTER 3

The Dynamic Demand for Inputs and the Evolution of Output

INTRODUCTION

In Chapter 2 we traced the macro economy's aggregate supplies of capital and labor to the life-cycle saving and labor supply decisions of households. We saw that these decisions depend on the income households can earn from working and saving. In this chapter we'll consider the decisions by firms to hire (to demand) the capital and labor supplied by the household sector. We'll see that firms' demands for labor and capital also depend on wage and interest rates, which represent the costs of hiring these inputs.

In the course of developing the demand side of our growth model, we'll learn about the size of U.S. firms and preview some of the issues raised in Chapter 16 by touching on the financial structure of firms—the way in which firms acquire or hire the capital they use in production. We'll also point out some of the challenges firms face in hiring, retaining, and motivating workers.

After describing the demand side of our life-cycle model, we'll combine it with the supply side to determine the time paths of the wage and interest rates that equate the supplies of labor and capital in each time period to the contemporaneous demands for these inputs. Thus, we'll describe the **general equilibrium** determination, through time, of wages and interest rates. The term "equilibrium" refers to the situation in which there is no upward or downward pressure on the wage or interest rate because the supplies of capital and labor equal the demands for these inputs. The adjective "general" refers to the simultaneous equilibrium of all of the economy's markets. Once we learn how the economy's wage and interest rates evolve over time, we'll also know how the equilibrium amounts of capital and labor evolve and how the economy grows.

General equilibrium *A situation in which supply equals demand in all markets simultaneously*

The goal of this chapter is to produce a complete model, albeit a very simple one, of economic growth. Although the model is simple, it is highly instructive. It allows us to answer the following types of questions.

- Do economies grow forever or do they settle down into some permanent (or steady) state?
- How does a country's saving behavior influence its wage and interest rates?
- How does our two-period life-cycle model explain economic growth?
- How are different generations affected by the growth process?
- Can the extraordinary postwar growth of Japan and Germany be explained as their "catching up" with the U.S.?
- How does a baby boom affect the economy over time?
- Why did real wages rise during the Middle Ages following the Black Death?

Throughout this chapter we'll continue to assume that the economy is closed to international trade and investment. In Chapter 6 we'll extend our simple model to allow residents of one country to invest their savings in another. In that chapter we'll see that the process of economic development can be much more rapid when developing countries import capital from abroad.

ADDING FIRMS TO OUR MODEL

So far we have made the simplifying assumption that the elderly—the owners of capital—invest their capital in their own firms and hire labor to work with that capital. In the corn economy metaphor, each person works on someone else's farm when young, but sets up her own farm when old, using her saving as seed for the young workers she hires to sow. The model is unaffected if we assume instead that some of the elderly combine their savings and invest them in bigger firms. The only thing we require is that there still be a large number of firms that compete with one another in hiring capital and labor. That is, we need perfect competition.

In the U.S., the number of firms depends on how we count them. If we count all the proprietorships, partnerships, and corporations, including those with no employees except the owners, the number is close to 20 million—roughly one firm for every nine adults. If we count firms with 20 or more employees, the number is about three-quarters of a million—roughly one firm for every 240 adults. Figure 3-1 points out that most U.S. business establishments—87 percent—are small, with fewer than 20 employees. But it also shows that most U.S.

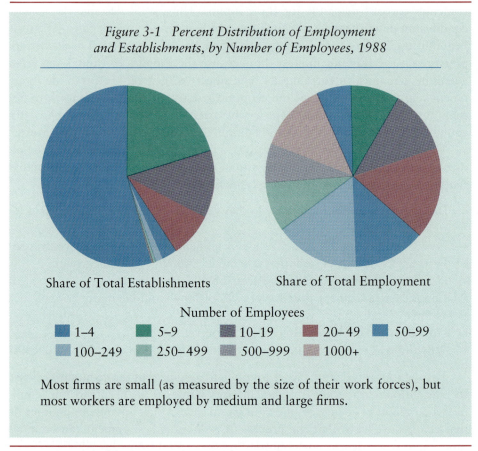

Figure 3-1 Percent Distribution of Employment and Establishments, by Number of Employees, 1988

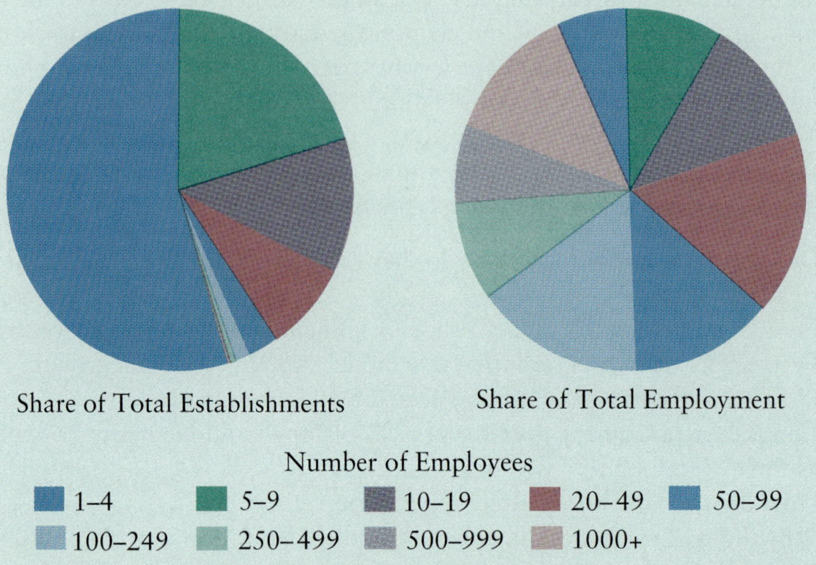

Most firms are small (as measured by the size of their work forces), but most workers are employed by medium and large firms.

Source: U.S. Bureau of the Census, 1989

workers—73 percent—work for medium and large establishments, those with 20 or more employees.

General Motors is the U.S. firm with the most workers—almost three-quarters of a million. That is a lot of people—more than reside in Alaska, Vermont, North Dakota, South Dakota, Delaware, or Wyoming. But GM's work force represents less than 1 percent of total U.S. employment. Indeed, the total employment of the Fortune 500 largest U.S. companies accounts for only about a tenth of U.S. employment. The very large number of U.S. firms hiring labor and capital make input markets in the U.S. highly competitive.

The Capital Structure of Firms

Whatever their number, the firms in our model need capital to operate. We can think of these firms as either borrowing capital from the elderly or selling shares of stock (issuing ownership rights to the firm) to the elderly in exchange for the use of their capital. Selling stock is also referred to as issuing *equity*. Those elderly who own and operate their own firms can be thought of as borrowing from themselves, or issuing equity to themselves.

In the case of borrowing, the elderly receive back, at the end of their old age, their initial capital (their principal) plus interest due on the borrowing. In the case of the sale of stock, the elderly recover their initial capital plus the return on that capital through the receipt of *dividends* paid out by the firms and by selling their shares of stock back to the firms or to the young, who are interested in acquiring assets.[1] Regardless of which method of finance firms use, the underlying outcome is the same. Each firm gets to use some capital for one period, but must return it along with the income earned on that capital at the end of the period. Hence, in our model the method of finance has no impact.[2] This discussion ties in with the point we made in the last chapter that no matter what form financial assets and liabilities take—whether stocks, bonds, rental agreements, or whatever—the net wealth of a country boils down to the value of its real capital assets.

In the real world the important difference between borrowing and selling shares of stock turns on the likelihood that the firm will make good on its commitment. Firms that suffer losses and can't repay their debts may go bankrupt, and the bankruptcy process can often tie up the use of the physical capital for long periods of time. In contrast, equity financed firms with losses will see the market value of their stock fall but will not necessarily have to close down operations.

Case Study: The Capital Structure of U.S. Nonfinancial Corporations

Capital structure *The division of a firm's liabilities between funds raised by borrowing and funds raised by issuing equity and retaining earnings*

Figure 3-2 shows recent trends in the **capital structure** of U.S. nonfinancial corporations. It shows the total value of corporate capital, the amount of that capital financed through corporate borrowing, and the amount financed through equity. In equity finance, funds are generated by selling new shares of stock and by retaining profits (known as *retained earnings*) within the firm. The ratio of the amount of capital acquired through borrowing to the amount acquired through equity finance is called the *debt-equity ratio*, or *leverage ratio*. The annual debt-equity ratio for U.S. corporations averaged .520, .633, .588, and .686 in the 1950s, 60s, 70s, and 80s, respectively. The debt-equity ratio changed dramatically in the 1980s. In 1980 it stood at .461—a 30-year low. By 1989 it had risen to .837. Many critics argue that businesses recklessly "overborrowed" in the 1980s. As we'll discuss in Chapter 16, there are other possible explanations for recent changes in U.S. debt-equity ratios. Whatever the cause, the increased leverage probably gave rise to higher rates of bankruptcies. So too did federal legislation that made it easier for businesses to file for bankruptcy.

1. Firms that do not pay out the return on capital as a dividend but instead, retain these earnings will raise the value of their stock. That is because the stock represents a claim, not only on the original capital invested in the firm, but also on the additional earnings retained by the firm. Stockholders who sell their stock will thus recover their return on capital in the form of a capital gain.
2. This is a simple example of the Modigliani-Miller theorem that plays an important role in the theory of corporate finance we discuss in Chapter 16.

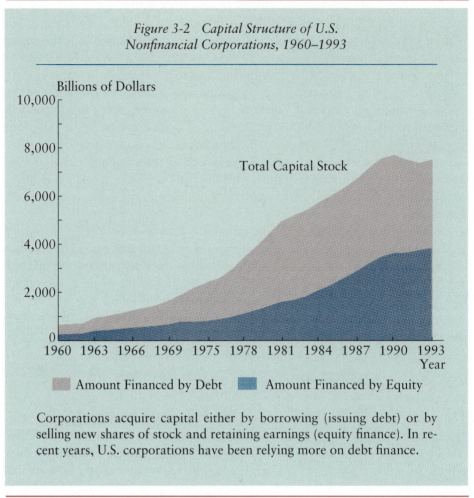

Figure 3-2 Capital Structure of U.S. Nonfinancial Corporations, 1960–1993

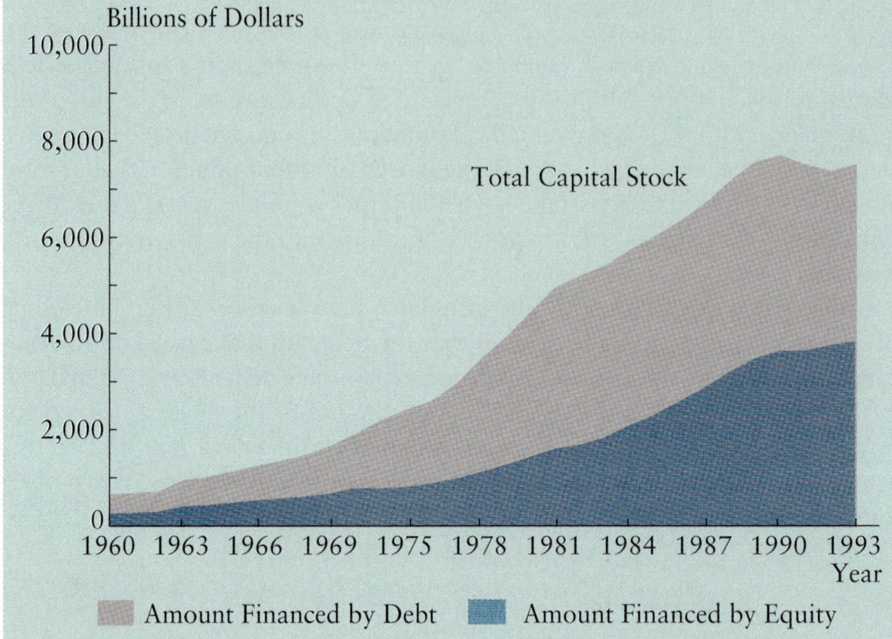

Corporations acquire capital either by borrowing (issuing debt) or by selling new shares of stock and retaining earnings (equity finance). In recent years, U.S. corporations have been relying more on debt finance.

Note: Equity finance is measured as total capital less debt.
Source: Board of Governors of the Federal Reserve System

THE HUMAN CAPITAL STRUCTURE OF FIRMS

To keep our model simple, we assume that firms hire labor—demand human capital—but do not improve its quality through on-the-job training. We also ignore any improvement in workers' skills through the accumulation of job experience. Although these omissions do not significantly affect the main message of our growth model, it is important to keep in mind that hiring (demanding) labor in the real world is more complex than simply signing up people to work on a moment's notice and letting them go the next day. Actually, with the exception of longshoremen and certain farm and construction workers, it is hard to think of workers who are hired on a daily basis. On-the-job training, the accumulation of experience, and the process of learning-by-doing all require a long-term relationship between workers and firms. As a result many firms structure their compensation packages to encourage workers to stay with them for many years.

They often do so by providing higher wages at the end of the worker's career than at the beginning. This wage structure also gives workers an incentive to work hard so as to ensure that they retain their jobs through the particularly lucrative end stages of their careers.

In the U.S., about half of workers eventually find jobs that last 20 years or more.[3] However, finding these successful long-term matches between employers and employees requires considerable searching by both parties. As a result, most jobs are of short duration, even though most workers spend a large part of their careers in a single job.

In addition to determining when and how much to train and compensate their workers during periods of normal economic activity, firms have to decide how to handle their work forces during recessions. Because of the costs of training new recruits once a recession is over, many firms are loath to lay off long-term employees.

PROFIT MAXIMIZATION

Financing decisions, incentive structures, layoff policy, and a number of other factors make the employment of capital and labor more complicated than it might first appear. However, the ultimate issue for competitive firms is whether acquiring these inputs means more or less profit. So now, in returning to our model, we'll sweep aside these complexities and consider the simplest setting in which firms choose the amounts of capital and labor to *maximize profit* (revenue minus cost). We'll revisit these considerations in Chapters 11 and 16 when we discuss the difficulties firms face in adjusting their demands for capital and labor over the business cycle.

Let's consider the collective profit of all firms in deriving their total input demands. These total input demands result from adding up the separate input demands of each of the economy's firms. The collective profit at time t is defined in the following equation:

$$\text{Profit}_t = Y_t - r_t K_t - w_t L_t$$

The first term on the right-hand side of this expression is Y_t, which continues to stand for the quantity of total output. Since the price of output (the price of corn) equals 1, Y_t also stands for total revenue (the price of corn times the quantity of corn is 1 times Y_t, or simply Y_t). As in Chapter 2, r_t is the interest rate, and K_t is the total amount of capital demanded by the firms. To keep our model simple, we assume that capital does not depreciate. Consequently, we do not include an adjustment for depreciation in our expression for profit.

The interest rate is the cost to the firm of using a unit of capital for one period. The product $r_t K_t$ stands for the total costs to all firms in the economy of

3. Robert E. Hall, "The Importance of Lifetime Jobs in the U.S. Economy," *American Economic Review* (September 1982): 716–724.

using capital in period t. The last term in the expression for profit represents the total costs of hiring labor; here, w_t still stands for the wage, and L_t stands for the total amount of labor demanded by firms in period t.

Our formula indicates that profit is the income left over after paying the costs of hiring capital and labor. Economists often refer to profit so defined as *pure profit*. They do so to distinguish what they mean by profit from the everyday use of the term. In everyday parlance the term "profit" refers to the normal income earned by owners of capital, r_tK_t, as well as any additional pure profit. For example, "corporate profits" refers to all the capital income earned by corporations, most of which simply represents a normal return on their investment.

In choosing values of K_t and L_t to make profit as large as possible, the firms in our model take the interest rate and wage as given. Each firm correctly assumes that its own decisions as to how much capital and labor to hire have no appreciable influence on the interest and wage rates. This is in keeping with the assumption of competitive input markets; there are a very large number of firms, each of which is too small to significantly shift the aggregate demands for inputs.

The Demand for Capital and Labor

Marginal product of capital
The change in total output arising from a one-unit increase in usage of capital, holding labor fixed

Marginal product of labor
The change in total output arising from a one-unit increase in usage of labor, holding capital fixed

Marginal cost of capital
The change in the total cost of production when usage of capital increases by one unit

Marginal cost of labor
The change in the total cost of production when usage of labor increases by one unit

The following reasoning may help you understand the profit-maximizing choice of capital and labor. Suppose firms have chosen quantities of capital and labor that yield the largest profit. Then, it must be the case that adding or subtracting a small amount of either capital or labor will leave profit unchanged. If adding or subtracting either a bit of capital or a bit of labor resulted in higher profit, it could not be the case that the firms had chosen the profit-maximizing combination of inputs in the first place.

Profit is defined as revenue minus cost, so the condition that changing either capital or labor leaves profit unchanged means that the change in revenue (the *marginal revenue*) from such adjustments must equal the change in cost (the *marginal cost*). With the price of output fixed at 1, marginal revenue from changing either of the two inputs simply equals the marginal output. The extra output from increasing capital is called the **marginal product of capital,** and the extra output from increasing labor is called the **marginal product of labor**. Since competitive firms take the interest rate and wage as given, increasing capital by one unit raises total costs by r_t, and increasing labor by one unit increases total costs by w_t. Hence, the interest rate is the **marginal cost of capital**, and the wage is the **marginal cost of labor**. Profit maximization requires that the marginal product of capital equals the interest rate and that the marginal product of labor equals the wage.

Cobb-Douglas Input Demands

For our Cobb-Douglas production function, the formulas for the marginal product of capital and labor are extremely simple. In the case of capital, the marginal product is $\beta Y_t/K_t$, which is the capital coefficient multiplied by output per unit of capital.[4] Given this formula, the condition that the marginal product of capital equals the interest rate can be written as

$$\beta \frac{Y_t}{K_t} = r_t$$

If we solve this equation for β, we find that it equals the ratio of total capital income, $r_t K_t$, to output, Y_t, which also equals the nation's income. Hence, β is capital's share of income, as we claimed in Chapter 1.

In the case of labor, the marginal product is $(1 - \beta)Y_t/L_t$. This is the labor coefficient multiplied by the amount of output per unit of labor. The condition that the marginal product of labor equals the wage rate is expressed as

$$(1 - \beta) \frac{Y_t}{L_t} = w_t$$

Solving this expression for $(1 - \beta)$ indicates that $(1 - \beta)$ equals labor's share of income, $w_t L_t/Y_t$.

If firms hire capital and labor according to these formulas, what will their total profit be? The answer is zero, as we can see by substituting for $r_t K_t$ and $w_t L_t$ from the above two equations into the expression for profit. The substitution yields the expression Profit $= Y_t - \beta Y_t - (1 - \beta)Y_t = 0$. Since the owners of capital (the elderly at time t) receive a share β of output, and since young workers receive a share $(1 - \beta)$ of output, all output is paid out to the two productive inputs, and nothing is left over as profit. Again, by saying that profit equals zero, we mean that pure profit equals zero, not that the income earned by capital is zero.

This zero profit condition is the result of perfect competition. If profits were positive, additional firms would enter the market and existing firms would expand their production. These actions would raise the demands for labor and capital, bidding up the wage and the interest rate until profits were zero. If profits were negative, existing firms would either leave the market or reduce their production. This would depress demands for labor and capital, driving down the wage and the interest rate until profits were zero.

4. If you are familiar with calculus, you can derive the marginal product of capital as the partial derivative of the production function with respect to K_t. In the case of capital, the partial derivative is $\beta A_t K_t^{\beta-1} L_t^{1-\beta}$, which is just $\beta Y_t/K_t$. In the case of labor, it is $(1 - \beta)A_t K_t^{\beta} L_t^{-\beta}$, which is just $(1 - \beta)Y_t/L_t$.

If you aren't familiar with calculus, you can generate these formulas using algebra and the fact that $(1 + \delta)^{\beta}$ is approximately equal to $1 + \beta\delta$ when δ is a number very close to zero. Take the marginal product of capital. We can write the increase in output, ΔY_t, from having δK_t more capital at time t as $A_t(K_t + \delta K_t)\beta L_t^{1-\beta} - A_t K_t^{\beta} L_t^{1-\beta}$. With a little algebra and the use of our approximation formula, we can write $\Delta Y_t = \beta\delta Y_t$. Dividing both sides of this equation by δK_t and replacing δK_t by ΔK_t (since δK_t is the change in K_t) gives $\Delta Y_t/\Delta K_t = \beta Y_t/K_t$. The left-hand side of this equality is the change in output for a small change in capital—capital's marginal product.

The Relationship of the Capital-Labor Ratio to the Wage and the Interest Rate

We can express the marginal products of capital and labor in terms of the input demands by substituting the Cobb-Douglas formula for Y_t, $A_t K_t^{\beta} L_t^{(1-\beta)}$, in the last two equations. With this substitution, the equation relating the marginal product of capital to the interest rate becomes

$$\beta A_t \left(\frac{L_t}{K_t}\right)^{(1-\beta)} = r_t$$

If capital is relatively scarce (the ratio of labor to capital is high), an additional unit of capital will be very productive in increasing output. In contrast, if capital is relatively abundant (the ratio of labor to capital is low), an additional unit of capital will be less productive, since there will be less labor available to use this additional capital. These ideas are reflected in the formula. It says that the larger the ratio of labor to capital, the larger the marginal product of capital. This is just the concept of diminishing returns, which we reviewed in Chapter 1.

Substituting the Cobb-Douglas formula for output into the equation relating the marginal product of labor to the wage rate yields

$$(1 - \beta) A_t \left(\frac{K_t}{L_t}\right)^{\beta} = w_t$$

Thus, the larger the ratio of capital to labor, the larger the marginal product of labor (the left-hand side of the equation). The more scarce labor is, the larger its marginal product.

DETERMINING THE EQUILIBRIUM VALUES OF THE WAGE AND THE INTEREST RATE

The last two equations tell us about the firms' demands for capital and labor when the interest rate equals r_t and the wage rate equals w_t. But they can also be used to determine what interest rate and wage rate must prevail at time t if the firms are to demand the available amounts of capital and labor. This way of viewing these equations can help you understand how the interest rate and the wage rate are determined at time t. In equilibrium the supplies of capital and labor must equal the demands. If we know the supplies of these inputs we can substitute those values into the above equations to determine the interest rate and wage rate at which firms' demands for capital and labor equal the available supplies.

Do we know the available supplies of capital and labor at time t in our model? Yes. From Chapter 2, we know that the labor supply at time t, and every other time period, is simply N, the number of young people. Hence, in the above two equations, we can set the firms' collective demand for labor, L_t, equal to the collective supply of labor, N. The capital stock at time t equals the assets of the elderly at time t, Na_t, where a_t still stands for assets per old person. Hence, in the above two equations we can set the firms' total demand for capital, K_t, equal to the elderly's collective supply of capital, Na_t.

Let's denote the equilibrium ratio of capital to labor at time t by k_t. Because the demands for inputs equal their supplies, k_t equals K_t/L_t, which equals Na_t/N. By substituting k_t for the capital-labor ratio in the last two equations, we can write the equilibrium wage and interest rates prevailing at time t more compactly:[5]

$$r_t = \beta A_t k_t^{\beta - 1}$$
$$w_t = (1 - \beta) A_t k_t^{\beta}$$

These equations tell us that a higher capital-labor ratio means a lower equilibrium interest rate and a higher equilibrium wage rate. Intuitively, larger supplies of capital relative to labor make capital more abundant relative to labor. This drives down the market price of using capital—the interest rate—and drives up the market price of using labor—the wage rate.

Are these formulas for the wage and interest rate consistent with the data? The answer, broadly speaking, appears to be yes. Take the wage. In Chapter 1 we pointed out that U.S. real wage growth has slowed in the past two decades. This slowdown in real wage growth has coincided with slower growth in U.S. productivity and capital intensity—precisely the elements that determine wage growth, according to our model's formula for the wage.

Diagramming Factor Market Equilibrium

Figures 3-3 and 3-4 show the demand curves relating the capital-labor ratio to the wage rate and to the interest rate, assuming the technology coefficient, A_t, is constant through time. The curves show that firms demand more capital relative to labor the higher the wage, and they demand less capital relative to labor the higher the interest rate. In equilibrium, the wage and interest rate are jointly determined so we can use either demand curve to calculate the demand for capital relative to labor and end up with the same answer.

To determine the equilibrium values of the wage and interest rates at time t, we need the supply curve of capital relative to labor. Since all the capital and all the labor available at time t are brought to market regardless of the prevailing values of the interest rate and wage, the time t supply curve of capital relative to labor is simply a vertical line in Figures 3-3 and 3-4.

Recall that t can stand for time 0 or time 1 or, indeed, any time period. Therefore, Figures 3-3 and 3-4 can be used to determine factor market equilibrium for any period we wish to consider. For example, in these two figures we

5. In the first equation we use the facts that $L_t/K_t = 1/k_t$ and that $(1/k_t)^{(1-\beta)} = k_t^{(\beta-1)}$. If you are rusty or unfamiliar with the algebraic manipulation of exponents, we recommend that you read the refresher on exponents at the end of this chapter.

Figure 3-3 The Dependence of the Wage Rate at Time t *on the Capital-Labor Ratio*

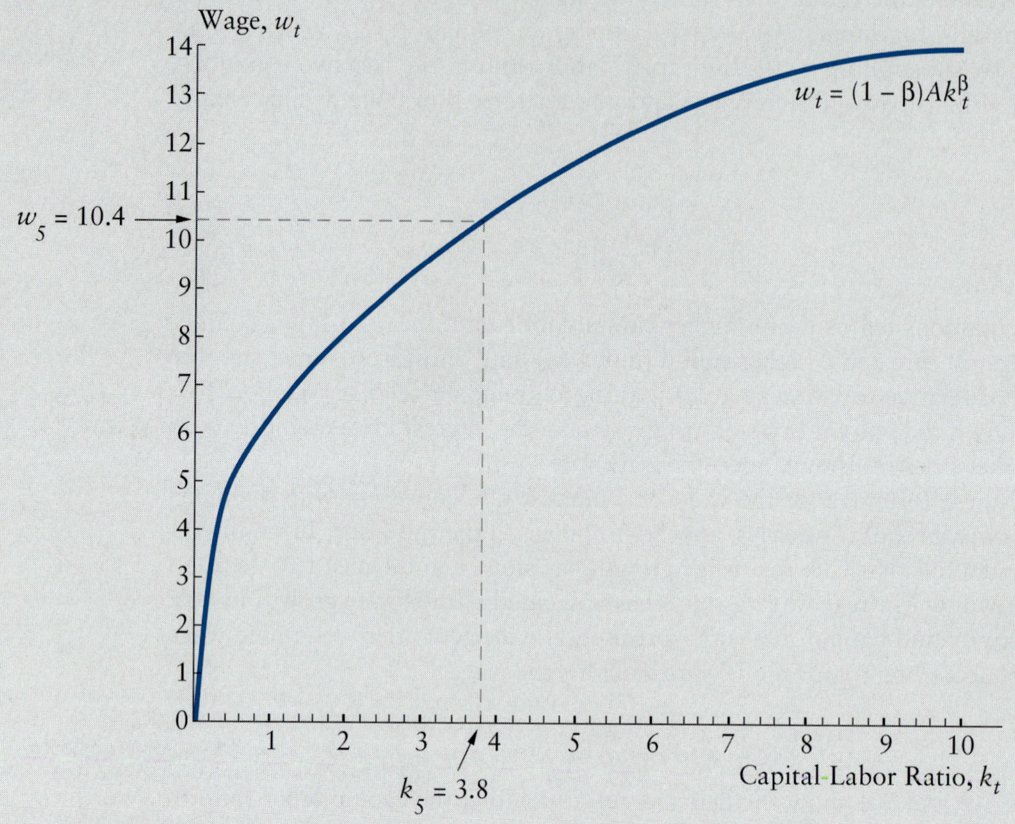

In equilibrium, a larger supply of capital makes labor more scarce (relative to capital) and raises the price of labor—the wage rate.

consider time 5 and assume that k_5 equals 3.8. Accordingly, we draw the supply curve for k_5 as a vertical line emanating from the value of 3.8 on the horizontal axis. The intersections of the supply and demand curves indicate the wage rate (10.4) and the interest rate (1.178) at time 5. We can use our formulas to confirm these values, assuming that A equals 10 and β equals .3.

MODELING GROWTH

We've just shown that the capital-labor ratio at time t is critical for determining the wage at time t. In Chapter 2 we showed that the wage rate at time t deter-

Figure 3-4 The Dependence of the Interest Rate at Time t on the Capital-Labor Ratio

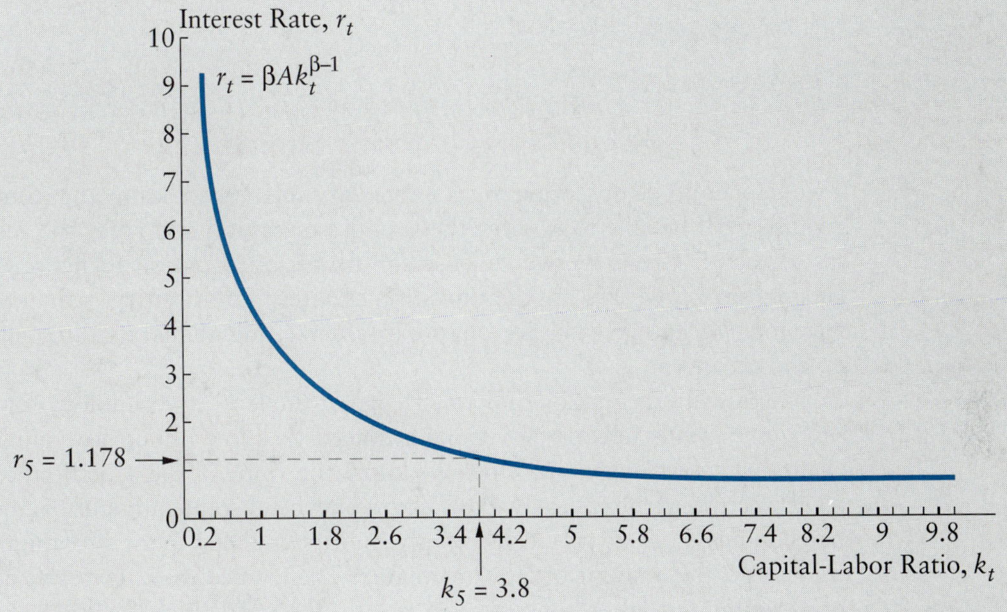

In equilibrium, a larger supply of labor makes capital more scarce (relative to labor) and raises the price of capital—the interest rate.

mines the supply of capital at time $t + 1$ and therefore, with labor supply fixed at N, the capital-labor ratio at time $t + 1$.[6] Hence, if we know the capital-labor ratio at time t, we know the wage at time t and can figure out the capital-labor ratio at time $t + 1$. And, since there is nothing special about periods t and $t + 1$, if we know the capital-labor ratio at time $t + 1$, we can proceed in the same manner to figure out the capital-labor ratio at time $t + 2$, and so on.

To derive the relationship between the capital-labor ratio at times t and $t + 1$, we start with the fact that $k_{t+1} = a_{t+1}$ (capital per worker at time $t + 1$ equals assets per old person). Next we replace a_{t+1} with $(1 - \alpha)w_t$ (assets per old person equals the saving they did when young). This leaves us with $k_{t+1} = (1 - \alpha)w_t$. Finally, we replace w_t by the marginal product of labor at time t, $(1 - \beta)A_t k_t^{\beta}$. This gives us

$$k_{t+1} = (1 - \alpha)(1 - \beta)A_t k_t^{\beta}$$

6. Recall that the assets owned by the old at time t + 1 equal the saving they did when young, i.e., $a_{t+1} = (1 - \alpha)w_t$, and that the total capital stock at time $t + 1$ equals Na_{t+1}.

Transition equation *An algebraic equation relating the economy's capital-labor ratio in two successive periods*

We call this the **transition equation** because it tells us how the economy's capital-labor ratio changes (transits) from one time period to the next. Since t can stand for any time period, we can use the transition equation to determine how the capital-labor ratio changes between any two consecutive time periods. For example, if we let t equal 3, the transition equation tells us that k_4 depends on k_3 according to $k_4 = (1 - \alpha)(1 - \beta)A_3k_3^{\beta}$.

Using the Transition Equation to Track the Economy's Growth Path

If we happen to be observing the economy at time 0, we'll know the value of k_0 because we'll be able to observe the supplies of capital and labor the economy has on hand. Given k_0, we can use the transition equation to figure out k_1. Then, given k_1, we can use the transition equation (after setting t equal to 1) to determine k_2, and given k_2 we can use it (after setting t equal to 2) to determine k_3, and on and on. . . .

The transition equation and knowledge of the level of technology for all future time periods tells us everything we need to know about how our simple economy evolves over time. Once we know the value of the capital-labor ratio in each period in the future, we can figure out the absolute amount of capital in the economy in each period by simply multiplying each period's capital-labor ratio by N, the amount of labor available. Then, since we know each period's total capital and labor supplies, we can use the production function to determine the economy's output in each period. Knowing the path through time of the capital-labor ratio is also sufficient to determine wage and interest rates at each future date. How? By applying the equations linking these factor prices to their marginal products, which depend, of course, on the prevailing capital-labor ratios.

From knowledge of the wage and the interest rate in each period we can also determine consumption by the young and the old in each period and, thus, aggregate consumption. Recall that total consumption by the young in any period equals α times the prevailing wage times the number of young people. Consumption by the old in any period equals principal plus interest on the economy's assets—the capital stock multiplied by one plus the interest rate. Finally, by subtracting each period's total consumption from that period's output, we can calculate the economy's total saving, which, as demonstrated in Chapter 2, also equals its total investment.

TRACKING THE ECONOMY'S GROWTH PATH: A NUMERICAL EXAMPLE

Let's use a numerical example to trace exactly how the economy evolves. We can start at time $t = 0$, insert some values for the parameters in the transition equation, and see how the economy evolves. In this calculation we'll adopt values of .5 for α and .3 for β. Let's also set the level of technology, A, equal to 10 in all time periods. By keeping technology fixed, we'll be able to concentrate solely on the process of capital accumulation. Finally, let's assume the population size of each generation (N) equals 100 and that the supply of capital at time 0, when we begin looking at our economy, equals 150. Hence, the capital-labor ratio at time 0 is 1.5 (1.5 units of capital for every worker). Since $(1 - \alpha)(1 - \beta)A$ equals $0.5 \times 0.7 \times 10 = 3.5$, the general form of our transition equation is $k_{t+1} = 3.5k_t^{.3}$. Application of our transition equation for periods $t = 1$ through $t = 7$ yields the following:

$$k_1 = 3.5 \times 1.500^{.3} = 3.953$$
$$k_2 = 3.5 \times 3.953^{.3} = 5.286$$
$$k_3 = 3.5 \times 5.286^{.3} = 5.768$$
$$k_4 = 3.5 \times 5.768^{.3} = 5.921$$
$$k_5 = 3.5 \times 5.921^{.3} = 5.967$$
$$k_6 = 3.5 \times 5.967^{.3} = 5.981$$
$$k_7 = 3.5 \times 5.981^{.3} = 5.985$$

We can use these results on the capital-labor ratio plus other equations from our model to determine the time paths of all of the other variables. Appendix Table A-1 lists the equations of our model. Table 3-1 uses these equations and the assumed values of A, N, α, and β to track all of the economy's economic variables for the periods 0 through 7. It also indicates the long-run (time $t = \infty$) values of our economy, which we'll explain later.

Examine the results in Table 3-1, starting with the values of the economy's variables at time 0. Plugging 150 for K_0 and 100 for N_0 into the production function, we find that total output at time 0 equals 1129.3. If we measure output in bushels of corn, we can say that the economy produces 1129.3 bushels at time 0. As discussed above, knowledge of the capital-labor ratio is crucial for determining the values of the wage and interest rate. Using our formulas for the marginal products of labor and capital, we find w_0 equals 7.905 (bushels of corn per worker) and r_0 equals 2.259 (bushels of corn per unit of capital).

Since we measure output and capital in the same units (bushels of corn), r_0 is a unit-free number (its units are bushels of corn per bushel of corn). By a unit-free number, we mean that r_0 is a percentage rate of return—an interest rate. In the real world we are used to annual interest rates in the single digits, such as 3 percent or 8 percent. So, at first glance, a value of 2.259 (225.9 percent) for r_0 seems very high. But although r_0 is an interest rate, it is not an annual interest rate.

Recall that each period in our model corresponds to roughly 30 years, so r_0 is roughly a 30-year rate. The corresponding annual interest rate is 4.017 percent. Here's why. With an annual interest rate of 4.017 percent, the 30-year interest rate is calculated by determining how much \$1.00 invested at 4.017 percent each year would yield at the end of 30 years. The answer is found by multiplying \$1.00 by 1.04017 30 times (multiplying \$1.00 by 1.04017 raised to the power 30). The resulting amount is \$3.259, which equals the initial \$1.00 invested plus \$2.259 in interest.

Table 3-1 An Illustrative Transition Path of the Two-Period Economy

Period	k_t	K_t	Y_t	w_t	r_t	c_{yt}	c_{ot}	S_t	I_t
0	1.500	150.0	1129.3	7.905	2.259	3.953	4.888	245.27	245.27
1	3.593	395.3	1510.3	10.572	1.146	5.286	8.484	133.34	133.34
2	5.286	528.6	1647.9	11.535	.935	5.768	10.230	48.17	48.17
3	5.768	576.8	1691.6	11.841	.880	5.921	10.843	15.29	15.29
4	5.921	592.1	1704.9	11.934	.864	5.967	11.035	4.66	4.66
5	5.967	596.7	1709.0	11.963	.859	5.981	11.094	1.41	1.41
6	5.981	598.1	1710.2	11.971	.858	5.986	11.112	0.42	0.42
7	5.985	598.5	1710.5	11.974	.857	5.987	11.117	0.13	0.13
.	.	.	.	.	.	.	.	.	.
.	.	.	.	.	.	.	.	.	.
.	.	.	.	.	.	.	.	.	.
∞	5.987	598.7	1710.6	11.975	.857	5.987	11.119	0.00	0.00

Assumptions: $k_0 = 1.500$; $\alpha = .5$; $\beta = .3$; $A = 10$; $N = 100$

Source: Board of Governors of the Federal Reserve System

The remaining variables in the first row of Table 3-1 are consumption by the young, c_{y0}; consumption by the old, c_{o0}; the economy's aggregate saving, S_0; and the economy's aggregate investment, I_0, all are measured at time 0. With $\alpha = 0.5$, the young always consume half their wages, so $c_{y0} = .5 \times w_0 = 3.953$. The old consume their capital plus interest on that capital. We've already determined that each old person at time 0 has 1.5 units of capital. At the end of the period, the elderly each consume $1.5(1 + r_0) = 1.5 \times 3.259 = 4.888$ units of output (their original capital plus interest earned on it). If we add together the consumption by all the young and all the old and subtract this value of aggregate consumption from the economy's output, we arrive at the economy's total saving at time 0. The value given in the table is 245.27 units of output. Note that this is the same value as the economy's total investment at time 0, where I_0 is calculated as $K_1 - K_0$. Indeed, our economy's saving equals its investment in each period. But this should come as no surprise. We learned in Chapter 2 that national saving (the nation's acquisition of additional real assets) equals national investment (the addition to its stock of real assets used in production).

Where Does the Economy Go and How Long Does It Take to Get There?

Now that you understand our simple economy at time 0, let's ask what happens to it over time. The short answer is that the economy grows. It enjoys an increasing stock of capital, which helps produce higher levels of output. Since the labor supply is fixed, the increase in capital also means an increase in the capital-labor ratio. This process of capital deepening raises the marginal product of labor and lowers the marginal product of capital, meaning higher wage rates and lower interest rates.

Each of the variables listed in Table 3-1 converges to specific long-run (time $t = \infty$) values. For example, the long-run value of output is 1710.6, and the level of output gets closer and closer to this value through time. This long-run level of output level is 51 percent larger than its initial level of 1129.3 at time 0. Over time, the economy's output grows in total by 51 percent.

Most of the growth in output occurs in the first few periods of the transition. Indeed, measured in terms of the number of periods, all of the economic variables of our economy converge quite rapidly to their long-run values. In the case of output, the absolute growth between times 0 and 1 is 381.0 units, which is 65 percent of the 581.3 units (1710.6 units – 1129.3 units) by which output ultimately grows. The growth in output between time 0 and time 2 is 89 percent of ultimate output growth.

Although convergence in terms of number of periods is quick, convergence in terms of years is rather slow. Again, each period corresponds to 30 years. So even after 30 years—the amount of real-world time between periods 0 and 1—completed output growth falls short—in this case, 35 percent short—of ultimate output growth.[7]

IS GROWTH A TEMPORARY PHENOMENON?

Another way of saying that output converges through time to a fixed (unchanging) value is to say that growth in our model slows down and ultimately ceases; growth is a temporary phenomenon. Should we be surprised by this convergence of the economy's capital stock and the eventual cessation of growth? Maybe and maybe not. First of all, by keeping the population size of each generation constant at $N = 100$ and keeping technology fixed at the value $A = 10$, we've eliminated two sources of growth—population growth and technological change—that could keep the economy's output growing forever.[8]

The only other source of growth of output is an increasing capital stock. But for the economy to continue to grow at a rate that does not diminish through time, the capital stock would have to grow larger and larger. The explanation for why the capital stock does not continually increase, but instead converges to a fixed value, runs like this. The capital stock in period 0 is small. As a consequence, the wage in period 0 is low, so saving by the young in that period is limited. But even this limited amount of saving is sufficient to make the capital

7. Fairly slow transitions are not simply an artifact of the current model. More realistic models in which each period corresponds to a year and people live for 75 or so periods also produce slow transitions.

8. We'll review the effects of population growth and technological change later in this chapter and in the Appendix.

stock at time 1 larger than the capital stock at time 0. This makes the wage at time 1 larger, facilitating even more saving by the young at time 1. But as each period passes, the amount by which the wage rises becomes smaller. The reason has to do with diminishing returns to additional capital. When capital is very scarce, adding one more unit has a big impact on increasing the wage. But when capital is very abundant, adding another unit has only a negligible effect on the wage. Hence, along the transition path the growth rate of the wage gets smaller and smaller until eventually the wage doesn't change at all. At that point, with the wage constant, every generation saves the same amount when young and brings the same amount of capital into old age. As a result the capital stock, as well as the wage, remains constant from one period to the next.

The Steady State

Steady state
The long-run position toward which the economy converges; a situation in which all economic variables grow at the same rate (which may be zero)

The long-run position, or state to which the economy converges, is called its **steady state.** As we've seen, our economy's growth rate in the long run is steady, albeit steady at the value of zero. Not only does output remain constant through time in our economy's steady state, but so do all other economic variables. We can find the long-run values of economic variables—the economy's steady state—by repeated use of our transition equation. This method of determining where the economy is ultimately headed works fine, but it is tedious. There is a quicker method that also uses the transition equation. It exploits the fact that if the economy is in its steady state in period t, the economy's capital-labor ratio a period later, at time $t + 1$, will be the same as at time t. Let's call the steady-state value of the capital-labor ratio $\bar{k}$. Then if the economy is in its steady state at time t, $k_t = \bar{k}$ and $k_{t+1} = \bar{k}$. Since our transition equation relating the capital-labor ratios in two adjacent periods holds whether or not we are in the steady state, we can replace k_{t+1} and k_t in the transition equation by $\bar{k}$ and write

$$\bar{k} = (1 - \alpha)(1 - \beta)A\bar{k}^{\beta}$$

The final step in deriving the steady-state value of the capital-labor ratio is to solve this equation for $\bar{k}$.[9] The solution is given by

$$\bar{k} = [(1 - \alpha)(1 - \beta)A]^{1/(1-\beta)}$$

To illustrate the use of this equation, let's plug in the values $\alpha = .5$, $\beta = .3$, and $A = 10$. This gives

$$\bar{k} = 3.5^{1.42857} = 5.987$$

which is the same value we eventually find by repeated use of the transition equation.

9. We do so by dividing each side of the equation by $\bar{k}^{\beta}$, so that $\bar{k}/\bar{k}^{\beta} = (1 - \alpha)(1 - \beta)A$, or $\bar{k}^{(1-\beta)} = (1 - \alpha)(1 - \beta)A$. Next we raise each side of this equation to the power $1/(1 - \beta)$.

We can use the value of the steady-state capital-labor ratio to calculate directly the steady-state values of all the other economic variables. Specifically, we can multiply $\bar{k}$ by N to calculate the steady-state capital stock, $\bar{K}$. Inserting the steady-state values of capital and labor into the production function determines the steady-state level of output, $\bar{Y}$. We can also use the steady-state capital-labor ratio to determine the marginal products of labor and capital that prevail in the steady state; they will equal the steady-state values of the wage and interest rate, $\bar{w}$ and $\bar{r}$, respectively. Finally, the steady-state values of consumption when young, $\bar{c}_y$, and consumption when old, $\bar{c}_o$, are calculated as $(1 - \alpha)\bar{w}$ and $\bar{k}(1 + \bar{r})$, respectively.

Steady-State Saving and Investment

Since the capital stock is fixed in the steady state—it's the same period after period—the change in the capital stock between any two time periods when the economy is in its steady state is zero. Since national investment is defined as the change over time in the economy's capital stock, the steady-state value of national investment is zero. So too is the steady-state value of national saving.[10]

A steady-state level of saving of zero may seem strange at first. After all, even when the economy is in its steady state there are still new generations coming along each period who save for their old age. True, but in the steady state the positive saving by the young just offsets the negative saving (the dissaving) by the old, leaving total saving equal to zero. In each period in the steady state, each old person receives income of $\bar{r}\bar{k}$, but consumes $\bar{k}(1 + \bar{r})$. Hence, each old person's saving is $\bar{r}\bar{k} - \bar{k}(1 + \bar{r}) = -\bar{k}$. But $\bar{k}$ not only equals the steady-state dissaving of each old person, it also equals the amount of capital being accumulated by each young person; i.e., it equals the amount of saving by each young person. Hence, the steady-state saving of the young is exactly offset by the steady-state dissaving of the old, and aggregate saving equals zero.

HOW GROWTH AFFECTS THE WELFARE OF DIFFERENT GENERATIONS

Now that we've seen how variables change and where they end up, let's go back to see how the welfare of different generations is affected along the way in the transition calculated in Table 3-1. The fact that the wage rate rises and the interest rate falls over this transition has important implications for the welfare of each generation. The rising wage shifts the budget constraints of successive generations outward; the lower interest rate rotates the budget constraints

10. If we were to include depreciation of the capital stock in our model, the steady state would feature positive gross investment, with the level of gross investment each period just sufficient to make up for the depreciation of capital in that period. Although gross investment would be positive, net investment—gross investment less depreciation—would be zero, as would net national saving, defined as total output minus depreciation minus total consumption.

Figure 3-5 Budget Constraints of Successive Generations

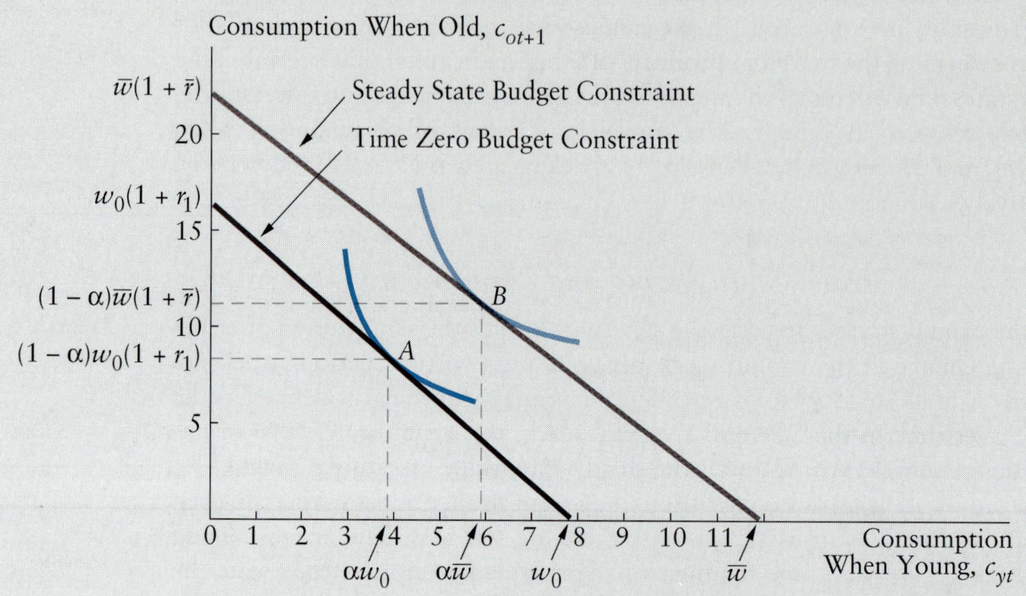

During the transition in which k rises to a higher steady-state value, the wage rate rises and the interest rate falls. That means that budget constraints shift outward and become flatter over time. Each successive generation is able to consume on a higher indifference curve, so that each is better off than its predecessor. The figure shows that generations born in the steady state, consuming at point B, enjoy more consumption when young and more when old than do those born at time 0 (point A).

inward and away from consumption when old. As we showed in Chapter 2, a lower real interest rate means a higher price of consumption when old. Thus, the budget constraints shift in response to changes in prices as well as changes in income.

The net impact of these changes on successive generations is indicated in Figure 3-5, which shows the budget constraint of the generation born at time 0 as well as those of generations born in the steady state. The budget constraints of other generations, such as the one born at time 3, lie in between the budget constraints shown in Figure 3-5. The diagram suggests that as the economy heads to its steady state, each successive generation is better off than its predecessor. Each successive generation ends up on a higher budget constraint, consuming more when young and when old than generations that came before. Compare, for example, the consumption levels when young and when old of the generations born at times 0 and 1, both of which are listed in Table 3-1. In reading the consumption values of these and other generations, keep in mind that a generation is old a period later than when it is young. Hence, the value of each generation's old-age consumption can be found in the row below the value of its consumption when young. In the case of generation 0, consumption when young is 3.953 and consumption when old is 8.484. For generation 1, consumption when young is 5.286 and consumption when old is 10.230. Thus, generation 1 consumes 33.7 percent more when young and 20.6 percent more when old than generation 0. The bigger percentage increase in consumption when young than when old across the two generations reflects generation 1's response to the lower interest rate. This lower rate leads generation 1 to substitute away from consumption when old and toward consumption when young. But the income effects of a higher wage lead it to consume more both when young and when old. The net impact of these income and substitution effects is higher consumption both when young and when old for generation 1 compared with generation 0, but a larger increase in consumption when young.

Let's make one more comparison of consumption levels—between generations born in the long-run steady state and the generation born at time 0. The generations born in the steady state enjoy 51.4 percent more consumption when young and 31.1 percent more consumption when old—as shown by point *B* in Figure 3-5. Thus, the process of economic growth described by this particular illustration of our model has a very powerful effect in raising the living standards of successive generations. Of course, the extent of improvement in economic welfare during the transition to the steady state depends on how far from steady state the transition begins. In our illustration, the economy was rather far from the steady state. Its capital-labor ratio at time *t* was only 25 percent of the steady-state capital-labor ratio.

Case Study: Post–World War II Japanese and German Capital Deepening

One question left unanswered about our illustrative transition (Table 3-1) is how it started. How did the capital stock at time 0 come to equal 150 units? If the capital stock at time 0 had instead been 598.7 units—the steady-state value—the capital stock at time 1 and all future dates would also have equaled 598.7 units. This is what the words "steady-state value of the capital stock" mean.

One way the transition may have gotten started is through a war. Suppose the economy had been in its steady state, but that at the beginning of period 0 (before production occurs) there was a war that destroyed almost three-quarters of the capital stock, leaving only 150 units of capital for production at the end of period 0. For purposes of discussion, also suppose there was no loss in life in the war, so the postwar labor force always equals *N*. Then the postwar (period 0 and beyond) growth of the economy would be exactly as shown by the transition in Table 3-1.

Let's further suppose the war was fought against another country with the same economic structure, but which suffered no damage to its capital stock or to its labor force and, in that sense, was victorious. (By the "same economic structure" we mean the same values of A, α, and β, and, thus, the same form of the transition equation.) Finally, let's assume the victorious country was also in a steady state prior to the war. Since the victor lost none of its inputs at time 0, it remains in its steady state in time 0 and thereafter. The victorious country thus experiences zero growth and has a zero saving rate in the postwar period. The losing country, whose economy is described in Table 3-1, experiences very rapid growth and exhibits a very high saving rate for several periods. The postwar growth and saving rates of the losing country always exceed those of the winning country. However, the catching-up process slows down over time, in the sense that the losing country's growth and saving rates are initially very high and then decline through time.

Citizens of the winning country may be distressed to observe that it is neither growing nor saving in the postwar period, while the losing country is doing a lot of both as it catches up. The winner can take solace from the fact that during the catching-up period its per capita income remains above the losing country's. How long does the catching up process take? Quite a while, according to Table 3-1. As mentioned above, even after two periods—60 years in real time—the losing country's per capita income is still less than the winning country's.

This discussion has some strong parallels to the post–World War II performances of the Japanese and German economies compared with that of the United States. Intense Allied bombing during World War II destroyed a large portion of the Japanese and German capital stocks. In contrast, the U.S. nonmilitary capital stock survived the war entirely undamaged. As a consequence, Japan and Germany started the postwar era with much smaller capital-labor ratios than the U.S.[11] To a certain extent the remarkable postwar growth and saving rates of the Japanese and German economies can be understood as a process of catching up with the U.S. through restoration of their steady-state capital-labor ratios. Figure 3-6 shows the post-1950 convergence of the Japanese and German living standards to that in the U.S. (measured by per capita income). The figure indicates that Japanese and German per capita incomes were only 14 percent and 36 percent of the U.S. level in 1950, respectively. By 1988, Japan and Germany had reached 66 and 68 percent of U.S. per capita income, respectively.

Figure 3-7 compares saving and growth rates in the three economies between 1960 and 1991.[12] Over this period the annual Japanese saving rate averaged 1.7 times the U.S. rate, and the German saving rate averaged 1.4 times the U.S. rate. The Japanese and German saving rates declined through the early 1980s, in accordance with the prediction of our simple model. Since the early 1980s Japanese and German saving rates have increased dramatically, while the

---

11. Postwar Japanese, German, and American capital-labor ratios depended not just on the amount of capital that survived the war, but also on the number of Japanese, German, as well as American workers who survived. Although a very large number of workers—or potential workers—in each of these countries were killed in the hostilities, there was a larger proportionate destruction of capital than of workers in Japan and Germany than in the U.S.

12. The saving rates in Figure 3-7 are based on Organization for Economic Cooperation and Development (OECD) data, which measure government consumption differently from the U.S. National Income and Product Accounts (NIPA). NIPA data are used in Figure 2-9, which explains why the U.S. saving rate differs in the two figures.

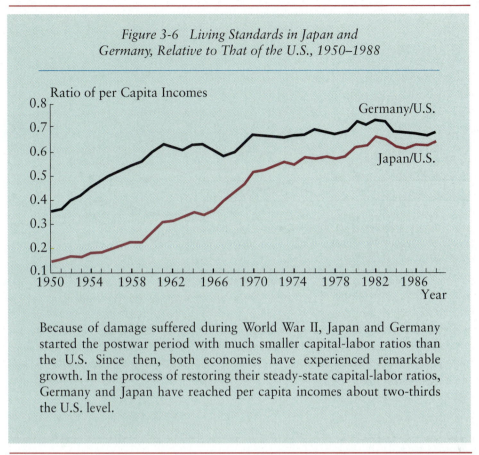

Figure 3-6 Living Standards in Japan and Germany, Relative to That of the U.S., 1950–1988

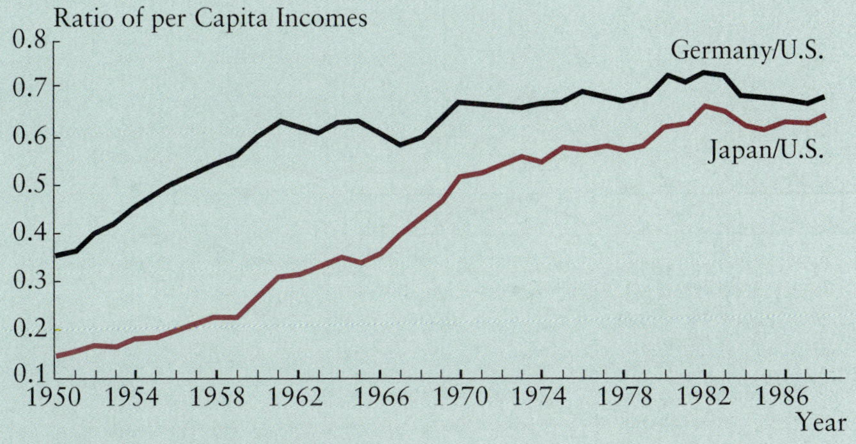

Because of damage suffered during World War II, Japan and Germany started the postwar period with much smaller capital-labor ratios than the U.S. Since then, both economies have experienced remarkable growth. In the process of restoring their steady-state capital-labor ratios, Germany and Japan have reached per capita incomes about two-thirds the U.S. level.

Source: R. Summers and A. Heston, *The Penn World Table,* Department of Economics, University of Pennsylvania

U.S. saving rate has plummeted. As a consequence, huge differences remain between the saving rates of Japan and Germany, on the one hand, and the U.S., on the other.

To summarize these postwar comparisons, the Japanese and German economies have been catching up to the American economy over the past several decades. But the American economy has not been a stationary target. Rather, its saving and growth rates have declined, thus causing the U.S. to play a form of "catch-down" with the Japanese and German economies.

Case Study: The Black Plague

If wars can produce a sudden decline in a country's capital-labor ratio, is there anything that can produce a sudden increase? One such mechanism is an epidemic that wipes out a large fraction of the labor force. Unfortunately, the world has experienced such epidemics off and on throughout recorded history. The current AIDS epidemic, left uncontrolled, has the potential for killing millions of people during their prime working years. As of 1993, the estimated

Figure 3-7 U.S., Japanese, and German National Saving Rates, 1960–1991

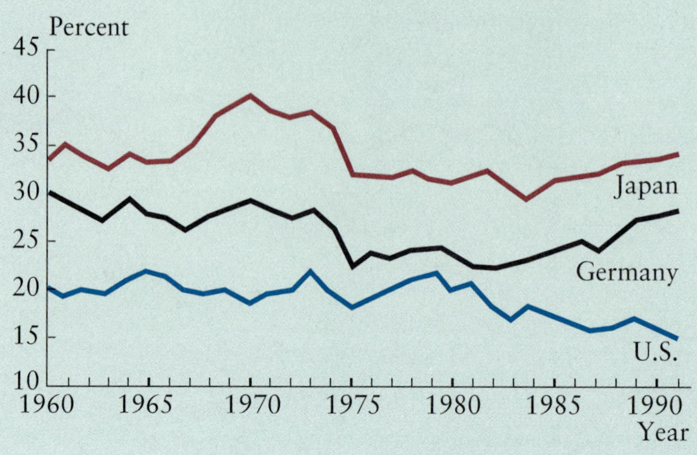

In the years since 1960, Germany and Japan have each saved a larger share of their national incomes than the U.S. has. The high saving rates in Germany and Japan have enabled them to approach the U.S. in terms of capital-labor ratios and per capita incomes. Meanwhile, U.S. saving and growth rates have declined.

Source: O.E.C.D.

number of people in the world with AIDS had reached 10.5 million, with projections of 30 million by the turn of the century. In the U.S. and a number of other countries, AIDS is now a leading cause of death among the middle-aged.

The most notorious epidemic in history was the Black Death—the scourge of bubonic and pneumonic plague that killed about one-third of Europe's population between 1348 and 1351. The plague's intensity differed across regions; in some areas almost half the population was wiped out. In England the plague returned in 1368, 1374, and 20 more times in the fifteenth century. The Black Death, combined with recurring wars, reduced England's population from 3.7 million in 1348 to 2.1 million in 1430.[13] The dramatic population declines in England and other regions were associated with equally dramatic increases in capital-labor ratios, since the principal form of capital—agricultural land—remained intact. Economic historians, studying commercial records of the period, report substantial increases in real wages in the aftermath of the plague. In

13. Robert Paul Thomas and Douglass North, *The Rise of the Western World* (New York: Cambridge University Press, 1973).

Table 3-2 The Transition Path Following an Epidemic

Period	k_t	K_t	Y_t	w_t	r_t	c_{yt}	c_{ot}	S_t	I_t
Pre-plague	5.987	598.7	1710.6	11.975	.857	5.987	11.119	0.00	0.00
0	8.936	598.7	1292.5	13.503	.648	6.752	9.864	–146.36[a]	–146.36
1	6.752	452.4	1188.2	12.414	.788	6.207	12.072	–36.48	–36.48
2	6.207	415.9	1158.6	12.105	.836	6.052	11.395	–10.36	–10.36
3	6.052	405.5	1149.9	12.014	.851	6.007	11.201	–3.06	–3.06
4	6.007	402.5	1147.3	11.986	.855	5.993	11.144	–0.91	–0.91
5	5.993	401.5	1146.5	11.978	.856	5.989	11.127	–0.27	–0.27
6	5.989	401.3	1146.3	11.976	.857	5.988	11.122	–0.08	–0.08
7	5.988	401.2	1146.2	11.975	.857	5.987	11.120	–0.02	–0.02
.	.	.	.	.	.	.	.	.	.
.	.	.	.	.	.	.	.	.	.
.	.	.	.	.	.	.	.	.	.
∞	5.987	401.2	1146.2	11.975	.857	5.987	11.119	0.00	0.00

[a]Note that in subtracting aggregate consumption from output to form aggregate saving in period *t*, we need to multiply the consumption of the old by 100 (the number of elderly at time *t*), whereas we need to multiply the consumption of the young by only 67 (the number of young survivors of the time *t* epidemic). At any point from time 1 onward, there are always 67 old and 67 young people.
Assumptions: $k_0 = 8.936$; $\alpha = .5$; $\beta = .3$; $A = 10$; $N = 67$

England, real wages rose by over one-quarter in the years after the Black Death.[14]

An increase in real wages as a consequence of a sudden rise in the capital-labor ratio is exactly what our model predicts. Table 3-2 illustrates the case of an epidemic that strikes our economy at time 0, when it is in its steady state with a capital stock of 598.7 units and a work force of 100 young people. When the epidemic hits, it wipes out a third of young workers, reducing their total to 67. The size of each generation born after the epidemic is also 67. This reflects our assumption that at the end of each period, the generation that is young gives birth to an equal number of children who constitute the young workers of the following period.

The epidemic kills people, not capital. So at time 0 there are still 598.7 units of capital on hand to be used by the 67 surviving workers. Thus, the capital-labor ratio at time 0 no longer equals the steady-state value of 5.987—598.7 units of capital divided by 100 workers. Instead it equals 8.936—598.7 units of

14. B. H. Slicher Van Bath, *The Agrarian History of Western Europe*, A.D. *500–1850* (London: Edward Arnold, 1963), 326–327.

capital divided by 67 workers. At time 0, the higher capital-labor ratio drives up the wage and drives down the interest rate. This makes the young survivors of the epidemic better off, at least on economic grounds, but makes the elderly survivors worse off; they have the same amount of capital, but earn less interest on it.

The wage at time 0 is driven up to 13.503—13 percent larger than the pre-epidemic steady-state wage. The interest rate is driven down to 0.648, about a quarter smaller than its pre-epidemic value. As the economy evolves, the capital-labor ratio falls back to its pre-epidemic, steady-state value. This produces a decline over time in the wage and an increase over time in the interest rate. Since the wage remains above its pre-epidemic value until the economy returns to its former steady-state capital-labor ratio, all generations born in the interim end up better off as a result of the epidemic.

The explanation for why the capital-labor ratio falls during the transition runs like this. The increase in the capital-labor ratio produced by the epidemic raises the wage of the generation that is young at time 0. This leads them to accumulate more capital for period 1 than would otherwise have been the case. But because of diminishing returns, the wage at time 0 increases by a smaller percentage than the capital-labor ratio. This means that the capital-labor ratio at time 1, which depends on the wage at time 0, increases by a smaller percentage than does the capital-labor ratio at time 0. So there is more capital relative to labor at time 1 than there would have been without the epidemic, but not as much as at time 0, immediately following the epidemic. Over time, the capital-labor ratio gets smaller each period, but the reductions in the capital-labor ratio between successive periods also get smaller, so the ratio ends up stabilizing at the steady-state value.

During the transition back to the steady state the national economy illustrated in Table 3-2 dissaves. The positive saving done by the young each period is more than outweighed by the dissaving of the old in the period. Again, this makes sense, because the old people alive in, say, period 5 are dissaving based on the saving they did out of the wages they earned when young—w_4. But since wages are falling over the transition, w_4 exceeds w_5—the wage out of which the young in period 5 save. So the wage underlying the dissaving of the old (last period's wage) exceeds the wage underlying the saving of the young (this period's wage).

The epidemic does not change the form of the transition equation for the capital-labor ratio, and that is why the economy ultimately ends up with the same steady-state capital-labor ratio, wage and interest rates, levels of consumption when young and old, and level of output per worker. But in permanently reducing the population size—the number of young suppliers of labor and the number of old suppliers of capital—the epidemic permanently reduces the total supplies of both capital and labor as well as the level of output. In Table 3-2 the steady-state levels of capital and output are precisely one-third less than their pre-epidemic steady-state values. The one-third reduction in capital and output is the same as that in the work force. That is what we expect, since the transition equation tells us that capital per worker and output per worker are the same as in the pre-epidemic steady state. In other words, the population size of each generation, N, ultimately determines the absolute scale of the economy, but not the level of capital per worker or any of the variables that depend on capital per worker.

THE TRANSITION PATH DIAGRAM

Now that we've described our simple economy algebraically and numerically, let's describe it graphically. The diagram we'll now develop shows the transition path for the capital-labor ratio as well as its steady-state value. It can be used to understand what happens in the aftermath of wars, epidemics, baby booms, and baby busts (sudden and dramatic reductions in the fertility rate). It can also be used to understand the economy's response to changes in saving preferences (changes in α), changes in the form of the production function (changes in β), and changes in the level of technology (changes in A). Finally, as we'll explore in detail in Chapters 7 and 8, it can be used to understand the saving and growth effects of fiscal and monetary policy.

The diagram is simply a plot of the capital-labor ratio at one point in time, say time $t + 1$, against the capital-labor ratio the period before, at time t. According to our transition equation and our assumed values for α, β, and A, we know that $k_{t+1} = 3.5k_t^{.3}$. Figure 3-8 plots this relationship. Specifically, we measure k_t on the horizontal axis and its associated value of k_{t+1}, given by $3.5k_t^{.3}$, on the vertical axis. For example, for k_t equal to 1.50, the value of k_{t+1} is 3.953 ($3.5 \times 1.50^{.3}$), so the height of the curve above the value of 1.50 is 3.953. For k_t equal to 4.00, $k_{t+1} = 3.5 \times 4.00^{.3} = 5.305$, and the height of the curve above the value of 4.00 is 5.305. And if k_t is 8.00, then k_{t+1} is $3.5 \times 8.00^{.3} = 6.531$, which is the height of the curve above 8.00.

The concave shape of the transition curve reflects the fact that the value of β, which determines the exponent of k_t, is a number less than 1. The larger the value of β, the less concave the shape of the curve. The curve passes through the origin, since when k_t equals zero, k_{t+1} also equals zero. Finally, the height of the curve for values of k_t greater than zero depends on the values of A, α, and β. For example, if we set A equal to 20, rather than 10, the transition equation becomes $k_{t+1} = 7.0k_t^{.3}$, and the graph of the k_{t+1} curve lies above the one shown in Figure 3-8.

Using the Transition Curve to Track the Time Path of the Capital-Labor Ratio

Since the transition equation holds for any two successive periods, the transition diagram holds as well. Figure 3-9 shows how we can use the transition diagram over and over again to determine the time path of the capital-labor ratio. Figure 3-9 is identical to Figure 3-8, except that it includes a straight line extending from the origin at a 45-degree angle. This 45-degree line will help us reuse the transition curve to follow the economy over time.

To see how this works, let's use the curve to plot the transition we calculated in Table 3-1. Specifically, let's start at time 0 with a value of k_0 equal to 1.500. This value is marked on the horizontal axis in Figure 3-9. Given this value, we

Figure 3-8 The Transition Diagram

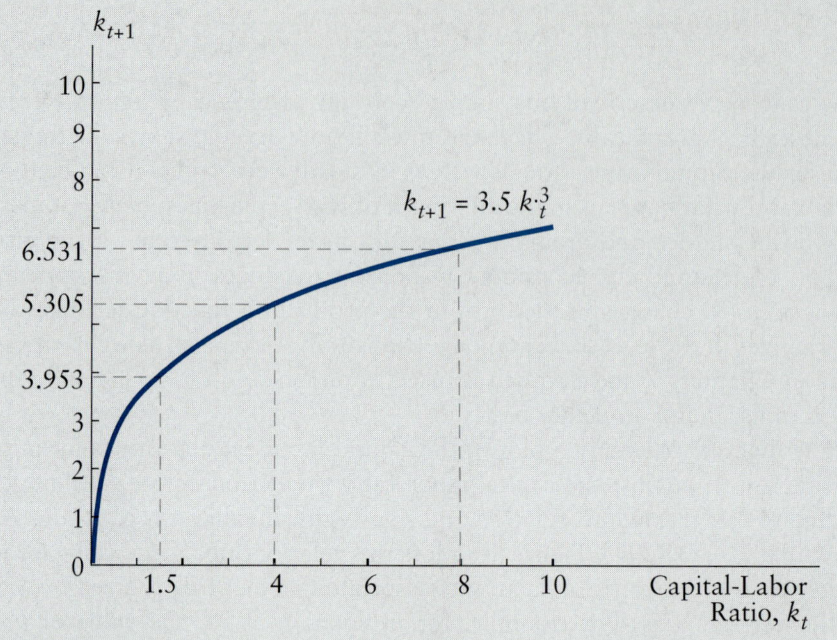

The transition curve depicted here relates the capital-labor ratio in any period, t, to the ratio in the next period, $t + 1$. For any value of the current ratio, k_t, measured on the horizontal axis, the height of the curve measures next period's ratio, k_{t+1}.

go up to the curve to find the value for k_1, which, as measured by the length of the segment *DF*, is 3.953. Now if we want to reuse the transition curve to find the value of k_2 given the value of k_1 of 3.953, we need to measure 3.953 along the horizontal axis. The 45-degree line helps us do that. We start at the value of 3.953 on the vertical axis (point *E*), then draw a horizontal line over to the 45-degree line at point *G*, and then draw a vertical from point *G* down to point *H*. The horizontal distance from the origin to point *H* is 3.953—the distance we wanted to measure on the horizontal axis. How do we know the distance from the origin to point *H* is 3.953? Because of the symmetry of the triangles 0*EG* and 0*HG*. A shortcut in getting from point *D* to point *H* is simply to start at *D*, go up to the curve to point *F*, across to *G*, and back down to point *H*.

Figure 3-10 shows the repeated use of this technique. Starting at $k_0 = 1.500$, we go up to the curve, over to the 45-degree line, and then down to find k_1. We do the same to find k_2, k_3, etc. To shorten our steps even further, we can skip the going down, and simply go up to the curve, over to the 45-degree line, up to the curve, over to the 45-degree line, and so on. The process of going up and over repeatedly is indicated by the arrows in the figure.

Figure 3-9 Adding the 45° Line to the Transition Diagram

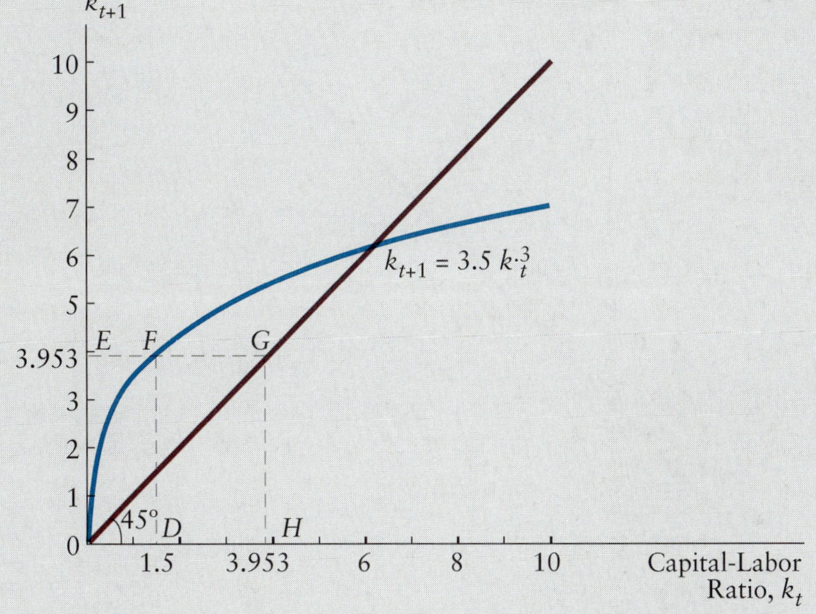

Adding a 45° line to the transition diagram makes determination of the time path of the capital-labor ratio easy. At any point along the 45° line, the horizontal distance from the origin equals the vertical distance from the origin. Starting at time 0 with a capital-labor ratio of 1.5 at point *D*, we see from this transition curve that the time 1 ratio is 3.953 at points *F* and *E*. By projecting this height over to the 45° line and then downward, we can find the value 3.953 on the horizontal axis. The properties of the 45° line ensure that distance *OH* equals distance *OE*. Thus, k_1 equals 3.953 at point *H* on the horizontal axis.

As Figure 3-10 makes clear, following the capital-labor ratio in this manner leads to convergence at the point where the curve intersects the 45-degree line. This intersection occurs at $\bar{k}$—the steady-state value of the capital-labor ratio. At the value of $\bar{k}$, going up to the curve, across to the 45-degree line, and then down puts us back at $\bar{k}$. So, when k_t equals $\bar{k}$, k_{t+1} equals $\bar{k}$ as well, which is the definition of the steady-state capital-labor ratio.

The transition we just described could well have been initiated at time 0 by a war that reduced the economy's capital-labor ratio from its steady-state value of 5.987 to a value of 1.500. Alternatively, it could have been initiated by a one-time baby boom occurring at time 0 that raised the value of *N*, the population size of each new generation, from 100 to 399. If the economy had previously been in its steady state, its capital stock would have equaled 598.7, and the

Figure 3-10 Using the Transition Diagram: A Shortcut

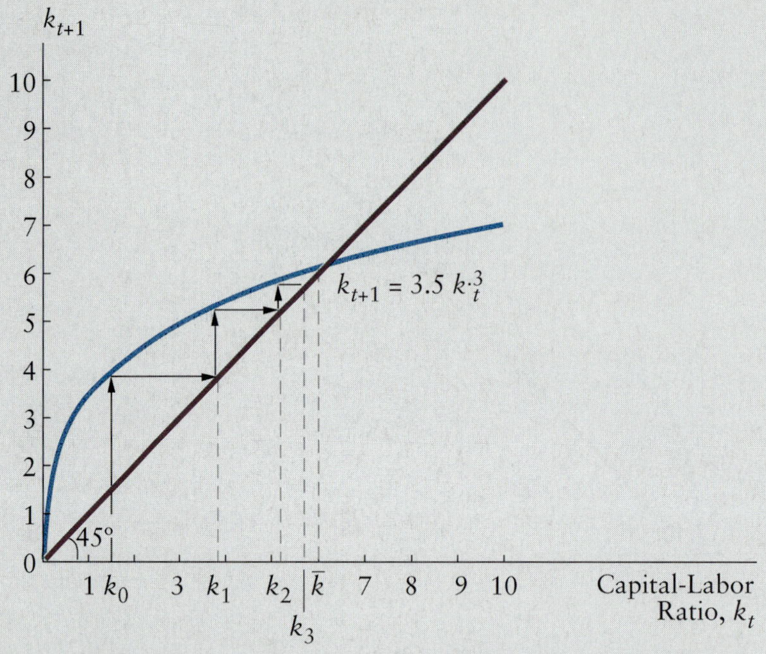

The transition diagram with a 45° line, can be used to trace the movement of the capital-labor ratio from any initial value to its ultimate steady-state value. Beginning at k_0, we read up to the transition curve to find k_1. We then move from that point over to the 45° line and downward, to locate k_1 on the horizontal axis. From that point, we read up to the 45° line to determine k_2. The arrows indicate a shortcut way of determining the capital-labor ratio in any period, and its ultimate steady-state value.

higher value of N would have lowered the time 0 value of the capital-labor ratio to 1.500.

We can also use the diagram to describe the transition following the epidemic illustrated in Table 3-2. We do so in Figure 3-11 by starting with $k_0 =$ 8.936, which is to the right of the steady-state capital-labor ratio of 5.987. To determine the value of k_1, we again go up to the curve. And to measure k_1 along the horizontal axis, we again go across to the 45-degree line and back down. The arrows in the figure show how we can trace the transition to the steady state by going over and down repeatedly. Whether we measure the capital-labor ratio each period on the vertical or horizontal axis, it is clear that Figure 3-10 shows a transition in which the capital-labor ratio rises through time to $\bar{k}$, and Figure 3-11 shows a transition in which the capital-labor ratio declines through time to $\bar{k}$.

Figure 3-11 The Transition Following an Epidemic

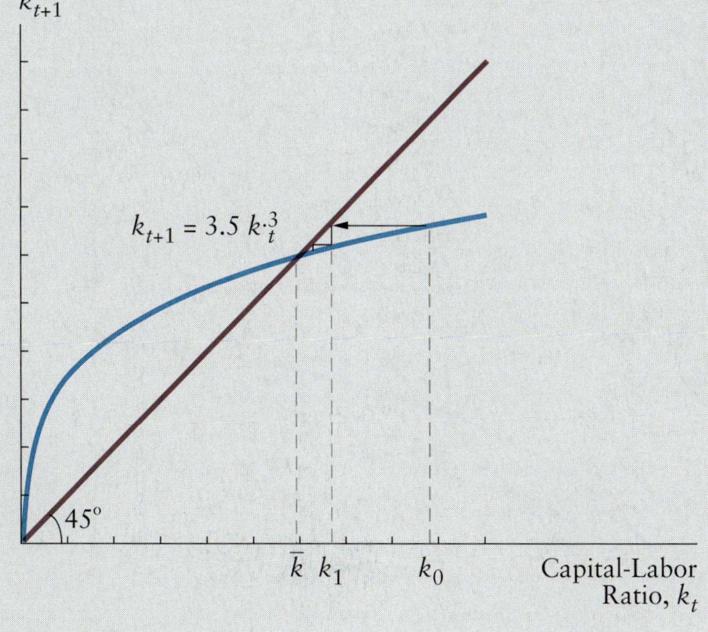

An epidemic that killed many young workers would initially raise the capital-labor ratio. Starting from this higher value of k_0, forces would be set in motion that would restore the capital-labor ratio to its steady-state value of $\bar{k}$. The arrows in the figure trace the transition.

Using the Transition Diagram to Study Changes in Saving Preferences

As described in Chapter 2, the U.S. rate of saving has declined dramatically over about the past 15 years. One possible explanation for this decline is a shift in preferences toward more consumption when young and less when old. In our model, these preferences are governed by the value of α, the propensity to consume when young out of the present value of lifetime income. The larger the value of α, the smaller the fraction of wages that each young person saves for old age. A decline in α has no permanent impact on saving in our model (steady-state saving is, as before, zero), but it does alter the steady state toward which the economy moves and lowers saving during the transition to this new steady state.

Figure 3-12 shows the transition curve before and after a rise in α. Unlike the war and epidemic examined in Figures 3-10 and 3-11, a rise in α does not involve moving along the historic transition curve. Rather, it causes a shift to a new transition curve, followed by a movement along that new curve. The reason

Figure 3-12 The Transition Following an Increase in the Propensity to Consume

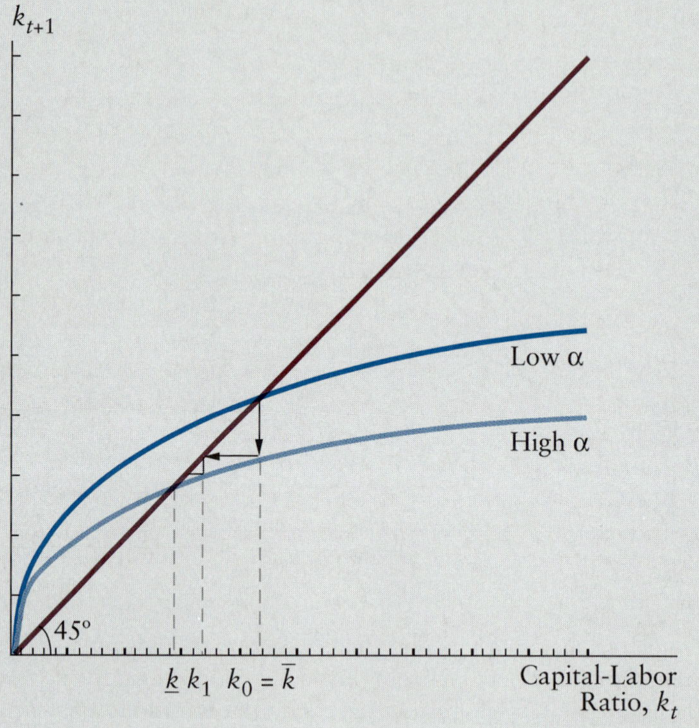

The transition curve is drawn for given values of A, the technology coefficient; β, capital's share of output; and α, the propensity to consume. Changes in any of these values will affect the transition curve. In the diagram, an increase in α has the effect of rotating the transition curve downward, triggering a transition to a new, lower steady state. Beginning at $k_0 = \bar{k}$, the capital-labor ratio falls over time until it reaches the new steady-state value $\underline{k}$ where the lower transition curve intersects the 45° line.

we need to deal with a new transition curve is that the formula for the transition curve, $k_{t+1} = A(1 - \alpha)(1 - \beta)k_t^{\beta}$, clearly depends on α. Hence, our plot of values of k_{t+1} for different values of k_t will depend on the value we choose for α. Larger values of α shift the curve downward.

Suppose the economy of Figure 3-12 is in its steady state with capital-labor ratio $\bar{k}$ at time 0, when the first generation to have a larger α appears. The transition path of the capital-labor ratio will be as indicated by the arrows. To find the capital-labor ratio prevailing at time 1, we start with the value of k_0 which, by assumption, equals $\bar{k}$, and go down to the new transition curve. Then we follow this new transition curve by going across and down, across and down, until we reach $\underline{k}$ the new steady-state capital-labor ratio.

Since $\underline{k}$ lies to the left of $\bar{k}$, we see that the increase in α causes a reduction over time in the capital-labor ratio. With the labor supply fixed each period, the decline in the capital-labor ratio means a decline over time in the absolute amount of capital. And since investment is the change over time in capital, national investment must be negative during the transition, as is national saving. Thus, an increased preference for consumption when young produces a temporary decline in national saving, but a permanent reduction in the capital stock. If, as some have claimed, today's young and middle-aged Americans are less saving-oriented than their parents' and grandparents' generations, the U.S. may be experiencing the kind of transitional decline in saving indicated in Figure 3-12.[15]

ADDING POPULATION AND TECHNOLOGICAL CHANGE TO OUR MODEL

So far we've assumed away population growth and technological change to focus attention on the process of capital accumulation. As we show in the Appendix, adding these elements back into the model requires only minor modifications of our transition equation. With population growth or technological change, the capital accumulation process described above remains basically the same. In particular, each period's capital stock continues to reflect the saving done by the young in the previous period. And if population growth or technological change proceeds at a constant rate, the economy eventually converges to a steady state, albeit not one in which all variables remain constant through time. Instead, some variables remain constant and others grow at a constant rate.

Consider first population growth, holding the level of technology fixed. Population growth means there are more young people saving each period than there were in the previous period. Consequently, were the amount of saving per young person to remain constant through time, the total capital stock would nonetheless grow simply because there are more young savers around each period. This is precisely what happens in our model in the steady state assuming a constant rate of population growth. The amount of saving per young person remains the same through time, but the absolute size of the capital stock grows at the same rate as the number of young savers grows. Since young savers are also the economy's young workers, this means the capital stock and the labor supply both grow at the same rate in the steady state. Consequently, the capital-labor ratio in the steady state is constant, just as in the case of no population growth.

So, in the steady state with population growth, we find that all variables that depend on the capital-labor ratio, such as the wage, the interest rate, and output per worker, remain constant. All aggregate variables, such as output, the capital stock, and the work force, grow at the rate of growth of the population. Thus,

15. Michael J. Boskin and Lawrence Lau, "An Analysis of Postwar U.S. Consumption and Saving," Parts I and II, National Bureau of Economic Research working papers 2605 and 2606, June 1988.

the absolute size of the economy grows through time, but in per capita terms it remains constant.

Next, consider technological progress, holding the population fixed.[16] With technological progress, even if the capital-labor ratio were to remain unchanged through time (it doesn't), the wage would grow because the technology coefficient (A_t), which enters the formula for the marginal product of labor, would be larger each period. But a higher wage each period means that the capital-labor ratio will increase each period as well. The reason is that each generation will save more (accumulate more capital) than the previous generation. Since we are assuming no growth in the work force, this means a higher capital-labor ratio through time. So technological progress, by raising the level of the wage each period, raises the capital-labor ratio each period.

If the rate of technological progress is constant, the economy will eventually converge to a steady state. This steady state features growth, at a constant rate, both in aggregate variables, such as output and the capital stock, and in per capita variables, such as capital per worker, output per worker, and the wage paid per worker. Thus, unlike the steady state with constant population growth, a steady state with constant technological progress means rising living standards through time.

Understanding Technological Change: The Study of Endogenous Growth

Chapter 1 stated that measured technological change "explains" a significant share of overall economic growth as well as growth in labor productivity. The chapter also revealed that there is considerable debate over the source of technological change. Some economists believe that what we measure as technological change is largely improvements in the quality of capital and labor. That is, they believe technological change is mostly embodied in inputs. Others believe that measured technological change primarily reflects pure technological breakthroughs—the discovery of ways to produce more products, better products, and new products with the same inputs.

The importance of technological change and the fact that its precise determinants are poorly understood has made its study a hot topic. Some economists have focused on the role of research and development, as influenced by government patent protection, in producing new technological breakthroughs. Others have studied learning-by-doing and the diffusion of production know-how among workers, industries, and countries, and even across generations. Still others have considered how better education becomes embodied in human capital and how better technology becomes embodied in physical capital.

What all of this new research has in common is that it makes technological change endogenous to (caused or produced by, and thus, responsive to) economic decisions. For this reason the growth processes under study are referred

16. In the Appendix we consider the effects of population and productivity growth together, but it is easy to separate the two effects.

to as **endogenous growth**. Endogenous growth models typically predict that the economy will experience a constant rate of technological progress, at least in the long run. But these growth models also show that the particular rate of technological progress the economy ends up with is not immutable. Instead, it reflects economic decisions, such as how much to invest in research and development or how much schooling to provide children.

Endogenous growth *A growth process in which the long-run rate of growth is determined by economic decisions, such as how much to invest in R&D or how much schooling to provide children*

Another feature common to all endogenous growth models is that the process producing technological change does not peter out over time. To sustain growth through the indefinite future, it is not enough for technology to improve by a fixed amount and then stay fixed. Instead, technology must continually improve. For this to happen the forces generating technological progress cannot be subject to diminishing returns. For example, if research and development is the critical input in technological progress one must assume that, regardless of the amount of R&D done in the past, an additional dollar spent on R&D will generate as much additional technological progress now as it did in the past.

We do not have space in this text to extend our life-cycle model to include endogenous growth, but be assured that such extensions can be made. Consequently, we should think of endogenous growth as providing an economic explanation for changes through time in A_t which, for convenience, we take in this book to be exogenous.

Chapter Summary

1. In this chapter we developed the demand side of our two-period life-cycle model. We then combined the demand and supply sides of our model to produce a simple model of economic growth.

2. We showed that firms' demands for capital and labor result from their maximization of profit. Firms hire these inputs up to the point at which their marginal revenues equal their marginal costs. The marginal cost of capital is the interest rate, and the marginal cost of labor is the wage.

3. In our simple model with its Cobb-Douglas production function, the formulas for the marginal products of capital and labor depend on the capital-labor ratio. If the capital-labor ratio is high, capital is relatively abundant and labor is relatively scarce. This makes the marginal product of capital low and the marginal product of labor high.

4. The values of capital and labor entering the marginal product formulas represent the demands by firms for these inputs. But in equilibrium the total demands by firms for capital and labor must equal the total supplies of these inputs by the household sector. At any one time the supply of capital is given by the past asset accumulation of those who are currently old. And the labor supply is given by the number of young people. Equating each period's input supplies and demands determines the period's equilibrium wage and interest rate.

5. In our model, knowledge of this period's wage is sufficient to determine next period's capital-labor ratio. But since this period's wage depends on this period's capital-labor ratio, there is a relationship (the transition equation) between this period's and next period's capital-labor ratio.

6. Given the value of the capital-labor ratio at some point, say time 0, we can use the transition equation to calculate the capital-labor ratio in all subsequent periods. And the time path of the capital-labor ratio is all we need to compute the time paths of all of the economy's other variables. The transition equation and its associated graph indicate that in the absence of population growth or technological change, growth as well as saving are temporary, or transitional, phenomena.

7. The fact that country A is growing faster and saving more than country B does not necessarily mean that country B will be left in the dust. Country A may simply be catching up with country B. According to our model, the catching-up process can take many years.

8. The process of transitional growth may be triggered by shocks to the economy's capital-labor ratio. Examples of such shocks are wars, epidemics, baby booms, and baby busts. Transitional growth may also be triggered by factors that alter the transition equation. These factors include changes in the propensity of the young to consume (α), in the level of technology (A), and in capital's coefficient in the production function (β). Once the transition curve shifts, the economy's transition is determined by that new curve.

9. Adding population and productivity growth to the model requires only minor modifications to the transition equation. If either the population growth rate or the productivity growth rate is constant, the economy will converge to a steady state, but one in which certain variables grow at a constant rate through time.

10. Economists are actively trying to understand the forces behind technological progress through their research on endogenous growth. Endogenous growth models assume that an economy's rate of technological progress is determined by economic factors, such as the extent of research and development.

Key Concepts

General equilibrium
Capital structure
Marginal product of capital
Marginal product of labor
Marginal cost of capital
Marginal cost of labor
Transition equation
Steady state
Endogenous growth

Review Questions

1. What are *equity* and *dividends*? Using notation from the life-cycle model, show how these factors relate to saving by the young and consumption by the elderly.

2. If the elderly lend their savings to firms instead of purchasing ownership in firms, how does that affect the amount of consumption they can enjoy when they are old?

3. What is *capital structure*, and how has it changed over recent history for U.S. nonfinancial corporations? Taking into account institutional factors such as bankruptcy laws, why might there be some differences between using debt finance and using equity finance?

4. How do the human capital assumptions used in the life-cycle model differ from human capital development in the real world?

5. To economists, what does the term *pure profit* mean? How does it differ from the term *profit* in everyday parlance? If pure profit is zero, are firms earning any return on their capital?

6. What is meant by *competitive input markets*? Specifically, what conditions lead input markets to be competitive, and what are the implications for factor prices?

7. What is *marginal revenue*? What is *marginal cost*? Why must they be equal if profit is being maximized?

8. What happens to the value of the marginal product of capital as more capital is employed? Illustrate your answer using the intensive-form formulas for the marginal product. What is the term given to describe this property? Show whether the same property holds for increasing labor. Also show what impact an increase in capital has on the marginal product of *labor*.

9. What information is provided by the *transition equation*? Explain what is meant by the *steady state*. How can the transition equation help us determine how the economy looks in the steady state?

10. Why does growth ultimately cease when the labor force and technology are constant?

11. How does the life-cycle model help explain changes in the standard of living over time and other phenomena such as adjustments following loss of capital or labor due to extraordinary events such as war and plagues?

12. What distinguishes *endogenous growth* models from variants of the life-cycle model considered thus far?

Numerical Questions

Assume the following values when answering questions 1 through 6: $A = 4$, $N = 200$, $K_0 = 300$, $\alpha = .5$, and $\beta = .3$.

1. a. Calculate the equilibrium values of w_0 and r_0.
   b. What happens to w_0 and r_0 if K_0 rises to 400?
   c. What happens to w_0 and r_0 if N rises to 250?
   d. What happens to w_0 and r_0 if β falls to 0.25?
2. a. Calculate the time path of k_t, K_t, Y_t, w_t, and r_t for periods 1 through 5.
   b. What are the steady-state values of these variables?
   c. What percent of the capital stock's transition to the steady state occurs between period 0 and period 1? between period 4 and period 5? Explain any difference.
   d. At what rate will k_t, K_t, Y_t, w_t, and r_t grow in the steady state? Why?
3. Suppose that the economy is currently in the steady state calculated in question 2. Congress suddenly alters immigration laws, causing an increase in N of 50.
   a. Calculate the time path of k_t, K_t, Y_t, w_t, and r_t for the five periods after the change in N.

b. What are the new steady-state values of k_t, K_t, Y_t, w_t, and r_t?
c. Compare the new steady-state values to those before the change in N. Explain any differences and similarities.

4. Once again, assume that the economy is currently in the steady state calculated in question 2. Suddenly a series of earthquakes destroys one-third of the capital stock.
   a. Calculate the new steady-state values of k_t, K_t, Y_t, w_t, and r_t.
   b. Compare the new steady-state values to those before the change in the capital stock. Explain any differences and similarities.
   c. Calculate the time path of k_t, K_t, Y_t, w_t, and r_t for the five periods after the change in the capital stock.
5. Suppose that β falls to 0.25.
   a. Compute the new steady-state values for k_t, K_t, Y_t, w_t, and r_t.
   b. Compare the new steady-state values to those computed in question 2. Explain any differences and similarities.
6. Using the initial values, graph the transition path. When drawing the graph, plot five points: two with k_t below its steady-state value, one with k_t equal to its steady state, and two with k_t above its steady-state value.
   a. Explain why a 45-degree line can be used to locate the steady-state value of k_t.
   b. How is an increase in α shown in the graph?
   c. How is a decrease in A shown in the graph?
   d. How is an increase in N shown in the graph?

Analytical Questions

1. Assuming that firms maximize profits and that the price of output is 1, why must the interest rate equal the marginal product of capital? Why must the wage rate equal the marginal product of labor?
2. Using the formulas from the Cobb-Douglas production function (i.e., using variables rather than numbers), show that if factor prices equal their marginal products, then pure profit must be zero.
3. In the life-cycle model, an increase in multifactor productivity has no effect on the steady-state value of r_t. Explain why this is so. (Helpful hint: A change in A_t has two effects on the marginal product of capital.)
4. "A country's standard of living can continue to rise only if there is ongoing technological change." Comment.
5. Many commentators have claimed that the high-spending, low-saving lifestyle of the 1980s will result in lower living standards for future generations. Use the life-cycle model to evaluate this claim.

APPENDIX

Population Growth

Rather than assume the number of people in each generation is constant through time, let's allow that number to increase each period at the rate n. Hence, if the number of young is 100 at time t, the number of young is $100 \times (1 + n)$ at time $t + 1$. The number of young at time $t + 2$ is $100 \times (1 + n) \times (1 + n)$, and so on. What's a reasonable value for n? Well, n is a 30-year population growth rate. In the U.S. the number of young and middle-aged adults increased by about 75 percent between 1960 and 1990, suggesting a value of $n = .75$. This corresponds to an annual growth rate of about 1.88 percent, since $(1 + .0188)^{30} = 1.75$.

Whatever the value of n, the important point for deriving our transition equation is that at any point in time there are $1 + n$ young workers for every old person. If we let N_t stand for the size of the generation born at time t, then at time $t + 1$ there are N_{t+1} young workers and N_t old people, where $N_{t+1} = (1 + n)N_t$. As we derive our modified transition equation, note that at time $t + 1$ the total capital stock equals the number of old people, N_t, multiplied by the assets per old person, a_{t+1}; that is, $K_{t+1} = N_t a_{t+1}$. To form k_{t+1}, we need to divide K_{t+1} by N_{t+1}, the number of workers at time $t + 1$. This gives us $k_{t+1} = N_t a_{t+1}/N_{t+1} = N_t a_{t+1}/N_t(1 + n) = a_{t+1}/(1 + n)$. Thus, because of population growth, the number of young workers differs from the number of old people. And capital per worker is no longer equal to assets per old person. Instead, it equals assets per old person divided by $(1 + n)$. We can now substitute $(1 - \alpha)w_t$ for a_{t+1} and plug in the marginal product formula for w_t, to arrive at our modified transition equation:

$$k_{t+1} = \frac{(1-\alpha)(1-\beta)Ak_t^{\beta}}{(1+n)}$$

Thus, with population growth, the modified transition equation just equals the original equation with the right-hand side divided by one plus the population growth rate.[17] We can use the same transition diagram as before, with the

17. The growth rate (n) in the number of young people each period is also the growth rate of the entire population. To see this, note that at any time $t + 1$ there are 1 + n as many old people than there were at time t and there are also $1 + n$ more young people than there were at time t. Hence, the growth rate of the entire population between the two periods is n.

caveat that we need to graph the transition curve based on the new formula that includes $(1 + n)$. We can use either the new formula or the transition diagram based on this formula to track the evolution of the economy's capital-labor ratio, as well as the evolution of other variables, like the wage and interest rate, that depend simply on the capital-labor ratio. To find the absolute quantity of capital in a particular period, we simply multiply the derived capital-labor ratio by the total number of young workers in that period. Knowledge of the total capital stock and total work force in each period can be coupled with the production function to determine total output. In the steady state, the absolute amounts of capital and labor rise through time at the population growth rate. Since the capital stock is increasing in the steady state, the steady state features positive national saving and, it follows, national investment.

As before, our modified model tracks the economy in per-worker terms. To find the economy's aggregates, we simply need to blow up the per-worker information by multiplying by the number of workers. In addition, we can still use our transition diagram to consider wars, epidemics (the one-time killing off of young people that leaves unchanged the future growth rate in the number of young people), changes in saving behavior, and changes in government policy. We can also use it to ask how a rise or fall in the rate of population growth affects capital intensity. As our modified formula makes clear, a higher population growth rate shifts the transition curve downward, meaning a lower steady-state ratio of capital to labor.

Technological Progress

It's easy to include technological progress in a more general transition equation that also includes population growth.[18] Consider the transition equation when technology varies through time, so that A is specific to a certain time, as denoted by the subscript t: $k_{t+1} = (1 - \alpha)(1 - \beta)A_t k_t^{\beta}/(1 + n)$. We can use this equation to track the transition of the economy's capital stock. To do so we need to know how A_t evolves. For example, if we start at time 0 knowing values of k_0 and A_0 as well as values for the parameters α, β, and n, we compute k_1 based on the equation $k_1 = (1 - \alpha)(1 - \beta)A_0 k_0^{\beta}/(1 + n)$. Given the computed value of k_1 and the value of A_1 we find k_2 from the equation $k_2 = (1 - \alpha)(1 - \beta)A_1 k_1^{\beta}/(1 + n)$. Given the computed value of k_2 and the value of A_2, we can find k_3. Proceeding in this manner gives us the values of the capital-labor ratio at all points in time in the future.

In the special case in which technology grows at a constant rate, say v, we can determine all future values of technology given our knowledge of A_0 and the value of v. How? By computing A_1 from $A_1 = A_0(1 + v)$, computing A_2 from $A_2 = A_1(1 + v)$, computing A_3 from $A_3 = A_2(1 + v)$, etc. With a constant growth rate of technology, our economy will converge over time to a steady state, but one in which the capital-labor ratio grows each period at a constant rate equal

18. Note that if we set the population growth rate, n, equal to zero, we end up with our standard transition equation that permits productivity growth but assumes zero population growth.

to $(1 + v)^{1/(1-\beta)} - 1$, rather than remaining fixed through time. The steady-state growth in the capital-labor ratio reflects the fact that technology raises the wage and thus, the amount of capital accumulated by each successive generation. In the steady state with a constant growth rate of technology, output per worker and the wage rate will also grow at the rate $(1 + v)^{1/(1-\beta)} - 1$, which exceeds v, the growth rate of technology. These variables grow more rapidly than technology because their growth depends on growth in the capital-labor ratio as well as growth in technology.

The one variable that does not change in the steady state is the interest rate. The reason is that opposing forces operate on the interest rate. The first is the increase in the capital-labor ratio, which would, by itself, lower the interest rate. The second is the increase in the level of technology, which, working alone, would raise the interest rate. In the steady state these opposing forces exactly offset each other, so the interest rate remains constant.

Refresher on Exponents

In stating the properties of exponents we let z, a, and b stand for three numbers. In our examples we let z equal 2, a equal 4, and b equal 3. Raising a number to the power zero gives 1.

General Form	Example
$z^0 = 1$	$2^0 = 1$

Raising a number to the power 1 gives the number.

General Form	Example
$z^1 = z$	$2^1 = 2$

Negative Exponents

General Form	Example
$z^{-a} = \frac{1}{z^a}$	$2^{-4} = \frac{1}{2^4} = \frac{1}{16} = .0625$

Addition of Exponents

General Form	Example
$z^a \times z^b = z^{a+b}$	$2^2 \times 2^3 = 2^5 = 2 \times 2 \times 2 \times 2 \times 2 = 32$

Subtraction of Exponents

General Form	Example
$\frac{z^a}{z^b} = z^a \times z^{-b} = z^{a-b}$	$\frac{2^4}{2^3} = 2^4 \times 2^{-3} = 2^1 = 2 = \frac{16}{8}$

Multiplication of Exponents

General Form	Example
$(z^a)^b = z^{a \times b}$	$(2^4)^3 = 2^{4 \times 3} = 2^{12} = 4096$

Division of Exponents

General Form	Example
$(z^a)^{1/b} = z^{a/b}$	$(2^4)^{1/3} = 2^{4/3} = 2^{1.333} = 2.519$

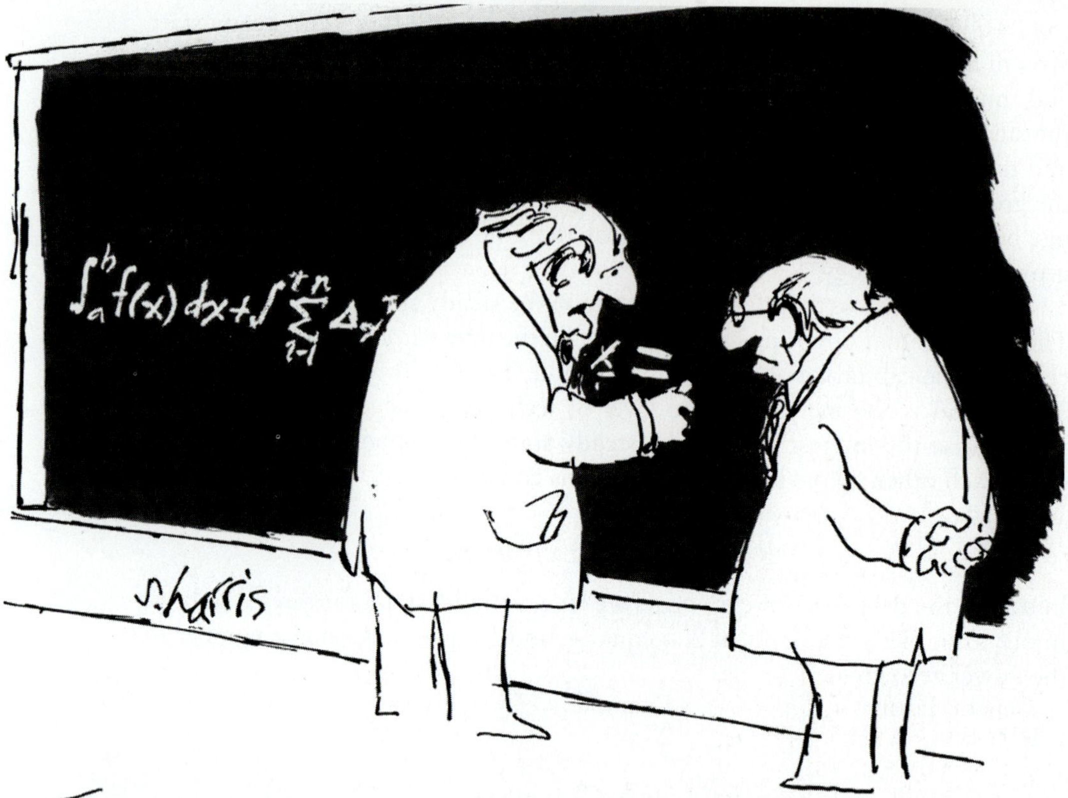

"THIS IS THE PART I ALWAYS HATE."

Table A–1 The Complete Model for Any Time t

Labor Supply Equals the Number of Young	$L_t = N$
Capital Supply Equals Assets of the Elderly	$K_t = Na_t$
Assets of the Elderly Equal Their Savings When Young	$a_{t+1} = (1 - \alpha)w_t$
Capital per Worker Is Denoted by k	$k_t = \frac{K_t}{L_t}$
Output	$Y_t = A_t K_t^{\beta} L_t^{(1-\beta)}$
Marginal Product of Labor Equals the Wage	$w_t = (1 - \beta)A_t k_t^{\beta}$
Marginal Product of Capital Equals the Interest Rate	$r_t = \beta A_t k_t^{(\beta-1)}$
Transition Equation	$k_{t+1} = (1 - \alpha)(1 - \beta)A_t k_t^{\beta}$
The Young Consume α of Their Wages	$c_{yt} = \alpha w_t$
The Old Consume Their Assets Plus Interest	$c_{ot} = a_t(1 + r_t)$
National Saving Equals Output Less Aggregate Consumption	$S_t = Y_t - Nc_{yt} - Nc_{ot}$
National Investment Equals the Increase in the Capital Stock	$I_t = K_{t+1} - K_t$

C H A P T E R 4

Economic Fluctuations

INTRODUCTION

Recession
A period of declining output and employment in many sectors of the economy, usually lasting from six months to a year

Expansion
A period between recessions characterized by economic growth

In July of 1990 the U.S. economy entered a **recession**—a period of negative growth and relatively low utilization of inputs—for the ninth time since the end of World War II. The recession ended eight months later, in March 1991. The 1990–1991 recession interrupted nearly eight years of economic growth that constituted the second longest **expansion** in this century. But how did the 1990 recession begin? What caused it? What distinguished the recession month of August 1990 from the expansion month of August 1989? How could we tell that the recession had ended? Why was the previous recession, during 1981–1982, more severe, and why did it last longer?

To many economists, short-run economic fluctuations are the most interesting and intriguing aspect of macroeconomics. The central question associated with fluctuations is simply their *cause*. We'll see in Chapter 10 that there are a number of suspects, but no clear culprit. But first, we need to understand the characteristics of economic fluctuations, to set the stage for the subsequent challenging (and at times perilous!) search for the explanation of economic booms and busts.

In the previous chapters, we developed a model in which the economy grows smoothly through time. However, as we saw in Chapter 1, economic growth is not always smooth. This chapter considers economic fluctuations—also called **business cycles**—in more detail and relates them to the model developed in Chapters 2 and 3. It begins by discussing business cycle measurement, then turns to some issues of business cycle theory. Among the questions we'll address are:

Business cycles *Periodic increases and decreases in output and employment around the economy's long-run growth path*

- How is the stage of the business cycle determined at any particular time?
- How is unemployment defined, and how does it vary over the business cycle?
- How does labor productivity behave over the cycle?
- What are the relative cyclical behaviors of consumption and investment?
- How strongly are economic fluctuations related across countries?
- What is the relationship between seasonal fluctuations and business cycle fluctuations?
- Can our dynamic life-cycle model help explain economic fluctuations?

To address the last question, we will use our model to describe one particular view of business cycles—namely, the theory of *real business cycles*. According to this view, economic fluctuations can be traced to periodic *shocks*, or disturbances, to the economy's production function. The real business cycle explanation of recessions is controversial. We present it here not because it is necessarily a more convincing explanation than others we'll describe in Chapter 10, but because it is easy to exhibit in the life-cycle model we've just developed. Furthermore, it is consistent with at least some of the phenomena this chapter describes.

WHAT ARE ECONOMIC FLUCTUATIONS?

Economic fluctuations are the ebbs and flows of macroeconomic activity. They are typically relatively short, measured in years and even months rather than the decades on which we focused in discussing dynamic transitions and long-run growth. Aggregate output, as measured by real gross domestic product, normally grows from one year to the next. So too does output per capita, even as population grows. But there are periods when growth does not occur and, roughly speaking, these periods are classified as recessions. Figure 4-1 shows the quarterly performance of real GDP since 1947, with the shaded areas indicating periods of recession. The upper panel of the figure shows the level of real GDP, and the lower panel presents the corresponding percent change in real GDP from its value in the previous quarter.[1]

The lower panel confirms that recessions are periods of negative, and at times quite negative, growth. Recessions normally begin with two quarters of consecutive decline in real GDP and end when output stops falling. However,

1. As is customary, the percent changes are expressed in annual terms. For example, a 4 percent rate of change from one quarter to the next indicates that if real GDP grew at its current rate for a full year (rather than just one quarter), it would rise by 4 percent.

Figure 4-1 Real GDP Since 1947

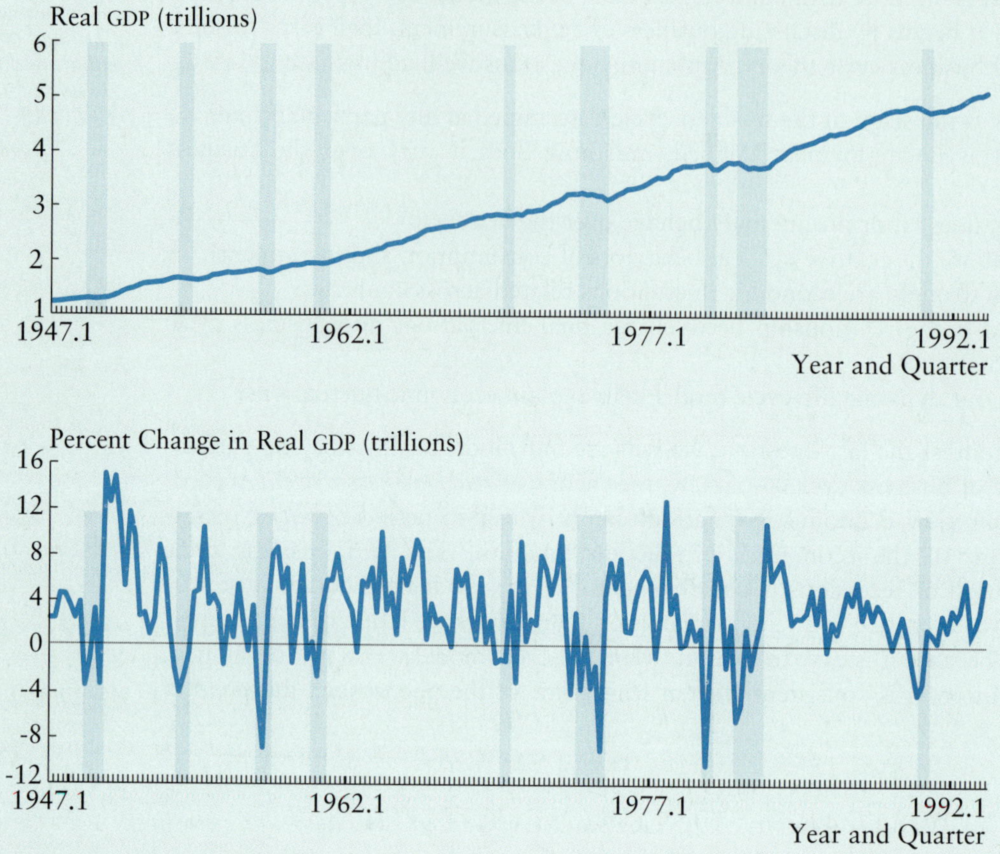

The upper panel of the figure shows quarterly real GDP since 1947, with shaded areas indicating recessions. The lower panel shows the corresponding percent changes (at annual rates) from one quarter to the next. It confirms that recessions are indeed periods of negative growth and that most quarters during which real output falls occur in recessions.

Source: *Economic Report of the President*, 1994

there is no precise rule for determining when a recession begins and when it ends.[2] The generally accepted formal dating of recessions, which was used to determine the shaded areas in Figure 4-1, is performed by the Business Cycle Dating Group of the National Bureau of Economic Research (NBER). The NBER announces the beginning date well *after* a recession has begun and the ending

2. For example, the 1957–1958 recession was deemed to have begun in August 1957, during the third quarter of that year. However, real GDP fell slightly in the *second* quarter of 1957 and *grew* slightly in the third quarter of 1957, before beginning two successive quarters of declining output in October 1957.

date well after the recession has ended. (The beginning date of a recession is called the business cycle *peak*; the end is called the *trough*.) The NBER does not automatically define a recession in terms of two consecutive quarters of decline in real GDP, preferring the more subjective, but closely related, definition of "a recurring period of decline in total output, income, employment, and trade, usually lasting from six months to a year, and marked by widespread contractions in many sectors of the economy."

Note that NBER's activity is *dating* business cycles, not *predicting* them. Its pronouncements are more useful to those wishing to understand how the economy functions than to employers, investors, workers, and others interested in knowing what's ahead. *Forecasting* business cycles is an entirely different activity (although one also pioneered by the NBER), and it is discussed below.

The Frequency, Duration, and Volatility of Business Cycles

Figure 4-1 clearly shows that expansions last longer than recessions. From October 1945, when the first expansion shown in the figure began, to March 1991, when the most recent recession ended, the nine expansions averaged nearly 50 months—over four years—whereas the nine recessions averaged just under 11 months. From trough to trough, therefore, the full business cycles since late 1945 have averaged about 61 months, or just over five years.

Interestingly, this pattern has changed over time. Table 4-1 presents data on all business cycles since 1854, divided into three subperiods of about equal length. We can see that, during the 11 cycles between 1854 and 1900, expansions averaged 27 months, recessions over 23 months, and full cycles about 50 months. From 1900 to 1945, the 11 expansions lasted an average of about 31 months and recessions about 18 months. Hence, in the period since 1945, expansions have become nearly twice as long and recessions less than half as long as before 1900. Indeed, the two longest expansions since the beginning of business cycle dating in 1854 have occurred since 1960.[3]

In addition, business cycle *volatility*, as measured by the magnitude of swings in the growth rate of output, has lessened over time. Between 1900 and the beginning of the depression in 1929, output fell by at least 6 percent in four separate years. On six occasions, it rose by at least 10 percent in a single year. No similar rise or fall in output has occurred since the early 1950s.[4]

Many macroeconomists attribute the declining frequency and severity of recessions to more active monetary and fiscal policy (the conduct of which we'll consider beginning in Chapter 7) after the Great Depression. It is true that there has been no recession so serious since then. However, the general trend toward shorter recessions predated the 1930s and extended into the 1980s, during the administrations of presidents who seemed to oppose monetary and fiscal

3. For further discussion see Francis X. Diebold and Glenn D. Rudebusch, "Have Postwar Economic Fluctuations Been Stabilized?" *American Economic Review* 82 (September 1992): 993–1005.

4. See R. J. Gordon, ed., *The American Business Cycle* (Chicago: University of Chicago Press, 1986), Appendix B. Gordon measures output in terms of gross national product (GNP), a statistic closely related to GDP. Many historical studies refer to GNP rather than GDP.

Table 4-1 Economic Fluctuations Since 1854

Business Cycle		Length (months)	
Peak	Trough	Expansion	Recession
	December 1854		
June 1857	December 1858	30	18
October 1860	June 1861	22	8
April 1865	December 1867	46	32
June 1869	December 1870	18	18
October 1873	March 1879	34	65
March 1882	May 1885	36	38
March 1887	April 1888	22	13
July 1890	May 1891	27	10
January 1893	June 1894	20	17
December 1895	June 1897	18	18
June 1899	December 1900	24	18
September 1902	August 1904	21	23
May 1907	June 1908	33	13
January 1910	January 1912	19	24
January 1913	December 1914	12	23
August 1918	March 1919	44	7
January 1920	July 1921	10	18
May 1923	July 1924	22	14
October 1926	November 1927	27	13
August 1929	March 1933	21	43
May 1937	June 1938	50	13
February 1945	October 1945	80	8
November 1948	October 1949	37	11
July 1953	May 1954	45	10
August 1957	April 1958	39	8
April 1960	February 1961	24	10
December 1969	November 1970	106	11
November 1973	March 1975	36	16
January 1980	July 1980	58	6
July 1981	November 1982	12	16
July 1990	March 1991	92	8

	Average Length		
	Expansion	Recession	Entire Cycle
1854–1900	27.0	23.2	50.2
1900–1945	30.8	18.1	48.9
1945–1991	49.9	10.7	60.6

activism. Moreover, recent research suggests that the apparent volatility of prewar cycles may be partially attributable to the poor quality of prewar data.

Case Study: How Much Has U.S. Business Cycle Volatility Declined?

Most controversies in macroeconomics center on how to interpret the data we observe. For example, economists differ on how to explain the severe drop in output observed during the Great Depression. However, one ongoing controversy is about the data themselves.

Before World War II, the collection of macroeconomic data was relatively haphazard. Since the war the U.S. Department of Commerce has been responsible for producing standard output measures such as GDP. The Commerce Department's annual series extend back to 1929. Until recently the most widely accepted output series for years before 1929 was based on that provided many years ago by Simon Kuznets, who was awarded a Nobel Prize for his efforts. It is the Kuznets series on which our conclusions about pre-1929 GNP volatility are based.

Because he lacked data about this early period, Kuznets had to make a variety of assumptions in order to arrive at his GNP estimates. For example, because he did not have information about production in some sectors of the economy, he essentially assumed a constant relationship between the output in these sectors and output in the sectors for which data were available. In a challenge to Kuznets' approach, Christina Romer of the University of California at Berkeley pointed out that, during the postwar years for which better data are available, the composition of output has varied over the business cycle.[5] She argued that output in the sectors not observed by Kuznets was less volatile than he had assumed. Adopting an alternative approach based on observed postwar patterns of output composition, as well as other modifications to the earlier methodology, Romer offered an alternative series for real GNP. Her series, presented in Figure 4-2, is considerably less volatile than Kuznets' original series.

According to Romer's data, real GNP growth exceeded 10 percent in just one year—not six years—during the period 1900–1929, and did not fall by even 5 percent in any year during this period. However, Romer's conclusions—that output fluctuations were only moderately more volatile before 1929 than after World War II—have themselves been challenged. For example, Nathan Balke and Robert Gordon of Northwestern University used data from other sources to broaden the industrial coverage of the original Kuznets data. They constructed a second alternative measure of real GNP for the years before 1929 that, although also different from Kuznets' series, is just as volatile.[6]

5. Christina D. Romer, "The Prewar Business Cycle Reconsidered: New Estimates of Gross National Product, 1869–1908," *Journal of Political Economy* 97 (February 1989): 1–37.
6. Nathan S. Balke and Robert J. Gordon, "The Estimation of Prewar Gross National Product: Methodology and New Evidence," *Journal of Political Economy* 97 (February 1989): 38–92.

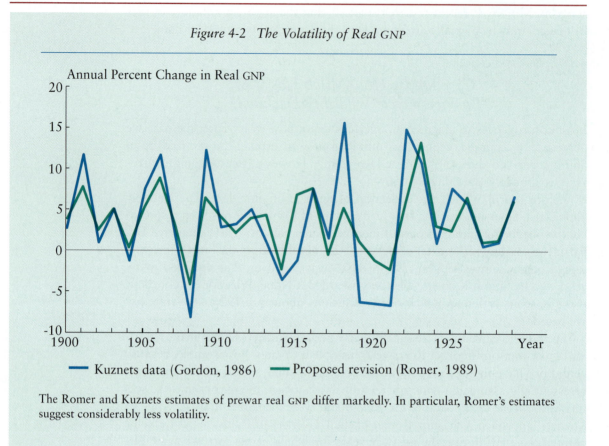

Figure 4-2 The Volatility of Real GNP

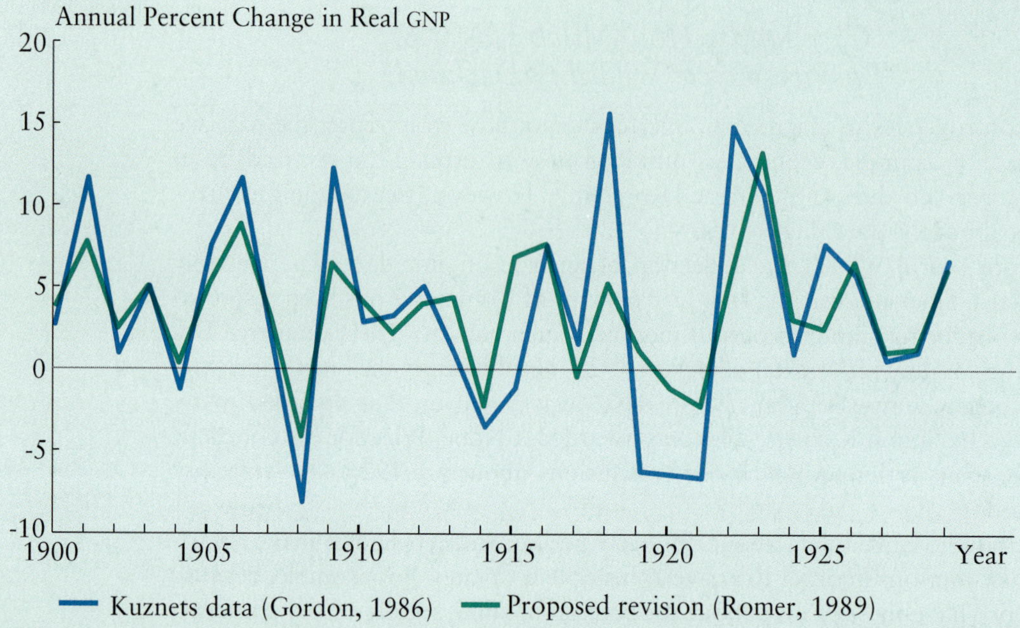

The Romer and Kuznets estimates of prewar real GNP differ markedly. In particular, Romer's estimates suggest considerably less volatility.

THE ANATOMY OF BUSINESS CYCLES

Economists have long studied economic fluctuations to gain insights into the fundamental relationships that determine macroeconomic dynamics. Focus has sometimes shifted away from the subject, as during the long expansion of the 1960s, when it was widely believed that the business cycle had been "solved." But the five recessions experienced since then have put business cycles back on the research agenda. A starting point for such research is understanding what business cycles look like.

Sectoral Versus General Effects

Modern economies experience continuous change in the industrial and geographic composition of output. As we discussed in Chapter 1, the U.S. made the transition from an agrarian to an industrial economy early in this century. More recently, it has been experiencing a shift from industrial production to the supply of services. Both population and production activity have shifted away from regions that specialized in agriculture (such as South Dakota, whose population rose by just 7 percent between 1950 and 1990, compared to 64 percent for the country as a whole) and heavy industry (such as Detroit and Pittsburgh, which lost almost half their populations over the same period). Although these industrial and regional declines are often loosely referred to as recessions, they are not recessions as economists define them. They are really more permanent and long-term changes, rather than economy-wide recessions of relatively short duration.

We distinguish broad, short-term fluctuations from longer-term declines in particular industries because the two phenomena stem from different causes. Longer-term declines usually reflect fundamental shifts in household tastes and firms' costs of production. Short-term cycles ordinarily stem from shocks to the economy or inherent macroeconomic instability. Distinguishing a recession from longer-term economic processes is not always easy. There are always significant differences in the severity of recessions across different regions and sectors of the economy, which raise the question of whether the underlying economic problems are really nation-wide and industry-wide.

From the perspective of potential government intervention, there is little to be gained by attempting to stem the tide of changing tastes and technology, but there may well be reason to attempt short-term stabilization. For a macroeconomist the distinction between broad and brief recessions and longer-term economic adjustments is, therefore, quite important. This does not mean that longer-term adjustments are not painful and cannot be mitigated by economic policies—it simply means that they do not present an obvious case for short-run macroeconomic policy intervention.

The Cyclical Volatility of Major Industries

Table 4-2 presents real annual GDP growth rates for the economy as a whole and the major industries into which it is divided, for the period 1981–1990. The first column shows each industry's share of total GDP in 1990. Note how the recession year 1982 was characterized by declines in output not only in the aggregate, but also in several industries. In other years, at least one industry experienced a decline in output (for example, construction in 1981 and wholesale and retail trade in 1987), but such declines lack the breadth of a recession. Similarly, certain industries, notably mining, experienced persistent declines in production over the period. These declines reflect long-term trends in these particular industries.

A final point that Table 4-2 illustrates is the varying degree of volatility across industries. Mining has experienced the widest swings in output growth in the past decade (with growth rates ranging from –11 percent to +15 percent). Production in agriculture and construction has also been quite volatile. At the other end of the spectrum, growth rates in finance, insurance, and real estate and in services have fluctuated in much narrower bands (between 0 and 5 percent and 1 and 6 percent, respectively). Government enterprises has experienced even smoother growth, with growth rates fluctuating within a band of less than 4 percentage points.

Table 4-2 Real GDP Growth Rates, by Industry

	Percent of 1990 GDP	1981	1982	1983	1984	1985	1986	1987	1988	1989	1990
Total	100.0%	1.8%	-2.2%	3.9%	6.2%	3.2%	2.9%	3.1%	3.9%	2.5%	0.8%
Agriculture	1.9	15.0	0.8	-6.7	4.5	14.5	3.2	4.7	-3.8	3.4	7.0
Mining	1.8	-7.1	-1.5	-2.5	15.0	1.6	-0.4	0.0	13.7	-11.3	4.8
Construction	4.3	-5.8	-5.6	3.1	12.3	9.5	0.0	1.9	-0.8	0.8	-2.0
Manufacturing	18.8	2.9	-4.8	3.2	7.8	2.4	1.1	7.3	5.2	0.8	-1.0
Transportation and Utilities	9.3	0.2	-1.7	6.2	7.4	1.1	1.3	8.5	2.8	2.7	2.9
Wholesale and Retail Trade	16.4	5.4	3.1	6.2	11.5	5.7	9.5	-2.2	4.9	4.2	-1.5
Finance, Insurance and Real Estate	17.7	1.7	0.5	2.8	4.7	1.9	0.0	4.3	4.6	2.5	-0.1
Services	17.8	2.5	0.8	3.2	5.9	5.0	4.1	4.2	3.9	4.1	3.1
Government Enterprises	11.9	0.5	-0.9	1.1	0.9	2.1	1.7	1.7	1.9	2.0	2.6

Source: *Survey of Current Business,* May 1993

Earlier, we saw that the U.S. business cycle has changed over time, with recessions becoming shorter and expansions longer. Part of this change is due to the shift in production from such volatile industries as agriculture and mining to more stable industries, including finance, services, and government. These shifts, in turn, mean that different regions and industries may experience a particular recession in different ways.

Case Study: The Massachusetts Miracle

In 1988, Governor Michael Dukakis of Massachusetts won the Democratic party's presidential nomination, largely on the strength of the Massachusetts economy's spectacular performance during his time in office. By 1990, when his Republican successor took over, Dukakis left an economy in the throes of an economic crisis: the Massachusetts miracle had become a disaster.

One measure of the well-being of a state's economy is the growth rate of its real personal income, an income concept closely related to GDP. Figure 4-3 compares real personal income in the United States and Massachusetts during the 1980s. It shows that in 1982, just before Dukakis was elected governor, Massachusetts began to lead the U.S. economy out of the 1981–1982 recession. As the GDP began to grow in 1983, the Massachusetts economy soared. Personal income in the state grew more rapidly than it did nationally in each of the next six years.

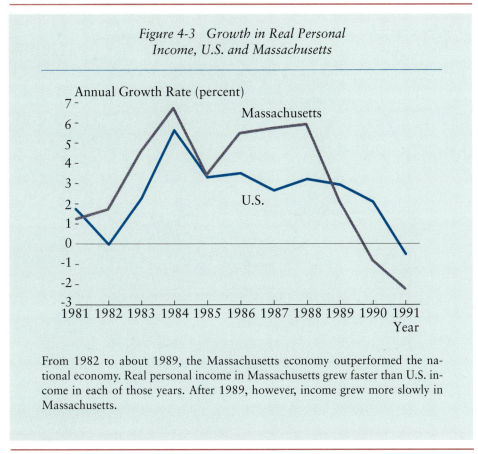

Figure 4-3 Growth in Real Personal Income, U.S. and Massachusetts

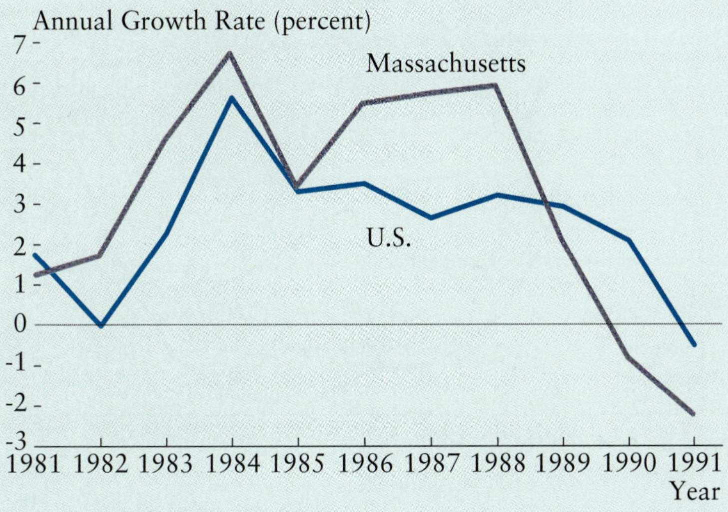

From 1982 to about 1989, the Massachusetts economy outperformed the national economy. Real personal income in Massachusetts grew faster than U.S. income in each of those years. After 1989, however, income grew more slowly in Massachusetts.

Source: *Survey of Current Business*, various issues

Figure 4-4 (page 130) graphs another measure of economic activity, the unemployment rate (which we will discuss more fully below), and this graph tells the same story. The Massachusetts unemployment rate rose more modestly in 1982 and fell more sharply in the mid-1980s than the national unemployment rate. In 1987, the 3.2 percent unemployment rate in Massachusetts was the lowest of *any* state in the country.

By 1989, however, the situation had changed for the worse. Though the national unemployment rate was still falling, the Massachusetts rate had already begun to rise. By the time the national recession finally hit in July 1990, the Massachusetts economy was already experiencing a shrinkage of personal income. Its 6 percent annual unemployment rate exceeded the national average for the first time in over a decade. By 1991, the Massachusetts unemployment rate had jumped to 9 percent.

The 1990–1991 recession was a bad one for the rest of the Northeast, too. By contrast, the 1981–1982 recession had been especially bad in many Midwestern states. Why the difference? Though recessions reflect a broad downturn in the economy, the timing and severity across regions and industries shift from

Figure 4-4 Unemployment Rate, U.S. and Massachusetts

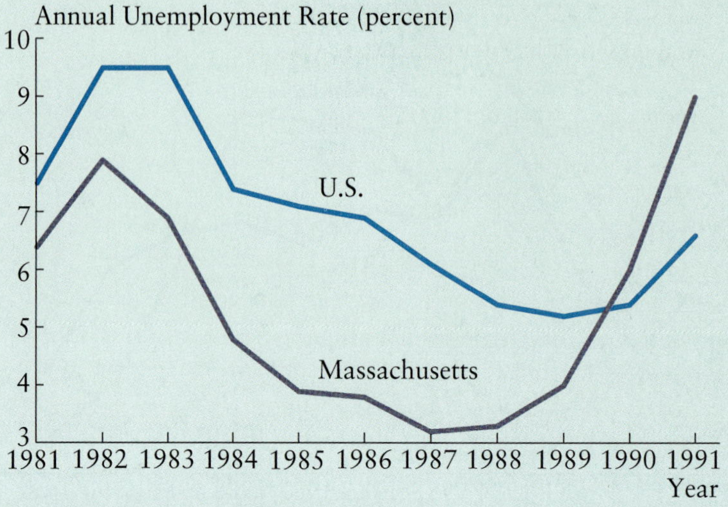

From 1982 to about 1989, the Massachusetts economy outperformed the national economy. The unemployment rate in Massachusetts was lower than the national rate in each of those years. After 1989, however, the Massachusetts unemployment rate exceeded the U.S. rate.

Source: *Employment and Earnings,* various issues

one recession to the next for reasons economists cannot always fully explain. In this instance, part of the explanation lies in regional differences in industrial composition. For example, Massachusetts depends more than the nation as a whole on finance, insurance, and real estate, which performed relatively worse in the more recent recession, and less on agriculture and mining, which fared relatively better. But even on an industry-by-industry basis, the Massachusetts economy grew more slowly than did the overall U.S. economy during the 1990–1991 recession.[7]

Timing of Turning Points: The Index of Leading Indicators

The beginnings and ends of recessions are referred to as *turning points* in the business cycle. They mark the points at which growth shifts from positive to negative or from negative to positive. Table 4-2 and Figures 4-3 and 4-4 indicate that turning points differ across regions and industries. For example, in the 1981–1982 recession, construction activity fell in 1981, whereas for some other

7. See Lynn E. Browne, "The Role of Services in New England's Rise and Fall: Engine of Growth or Along for the Ride?" *New England Economic Review* (July/August 1991): 27–44.

Table 4-3 Components of the Index of Leading Indicators

Average Weekly Hours of Production Workers in Manufacturing
Average Weekly Initial Claims for Unemployment Insurance
New Orders for Consumer Goods and Materials (in 1987 dollars)
Vendor Performance Index: Percent of Companies Reporting Slower Deliveries
Contracts and Orders, Plant and Equipment (1987 dollars)
Building Permits Index, New Private Housing Units
Change in Unfilled Orders, Durable Goods (1987 dollars)
Percent Change in Sensitive Materials Prices
Stock Price Index (Standard and Poors 500)
Money Supply, M2 (1987 dollars)
Index of Consumer Expectations (from the University of Michigan)

industries, production began to fall only in 1982. Similarly, Massachusetts moved into the 1990 recession well before the rest of the economy.

Construction's decline in 1981 did not necessarily indicate that the economy was headed toward recession. In earlier years, construction activity often declined without presaging a recession. However, there are some industries and types of activity whose business cycle patterns do normally foreshadow the overall business cycle. Because they *lead* the business cycle, we call them **leading indicators**. A decline in a leading indicator suggests that a recession may be on the way.

Leading indicator *An economic statistic whose movements foreshadow future changes in economic activity*

Not only do they represent but one method economists use to forecast business cycles, the leading indicators also tell something about the pattern of activity within business cycles. Because of this, the leading indicators are interesting in their own right, even if we ignore their usefulness in predicting recessions.

Leading indicators have been a popular measure of macroeconomic health since they were first developed in 1937. The Composite Index of Leading Indicators is produced by the Bureau of Economic Analysis of the U.S. Department of Commerce. This index is constructed by combining the eleven monthly macroeconomic time series listed in Table 4-3. The Composite Index is the one reported periodically by the press.

Some of these eleven series lead the business cycle because they are closely related to subsequent production activities. For example, building permits for housing must be obtained before housing construction occurs. New orders for plant and equipment and consumer goods and materials lead to the production and delivery of such goods. Unfilled orders and slow vendor performance indicate that producers have high demand that will eventually be met.

Figure 4-5 Index of Leading Indicators, 1948–1993

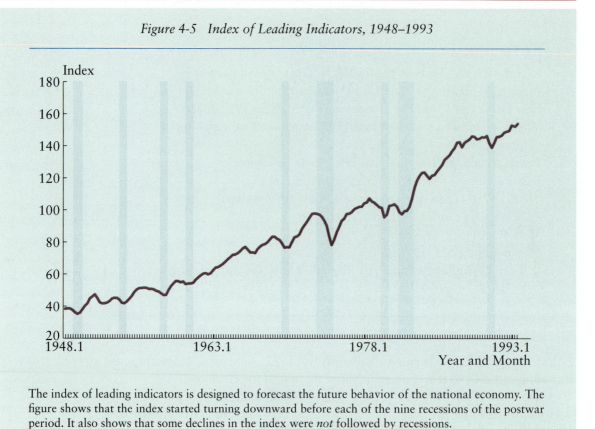

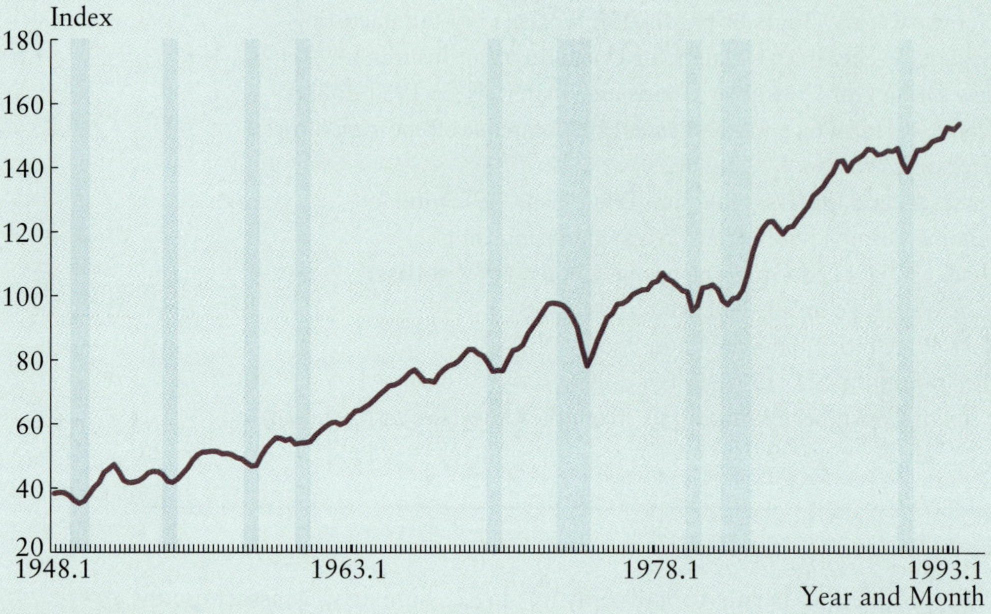

The index of leading indicators is designed to forecast the future behavior of the national economy. The figure shows that the index started turning downward before each of the nine recessions of the postwar period. It also shows that some declines in the index were *not* followed by recessions.

Source: *Survey of Current Business,* various issues

The inclusion of the index of consumer expectations reflects the fact that consumers are forward-looking. Their anticipations of changes in economic conditions are useful in predicting what actually will occur. As we'll see in Chapter 16, stock prices act as a leading indicator for much the same reason: they indicate investors' optimism or pessimism about the prospects of those firms whose stock prices are included in the index. The four remaining series in the index relate to employment, whose connection to the business cycle we will discuss shortly, and to money and prices, which we will discuss beginning in Chapter 8.

Figure 4-5 graphs the Index of Leading Indicators for the period since 1948, with recession periods shaded. Each recession during this period was preceded by a decline in the index. Even so, there are at least three problems with using the index to predict turning points.

1. *For how long?* The index often drops for a month or more. After how many months of successive drops should we conclude that a recession is coming?

A customary rule of thumb is that a recession is on the way once there have been three successive monthly declines in the index.

2. *How soon?* But even after three successive declines in the index occur, thus indicating a recession, *when* is that recession going to occur? The index doesn't always lead the business cycle by the same number of months. It led the January 1980 downturn by 15 months but the July 1981 downturn by just 2 months.
3. *Whoops!* Regardless of the rule used, the index predicts some recessions that *don't* happen in addition to those that do. For example, the index declined for several successive months in 1984 when no recession was imminent.

Although the leading indicators remain a popular index of the state of the economy, macroeconomists can't completely rely on them to forecast business cycle turning points.

Drawing by Shanahan; © 1993 The New Yorker Magazine, Inc.

UNEMPLOYMENT

Figure 4-4 shows that recessions are associated with increases in the unemployment rate. For example, near the trough of the 1981–1982 recession, the U.S. unemployment rate soared briefly to over 9 percent. This helps explain why new claims for unemployment insurance, a program that pays benefits to unemployed workers, appears in the index of leading indicators. But what is **unemployment**? It is quite different from simply not being employed. In 1993, over 72 million U.S. adults (persons over age 16) were not employed. Of these, only 8.7 million, or 12 percent, were classified as unemployed. The remainder were considered neither employed nor unemployed.

Unemployment *The state of seeking work but not having a job*

The Household Survey

How should unemployment be defined? The U.S. and most other countries define unemployment as the condition of actively seeking work but not having a job. In the United States, the tool used to measure the unemployment rate is the Current Population Survey, conducted by the Census Bureau. Each month, a sample of households is surveyed, and adult members are asked about their employment status. There is a three-way classification: employed, unemployed, and not in the labor force. The precise definitions are as follows:

- *Employed:* All persons who worked for 15 or more hours in the past week or were absent from a job for reason of illness, vacation, bad weather, etc.
- *Unemployed:* All persons who were not employed but were available for work and had looked for work in the past 4 weeks, or were awaiting recall from a job layoff, or were awaiting the start of a new job within 30 days

The sum of employed and unemployed individuals is the *labor force*. It includes about two-thirds of the adult population. All other adults, including students, retired persons, and those doing housework, are considered to be out of the labor force.

At first blush it may seem natural to define unemployment in this way, as a state of seeking work but not having a job. But, in practice, many cases are difficult to classify. For example, should an aerospace engineer who had previously worked for $25 an hour be considered available for work if she declines an offer to work for $6 an hour? (She is.) Should a college basketball player who would drop out of college for the right pro contract be considered unavailable for work? (He is.)

Unemployment, as we define it, suggests the lack of a job at an individual's "normal" wage rate and working circumstances, but these are not well-defined concepts. Their meaning has a tendency to shift over the business cycle as workers' perceptions of employment prospects change. Some so-called *discouraged workers* eventually abandon their job search and shift from the category "unemployed" to "not in the labor force." As a result, the fraction of the adult population in the labor force—the **labor force participation rate**—tends to decline slightly during recessions.

Labor force participation rate
The fraction of the adult population that is either employed or unemployed

Employment and Hours

Changes in the number of people working is just one cause of variation in labor input, measured by total hours worked, over the business cycle. As we discussed in Chapter 1, total hours worked in a given period equals the adult population times the fraction of adults employed times the average number of hours each employee works. As recessions hit, not only is the rate of employment affected, but so is the number of hours the average employee works. The index of leading indicators also includes the average weekly hours of manufacturing workers (see Table 4-3).

One of the categories of work most sensitive to the business cycle is overtime hours—the hours employees work beyond their normal weekly hours. Figure 4-6 shows the average number of overtime hours per week for manufacturing workers for the period since 1970. The series moves with the business cycle, dipping during each shaded recession period.

During recession, there are two ways in which the economy's measured labor input declines: the number of people employed declines and the number of hours worked by those still employed declines. There is yet a third source of decline in *effective* labor input during recessions. Labor productivity is **procyclical**: output per worker-hour declines, or grows more slowly, during recessions. One interpretation of this fact is that firms tend to use their work forces less intensively during recessions, reducing the measured productivity level. This phenomenon is often called *labor hoarding* because it suggests that firms have more labor on hand than is needed to produce current output levels.

Procyclical behavior
The behavior of any economic variable that increases when GDP increases and falls when GDP falls

Capital Becomes Unemployed, Too

Although it is customary to think of recession as a phenomenon that affects workers, it also has an impact on the other input of our production function, capital. When businesses operate with fewer workers than normal, they don't necessarily use all the plant and equipment they have on hand as intensively.

Figure 4-6 Overtime Hours, Manufacturing, 1970–1993

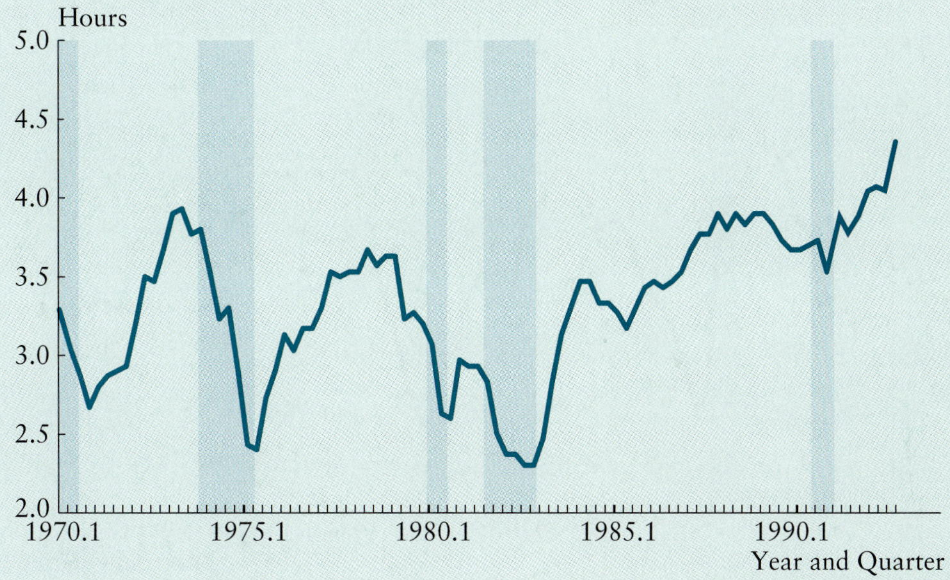

During and immediately before recessions, firms reduce the amount of labor they employ. One way of doing this is to reduce the average number of hours each employee works. As a result, overtime hours in manufacturing fall during recessions; average overtime hours is a *procyclical* variable.

Source: *Economic Report of the President,* 1994

The most important measure of capital utilization is constructed by the Federal Reserve System ("the Fed"). The Fed's index is calculated in two stages. In the first stage, an industry's capacity to produce is estimated, based on past production levels. Then this estimate is compared to current production levels to derive the rate of **capacity utilization**. Like unemployment, capacity utilization does not have a clear, unambiguous definition. For example, it might be possible, in wartime or other periods of extreme demand, for industries to exceed measured capacity by running machines for longer periods each day than would be the normal maximum.

Capacity utilization *The ratio of current production in an industry to that industry's measured capacity to produce*

Figure 4-7 presents the Fed's capacity utilization measure for U.S. manufacturing since 1970. Like the overtime hours shown in Figure 4-6, capacity utilization has been procyclical, falling during recessions and rising during expansions. Indeed, the two series have strikingly similar patterns.

Bankruptcies and the Business Cycle

Capital that is not utilized does not produce income for its owner. Hence, as capacity utilization falls, the incomes of businesses owning capital fall too. As a

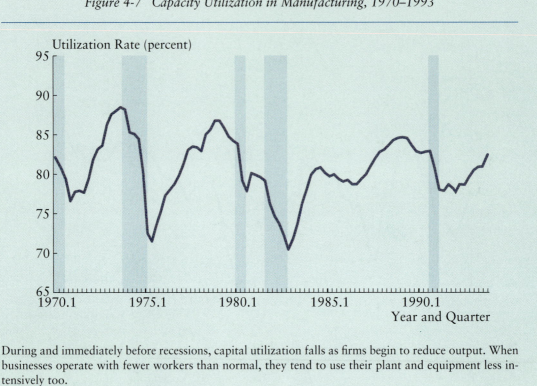

Figure 4-7 Capacity Utilization in Manufacturing, 1970–1993

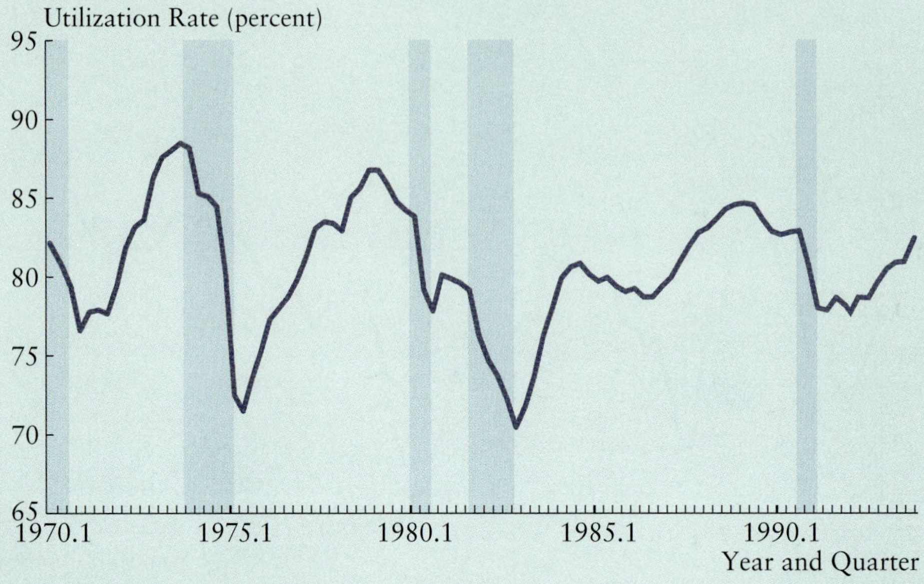

During and immediately before recessions, capital utilization falls as firms begin to reduce output. When businesses operate with fewer workers than normal, they tend to use their plant and equipment less intensively too.

Source: Board of Governors, Federal Reserve System

result, more businesses fail—go bankrupt—during recessions. This cyclical pattern is evident in Figure 4-8, which plots the annual failure rate per 10,000 businesses over time, with recession periods superimposed on the graph. However, recessions are not the only cause of rising business failures. There was also a striking increase in the failure rate during the long expansion of the 1980s, when capacity utilization was relatively high. We will discuss this interesting phenomenon in Chapter 16.

UNDERSTANDING ECONOMIC FLUCTUATIONS

So far, we have described the patterns of output and employment changes over the business cycle. But identifying such cyclical regularities does not *explain* them. What causes output to fluctuate? To gain some insight we'll consider three issues: the uses of output over the business cycle, the relationships among different countries' business cycles, and the relationship of the business cycle to other dynamic behavior, including seasonal shifts in production.

Figure 4-8 Business Failure Rate, 1946–1992

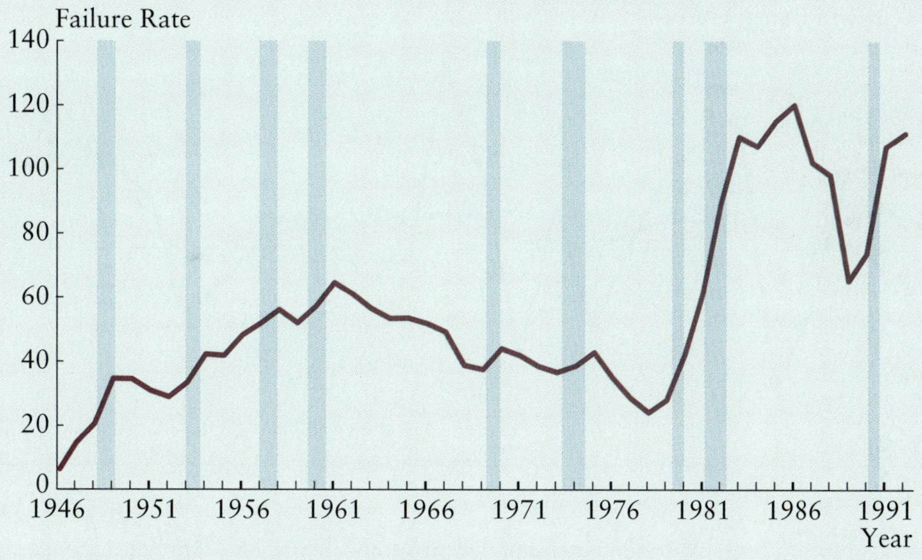

More businesses fail during recessions than during more normal times. This pattern is reflected in the figure: the business failure rate increases during the shaded recession periods. The figure also shows a sharp rise in failures during the first half of the expansion of the mid-1980s.

Source: *Economic Report of the President,* 1994

Uses of Output over the Cycle

An economy's production can be categorized in several ways. One approach distinguishes output by the industry that produces it. Table 4-2 described the business cycle behavior of the output of different industries. We have seen that although most industries are procyclical, their sensitivity to the business cycle varies. For example, the services sector normally experiences smaller swings in production than do manufacturing and construction. Why does the output of some industries fluctuate so severely? An important part of the answer lies in how their output is used.

Rather than distinguishing production by its industry—where it comes from—we can divide output by its use—where the output goes. We normally distinguish four different *uses*: consumption by households, investment by businesses, *exports* to foreigners, and *government purchases*. We discussed consumption and investment in detail in previous chapters. Exports are those goods produced domestically but sold abroad, and government purchases are goods and services bought by the government.

These divisions into uses are related to the breakdown by industry. Goods purchased for investment, which add to the economy's capital stock, are

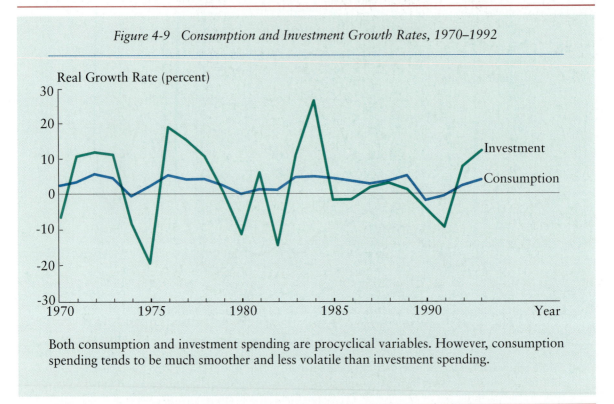

Figure 4-9 Consumption and Investment Growth Rates, 1970–1992

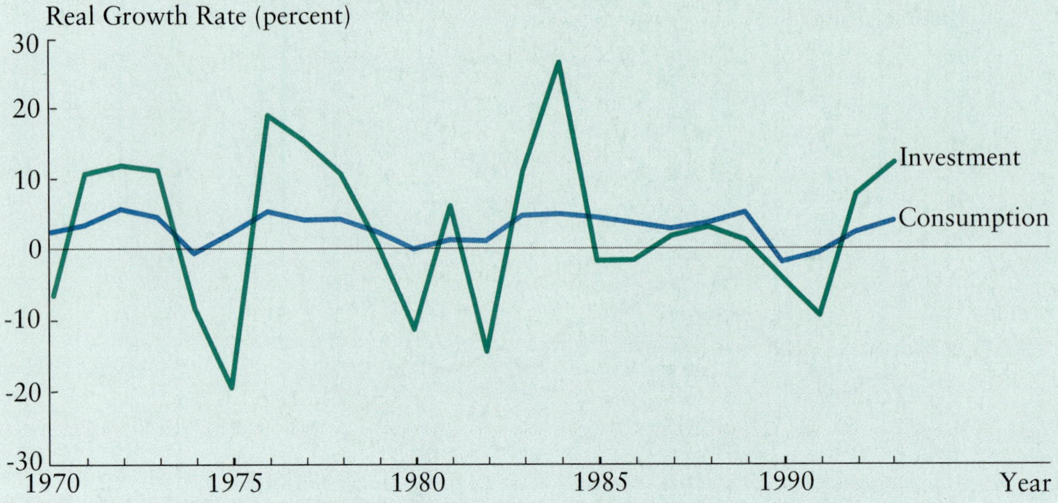

Both consumption and investment spending are procyclical variables. However, consumption spending tends to be much smoother and less volatile than investment spending.

Source: *Economic Report of the President,* 1994

primarily *durable goods*—they last longer than a year—and are produced mainly in two sectors. Machinery and equipment come primarily from manufacturing, whereas structures (factories, office buildings, and so forth) are produced by the construction industry. Consumption, on the other hand, which accounts for about two-thirds of GDP, draws on the outputs of several industries.

Not surprisingly, the business cycle behavior of various industries mirrors fluctuations in the sources of demand for their output. Because investment demand is more volatile than consumption, the construction and manufacturing sectors are more volatile than most other industries.

Figure 4-9 shows the annual percent changes in consumption and investment since 1970. Although both series exhibit procyclical behavior, consumption has been much less volatile. During the 70s and 80s, consumption grew at annual rates ranging from –2 percent to +6 percent. Investment declined by nearly 20 percent in 1975 and grew by over 26 percent in 1984. Why do the patterns differ so much? We'll return to this question below, as we begin to relate business cycle behavior to the life-cycle model developed in Chapters 2 and 3. Like consumption, exports and government spending are far less volatile than investment. Thus, we can trace an important part of the variation in output over the business cycle to fluctuations in investment.

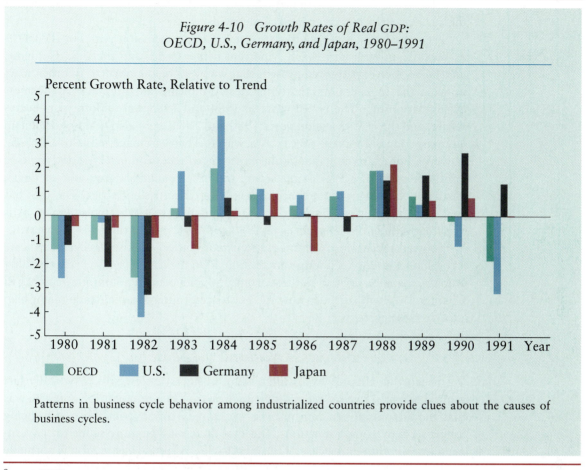

Figure 4-10 Growth Rates of Real GDP: OECD, U.S., Germany, and Japan, 1980–1991

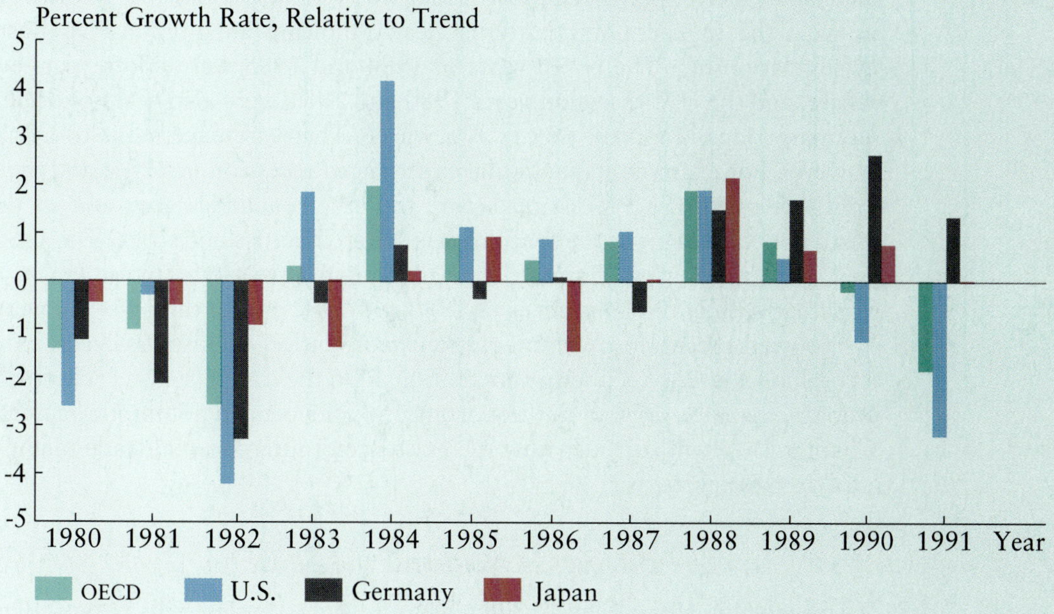

Patterns in business cycle behavior among industrialized countries provide clues about the causes of business cycles.

Source: OECD

International Spillovers

Fluctuations in investment, as well as in other uses of output, have many causes. One way of narrowing the list of suspects is to look at contemporaneous business cycle behavior in other countries. If a recession occurs in the U.S. but not in Japan, that may rule out certain causes, such as a sharp increase in oil prices that affects all oil-importing countries. If a U.S. recession begins just after the outbreak of a worldwide recession, other causes, such as monetary and fiscal policy mismanagement in the U.S., may be ruled out.

We saw in Chapter 1 that during the past several decades the U.S. growth rate has been lower than those of Japan, Germany, and the other OECD countries. But what about these countries' business cycle performance? Figure 4-10 presents the annual growth rates of real GDP, as deviations around their trends, for the U.S., Germany, Japan, and the entire OECD. By subtracting the trend, we control for the differences in growth rates among the countries, i.e., we look at the cyclical performance around these trends.

From the figure it is easy to pick out 1982 as a recession year. For the OECD as a whole, growth was nearly 3 percent below trend, and the U.S., Germany, and Japan each experienced growth that was well below normal. In other years as well, the cross-country patterns clearly indicate an international business cycle relationship. The boom years of 1984 and 1988 were boom years everywhere, and the U.S. recession years 1980 and 1981 were also years of decline in Germany, Japan, and the OECD as a whole. There are exceptions to this rule, however. For example, Japan alone experienced recession in 1986, and the U.S. grew out of its 1982 recession before the other countries grew out of theirs. Also, the *magnitude* of fluctuations has differed across countries. The U.S. has generally experienced sharper fluctuations than have Germany or Japan, as is apparent both in the downturns of 1980 and 1982 and in the 1984 recovery.

To what extent does the international correlation of business cycles indicate a common source of economic fluctuations? Do the differences in cycle volatility among countries suggest the importance of independent domestic factors? In Chapter 6 we will consider how the existence of international trade might help explain these patterns.

The Business Cycle and the Seasonal Cycle

We began this chapter by distinguishing business cycles, which typically last around five or six years, from long-run growth. The argument for doing so was that the factors influencing business cycles may differ from those influencing longer-term dynamic transitions, and that there may be more scope for government intervention in the case of business cycles. A similar distinction is normally made with respect to economic fluctuations of an even shorter duration: the *seasonal* cycle.

It is easy to identify the factors causing fluctuations in output over the seasons and hard to argue that government policy should be used to offset these fluctuations. People spend more in December because of Christmas, and produce less in August in order to take vacations. The seasonal fluctuations these phenomena induce are *desirable*—they reflect households' tastes.

Some seasonal fluctuations are associated with the nature of technology. For example, there is more construction activity in the fall than in winter, and more agricultural production in the summer. These seasonal fluctuations reflect a desirable allocation of social resources. There is nothing to be gained, and clearly something to be lost, in attempting to induce people to do their Christmas shopping in July or their crop harvesting in January.

Seasonal adjustment *An attempt to isolate and remove seasonal movements from economic time series*

Because seasonal cycles are easier to understand than business cycles, and of less concern from a policy perspective, it is common to subject data to **seasonal adjustment**—the elimination from those data of seasonal fluctuations. (This technique is not appropriate for use with annual series, only for those with a higher frequency, such as quarterly or monthly.) The quarterly GDP series shown in Figure 4-1 are seasonally adjusted, as are most quarterly data provided by the Commerce Department. Eliminating seasonal variation, like eliminating long-term trends (as we did in Figure 4-10), allows us to study the business cycle

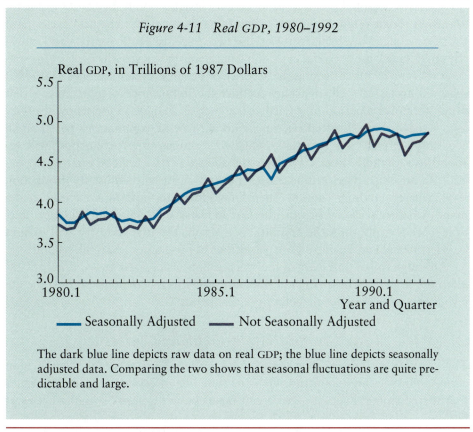

Figure 4-11 Real GDP, 1980–1992

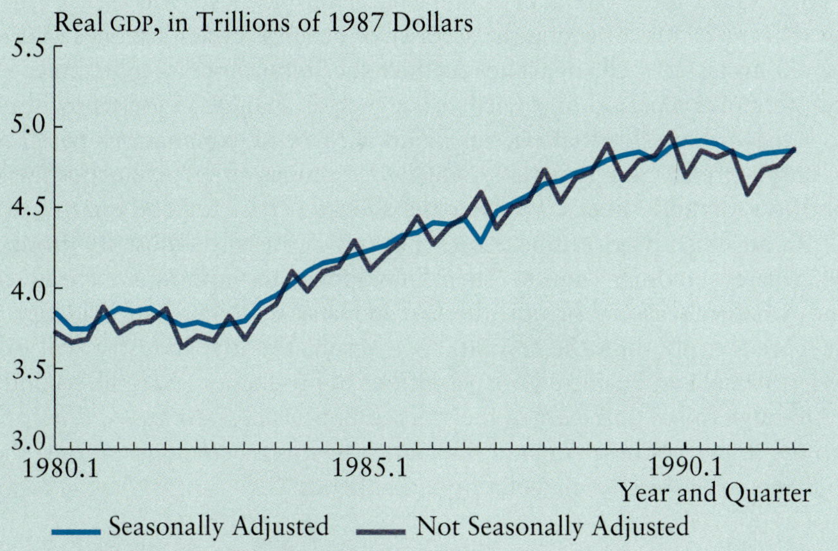

The dark blue line depicts raw data on real GDP; the blue line depicts seasonally adjusted data. Comparing the two shows that seasonal fluctuations are quite predictable and large.

Source: *Survey of Current Business,* various issues

properties of a macroeconomic time series. If we did not perform a seasonal adjustment, the seasonal variation in some series would swamp the variation associated with the business cycle.

Figure 4-11 shows the effect of seasonal adjustment on GDP since 1980. The solid line shows the quarterly values of real GDP (in 1987 dollars). This series—repeated from the upper panel of Figure 4-1—has been seasonally adjusted. The second series is also real quarterly GDP, but it is not seasonally adjusted.[8] As the figure shows, seasonal fluctuations are much more regular than business cycle fluctuations, consistent with the view that they are more predictable and are part of an equilibrium path. Still, these seasonal fluctuations are large. With output typically falling at an annual rate of about 19 percent from the peak of one year (the fourth quarter, October through December) to the trough of the next (the first quarter, January through March), the seasonal drop in output during the normal year far exceeds the drop in seasonally adjusted output of any recession quarter shown in the lower panel of Figure 4-1.

8. Because no series on real, seasonally unadjusted quarterly GDP is readily available, our series is derived by dividing seasonally unadjusted nominal GDP (not adjusted for price-level changes) by the *Consumer Price Index* (CPI), a seasonally unadjusted price series that is similar (in other respects) to the GDP price deflator. Both series are discussed in Chapter 5.

We study seasonal cycles in order to gain insights about the causes of fluctuations. In recent years, economists examining seasonal and business cycles have found a strong relationship between the two. In particular, countries and industries that have large seasonal cycles have large business cycles as well.[9] This suggests that the factors affecting the severity of business cycles are ones that affect seasonal cycles as well. It argues against the importance of phenomena that occur only over a period of several years, such as changes in government policy associated with presidential elections, and in favor of explanations based on an economy's production structure, which determines how production will respond to economic shocks, whether the shocks persist for one quarter or several. As an illustration, suppose one industry can easily adjust its production level, whereas another cannot. Then, in response to variations in product demand, whether seasonal or not, the first industry will alter its level of production more sharply than the second. As a result, the first industry will exhibit larger seasonal and business cycle variations in production than the second.

Although this is only part of the story about business cycles—it does not explain the source of these demand fluctuations—it is a useful insight into the determinants of business cycle volatility nonetheless.

Are Business Cycles Actually Cycles?

This chapter has shown that the business cycle is an important phenomenon across industries and countries. Or is it? One line of economic research argues that the economic fluctuations we call business cycles aren't actually cycles at all.[10]

The argument is subtle, because of the statistical difficulty in distinguishing between two situations. In the first, the economy follows a long-run dynamic path that is disturbed by temporary cyclical fluctuations in which periods of greater-than-average output growth tend to be followed by periods of less-than-average growth. In the second, the economy does not have temporary cycles that are distinct from its long-run path. Instead, its long-run dynamic path is itself subject to upward and downward shocks—following what is known as a **random walk**, in which each shock to output is a permanent one, but some shocks are positive and some negative. In this case, there is no underlying cycle—output is no more likely to fall after a period of positive growth than after a period of negative growth. However, there will occasionally, by chance, be runs of negative or positive shocks that give the *appearance* of cycles.

Random walk theory
The view that economic fluctuations result from permanent shocks to the economy's growth path, rather than temporary cycles around a long-run path

The random walk theory can be explained using an analogy to flipping a coin. Imagine that output rises one unit for each head and falls one unit for each tail. When you flip a coin several times, each flip is independent, with equal probability of being a head or a tail. Yet you are likely to get some runs of successive heads followed by runs of successive tails among your flips. These runs of heads and tails will provide an up-and-down pattern of output fluctuations

9. This evidence is presented in J. Joseph Beaulieu, Jeffrey K. MacKie-Mason, and Jeffrey A. Miron, "Why do Countries and Industries with Large Seasonal Cycles also Have Large Business Cycles?" *Quarterly Journal of Economics* 107 (May 1992): 621–656.

10. See Charles R. Nelson and Charles Plosser, "Trends and Random Walks in Economic Time Series," *Journal of Monetary Economics* 10 (1982): 139–162, and John Campbell and N. Gregory Mankiw, "Are Output Fluctuations Transitory?" *Quarterly Journal of Economics* 103 (November 1987).

Figure 4-12 Business Cycles or Random Walks? A Comparison

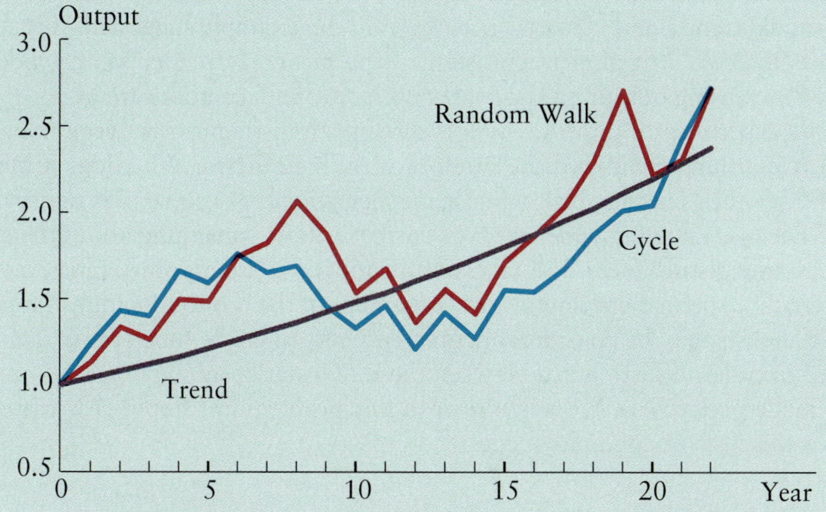

The burgundy line shows the simulated behavior of output assuming that it follows a random walk—that is, assuming that random shocks to GDP are permanent in the sense that they influence output in all subsequent years. The blue line labeled "Cycle" shows the simulated behavior of output as fluctuations around a long-term trend. Notice that the behavior of the two series appears to be quite similar, meaning that it is difficult to know which theory better describes the facts.

that resembles a cycle, even though no cycle exists. Now, suppose instead that output rises by a bit more than one unit when a head occurs, and falls by a little less than one unit when a tail occurs. Then, in addition to the apparently cyclical behavior in output represented by the coin flips, there will also be a tendency for output to grow over time. Thus, through independent flips of this coin, we could produce a pattern of output that appears to exhibit cyclical behavior around a growing trend.

Figure 4-12 illustrates the results of such an experiment. The graph shows three curves. One, labeled "Trend," depicts smooth growth at a rate of 4 percent per period. The second curve, labeled "Cycle," is the result of adding a cycle to the first curve. The cycle, in turn, has two components: a sine wave that causes output to oscillate smoothly, plus an annual random shock that is purely *transitory*, in that each year's random shock to output lasts for just that year.[11] This curve represents the business cycle as we have described it: fluctuations around a long-run trend.

11. The curve's formula is $y_t = (1.04)^t + .4\sin(.1\pi t) + .15x_t$, where x_t is drawn randomly from a uniform distribution between –1 and 1. That is, the likelihood of year t's shock, x_t, taking any particular value between –1 and 1 is the same as that for every other value in the range.

The third curve, labeled "Random Walk," starts in year 0 at the same income level as the other curves and grows each year at a rate that is random and has an average value of 2 percent. In this case random shocks to the level of output are *permanent* in the sense that they influence output in all subsequent years. Unlike the case of the cycle, there is no tendency for output to return to the original trend line.[12] However, as the coin flip example suggested, this curve exhibits the two central characteristics of the business cycle curve: a tendency toward increasing output and *apparent* cycles around a smooth trend.

This experiment indicates why it is difficult to distinguish between the business-cycle-around-trend and the random-walk hypotheses. Why does it matter which hypothesis is true, if the time series behavior looks so similar under each view? Because knowing which story is correct tells us something about the costs of economic disturbances. If a recession is not really a temporary phenomenon but actually a permanent downward movement of the economy's long-run path, its social costs may be considerably greater. Unfortunately, much more data are needed in order to distinguish between these two statistical hypotheses—but we must make policy now. We will return to this problem in Chapter 12, when we discuss the costs of unemployment.

HOW DO ECONOMIC FLUCTUATIONS FIT INTO OUR MODEL?

This chapter has focused on the nature and measurement of economic fluctuations. In previous chapters, we developed a model of the economy's equilibrium output path. We can illustrate how economic fluctuations arise in the model using one particular approach to explaining business cycles, the **real business cycle theory.**

Real business cycle theory
A macroeconomic theory that traces economic fluctuations to shocks to the level of technology

According to real business cycle theory, fluctuations are simply part of the economy's equilibrium path, in much the way seasonal cycles are.[13] One real business cycle approach argues that business cycle fluctuations are caused by disturbances to the economy's production function through the technology parameter, which we have labeled A_t. Consider what happens if A_t temporarily increases, perhaps because of a reduction in oil prices, a good harvest, or a new scientific breakthrough. This increases both output and labor productivity (output per worker), since (as we learned in Chapter 1) the ratio of output to labor equals

12. This curve's formula for output is $y_t = y_{t-1}(1.02 + .2x_t)$, where x_t is the same random variable used to construct the "cycle" curve. Here, though, the value of x_t affects not only the current value of output, y_t, but every subsequent value of output $(y_{t+1}, y_{t+2}, \ldots)$ as well.

13. A good introduction to real business cycle theory is Charles I. Plosser, "Understanding Real Business Cycles," *Journal of Economic Perspectives* 3 (Summer 1989): 51–78. Three important articles in this literature are Finn E. Kydland and Edward Prescott, "Time to Build and Aggregate Fluctuations," *Econometrica* 50 (November 1982): 1345–1370; John B. Long and Charles Plosser, "Real Business Cycles," *Journal of Political Economy* 91 (February 1983); and Edward Prescott, "Theory Ahead of Business Cycle Measurement," *Carnegie-Rochester Conference Series on Public Policy* 25 (Autumn 1986): 11–44

$$y_t = A_t k_t^{\beta}$$

where β is the production function parameter, y is output per worker, and k is capital per worker. Moreover, the increase in A also leads to an increase in capital accumulation between period t and period $t + 1$. As we found in Chapter 3, $k_{t+1} = (1 - \alpha)w_t$. That is, the economy's capital-labor ratio next period equals the amount saved by each young person this period which, in turn, is a fraction $(1 - \alpha)$ of that young person's wage. Since the wage equals the worker's marginal product, $(1 - \beta)A_t k_t^{\beta}$, the capital-labor ratio evolves according to the transition equation,

$$k_{t+1} = (1 - \alpha)(1 - \beta)A_t k_t^{\beta} = (1 - \alpha)(1 - \beta)y_t$$

where α is the share of labor income young people consume and, in the case of the second equality, we have replaced $A_t k_t^{\beta}$ by y_t. If technology improves in period t, the capital-labor ratio will be higher in the following period. This increase in k_{t+1} will then increase output in period $t + 1$, as well as the capital-labor ratio in period $t + 2$, and so on in successive periods, although the increases in k and y become smaller and smaller.

Let's confirm this behavior by considering a concrete example, with $\alpha = .5$, $\beta = .3$, A initially equal to its long-run value of 10, and the economy at its steady-state value of output per worker and capital per worker.[14] Suppose A rises temporarily by 20 percent—to a value of 12—in period 2, and then falls back to 10 in period 3. The response of output to this one-period shock to A_t is presented in the column labeled y_t in Table 4-4, and shown by the curve labeled "Output" in Figure 4-13.

As indicated in the table, output increases by 20 percent in the period of the shock, from 17.107 to 20.528. This makes sense because all that happens initially is that the existing resources are 20 percent more productive than in the previous period. In periods 3, 4, and thereafter, output per worker drops back toward its original level. However, it does not fall all the way immediately. The reason why output remains above its long-run level even after the technology shock abates is that higher productivity in period 2 raises workers' wages in that period.[15] These workers, in turn, save a share α (in this case, one-half) of the increase. This increase in saving—and hence investment—increases the capital stock in period 3, causing output to be higher than its long-run level even though $A = 10$. That is, output is higher in period 2 as a direct result of the technology shock, and in subsequent periods as an *indirect* result of the shock, through the increase in capital. Eventually, the economy does make its transition back to its steady state, following the transition process described in Chapter 3. However, if we combined this shock with other positive and negative shocks

14. We can calculate this steady-state value of k using the following formula, which was derived in Chapter 3: $\bar{k} = [(1 - \alpha)(1 - \beta)A]^{1/(1 - \beta)}$. Given the values of α, β, and A chosen here, the solution is $\bar{k} = 5.987$.

15. Recall from Chapter 3 that, according to the Cobb-Douglas model, wages are a fixed share, $(1 - \beta)$, of output. Hence, workers receive the same share of any increase in output caused by the productivity shock, and owners of capital receive the rest.

Table 4-4 Response to a Technology Shock

Period	A_t	k_t	y_t	i_t	c_t
0	10	5.987	17.107	0.000	17.107
1	10	5.987	17.107	0.000	17.107
2	12	5.987	20.528	1.197	19.331
3	10	7.185	18.069	–0.861	18.930
4	10	6.324	17.390	–0.238	17.628
5	10	6.086	17.191	–0.070	17.261
.	.	.	.	.	.
.	.	.	.	.	.
.	.	.	.	.	.
∞	10	5.987	17.107	0.000	17.107

Lowercase variables are expressed per young person; $c_t = c_{yt} + c_{ot}$. Parameter values: $\alpha = .5, \beta = .3$.

every few periods, it would clearly be possible to produce a pattern of output fluctuations similar to those observed in the actual economy.

The Response of Consumption and Investment to a Technology Shock

In addition to per capita output, Figure 4-13 and Table 4-4 also show the behavior of investment and consumption during the transition. As the table and figure demonstrate, investment and consumption behave quite differently in response to the technology shock. Consumption rises by a smaller percentage than output in period 2, and falls by a smaller percentage than output in period 3. In contrast, investment jumps immediately from its initial value of zero and then falls quickly back, becoming negative as output falls in subsequent periods. Fully 35 percent of the initial increase in output is accounted for by increased investment, despite the fact that in the steady state, investment accounts for literally none of output. Thus, the simulation reproduces the volatility of actual investment relative to actual consumption that we documented earlier, in Figure 4-9.

Let's see why the model produces this pattern of investment and consumption, looking first at investment. Table 4-4 shows that investment also equals 35 percent of the corresponding output change in each succeeding period. This is no coincidence. Consider the expression that relates the next period's capital-labor ratio, k_{t+1}, to output per worker, y_t. This relationship holds for every pe-

Figure 4-13 An Increase in the Level of Technology

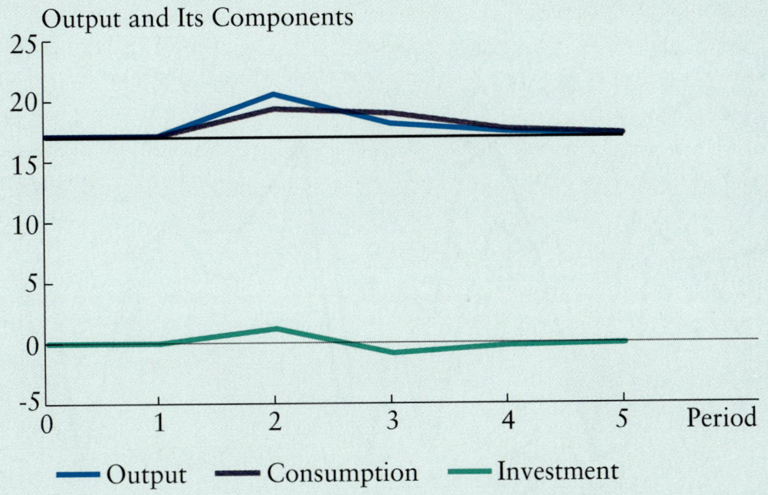

According to the real business cycle theory, business cycle fluctuations result from shocks to the economy's technology. This figure depicts the responses of output, consumption, and investment to a temporary improvement in technology, assuming the real business cycle theory is valid. Output remains above its long-run level for some time after the technology shock abates. Consumption follows the pattern of output, but is less volatile. Investment is more volatile than output, jumping immediately after the shock, then turning negative.

riod t, so we may subtract the expression for k_t from that for k_{t+1} to obtain an expression for $k_{t+1} - k_t$, which equals investment per worker, i_t:

$$i_t = (1 - \alpha)(1 - \beta)\,(y_t - y_{t-1})$$

In the simulation, $\alpha = .5$ and $\beta = .3$. Therefore, investment equals exactly $(1 - .5)(1 - .3) = .35$ times the change in output, for every period t. This change in output may be large, small, or even negative, so we can readily see why the model predicts wide swings in the level of investment.

Accelerator *The relationship whereby the level of investment is determined by the change in output*

This important relationship—between the *level* of investment and the *change* in the level of output—is known as the **accelerator**.[16] How well does the

16. What explains the name? In physics, the rate of change of an object's position is called its velocity, and the rate of change of this rate of change is the object's acceleration. Here, the *level* of investment depends upon the *change* in the level of output—output's velocity. That means a change in the level of investment will be caused by a change in output's velocity—its acceleration.

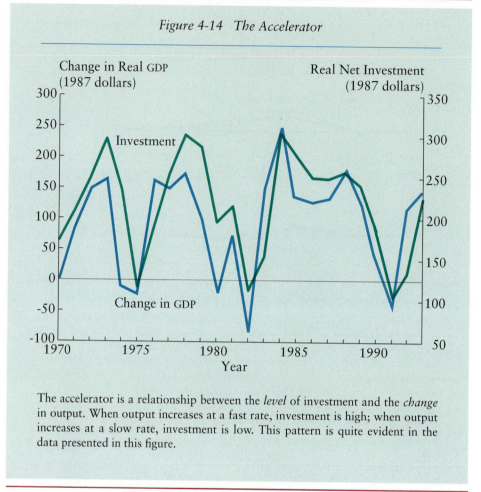

Figure 4-14 The Accelerator

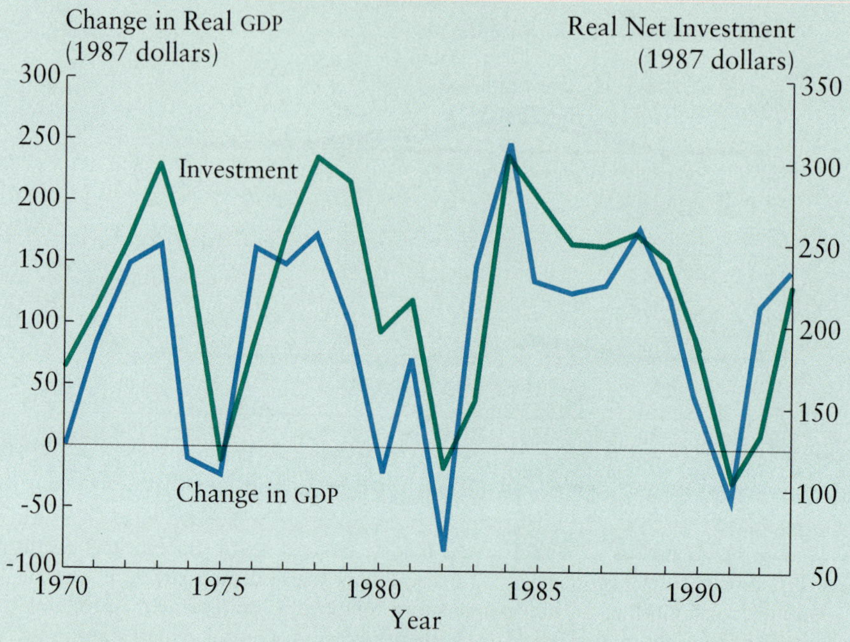

The accelerator is a relationship between the *level* of investment and the *change* in output. When output increases at a fast rate, investment is high; when output increases at a slow rate, investment is low. This pattern is quite evident in the data presented in this figure.

Source: *Economic Report of the President,* 1994

accelerator theory explain movements in investment? Figure 4-14 plots annual U.S. net investment against changes in GDP and shows that the two series move closely together, as predicted. As we will see further in Chapter 16, a variety of additional factors influence the pattern of investment over the business cycle. However, this basic accelerator relationship is very useful in helping us understand the volatility of investment.

The model predicts that investment will be more volatile than output and it predicts that consumption will be less volatile. Output rises by more than consumption in the period of the shock and falls more rapidly thereafter. This is a result of the life-cycle model of consumption. When income rises initially in period 2, the old consume all the additional income they receive in the form of higher returns to capital. However, the young consume only a fraction, α, of their increase in income and save the rest. This explains not only why consumption rises by less than output initially, but also why it falls by less in period 3. The increase in saving by the young in period 2 provides them with additional consumption in period 3, regardless of the level of income in that period. We refer to this behavior as **consumption smoothing**, because it spreads the impact of single-period shocks to income over more than one period's consumption.

Consumption smoothing *The tendency of consumption spending to be less volatile than output*

Does the Real Business Cycle Model Explain Economic Fluctuations?

There are limitations to the simple real business cycle model we have just considered. Although it produces output fluctuations, the model does not produce employment fluctuations, which are an important feature of the business cycle. But employment fluctuations will arise in response to technology shocks if we expand the utility function to include utility for leisure when young and old. As we saw in Chapter 2, with this utility function the ratio of labor supplied when young to labor supplied when old depends on the ratio of wages when young to wages when old. Intuitively, we assume that people take advantage of periods of high wages to work harder and longer and take more leisure during periods when wages are depressed. A second issue is that our model involves periods that, in the real world, are many years in length, much longer than the periods over which business cycles occur. A more realistic, but also more complex, multiperiod version of the model could explain the short-run fluctuations in employment and hours we actually observe during business cycles. Thus, some of the model's limitations are merely the result of its simple nature.

Still, there is considerable dispute about the importance of technology shocks in causing fluctuations. Do the increase in unemployment and the drop in hours worked observed during recessions really reflect voluntary choices by workers to supply less labor? Undoubtedly, technology shocks and voluntary variations in labor supply over the business cycle are part of the story. But many economists find it implausible that the Great Depression could have been caused by a negative technology shock, or that voluntary withdrawals from employment explain the 25 percent unemployment rates during that period. As late as 1939, fully ten years after the depression began, the civilian unemployment rate exceeded 17 percent, a level that has not even been approached during the postwar period. Could so many workers have been so patiently awaiting a return to "normal" productivity levels? Even in the more normal recessions that have occurred in recent decades, much unemployment is difficult to characterize in terms of optimal responses to wage variations over time.

In any event, the real business cycle theory is certainly a useful first step to understanding how economic fluctuations may arise in the model we have developed. Moreover, although economic fluctuations may be more than equilibrium responses to technology shocks, certain aspects of the model we have just discussed, such as consumption smoothing and the accelerator, are consistent with other theories of economic fluctuations as well.

Chapter Summary

1. Although aggregate output, measured by real GDP, normally grows over time, there have been recurrent periods of negative growth, called recessions. Since World War II, recessions have averaged just less than one year in length. Recessions combined with expansions (periods of growth, which typically last about four years) are called business cycles. Since the end of World War II, there have been nine full cycles. The frequency and severity of recessions have declined since the prewar years. Some economists see this as the result of a more active government economic policy. Changes in the composition of output and measurement problems with earlier data also appear to be explanatory factors.

2. Economic fluctuations affect different regions and industries differently, but still are characteristically broad in their impact. Though each business cycle is different, it is still possible to use certain recurring relationships in the timing of macroeconomic variables to form the Composite Index of Leading Indicators, which normally begins to decline several months before a recession begins. Postwar recessions in the United States have been more severe than recessions in Germany and Japan, but the timing of the cycles has been similar, reflecting connections among these three economies through international trade and other factors.

3. The breadth and brevity of recessions distinguishes them from longer-run shifts in regional and industrial development, which have more to do with changing consumer tastes and production methods than with any kind of macroeconomic instability. Likewise, business cycles differ from the shorter, more volatile, but also more predictable, seasonal variations in production that occur each year.

4. When recessions hit, the use of both labor and capital declines. The reduction in labor input occurs through reductions in the number of workers employed, in the average number of hours worked, and in the intensity of such work. The reduction in capital input is evident in the falling rate of capacity utilization, as well as in the increasing rate of business failures. Some industries, such as construction, experience more volatile swings in output over the business cycle than do others, such as services. Part of the explanation lies in the relative volatility of the uses to which different industries' products are put. In particular, investment is subject to much sharper swings than consumption.

5. There is great controversy about what causes economic fluctuations. One theory explains fluctuations in output and employment as equilibrium phenomena by subjecting a model (like the one developed in previous chapters) to recurring shocks to the economy's productivity level. This real business cycle approach is also consistent with the observed volatility of investment and smoothness of consumption over the business cycle. However, it is not the only approach capable of explaining consumption and investment behavior. It also characterizes unemployment as voluntary, a conclusion difficult for many economists to accept.

6. It is even possible that economic fluctuations are not really cycles at all, but simply the random combinations of negative and positive permanent shocks to the economy's level of output. In this case, the drop in output during recessions has a permanent impact on the economy: there is no tendency for the economy to get back on its previous growth path. Under this hypothesis, stabilization policy becomes even more important, for such policy may provide permanent benefits.

Key Concepts

Recession
Expansion
Business cycles
Leading indicator
Unemployment
Labor force participation rate
Procyclical behavior
Capacity utilization
Seasonal adjustment
Random walk theory
Real business cycle theory
Accelerator
Consumption smoothing

Review Questions

1. Define the terms *expansion* and *recession*. How is the existence of a recession determined?
2. What are the relative lengths of expansions versus recessions? How have the average lengths of each changed over time?
3. How is business cycle *volatility* measured? Has volatility changed over time?
4. Why do macroeconomists try to distinguish broad-based, short-term cyclical fluctuations from long-term sectoral declines?
5. To what does the term *leading indicators* refer? What is the *Composite Index of Leading Indicators*? What shortcomings does the index have as a forecasting tool?
6. Define the terms *employed, unemployed, labor force, discouraged workers*, and *labor force participation rate*.
7. Identify three ways in which the economy's measured labor input declines during a recession.
8. How is the *utilization of capital* over the business cycle measured?
9. Are the timing and magnitude of business cycles similar across major industrialized countries?
10. What is *seasonal data adjustment*, and why do macroeconomists prefer to study seasonally adjusted data?
11. How does the *real business cycle theory* explain economic fluctuations?
12. What is the *accelerator*, and how does it arise in the life-cycle model?
13. What is *consumption smoothing*, and how does it arise in the life-cycle model?

Numerical Questions

1. Suppose that you are given the following information about the labor market. The amounts shown are in thousands.

Year	Population	Employment	Unemployment
1990	188,049	117,914	6874
1991	189,765	116,877	8426
1992	191,576	117,598	9384

   a. For each year, calculate the size of the labor force.
   b. For each year, calculate the labor force participation rate.
   c. For each year, calculate the unemployment rate.
   d. Do the data suggest that the number of discouraged workers might have increased in a particular year? If so, which year?
2. Assume that the economy starts out in a steady state characterized by the following values: $A = 4$; $N = 200$; $\alpha = .5$; and $\beta = .3$. Suppose that A rises *for only one period* to 4.5, and then returns to its initial value of 4.
   a. Trace out the resulting time path for output over the next five periods.
   b. What is the new steady-state value of output?
   c. In what sense does the path of output constitute a "business cycle"? In what sense does the output path not constitute a "business cycle"?
3. Assume that output follows the same path as calculated in question 2.
   a. For each of the five periods, compute investment per worker, i_t, and the percentage change from the preceding period.
   b. For each of the five periods, compute c_t, total consumption divided by the number of young persons, and the percentage change from the preceding period.
   c. Compare your answers in parts a and b to the percentage change in output per worker. Does investment per worker change by a greater or lesser amount than output per worker? What about consumption per person? Are your answers consistent with the concepts of the accelerator mechanism and consumption smoothing?

Analytical Questions

1. Suppose that recent unemployment reports from the U.S. Department of Labor indicate that the unemployment rate has held steady at 7 percent for several months. Is it possible to draw firm conclusions about the health of labor markets from these reports? That is, is it possible that labor market conditions are actually improving despite the lack of change in the unemployment rate? Why or why not?
2. You are a member of the President's Council of Economic Advisers and a strong believer in real business cycle theory. For the past several months, economic and financial data have indicated that real GDP is falling. The president has asked for your opinion about the correct policy response. What do you tell him?
3. Assume that a country's economy is in a steady state. The country enters a war in period 1 which requires a fraction of the labor force to leave the

country for one period. After that, the labor force returns to its original level. Answer the following without using numbers; it may help to refer to the transition diagram (Figure 3.9, page 105).

a. What happens in period 1 to the capital-labor ratio? to the level of output? to saving by the young and therefore next period's capital stock?

b. In period 2, given the new value of the capital stock and the return of the labor force to the initial level, what happens to the capital-labor ratio? to the level of output relative to its steady-state value?

c. Subsequent to period 2, what will the path of the capital-labor ratio look like?

d. What will the path of output between the old steady state and the new steady state look like?

C H A P T E R 5

The Measurement of Output

INTRODUCTION

As you've learned, gross domestic product (GDP) is a country's total production of goods and services. GDP per capita measures the country's standard of living. The growth rate of GDP measures its development, and fluctuations in GDP chart its business cycles. Having an accurate estimate of GDP is quite valuable in macroeconomic analysis—a point illustrated by the controversy over pre-1929 U.S. output volatility discussed in the last chapter.

The measurement of GDP, its components, and alternative definitions of output is called *national income accounting*. In addition to clarifying how to measure macroeconomic variables, national income accounting helps us understand underlying macroeconomic relationships. As we'll see, there are several ways to measure GDP. However, the *national income identity* tells us that these different ways must yield the same result. This requirement not only provides a check on the national income accountants' GDP estimates but also provides information about how the components of these alternative measures relate to one another.

Many relationships that arise in national income accounting will be familiar from earlier chapters. In those chapters we discussed economic variables without worrying about their measurement. But discussing and measuring economic variables are two different things. Much of national income accounting is concerned with the host of difficult problems their measurement presents. Perhaps the most important of these problems is determining the extent to which increases in nominal magnitudes, such as nominal GDP, are due to increases in prices as opposed to increases in quantities.

Empirical resolution of the problems of national income accounting has important implications for macroeconomic analysis. As you will see, attributing more of the increase in expenditures on computers to quality improvements than to price increases raises measured growth in real GDP but lowers measured growth in the price of computers. Treating household purchases of durable goods as investment rather than consumption would raise the nation's measured rates of saving and investment. Ignoring production that takes place in the household leads to an overestimate of real GDP growth during periods when people engaged in household production leave the home and enter the work force. Closing inefficient industries in Eastern Europe may lead to an overstatement of the associated decline in real GDP there if the goods sold by those industries were produced at artificially high prices.

Among the questions we'll address in this chapter are:

- How do we distinguish increases in nominal output due to price increases from those due to increases in real output?
- What is the correct measure of overall price inflation when prices of different commodities rise or fall at different rates?
- What types of measurement problems lead to understatements or overstatements of GDP?
- How should we calculate the true amount of consumption services arising from the ownership of durable goods such as houses and refrigerators?
- How does the national income identity help us relate *exports* and *imports*—the sales and purchases of commodities from foreigners—to the levels of national saving and investment?
- As the countries of Eastern Europe make the economic transition to a market system, how is the measurement of their GDP affected?

We begin the chapter by describing three different ways of measuring GDP. This will lead us into a discussion of derivative measures of output, such as gross national product (GNP), and the difficulties of distinguishing among the components of output, notably consumption and investment. After that, we will use the national income identity to study the relationship among saving, investment, and international trade. Next, we will turn to the problem of determining how much of the increase in nominal GDP from one year to the next is due simply to price level increases rather than changes in actual output. Finally, we will consider a variety of other problems encountered in measuring the true value of an economy's production.

MEASURING GROSS DOMESTIC PRODUCT

Gross domestic product is the total value of the *final goods and services* produced in a country in a particular year, no matter who owns the capital and labor used to produce them. The term "final" here refers to the fact that the commodities are not resold to other producers during the year.

If some of a country's productive inputs are located abroad, GDP will not include the value of the goods and services produced abroad by those inputs. The salary earned by U.S. first baseman Cecil Fielder when he played for a Japanese baseball team did not contribute to U.S. GDP. On the other hand, if some of the inputs at home are foreign-owned, GDP will include goods and services produced by those inputs. The Pittsburgh Penguins' payments to Canadian hockey player Mario Lemieux, for example, are included in U.S. GDP.

As we saw in Chapter 2, there is a fundamental relationship between the value of output and the income this production generates. Each dollar of output generated by firms provides a dollar of income for some input supplied by households. This income, in turn, is spent on output. Hence, income must equal output. We can think of this process in terms of the circular flow of income, depicted in Figure 5-1. Dollars flow from households to firms to purchase output, and from firms back to households to pay the inputs that produce output. Flowing in the opposite direction are the goods and inputs associated with these payments—goods flow from firms to households and inputs from households to firms. It might seem natural to think of production as occurring first in this circular flow, followed by the payment of income. However, we actually measure the income as soon as it is earned, which is precisely when the production occurs. Thus, all happens simultaneously at each point in time—there is no place where the circular flow "starts."

National income identity
The logical requirement that the value of national output must equal the value of factor incomes as well as the sum of values added

The equality between income and output is called the **national income identity**. Although output and income are certainly different concepts, we can think of GDP as a measure of total national output or total national income, since the two are always equal. We can also measure GDP either by adding up all incomes earned or by adding up the value of all final production. Indeed, these are two of the three distinct methods used to calculate GDP. They are called the *final sales method* and the *factor incomes method*.[1]

Value added
The difference at a stage of production between the sales of a product and the value of intermediate inputs used to produce it

The third method of calculating GDP is the *value added method*. It differs from the final sales method in cases where production occurs in several stages, with one firm selling *intermediate goods* to another before the final product is sold. Examples of intermediate goods are the steel purchased by car manufacturers to make automobiles and the fertilizer used by farmers to stimulate crop growth. When a firm uses intermediate goods, the value of its output exceeds its payments to capital and labor by the amount it pays for the intermediate goods. We define **value added** as sales minus payments for intermediate goods; it also equals payments to the primary inputs of capital and labor. Since each firm's

1. The word "factor" here reminds us that "factor of production" is a commonly used synonym for what we have called "inputs."

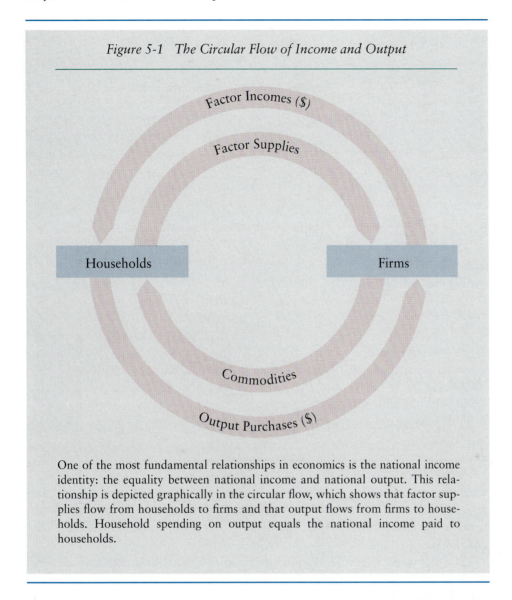

Figure 5-1 The Circular Flow of Income and Output

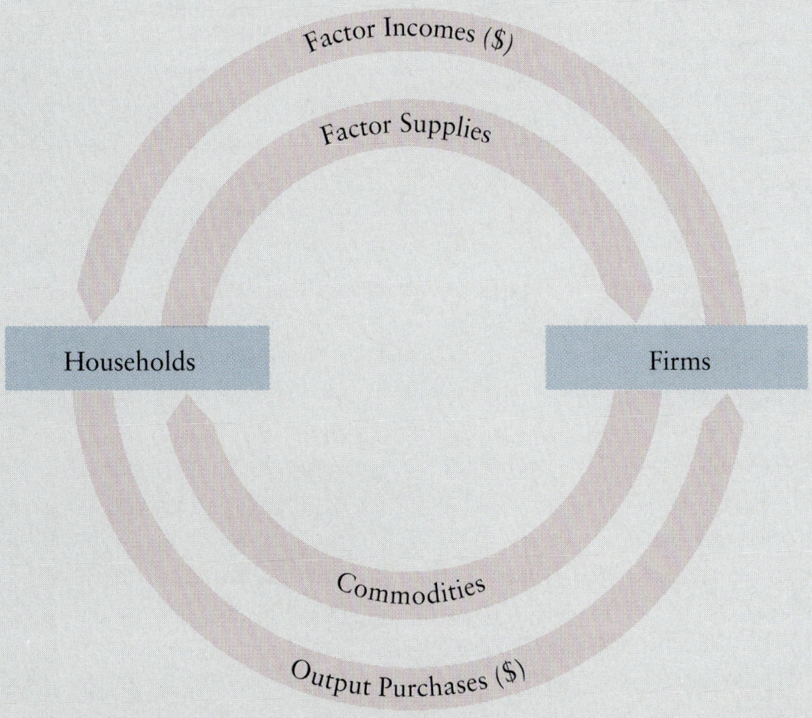

One of the most fundamental relationships in economics is the national income identity: the equality between national income and national output. This relationship is depicted graphically in the circular flow, which shows that factor supplies flow from households to firms and that output flows from firms to households. Household spending on output equals the national income paid to households.

output will generally exceed the sum of its payments to capital and labor, adding the output of all firms together yields a total that exceeds the sum of all factor incomes, and hence GDP.

When firms use intermediate goods, we cannot add the output of each firm to obtain a measure of GDP. The problem encountered in doing so is called "double counting"—the sum of outputs exceeds GDP because some production is counted more than once. Steel would be counted when produced by the steel company and again as part of the automobile. The final sales method and the value added method deal with this problem in different ways. The final sales method counts only the last sale, whereas the value added method subtracts each firm's payments for intermediate inputs. Both approaches ensure that every dollar of production is counted exactly once, so that the resulting total equals

Table 5-1 National Income Accounting: An Example

		Farmer	Manufacturer	Retailer	
(1) Sales		100	150	170	
(2) (For final use)		0	0	170	
Less:					
(3) Materials used		0	100	150	
(4) Wages		20	25	10	
(5) Rent		0	10	5	
(6) Interest		30	0	0	
Equals:					
(7) Business income		50	15	5	
(Proprietors' income)		50	0	5	
(Corporate profits)		0	15	0	
GDP					Total
Factor payments	(4 + 5 + 6 + 7)	100	50	20	170
Value added	(1 – 3)	100	50	20	170
Final sales	(2)	0	0	170	170

GDP. Since value added equals factor income for each firm, the sum of values added must equal the sum of factor incomes, or GDP. Likewise, final sales by firms to purchasers must equal the income that such purchasers spend—once again, GDP.

The following example, detailed in Table 5-1, illustrates the three methods of calculating GDP. Take the case of the production and sale of popcorn, involving a farmer, a popcorn manufacturer, and a retail convenience store.

The production process begins with a farmer, who harvests corn using a tractor he owns and a worker he has hired. The farmer sells the crop for $100 to a popcorn manufacturer, pays his employee $20, and pays the bank mortgage interest on his farm of $30. This leaves $50 of income for the farmer. The farmer's value added is $100—he has produced $100 worth of corn without using (in this simple example) any intermediate goods. His final sales are zero, since the manufacturer is not the ultimate user of the corn—it will be turned into popcorn for resale. His factor payments equal total payments to labor and capital. Payments to labor equal $20. Payments to capital equal all payments to owners of real or financial assets. This includes not only the $30 of interest the farmer pays to the bank, but also the $50 of profit he clears in the transaction. We classify this profit according to whether the business is a corporation or not.

In the case of a corporation, the profits are called *corporate profits*. In the case of proprietorships, such as the farmer's, profits are classified as *proprietors' income*.[2]

At the second stage of production, the popcorn manufacturer owns a popping machine and rents a factory building for his operations. After buying the farmer's corn for \$100, he hires a master popcorn popper to pop it. Selling the popcorn to the retailer, the manufacturer receives \$150, of which \$25 goes for the popper's wages and \$10 for the building rental, a category of capital income that is classified, not surprisingly, as *rental income*. This leaves \$15, after the cost of the corn itself. The manufacturer is a corporation, and so this income is counted as corporate profits. Since the manufacturer's sales of popcorn are not to the ultimate user, final sales are zero. Value added equals sales less the cost of materials, or \$50. Factor income to labor and capital is also \$50.

The retail store owner rents space for \$5, employs a store clerk for \$10, and, after buying the popcorn for \$150, sells it to her customers for \$170. This leaves the owner, who is not a corporation, with \$5 of proprietors' income. Final sales are \$170, value added \$20, and factor income \$20.

We can now see that all three methods of calculating GDP give the same result. The factor income method adds the \$100 of factor income paid by the farmer to the \$50 paid by the manufacturer and the \$20 paid by the retailer to obtain a GDP of \$170. The values added at these three stages of production also sum to \$170, which equals final sales at the last stage of production.

This example also shows why we do not wish to count the sales of all three businesses in calculating GDP. The retailer does not produce the popcorn she sells, but does create additional output by providing the service of distributing the finished product. If we count the entire value of the popcorn when the retailer sells it, we cannot also count it when the manufacturer sells it to the retailer, for the popcorn itself is produced only once, not twice. Another way of seeing the logic behind the final sales approach is to consider the case in which the retailer and the manufacturer merge. The combined entity would buy the raw corn for \$100 and sell popcorn to consumers for \$170. This merger has no effect on the nature of production or the level of GDP, and the final sales approach would still yield the correct answer of \$170 for GDP; so would the value added method (\$100 + \$70 = \$170). However, the procedure of adding all sales together would provide a smaller measure than before (\$100 + \$170 = \$270 versus \$100 + \$150 + \$170 = \$420), a nonsensical result, since there has been no change whatsoever in production.

Case Study: How Not to Impose a Sales Tax

This difference between total sales on the one hand and final sales and value added on the other has an important application to fiscal policy. A government wishing to tax output may tax final sales, as many states in the U.S. do through

2. Actually, a portion of proprietors' income is really labor income. In this case, the farmer's "profit" is partially a return to his farm's assets, but also a return to his own labor. The national income accounts do not separate proprietors' income into these two components.

their retail sales taxes, or value added, as many European countries do. Our study of national income accounting shows that these two methods should be equivalent, and they are generally recognized to be so.

Taxes on *all* sales, called *turnover taxes*, apply to more than total output. They are especially hard on production processes involving several stages of production, because the same output is taxed several times. In our popcorn example, a turnover tax on all sales at the rate of 5 percent would generate \$21 in revenue on total sales of \$420, equivalent to a tax rate of over 12 percent on GDP. For this reason, turnover taxes have been abandoned in most countries as a tool of fiscal policy.

RELATED MEASURES OF PRODUCTION AND INCOME

Now that you have an intuitive understanding of the three approaches to national income accounting and the measurement of GDP, let's consider some related measures of production and income.

GDP Versus GNP

In previous chapters we presented data for an output measure called gross national product (GNP), which is closely related to GDP. The two differ, in a sense, in their drawing of national boundaries. U.S. GNP counts all output produced by U.S.-owned inputs no matter where those inputs are situated in the world. GDP counts all output produced in the U.S. regardless of who owns the inputs involved. Thus, GNP includes the output of U.S.-owned inputs located in foreign countries and excludes the output produced in the U.S. by foreign-owned inputs.[3] For example, if a U.S. business invests in France, the corporate profits it earns there would be included in U.S. GNP but not U.S. GDP. If a French business invests in the United States, its earnings in the U.S. would count in U.S. GDP but not U.S. GNP. Whereas GNP is a measure of what U.S.-owned inputs produce, GDP measures what is produced in the U.S. Similar conclusions apply to wages earned by U.S. workers in France and by French workers in the U.S.

The relationship between GNP and GDP is written as

$$\text{GNP} = \text{GDP} + E$$

where E equals net factor income earned abroad: the income of U.S. inputs abroad minus the income of foreign inputs earned in the U.S. In our example in Table 5-1, GNP and GDP are equal—there are no foreign transactions.

In 1993, U.S. inputs earned \$131.7 billion dollars abroad, and foreign inputs earned \$131.6 billion in the U.S. To go from GDP to GNP, we add the first number and subtract the second. Hence, GNP exceeded GDP by \$0.1 billion—

3. Until 1991, the U.S. Department of Commerce, which produces the national income accounts, placed more emphasis on GNP than GDP as a measure of output. The switch to GDP was motivated by the desire to make U.S. statistics comparable to those of other countries and by the view that GDP is better suited to tracking domestic economic activity during business cycles.

less than .002 percent of GDP. This discrepancy, though never large, has fallen over time because of the increasing relative importance of foreign inputs in the U.S. (whose income is included in GDP but not GNP). The distinction between GDP and GNP is more important for other countries, such as Canada, where net foreign ownership of industry is more significant.

Net Domestic Product and National Income

As we discussed in Chapter 1, most physical assets depreciate. Some assets, such as buildings, depreciate slowly; others, computers for example, depreciate quite rapidly.[4] Depreciation represents a decline in the value of existing capital. Part of GDP must be used to offset depreciation if the nation is to maintain its productive capacity. *Net domestic product (NDP)*,[5] GDP minus depreciation, measures what's left over. It is the net amount that we have available, once we have replaced the capital that depreciated since the accounting period (the year, the quarter, etc.) started.

Figure 5-2 shows how the ratio of depreciation to GDP has grown since 1960. The reason for this increase in the ratio is the increasing share of equipment in the economy's capital stock. In 1960, equipment represented 19.2 percent of all fixed capital, and structures the other 80.8 percent. By 1991, equipment's share had risen to 24.1 percent. Since equipment depreciates more rapidly than structures, the average depreciation rate of the capital stock has increased as well.[6]

To account for depreciation in our popcorn example, we must consider each of the real assets owned by the businesses: the farmer's tractor and the manufacturer's popping machine. (The farmer's land doesn't depreciate.) The result of including depreciation is shown in Table 5-2. Taking account of the $10 of depreciation on the farmer's tractor reduces his income by $10. Likewise, the $5 of depreciation on the popping machine reduces the manufacturer's corporate profits by $5. But now, it appears that we have a problem equating our different measures of gross output. Factor incomes have declined but GDP has not. Adding together all factor incomes now results in a measure of NDP, not GDP. As a result, it is necessary to add depreciation back to the factor income measure to obtain GDP once again.

A second accounting adjustment involves *indirect taxes*, such as retail sales taxes, paid on business transactions. In Table 5-2, we have assumed the retailer

4. Depreciation does not arise just from assets wearing out and becoming less productive. We measure depreciation by asking how much less an asset produces than a comparable new one. In the case of computers, for example, machines that are several years old may be just as productive as they were when they were produced. However, relative to the current state of technology, these machines have very low productivity, and are viewed as having depreciated considerably.

5. A related measure is *net national product*, or NNP, which is calculated by subtracting depreciation from GNP, rather than GDP.

6. For a *given* level of GDP, higher depreciation means lower NDP. But the trend toward increased depreciation does not necessarily indicate a lower level of NDP, because GDP is not invariant with respect to the types of investment firms have made in the past. NDP might well be lower had firms invested more in buildings and less in equipment. The fact that firms chose to invest more in equipment suggests that they believed that their incomes (and hence NDP) would be higher by doing so.

Figure 5-2 Depreciation as a Share of Output, 1960–1993

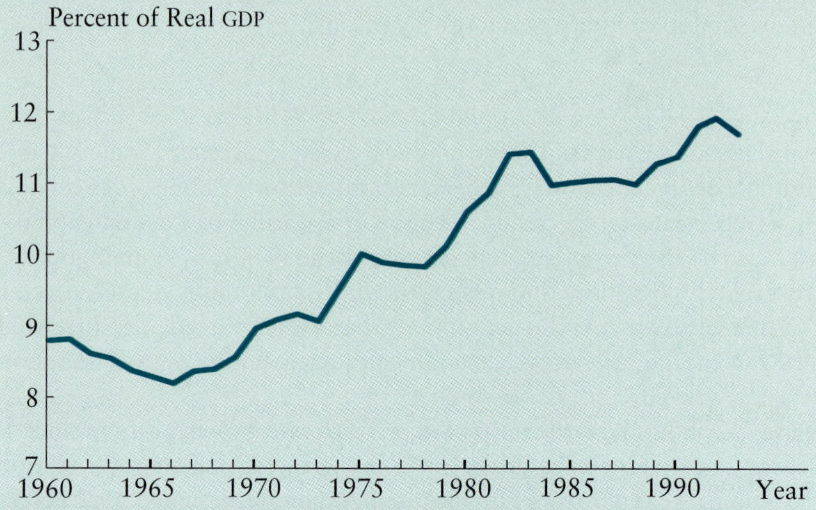

Depreciation is the decline in the value of existing capital. The figure shows that depreciation has grown as a share of GDP since 1960, reflecting the increased share of equipment in the U.S. capital stock. Since equipment depreciates more rapidly than structures, the growing importance of equipment has raised the average depreciation rate over the past several decades.

Source: *Survey of Current Business,* various issues

must pay the government 1 percent of all sales, which (to the nearest dollar) equals \$2. This leaves her with a net profit of just \$3, rather than \$5.[7] Once again, factor income declines with no reduction in GDP. To offset this decline and maintain consistency between the factor income measure of GDP and the other two measures, it is necessary to add indirect business taxes back to the factor income measure.

National income GNP *less the sum of depreciation and indirect business taxes*

Although consistency is important, it is not especially intuitive to think of depreciation or indirect business taxes as income accruing to any input, since no owner of capital or labor ever receives them. Therefore, we define a third measure of aggregate income, **national income** (NI), equal to the sum of factor incomes, that excludes these two terms. In 1993, NDP was 89.5 percent of GDP, and NI was 81.1 percent of GDP.

7. Here, we have assumed that the imposition of the sales tax simply reduces the profits of the retailer by the amount of the tax. Alternatively, the retail price of popcorn might rise by enough to allow the retailer to "shift the tax forward" to purchasers, by selling the same popcorn for \$172 rather than \$170. Can you trace through how this difference would affect the rest of our example, and verify that the national income identity would still be satisfied?

Table 5-2 National Income Accounting: A Further Example

	Farmer	Manufacturer	Retailer	
(1) Sales	100	150	170	
(2) (For final use)	0	0	170	
Less:				
(3) Materials used	0	100	150	
(4) Wages	20	25	10	
(5) Rent	0	10	5	
(6) Interest	30	0	0	
(8) Depreciation	10	5	0	
(9) Indirect business taxes	0	0	2	
Equals:				
(7) Income	40	10	3	
(Proprietors' income)	40	0	3	
(Corporate profits)	0	10	0	
GDP				**Total**
Factor payments (4 + 5 + 6 + 7 + 8 + 9)	100	50	20	170
Value added (1 – 3)	100	50	20	170
Final sales (2)	0	0	170	170

Table 5-3 presents 1993 figures for GDP, NDP, and NI, as well as the breakdown of NI into the various types of factor income: wages and salaries, rent, interest, corporate profits, and proprietors' income. As we learned in Chapter 1, wages and salaries—labor income—account for the vast majority of all income.

In constructing NI, we measure the national income of the U.S., including income earned abroad. Therefore, as the table shows, we include the income that U.S. inputs earn abroad, net of income generated in the U.S. that does not go to U.S.-owned inputs.[8] The table also indicates three minor, additional adjustments made in computing national income.[9]

8. This is the same adjustment we make in going from GDP to GNP, as discussed above.

9. The first two adjustments are to exclude both net operating profits of government enterprises, such as the Bonneville Power Administration, which sells hydroelectric power in the Pacific Northwest (because such profits are never received by any individual or business) and transfer payments, such as charitable contributions, made by businesses to households (since these reduce business profits without increasing any other form of factor income). The last adjustment is called the *statistical discrepancy*. According to the national income identity, the output and factor incomes approaches to computing GDP should give exactly the same answer. Inevitably, however, there are small differences that arise from measurement errors. The statistical discrepancy accounts for these differences.

Table 5-3 GDP, NDP, and National Income: 1993 (billions of dollars)

Gross Domestic Product		6,379.4
Less depreciation	671.1	
Equals		
Net Domestic Product		5,708.2
Plus		
Net receipt of foreign factor income	0.1	
Less		
Indirect business taxes	530.6	
Business transfer payments	28.0	
Net surplus of government enterprises	–7.0	
Statistical discrepancy	14.6	
Equals		
National Income		5,142.1
Wages and salaries	3,772.1	
Proprietors' income	442.1	
Rent	13.0	
Corporate profits	467.3	
Interest	447.6	

Source: *Economic Report of the President,* 1994

National Income Versus Personal Income

Different measures of income have different uses. GDP measures total domestic production, whereas NDP tells us how much of that production is available after we replace capital that has worn out. GNP measures total production by domestic-owned inputs. We also need measures of household income, which may be more relevant to household behavior. One example is national income, which is the income earned by capital and labor. It excludes components of NDP not received as factor incomes and includes factor incomes earned abroad that NDP omits.

Personal income *The amount of before-tax income received by households; national income minus income earned but not received plus income received but not earned*

For some purposes, it is useful to know how much income households actually *receive* during a particular year. **Personal income** is the relevant measure of income receipts. It excludes certain elements of national income that households earn but do not receive directly. At the same time, personal income *includes* certain household receipts that are *not* components of national income. As a result, personal income may sometimes exceed national income, as it did in 1993.

Table 5-4 shows the differences between national income and personal income for 1993. The primary exclusion from national income is *retained earnings*, those corporate earnings not actually distributed in cash as *dividends* to

Table 5-4 From National Income to Personal Income, 1993 (billions of dollars)

National Income		5,142.1
Less		
Corporate profits not paid as dividends to households	309.0	
Plus		
Government transfer payments in excess of social insurance contributions	304.4	
Interest not in GDP	248.2	
Business transfer payments to persons	21.9	
Wage payments less accruals	–20.0	
Equals		
Personal Income		5,387.6
Less		
Individual Income Taxes	681.6	
Equals		
Disposable Personal Income		4,706.0

Source: *Economic Report of the President*, 1994

the owners, or shareholders, of corporations. Why exclude retained earnings? The notion is that households don't respond to income not actually received in cash. However, this is not as logical as it may seem. When corporations retain earnings, these earnings still belong to households, through their ownership of corporations. The relevant question is whether households "pierce the corporate veil," taking rational account of the value of the firms they own. Evidence suggests that they do, which calls this exclusion into question.[10]

The primary additions made in going from national income to personal income are *transfer payments* from the government to households. Unlike other payments to households already included in national income, transfer payments are not compensation for supplying inputs to the production process. The first category of transfer payments includes payments made under programs like Social Security and unemployment compensation, net of Social Security taxes paid by households. The second category is the interest households receive in excess of that generated by production, primarily the interest paid by the government on the national debt. This interest is classified in the national income accounts

10. For further discussion and statistical evidence, see Alan J. Auerbach and Kevin Hassett, "Corporate Savings and Shareholder Consumption," in B. Douglas Bernheim and John Shoven, eds., *National Saving and Economic Performance* (Chicago: University of Chicago Press, 1991).

as a government transfer to households, since it does not arise from the production of output.[11]

From personal income, we take one additional step to get to *disposable income*, the income households receive *and* have available to them after they pay income taxes. That is,

Disposable Income = Personal Income − Individual Income Taxes

In 1993, disposable income was $4,706.0 billion, or 87.3 percent of personal income and 73.8 percent of GDP. Disposable income is the measure of income often cited in the press as an indicator of household well-being and purchasing power.

COMPONENTS OF GDP

The goods and services that comprise GDP are either used to satisfy domestic demand for private consumption (C), government spending (G), and domestic investment (I) or shipped abroad as exports, X. Of course, domestic demand for $C + G + I$ can also be met through imports, M. Hence, we have

$$\text{GDP} + M = C + I + G + X$$

or,

$$\text{GDP} = C + I + G + X - M$$

In words, this expression says that U.S. domestic output equals the sum of domestic U.S. consumption, investment, and government purchases, plus net sales to foreign purchasers. The upper panel of Table 5-5 gives a breakdown of 1993 GDP into its output components, with some further divisions of the components themselves.

Consumption Versus Investment

The decomposition of GDP into components of output distinguishes consumption from investment. In the two-period model developed in earlier chapters, it is easy to distinguish consumption from investment. Consumption is the output consumed by the household today; investment is the output set aside for use in production in subsequent periods. Making the distinction in the real world is more difficult. Businesses may unintentionally carry over some output into the future, and some of the household purchases labeled as consumption may really constitute investment, as we have just defined it.

11. Personal income also includes transfer payments made to households by businesses and an adjustment for the fact that the wages households actually receive in a given year may differ slightly from those earned during that year.

Table 5-5 Components of GDP: Types of Output and Uses of Income, 1993 (billions of dollars)

Output			
GDP	6,374.0		
Consumption (C)		4,390.6	
Durable goods			537.7
Nondurable goods			1,350.2
Services			2,502.7
Investment (I)		892.0	
Nonresidential equipment			444.4
Nonresidential structures			178.6
Inventory accumulation			16.8
Residential structures			252.3
Government purchases (G)		1,157.1	
Net exports (net foreign investment)		–65.7	
Exports (X)			660.1
Imports (M)			725.8
Income			
GDP	6,374.0		
Plus net foreign factor income (E)	0.1		
Equals GNP	6,374.1		
Consumption (C)		4,390.6	
Government purchases (G)		1,157.1	
Net transfers abroad (J)		33.0	
National saving (S)		793.4	

Note: Net foreign investment (I^f) = –98.6

Source: *Economic Report of the President,* 1994

The national income accounts treat business purchases carried into the next year as investment. This includes not only durable goods—equipment and structures (photocopiers, office buildings, factories, buses, etc.) but also inventories—goods that will eventually be sold. Although inventory accumulation is always classified as investment, it is not necessarily intentional. Some firms may plan to accumulate inventories of goods they wish to resell. Others may find themselves in possession of unwanted inventories if current sales fall short of expectations during a particular year.

Refer again to the popcorn example given in Tables 5-1 and 5-2. Here, all output is consumption—the $170 worth of popcorn bought by consumers. Suppose, however, that video stores were closed and the demand for popcorn dropped suddenly, so there was $50 worth of popcorn left in the convenience store at the end of the year. The national accounts would record this as a $50 investment in popcorn inventories by the retailer. This makes sense, because the $50 must be accounted for as output in the year it was produced. Still, if the retailer has trouble selling the popcorn, this particular investment may prove to be quite unproductive, unlike the capital accumulated in our two-period model.

The Treatment of Housing

Table 5-5 gives the level of each investment component in 1993. Note that the majority of structures built in that year were *residential* structures—both multifamily units (apartment buildings, condominiums, and cooperatives) and single-family houses. About two-thirds of this housing investment was made by households, through the purchase of owner-occupied housing; households, as well as businesses, can invest. But what does investment in owner-occupied housing produce in the future? It produces the money its owner saves by not having to rent from someone else. In a sense, the owner rents the housing from himself, so we call the income **imputed rent**. Since there is no market transaction to use in measuring imputed rent, it must be estimated by national income accountants. Their estimate of imputed rent is included in the rent component of factor income and in the consumption of services.

Imputed rent
An estimate of the value of housing services enjoyed by homeowners in a given year

To understand how national income accountants impute rent on owner-occupied housing, let's add home ownership to our two-period model. We'll assume that individuals purchase houses at the end of their youth and sell them at the end of their old age. Let's take h_{t+1} to be the price of the house purchased by the generation that is young at time t and old at time $t + 1$. In our simple model, members of this generation earn a wage w_t at time t. A portion of this wage is spent on consumption when young, c_{yt}, a portion is spent on housing to be occupied in old age, h_{t+1}, and the rest represents the non-housing assets, a_{t+1}, brought into old age; that is,

$$c_{yt} + h_{t+1} + a_{t+1} = w_t$$

When members of generation t are old at time $t + 1$, they finance their consumption, c_{ot+1}, from the return of principal plus interest on their assets and the sale of their houses. As tangible assets, the houses have depreciated in the intervening period; let's assume each has lost a fraction δ of its value and can now command a price of just $h_{t+1}(1 - \delta)$. Then old-age consumption is

$$c_{ot+1} = a_{t+1}(1 + r_{t+1}) + h_{t+1}(1 - \delta)$$

If we combine these two equations to eliminate a_{t+1}, we obtain a revised lifetime budget constraint:

$$c_{yt} + \frac{c_{ot+1}}{1 + r_{t+1}} + \frac{(r_{t+1} + \delta)h_{t+1}}{1 + r_{t+1}} = w_t$$

This equation says that the present value of spending (on consumption when young and old and on housing services when old) equals the present value of the individual's lifetime income. The product $(r_{t+1} + \delta)h_{t+1}$ represents the imputed rent on housing services when old. This makes sense. In residing in a house worth h_{t+1} units for one period, the individual isn't forgoing the principal of the investment in housing, because she can sell the house at the end of the period. However, she is forgoing the interest she could otherwise have earned by investing the resources. She is also bearing the additional loss in the value of the house that arises from depreciation.[12]

Housing is not the only durable commodity households purchase. As Table 5-5 shows, the national accounts divide consumption into three categories: services, nondurable goods, and durable goods. The distinction between goods and services separates commodities into those that are tangible (potato chips, for example) and those that are not (e.g., medical treatment). Durable goods are items that last for more than a year, like automobiles and washing machines. In principle, they should be treated just like owner-occupied housing, as an investment by households. The services produced by these durables should be treated as consumption and measured as the imputed rent on the durables. Although this is possible, it isn't done in the official national income accounts.

The effect of omitting this correction is to overstate consumption and understate investment and saving. An even more serious omission of this type is made in accounting for government purchases of durable goods: all government purchases, regardless of their nature, are treated as expenditures for current consumption; none are treated as investment. We will discuss this omission in more detail in Chapter 7, once we have considered the nature of government spending more fully.

USING THE NATIONAL INCOME IDENTITY

The national income identity tells us that different ways of measuring GDP must yield the same answer. In particular, GDP measured as output must equal GDP measured as the sum of factor incomes. That is,

$$\text{GDP}_{\text{output}} = \text{GDP}_{\text{income}}$$

12. The actual formula for imputed rent used by the national income accountants is more complicated. It also takes account of the possibility that house prices increase or decrease relative to other prices in the economy.

This identity, and the breakdown of each GDP measure into its components, offers a number of useful insights. A particularly important insight involves how international trade, national saving, and domestic investment are related.

National Saving and the Trade Deficit

Trade deficit *The difference between the values of imports and exports in a given year*

The difference between exports and imports, $X - M$, is called the *trade surplus*, since it indicates how much more a country is exporting than it is importing. This measure can also be expressed in terms of the **trade deficit**, which is equal to $M - X$. There has been much concern in the U.S. in recent years about the size of the trade deficit. In 1987, for example, imports exceeded exports by $143.1 billion—more than 3 percent of GDP. We can use the national income identity to help understand the relationship between national saving and the trade deficit.

We begin by recalling that GDP is either consumed by the private and government sectors, invested at home, or sent abroad as net exports. Hence,

$$\text{GDP} = C + I + G + X - M$$

Let's add net foreign income, E, to both sides of this identity and recall that GDP plus net foreign income equals gross national product, GNP:

$$\text{GNP} = C + I + G + X - M + E$$

Next, subtract consumption and government purchases from both sides of this formula for GNP:

$$\text{GNP} - C - G = I + X - M + E$$

Now GNP is a measure of the economy's income, including the income it earns abroad. GNP minus private and government consumption in our model just equals S, national saving. But in the real world, some of GNP that is not consumed is transferred abroad. If we let J stand for net transfers abroad, then we can replace GNP $- C - G$ by $S + J$, rearrange terms, and write

$$S - I = X - M + E - J$$

Finally, note that the difference between national saving and domestic investment, $S - I$, is simply the amount of saving invested abroad, which we call *net foreign investment*, F. Hence, replacing $S - I$ by F gives

Capital account balance *Minus net foreign investment*

$$I^f = (X - M) + E - J$$

Current account balance *Net exports plus net foreign income minus net transfers abroad*

In this expression, the left-hand side—net foreign investment—is also referred to as minus the **capital account balance** in international transactions, and the right-hand side is called the **current account balance**. This terminology reflects the respective sides' dependence on investment and current expenditures. Subtracting

I^f from both sides of the expression shows that the current and capital account balances sum to zero.

It may seem strange that a country's net exports and its net foreign investment are so closely linked, but the relationship is easy to understand from the perspective of our simple two-period model in which a single good, say corn, serves as both a consumption and an investment good. In our model, the home country invests abroad when it plants some of its corn in the foreign country. If we ignore transfer payments to foreigners, then net foreign investment—the increase in the amount of corn the home country plants abroad—equals the flow of corn to the foreign country—the net export of corn—plus the amount of corn earned by the home country and kept abroad—the net factor income earned abroad. The intuition that investing abroad means exporting some of a country's domestic output or reinvesting its foreign earnings abroad also holds in the real world, in which there are many different kinds of investment and consumption goods. When a country exports goods, for example, it can be thought of either as placing some of its own capital goods in the foreign country—in which case the exports translate directly into the foreign investment—or as selling some of its consumption goods and services in the foreign country and using the proceeds to buy capital goods in the foreign country which it leaves (invests) there.

Table 5-5 indicates that net foreign investment was –$98.6 billion in 1993, which means that foreigners' investment in the U.S. exceeded U.S. investment abroad. As we have just learned, this number can be arrived at in more than one way. It equals the difference between national saving and domestic investment, $S - I$, as well as the current account balance, $(X - M) + E - J$.

Case Study: Operation Desert Storm and the Current Account Balance

Normally, most of the year-to-year fluctuations in the current account balance are due to shifts in net exports, also called the **trade balance**. Net factor incomes from abroad (E) and net transfer payments to foreigners (J) tend to vary far less over the short run. However, this rule of thumb was violated for the U.S. in 1991. Figure 5-3 plots net transfer payments abroad as a share of GDP, along with the current account deficit—equal to minus the current account balance. As the figure illustrates, net foreign transfer payments have typically been quite stable relative to the current account. However, in 1991, these transfers dropped suddenly by about 0.75 percent of GDP for one year, becoming negative and causing the current account to shift temporarily into surplus. The negative net transfers indicate the U.S. was a net recipient of foreign transfer payments during this year.

Trade balance *The difference between a country's exports and imports in a given period; a synonym for net exports*

What happened in 1991? Quarterly data indicate that this anomalous behavior was confined to the first two quarters of 1991, particularly the first—during Operation Desert Storm in Kuwait. The U.S. supplied much of the military might and many of our allies, who were militarily less active, supplied a considerable amount of cash to help finance the operation.

Figure 5-3 Operation Desert Storm and the Current Account

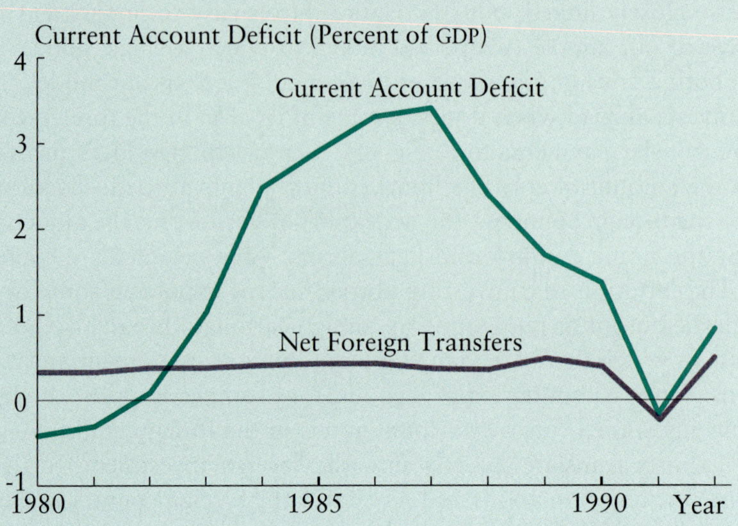

Since 1980, the current account deficit has first increased, then decreased. Net foreign transfers, however, have been quite stable. The exception was during the first two quarters of 1991 when the U.S. experienced a net inflow of cash from its allies in the Gulf War. That inflow made net transfers negative for the year and caused the current account to shift temporarily into surplus.

Source: *Economic Report of the President,* 1994

Case Study: The Trade Deficit since 1980

Aside from unusual circumstances, such as those of 1991, the trade surplus, $X - M$, and net foreign investment, I^f, move quite closely together. For given levels of E and J, reductions in the trade surplus—or increases in the trade deficit—will also reduce net foreign investment, meaning that U.S. residents will be investing less abroad, foreigners will be investing more in the U.S., or both.

Is it a bad thing to run a trade deficit and have foreigners adding to the capital stock in this country? Quite the contrary. As we saw in Chapter 1, having more capital per worker raises labor productivity and real wages.[13] The employees of Honda of America in Marysville, Ohio would surely confirm this point. They would be considerably worse off if Honda had not invested over $3 billion in plant and equipment in Marysville. Indeed, Honda of America has already become the largest exporter of American-made cars to Japan.

13. Having more capital lowers the real return on capital, which hurts domestic owners of capital. But it can be shown that the benefit to workers (the young in our model) exceeds the loss to owners of capital (the old in our model), implying that everyone in society could be made better off by permitting foreign investment.

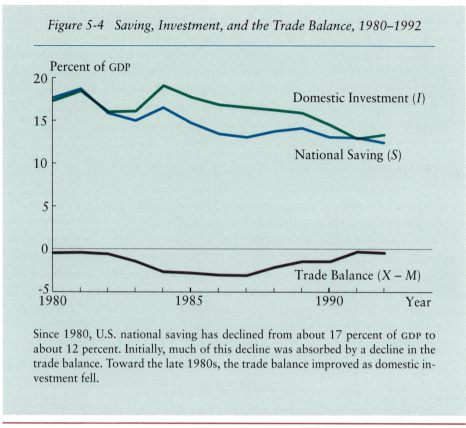

Figure 5-4 Saving, Investment, and the Trade Balance, 1980–1992

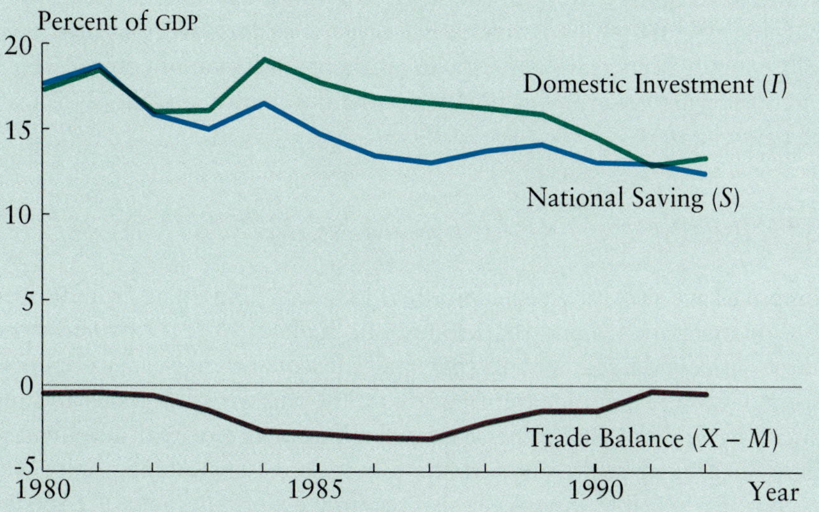

Since 1980, U.S. national saving has declined from about 17 percent of GDP to about 12 percent. Initially, much of this decline was absorbed by a decline in the trade balance. Toward the late 1980s, the trade balance improved as domestic investment fell.

Source: *Economic Report of the President,* 1994

If having foreigners invest in this country is a good thing, why is there so much concern about trade deficits? The answer can be understood by recalling that national saving, S, equals the sum of domestic investment, I, and net foreign investment, I^f. When a country's saving falls, either its domestic investment or its net foreign investment must also fall. As we will see in Chapter 6, when capital is internationally mobile, it may be net foreign investment that falls (is **crowded out**) when saving declines. Hence, one reason we ought to be concerned about an increase in inbound foreign investment, and the associated increase in the trade deficit, is that they may reflect a decline in the nation's saving. We can, of course, look directly at the nation's saving behavior, but trade deficits seem to attract more attention from the media than does the national saving rate.

Crowding out *A reduction in domestic investment as a result of a decrease in national saving*

Figure 5-4 plots the ratios to GDP of national saving (S), domestic investment (I), and the trade balance ($X - M$) since 1980. As the figure shows, national saving declined from around 17 percent of GDP in 1980 to 12 percent in 1992. During the early part of this decline in saving, most of the crowding out caused by the decline in national saving was of net exports. Indeed, domestic investment actually *rose* as a share of GDP into the mid-1980s. By the late 1980s, however, the pattern of crowding out had shifted. The rate of domestic investment declined, and net exports began to improve. By 1991, the trade deficit had fallen below 1 percent of GDP, from its high of over 3 percent in the mid-80s. Explaining why national saving fell and the precise response of net exports is beyond the realm of national income accounting. Still, national income accounting tells us that it is essentially impossible to increase net exports without increasing national saving or decreasing domestic investment—a lesson of considerable value when considering government policy toward international trade, as we will see in the next chapter.

DISTINGUISHING REAL FROM NOMINAL MAGNITUDES

Price level
A weighted index of prices of individual goods and services at a particular point in time

Inflation rate
The percentage increase in the price level from one period to the next

In Chapter 2 we saw how per capita real GDP can be used as an indicator of a nation's living standard and that changes in the level of real GDP show the rate at which an economy grows. In that and subsequent chapters we ignored the question of how to combine information on the vast array of goods and services produced by modern economies into a single measure of real output. As we'll see here, measuring real GDP quite literally requires combining apples with oranges, but in a sensible way. We'll also see how economists measure the level of prices—**the price level**—and the rate of change over time in the price level—the **rate of inflation**.

Measuring Real GDP

To understand the calculation of real GDP, let's first think about *nominal GDP*—GDP not adjusted for changes in prices. To determine nominal GDP in, say, 1995, we just add together the *values* of the sales of all final goods and services produced in 1995. The value of a good or service is just its price times the quantity sold. In the case of 1995 nominal GDP, the quantities of final goods and services sold in 1995 are valued at *prevailing* prices, which, in this case, are 1995 prices. Thus,

$$\text{1995 Nominal GDP} = \sum_{i=1}^{M} p_{i,1995} \times q_{i,1995}$$

In this equation, the symbol Σ means summation. The equation says that 1995 nominal GDP is the sum, for commodities from 1 to M (the total number of commodities), of the products of their prices in 1995 times their quantities in 1995. The term $p_{i,1995}$ stands for the price of commodity i in 1995 and $q_{i,1995}$ stands for the quantity of commodity i sold to its end users in 1995. Thus, 1995 GDP is the 1995 price of apples sold to the public times the quantity of apples sold, plus the 1995 price of oranges sold to the public times the quantity of oranges sold, plus the 1995 price of Dodge Caravans sold to the public times the quantity of Caravans sold, plus the 1995 price of Boeing 777s sold to airlines, times the quantity of 777s sold, and so on.

As the formula shows, nominal GDP can change either because the prices of commodities change or because the quantities of final goods and services change. If we want to consider only the change in quantity of the economy's output we must control for price changes. This is what happens in the calculation of real GDP: we still add together the value of final goods and services, but we use a *time-invariant* set of prices in valuing the quantities sold. In the U.S. the prices used to calculate real GDP are the ones that prevailed in 1987. The year 1987 is called the *base year* for calculating real GDP. To better understand the calculation of real GDP, compare the formulas for real GDP in two years, say, 1993 and 1960:

$$\text{1993 Real GDP} = \sum_{i=1}^{M} p_{i,1987} \times q_{i,1993}$$

$$\text{1960 Real GDP} = \sum_{i=1}^{M} p_{i,1987} \times q_{i,1960}$$

Since the same set of 1987 prices is used in determining real GDP for 1960 and 1993, any difference in real GDP can only reflect differences in quantities of goods produced in the two years. Real GDP is a *quantity index* because it values quantities at a common base-year set of prices.

Let's now compare some actual values of nominal and real GDP. U.S. nominal GDP in 1993 was $6.374 trillion, which is over 12 times larger than the $513 billion value of nominal GDP in 1960. But how much of the increase in nominal GDP between the two years reflects an increase in output and how much simply reflects increases in prices? The answer can be determined from the values of real GDP. Since real GDP in 1993 was $5.133 trillion and real GDP in 1960 was $1.971 trillion, real output was 2.6 times larger in 1993 than it was in 1960. Hence, most of the increase in nominal GDP between 1960 and 1993 reflects an increase in prices rather than an increase in the production of final goods and services. As we will see, we use the relative movements of nominal and real GDP to measure the rate at which prices are increasing.

Measuring Inflation

Economists measure inflation—the rate of increase in prices—by determining how much a given bundle of goods would cost at different times. The value of a given bundle of goods at different points in time is called a *price index*. A price index is like a quantity index, except that rather than holding prices fixed at base-year values and letting quantities vary, we hold quantities fixed at base-year values and let prices vary. For example, if the base year is 1980, we construct the price index for, say, 1960 and 1993 by substituting these years' prices for those of 1980:

$$\text{1960 Value of Price Index} = \sum_{i=1}^{M} p_{i,1960} \times q_{i,1980}$$

$$\text{1993 Value of Price Index} = \sum_{i=1}^{M} p_{i,1993} \times q_{i,1980}$$

In both of these formulas the bundle of goods is the same, namely the 1980 bundle. The 1960 index value tells us what it would have cost to purchase that bundle in 1960. The 1993 value measures the cost of that same bundle in 1993. The only reason the two values of the price index differ is because the prices of commodities in the two years differed. Which goods we include in the bundle of commodities depends on what kinds of price changes we want to consider.

Consumer Price Index
A measure of the price of a fixed "market basket" of consumer goods and services

Perhaps the most frequently used price index in the U.S. is the **Consumer Price Index** (the CPI), which has a base year of 1982—it holds quantities fixed at the 1982 bundle of final goods and services sold to consumers. The CPI is useful because it provides an indication of the price changes households face in their daily lives. The CPI is basically computed as just indicated, but an additional step is taken so that the annual values of the index will be in units that are easier to deal with than billions or trillions of dollars. This additional step is called normalizing the index. Each year's value of the CPI (such as the sums determined in the above two formulas) is divided by the average of its values in 1982, 1983, and 1984 and then multiplied by 100. This makes the value of the CPI average 100 during the period 1982–1984, and makes the values of the CPI in other years equally easy to consider. For example, in 1993, the normalized CPI was

$$\text{1993 Value of CPI} = \frac{\sum_{i=1}^{M} p_{i,1993} \times q_{i,1982}}{\sum_{i=1}^{M} p_{i,1982-1984} \times q_{i,1982}} \times 100$$

The choice of year to use in normalizing a price index is not significant. Even though the level of each year's index is influenced by the normalization, the ratio of the normalized values of the CPI in any two years is unaffected. It is such ratios that are of interest, because they tell us about the increase in prices between two years. For example, normalizing the CPI to its value in 1980, rather than 1982–1984, would increase the value of the normalized CPI in every year (because prices were lower in 1980 than during the period 1982–1984) but would not change the ratio of any two years' values of the normalized CPI.

Figure 5-5 shows the annual rates of inflation since 1960, derived by taking the rate of change of the CPI in each year. How much did consumer prices increase between 1960 and 1993? Since the respective values of the CPI in 1960 and 1993 are 29.6 and 144.5, the consumer price level rose by a factor of 4.88 (144.5 divided by 29.6). However, this 388 percent increase in the price level between 1960 and 1993, an average of 4.92 percent a year, did not occur smoothly over the period. The average annual rate of inflation was only 2.35 percent in the 1960s. It was 7.06 percent in the 1970s, and 5.50 percent in the 1980s. During the entire period, 1962 had the lowest inflation rate, just 1.00 percent, and 1980 was the high-water mark, with inflation registering 13.50 percent.

Although the CPI rose by 388 percent between 1960 and 1993, there was considerable difference in the rate of price increases among the different types of consumer goods included in the CPI. For example, medical prices rose by 803 percent, whereas clothing prices rose by only 193 percent. The prices of some

Figure 5-5 Inflation Rates Since 1960

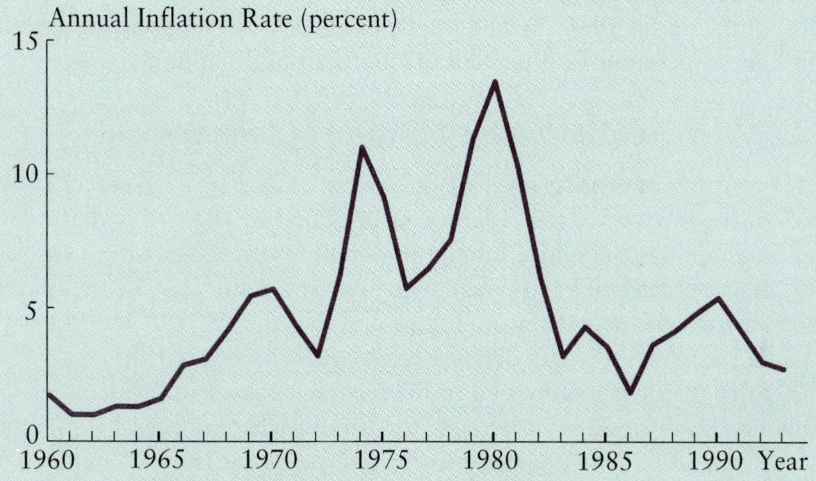

The inflation rate, measured by annual changes in the Consumer Price Index, has varied markedly in the years since 1960. Over the entire period, the price level increased by 388 percent, an average of about 5 percent per year. However, the average rate was 2.35 percent during the 1960s, about 7 percent during the 1970s, and 5.5 percent during the 1980s. The lowest inflation rate, 1 percent, occurred in 1962; the highest rate, 13.5 percent, in 1980.

Source: *Economic Report of the President,* 1994

consumer goods and services actually fell. For example, energy prices fell by 12.8 percent between 1985 and 1987.

Using the CPI

The CPI is often used to adjust nominal sums of money for the price changes that occur between two periods of time. Take, for example, the \$297 billion and \$345 billion of compensation paid to employees in 1960 and 1963, respectively. The nominal amount paid to employees rose by 16.2 percent during this period, but how much did the real purchasing power of employee compensation increase?

One way to answer this question is to convert the 1960 nominal amount of \$297 into 1963 dollars and then compare the converted amount with \$345 billion. We do this by first dividing the \$297 billion by the price level, the CPI, for 1960. This neutralizes the price units of 1960. Then, we multiply by the CPI for 1963 to express this price-free magnitude in terms of 1963 dollars. Since the CPI for 1960 was 29.6 and the CPI for 1963 was 30.6, the value of 1960 compensation expressed in 1963 dollars is \$307 billion (\$297 divided by 29.6, then multiplied by 30.6). That amount can now be compared with \$345 billion, since both are expressed in 1963 dollars. The 12.4 percent difference reflects only the increase in real compensation.

An alternative to converting the 1960 nominal sum into 1963 dollars is to convert the 1963 sum into 1960 dollars. In this case we multiply $345 billion by the ratio of the CPI in 1960 divided by the CPI in 1963. The resulting amount of $334 billion is the same 12.4 percent greater than $297 billion.

An Alternative Measure of Inflation

GDP deflator
A current-weights index used to correct GDP for price changes

The CPI measures the price level of goods purchased by consumers. Another measure of the price level and inflation is provided by the **GDP deflator**, which uses as its quantities the entire bundle of commodities comprising GDP. Unlike the CPI, the GDP deflator's base year is the *current* year. That is, the quantities used to construct the GDP deflator are those of the current year. The year of normalization, for which the GDP deflator is set equal to 100, is 1987.

The GDP deflator is closely tied to the measure of real GDP discussed above. Multiplying the normalized GDP deflator for the current year by the current year's measure of real GDP yields the current year's measure of nominal GDP, multiplied by 100.[14] Drawing an analogy to a household's expenditure decision, we may think of nominal GDP as the total amount spent, real GDP as the quantity purchased, and the GDP deflator as the price of real GDP. For example, in 1993, nominal GDP was $6.374 trillion, which equals the product of that year's GDP deflator, 123.6, and its real GDP, $5.133 trillion, divided by 100. Since the GDP deflator had a value of 100.0 in 1987, we see that prices rose by 23.6 percent between 1987 and 1993—an average annual rate of inflation of 3.6 percent.

Choosing the Base Year for Price Indices

We have now considered two price indices, the consumer price index and the GDP deflator. These indices differ in three respects. One difference of little importance is the year of normalization (when the index equals 100)—1982–1984 for the CPI, 1987 for the GDP deflator. A second difference is the bundle of commodities: the CPI is based on consumer purchases and the GDP deflator is based on all components of GDP. The remaining difference concerns which year's quantities are used in constructing the index—the choice of base year. Using the quantities purchased in some past year produces what is called a *Laspeyres index*. This tells us how much the cost of goods purchased in the base year has risen. The CPI is a Laspeyres index; it uses the quantities from 1982 and tells us how much those quantities would cost today.

Using current year quantities to estimate the price level produces a *Paasche index*, which tells us how much the goods produced this year would have cost in the past. The GDP deflator, derived by dividing any year's nominal GDP by

14. You can verify this by constructing the formula for the GDP deflator. Using the formula for the CPI given above, replace the base year of 1982 with the current year, and the 1982–1984 years of normalization with 1987. Then multiply the resulting expression for the GDP deflator by the expression for real GDP, given in the previous section, for the current year.

the same year's real GDP, is an example of a Paasche index—it is based on the current year's quantities, and tells us how much more those quantities cost than they would have in 1987.

Unless the same bundle of goods was produced in past years as in the current year, a Laspeyres index and a Paasche index will provide different measures of the historic course of price increases. Neither index tells us precisely how price increases affect economic welfare. The Laspeyres index tends to overstate the impact of price increases, the Paasche index to understate them.[15] But together, they provide bounds to the right answer.

Accounting for Quality Change and New Commodities

Because of technological change, the price changes of many commodities are difficult to measure. A perfect example is computers. We encounter two related problems in trying to incorporate computer price changes in a price index. First, some models have only recently been invented or introduced. What price should be used for these goods in the base year? For example, if a certain type of computer was invented in 1985, what was its price in 1982? One answer might be "infinity," since it was not available at any price. However, this overstates the price in that year if some substitute goods, however inferior, were available.

The second problem involves changes in quality. The best personal computers commonly available in 1982 took much longer to perform calculations than their counterparts in 1989. In a sense, the 1989 models were new goods: the versions available in 1982 were inferior substitutes.

Part of the solution to these problems is to change the base year frequently, to reduce the number of cases of new products and significant changes in technology that must be dealt with. However, base-year changes only reduce the problem, because quality changes and product innovation occur continuously. We can deal with the problem only by attempting to measure quality changes directly, by converting the 1982 and 1989 computers into comparable units. This is done by measuring not the quantity of computers produced, but the quantity of computing power. Although the 1982 computer may have borne a superficial resemblance to the 1989 computer, we might say it contained only about one-tenth the computing power of its 1989 counterpart. Using computing power as a measure of output overcomes the problem of quality change and, because it permits us to compare different generations of computers, it overcomes the problem of new commodities as well.

The effect of accounting for quality change has been to magnify the price decreases that have been observed for computers in recent years: the price of computers has fallen, but the price of computing power has fallen even more. In fact, the price of personal computers (adjusted for quality change) in 1989 was just 32 percent of the price in 1982, which amounts to an average annual rate of price *deflation* of 15 percent.

15. The Laspeyres index ignores the fact that households substitute away from commodities that become relatively expensive. The Paasche index, on the other hand, fails to account for the fact that the substitution was necessary.

ADDING NOMINAL QUANTITIES TO OUR MODEL

The model developed in Chapters 1 through 4 is expressed in real terms—in units of corn. However, it is easy to express the same model in nominal terms (in units of money, such as dollars) by accounting for differences in the price level—the price of corn in terms of units of money—over time. We simply multiply each period's real quantities by the price level that prevails in that period.

Recall that the young household in period t earns a wage w_t, consumes c_{yt}, and saves a_{t+1}. We write this relationship in nominal terms by multiplying both sides by the year t price level, p_t:

$$p_t a_{t+1} = p_t w_t - p_t c_{yt}$$

(We refer to $p_t w_t$ as the *nominal* wage rate.) The expression relating the same person's consumption and assets one period later (when the person is old) is recast in nominal terms by multiplying it by the current price level, in this case p_{t+1}:

$$p_{t+1} c_{ot+1} = p_{t+1} a_{t+1}(1 + r_{t+1})$$

Real interest rate
The nominal interest rate adjusted for inflation; approximately the nominal interest rate minus the expected rate of inflation

where c_{ot+1} is consumption when old and r_{t+1} is the **real interest rate**, the percent increase in resources the household gets in exchange for its saving. Note that on the right-hand side of this expression the assets acquired in year t are now multiplied by p_{t+1}, rather than p_t. If we wish to express the nominal amount spent in period $t + 1$ in terms of the nominal amount saved in period t, $p_t a_{t+1}$, we rewrite the second-period budget constraint as follows:

$$p_{t+1} c_{ot+1} = p_t a_{t+1}(1 + i_{t+1})$$

Nominal interest rate
The interest rate paid on financial assets

where i_{t+1} stands for the **nominal interest rate** at time $t + 1$, the percent return in *dollars* the household earns on its assets. Comparing these two expressions, we can see that $1 + i_{t+1}$ equals $1 + r_{t+1}$ multiplied by the price ratio, p_{t+1}/p_t. From this relationship, we derive the following one relating the two interest rates and the inflation rate, $\pi_{t+1} = (p_{t+1} - p_t)/p_t$:

$$i_{t+1} = r_{t+1} + \pi_{t+1} + r_{t+1}\pi_{t+1}$$

As this expression shows, the nominal interest rate equals the real interest rate, r_{t+1}, plus the inflation rate, π_{t+1}, plus the product of the real interest rate and the inflation rate. Over relatively short periods of time (such as one year), the third term will be quite small compared to the other terms, and can be ignored. Thus, the nominal interest rate exceeds the real interest rate by approximately the rate of price inflation:

$$i_{t+1} = r_{t+1} + \pi_{t+1}$$

This is known as the **Fisher equation**, after Irving Fisher of Yale, one of the world's leading economists during the years leading up to World War II.

Fisher equation *The proposition that the nominal interest rate (i_t) approximately equals the sum of the real interst rate (r_t) plus the expected rate of price inflation (π_t)*

Economists call the difference between the two interest rates the *inflation premium*. To understand why the nominal interest rate incorporates an inflation premium, consider the return received in our model by a young person who saves by purchasing a financial instrument that pays off in a nominal amount of dollars, rather than directly in the form of commodities, such as corn. Specifically, let's assume that rather than use their dollar savings to purchase real assets (corn) and invest (plant) their capital directly, young people at the end of their youth lend their dollar savings to firms and receive in exchange a bond—a piece of paper—which promises to pay, in dollars, principal plus nominal interest on the loan at the end of the period. What do the firms do with the dollars they receive in exchange for their bonds? They turn around and use them to purchase corn, which they plant. At the end of the period the firms sell off the crop for dollars and use the dollar proceeds to pay nominal wages to their young workers and to pay principal plus interest on the bonds.

Since people have the option of using their savings to purchase and plant corn themselves, the real return they receive from lending their savings to firms can't be any lower than what they can earn investing on their own. In calculating their real return from buying a bond, young workers will take into account that when they are repaid in dollars at the end of their old age, the real value of their principal will have declined if prices have risen during the period. Thus, in order to protect the real principal of young people's financial investments, firms will have to promise to pay a premium to take account of the inflation over the period. This is why the nominal interest rate equals the real interest rate plus the rate of inflation. How do firms get the extra dollars to pay a nominal interest rate in excess of the real interest rate? They sell their output at the end of each period at the prevailing price of output. If the price of output has risen, firms will earn more dollars, some of which they will use to pay the inflation component of their interest obligations.

Measuring the Real Interest Rate

In most financial markets, transactions are in nominal terms; we observe the nominal interest rate and must compute the real interest rate by subtracting the inflation rate from the nominal interest rate. Figure 5-6 shows the nominal and real interest rates on U.S. government Treasury bills since 1970, with the inflation rate calculated based on the GDP deflator. The figure shows that nominal interest rates peaked in 1981 at around 14 percent. Real interest rates, on the other hand, were highest in 1984, at just over 5 percent, and were actually negative for much of the 1970s.

In earlier chapters, we discussed some of the supply and demand factors that cause real interest rates to fluctuate. However, some of the fluctuations in real interest rates shown in Figure 5-6 may be due simply to the fact that only nominal interest rates are established by financial markets. Because no one can know

Figure 5-6 Nominal and Real Interest Rates, 1970–1993

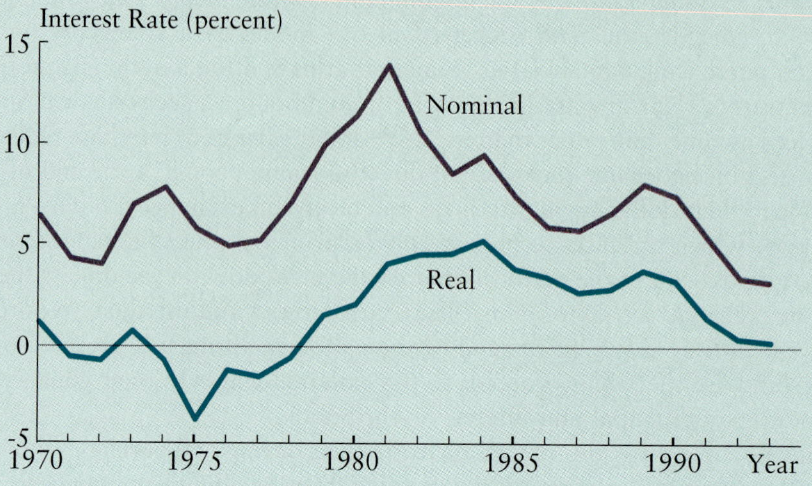

According to the Fisher equation, the nominal interest rate is approximately equal to the real interest rate plus the expected rate of inflation. In this figure, the real interest rate is estimated by subtracting the known rate of inflation from the known nominal interest rate. The graph shows that the estimated real interest rate was negative during the mid-1970s, then positive during the 1980s. Some of the fluctuations exhibited here may be due to errors in forecasting the rate of inflation.

Source: *Economic Report of the President,* 1994

exactly what the inflation rate will be over a given period, no one can know what the real interest rate will be. Presumably, the nominal interest rate is set in accordance with the expected inflation rate, to deliver an appropriate real interest rate, should that expected inflation rate actually prevail. However, if inflation turns out to be higher (or lower) than expected in one year, the corresponding real interest rate will be lower (or higher). For example, suppose the expected inflation rate is 5 percent and that the nominal interest rate is set at 8 percent to provide an expected real interest rate of 3 percent. If the inflation rate turns out to be 9 percent, the observed real interest rate will be –1 percent; if the inflation rate is 2 percent, the observed real interest rate will be 6 percent. Thus, some of the variation in observed real interest rates over time is due to unfulfilled expectations with respect to inflation rather than changes in *expected* real interest rates.

The distinction between expected and actual real interest rates may help explain why real interest rates were negative in the 1970s, when inflation was high, and why real interest rates rose in the early 1980s, as the inflation rate fell.

In later chapters, we will discuss alternative explanations for the rise in real interest rates during the early 1980s.

ADDITIONAL PROBLEMS OF MEASUREMENT

The factor income and output measures of GDP differ by a very small statistical discrepancy, because of problems of measurement. Beyond that statistical discrepancy there are a number of more fundamental problems that national income accountants must deal with in measuring GDP. These include some issues discussed above, such as distinguishing consumption from investment and accounting for changes in quality when estimating price changes.

In measuring GDP, we rely heavily on our ability to value production by observing prices paid in market transactions. Absence of markets presents several additional challenges that make accurate measurement and comparisons of GDP across countries more difficult.

Nonmarket Activities

In Chapter 1, we learned that the labor force participation rate of women has increased during the postwar period. What effect did this have on GDP? It increased measured GDP. However, the increase in measured GDP overstates the true increase in output, because it has been coupled with a decline in nonmarket activity, production that occurs outside of formal markets and is therefore omitted from GDP calculations.

As women left the home for formal employment, families needed to rely more on others to provide services, such as day care, that previously might have been provided by a mother. When a mother leaves the home to accept formal employment, our measure of GDP includes not only her labor income, but also the income earned by the day care provider she uses. In the past, however, if a mother provided "day care" directly for her own children, this failed to show up in GDP. Hence, the shift of day care from the nonmarket sector to the market sector increases the extent to which day care provision is included in GDP.

Another problem resulting from the lack of markets is the difficulty of valuing government expenditures. A considerable share of government spending goes to provide services to the public, through police and fire protection, education, garbage collection, and so on. If these services were provided by the private sector, we could measure GDP using the final sales method based on sales prices. However, governments typically do not sell these services, so we have no market measure of their value. Instead, we value the production at the cost of inputs, e.g., we measure the police payroll instead of the value of police services.[16]

16. Isn't this just the factor incomes approach, which should yield the same answer as the final sales approach? Not exactly. If a government service is more or less highly valued than the sum of associated factor payments, we ought to include an additional term to account for the "profit" the service generates for the economy (which is negative when factor payments fall short of the value of the service).

Unreported Income

Not all unmeasured income is nonmarket income. Some income is earned in markets but simply not reported, for tax reasons. If parents provide day care for their own child, this is not counted as income, either by national income accountants or the Internal Revenue Service, which is charged with collecting income taxes. If another person provides day care to the family, for cash, and does not report the income, this transaction will not be included in GDP, although in principle it is supposed to be. Some of this unreported income shows up in GDP because it can be measured indirectly, but not all does.

Distorted Markets

A related problem arises when markets are distorted. The formerly planned economies of Eastern Europe did not rely very heavily on market forces to determine prices. As a result, the prices of different goods and services often varied considerably from the values households placed on these commodities. In the process of transition, these economies have experienced significant shifts in prices and resource allocation. How should we account for the sharp reductions in the production of certain industries?

Consider the case of the Trabant, once the pride of East Germany. This automobile was forced on East German consumers for a price far in excess of its value on the world market. As soon as German unification occurred, and East Germans could purchase other cars, production of Trabants ceased—consumers placed such a low value on them that they were not worth producing. How much output was lost when the Trabant factories closed? Based on the prices for which Trabants had been sold, a lot. Based on the value of Trabants in the world market, far less.

Pollution and Other Environmental Damage

The quality of life is affected by more than the amount of commodities produced in markets or in the home. Air and water quality, for example, are important determinants of health and life expectancy. However, the maintenance of a good environment or, conversely, the destruction of the environment, do not enter into GDP calculations.

This omission has two effects. First, it makes GDP an inadequate measure of national well-being. Second, and perhaps more important, it makes the evaluation of the benefits of environmental programs more difficult. For example, in the 1970s, U.S. companies devoted a considerable share of their investment expenditures to pollution control, in order to meet standards imposed by the U.S. government for clean air and water. Based on national income accounting measures, these expenditures were entirely unproductive—the cleaner air and water they produced do not show up in GDP. But it is clearly a mistake to view pollution abatement expenditures as unproductive. They may very well have been of great social value, but we lack a precise measure of their contribution to national welfare. It is useful to keep this in mind when comparing U.S. GDP with those of other countries with more severe pollution problems.

Chapter Summary

1. National income accounting is the process by which we measure how much the economy produces, the form this production takes, who buys it, and how much it costs. There are three alternative approaches to the measurement of gross domestic product (GDP), which is the primary measure of national production: final sales, value added, and factor incomes. According to the national income identity, these three approaches must produce the same measure of GDP.

2. Other measures of aggregate production include net domestic product, which excludes depreciation; national income, which measures income directly earned by suppliers of labor and capital; and personal income, which distinguishes receipts of households from those of corporations. Although GDP is now the most widely used measure of output, a common alternative is gross national product (GNP), which adds to GDP the foreign earnings of domestic inputs, but excludes the domestic earnings of foreign inputs.

3. Among the components of GDP, it is important to distinguish consumption from investment, which we do for purchases of houses, but not for other purchases of durable goods by households or the government. These omissions understate the levels of national saving and investment.

4. The national income identity has several applications. For example, it may be used in the design of tax policy (to understand why a turnover tax is undesirable) and in understanding the relationship among national saving, domestic investment, and net foreign investment.

5. We seek to distinguish changes in the real quantity of goods and services produced, real GDP, from those changes in nominal GDP that are due to changes in the price level, through the construction of quantity and price indices. Real GDP, currently measured in 1987 dollars, is an example of a quantity index, which measures the actual increase in output over time. The GDP deflator is the corresponding price index that measures the change in the aggregate price level. An alternative price index is the consumer price index (CPI).

6. In the presence of inflation, we must subtract the inflation rate from the nominal interest rate to obtain a measure of the real interest rate. One reason why real interest rates fluctuate over time is that inflation rates turn out to be higher or lower than expected.

7. Output measurement presents several problems, including how to account for technological innovation and new commodities and how to value production that occurs in distorted markets or markets for which sales are not measured or reported. These omissions are especially important for economies in transition, whether it be away from distorted markets, toward a cleaner environment, or toward a higher labor force participation rate.

Key Concepts

National income identity
Value added
National income
Personal income
Imputed rent
Trade deficit
Capital account balance
Current account balance
Trade balance
Crowding out
Price level
Rate of inflation
Consumer Price Index
GDP deflator
Real interest rate
Nominal interest rate
Fisher equation

Review Questions

1. How does the *circular flow of income* diagram help to explain the *national income identity*? Explain how the *final sales method* and the *factor incomes method* of computing GDP relate to your answer.
2. What is the difference between *final* and *intermediate* goods? Why aren't all sales by businesses included in GDP? What is the *value added method* for computing GDP?
3. What is the difference between *GDP* and *GNP*? Which one more closely reflects domestic business cycle behavior (i.e., within U.S. borders)? How large is the numerical difference between the two measures?
4. Explain how *gross domestic product*, *net domestic product*, *national income*, *personal income*, and *disposable income* are related. How is each useful in observing or analyzing economic activity?
5. How are corporate profits, retained earnings, and dividends related? It has been stated that households "pierce the corporate veil." What is meant by this and how might it affect economic activity?
6. What are the (expenditure) components of GDP? Why are imports subtracted from expenditures in summing to GDP? How are expenditures by individuals further broken down? What are some of the current inconsistencies in categorizing actual expenditures?
7. What is meant by *imputed rent*? How is it treated in the national income accounts? Notationally, how is it captured in the life-cycle model?
8. What are the *current account balance* and the *capital account balance*? Why must they always sum to zero?
9. Explain what is meant by a *quantity index* and why *real GDP* is an example of one. How does real GDP differ from *nominal GDP*?
10. Explain what is meant by a *price index*. What is the difference between a *Laspeyres index* and a *Paasche index*, and how might they tend to underestimate or overestimate the impact of price increases on economic welfare?
11. What is the *GDP deflator* and in what ways does it differ from the *Consumer Price Index*?
12. Explain the *Fisher equation* and each of its components. Which of the components are generally observed and which are computed?
13. What measurement problems arise in quantifying the value of production? Briefly explain each.

Numerical Questions

1. The table below gives information from the national income accounts for a small country.

Values expressed in current 1993 dollars

Personal consumption expenditures	$1,000	Corporate profits	$200
Gross private domestic investment	250	Dividends	50
Net private domestic investment	220	Transfer payments	300
Government purchases of goods and services	500	Contributions for social insurance	200
Net exports	−30	Disposable income	1,585
Imports	50	Proprietors' income	150
Net factor income earned abroad	5	Rental income	10
National income	1,685	Interest income	140
Interest not in GDP	150		

All information needed to answer the following questions is given in the table. All values not shown there either can be computed from other values in the table (e.g., depreciation and retained earnings) or are assumed to be zero (e.g., business transfers, net surplus of government enterprises, and the statistical discrepancy). Compute values for the following items:

a. GDP
b. NDP
c. Exports
d. GNP
e. Indirect business taxes
f. Retained earnings
g. Personal income
h. Personal tax and nontax payments
i. Wages and salaries

2. Answer each of the following questions based on the incomplete information supplied in the table below.

a. Compute nominal GDP in period 1.

Period	Implicit Price Deflator for GDP (period 1 = 100)	Nominal GDP (current $)	Real GDP (period 1 $)
1	100	?	300
2	?	900	600
3	300	1,500	?
4	200	1,200	?

b. Compute the price deflator in period 2.
c. Compute real GDP in periods 3 and 4.
d. Was there a recession in any of the periods? Explain.
e. Was there deflation in any of the periods? Explain.

3. The following table includes price and quantity information on the only two goods produced in an economy. Answer each of the following questions based on that information.

	Food		Clothing	
Year	Price	Quantity	Price	Quantity
1992	$30	10	$20	5
1993	$45	20	$25	7

a. What are the individual inflation rates for both food and clothing?
b. Using 1992 as the base year (for weights and normalization), compute the value of the Consumer Price Index for both years.
c. What was the average rate of inflation between 1992 and 1993? Is it the arithmetic average of the two rates in part a above? Why or why not?
d. Assume that over the same periods your income jumped by 60 percent, from $10,000 to $16,000. Express those values in 1992 dollars and compute the percentage change in your *real* income.

4. Answer each of the following questions using the table given in question 3, again assuming that food and clothing are the only two goods in the economy.
a. Calculate nominal GDP in each year.
b. Using 1992 as the base year, calculate real GDP in each year. What was the percent change in real output?
c. Compute the GDP deflator for each period and its percentage change between 1992 and 1993. Is this the same as the change in the Consumer Price Index computed in part b of question 3? Why or why not?

5. Answer each of the following questions regarding the relation of interest rates and inflation.
a. Suppose that in 1992 you loaned out $100 at 5 percent interest, to be paid back one year later. Over the year, inflation was 8 percent. Compute the real value, expressed in 1992 dollars, of the money paid back in 1993, as well as the percent change in the real value. (Helpful hint: Use a deflator based in 1992, *not* the Fisher equation.)
b. Using the values in part a above and the Fisher equation, compute the real rate of return on the money loaned out. Does it (approximately) equal the percent change in the money's real value, calculated above?
c. If you require a real rate of return of 4 percent and the inflation rate is expected to be 3 percent, what interest rate would you charge? Compute the real rate of return if the inflation turns out to be 1 percent, 7 percent, and 10 percent.

Analytical Questions

1. Which of the following events would be included in this year's gross domestic product?

a. You buy a ticket to a Boston Red Sox baseball game.
b. You buy a 1960 Mickey Mantle baseball card.
c. You buy a Treasury bill.
d. You buy a General Motors corporate bond.
e. You buy a new General Motors car that was made in Mexico.
f. A Mexican citizen buys a new General Motors car made in Detroit.
g. You buy a 1987 Chevrolet.
h. You prune the trees in your front yard.
i. You hire a tree service to prune the trees in your front yard.
j. You win a $50 bet with your friend on a football game.
k. You borrow $100 from your parents.

2. Suppose that you are comparing the standard of living in two countries. One is a developed country with per capita income equal to $17,000 per year; the other is a developing country with per capita income equal to $1,000 per year. Can you conclude that the standard of living in the developed country is 17 times that of the developing country?

3. There has been tremendous concern in the United States about the rapid increase in the price of health care. Indeed, rising medical costs are a major factor in recent calls for an overhaul of the health care system. Despite the great concerns that have been voiced, is there reason to believe that the measured price increases have overstated the true rise in the cost of medical services?

C H A P T E R 6

Saving and Growth in the International Economy

INTRODUCTION

Exports
Goods and services sold to foreign buyers

Imports
Goods and services purchased from foreign sellers

Issues of international trade and finance have preoccupied U.S. policy makers in recent years. One reason is the increased "openness" of the U.S. economy, measured by its increasing participation in foreign trade and investment. Figure 6-1 shows that both **exports** (U.S. goods and services sold to foreign countries) and **imports** (foreign goods and services sold to the U.S.) have grown sharply in recent years. This growth in U.S. trade reflects a number of factors, including reduced trade barriers and improved transportation methods.

Past decades have witnessed not only an increase in U.S. exports and imports but also a change in their relative magnitudes. Exports accounted for less than 5 percent of GDP in 1960 and rose to over 10 percent of GDP by 1993. But over most of this period, imports grew even faster than exports. As a result, by the mid-1980s imports exceeded exports by more than 3 percent of GDP. It is this *imbalance* in U.S. trade that has attracted the attention of macroeconomists as well as the general public.

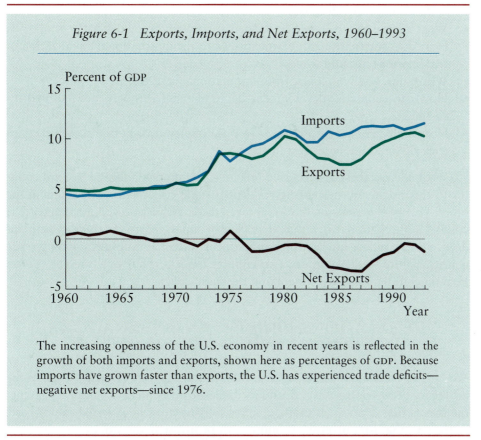

Figure 6-1 Exports, Imports, and Net Exports, 1960–1993

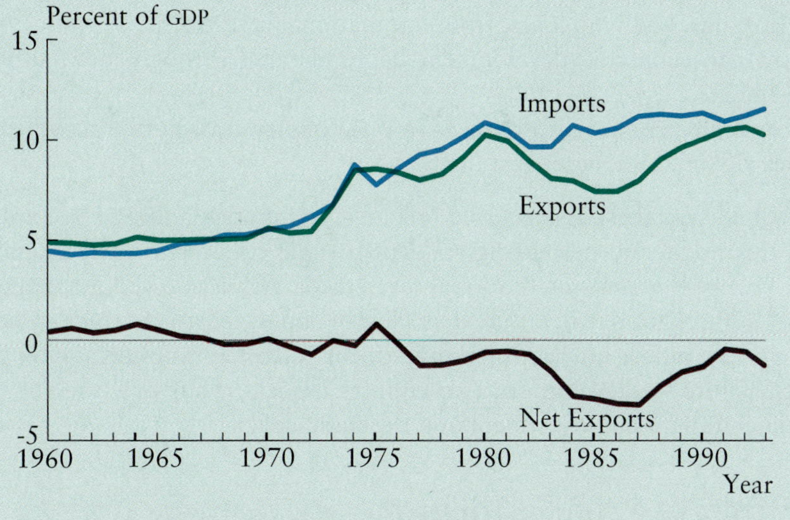

The increasing openness of the U.S. economy in recent years is reflected in the growth of both imports and exports, shown here as percentages of GDP. Because imports have grown faster than exports, the U.S. has experienced trade deficits—negative net exports—since 1976.

Source: *Economic Report of the President*, 1994

Much popular discussion pictures the *trade deficit* (the excess of imports over exports) as bad for an economy and its workers. But, as we'll see, this characterization misses the mark. Trade deficits may arise as the *result* of other economic problems, such as a low national saving rate, and they can actually serve to lessen the impact of such fundamental economic problems. We will see this quite clearly when we consider the economic effects of trade restrictions.

Moreover, trade deficits need not result from economic weakness at all—they may also result from economic strength. Although the trade deficits of the 1980s occurred during a period of economic difficulties, the U.S. was also a net importer during the late nineteenth century, while it was becoming a world economic power. And, as Figure 6-1 shows, our only trade surpluses since the mid-1960s occurred in 1970, 1973, and 1975, two of which were *recession* years. Clearly, a trade deficit can occur in good times or bad, and a trade surplus needn't be a sign of a robust economy.

Why do trade deficits sometimes signal strength and at other times weakness? Can running a trade deficit actually help the economy? Our goal in this chapter is to sort out these and other issues of international trade and investment. Among the questions to be answered are:

- What causes trade deficits?
- What are the effects of policies aimed at reducing trade deficits?
- How does international investment lead to the international equalization of real interest rates and wages?
- Who gains, and who loses, from international investment?
- How can economic development be accelerated through international investment?
- How are economic disturbances in one country transmitted to other countries via international investment?

We'll address these issues using our life-cycle model, adding a second country to the model and permitting residents of one country to own assets in the other; i.e., we'll permit international investment. As we showed in Chapter 5, a country's international investment is closely connected to its trade deficit. Indeed, understanding international investment is the key to understanding trade deficits. Before we develop our two-country model, let's review the connection between international investment and the trade deficit.

THE RELATIONSHIP BETWEEN INTERNATIONAL INVESTMENT AND THE TRADE DEFICIT

Domestic investment
The increase in the domestic capital stock; it equals national saving minus net foreign investment

We start by recalling that the net amount a country invests abroad, I^f, equals the difference between its saving, S, and its **domestic investment**, I. Simply speaking, the reason that $I^f = S - I$ is that a country's saving must be invested somewhere, so the part that isn't invested at home must be invested abroad.

For a country to invest internationally, it must add to the amount of capital it owns abroad. This can happen in one of several ways. The first is for the country to increase its net exports, $X - M$ (or reduce its trade deficit, which is measured as $M - X$). Specifically, the country can either export capital goods abroad directly, or it can export consumption goods abroad and use the proceeds from these exports to purchase capital goods in the foreign country. Another way is for the country to use the income, E, that it earns on its foreign capital to purchase additional foreign capital.[1]

Net foreign investment
The difference between national saving and domestic investment

The point that a country's **net foreign investment** equals its net exports plus its net foreign income ($I^f = X - M + E$) is particularly easy to understand when the international economy features only one commodity. As in previous chapters, imagine that this commodity is corn, which can be both a capital good (it can be planted) and a consumption good (it can be eaten). For a country to engage in net foreign investment in a given period, it must add to the quantity of corn it owns abroad. This means it must either export more corn during the period than it imports or simply leave some of the corn it receives during the

1. A third way, which we'll ignore for the rest of this chapter, is for the foreign country simply to donate some of its capital to the domestic country. Such a donation of capital would reduce net transfers abroad (denoted as J in Chapter 5).

period in the foreign country in the form of capital income earned on its net foreign assets.

To summarize, we've reiterated that

$$S - I = I^f = X - M + E$$

As these identities make clear, for a given level of net foreign income, E, reducing the trade deficit (making $X - M$ less negative) requires increasing net foreign investment, I^f. But since I^f equals national saving less domestic investment ($S - I$), reducing the trade deficit can only be accomplished by increasing the difference between national saving and domestic investment. Thus, if a country saves more but chooses not to invest the additional saving at home, its trade deficit will fall. Alternatively, its trade deficit will fall if its saving remains the same but it decides to invest less at home. The size of the trade deficit depends on both saving and domestic investment decisions, which, as we'll see, are influenced by quite different factors.[2]

As in previous chapters, we study a country's saving by considering changes over time in its citizens' ownership of assets. We study its domestic investment by considering changes over time in the domestic capital stock. The difference between a country's ownership of assets and its domestic capital stock equals its net foreign assets. Changes over time in a country's net foreign assets is what we mean by the term net foreign investment. Hence, our strategy for understanding a country's net foreign investment is to examine its net foreign asset position and how that position changes over time.

A Two-Country Model

We now want to expand our model to consider cross-border ownership of assets. That will tell us about international investment flows and, ultimately, the trade deficit. But first, let's briefly review our single-country model. Recall that, when young, each individual consumes α of his wages and saves the rest, using principal plus interest on these savings to finance old-age consumption. The wage and interest rates the individual receives during his lifetime depend on the prevailing relative supplies of labor and capital. The higher the capital-labor ratio in a given period, the higher the wage rate and the lower the interest rate.

Because next period's capital-labor ratio is determined by the amount of his wages that each young person saves this period, and because this period's wages depend on this period's capital-labor ratio, we can derive a transition equation relating the capital-labor ratio next period to the capital-labor ratio this period:

$$k_{t+1} = (1 - \alpha)(1 - \beta)Ak_t^{\beta}$$

2. By adding domestic investment to both sides of the expression, we can also express the identity relating saving, investment, and trade deficit as $S = I + (X - M) + E$. As we saw at the end of Chapter 5, the decline in U.S. national saving that occurred in the 1980s initially affected primarily the trade balance, $X - M$. However, by the early 1990s, the trade deficit had declined as a fraction of GDP ($X - M$ had risen), and so had domestic investment.

Figure 6-2 Equilibrium in Autarky

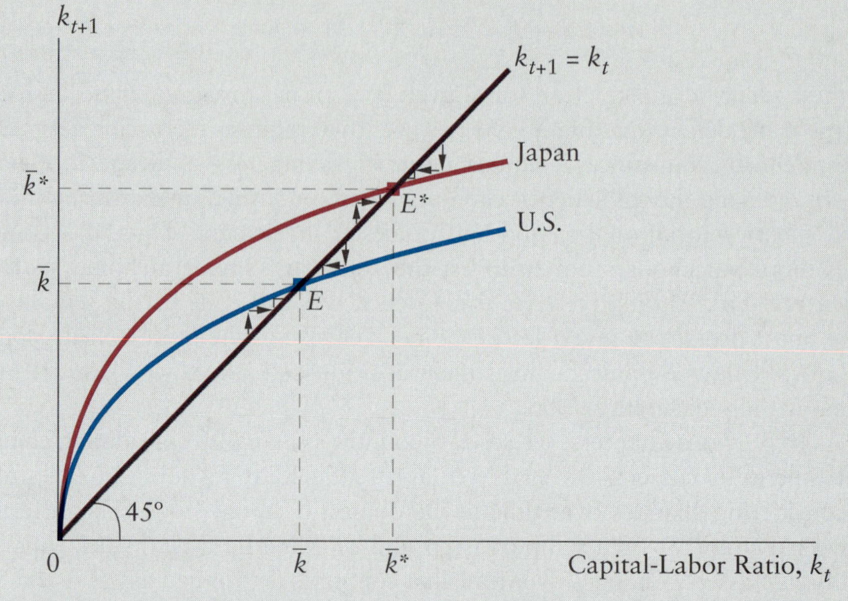

In the absence of international trade, each nation's steady-state capital-labor ratio is determined by the intersection of its transition curve with the 45° line. In this figure, the U.S. capital-labor ratio, $\bar{k}$, is determined at point E. Because Japan has a higher propensity to save—a lower value of α—its transition curve is higher. The Japanese steady-state capital-labor ratio is $\bar{k}^*$, at point E^*.

where A is the economy's level of technology,[3] β is the share of capital in national output, and k_t is the economy's capital-labor ratio at time t. This equation is represented by the lower curve in Figure 6-2, labeled "U.S." As we learned in Chapter 3, the capital-labor ratio eventually reaches a steady state when $k_{t+1} = k_t$, as depicted at point E in the figure.

Now that we have reviewed our model of one country, say the U.S., how can we add a second country, say Japan, to the model? Let's first consider this second economy by itself, as a closed economy. If Japan also has a Cobb-Douglas production function and a Cobb-Douglas utility function, the same kinds of equations and analysis apply. We can solve for Japan's transition equation and its steady-state capital-labor ratio, wage rate, and interest rate, just as we have for the U.S. If Japan's economy has the same technology (A and β) and taste (α)

3. As we discussed in earlier chapters, A increases over time when there is technological progress. In most of this chapter, we'll assume A is constant. We'll also assume that the population is constant.

parameters, it will have the same transition equation, the same steady-state capital-labor ratio, $\bar{k}$, and hence the same long-run wage and interest rates.

Yet we know from observation that the economies of the two countries *do* differ in several respects. One important difference is that the Japanese appear to have a higher propensity to save than Americans do. In our model, this means the Japanese have a lower value of α than do the Americans. Let's assume, for the sake of argument, that this is the only difference between the two economies, and take α to be the American propensity to consume and α^*, which is less than α, to be the Japanese propensity to consume.[4] Since their consumption propensities differ, the U.S. and Japanese transition equations will differ. Figure 6-2 makes this clear. It shows that the Japanese transition curve lies above the U.S. curve. It also indicates that, in the long run, Japan ends up at point E^* with a larger steady-state capital-labor ratio than the U.S. ($\bar{k}^*$ is larger than $\bar{k}$). As a result, the Japanese steady-state wage rate is higher than that of the U.S. and the steady-state interest rate is lower.

Factor Price Equalization

The analysis up to this point focused on each country in isolation, with no international trade or investment. Economists call this a state of **autarky**. Can the steady-state differences observed in autarky persist if the economies are open to international trade and investment? In short, the answer is no.

Autarky
A state of economic self-sufficiency; a situation in which a nation is isolated from trade with other nations

If the interest rate is higher in the U.S., wouldn't Japanese savers wish to invest in the U.S.? They would, and they do. We know from Chapter 5 that net U.S. foreign investment has been negative in recent years. In 1993, for example, it was –$98.6 billion, meaning that $98.6 billion more capital flowed into the U.S. than flowed out of the U.S. to foreign countries. A considerable share of this net inbound investment came from Japan.

In our model the flow of investment from Japan to the United States affects the capital-labor ratio in each country, lowering it in Japan and raising it in the U.S. This, in turn, reduces the interest rate in the U.S. and raises it in Japan, with the process continuing until interest rates are equalized. At this point, Japanese investors (the Japanese elderly in our model) will be just as happy to invest in Japan as in the U.S.

In our open-economy model, wage rates as well as interest rates will be equalized. The reason is simple. Since the interest rate in each country depends on its capital-labor ratio, and since the two countries' interest rates are equalized, their capital-labor ratios are equalized as well. But since each country's wage also depends on its capital-labor ratio, it follows that each country will have the same wage.[5] Therefore, cross-border investment serves to equate not only returns to capital—the interest rates in the two countries—but also returns

4. Throughout the analysis that follows, we'll use a * superscript to denote variables of the foreign country.

5. This unique relationship between the interest rate and the capital-labor ratio *does* depend on our assumption that the two countries have the same production function. As we saw in Chapter 3, an increase in A, the technology parameter, would increase the interest rate corresponding to a particular capital-labor ratio.

Figure 6-3 Factor Price Equalization

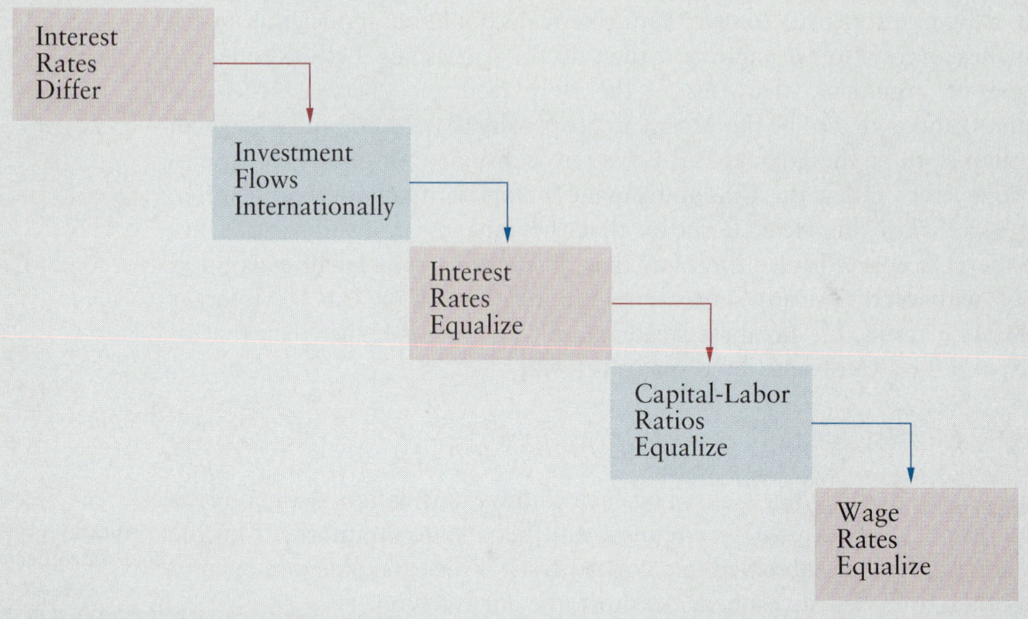

With the opening of international trade, forces are set in motion that tend to equalize wage and interest rates. Differences in interest rates trigger cross-border investment flows as capital suppliers seek the highest possible rates of return. These flows tend to eliminate interest rate disparities by increasing the supply of capital to high interest rate nations while decreasing it in the low interest rate, capital-exporting nations. Equal interest rates imply equal capital-labor ratios, and thus equal wage rates (for labor of equivalent skills and experience). Thus, cross-border investment drives wage and interest rates into equality world-wide.

Factor price equalization
A tendency for interest rates and wage rates to equalize between two nations

to *labor*—the wage rate in each country. Economists refer to this outcome (depicted in Figure 6-3) as **factor price equalization.**[6]

Evidence on Factor Price Equalization

Does investment flow freely enough among countries to produce factor price equalization? Figure 6-4 shows the real interest rates on government-issued bonds for the five major Western economies (the U.S., Japan, Germany,[7] France, and the United Kingdom)—known as the *G-5 countries*—over the period since 1978, with the U.S. rate highlighted.

6. In more complex models of international trade, factor-price equalization can occur even without capital flows, through changes in the mix of commodities that different countries produce. See, for example, Wilfred J. Ethier, *Modern International Economics*, 2nd ed. (New York: Norton, 1988).
7. Before 1991, the German data are those for the former West Germany.

Figure 6-4 Real Interest Rates for the G-5 Nations, 1978–1992

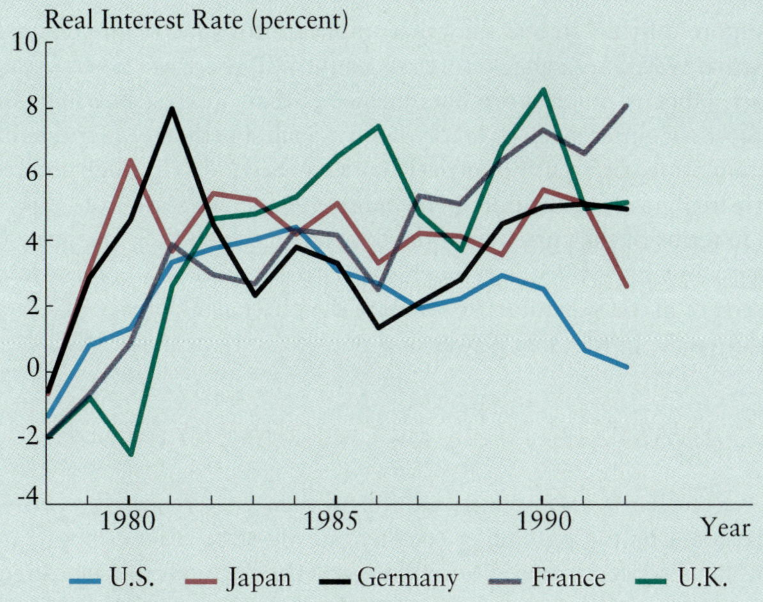

Some evidence suggests that real interest rates do move together in different countries. In 1978, for example, the U.S., Japan, Germany, France, and the U.K. all experienced negative rates. In 1984, all rates clustered around 4 percent. However, in other years, such as 1980 and 1990, there were large disparities among the five nations. In part, these observed differences may reflect errors in forecasting inflation rates.

Source: OECD

There is some evidence that interest rates do move together. In 1978, for example, all five countries had negative real interest rates. In 1984, when the U.S. real interest rate peaked near 6 percent, all five countries had real interest rates of almost 4 percent or more. On the other hand, there are significant differences among the countries in other years. These differences do not necessarily represent a contradiction of factor price equalization. According to the Fisher equation we encountered in Chapter 5, the real interest rate equals the nominal interest rate minus the inflation rate:

$$r = i - \pi$$

When investors compare interest rates in different countries, they know only the nominal interest rate. If inflation turns out to be higher than expected in one country, the corresponding real interest rate will be lower. If inflation is lower than expected, the real interest rate will turn out to be higher. Thus, cross-country differences in *observed* real interest rates could be due to differences in errors in forecasting the inflation rate rather than differences in *expected* real interest rates.

It is more difficult to test the other implication of factor price equalization theory—that wages are equalized across countries. There are several reasons for this. First, labor is much more heterogeneous than interest-bearing assets. We must adjust for differences in labor quality, such as education and skill levels, when comparing different countries' workers. Second, although interest rates are "unit free" (they are simply percentages), wage rates are not—they are expressed in terms of the currency of the country in which they are earned. As we will discuss in Chapter 13, it is much easier to compare 4.5 percent in the U.S. to 5.2 percent in the U.K. than to compare the purchasing power of \$11 an hour in the U.S. to the purchasing power of 6 pounds an hour in the U.K.

ANALYZING THE TWO-COUNTRY MODEL

We have seen that if two countries differ in their preferences for consumption (as represented by the parameter α), their steady-state capital-labor ratios will differ in the absence of international investment. Through this investment, factor prices and capital-labor ratios are equalized. Let's analyze this process using our model, by bringing together the two countries represented in Figure 6-2.

Figure 6-5 repeats the capital accumulation paths followed in autarky by low-saving (high α) and high-saving (low α) countries, which we have labeled "U.S." and "Japan," respectively. As discussed, the lower the value of α, the higher the long-run capital-labor ratio for any particular country in autarky. In the figure, the steady-state capital-labor ratio for the U.S. has a value $\bar{k}$, at point E; for Japan, the corresponding value is $\bar{k}^*$, at point E^*.

If investment can occur between the countries, neither point represents a long-run steady state. Different capital-labor ratios imply different interest rates. That situation would trigger international investment, leading to the equalization of capital-labor ratios as well as factor prices in the two countries.

What is the common, world-wide capital-labor ratio at any point in time? Since it is the same in both countries, it must equal the sum of assets accumulated in the two countries, divided by the sum of their working populations. That is, in period $t + 1$,

$$k_{t+1} = \frac{Na_{t+1} + N^*a^*_{t+1}}{N + N^*}$$

where N^* is the population of each generation in Japan and a^*_{t+1} is asset accumulation per young person there.

For the U.S., the accumulation of assets by young people remains the same as before, namely,

Figure 6-5 Two-Country Equilibrium

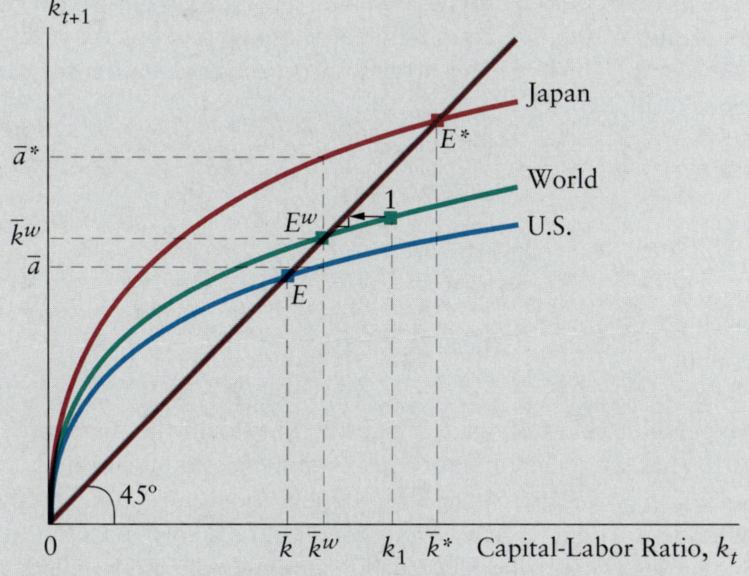

In autarky, the capital-labor ratios in Japan and the U.S. are determined where their respective transition curves intersect the 45° line—at E^* and E. Once trade begins, the evolution of the common, world-wide capital-labor ratio is governed by the world transition curve, which is a weighted average of the two countries' curves. The steady-state world ratio is shown at E^w.

Given transborder investment, the U.S. and Japanese curves measure assets owned by domestic residents, not the domestic capital stocks. Because the U.S. asset curve lies below the world transition curve, U.S. asset ownership falls short of the U.S. capital stock. Some of that stock is owned by the Japanese.

$$Na_{t+1} = N(1 - \alpha)w_t$$

For Japan, we have a corresponding equation describing saving by the young:

$$N^*a^*_{t+1} = N^*(1 - \alpha^*)w_t$$

where α^* is the fraction of first-period earnings not saved. We do not need a superscript for the wage rate, w_t; factor price equalization ensures that it is the same in both countries:

$$w_t = (1 - \beta)Ak_t^{\beta}$$

The Worldwide Transition Equation

We have seen that the world-wide capital-labor ratio in period t determines the world wage rate, which then separately determines the amount of assets the young in each country bring into period $t + 1$. The total of those assets, when divided by the sum of the two countries' populations, gives us the next period's capital-labor ratio. Thus, we end up with a transition equation for the world capital-labor ratio, namely,[8]

$$k_{t+1} = (1 - \bar{\alpha})(1 - \beta)Ak_t^{\beta}$$

where

$$\bar{\alpha} = \frac{N\alpha + N^*\alpha^*}{N + N^*}$$

This expression indicates that the transition equation for world-wide capital accumulation has the same form as the transition equation for a single economy. In place of a single country's value of α, though, it depends on a weighted average of the values α and α^*, with weights equal to the relative population sizes of the two countries. This is the relationship shown as the intermediate curve in Figure 6-5, labeled "World." At point E^w, the world capital stock reaches a long-run steady state, with a world-wide capital-labor ratio, $\bar{k}^w$ (for "world"), that is larger than the capital-labor ratio prevailing in autarky in the U.S., $\bar{k}$, but smaller than the capital-labor ratio prevailing in autarky in Japan, $\bar{k}^*$. As before, if the world capital-labor ratio begins at a value less (greater) than $\bar{k}^w$, capital will accumulate (decumulate) world-wide until it reaches $\bar{k}^w$.

Asset Accumulation along the Transition Path

Now that we have characterized the evolution of the world capital-labor ratio, we can go back and consider the evolution of assets in each country. Comparing the two tells us about the pattern of international capital ownership, changes in which determine international investment flows.

Combining the asset accumulation equation for the U.S. (how much of their wages the young wish to save) with the expression relating the U.S. (and world-wide) wage rate to the world-wide capital-labor ratio yields the expression for U.S. assets per old person (or per young person, since the number of young Americans equals the number of old Americans):

$$a_{t+1} = (1 - \alpha)(1 - \beta)Ak_t^{\beta}$$

8. This expression is obtained by dividing the sum of the expressions for net assets in each country, namely $Na_{t+1} = N(1 - \alpha)(1 - \beta)Ak_t^{\beta}$ for the U.S. (and the same for Japan but with N^* and α^* in place of N and α) by the sum of the two countries' populations, $N + N^*$, and factoring out the common terms in the numerator and denominator.

For Japan, the comparable expression is:

$$a^*_{t+1} = (1 - \alpha^*)(1 - \beta)Ak_t^\beta$$

These expressions correspond to the bottom and top curves in Figure 6-5—the curves that describe capital accumulation in each country in autarky, *without* international investment. With international investment, these curves simply describe assets owned by domestic residents, not the domestic capital stock. For any world-wide capital-labor ratio in period t, k_t, we move vertically to the appropriate curve to determine the level of assets per old person in period $t + 1$ in the U.S. (a_{t+1}) and Japan (a^*_{t+1}). Since the capital-labor ratio in period $t + 1$, k_{t+1}, is determined by the middle curve in the diagram, U.S. assets per old person always fall short of the U.S. capital-labor ratio ($a_{t+1} < k_{t+1}$), whereas Japanese assets per old person always exceed the Japanese capital-labor ratio ($a^*_{t+1} > k_{t+1}$).

The level of assets Americans own abroad—the U.S. **net foreign asset position**, sometimes also referred to as the international investment position of the U.S.—equals the difference between U.S. assets and U.S. domestic capital. Denoting it by K^f_t, we find this means that $K^f_t = Na_t - Nk_t$. In the case of Japan, its net foreign asset position is its assets less its domestic capital, so $K^{f*}_t = N^*a^*_t - N^*k_t$. In the long-run steady state, when U.S. assets per old person equal $\bar{a}$ and the world-wide capital-labor ratio equals $\bar{k}^w$, $\bar{K}^f = N\bar{a} - N\bar{k}^w$. Similarly, $\bar{K}^{f*} = N^*\bar{a}^* - N^*\bar{k}^w$.[9]

Net foreign asset position
The difference between a nation's world-wide ownership of assets and its domestic capital stock

Tracing the World Economy's Transition

Now that we've presented the two-country model, let's use it to trace the world economy's transition starting from autarky. Specifically, let's suppose that at time 0 the world economy is in its steady-state autarkic position denoted by points E and E^* in Figure 6-5. Now suppose that during period 0 the Japanese and U.S. governments permit free international investment. What will happen? The answer is that investment will immediately flow from Japan to the U.S. during period 0 so as to equalize the capital-labor ratios in the two countries at time 1.

This world-wide capital-labor ratio at time 1, k_1, is calculated by dividing total world assets at the beginning of time 1 by the total world labor force. In Figure 6-5, k_1 lies to the right of $\bar{k}$.[10] Starting with k_1 we now use the world capital-labor transition curve (labeled "World" in the figure) to trace the transition

9. What share of the U.S. capital stock does Japan own at each point in time, in this example? At time t, total U.S. assets equal Na_t and the total U.S. capital stock equals Nk_t. Since $a_t = (1 - \alpha)w_{t-1}$ and $k_t = (1 - \bar{\alpha})w_{t-1}$, the ratio of U.S. assets to the U.S. capital stock is $(1 - \alpha)/(1 - \bar{\alpha})$ at each point in time. For example, suppose that $\alpha = .5$ and $\alpha^* = .35$. Given that the U.S. population is roughly twice that of Japan, the value of $\bar{\alpha}$ (the average of α and α^*, weighted by relative populations) is .45 (2/3 times .5 plus 1/3 times .35). In this case—the one actually depicted in Figure 6-5—the ratio of U.S. assets to U.S. capital will equal .5/.55, or about .91—the U.S. has only enough wealth to purchase 91 percent of its domestic capital stock; the rest must be owned by Japan.

10. Mathematically, it is possible to show that k_1 must be larger than $\bar{k}$.

path of the world's capital-labor ratio to its final steady-state value of $\bar{k}^w$ (the value of the world's capital-labor ratio at point E^w).

During the transition we can measure each period's capital-labor ratio on the horizontal axis. We can read up to the U.S. and Japanese asset curves to find the respective asset holdings of the two countries in that period. Doing so, we observe that in each period Japanese assets per young person exceed its capital per young person, whereas the opposite is true for the U.S. Hence, during the transition as well as in the final steady state, Japan has positive net foreign assets and the U.S. has negative net foreign assets.

Net Foreign Investment During the Transition

Recall that U.S. net foreign investment during any two periods equals the change in U.S. net foreign assets between the periods. Thus,

$$I_t^f = K_{t+1}^f - K_t^f$$

Let's first think about I_0^f, net foreign investment during period 0. Since the world economy is in autarky in period 0, we know that K_0^f equals zero. We also know that K_1^f is negative—U.S. assets at time 1 are less than the U.S. capital stock at time 1.[11] That means U.S. net foreign investment at time 0, when the transition begins, is negative; i.e., the U.S. imports capital from abroad. Next, consider I_t^f when t is large enough so the economy has reached its steady state. In the steady state, the U.S. net foreign asset position does not change from one period to the next, so K_{t+1}^f equals K_t^f, and net foreign investment is zero.

Thus, we've learned that during the transition from autarky, U.S. net foreign investment starts out negative and ultimately becomes zero. As may be confirmed with numerical calculations, U.S. net foreign investment is a smaller negative value during each period of the transition, ending up at zero in the long-run steady state.

The Trade Balance During the Transition

Now that we know about the qualitative pattern of U.S. net foreign investment during the transition, let's use this knowledge to understand how the trade balance evolves. Recall that net foreign investment equals the sum of the trade balance plus net foreign income, i.e.,

$$I_t^f = X_t - M_t + E_t$$

E_t simply equals the interest rate at time t multiplied by U.S. net foreign assets, K_t^f, so we can write

$$I_t^f = X_t - M_t + r_t K_t^f$$

11. In terms of Figure 6-5, K_1^f is given by $Na_1 - Nk_1$, where a_1 equals $\bar{k}$.

Let's use this expression to think about the trade deficit at time 0. First, we know that K_0^f equals zero and that I_0^f is negative. Hence, it follows that $X_0 - M_0$ is negative—the U.S. runs a trade deficit at time 0. Next, consider the U.S. trade deficit in the long-run steady state. We know that in the steady state, I_t^f equals zero. We also know that K_t^f is negative because the transition curve lies above the U.S. asset curve. Consequently, we can infer from the above formula that in the long run, $X_t - M_t$ is positive, i.e., in the long run the U.S. runs a trade surplus.

Thus, the U.S. trade balance starts off negative and ultimately becomes positive. What explains this pattern? The answer is that at the beginning of the transition, the U.S. runs a trade deficit in order to import additional capital from abroad. But in the long run, it runs a trade surplus as the Japanese **repatriate** back to Japan the capital income on their U.S. investments.

Repatriation of foreign income
The return to foreign owners of domestic capital of income earned on this capital

A Transition Arising from a Decline in the U.S. Propensity to Save

To continue building your intuition and understanding of international investment and the trade balance, examine Figure 6-6 and Table 6-1, which consider a transition from a different steady state in which the U.S. and Japan initially have the same propensity to save. In terms of Figure 6-6, both countries initially have the same asset accumulation curve—the one labeled "Japan." Then, even with the opportunity for world trade, there is no net trade or foreign investment—input prices are already equal.

In Figure 6-6, the initial capital-labor ratio is $\bar{k}^*$. That value (given in the first line of Table 6-1) for year 0 is 8.71. It is based on the same parameter values for production (A = 10 and β = .3) used in the first examples in Chapter 3, but a higher propensity to save, i.e., a lower value of α (.35 instead of .50). The higher propensity to save produces a higher steady-state capital-labor ratio (8.71 instead of 5.99). Note that in the table each country's saving and investment are initially zero, as are net foreign investment by the U.S. in Japan (i^f) and net Japanese assets owned by the U.S. (k^f)—the lowercase letters indicating that each is expressed relative to the number of people per generation. Thus, net exports from the U.S. (nx) also equal zero.

Suppose that, during period 1, the desire for consumption when young, as represented by α, rises permanently in the U.S. above the value that continues to prevail in Japan.[12] In Figure 6-6, the increase in α causes a downward shift in the asset accumulation curve, to the one labeled "U.S." As a result of the reduced U.S. asset demand, the world economy's transition is now governed by the middle curve, labeled "World," and has a capital-labor ratio less than k^* entering period 2—as determined by the height of the initial point labeled 1 on the middle curve.

12. A change in preferences is only one of many possible explanations for the decline in national saving that occurred in the U.S. during the 1980s. As we'll see when discussing fiscal policy in Chapter 7, government may affect national saving through its influence on household consumption and by the amount it chooses to spend on *government* consumption.

Figure 6-6 An Increase in U.S. Consumption

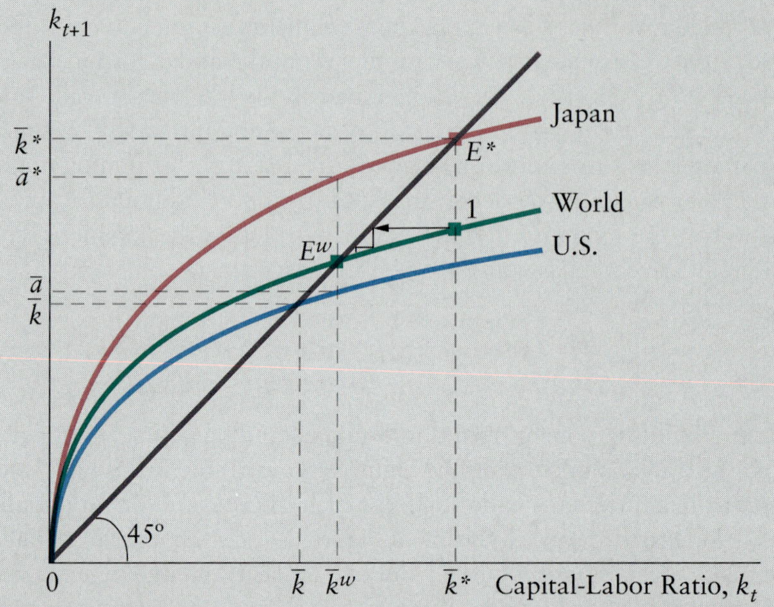

Initially, the U.S. and Japan have the same propensity to save and so share a common asset curve—the one marked "Japan." There is no net trade or foreign investment. If the desire for consumption when young then rises permanently in the U.S., the country's asset accumulation curve rotates downward to the one marked "U.S." From that point on, the world economy's transition is governed by the middle "World" curve. Ultimately, the world capital-labor ratio converges to $\bar{k}^w$ at E^w.

Ultimately, the world capital-labor ratio will converge to a value of 6.86 at E^w. Figure 6-6 shows that in the steady state the U.S. capital stock exceeds U.S.-owned assets (since $\bar{k}^w > \bar{a}$), so $\bar{k}^f$ is negative, as indicated in the last row of Table 6-1. As we have already noted, even though each country's domestic investment must be zero in the steady state (for k is not changing), the U.S. trade balance must be positive and precisely equal to the interest payments on the Japanese-owned capital in the U.S.[13]

As the table shows, however, the U.S. must first import the Japanese capital. This initial capital importation occurs in period 1, when U.S. preferences change. The increased preference for first-period consumption in the U.S.

13. This can be verified from Table 6.1 using the formula for r_t, $\beta A k_t^{\beta-1}$, the assumed values of β and A, .3 and 10, and the steady-state value of k, 6.86. The solution for r, .78, multiplied by the steady-state value of $\bar{k}^f$, −.62, equals minus the trade balance, −.49 (actually, −.484, due to rounding error).

Table 6-1 The Transition Arising from Increased U.S. Consumption

		U.S.			Japan						
Period	k	c_y	c_o	s	c_y^*	c_o^*	s^*	i	i^f	k^f	nx
0	8.71	4.69	14.45	0.00	4.69	14.45	0.00	0.00	0.00	0.00	0.00
1	8.71	6.70	14.45	−2.01	4.69	14.45	0.00	−1.34	−0.67	0.00	−0.67
2	7.37	6.37	11.67	−0.33	4.46	15.17	−0.43	−0.36	0.03	−0.67	0.53
3	7.01	6.28	11.26	−0.10	4.39	14.64	−0.12	−0.10	0.01	−0.64	0.50
4	6.91	6.25	11.15	−0.03	4.37	14.49	−0.04	−0.03	0.00	−0.63	0.49
5	6.87	6.24	11.11	−0.01	4.37	14.45	−0.01	−0.01	0.00	−0.62	0.49
6	6.86	6.24	11.10	0.00	4.37	14.43	0.00	0.00	0.00	−0.62	0.49
.	.	.	.	.	.	.	.	.	.	.	.
.	.	.	.	.	.	.	.	.	.	.	.
.	.	.	.	.	.	.	.	.	.	.	.
∞	6.86	6.24	11.10	0.00	4.37	14.43	0.00	0.00	0.00	−0.62	0.49

Assumptions regarding production: $\beta = .3$; $A = 10$. Assumptions regarding preferences in the U.S.: $\alpha = .5$, $N = 200$; in Japan: $\alpha^* = .35$, $N^* = 100$

increases actual first-period consumption. Rather than consuming 4.69 units each (.35 times their wages), young people in period 1 consume 6.70 units per person—half of their wages. Since the behavior of the elderly does not change (they consume all their income plus their assets), U.S. saving declines by the same amount: 6.70 – 4.69 = 2.01 units per each young person.

In a closed economy, U.S. investment would fully reflect this decline and produce a higher interest rate in the U.S. than in Japan. But in an open economy, factor price equalization brings enough Japanese investment into the U.S. to keep the U.S. interest rate from rising above the Japanese rate. Net U.S. foreign investment equals –.67 units per worker in period 1, reflecting the investment from Japan.[14]

As described in detail in the Appendix, we can solve the transition equation and predict behavior in each successive period in a systematic way. Given the initial capital-labor ratio, we can determine the wage rate. Consumption by each young person is this wage rate multiplied by the appropriate value of α. Consumption by the young in period 2 is smaller than in period 1 because of the lower wage rate following the decline in the world capital-labor ratio. Consumption by the elderly equals domestic assets multiplied by 1 plus the interest

14. The decline in Japanese investment per worker is twice the Japanese foreign investment per U.S. worker because the U.S. is assumed in the example to have twice the population of Japan.

rate. We calculate the interest rate, like the wage rate, using the world capital-labor ratio.

The level of assets equals the previous period's saving by the young. National saving in each country is the difference between its national income and the combined consumption by its young and old. World investment is the sum of the two countries' saving and is divided between the countries in a way that maintains equal capital-labor ratios. Each country's net foreign asset position equals its domestically owned assets minus its domestic capital stock. Finally, its trade balance equals its net foreign investment less its net foreign income.

Returning to the question of how the trade balance evolves over time, recall the model's prediction that a decline in the U.S. propensity to save leads it to run a trade deficit initially, but ultimately a trade surplus. Table 6-1 shows that the turnaround in the trade balance occurs in period 2. In period 2, the U.S. runs a trade surplus, reflecting the interest on the Japanese-owned U.S. capital stock that is flowing back to Japan.

Case Study: U.S. Trade Deficits and Saving in the 1980s

Is Table 6-1 consistent with the U.S. experience as its national saving declined in the 1980s? Could that decline have reflected a decreased propensity to save? Initially, as shown in Figure 5-4 (page 173), the decline in U.S. saving was almost fully reflected in the trade deficit; domestic investment fell little relative to GDP. Toward the late 1980s, though, the gap between U.S. saving and investment narrowed, as the trade balance improved. This is precisely the pattern the model predicts will result from a decreased propensity to save—initially, a significant part of the decline in saving is absorbed by a decline in net exports. Later, net exports recover.

Is such a reversal in the pattern of net exports necessary? Indeed it is, as some basic logic reveals. The relationship between the trade deficit and net foreign investment, $(X - M) = I^f - rK^f$, implies that a country with a negative net foreign asset position ($K^f < 0$) can avoid a trade surplus only if additional inbound foreign investment exceeds the earnings on existing foreign-owned domestic capital—I^f must exceed rK^f in absolute value. In other words, the growth rate of K^f, equal to I^f divided by K^f, must exceed the interest rate. Although this can happen for a time, such rapid growth would eventually put the entire domestic capital stock in the hands of foreigners. At some point—in our example, after just one period—the foreign appetite for additional domestic assets no longer keeps up with the growth of earnings on existing foreign-owned domestic assets.[15] When this happens, a trade surplus results.

15. In the real world, there are additional brakes on international investment that stem from the risks associated with such investment. For example, a significant share of inbound foreign investment in many nations takes the form of government borrowing. The fear that governments, having gone deeply into debt, might simply default may lead foreign investors to limit their exposure to such a risk. Default risk, and foreign lenders' response to it, played an important role in the "debt crisis" in Latin America in the 1980s.

UNDERSTANDING THE EFFECTS OF TRADE AND TRADE POLICY

Our model predicts that a decline in a nation's propensity to save leads it to import capital from abroad. Though the nation's trade balance ultimately turns around, the share of its capital that is foreign-owned ends up permanently higher. Like other predictions of the model, this also is consistent with recent U.S. experience. The increased foreign ownership of the U.S. capital stock has caused considerable alarm in some circles.

There are really two issues here. One concerns the level of assets owned by foreigners in the U.S. The second relates to the difference between this level and the level of assets owned abroad by U.S. investors—the U.S. net foreign asset position. It is the behavior of this second measure that our model analyzes.

As the world capital market has become more integrated over time, making it easier for individuals in one country to invest in another, there have been increases in cross-border ownership. Just as foreign holdings in the U.S. have risen, Americans have increased their holdings abroad, to nearly $2 trillion at the end of 1992. Foreign investment takes two forms. Some is *foreign direct investment*, whereby the investor makes an investment abroad by putting capital goods in place (building a factory, for example) or buying a company directly. The rest is *portfolio investment*, whereby the investor buys stocks or bonds issued by a foreign company or government.

There may be nationalistic reasons to be concerned about the increased foreign ownership of domestic assets. From a macroeconomic perspective, however, what is of greater concern is the trend in the U.S. net foreign asset position. The bigger this gap, the more U.S. national wealth falls short of the value of its national capital stock.

In recent years foreign-owned assets in the U.S. have grown more rapidly than U.S.-owned assets abroad. Figure 6-7 shows the trends in these two series since 1978. In fact, in 1987, the U.S. crossed the line from being a net *creditor* nation—owning more abroad than foreigners owned in the U.S.—to being a net *debtor* nation—owning less abroad than foreigners own here. By 1992, foreigners owned $2.5 trillion—about one-ninth—of U.S. assets, which exceeded U.S. holdings abroad by over $500 billion.

Americans would certainly be better off if they were wealthy enough to own all the capital in the U.S., but this is not a feasible alternative. It is possible to restrict foreign ownership, but not if the U.S. wishes to maintain its domestic capital stock at its present level. As we will see, eliminating foreign ownership would cause a decline in the U.S. standard of living. Enacting restrictions on capital inflows *would* be a way to increase the share of the U.S. capital stock owned by U.S. citizens and companies, but it wouldn't work the way its champions envision. Rather than U.S.-owned assets increasing as a share of a given U.S. capital stock, the capital stock itself would *decrease* to the point that it could all be owned by U.S. citizens, given their pattern of saving.

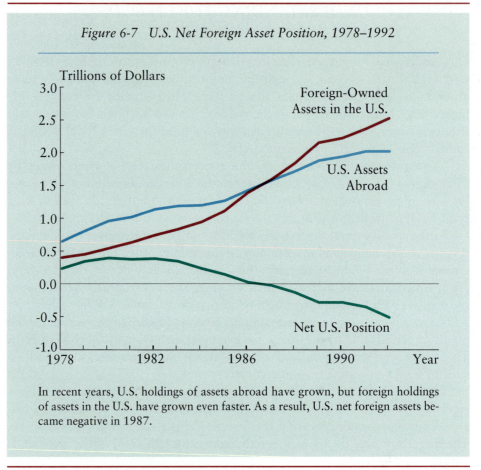

Figure 6-7 U.S. Net Foreign Asset Position, 1978–1992

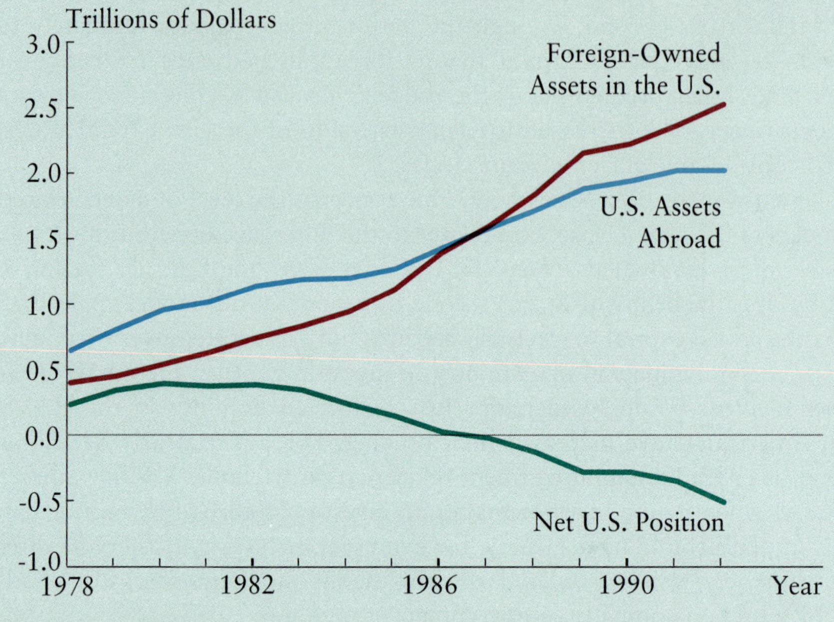

In recent years, U.S. holdings of assets abroad have grown, but foreign holdings of assets in the U.S. have grown even faster. As a result, U.S. net foreign assets became negative in 1987.

Source: *Survey of Current Business*, June 1993

The Costs of Restricting Foreign Investment

Suppose the conditions discussed in previous examples prevail, so the U.S. young have a higher propensity for first-period consumption than their Japanese counterparts. With the world economy open to trade, the long-run steady state will be at point E^w in Figure 6-8, with a world (and U.S.) capital-labor ratio equal to $\bar{k}^w$. At this capital-labor ratio, U.S. assets per worker will be $\bar{a}$—a number less than $\bar{k}^w$, since part of capital stock located in the U.S. will be Japanese-owned. If the U.S. owned all *this* capital stock, its citizens clearly would be better off. This improvement would require moving the U.S. economy's asset position from point U to point E^w. But this is not feasible, as long as U.S. saving preferences are described by the lower asset accumulation curve.

If the world economy were initially at point E^w, closing the U.S. economy to foreign ownership—enforcing autarky—would drive the U.S. out of the steady state. The U.S. would find its capital stock higher than the level of assets its young generation wished to accumulate, $\bar{a}$ per individual. In a closed economy the U.S. capital-labor ratio would evolve according to the lower curve, labeled

Figure 6-8 The Impact of Restricting Foreign Investment

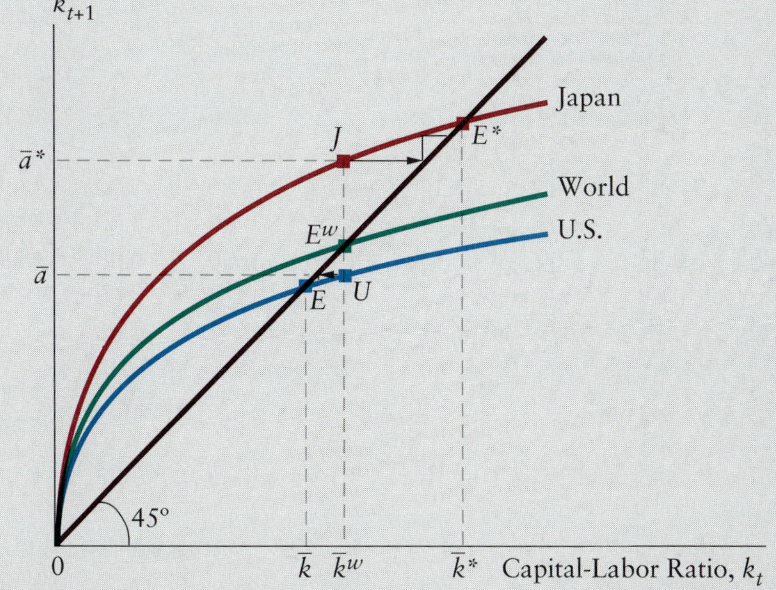

In the steady state with international investment, U.S. assets per worker are $\bar{a}$, which is less than $\bar{k}^w$ because part of the capital located in the U.S. is Japanese-owned. Closing the U.S. economy to foreign ownership would drive the U.S. out of the steady state. As a closed economy, the U.S. capital-labor ratio would evolve along the lower curve labeled "U.S." In the new steady state, at point E, all U.S. capital would be domestically owned, but national wealth per capita would be smaller—$\bar{k}$ rather than $\bar{a}$.

"U.S." Starting from the world-wide capital-labor ratio $\bar{k}^w$ in period 1, the U.S. would have a capital-labor ratio of just $\bar{a}$ in the first period after the return to autarky, period 2. However, even this lower capital-labor ratio would be unsustainable. Starting from $\bar{a}$ as the period 2 capital-labor ratio on the horizontal axis in the figure, we obtain a still lower value for the period 3 capital-labor ratio based on the U.S. curve.

As each successive U.S. generation saved less than the previous generation, the capital stock would fall over time to a new, lower steady-state value. This would bring the U.S. not to point E^w—with its original level of capital all U.S.-owned—but to point E, with capital and assets per worker equal to $\bar{k}$—lower than $\bar{k}^w$, but also lower than $\bar{a}$. By requiring all its domestic capital to be domestically owned, the U.S. would lose not only the capital that had initially been owned by foreigners—dropping from $\bar{k}^w$ to $\bar{a}$—it would lose more, suffering a decrease in its own national wealth, from $\bar{a}$ to $\bar{k}$.

Table 6-2 The Transition Path After Prohibiting Foreign Investment

	U.S.								
Period	k	w	r	c_y	c_o	u	i^f	k^f	nx
0	6.86	12.5	0.78	6.24	11.10	8.32	0.00	−0.62	0.49
1	6.86	12.5	0.78	6.24	11.10	8.44	0.62	−0.62	1.11
2	6.24	12.1	0.83	6.06	11.43	8.24	0.00	0.00	0.00
3	6.06	12.0	0.85	6.01	11.21	8.18	0.00	0.00	0.00
4	6.01	12.0	0.85	5.99	11.15	8.17	0.00	0.00	0.00
5	5.99	12.0	0.86	5.99	11.13	8.16	0.00	0.00	0.00
6	5.99	12.0	0.86	5.99	11.12	8.16	0.00	0.00	0.00
.	.	.	.	.	.	.	.	.	.
.	.	.	.	.	.	.	.	.	.
.	.	.	.	.	.	.	.	.	.
∞	5.99	12.0	0.86	5.99	11.12	8.16	0.00	0.00	0.00

	Japan						World Consumption
Period	k^*	w	r	c_y^*	c_o^*	u^*	
0	6.86	12.5	0.78	4.37	14.43	9.49	5348
1	6.86	12.5	0.78	4.37	14.43	9.19	5348
2	8.11	13.1	0.69	4.59	13.73	9.58	5330
3	8.52	13.3	0.67	4.66	14.23	9.70	5333
4	8.65	13.4	0.66	4.68	14.39	9.73	5335
5	8.69	13.4	0.66	4.69	14.43	9.74	5336
6	8.70	13.4	0.66	4.69	14.45	9.75	5336
.	.	.	.	.	.	.	.
.	.	.	.	.	.	.	.
.	.	.	.	.	.	.	.
∞	8.71	13.4	0.66	4.69	14.45	9.75	5336

Assumptions: $\alpha = .5$; $\alpha^* = .35$; N = 200; N* = 100

Table 6-2 provides a numerical simulation of this transition. Initially, in period 0, the U.S. and Japan have the same capital-labor ratio, as dictated by the long run steady state at point E^w—the one given in the last line of Table 6-1. Table 6-2 shows that in this steady state U.S. citizens consume more in the first period of life and less in the second period than their Japanese counterparts. In order to compare the well-being of different generations over time in each country, we calculate each generation's lifetime utility using the expression for Cobb-Douglas utility introduced in Chapter 3. For the U.S., utility for the generation born in period t is

$$u_t = c_{yt}^{\alpha} c_{ot+1}^{1-\alpha}$$

The expression for Japan is similar, but with all variables carrying the * superscript.

The column labeled "u" in Table 6-2 gives the utility for individuals in each country who are born in each period, based on these expressions for lifetime utility and the consumption levels shown in the adjoining columns. The utility of a young person born in the U.S. in period 0, for example, is based on his consumption when young in period 0, 6.24, and when old in period 1, 11.10.

The transition in Table 6-2 is based on the assumption that, after period 1, all capital in the U.S. must be owned by U.S. citizens. As a result, the U.S. loses the .62 unit of capital per worker that was owned by Japan, shown in the column labeled k^f. Indeed, the U.S. runs an enormous trade surplus in period 1 (as indicated in the column labeled nx), for it sends to Japan not only all the interest on the capital the Japanese own in the U.S., but all of the capital itself. In subsequent periods, both its trade balance and its net foreign investment are zero, since the U.S. has ceased economic contact with Japan. We solve for these subsequent periods of the transition using the single-country approach developed in Chapter 3, because the two countries' economies in autarky are entirely independent of one another.

The table indicates that, initially, elderly Americans are made better off by the prohibition of inbound investment. Having already "locked in" their wages in period 1, the elderly in period 2 benefit from the higher interest rates that accompany a lower capital-labor ratio. Thus, they get the best of both worlds: a high capital-labor ratio when working (and hence a high wage) and a lower capital-labor ratio when retired (and hence a higher interest rate). However, this benefit does not accrue to subsequent generations, who must first work and earn lower wages as the result of the lower capital-labor ratio before they can benefit from higher interest rates. As the capital-labor ratio falls in each successive period, so does the utility achieved by that period's young generation. By period 5, the U.S. capital-labor ratio has fallen to its steady-state level in autarky.

But what of Japan? If the U.S. loses so much from prohibiting inbound investment from Japan, does Japan gain? Most, but not all, Japanese generations do benefit. This is the reverse of the U.S. pattern. From Figure 6-8, we see that if Japan were forced to accumulate all its assets domestically, it would have a level of assets per worker greater than $\bar{k}^w$, determined by the higher Japanese asset accumulation curve, at point J. Just as the U.S. in autarky would eventually move to point E, Japan would move to point E^*, with its capital-labor ratio and its assets per individual equal to $\bar{k}^*$. In Table 6-2, the Japanese capital-labor ratio moves from 6.86 to 8.71.

Initially, this capital deepening makes the elderly Japanese worse off. After working during a period in which some Japanese assets were invested in the U.S., the elderly in period 2 are permitted to invest only in Japan. That drives up the capital-labor ratio there and drives down the interest rate those elderly individuals can obtain. Subsequent generations, however, benefit from the successively higher wages produced by increasing domestic capital-labor ratios. On balance, the Japanese gain from trade restrictions, just as Americans lose. But, in the short run, the opposite is true: for a time, the hypothetical U.S. strategy of limiting inbound investment appears to "work," at least for one generation of Americans—those who are old at the time of the investment limitations.

Thus, there are winners and losers between countries and among generations within each country. As a consequence, we cannot say simply that the "world" is better off or worse off because of the restriction of inbound investment. In one sense, though, the world is worse off. We can show that the winners' gains are smaller than the losers' losses. Put another way, trade expands the size of the social "pie" to be divided among different individuals. We refer to this expansion of the social pie as the **gains from trade**. Restricting trade reduces the size of this pie. To see this, consider the total consumption by both generations in both countries—total world consumption—in any given year. In period 1, this value is 5348 (check this for yourself). With the closing of the U.S. to foreign asset ownership in period 2, it drops to 5330. By period 5, it has recovered to 5336, but it rises no higher thereafter—world consumption is permanently lower.[16]

Gains from trade *The improvement in economic well-being resulting from specialization and exchange*

Why does trade improve welfare? Because it makes capital more productive. When borders close, all Japanese capital must be invested in Japan, where it earns a lower rate of return than it would in the U.S. In autarky, Japanese capital earns a rate of interest of .66 and U.S. capital earns .86. Recall that the interest rate is the marginal product of capital in a competitive market environment. Thus, the productivity of Japanese capital would improve if some of it were taken from Japan and invested in the U.S. This happens automatically when world markets are open (through the factor price equalization process discussed above), but it can be prevented through protectionist policies that limit foreign investment.

FOREIGN INVESTMENT AND GROWTH

In Chapter 3 we discussed the transition process for an economy after part of its capital stock has been destroyed by war. We saw that such an economy experiences a higher rate of saving and economic growth than other countries that did not experience such a loss. We also learned that the damaged economy eventually approaches the standard of living it would have achieved in the absence of war. Our analysis of this transition was of a single economy in autarky. How is

16. This difference is small, but in more complex models in which the two countries can specialize in the production of different commodities, the gains from international trade and investment can be much larger.

the recovery from a capital "shortage" (a level of capital below the steady-state value) affected by trade and capital flows, and what pattern will these flows take over time?

As we will see, an economy with a capital shortage can grow more rapidly by importing that capital from abroad. The high interest rate associated with the low capital-labor ratio in a war-ravaged economy will attract foreign investment. The capital inflow will make workers in the recovering country more productive; their higher wages will allow them to accumulate more capital on their own. Once this occurs, they no longer will need the capital from abroad. Hence, the postwar world will see a pattern of foreign capital flowing into the capital-poor country initially and then *from* this country later.

Indeed, although we will characterize the transition process as the recovery from a war, it applies equally well to any case in which one country, or one region, has a considerably smaller capital-labor ratio than another. It applies to Eastern Europe today, which has an educated labor force but an outmoded capital stock. It applies to the historical experience of the U.S., which imported capital in the nineteenth century in order to speed its industrial expansion.

Capital Deepening in an Open Economy

Figure 6-9 shows the impact of foreign investment on the development of a country with little initial capital. It compares the recovery of a country ("Japan") from a decimated capital stock with and without foreign investment from a second country ("U.S."). In the open economy case, we assume the U.S. has the same saving propensity as Japan but suffers no loss of capital. For simplicity, we assume the initial U.S. capital-labor ratio takes on its steady-state value $\bar{k}$.

The figure presents two alternative transition paths beginning in period 1, each based on Japan's period 0 capital-labor ratio of k_0^*. For the closed economy case, we simply move vertically from this capital stock to point J to locate the period 1 capital-labor ratio Japan is capable of generating through its own saving, k_1^*. Then, we follow the usual transition process from this capital-labor ratio to $\bar{k}$, at point E. For the open economy case, we combine Japan's assets in period 1, $N^*k_1^*$, with those generated by the U.S., $N\bar{k}$, to achieve a world-wide capital-labor ratio that falls between k_1^* and $\bar{k}$, k_1^w. The *world-wide* transition—for the U.S. as well as for Japan—then proceeds to point E from point W, thus beginning at a much higher capital-labor ratio than the closed economy process.

Table 6-3 gives a numerical comparison of these transitions, with $\alpha = \alpha^* = .5$. (The closed economy case repeats the simulation given in Table 3-1, page 92.) In each case, Japan saves 2.45 units per young person in period 0 because of its very low initial capital-labor ratio. Even with this high level of saving, though, Japan still has lower assets per worker than the U.S.—3.95 versus 5.99—at the beginning of period 1. If the Japanese economy is closed, this gap in assets per worker translates into a continuing gap between the capital-labor ratios of the two countries. In the open economy case, however, U.S. residents invest enough of their saving in Japan during period 0 that the capital-labor

Figure 6-9 Recovery from War: Closed Versus Open Economy

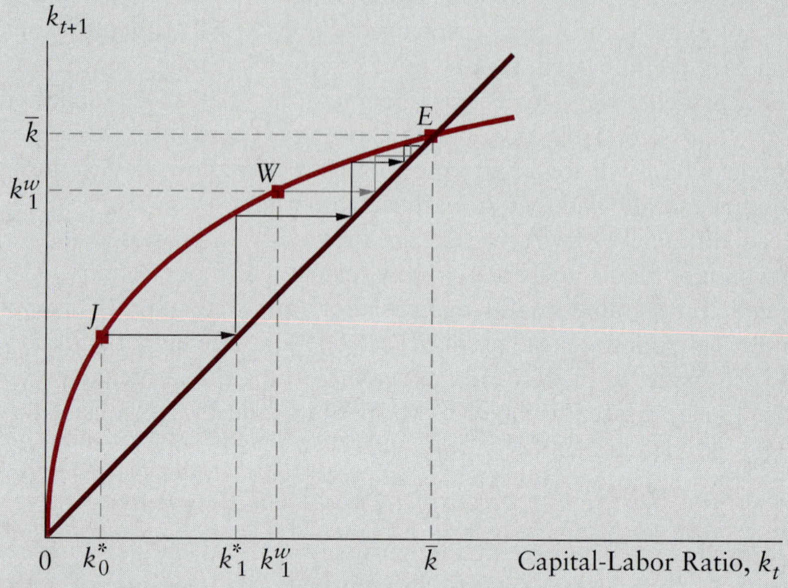

This figure presents alternative transition paths for the Japanese economy whose capital stock was decimated during World War II. For an economy closed to foreign trade, the transition begins with the postwar capital-labor ratio, k_1^*, at point *J* and ends in the steady state at point *E*. However, if Japan imports capital from the United States, the world-wide transition begins from k_1^w at point *W*. In this second case, Japan's transition starts from a much higher capital-labor ratio and attains the steady state more quickly.

ratios, and hence interest rates, in the two nations are equalized in period 1. This means 1.36 units of capital per Japanese worker must be imported from the U.S. This number appears as Japan's trade deficit in period 0.

In the open economy scenario, once Japan has the same capital-labor ratio as the U.S. at the beginning of period 1, it has the same productive potential. Each country has the same output per young person in period 1. The young in period 1 have the same wages and the same consumption per capita in each country. The old generations of period 1 do differ in their consumption, however, because part of the Japanese capital stock is owned by U.S. citizens. Each old person consumes her assets plus the interest on these assets. The interest rate is the same world-wide, but U.S. assets per old person include the capital shipped to Japan in period 0. Hence, consumption by the elderly in the U.S. exceeds that of their counterparts in Japan. In order to consume their foreign-

Table 6-3 The Transition Following a War: Closed Versus Open Economies

Japan, Closed

Period	k	y	c_y	c_o	s	i	i^f	k^f	nx
0	1.50	11.29	3.95	4.89	2.45	2.45	0.00	0.00	0.00
1	3.95	15.10	5.29	8.48	1.33	1.33	0.00	0.00	0.00
2	5.29	16.48	5.77	10.23	0.48	0.48	0.00	0.00	0.00
3	5.77	16.92	5.92	10.84	0.15	0.15	0.00	0.00	0.00
4	5.92	17.05	5.97	11.04	0.05	0.05	0.00	0.00	0.00
5	5.97	17.09	5.98	11.09	0.01	0.01	0.00	0.00	0.00
6	5.98	17.10	5.99	11.11	0.00	0.00	0.00	0.00	0.00
.	.	.	.	.	.	.	.	.	.
.	.	.	.	.	.	.	.	.	.
.	.	.	.	.	.	.	.	.	.
∞	5.99	15.54	5.99	11.12	0.00	0.00	0.00	0.00	0.00

Japan, Open

Period	k	y	c_y	c_o	s	i	i^f	k^f	nx
0	1.50	11.29	3.95	4.89	2.45	3.81	–1.36	0.00	–1.36
1	5.31	16.50	5.78	7.64	1.82	0.47	1.36	–1.36	2.62
2	5.78	16.92	5.92	10.85	0.15	0.15	0.00	0.00	0.00
3	5.92	17.05	5.97	11.04	0.05	0.05	0.00	0.00	0.00
4	5.97	17.09	5.98	11.10	0.01	0.01	0.00	0.00	0.00
5	5.98	17.10	5.99	11.11	0.00	0.00	0.00	0.00	0.00
6	5.99	17.11	5.99	11.12	0.00	0.00	0.00	0.00	0.00
.	.	.	.	.	.	.	.	.	.
.	.	.	.	.	.	.	.	.	.
.	.	.	.	.	.	.	.	.	.
∞	5.99	15.54	5.99	11.12	0.00	0.00	0.00	0.00	0.00

U.S., Open

Period	k	y	c_y	c_o	s	i	i^f	k^f	nx
0	5.99	17.11	5.99	11.12	0.00	–0.68	0.68	0.00	0.68
1	5.31	16.50	5.78	11.57	–0.21	0.47	–0.68	0.68	–1.31
2	5.78	16.92	5.92	10.85	0.15	0.15	0.00	0.00	0.00
3	5.92	17.05	5.97	11.04	0.05	0.05	0.00	0.00	0.00
4	5.97	17.09	5.98	11.10	0.01	0.01	0.00	0.00	0.00
5	5.98	17.10	5.99	11.11	0.00	0.00	0.00	0.00	0.00
6	5.99	17.11	5.99	11.12	0.00	0.00	0.00	0.00	0.00
.	.	.	.	.	.	.	.	.	.
.	.	.	.	.	.	.	.	.	.
.	.	.	.	.	.	.	.	.	.
∞	5.99	15.54	5.99	11.12	0.00	0.00	0.00	0.00	0.00

Assumptions: $\alpha = \alpha^* = .5$; $N = 200$; $N^* = 100$

owned assets plus accrued interest, the U.S. elderly must bring all of this back from Japan—Japan runs a trade surplus big enough to reduce foreign ownership of its capital stock to zero.

In subsequent periods of the open economy transition, the two countries grow together back to the steady-state capital-labor ratio, but there is no further foreign investment or capital ownership. Since the young behave identically in the two countries, asset accumulation per capita, and hence the next period's capital per worker, is equal without international investment.

The numerical simulation in Table 6-3 shows how access to the world capital market speeds the developing country's ability to recover its prewar living standards. Whereas just over half the gap in the capital-labor ratio is erased during the first period if Japan's economy is closed, over 90 percent of the gap is eliminated with the aid of imported capital.

Does the developed country gain, too? Yes and no. As with the previous example of a move to autarky, there are winners and losers. The younger U.S. generation in period 1, for example, suffers a loss of wages due to the lower U.S. capital-labor ratio. As in the previous example, however, the gains exceed the losses—the extra capital Japan imports is much more productive there than it would have been in the U.S.

Case Study: Japan after World War II

Our model predicts that a country recovering from the wartime destruction of its capital should run a trade deficit for a time (one period in our model) in order to import foreign-owned capital. That's followed by a trade surplus (again, for one period in the model) to reverse the pattern of foreign ownership, followed by balanced trade. Did Japan actually experience this pattern after World War II? To a certain extent, it did. Figure 6-10 shows that Japan ran trade deficits during much of the 1950s and early 1960s—its average trade balance during the period 1952–1964 was negative. In the years since 1965, it has usually run trade surpluses, with the average annual surpluses growing from just under 1 percent of GDP between 1965 and 1980 to over 2 percent of GDP since then.[17] Although Japan has not yet returned to balanced trade, its recent trade surpluses have been lower than during their peak of the mid-1980s.

Given this recent moderation of Japan's trade surpluses, why do they still receive so much attention in the U.S. popular press? One reason is that Japan has continued to run large trade surpluses *with the U.S.*, even as the U.S. trade deficit has fallen. In 1992, for example, Japan's trade surplus with the U.S. was \$36.8 billion, accounting for *more* than all of the U.S. trade deficit. In other words, the U.S. ran a trade surplus with the rest of the world. At the same time,

17. In addition to the general trend toward increased surplus, Figure 6-10 reveals large annual variations, notably the trade deficits of 1974 and 1979–1980. Although we have not focused in this chapter on very short-run fluctuations in the trade balance, these movements are not difficult to explain. Each of these periods corresponds to an "oil shock" during which the price of crude petroleum rose significantly. Because Japan is a major oil importer, oil price increases mean an increase in the share of national income it must devote to consumption expenditures, and a decrease in the share that goes to national saving. From the national income identity, we know that this means a decline in the trade balance.

Figure 6-10 Japan's Trade Balance, 1952–1992

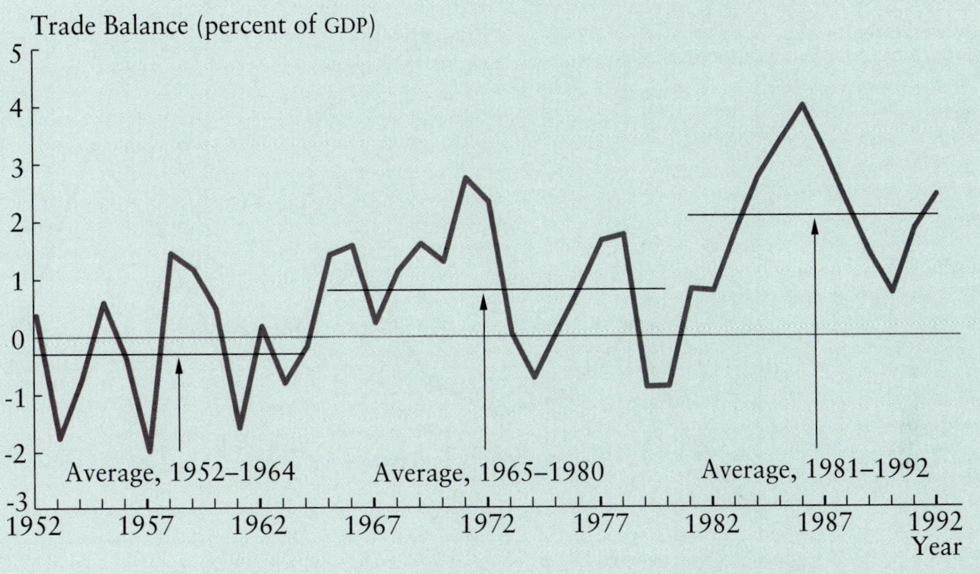

Our model predicts that an economy recovering from wartime destruction of its capital stock should run a trade deficit for a time in order to import capital. Later, it should experience a trade surplus to reverse the pattern of foreign ownership, followed by balanced trade in the steady state. To a certain extent, the Japanese experience since 1952 follows this pattern. During the 1950s and early 1960s, Japan's trade balance was negative, on average. Since the mid-1960s, Japan has usually run trade surpluses. Japan's trade is not yet balanced, but its recent surpluses have been lower than their peak value.

Source: OECD, National Accounts

Japan has run trade deficits with other regions, notably the oil-producing countries from which it imports fuel.

This distinction between a *bilateral* (between two countries) trade balance and a country's overall trade balance with the rest of the world does not arise in our two-country model, where the rest of the world is just one country. As the case of U.S.-Japan trade shows, however, the distinction is important in the real world, in which many countries trade simultaneously. In this context, our two-country model really tells us about a country's overall trade balance, not about its bilateral trade balances with particular countries. The latter will be determined by the types of goods and services different countries produce, and is more a question of international trade theory than macroeconomics.

Case Study: U.S. Industrialization in the Nineteenth Century

Like Japan recovering from World War II, the U.S. in the nineteenth century was a country with access to the latest technology but, in part because of immigra-

Figure 6-11 Net U.S. International Investment, Percent of GNP, *1873–1931*

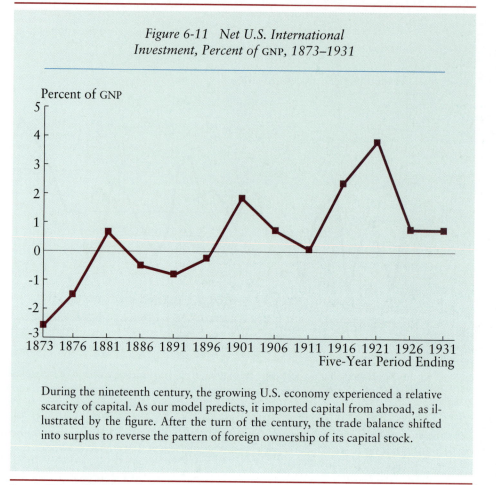

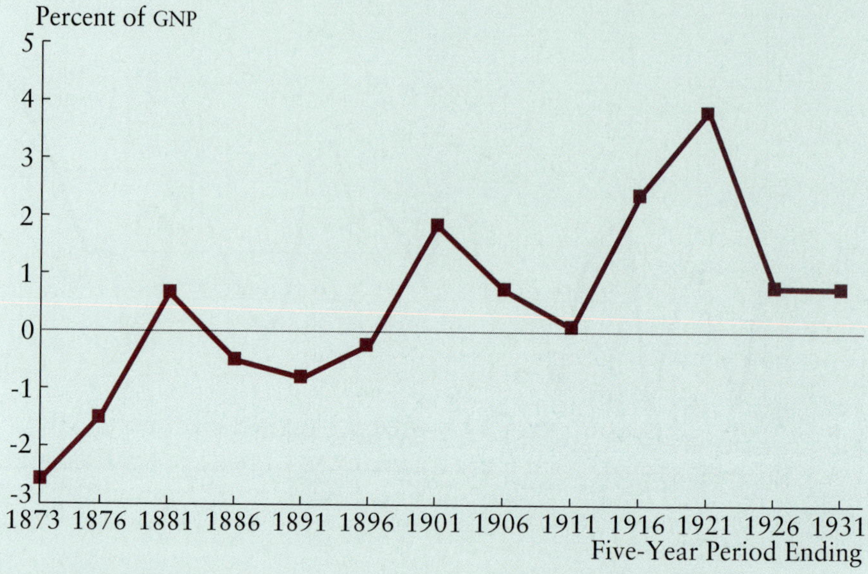

During the nineteenth century, the growing U.S. economy experienced a relative scarcity of capital. As our model predicts, it imported capital from abroad, as illustrated by the figure. After the turn of the century, the trade balance shifted into surplus to reverse the pattern of foreign ownership of its capital stock.

Source: *Historical Statistics of the U.S.*, Part 1

tion, a relative scarcity of capital. As our model predicts, the U.S. imported capital for a time before reversing the pattern of foreign ownership. Figure 6-11 shows net foreign investment relative to GNP for successive five-year periods between 1868 and 1931. It indicates that net foreign ownership of the U.S. capital stock rose for most of the period until 1896 but fell thereafter.

For the U.S. in the last century, Japan in the 1950s, and Eastern Europe today, trade deficits have not signified weakness, but the recovery from weakness. The trade surpluses run by Japan in the 1980s coincided with the arrival of prosperity and the ability to repay foreign borrowing. As in the example based on a decline in a country's propensity to save (see Table 6-1), there is a pattern of trade deficits followed by trade surpluses. However, the implications for national welfare of a postwar transition are quite different from those in the previous case, in which trade deficits arose from increased consumption, not increased investment. In that case, trade deficits coincided with a reduction in national output. In the case of a postwar transition, the opposite is true. Yet in each case, the opportunity to import capital improves the welfare of the importing country *relative to* its position without international trade and investment.

Chapter Summary

1. International trade has been of increasing importance to the U.S. economy, as both imports and exports have grown relative to GDP. This higher *level* of trade derives from factors not necessarily of a macroeconomic nature, such as improvements in the technology of transportation and reduced trade barriers. It is the trade *balance*, the difference between exports and imports, that is more directly relevant to our study of macroeconomics.
2. According to the national income identity, the trade balance must equal net foreign investment less net factor payments earned abroad. Net factor payments earned abroad themselves depend on past foreign investment. Net foreign investment is the difference between national saving and domestic investment.
3. In a closed economy, saving equals domestic investment. In a world of open economies, this identity holds for the world *as a whole*, but not necessarily for individual economies. Although each country determines its national saving, the level of investment taking place in a given country will depend on the relative returns to investment there and abroad. When investment can flow from one country to another, it will do so as long as rates of return to capital differ. Investment flows drive these rates together. This process of factor price equalization (which leads not only to equal interest rates but also to equal wage rates for comparably skilled and educated workers) determines how much investment takes place in each country. The combination of the level of investment and the amount of saving each country wishes to undertake determines each country's net foreign investment and hence its trade deficit or surplus.
4. Trade deficits can arise from increases in domestic investment or reductions in national saving, with very different implications in the two cases. Trade deficits induced by reductions in national saving, as in the U.S. in the 1980s, are associated with a decline in a nation's standard of living. Even though they do not cause this decline, trade deficits are often blamed. Yet the ability to run trade deficits actually lessens the magnitude of the decline. Trying to eliminate increased foreign ownership of domestic capital only reduces living standards further. Trade deficits resulting from increased investment, such as those incurred during Japan's recovery from World War II and the U.S. industrial expansion of the nineteenth century, demonstrate that trade deficits can signify growth, rather than economic decline.
5. Just as a trade deficit need not be bad, a trade surplus need not be good. As we demonstrated in one of our exercises, a country borrowing capital to offset a decline in its saving rate must eventually run trade surpluses to pay the interest on this foreign debt. The trade surplus in this case simply represents the share of GDP the country does not have available for its own uses—the legacy of having "mortgaged" its future.

Key Concepts

Exports
Imports
Domestic investment
Net foreign investment
Autarky
Factor price equalization
Net foreign asset position
Repatriation of foreign income
Gains from trade

Review Questions

1. What is a *trade deficit*?
2. What is *net foreign investment*? Explain two ways that a country can invest internationally.
3. How is the common, world-wide capital-labor ratio at any point in time expressed in variables?
4. Suppose that there are only two countries that are alike in every respect except their time preference parameter, α. How is the world-wide transition equation written and what value will the world-wide α have?
5. Where does the asset curve of a country with a high saving propensity lie in relation to that of a country with a low saving propensity? Where does the world-wide transition curve lie in relation to the curves for the individual countries?
6. What is *factor price equalization* and what is the mechanism by which it occurs? Does empirical evidence support the idea of factor price equalization?
7. What is a country's *net foreign asset position* and how is it shown in a transition diagram?
8. How does the net foreign asset position of a low-saving country change as the country moves from autarky to free trade?
9. How does the trade balance of a low-saving country change as the country moves from autarky to free trade?
10. What is *foreign direct investment*? What is *foreign portfolio investment*?
11. Who wins and who loses as a result of *trade restrictions*?
12. Why do trade restrictions reduce world consumption?

Numerical Questions

Suppose that the world consists of only two countries, Savum and Spendum. The following values apply to the Cobb-Douglas production functions and utility functions of each country. Use these values to answer questions 1 through 3 about each country's *steady state*.

Parameter	Savum	Spendum
A	4	4
α	0.3	0.6
β	0.25	0.25
N	100	200

1. a. Calculate the steady-state values of k, w, and r for each country under autarky.
   b. Compare the steady-state values calculated in part a. Do the differences make economic sense?
   c. Calculate the world-wide value of α.
   d. Calculate the steady-state values of k, w, and r for each country under free trade.
   e. Compare Savum's steady-state values under autarky to those under free trade. Explain any differences.
2. a. What are the *net foreign asset positions* of Savum and Spendum in autarky?
   b. Calculate the *total capital stocks* of Savum and Spendum under free trade.
   c. Calculate the *total amounts of assets owned* by Savum and Spendum under free trade.
   d. What are the *net foreign asset positions* of Savum and Spendum under free trade?
   e. Does the net foreign asset position of each country under autarky versus free trade make economic sense in terms of the countries' behavioral differences?
3. a. What are the steady-state net foreign incomes of Savum and Spendum under autarky?
   b. What are the steady-state trade balances for each country under autarky?
   c. What are the steady-state net foreign incomes of Savum and Spendum under free trade?
   d. What are the steady-state trade balances for each country under free trade?
4. a. Calculate the steady-state levels of consumption per person for old people and young people in each country under autarky.
   b. Calculate the steady-state utility of each young person in each country under autarky.
   c. Calculate the steady-state levels of consumption per person for old people and young people in each country under free trade. Compare them to the values under autarky and explain any differences.
   d. Calculate the steady-state utility of each young person in each country under free trade. Compare this to the utility value under autarky and explain any differences.
   e. Calculate world consumption under autarky and free trade. Provide an economic rationale for the difference.

Analytical Questions

1. Suppose that Savum and Spendum are in steady-state positions under free trade based on the parameters given in the table in the previous section. Suddenly, Spendum's value of α falls to 0.25. Give *qualitative* answers to the following questions, using transition diagrams to aid your reasoning.

a. What is the impact on the capital-labor ratios in Savum and Spendum in the period following the change? on the world-wide capital-labor ratio?
b. What is the impact on interest rates and capital flows in each country in the period following the change?
c. What is the impact on the net foreign asset positions of each country in the period following the change? on each country's trade balance?
d. In the new steady state, which country will be a net debtor? a net creditor?
e. In the new steady-state, which country has a trade surplus? a trade deficit?

2. Suppose that a developed country with a high saving propensity were to donate part of its capital stock to a low-saving, underdeveloped country. Assume that neither technology nor the size of the labor force in each country changes. Analyze whether the donation of capital stock would raise the standard of living in the underdeveloped country either temporarily or permanently. Does your answer depend on whether the donation occurs under autarky or free trade? (Helpful hint: Use transition diagrams to help your reasoning.)

3. Suppose that the United States and Japan are in steady-state equilibrium under autarky, as pictured in Figure 6-2. Assume that all trade restrictions are lifted and that *both labor and capital are mobile*, although the total amount of labor is fixed.

a. What will the capital and labor flows look like as the countries move to the new free-trade, steady-state position? (Helpful hint: What happens to the relative interest rates *and* wages after the change, and how are labor and capital likely to respond?)
b. Will the steady-state capital-labor ratio be different from the ratio that prevails when labor is not mobile? What about the steady-state wage and interest rate?
c. Will the steady-state net foreign asset position and steady-state trade balance of each country be different from those that prevail when labor is not mobile?

APPENDIX

Tracing the Path of the World Economy

1. Wages and interest rates are based on the world capital-labor ratio:

$$w_t = (1 - \beta)Ak_t^{\beta} \qquad r_t = \beta Ak_t^{(\beta - 1)}$$

2. Domestic assets per old person equal last period's saving by the young:

$$a_t = (1 - \alpha)w_{t-1}$$

3. Calculate consumption by the young and old:

$$c_{yt} = \alpha w_t \qquad c_{ot} = a_t(1 + r_t)$$

4. National saving equals national income less consumption:

$$S_t = Nw_t + r_t Na_t - Nc_{yt} - Nc_{ot}$$

5. The world capital stock evolves according to:

$$k_{t+1} = (1 - \bar{\alpha})(1 - \beta)Ak_t^{\beta}$$

6. Domestic investment is the change in domestic capital; net foreign investment is the difference between national saving and domestic investment:

$$I_t = Nk_{t+1} - Nk_t \qquad I_t^f = S_t - I_t$$

7. Net foreign assets equal domestic assets less domestic capital; net exports equal net foreign investment less net foreign capital income:

$$K_t^f = Na_t - Nk_t \quad X_t - M_t = I_t^f - r_t K_t^f$$

PART TWO

Fiscal and Monetary Policy

C H A P T E R 7

Fiscal Policy, Saving, and Growth

INTRODUCTION

Throughout the past six chapters we have frequently alluded to the behavior of government. Government, of course, is a major player in all modern-day national economies. One measure of the scope of government's activity is its direct spending on goods and services. As we learned in Chapter 5, government purchases represent one use of output, competing for GDP with investment, private consumption, and net exports. The size and composition of government purchases and the ways of paying for this spending are determined by **fiscal policy**.

Fiscal policy
The use of government purchases, taxes, transfers, and borrowing to influence aggregate economic activity

Fiscal policy is the means by which governments provide the expenditures citizens wish them to make. From a macroeconomic perspective, fiscal policy is also a tool for affecting the economy's performance in the short and long runs. Many economists believe that fiscal policy can and should be used to lessen the severity of business cycles. Others focus on the effects of fiscal policy, particularly the size of the government *budget deficit*, on long-term economic growth.

This chapter discusses the ways in which fiscal policy influences macroeconomic performance. We'll see that fiscal policy affects both resource *allocation* (how resources are used) and resource *distribution* (who gets them). The analysis here provides a basis for our study of countercyclical fiscal policy, which begins in Chapter 9.

We'll focus primarily on two types of fiscal policy: the level of government purchases and the distribution of the fiscal burden across generations (the **intergenerational distribution**). We will also touch on two other issues that will be taken up more fully in later chapters: the redistribution of resources among individuals *within* any particular generation (*intragenerational redistribution*) and the distortion of private sector incentives (for example, the incentive to save for the future). We'll consider a variety of examples of fiscal policy to illustrate its effects, showing how different means of financing governmental activities can have dramatically different effects on the economy.

Intergenerational redistribution *Shifting of fiscal burdens among different generations*

Among the questions addressed in this chapter are:

- How has fiscal policy in the U.S. changed over time?
- How does fiscal policy influence household behavior?
- What is the relationship between current and future fiscal decisions?
- How does fiscal policy redistribute resources among individuals in different generations?
- What impact does this intergenerational redistribution have on macroeconomic performance?
- Why is the government budget deficit an ambiguous measure of the state of fiscal policy?
- How might fiscal policy influence the trade deficit?
- How large is government investment, and how has it changed over time?
- Why might national saving be influenced by the types of taxes collected from individuals and firms?

After discussing the features of U.S. fiscal policy, we'll describe the constraint a government faces in setting fiscal policy through time. Next, we'll consider the macroeconomic effects of government purchases and how they are financed, demonstrating the central importance of which generations pay for these government purchases. As in earlier chapters, our basic tool for analyzing economic behavior over time will be the transition equation that determines how the economy's capital-labor ratio evolves. After revising the transition equation to incorporate government actions, we'll be able to study the effects of various elements of fiscal policy, such as the social security system and government investment.

GOVERNMENT EXPENDITURES AND FINANCE

In 1993, real spending on goods and services in the U.S. by all levels of government accounted for 18 percent of real GDP. In addition to purchasing goods and paying interest on borrowed funds, governments provide **transfer payments** to households and firms.[1] We refer to the sum of transfer payments and government purchases as the *government budget*. In 1993, governments in the U.S. at

Transfer payments *Cash or in-kind benefits given to individuals by the government*

1. Recall that transfer payments are not part of GDP because they are not directly associated with the creation of any goods or services.

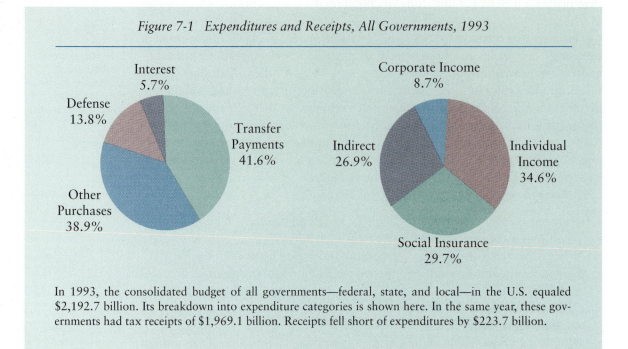

Figure 7-1 Expenditures and Receipts, All Governments, 1993

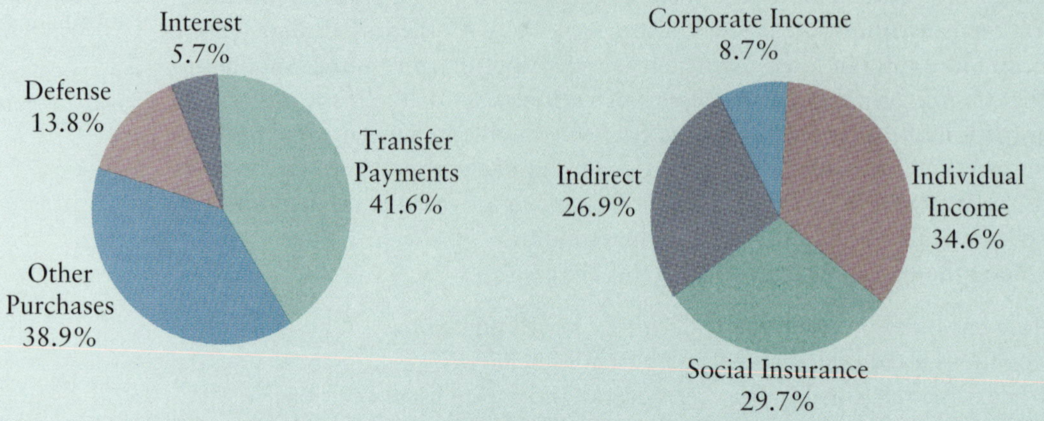

In 1993, the consolidated budget of all governments—federal, state, and local—in the U.S. equaled \$2,192.7 billion. Its breakdown into expenditure categories is shown here. In the same year, these governments had tax receipts of \$1,969.1 billion. Receipts fell short of expenditures by \$223.7 billion.

Source: *Economic Report of the President*, 1994

all levels (federal, state, and local) had an aggregate budget of \$2.19 trillion—slightly more than one-third the size of GDP. The left side of Figure 7-1 shows how this aggregate government budget was allocated among expenditure categories.[2]

In a market economy, the government must first obtain funds in order to make these purchases and transfers. It may do so in three ways. The simplest method is literally to create them, by printing money. Printing money has important effects on the economy, but it deserves separate consideration. Hence, we'll defer our discussion of money and monetary policy until Chapter 8.

If the government does not print the money needed to finance its budget, it must raise the funds from private sector households and firms. One way to obtain such funds is to borrow from the private sector—to issue bonds—which gives the government funds today in exchange for its promise to repay these funds, with interest, in the future. Interest payments are counted as transfer payments in the government budget. Bonds issued by the government are included

2. This calculation counts only once the transfers that are made from one level of government to another and then spent by the recipient government. For example, if the federal government provides funds to a state government for highway construction, this shows up as a transfer in the federal budget and as a purchase of goods and services in the state budget, but it is counted only once (and classified by its ultimate use, the purchase of goods and services) in Figure 7-1.

in the financial assets of the private sector, which we discussed in Chapter 2. Like financial assets issued by private businesses, government bonds provide future income to the owner. And, as with other financial assets, the rate of interest on these bonds is determined in the market for financial assets.[3]

The other way the government raises funds is by collecting taxes from households and businesses. The right side of Figure 7-1 gives a breakdown of the tax revenues raised in the U.S. in 1993 by all levels of government. Unlike the printing of money, which in the U.S. and virtually all other countries is a financing method used only by the central government, collecting taxes and issuing debt are used to finance expenditures by state and local governments as well.

Note from Figure 7-1 that tax revenues fell $223.7 billion short of expenditures in 1993. This is the amount, in the aggregate, that governments financed by issuing bonds. The difference between expenditures and taxes in the government budget is referred to as the government's **budget deficit**. The deficit, denoted DEF_t, is the amount of additional debt the government issues to meet its budget needs. It represents the increase in the **national debt**, B, from one year to the next:

Budget deficit *The difference between government expenditures and tax revenues in a particular period*

National debt *The value of the outstanding stock of government bonds held by the public*

$$B_{t+1} = B_t + \text{DEF}_t$$

Looked at another way, the national debt is the sum of all previous deficits (minus any surpluses).

Case Study: Postwar U.S. Budget Deficits

How has the U.S. budget deficit behaved in recent decades? Figure 7-2 graphs the ratios of federal receipts and expenditures to GDP for the period since 1960.[4] Superimposed on the figure are shaded areas to indicate periods of recession. The figure shows that the ratio of federal expenditures to GDP typically rises during recessions, whereas the ratio of taxes to GDP falls. Together, these patterns imply that the budget deficit rises or, as shown in the diagram, the budget surplus (equal to the deficit but with the opposite sign) falls.[5]

Why do deficits go up during recessions? Fiscal policy undergoes continual revision, as changes in economic conditions lead to changes in revenues and expenditures. During the 1990–1991 recession, for example, Congress voted to extend the number of weeks after becoming unemployed that workers could receive *unemployment compensation*, which replaces a fraction of the wages they would have received on the job. This action increased government transfer payments.

3. Figure 5-6 provided an historical picture of the *real* and *nominal* interest rates paid on *Treasury bills,* one type of bond that the U.S. federal government issues.

4. Even though the federal budget accounts for only about two-thirds of total government budgets in the U.S., macroeconomists typically focus on fiscal policy at the federal level. The reason is that there are too many separate decision makers and competing interests at the state and local levels for these governments to coordinate macroeconomic policies. State and local fiscal policies taken together have macroeconomic effects, but they are typically not shaped by individual governments with these effects in mind. One of the jobs of federal fiscal policy is to take account of the macroeconomic side effects of the fiscal policies of state and local governments.

5. An exception to this pattern is the recession of the early 1990s, when both expenditure and revenue shares of GDP were relatively constant.

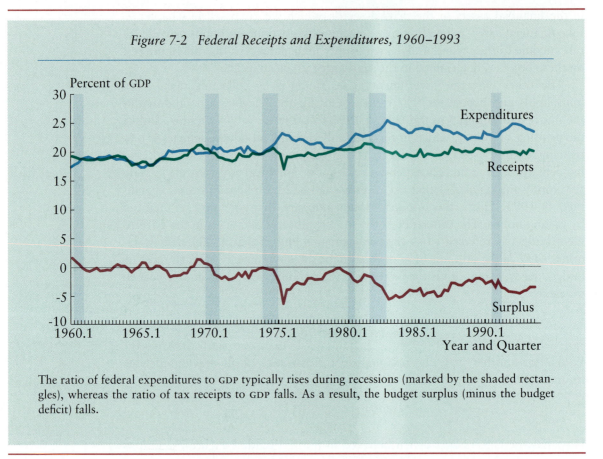

Figure 7-2 Federal Receipts and Expenditures, 1960–1993

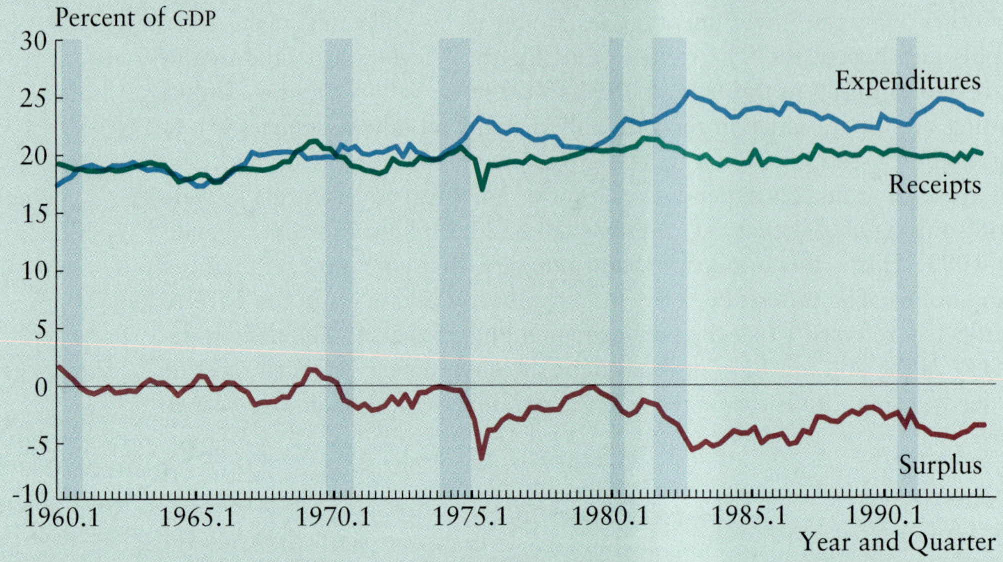

The ratio of federal expenditures to GDP typically rises during recessions (marked by the shaded rectangles), whereas the ratio of tax receipts to GDP falls. As a result, the budget surplus (minus the budget deficit) falls.

Source: *Economic Report of the President*, 1994

However, even had these benefits not been extended, unemployment compensation transfers would still have risen during the recession, as the *number* of unemployed workers grew.

Similar changes occur in tax revenues. During the 1974–1975 recession, for example, individuals were given an income tax rebate of $50 per person to increase disposable income and, it was hoped, household spending. However, even had no such change been adopted, tax revenues would still have fallen as the result of the recession, because the income taxes that individuals and businesses pay fall as income falls.

The effects of both legislated and built-in cyclical changes in the U.S. federal budget are evident in Figure 7-2. However, a second noticeable pattern in the figure is the trend in the budget surplus over the period. After hovering around zero through the 1960s, the surplus became negative (and the deficit positive) in the 1970s. Since the early 1980s, the deficit has been in the range of 4 percent of GDP. This budget gap reflects the fact that federal expenditures have grown as a share of GDP, while federal revenues have remained at roughly 20 percent of

GDP throughout the period. However, the figure does not explain the reasons for these trends, or their economic implications.

FISCAL POLICY AND THE GOVERNMENT BUDGET

Trends in the budget and the deficit in recent years have received more attention than their cyclical movements. To understand the impact of these trends, we must consider how current fiscal policy decisions affect future decisions. We begin by discussing the constraints that the government budget places on the design of fiscal policy.

The Intertemporal Budget Constraint

As we have seen, the government may finance its budget using a mixture of taxes and deficits, with deficits increasing the size of the national debt. But this does not mean that governments can simply avoid taxation by issuing more debt. As the national debt grows, so do the interest payments that the government must make on this debt. We observed in Figure 7-1 that such interest payments accounted for 5.7 percent of all government budgets in the U.S. in 1993; for the federal government alone, the figure was 12.1 percent. It is the growth in these interest payments that ultimately limits deficit finance. As we will now see, each government, like each household in our two-period model, faces a budget constraint that limits the purchases it can make.

To derive the government's budget constraint, let's rewrite the expression that relates the deficit to the change in government debt by breaking the deficit into its component parts. The deficit equals government expenditures less tax receipts. Expenditures, in turn, include purchases (denoted as G), transfer payments, and interest on the government debt. If we define Z to be *net* tax receipts—tax receipts less transfer payments—then the deficit equals $G - Z$ plus interest payments, which are equal to the interest rate, r, times the stock of outstanding government debt, B. Thus, in period $t + 1$, the stock of government debt equals

$$B_{t+1} = G_t - Z_t + (1 + r_t)B_t$$

The first two terms on the right-hand side of this expression equal the government's **primary deficit**. We can see from this expression that if the primary deficit is zero (government purchases, G_t, equal *net* tax receipts, Z_t), the real value of the debt still increases in period $t + 1$. In this case the government receives just enough tax receipts from the private sector to pay for its current purchases. But it must create still more debt to cover the interest on the debt already in existence. If the primary deficit is positive, then debt grows even faster than the interest rate.

Primary deficit *Government purchases of goods and services in a particular period minus the government's net tax receipts in that period; the period's budget deficit minus interest payments on outstanding government debt*

As we can see from this expression, if the government continually runs primary deficits, the national debt will grow at a rate higher than the interest rate.

Although this is feasible for a time, eventually it would lead to a national debt so large that the interest payments on it would exceed GDP, and hence any ability of the government to make them. At some point, then, government debt must begin growing at a rate lower than the interest rate.[6] For this to occur, the government will have to run negative primary deficits, i.e., *primary surpluses*.[7]

This restriction on the growth rate of the national debt quite literally imposes a budget constraint on the government. To obtain an expression for this constraint, we combine the expression above relating B_{t+1} to B_t for several successive periods. This produces a relationship between the national debt indefinitely far into the future, the initial stock of debt, B_t, and the primary surpluses or deficits in the intervening years. Requiring that the national debt eventually grow at a rate below the interest rate allows us to eliminate the term involving the future level of debt and write this expression as

$$0 = B_t + \frac{(G_t - Z_t)}{R_t} + \frac{(G_{t+1} - Z_{t+1})}{R_t R_{t+1}} + \ldots$$

where R_t equals $(1 + r_t)$, $R_{t+1} = (1 + r_{t+1})$, and so on.[8] The discount factors R are used to convert future values of $G - Z$ into their present values. We call this expression the **government intertemporal budget constraint** (GIBC). The GIBC says that the present value of all future primary deficits plus the initial stock of national debt must sum to zero. It *does not* require that the government ever repay the national debt itself. It *does* require that the government (eventually) run primary *surpluses* in order to meet interest payments on its debt.

Government intertemporal budget constraint (GIBC) *The requirement that the current value of national debt plus the present value of future government purchases equal the present value of the government's net tax receipts*

To relate the GIBC to the familiar household budget constraint, we can split up the terms in the primary deficit to obtain

$$\underbrace{\frac{G_t}{R_t} + \frac{G_{t+1}}{R_t R_{t+1}} + \ldots}_{\text{PV of Purchases}} = -B_t + \underbrace{\frac{Z_t}{R_t} + \frac{Z_{t+1}}{R_t R_{t+1}} + \ldots}_{\text{PV of Net Taxes}}$$

This version of the GIBC says that at the beginning of period t, the present value of all the government's future purchases equals the present value of its future net tax receipts minus the value of its outstanding debt. This budget constraint is like the household's intertemporal budget constraint, but with the net tax payments, Z_t, in place of wages and government purchases, G_t, in place of consumption

6. In our model, with A_t fixed, no population growth, and output constant in the steady state, the debt must eventually stop growing.

7. This is precisely the logic we used in Chapter 6 to demonstrate why the accumulation of foreign-owned domestic capital (like the growth of the national debt) will prevent a country from running trade deficits (or primary budget deficits) forever.

8. This expression is derived by substituting the equation for B_{t+1} into that for B_{t+2}, the resulting equation for B_{t+2} into that for B_{t+3}, and so on, each time dividing by the period's discount factor, R_t. For example, we divide the expression for B_{t+1} by R_t to obtain $B_{t+1}/R_t = (G_t - Z_t)/R_t + B_t$, and then substitute this into the expression for B_{t+2} divided by R_{t+1}, $B_{t+2}/R_{t+1} = (G_{t+1} - Z_{t+1})/R_{t+1} + B_{t+1}$, to obtain $B_{t+2}/R_t R_{t+1} = (G_{t+1} - Z_{t+1})/R_t R_{t+1} + (G_t - Z_t)/R_t + B_t$. As we continue this procedure, the left-hand side of the expression is the limit of the ratio $B_{t+T}/R_t R_{t+1} \ldots R_{t+T-1}$ as T increases. That limit is equal to zero because debt grows at a rate below the interest rate.

expenditures. Like the household, which by consuming more in the first period must consume less in the second, the government's current decisions affect its future ones. For example, if it spends a dollar more on goods and services in the current period without raising net tax payments concurrently, it must reduce future spending or increase future net tax payments by an amount with a present value of one dollar. Unlike the household, which has a finite lifetime, the government's budget constraint takes account of government purchases, G_t, and net tax payments, Z_t, into the distant future.

The relationship between the government intertemporal budget constraint and the budgets of individual periods illustrates an extremely important point: fiscal policy consists of a series of interdependent decisions made over time. When the government takes actions today, it commits itself to take compensating actions in the future. As long as the government makes these compensating changes, its *intertemporal* budget is balanced. But intertemporal balance can be achieved in a variety of ways, with very different implications for macroeconomic performance. To see why, let's consider how fiscal policy affects the economy.

Fiscal Policy and Household Behavior

As we'll see, many macroeconomic effects of fiscal policy turn on the difference in spending propensities between old and young—the fact that the old tend to consume a greater fraction of the resources available to them than the young do. To sharpen the conclusions and simplify the exposition, we will demonstrate the effects of fiscal policy using a simplified version of our model. Rather than have households consume when young and old, we'll assume that households consume only when old. That is, we'll set the parameter α that determines first-period consumption equal to zero. The analysis would be a bit more complicated if we used our more general model, but the same kinds of conclusions would follow.

Since c_{yt} equals zero in the simplified model, the lifetime budget constraint for the generation born in period t becomes

$$c_{ot+1} = (1 + r_{t+1})w_t$$

Because we are now assuming that households save all their wages when young, their consumption when old equals their wages, plus interest earned on this savings.

Now, let's add government fiscal policy to the picture, in the form of government spending, G_t, and net tax payments, Z_t. Fiscal policy affects household behavior through the level and timing of net tax payments. Even if we know the entire time path of net tax payments, Z_t, though, we also need to know how each period's payments are divided between the young and the old, in order to identify the fiscal policy impact on each generation. If each of the N members of the younger generation in period t makes net tax payments of z_{yt}, and each of the N older people pays z_{ot}, aggregate net tax payments in period t are

$$Z_t = Nz_{yt} + Nz_{ot}$$

In period t, the young generation's net tax payment will reduce its saving dollar for dollar—each young household will acquire assets equal to its wages less its payment when young, $a_{t+1} = w_t - z_{yt}$. When this same generation is old, in period $t + 1$, the amount each member can consume, c_{ot+1}, equals the income and principal from her assets less the payment she must make when old, i.e., $(1 + r_{t+1})a_{t+1} - z_{ot+1}$. Combining these expressions yields the household budget constraint for a member of generation t

$$c_{ot+1} = (1 + r_{t+1})(w_t - z_{yt}) - z_{ot+1} = (1 + r_{t+1})(w_t - \hat{z}_t)$$

where $\hat{z}_t$ is the *present value* of the individual's net tax payments, i.e., $\hat{z}_t = z_{yt} + z_{ot+1}/(1 + r_{t+1})$. Thus, the consumption behavior of households does not depend on the timing of net tax payments made when young or old, but simply on their combined present value.[9] This fact is key to the analysis presented elsewhere in this chapter. As we will see, two seemingly different policies that imply the same present value of net tax payments will have the same impact on household behavior.

Generational account
The present value of net tax payments made by a particular individual over his or her lifetime

We refer to this present value $\hat{z}_t$ as a **generational account**. It represents, so to speak, the "price of admission" that each member of generation t must pay to receive the benefits of the government's purchases.[10] The generational account has an important impact on different fiscal policies, because it determines how these policies affect household decisions. Moreover, we could have expressed the government intertemporal budget constraint in terms of these accounts, rather than in terms of each period's aggregate net tax payments, Z_t. That is, the present value of all future net tax payments equals the payments by the old in period t plus the present value at time t of the future generational accounts for all individuals born in or after period t. Thus, we can think of the government intertemporal budget as placing direct restrictions on the allocation of the fiscal burden among different generations.

Case Study: Generational Accounts, Now and in the Future

How large are the generational accounts faced by young Americans? Without knowing the future, we cannot be sure. However, we can make projections based on the assumption that current tax rules and transfer programs will be maintained. A recent calculation suggests that a typical newborn male in 1990 faces a net lifetime present-value tax burden of $76,400; a typical female's burden

9. This result is straightforward in the present case, in which households save everything for consumption when old. More generally, if households wish to consume more than $w_t - z_{yt}$ when young, our conclusion about only $\hat{z}$ being relevant (rather than its breakdown between z_{yt} and z_{ot+1}) rests on the assumption that households can borrow the additional money desired for consumption when young (to be repaid when old). If households cannot borrow, they are said to face *liquidity constraints*. We discuss this further in Chapter 15.

10. The concept of generational accounting is developed in Alan J. Auerbach, Jagadeesh Gokhale, and Laurence J. Kotlikoff, "Generational Accounting: A Meaningful Alternative to Deficit Accounting," in David Bradford, ed., *Tax Policy and the Economy*, vol. 5 (Cambridge: MIT Press, 1991) and Laurence J. Kotlikoff, *Generational Accounting* (New York: Free Press, 1992).

is \$29,400. The differences are due primarily to differences in life expectancy and labor force participation.[11]

The figures underlying these accounts come from tax and transfer components with very different patterns. Figure 7-3 shows the patterns of the different tax and transfer components over the lifetimes of the typical male and female. For each age in 1990, the figure shows the taxes each individual paid, the transfers he or she received, and the difference—the net tax payment—at that age. The generational account equals the present value of a generation's net tax payments from age 0 to age 90. The figure also shows the lifetime pattern of two important components of net tax payments, income and payroll taxes.[12] Evidently, a greater fraction of payroll taxes (which apply only to labor income) are paid earlier in life than is the case for income taxes (which apply to both labor and capital income). This is what we would expect from our life-cycle model, in which individuals work when young but receive income both when young and when old. Thus, raising current net tax payments, Z_t, through the payroll tax hits younger generations harder than raising the same amount through the income tax. In terms of our model, the relative values of z_{yt} and z_{ot} would differ under the two types of tax increase, with z_{yt} being higher for the payroll tax.

Transfer payments occur typically later in life than taxes do. In fact, once males reach age 76 (and females age 70), transfer payments exceed taxes. We describe this in our model by making z_{yt} positive and z_{ot} negative. As we will see, this difference in net tax payments is due primarily to the public provision of health and retirement benefits for older individuals. These different patterns of taxes and transfers suggest that raising Z_t through higher taxes will likely hit a younger population than raising Z_t through lower transfers. That is, raising taxes will increase z_{yt} relative to z_{ot} more than reducing transfers will.

What will generational accounts look like for future generations? Once again, it is hard to know exactly. However, the future streams of government purchases, G_t, and net tax payments, Z_t, projected on the basis of the continuation of current fiscal policy, do not satisfy the government's intertemporal budget constraint. If current policy is maintained, the present value of net tax payments will fall short of the present value of government purchases plus the current national debt. How short? To make up the difference from future generations alone would require their generational accounts to be 79.2 percent higher than those of present generations[13]—the accounts would rise from roughly a third of the present value of their lifetime labor income to well over one-half!

FISCAL POLICY AND ECONOMIC TRANSITIONS

Now that we have seen how fiscal policy affects household behavior, we can trace the impact of fiscal policy on the economy. A fiscal policy consists of a

11. See *Budget of the United States Government, Fiscal Year 1993,* February 1992, Chapter 26. The present value calculations use a real interest rate of 6 percent.
12. The amounts include not only income and payroll taxes paid directly by individuals but also those paid by businesses. Ultimately, all taxes on firms are borne by individuals in their capacity as owners, employees, and customers of the firms.
13. More recent estimates, in *Budget of the United States, Analytical Perspectives, Fiscal Year 1995,* chapter 3, suggest that the intergenerational imbalance is even higher.

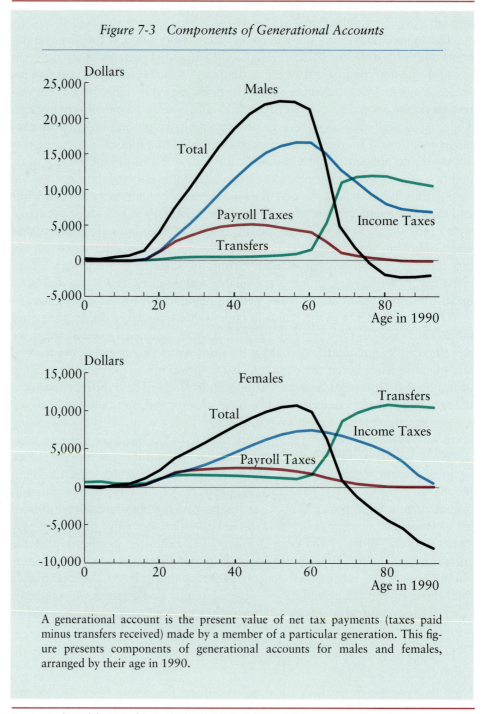

Figure 7-3 Components of Generational Accounts

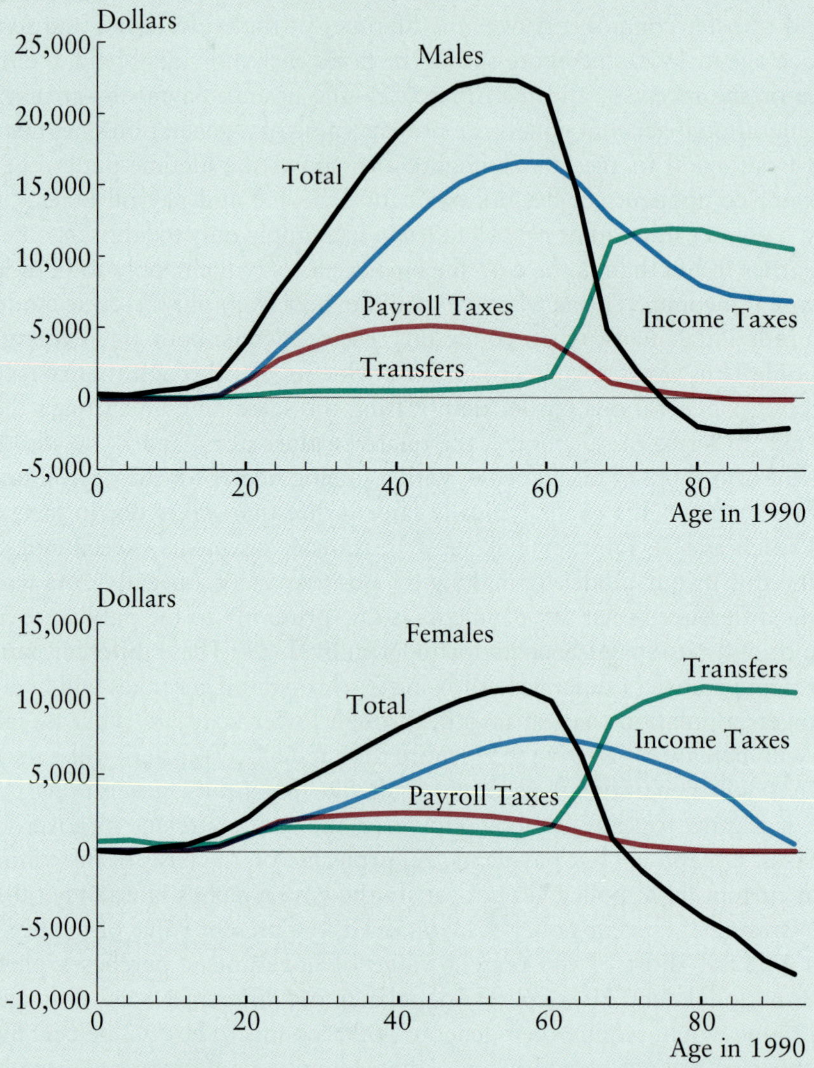

A generational account is the present value of net tax payments (taxes paid minus transfers received) made by a member of a particular generation. This figure presents components of generational accounts for males and females, arranged by their age in 1990.

Source: *Budget of the United States Government*, Fiscal Year 1993

time pattern of government spending (G_t), net tax payments (Z_t), and the breakdown of Z_t in each period into payments by the young and payments by the old. For a given pattern of government purchases, the government must ultimately

"What's this I hear about you adults mortgaging my future?"

By permission of the cartoonist, Dave Carpenter.

choose a corresponding time pattern of net tax payments that satisfy the government intertemporal budget constraint. Simultaneously, it must determine how much of each period's net tax payments will be borne by young and old generations. Both decisions (each period's Z_t and its division between z_{yt} and z_{ot}) affect the consumption by households and hence the path of the macroeconomy.

The Transition Equation with Fiscal Policy

Throughout most of this chapter we'll use the single-country, closed economy model developed in Chapters 2 and 3. We begin by characterizing the transition equation with no government, under our assumption that $\alpha = 0$. As before, we consider the acquisition of assets by each generation. Since $\alpha = 0$, each member of generation t wishes to save all its wages. These savings, in turn, are used to purchase capital. Thus, we have an equation relating the capital-labor ratios in successive periods:[14]

$$k_{t+1} = w_t = A(1 - \beta)k_t^{\beta}$$

14. We will assume throughout the chapter that the level of technology, A, is constant over time.

Figure 7-4 The Transition Equation with Fiscal Policy

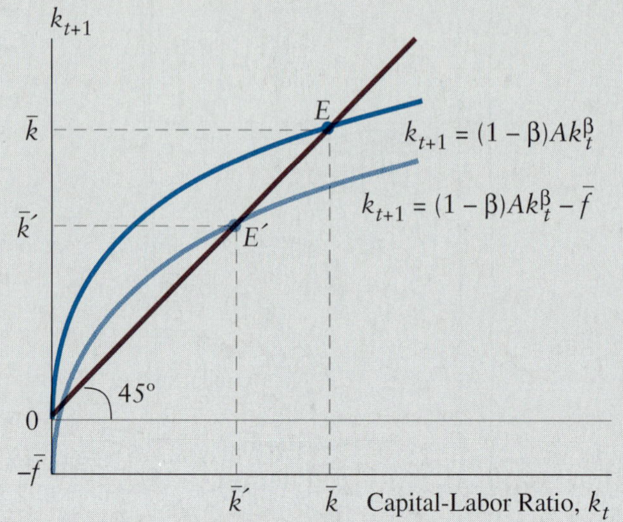

Our typical transition curve without fiscal policy is shown as the upper curve in the diagram. In the presence of fiscal policy, some of what each worker earns goes to the government in the form of net tax payments or bond purchases and is not available to purchase capital. The sum of these two payments is $\bar{f}$ for a member of generation t. The introduction of fiscal policy has the effect of shifting the entire transition curve downward.

The familiar diagram depicting this transition curve and its steady-state capital-labor ratio, $\bar{k}$, at point E, is shown by the upper curve in Figure 7-4.

We derived this transition equation by setting capital purchased equal to wages earned. But in the presence of fiscal policy, some of what each worker earns will go to the government in the form of net tax payments, z_{yt}. Hence, the assets a worker accumulates, a_{t+1}, will equal his wages, w_t, less z_{yt}. But not all of the worker's assets will be invested in capital. Some will be used to purchase government debt. If we let b_{t+1} stand for the amount of government debt a worker at time t purchases, then the capital a worker accumulates, k_{t+1}, will equal his total assets, a_{t+1}, less the amount of debt that he purchases, b_{t+1}. To summarize, we have $k_{t+1} = a_{t+1} - b_{t+1} = w_t - z_{yt} - b_{t+1}$.[15] Letting the term f_t (for fiscal) stand for $z_{yt} + b_{t+1}$, the sum of all payments the worker makes to the government in net taxes and bond purchases, we can write our formula for k_{t+1} compactly as

15. Even though the net payment, z_{yt}, and the debt purchase, b_{t+1}, occur at precisely the same time—the end of period t—the debt has the time subscript $t + 1$ because it is the debt that will be held during period $t + 1$.

$$k_{t+1} = A(1 - \beta)k_t^{\beta} - f_t$$

which, in graphical terms, is the basic transition equation shifted vertically downward by a distance f_t. The lower curve in Figure 7-4 provides one example, for the case in which f_t equals some positive value, $\bar{f}$. As the figure indicates, a positive value of $\bar{f}$ implies a lower steady-state capital-labor ratio, in this case $\bar{k}'$. We'll see shortly why this is so.

This transition equation applies to every fiscal policy we will consider. Although it can be simplified in each case, we can draw an important conclusion simply by looking at the general expression: it is the *sum* of the terms b_{t+1} and z_{yt}, and not their individual values, that determines the effect of fiscal policy. Whether the young acquire debt or pay taxes, they are left with less income with which to acquire capital. A policy that changes a single component of this sum will start a transition. Policies that imply offsetting changes in the two components will have no effect.

With this transition equation in hand, we can consider the impact of a range of government fiscal policies. We begin with the issue of how to finance government consumption purchases.

Financing Government Consumption Purchases

Suppose the economy is initially in a long-run steady state in which there is no government activity. The government now wishes to purchase a constant amount, say $\bar{G}$, for government consumption in each period. To measure the impact of government behavior, we must also specify how the government will finance this spending—how it will satisfy its intertemporal budget constraint. Perhaps the simplest way is to require that in each period the older generation make net tax payments to the government to cover that year's government purchases.[16] How would the government target the elderly for taxation? In terms of our model, a tax on consumption would suffice, since only the old consume. Even in the real world, consumption taxes tend to fall more heavily on the elderly than, say, payroll taxes do. Increasing the taxation of Social Security benefits, as the government did in 1993, would also do the trick.

The required payment from each elderly individual would be $z_{ot} = \bar{g} = \bar{G}/N$, beginning in the first period that the government purchases are made, say period 0. We can easily see that this policy will satisfy the government budget constraint: the government has no debt ($B_0 = 0$), and government purchases, $\bar{G}$ (which are equal to $N\bar{g}$), equal net tax payments, $Z_t = Nz_{ot}$, in each period and, hence, in present value as well.

Despite the change in government purchases, this policy has no impact on the level or path of aggregate output. Checking the general formula for the transition equation, we see that setting $f_t = 0$, as this policy does (the young pay nothing to the government), leaves us with the same transition equation that

16. All that matters in our model is the net tax payment each generation makes. There could be a tax equal to z_{ot} per person or a tax larger than z_{ot} and some government transfers made to the same individuals, with the difference between the tax and transfers equal to z_{ot}. For example, a positive value of z_{ot} = 10 might be the difference between income taxes of 12 and Social Security benefits of 2.

prevails in the absence of fiscal policy. Because it has no effect on the capital-labor ratio, this fiscal policy causes no change in either output or investment, the change in the capital stock from one period to the next.

Why is there no change in investment in this example? Beginning in period 0, consumption by elderly individuals will fall, since they each must now make a net tax payment of $\bar{g}$ before consuming. But as aggregate consumption by the elderly falls by the full amount of the net tax payment, Z_t, government purchases increase by exactly the same amount. Hence, overall spending on private *plus* public consumption remains unchanged, and so does national saving which, as we learned in Chapter 5, is the difference between output and total (government plus household) consumption. Since we know from Chapter 3 that national saving equals national investment, there is no change in investment, either. As a result, output in the following period is the same, and so on. There is no change over time in the economy's capital-labor ratio—it remains at $\bar{k}$.

We conclude that introducing government consumption purchases need not affect national investment—*if* the purchases are financed in a way that reduces private consumption to the same extent that government consumption increases. As we will now see, this condition will not be met if the burden of paying for each period's government spending is shifted from the old to the young.

Generational Policy

Let's suppose that the fiscal policy just discussed, in which each period's government spending is paid for by that period's elderly, is in place. Now, the government decides to shift the burden of paying for its purchases to later generations. How can this be accomplished, and what will its macroeconomic effects be?

The government can also satisfy its intertemporal budget constraint by charging each *young* person $\bar{g}$ to pay for contemporaneous government purchases. (As Figure 7-3 suggests, it might shift the tax burden from the old to the young by reducing income taxes and raising payroll taxes.) Whereas the previous policy set $z_{ot} = \bar{g}$ and $z_{yt} = 0$, the new policy of setting $z_{yt} = \bar{g}$ and $z_{ot} = 0$ will also satisfy the government intertemporal budget constraint—Z_t still equals $\bar{G}$ in each period. However, the burden on each generation changes. If the shift occurs in period 1, then the generation that is old in period 1 bears no burden *at all*, since it paid no tax when young and, as a result of this shift, none when old, either. The generation that is young at time 1 and subsequent generations have to pay a tax of $\bar{g}$ when young, rather than in old age. Though members of these generations pay $\bar{g}$ under both regimes, having to pay the tax one period earlier raises the present value of their lifetime net tax payments from $\bar{g}/(1 + r_{t+1})$ to $\bar{g}$. Hence, one generation gains and all subsequent generations lose as a result of this shift in fiscal burden.

The shift from taxing the old to taxing the young also has macroeconomic effects. Setting $z_{yt} = \bar{g}$ and $b_{t+1} = 0$ (there is still no government debt) yields a value of $f_t = \bar{g}$. Inserting this value in the general transition equation yields

$$k_{t+1} = A(1 - \beta)k_t^{\beta} - \bar{g}$$

Figure 7-5 Government Purchases Financed by the Young

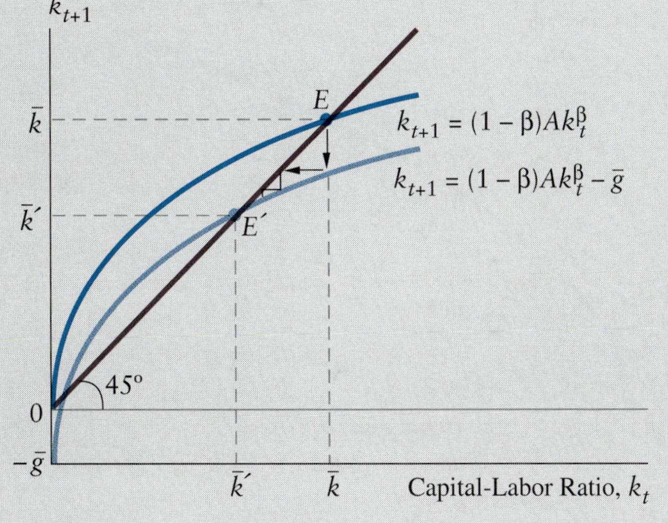

Beginning in the steady state at point E, the introduction of government purchases ($\bar{g}$) financed by taxing the young shifts the transition curve downward by the distance $\bar{g}$. The transition to the new steady state at point E' is governed by the new, lower transition curve. The result is a lower capital-labor ratio, $\bar{k}'$.

The equation tells us that for any given value of the current capital-labor ratio, the next period's capital-labor ratio is now lower by the amount $\bar{g}$. Why? Because the young use some of their wages, wages that otherwise would be saved, to pay taxes.

This change in the transition equation causes the economy to move to a lower level of capital and output. The transition process is governed by a curve that lies a distance $\bar{g}$ below the original curve, as shown in Figure 7-5. From $\bar{k}$, at point E, the economy moves to the new steady-state capital-labor ratio $\bar{k}'$, at point E', as depicted by the arrows in the figure.

As the capital-labor ratio falls, so does the level of output. This is depicted by the drop from $\bar{y}$ to $\bar{y}'$ in Figure 7-6, which graphs the production function: the relationship of output per worker to the capital-labor ratio. As we saw in Chapter 3, less capital per worker means lower labor productivity—and hence lower wages. At the same time, the relative scarcity of capital causes the real interest rate to rise.

The top panel of Table 7-1 provides a numerical illustration of this transition process, assuming values of $\beta = .3$, $A = 6$, and $\bar{g} = 2$. In the initial steady state, in period 0, output per worker is 11.10. There is no net investment, and

Figure 7-6 The Effect of Government Purchases on Output

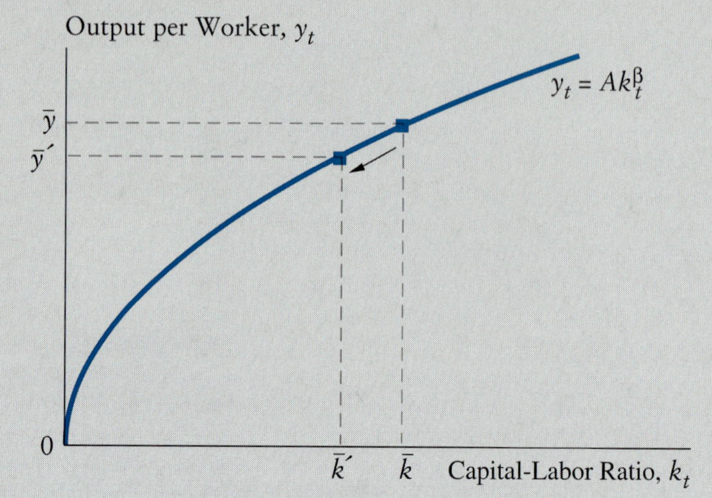

As depicted in Figure 7-5, the introduction of government purchases financed by taxes on the young has the effect of reducing the economy's steady-state capital-labor ratio from $\bar{k}$ to $\bar{k}'$. As the capital-labor ratio falls, per worker output falls along with it, from $\bar{y}$ to $\bar{y}'$.

consumption by the elderly is 9.10. The remaining output is absorbed by government purchases ($\bar{g} = 2$) and paid for by taxes on the elderly, whose generational account has a value 1.40—the discounted value of the tax paid when old. In period 1, the next generation of elderly are relieved of the need to pay taxes, and can now consume an extra 2 units per person. But government purchases don't change. Hence, consumption by households *and* government rises in the aggregate. The savings of each young person, equal to the next period's capital-labor ratio, is reduced by the taxes they must now pay, again 2 units per person. (Their generational account rises to 2 because the tax now must be paid in the first period of life.) As a result, there is an immediate drop in period 2 in the capital-labor ratio. This drop, in turn, leads to lower wages and still lower savings of the young. The process continues until a new steady-state capital-labor ratio is reached. The transition equation is

$$k_{t+1} = 4.2k_t^{.3} - 2$$

Requiring the young to finance government purchases leads to a decline in investment and the capital-labor ratio. Why? Because it is the young who save and provide funds for investment. Indeed, in our simplified two-period model,

Table 7-1 Requiring the Young to Pay for Government Purchases (All variables expressed in per worker terms)

Tax Finance

Period	k	y	c_o	b	z_y	z_o	$\hat{z}$	w	r
0	7.77	11.10	9.10	0.00	0.00	2.00	1.40	7.77	0.43
1	7.77	11.10	11.10	0.00	2.00	0.00	0.00	7.77	0.43
2	5.77	10.15	8.81	0.00	2.00	0.00	2.00	7.11	0.53
3	5.11	9.78	8.04	0.00	2.00	0.00	2.00	6.85	0.57
4	4.85	9.64	7.74	0.00	2.00	0.00	2.00	6.74	0.60
5	4.74	9.57	7.62	0.00	2.00	0.00	2.00	6.70	0.61
6	4.70	9.55	7.56	0.00	2.00	0.00	2.00	6.68	0.61
.	.	.	.	.	.	.	.	.	.
.	.	.	.	.	.	.	.	.	.
.	.	.	.	.	.	.	.	.	.
∞	4.67	9.53	7.53	0.00	2.00	0.00	2.00	6.67	0.61

Debt Finance

Period	k	y	c_o	b	z_y	z_o	$\hat{z}$	w	r
0	7.77	11.10	9.10	0.00	0.00	2.00	1.40	7.77	0.43
1	7.77	11.10	11.10	0.00	0.00	0.00	0.00	7.77	0.43
2	5.77	10.15	8.81	2.00	0.00	3.06	2.00	7.11	0.53
3	5.11	9.78	8.04	2.00	0.00	3.15	2.00	6.85	0.57
4	4.85	9.64	7.74	2.00	0.00	3.19	2.00	6.74	0.60
5	4.74	9.57	7.62	2.00	0.00	3.21	2.00	6.70	0.61
6	4.70	9.55	7.56	2.00	0.00	3.22	2.00	6.68	0.61
.	.	.	.	.	.	.	.	.	.
.	.	.	.	.	.	.	.	.	.
.	.	.	.	.	.	.	.	.	.
∞	4.67	9.53	7.53	2.00	0.00	3.22	2.00	6.67	0.61

Note: Values of $\hat{z}$ correspond to those of the elderly in each respective period. Parameter values assumed: $\alpha = 0$, $\beta = .3$, $A = 6$, $\bar{g} = 2$

the young save everything they have, whereas the old consume everything they have. Even in the much more complicated real world, the same phenomenon—the young consuming a smaller share of their remaining resources than the old—is observed. Shifting the tax burden from the old to the young shifts resources from those who save to those who consume, with the predictable result: consumption increases.

From this comparison, we may draw two conclusions. First, government spending, by itself, need not affect the economy's capital stock. We saw this in the case in which the elderly were taxed. Second, there can be quite different macroeconomic outcomes associated with the same aggregate government financing pattern. In particular, we have seen that pure tax finance ($Z_t = G_t$ for every period t) *can* reduce capital accumulation, depending on how each period's net tax payments are divided between young and old.

THE IMPACT OF GOVERNMENT DEBT

So far, we've considered alternative ways of using taxes to pay for government purchases: taxes on the old and taxes on the young. In neither case, nor in the transition from the first case to the second that we just considered, was the other method of raising funds—government borrowing—used. Now, let's consider a policy of debt finance.

Suppose that, as in the previous example, the government wishes to relieve the old in period 1 of the burden of paying for government purchases. Rather than imposing taxes on the young, the government decides to finance its purchases from period 1 onward by selling bonds. In each period it sells $\bar{g}$ worth of bonds to each young person to raise the funds needed to pay for that period's government purchases. In so doing, it promises to repay these funds with interest in the following period. Hence, beginning in period 2, the government also needs funds to repay the principal and interest on the debt issued in the previous period.

Let's consider the case in which the funds needed to repay the debt in each period come from the old—the same group receiving the principal and interest. In this case, in period 2, the government raises taxes of $\bar{g}(1 + r_2)$ from each old person to cover the interest and principal on outstanding debt while at the same time issuing new debt of $\bar{g}$ to each new young person to pay for that period's government purchases.

We can verify that this fiscal policy satisfies the government intertemporal budget constraint. There is no debt outstanding at the beginning of period 1 and no net tax payments in period 1. We can pair government purchases in period 1 with taxes in period 2, government purchases in period 2 with taxes in period 3, and so forth, to see that for each period's government purchases there are corresponding tax payments that occur one period later but have the same present value. Since each component has the same present value, the sums of the two series will, too—the present value of government purchases will equal the present value of tax payments.

What will the transition look like for this fiscal policy? Recall that in the general transition equation above, all that matters is the sum of z_{yt} and b_{t+1}. In the previous case, in which the young paid taxes, $z_{yt} = \bar{g}$ and $b_{t+1} = 0$. In the present case, in which the young pay no taxes but purchase government debt, $z_{yt} = 0$ and $b_{t+1} = \bar{g}$. In each case f_t, the sum of z_{yt} and b_{t+1}, equals $\bar{g}$. Hence, as before, the transition equation is

$$k_{t+1} = A(1 - \beta)k_t^{\beta} - \bar{g}$$

Since the initial capital-labor ratio is also the same as before, this implies that the entire transition path, including the new steady state, must be the same as well. We can verify this for the specific numerical simulation considered before, in which $\bar{g} = 2$. The bottom panel of Table 7-1 shows that, indeed, nothing is different about the transition except the fiscal variables b_t, z_{yt}, and z_{ot}.

Why do the two policies lead to the same economic behavior? Although the *timing* of tax payments is different for each generation after period 1, there is no difference between the two policies in the time path of generational accounts. For each policy, the generation born in period 0 pays no taxes and each subsequent generational account equals 2, regardless of whether the generation's taxes occur when it is old or young. Because it is the generational account that governs household consumption, there is no difference in consumption in the two cases. Since government purchases are also the same in the two cases, there is no difference in national saving, which is equal to income less consumption and government spending, or in investment, which equals national saving.

At first glance, we might have expected investment to differ in the two cases. When government taxes the young, each young person saves $\bar{g}$ less and buys less capital. Under the fiscal policy that sells debt to the young, the young pay no taxes and can purchase more assets. But not all of this asset acquisition translates into the purchase of productive capital. There is $\bar{g}$ of government debt per young individual that must be purchased as well. Hence, the increase in assets purchased, $\bar{g}$, is just offset by the increase in debt issued, and the capital-labor ratio in period $t + 1$ is exactly the same as in the case of pure tax finance.

The equivalence between these two cases is quite basic. Not only does each household face the same lifetime burden of fiscal policy, the resources it sends to or receives from the government in each period is the same as well. Put simply, if we examined each household's checkbook, we would not be able to tell which policy was in effect. Under the tax-finance policy, each young person pays $\bar{g}$ to the government when young and nothing when old. Under the debt-finance policy, each young person pays no taxes when young but buys $\bar{g}$ worth of debt from the government—it still sends $\bar{g}$ to the government, even if this payment is not referred to as a tax. In old age, the bondholder receives a repayment of principal and interest, $\bar{g}(1 + r_{t+1})$, but must also pay the same amount in taxes. Net receipts from the government are zero, as in the case of tax finance. Hence, in both instances, each person sends the government $\bar{g}$ when young and receives on net nothing when old. How we describe the flows between households and the government influences how we measure national debt; it does not affect household behavior.

Thus, a fiscal policy that shifts the burden of paying for government purchases from earlier to later generations places the economy on a transition path to a lower level of capital and output per worker. This policy *may* be accomplished using government debt. But it is the distribution of the fiscal burden among generations (which can be measured by generational accounts) rather than government debt per se that determines a fiscal policy's effect on national saving and capital accumulation. Concerns that fiscal policies relying on the accumulation of national debt will depress saving and investment may well be valid. But such concerns can be valid even in cases in which there is no government borrowing at all, if the generational pattern of taxation is similar.

Distinguishing Private from Public Saving

The fact that equivalent fiscal policies can be achieved with and without the use of national debt has implications for our measurement of saving. We learned in earlier chapters that national saving equals national investment. Since investment is exactly the same under the tax-financed and debt-financed government spending policies just considered, national saving must also be the same. But the division of national saving between *private saving* and *government saving* differs.

Private saving refers to the increase in household net worth from one period to the next (the change in households' assets minus their liabilities). Government saving refers to the increase in government net worth (government assets minus government liabilities). In the shift from taxing the young each period to pay for $\bar{g}$ to borrowing from the young each period (and taxing them more when they're old), there is an increase in private net worth and an equally large decrease in government net worth. This leaves the country's total (private plus government) net worth unchanged.

Here's why. After the shift to debt finance, each young person spends all of his wages, rather than his wages less taxes, to acquire assets, which raises the net worth he brings into old age. But the government, rather than collecting taxes from the young, borrows from them, which increases its liabilities and reduces its net worth. The increase in private net worth in the period when the transition from tax finance to debt finance occurs is recorded as private saving; the decrease in government net worth is recorded as government dissaving. These changes in private and government saving offset one another, so national saving remains the same. This result provides an important lesson: we must look at *national* saving, and not at private saving or government saving separately, to get an accurate picture of saving behavior.

FISCAL POLICY IN THE OPEN ECONOMY

Until now, this chapter's analysis has been based on the one-country version of our model, in which changes in national saving lead to equal changes in domestic investment. However, it is not hard to extend the results from Chapter 6 to study fiscal policy in the open economy as well.

As an example, let's continue to examine the two equivalent policies under which the fiscal burden is shifted from the old to the young in period 1. As we saw in Figure 7-5, these policies move the entire transition curve downward. In an open economy, the same downward shift would occur but, as we learned in Chapter 6, the similar curve in this case tells us just the country's asset holdings per elderly individual in the following period, not that period's capital-labor

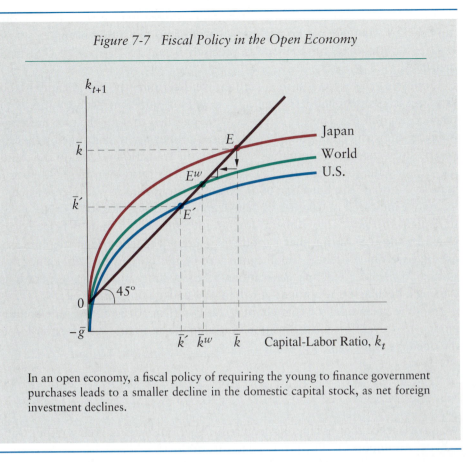

Figure 7-7 Fiscal Policy in the Open Economy

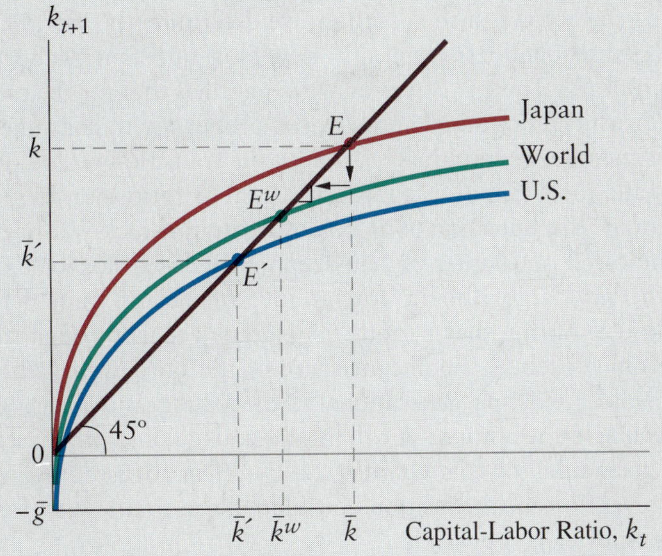

In an open economy, a fiscal policy of requiring the young to finance government purchases leads to a smaller decline in the domestic capital stock, as net foreign investment declines.

ratio.[17] For the sake of concreteness, let's assume that a second country, say Japan, initially has the same transition curve and equilibrium as the U.S., and that both countries begin in the long-run steady state. With two identical countries, the steady state is the same as in the one-country model and is located at point E in Figure 7-7. In such a steady state, as we discussed in Chapter 6, there is no net foreign ownership of either country's capital stock and neither country has a trade deficit or surplus.

When the U.S. policy changes, and its asset curve shifts downward, the transition follows the process illustrated in Figure 7-7. There is now a world transition curve (labeled "World") that lies between the asset curves for the U.S. and Japan, because it indicates the average of the two countries' assets per elderly individual, weighted by their respective populations. We determine each country's asset holdings in period 1 by moving vertically from the initial, period 1 capital-labor ratio $\bar{k}$ to that country's asset curve. This exercise indicates that U.S. assets fall short of U.S. capital in period 2 (as indicated by the height of the world

17. Assets refer here to capital owned either directly or indirectly through financial assets. They do not include government bonds.

transition curve), so there must be foreign investment by Japan in the U.S. during period 1. As there are no net foreign assets initially, at the beginning of period 1, this inbound investment is precisely equal to period 1's U.S. trade deficit.[18]

Following the arrows in the diagram, we determine the world capital-labor ratio in each subsequent period until the new long-run capital-labor ratio, $\bar{k}^w$, is reached at point E^w. This transition analysis parallels that for the case presented in Figure 6-6, which considered an increased propensity to consume by the U.S. young. Investment flows into the U.S. during the transition period. In the resulting steady state, the U.S. has a higher capital-labor ratio than it would have in autarky (at point E'), but some of its domestic capital stock is foreign-owned.

As we indicated in Chapter 6, many economists used this logic in the 1980s to explain the very large inbound foreign investment and trade deficits experienced by the U.S. during that period. They argued that, through the increased use of government debt, a significant share of the burden of fiscal policy was shifted from older existing generations to the young and future generations, causing a decline in the amount of capital the young could purchase.

For the remainder of this chapter, we'll return to using the one-country model. However, for each transition considered, the same type of extension to the open economy case is possible.

THE NATIONAL DEBT AND SOCIAL SECURITY

We have learned that fiscal policy can reduce national saving even without using deficits. An important illustration comes from the U.S. Social Security system.

The U.S. Social Security System

The most important transfer program in the United States is the federal government's Social Security system, which encompasses three major programs: Old Age and Survivors' Insurance (OASI), Disability Insurance (DI), and Health Insurance (HI)—Medicare. (The first two programs are sometimes considered together, as OASDI. All three programs combined are represented by the acronym *OASDHI*.) In recent years, nearly half of the federal, state, and local government transfer payments (other than interest and subsidies to government enterprises) were benefits paid by the federal government through these three programs.

Enacted in 1935, OASDI in 1993 paid $304.6 billion to retired and disabled workers and their surviving spouses and dependent children. The fastest-growing component of OASDHI is Medicare, introduced in 1965. By 1993 it accounted for $130.6 billion in transfers. During the period 1980–1993 alone, Medicare payments relative to GDP grew from 1.3 percent to 2.0 percent.

---

18. Recall that the trade surplus $X - M$ equals net foreign investment I^f minus earnings on net foreign assets, E, which in this case are zero.

The transfer payments made by the Social Security system are financed through *payroll taxes*: taxes deducted directly from wages and salaries by employers. Until the mid-1980s, the Social Security system operated basically as a tax-transfer system, with payroll taxes on working people roughly equal to the benefits of older retirees—a financing approach known as *pay-as-you-go (PAYG)*. This PAYG approach persisted through the years even as Social Security benefits rose.

Yet, even though no surplus or deficit was involved, these increases in the size of the Social Security program involved shifts in the fiscal burden. Each increase in benefits transferred additional resources to older generations and required additional net tax payments from younger ones.

Adding Social Security to the Model

In terms of our model, introducing Social Security benefits of, say, s per old individual provides the first generation that receives them with additional lifetime resources. However, members of each subsequent generation t are worse off. They receive an additional transfer payment when old ($z_{ot+1} = -s$), but (since there are the same number of people in each generation) must pay $z_{yt} = s$ more when young to satisfy PAYG balance. The generational account is therefore

$$\hat{z}_t = s - \frac{s}{(1 + r_{t+1})} = \frac{r_{t+1}s}{(1 + r_{t+1})}$$

The account equals the interest that each young person loses by having to pay the amount s when young before getting it back when old. For example, a payroll tax of s = \$3,000 today, even if offset by Social Security benefits of \$3,000 in old age, still deprives the individual of the opportunity to earn interest on that \$3,000. The present value of this loss is the interest on \$3,000, discounted because the loss occurs in old age.

We saw earlier that shifting the burden of government spending from the old to the young can reduce national saving. This is also the case for a policy that transfers resources directly from the young to the old. Setting $b_{t+1} = 0$ and $z_{yt} = s$ in the general closed-economy transition equation yields $f_t = s$ and

$$k_{t+1} = A(1 - \beta)k_t^{\beta} - s$$

This equation is the same expression as in the case of government consumption purchases but with transfers to the old, s, substituted for government consumption, $\bar{g}$. As before, the resources of the old, who have a high propensity to consume (in our model, they consume everything they have), are being increased at the expense of the young, who would have invested the funds they must now give up.

As in the case of paying for government purchases, this policy of increasing Social Security transfers to the old (which, in the U.S., has been accomplished through taxes on the young) *could* have been accomplished using government debt. In the period the transfers were introduced, say period 1, the government could have sold an amount s worth of debt to each young person rather than levying taxes immediately. It would then require those born in period 1 to pay taxes when old in period 2 to meet the principal and interest on that debt, $s(1 + r_2)$ per person. Then, in period 2, the transfers to this old generation of s per individual would be financed by debt sold to the young in period 2, to be repaid with interest using taxes on the same generation when old, in period 3. The same pattern would be followed in subsequent periods. The net fiscal burden on each generation would be the same as with direct tax finance (since a tax of s in the first period of life has the same present value as a tax of $s(1 + r_{t+1})$ in the second period), but this version of the policy would result in the creation of government debt.

Because it would shift resources from the young to the old, such debt creation would be associated with a decline in national saving. However, as in the previous case of financing government purchases, it is the underlying shift in the fiscal burden across generations, and not the presence or absence of national debt, that causes the decline in saving. Indeed, in the case of Social Security, economists have long emphasized the equivalence between the actual policy of tax-financed transfers and a hypothetical one using debt, by constructing a measure of the unfunded liability of the Social Security system, indicating how large the debt would be under the equivalent debt-finance policy.[19]

Case Study: Social Security and the Baby Boom

The concept of Social Security's unfunded liability helps illustrate why the Social Security system has been a source of concern in recent years. At present, the working population is relatively large, thanks to the post-World War II "baby boom." In exchange for contributing to the Social Security system over the years, these workers have been promised substantial health and old-age benefits when they retire. These promises have greatly increased Social Security's unfunded liabilities.

But who will pay these benefits? In the next century, when the baby boom generation is retired, the working population will be smaller relative to the retired population than it is now. If these future workers must pay all the Social Security benefits for those presently working, their burden will be very large. To avoid placing a large burden on these workers, the federal government recently has deviated from the general historical practice of PAYG finance. In 1983, it

19. The concept and measurement of this liability was described by Martin Feldstein in "Social Security, Induced Retirement and Aggregate Capital Accumulation," *Journal of Political Economy* 82 (1974): 905–926.

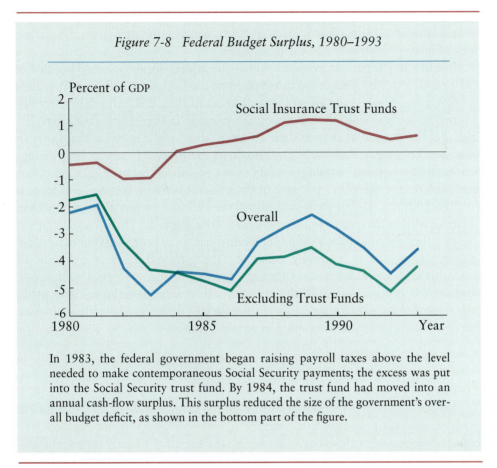

Figure 7-8 Federal Budget Surplus, 1980–1993

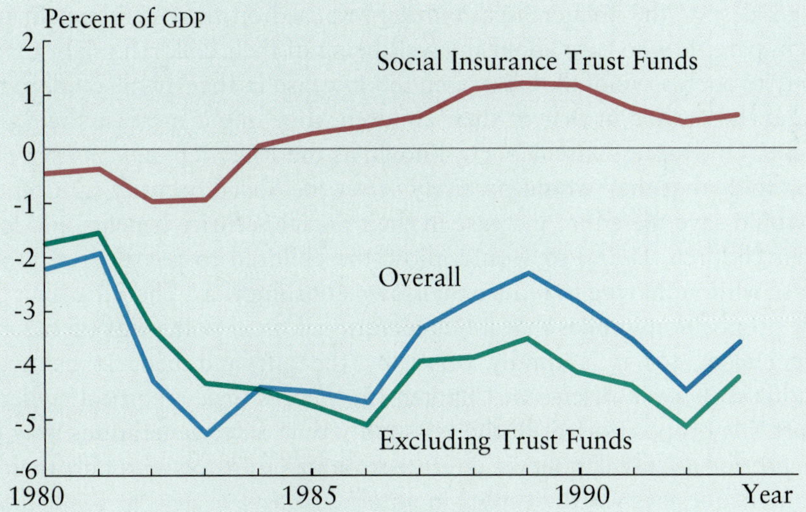

In 1983, the federal government began raising payroll taxes above the level needed to make contemporaneous Social Security payments; the excess was put into the Social Security trust fund. By 1984, the trust fund had moved into an annual cash-flow surplus. This surplus reduced the size of the government's overall budget deficit, as shown in the bottom part of the figure.

Source: *Survey of Current Business*, various issues

began raising payroll taxes above those needed for contemporaneous benefits, putting the extra funds in a social insurance *trust fund* to be used to help pay retirement benefits for the baby boom generation. In terms of the government's annual budget, this policy shift has put the Social Security system in an annual cash flow *surplus*. This surplus has reduced the government's overall budget deficit to a considerable extent in recent years, as Figure 7-8 shows.

Put simply, the Social Security trust fund is being accumulated to help offset the very large Social Security liability currently outstanding. Unfortunately, the projected growth of the trust fund appears to fall far short of the amount needed to cover this liability to the baby boom and other generations.

A Caveat: Ricardian Equivalence

This chapter's analysis has emphasized how a shift in the fiscal burden among generations alters capital accumulation and output. But what if those who must pay more are related to those who pay less? How, for example, will parents behave knowing that increased Social Security benefits for their own generation mean higher payroll taxes on their children?

In our model, parents consume all of the added Social Security benefits in old age, despite the greater fiscal burden imposed on their children. In reality, though, parents who care about the well-being of their children might react differently to such a windfall. Observing the increase in their own standard of living, and the decline in that of their children, they might increase their gifts or bequests. One rather extreme view, known as the *Ricardian equivalence proposition*, holds that they would *precisely offset* the Social Security transfers. Parents would save the entire increase in their Social Security benefits and leave it to their children. Doing so would allow the children to pay their payroll tax increase without having to reduce their own consumption. The Ricardian equivalence proposition implies that intergenerational fiscal policy has no macroeconomic effects, for it is simply offset by the gift and bequest behavior of individuals. As we'll discuss in Chapter 15, there is little empirical evidence to support this proposition. Still, the possibility that older generations may offset some portion of fiscal policy's intergenerational transfers through their own gifts and bequests is worth keeping in mind.

GOVERNMENT CAPITAL FORMATION

To this point, we have focused primarily on the revenue side of the government budget: how governments raise money to pay for government purchases or transfer programs to the elderly. Whatever the use of the funds raised, the distinction on the expenditure side between government purchases and transfers has not appeared particularly important. This is largely due to our assumption that government expenditures, whether for direct purchases or transfers to the elderly, do not contribute to capital accumulation. We have assumed that elderly households consume all resources at their disposal, and, implicitly, that all government purchases are for consumption, rather than being invested in capital. In reality, governments do purchase capital goods, such as roads and buildings. Government capital goods, like those purchased by households or firms, add to the nation's productive capacity.[20]

How is government capital added to our model? The nation's capital stock includes government-owned capital as well as that owned by households. Adding government capital, say k^g_{t+1} per worker at the beginning of period $t+1$, to capital purchased by households leads to the following transition equation:

$$k_{t+1} = A(1 - \beta)k_t^{\beta} - f_t + k^g_{t+1}$$

20. Indeed, some research has even suggested that government investment is more productive than private investment. See, for example, David A. Aschauer, "Is Public Expenditure Productive?" *Journal of Monetary Economics* (1989): 177–200.

Using this transition equation, let's return to the case in which government purchases an amount $N\bar{g}$ in each period, financed by the young. But now, suppose that these government purchases are capital goods that are added to the economy's overall productive capital stock. Since the purchases of capital are financed by the young, both f_t and k^g_{t+1} equal $\bar{g}$. Hence, all the fiscal terms in the transition equation disappear, leaving us with our basic no-fiscal-policy transition equation. This result makes sense: taking resources from the young causes them to purchase less capital, but the government offsets this reduction through its own capital purchases.

Case Study: Government Investment in the U.S.

As we have just seen, government capital purchases have a different effect on the macroeconomy than do purchases for immediate consumption. To measure national capital formation, we should add government investment to saving by the private sector when computing national saving. We should, but the government budget does not.

Although government statisticians do track the level of government investment, the national income accounts do not treat government investment any differently than government purchases for immediate consumption. As a result, national saving (as defined in Chapter 5 and measured by GDP less consumption and government purchases) and domestic investment, which normally focus only on private sector capital accumulation, are both understated by the extent of government investment. Because of this, the impact of changes in government spending on national capital formation may be misinterpreted. Taking account of government investment suggests that the recent decline in domestic investment discussed in Chapter 2 is even more significant than was indicated there, because government investment has declined sharply.

The capital stock growth rates (equal to net investment divided by the capital stock) since 1960 of both the U.S. private and government sectors are shown in Figure 7-9. The figure shows a decline in the growth rate of the private capital stock in the 1970s and 1980s, but a sharper decline in the growth rate of government capital. Government capital grew faster than private capital in the 1960s, but it grew more slowly throughout the 1970s and 1980s.[21] During the 1980s, the government's net capital stock grew in real terms at an annual rate of just 1.4 percent, compared to 2.5 percent for the private capital stock. Since real GDP grew by 2.6 percent annually over the same period, this means that the government capital stock failed to keep pace with GDP. There was no comparable drop in total government *purchases* relative to GDP, which grew at 2.8 percent during the 1980s. Thus, the lack of distinction between government investment and consumption in the national income accounts masked a shift away from government investment.

21. It is also interesting to note that government investment has tended to be less volatile than private investment, varying more gradually from year to year. Thus, whereas private investment dropped sharply as a share of GDP in the early 1990s, government investment remained relatively stable. We saw in Chapter 4 that the volatility of private investment plays a major part in the overall output fluctuations of business cycles.

Figure 7-9 Growth Rates of Net Capital Stocks, 1960–1992

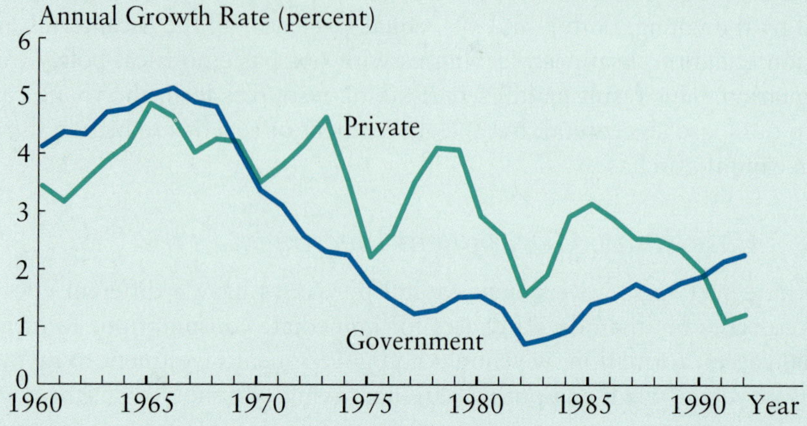

The economy's productive capital stock includes government capital as well as private capital. Since 1965 the growth rate of the private capital stock has declined. Over that same period, the growth rate of the government capital stock has fallen even faster. In recent years, the government capital stock has failed to keep pace with the growth of GDP.

Source: *Survey of Current Business*, various issues

FURTHER EFFECTS ON SAVING: INTRAGENERATIONAL TRANSFERS AND DISTORTIONS

Each of the previous case studies showed a way in which the composition of the government budget can influence national saving. Increases in transfer programs will depress saving if they redistribute resources from the young to the old. Increases in the share of government purchases devoted to immediate consumption reduce national saving even more directly.

In this section, we consider two additional channels through which fiscal policy affects saving. These are intragenerational transfers—the redistribution of funds among members of the same generation, rather than across generations—and the use of distortionary fiscal policy.

Intragenerational Redistribution: The Safety Net and Its Effects

Government transfer programs serve to transfer resources not only among different generations but also among members of given generations. We may think of such intragenerational redistribution as providing a "safety net" for the less fortunate members of each generation. Even though the transfers may occur within a single generation, there can still be an impact on overall saving.

There are two possible effects on saving of such intragenerational transfers, one associated with the transfers themselves and the other simply with the knowledge that they exist. First, transfers will increase consumption and reduce saving if those who receive the transfers consume a higher fraction of their resources than do those who pay for the transfers. As we'll see in Chapter 15, there is evidence that some poorer households consume whatever resources are available to them, rather than saving for the future as our two-period life-cycle model would suggest.

In addition, the presence of a social safety net may lead individuals not to save for the "rainy day"—not to protect themselves in the event of unemployment or illness. Such protection is, after all, one rationale for having the safety net. Some observers have suggested that this increased sense of government protection may have contributed to the decline in U.S. saving in the 1980s that was documented earlier.

In our general two-period life-cycle model (with consumption when young as well as when old), each of these reductions in the propensity to save increases the amount that the average individual consumes when young—like an increase in the parameter α. As we discussed in Chapter 3, such a change lowers the transition curve and leads to a lower steady-state capital stock.

Distortionary Fiscal Policy

To this point, we have analyzed government taxes largely as if they were *lump-sum* taxes—simply assessments on individuals requiring them to pay a certain amount to the government. We have treated transfers in the same way, simply as sums given to individuals. Some taxes and transfers actually do work in this way, but most do not. Instead, they are tied to some aspect of the individual's (or firm's) economic behavior. For example, a sales tax is tied to purchases of goods and services, an income tax to the amount of income earned. In most cases, taxing a particular activity distorts behavior. As intuition suggests, a taxpayer will tend to reduce whatever activity is subject to tax. Less of the taxed activity will take place than if the government collected an equivalent amount of tax independent of the level of that activity.

The appendix shows how a tax on capital income can distort and discourage household saving behavior. The impact is similar to an increase in the parameter α that determines how much households consume when young and how much they save. The result is a lower transition curve and a lower steady-state capital stock. Other taxes distort other household decisions. Taxes on labor income—both the income tax and the payroll tax used to finance the Social Security system—distort the household's decision about how much to work and when to retire. Taxes on individual commodities, such as liquor, gasoline, tobacco, or telephone calls, discourage the purchase of these commodities. Long studied by economists, these effects received heightened emphasis during the 1980s under the rubric of **supply-side economics**. Interpretations of this doctrine range from the generally accepted view that taxes distort behavior, sometimes in important ways, to the much more extreme view that reductions in distortionary taxation

Supply-side economics
The view that marginal tax rates exert an important influence on the behavior of households and firms

actually raise revenue by bringing forth more of the taxed activity, be it work effort or saving.

Case Study: Tax Policy in the 1980s

Whatever its exact meaning or its merits, supply-side economics did exert a considerable influence on policy making during the 1980s. Perhaps its most significant impact was on the *marginal tax rate*—the additional tax due per additional dollar of household income.

Through two major and controversial pieces of tax legislation enacted during the Reagan administration, the Economic Recovery Tax Act of 1981 and the Tax Reform Act of 1986, the maximum marginal tax rate on household income was reduced by more than half—from 70 percent in 1980 to 33 percent in 1988. Figure 7-10 shows the marginal tax rates faced by a married couple at different levels of real (1987 dollars) income in 1980, 1984, and 1988. The figure shows quite clearly that the biggest reductions in marginal tax rates occurred at higher income levels, where marginal rates and their distortions are the highest.[22] In fact, the tax system moved much closer to what is called a *flat rate tax*—an income tax with a single marginal tax rate—which its supporters have argued is simpler as well as less distortionary.[23]

If income taxes distort behavior, what is so controversial about lowering them? The problem is that simply reducing income taxes is not a feasible fiscal policy change. If the government intertemporal budget constraint is initially in balance, lowering income taxes reduces the government's net tax receipts and throws the intertemporal budget constraint out of balance. Restoring balance would require a reduction in government purchases or an increase in net tax payments, either immediately or in the future. Deferring the decision of how to respond until some future period makes the decision no less inevitable, although it may shift the burden (*and* the tax distortions) to future generations. Responding immediately by raising other taxes may simply replace the distortions of the income tax with the distortions of some other tax.

It *is* possible to reduce high marginal income tax rates *without* reducing income tax collections—by making the tax system less progressive. By 1993, for example, after some additional changes in 1990, the U.S. federal income tax consisted of three rates—15 percent, 28 percent, and 31 percent—depending on an individual's income level. Low-income individuals faced a marginal tax rate of 15 percent, high-income individuals a marginal tax rate of 31 percent. It would have been possible to eliminate the top rate, taxing no income at more than 28 percent, if we were willing to raise the first rate above 15 percent. This would have prevented the most serious income tax distortion, but would also have shifted some of the tax burden from the rich to the poor. What policy did

22. Indeed, in 1988, the highest levels of income did *not* face the highest marginal tax rate of 33 percent. This doesn't mean that the wealthy paid a smaller share of their total income in taxes; it simply means that they paid less tax on their last dollars of income earned than individuals in the 33 percent tax bracket.
23. See, for example, Robert Hall and Alvin Rabushka, *Low Tax, Simple Tax, Flat Tax* (New York: McGraw-Hill, 1982).

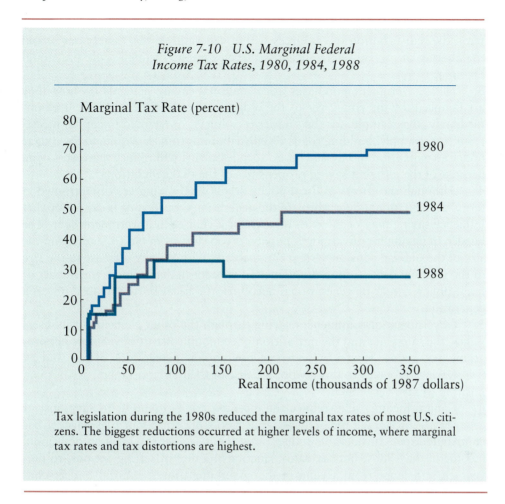

Figure 7-10 U.S. Marginal Federal Income Tax Rates, 1980, 1984, 1988

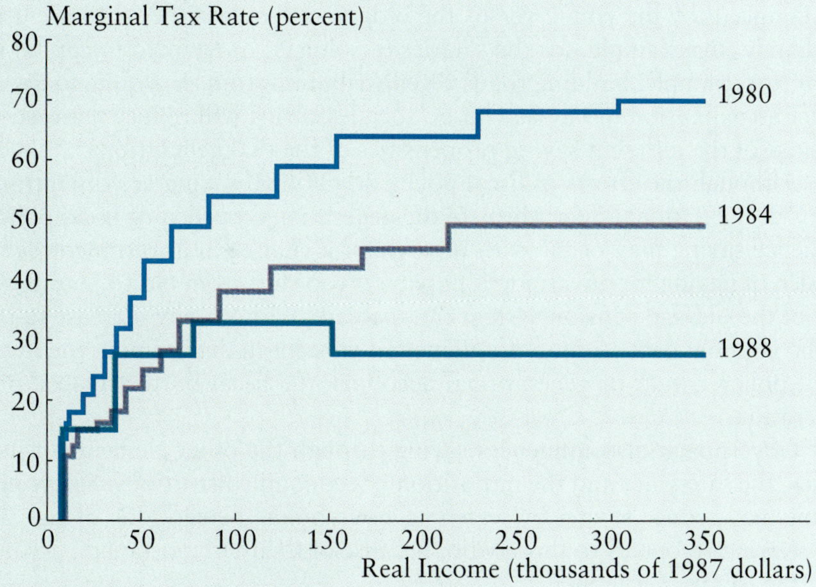

Tax legislation during the 1980s reduced the marginal tax rates of most U.S. citizens. The biggest reductions occurred at higher levels of income, where marginal tax rates and tax distortions are highest.

government actually follow? Based on the judgment that too much attention had been paid to distortions and too little to the distribution of the tax burden, President Clinton proposed and Congress agreed to an *increase* in the top marginal rate to 39.6 percent, combined with a reduction in the taxes faced by the working poor.

Chapter Summary

1. This chapter has discussed the nature of fiscal policy—how government borrowing and taxation are used to raise resources and how these resources are spent on government purchases and transfer payments. Fiscal policy is dynamic because current and future decisions are linked through the government intertemporal budget constraint, which requires the present value of net tax payments (taxes less transfers) to equal the current level of government debt plus the present value of government purchases.

2. Our analysis identified the macroeconomic effects of four types of government policy: the financing of government purchases, the redistribution of resources among generations (as through a pay-as-you-go social security system), the redistribution of resources within generations (the "safety net"), and the altering of private sector incentives (for example, through a tax on capital income).

3. How government purchases affect national saving depends on how they are financed (by the young versus the old) as well as whether they are used immediately (for example, for the salaries of soldiers) or devoted to capital investment (for example, building roads). Redistribution from the young to the old, as under an expansion of pay-as-you-go social security, will reduce national saving because of the different saving propensities of the two generations.

4. Although the effects of fiscal policy on national saving are often framed in terms of the national debt, shifts in the generational burden of fiscal policy that influence saving may occur with or without a change in government debt. The burden of paying for government purchases can shift from old to young, and the size of the old-age pension system can increase, without any increase in the size of the national debt. A more fundamental concept in determining the impact of fiscal policy is that of generational accounts, the fiscal burden placed on each generation.

5. Government also influences saving through the other elements of its fiscal policy, the safety net and the imposition of economic distortions. Safety net programs may reduce saving by lessening households' perceptions of risk and by transferring resources to those who, because of their circumstances, are not in a position to save very much.

6. Capital income taxes reduce the incentive for households to save, just as other taxes discourage the activities they tax. Concern about these distortions contributed to a considerable reduction in the marginal tax rates on household income in the 1980s, but tax rate reductions require offsetting actions, to prevent an imbalance from arising in the government intertemporal budget constraint. Recent increases in marginal tax rates arose from a need to balance the GIBC and from a belief that too much of the tax burden had been shifted to those in lower tax brackets.

7. In an open economy, reductions in national saving that arise from government action have an impact similar to those caused by changes in private behavior. In each instance, reductions in national saving lead to a temporary inflow of foreign investment and a trade deficit. Many economists argued that the trade deficits of the 1980s arose from government fiscal policies adopted during the period.

Key Concepts

Fiscal policy
Budget deficit
Intergenerational redistribution
Transfer payments
National debt
Primary deficit
Government intertemporal budget constraint (GIBC)
Generational account
Supply-side economics

Review Questions

1. What is the *government budget*? What is the *budget deficit*? How has the federal budget deficit behaved in recent decades?
2. Describe the ways in which the government can finance its expenditures.
3. What is the *national debt*? Write the formula for the stock of government debt. Explain the difference between government expenditures and government purchases of goods and services. What are *net taxes*? What is the *primary deficit* and why might the national debt grow even if the primary deficit is zero?
4. Explain the *government intertemporal budget constraint*. Why can it be said that fiscal policy consists of a series of interdependent decisions over time?
5. Explain the "simplified model" adopted in this chapter. That is, even prior to the inclusion of fiscal policy, how is consumption behavior in the two-period life-cycle model modified in the present chapter? How is the household budget constraint modified to include individual net taxes? What is the expression for aggregate tax payments?
6. What is a *generational account*? Which generational account is larger, a one-period tax imposed on the young or the same amount of tax imposed on the same individuals when they are old? Why? What is the typical lifetime pattern of the components of generational accounts?
7. How is the transition equation modified to reflect the simplified consumption decision assumed in this chapter? How is the transition equation modified to include fiscal policy? Explain what is included in the fiscal policy term and why it makes sense for them to be included.
8. Explain the difference between a payroll tax and a consumption tax. In this model, on whom does each fall? What are their effects on the transition equation?
9. What conclusions were reached in the chapter regarding the effect of government consumption on the level of national investment? In particular, does the method of finance matter? Why or why not?
10. Explain each of the following concepts of saving: *private saving*; *public saving*; and *national saving*. What effect does government consumption have on the *level* of national saving? What effect does the method of finance have on the *composition* of that national saving between public and private sources?
11. What three major programs does the *Social Security system* encompass? Historically, how were Social Security transfer payments financed? How and why has the method of financing changed more recently? Does a $4,000 payroll tax payment when young offset by a $4,000 Social Security benefit when old have any impact on the generational account? Why or why not?
12. What is *Social Security's unfunded liability*? To whom is it an asset and to whom is it a liability?
13. What are examples of *government capital formation*? Write the formula for the transition equation assuming that government capital is added to the nation's productive capital stock. How does government investment financed by taxes on the young affect the transition path?
14. How is government investment treated in the national income accounts? How *should* it be treated? Why? What is the effect of the accounting practice on estimates of overall capital formation?

15. Under what circumstances will intragenerational transfers (e.g., providing a *safety net* to poorer individuals within the same generation) affect capital formation? What will the effect(s) be?
16. What is a *distortionary tax* and what implications would such a tax have for the two-period life-cycle model?
17. Define *marginal tax rate* and *flat rate tax*. Assuming that marginal tax rates rise with income level, explain how it is possible to reduce high marginal tax rates while leaving tax collections unaltered. What are the implications for tax progressivity?

Numerical Questions

1. Suppose that the government initially has no debt, but suddenly decides to spend \$500 each year while collecting only \$450 in tax revenue each year. Also suppose that the interest rate, r, is expected to remain at 5 percent for the foreseeable future.

- **a.** Compute the *primary deficit* in each of the next four years.
- **b.** Compute the national debt in each of the next four years.
- **c.** Compare the growth rate of the national debt to the interest rate. Does the government's fiscal policy satisfy the GIBC? Why or why not?
- **d.** How might the government change its policy so that the GIBC is satisfied?

2. Suppose that the government enacts a new tax scheme whereby it collects \$60 each period from young people and \$40 each period from old people. Also, suppose that the interest rate per period, r, is expected to remain at 200 percent for the foreseeable future.

- **a.** What is the generational account of the old immediately after the tax scheme is implemented?
- **b.** What is the generational account of the young immediately after the tax scheme is implemented?
- **c.** Suppose that the government continues to collect \$100 each period in total, but now makes the young pay only \$30 each period. What happens to the generational account of the old immediately after the change? to the generational account of the young?

3. Suppose that output and production are described by Cobb-Douglas functions, and that the following parameter values hold:

Parameter	**Value**
A	4
α	0
β	0.3
N	100

- **a.** Calculate the steady-state capital-labor ratio and level of output.

b. Suppose that the government decides to purchase 1 unit of output for government consumption each period. To pay for it, the government collects taxes equal to 1 from the old each period. What will the steady-state capital-labor ratio and output level be? Compare these answers to those calculated in part a. Explain any differences or similarities.

c. Now suppose that the government changes its policy and pays for its spending by collecting taxes equal to 1 from the young each period. Calculate the capital-labor ratio and output level for the two periods following the policy change. Compare these answers to the steady state values calculated in part b. Explain any differences or similarities.

d. Finally, suppose that the government continues to collect taxes equal to 1 from the young each period. Now, however, the government uses the tax revenue to purchase 0.5 unit of capital and 0.5 unit of consumption instead of 1 unit of consumption. What will be the impact of the policy change on the capital-labor ratio and output level in the two periods after the change? Do these differ from the values calculated in part c? Why or why not?

4. Assume that the economy is in a steady state described by the parameters given in question 3. The government embarks on a fiscal policy whereby it purchases 3 units of output each period and finances its spending by collecting taxes of 3 from the young.

a. What values do the capital-labor ratio and interest rate take in the two periods after the change?

b. What is the generational account in the two periods after the change?

c. Suppose again that the economy is in the steady state described by the parameters in question 3. The government then decides to finance spending of 3 each period by borrowing 3 from the young and then taxing the old in the following period by an amount sufficient both to pay back the 3 and to pay interest on the borrowing. What values does the capital-labor ratio take in the two periods following the change? Do they differ from the ratios calculated in part a?

d. What values does the interest rate take in the two periods after the change described in part c, and how much tax will be collected from the old in each period?

5. Assume that the economy is in a steady state described by the parameters given in question 3. Starting today, the government implements a pay-as-you-go tax/transfer program whereby young people pay 2 each period to finance a payment of 2 to each old person.

a. What is the capital-labor ratio and output level in the two periods after the change? How do these values differ from the initial steady-state values? Why?

b. Calculate the impact of the pay-as-you-go plan on national saving in the two periods after the change. What is the plan's impact on private saving in these periods? on public saving?

Analytical Questions

1. If the government imposes a tax on the young to finance government consumption, what happens to the steady-state capital-labor ratio, private saving, public saving, and national saving? Now suppose that the elderly care enough about their children to provide them with a gift equal to the amount of the government tax. Relative to the initial steady state (i.e., with no fiscal policy), what will be the effect on the steady-state capital-labor ratio, private saving, public saving, national saving, and the composition of consumption?
2. In an open economy with two identical countries, what effect does a payroll tax in one country (to pay for government consumption) have on the worldwide capital-labor ratio and on that country's own net foreign asset position? What happens to its trade balance?
3. The government issues bonds to the young in order to finance a large one-time government consumption expenditure (e.g., for a war). When the bonds come due in the next period, they are reissued to the young at that time in the amount of the initial principal. The interest is obtained by a tax on the elderly at that time. The same procedure is followed in every subsequent period. Explain why this fiscal policy and method of finance satisfy the government intertemporal budget constraint. What is the effect of this fiscal policy on the generational account? Why? What is the effect on the steady-state capital-labor ratio, personal saving, public saving, and national saving? In what way(s) is this policy similar to a pay-as-you-go Social Security system? In what way(s) is the policy different?
4. Assume the same one-time government consumption expenditure and financing scheme described in question 3. After some number of years, the government repudiates the debt—that is, it unilaterally cancels its obligation to pay back either the principal or the interest due on the national debt. Because it no longer needs to raise revenue to make interest payments, it ceases to tax the elderly. What happens to personal saving, national saving, and the steady-state capital-labor ratio? Why don't governments typically adopt such a strategy?
5. During the 1980s, large federal budget deficits coincided with large trade deficits. Some analysts described this situation as "the twin deficits." The implication was that the simultaneous increase in the deficits was not a chance event. Rather, the large budget deficits *caused* the large trade deficits. Is it reasonable to argue that high budget deficits lead to high trade deficits? Will the deficits always, sometimes, or never be "twins"?

APPENDIX

The Analysis of Distortionary Taxation

In the text, we discussed the fact that taxes can distort behavior. An important example of distortionary taxation is the *capital income tax* imposed on the return to saving—claiming for the government a fraction of each additional dollar of interest income the household earns. By reducing the rate of return households earn from additional saving, the capital income tax discourages saving. We can see this by comparing the household's saving behavior in response to a capital income tax to its response to lump-sum taxation. To do so, we need to go back to our original two-period model of the household, in which the household does not automatically save everything it can, but instead consumes a fraction α of its resources in the first period—its wages—and saves the rest. Its assets when old equal

$$a_{t+1} = \alpha w_t$$

How would this asset accumulation be affected by a capital income tax? We can think of such a tax as equivalent to lowering r_{t+1}, the rate of return to saving. We have already seen, in Chapter 2, that for the Cobb-Douglas model, a reduction in the rate of return does not affect first-period consumption or asset purchases. Hence, a capital income tax *does not affect* the level of assets acquired by households.

The impact of capital income taxation is shown in Figure 7-11, which uses the indifference curve analysis we developed in Chapter 2. At point 0, in the absence of taxation, the household consumes a fraction α of its wages w_t when young, saving the rest for consumption when old. The imposition of a capital income tax is equivalent to a reduction in the interest rate. Because the slope of the budget line equals $-(1 + r_{t+1})$, this tax causes the budget line to become flatter. The result, as we have already noted, is that the household still chooses to consume αw_t when young, letting the capital income tax it must pay come entirely at the expense of consumption when old. This choice is shown at point 1 in the figure.

Is this inconsistent with the previous claim that capital income taxation reduces saving? Not really. To see why, we need to make the right comparison—to a tax that is not based on capital income. At point 1 in Figure 7-11, the household's capital income taxes amount to T. This is the vertical distance between

Figure 7-11 The Impact of Capital Income Taxation

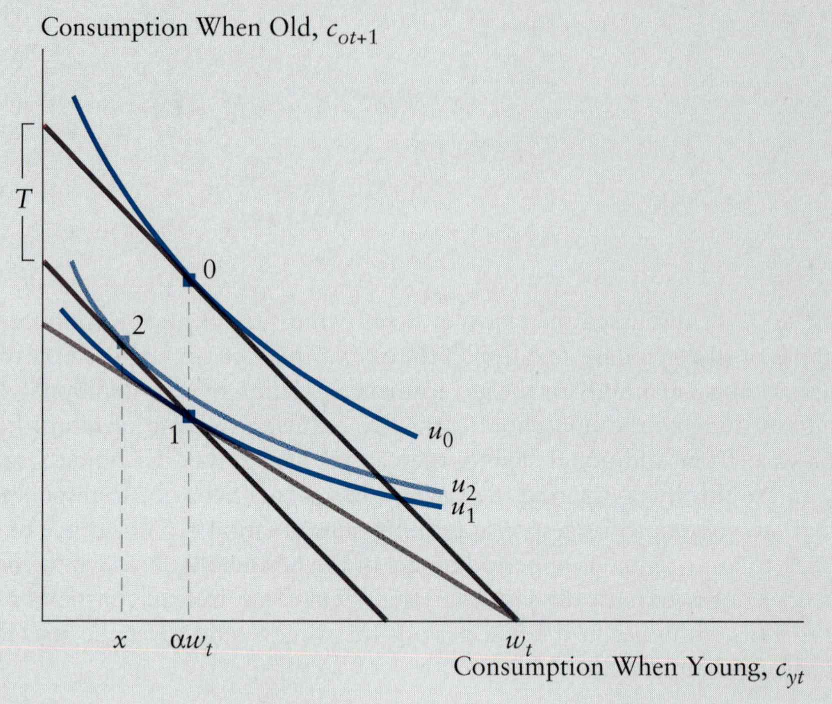

In the absence of taxation, a typical household consumes a fraction α of its wages, w_t, when young and saves the rest for consumption when old. The utility-maximizing consumption combination is determined at point 0, where the indifference curve marked u_0 is tangent to the household's budget constraint.

Imposition of a capital income tax is equivalent to a reduction in the interest rate; the effect is to flatten the budget constraint. The new utility-maximizing combination is determined at point 1. Does the capital income tax reduce saving? The answer is yes, if we compare it with a lump-sum tax that raises the same amount of revenue. Such a tax would cause a parallel inward shift of the original budget constraint and reduce its vertical axis intercept by T—the amount of taxes collected from each household. Along *that* budget constraint, the optimal combination is at point 2. By comparing points 1 and 2, we can see that the capital income tax leads to more consumption—αw_t rather than x—and less saving than a revenue-equivalent lump sum tax.

points 0 and 1, the amount by which second-period resources have shrunk because of taxation. Suppose that this same burden T had simply been imposed on the household by the government—not as a tax on capital income, but as a second-period lump-sum tax. In that case, the household's lifetime resources would have shrunk to less than w_t (can you calculate by how much?), as shown by the budget line that is parallel to the original one, but closer to the origin. The resulting choice, at point 2, indicates reduced first-period consumption—equal to x—as well as reduced second-period consumption.

We can summarize this comparison as follows. If it is simply presented with a lump-sum tax that must be paid when household members are old, the household will reduce its consumption both when young and when old in order to pay the bill. Faced instead with a capital income tax that ultimately raises the same amount of revenue, the taxpayer will elect to consume less only in the second period. Relative to the lump-sum tax, then, the capital income tax reduces household saving.

Hence, a capital income tax has an impact similar to that of a decline in the desire to save: an increase in α. Given the amount it must pay to the government when old, the household consumes more when young if the tax payment takes the form of a capital income tax. Like an increase in α, a switch from lump-sum taxation to capital income taxation causes a decline in the level of assets acquired by the young and, as a result, a transition to a lower capital stock.

C H A P T E R 8

Money and Prices in the Closed Economy

INTRODUCTION

Previous chapters focused on the real side of the economy—how real wages and interest rates are determined, how capital is accumulated, how output grows, etc. This chapter incorporates the economy's nominal side. It shows how the demand for and supply of money jointly determine the *price level*—the value of output measured in units of money. It also shows how the government can affect nominal and, potentially, real variables by changing the money supply.

We begin our analysis by asking: What is money? The answer is less obvious than one might think. Money is a commonly used means of payment, but what constitutes money has varied enormously across different societies. Even within a particular society, it's often hard to say exactly what is and is not money. The reason is that the basic properties of money are consistent with narrow as well as broad definitions.

In the U.S., pieces of paper printed in green and black serve as money as do copper, nickel, and copper-steel coins. But this official currency is not the only commonly used means of payment. Personal checks are also accepted in most

Figure 8-1 The Money Stock (M1) and the Price Level, 1960–1993

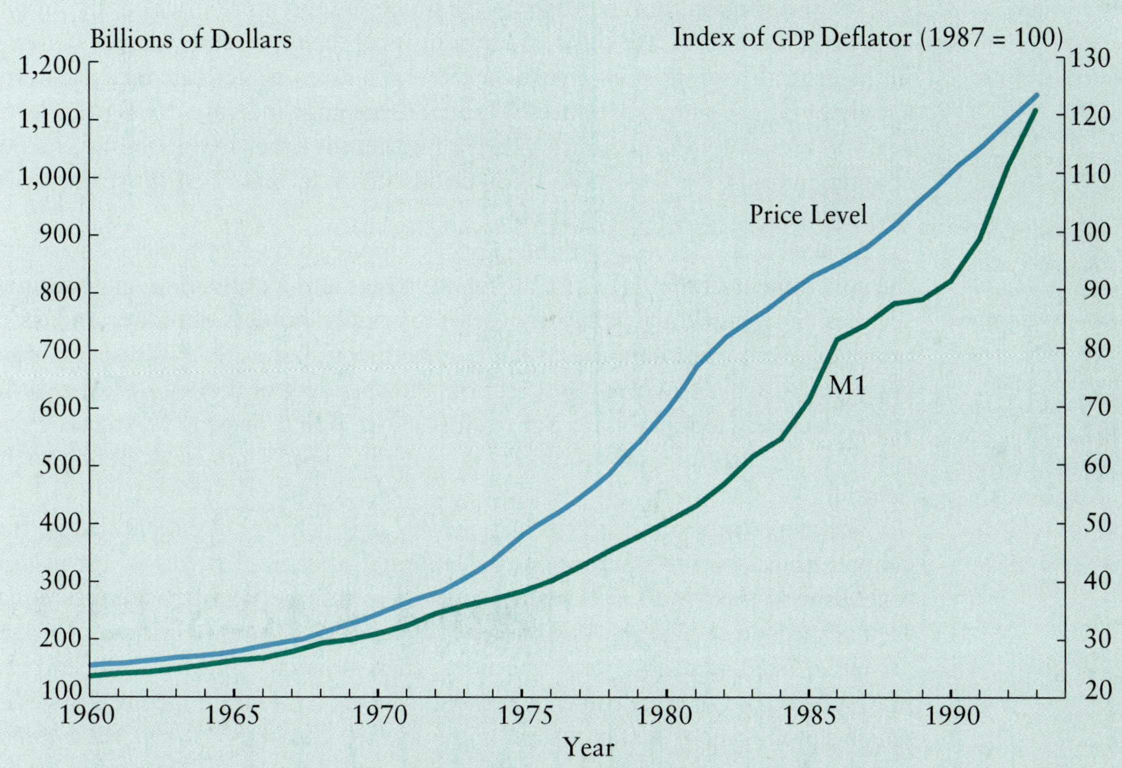

Since 1960, the M1 money stock has grown every year; so has the price level.

Source: *Economic Report of the President*, 1994

transactions. Indeed, most checking accounts are technically referred to as **demand deposits**, because deposited funds can be accessed immediately (upon demand) simply by writing a check. The value of all circulating currency plus the value of all demand deposits—called M1—is the measure of money most frequently cited by the Federal Reserve—the government agency responsible for determining the U.S. money supply.[1] But this is just one of the Federal Reserve's measures. In addition to M1, the Fed (short for Federal Reserve) keeps track of two other definitions of money, M2 and M3. M2 equals M1 plus, primarily, savings accounts, small time deposits, and money market mutual funds. M3 equals M2 plus, primarily, large time deposits.

Demand deposits *Accounts at financial institutions that pay little or no interest and against which depositors can write checks to obtain their deposits at any time*

Beyond the question of how to define money is the issue of its impact on prices. Figure 8-1 shows post-1960 growth in M1 together with the growth over

1. We'll discuss the Federal Reserve in detail in Chapter 14.

the same period in the price level, measured by the GDP deflator—the price index for all final goods and services discussed in Chapter 5. Both the M1 money stock and the price level have grown dramatically over the period.

Neutrality of money *The proposition that a one-time change in the money supply has no effect on any real variable and leads to a proportional change in the level of prices*

Monetary policy *The creation and spending of money by the government*

The proposition that increases in the money supply raise prices is an old one in economics. Indeed, the classical economists of the nineteenth century believed in the **neutrality of money**—they believed that a given percentage increase in the supply of money simply produces an equal percentage increase in the price level, with no impact on the economy's level of output or other real variables. As our chapter unfolds, we'll use the two-period life-cycle model to illustrate when money is neutral and when it is not.

As we'll show, increases in the supply of money represent a means by which the government can finance its transfer payments and its spending on goods and services. Such **monetary policy** imposes a tax on the holders of money and other nominal government liabilities, such as government bonds. In this respect, monetary policy, which involves the creation and spending of money by the government, is closely akin to fiscal policy. Just as we don't, in general, expect fiscal policy to be neutral, we shouldn't, in general, expect monetary policy to be neutral.

The close connection between monetary and fiscal policy identified in this chapter hinges on the assumption that nominal prices and wages adjust instantaneously to their market-clearing values (the values at which supplies equal their respective demands). As Chapter 9 will clarify, if nominal prices or wages are either fixed or *sticky* (slow to adjust), then monetary and fiscal policies can play special, but distinct roles, in helping markets equilibrate (achieve prices at which supplies equal demands) and in moving the economy toward *full employment*—where all those seeking employment at the going wage have jobs.

Here are some of the questions addressed in this chapter:

- What is money?
- What determines the demand for money?
- How do the supply of money and demand for money jointly determine the time path of the price level?
- Under what circumstances are changes in the money supply neutral?
- What is the relationship between inflation and the growth of the money supply?
- What is the relationship between fiscal and monetary policy?
- What are the costs of inflation?

WHAT IS MONEY?

Barter *The direct exchange of one commodity for another without the use of money*

Economists traditionally define money as those objects, whether rectangular pieces of paper, round pieces of metal, cigarettes, or animal pelts, that are generally accepted in payment for goods and services. Without money, goods would have to be exchanged through **barter**—the direct exchange of one good for another. This would be very inefficient, because barter requires a double coincidence of wants.

Source: B.C. by Johnny Hart. By permission of Johnny Hart and Creators Syndicate.

To see this, consider Milton, a barber, who wants to take juggling lessons, Paul, a juggler, who wants to hire a gardener, and James, a gardener, who needs a haircut. In a barter economy, Milton, James, and Paul won't be able to trade with each other. Instead, Milton will be forced to find a juggler who needs a haircut, James will need to find a barber who needs gardening, and Paul will have to find a gardener who wants to learn how to juggle—potentially, three very hard things for them to do. In contrast, with money, Milton can give James a haircut in exchange for money and use the money to pay Paul for juggling lessons, and Paul can use the money to hire James to work on his garden.

Although money makes an economy more efficient by reducing the time and other transactions costs of exchange, it can't work its magic unless participants in the economy are willing to accept it. That willingness, in turn, depends upon a number of factors including the physical properties of money and faith in the regulation of its supply.

Properties of Money

Most monies perform three crucial functions. First, they are used as *means of payment*, or *media of exchange*. In the United States, currency, coins, and checks can be used to pay for the immediate purchase of goods and services. They are media of exchange. Second, they represent *stores of value* that can be used to maintain purchasing power over time. Dollar bills, for example, can be kept in your pocket or under the mattress and used later to purchase goods and services of intrinsic value. Third, they are *units of account,* meaning that they are the units in which the prices of goods and services are quoted.

It's worth reflecting on why dollar bills are considered money whereas most other objects, such as houses, are not. It's conceivable, though far-fetched, that houses could be used as money. You could pay for a particular commodity by handing over possession of your house or apartment for a fixed time period. A house is also an asset—a store of value. You could hold onto it for a period of time and then, at some future date, exchange it for other goods and services. Also, you could quote prices of commodities in terms of, say, the number of days of use of your house—that is, your house could be a unit of account. So, if we were to define money strictly based on the above three properties—medium of exchange, unit of account, and store of value—we might include houses as well.

Liquidity
A measure of the ease with which an asset can be converted into money without significant loss of its value

The reason houses are not considered money and dollar bills are is that dollar bills are generally acceptable in exchange; i.e., they are a highly **liquid** means of payment. Liquidity refers to the ease and speed with which an object can serve as a medium of exchange. Some of the liquidity properties of dollar bills stem from their physical characteristics—they are light and easy to carry, whereas houses are not. Some stem from their divisibility—money comes in large and small denominations, so there's no problem in providing change in transactions. And still others stem from their homogeneity—one dollar bill is like any other, so everyone knows what he is getting when he accepts one. To appreciate the importance of liquidity, imagine the time it would take to purchase a car by offering the use of your house in exchange.

To summarize, it's pretty easy to include dollars and exclude houses in defining money. But in considering why we want to exclude houses, we also learn that defining money is not as easy as it might at first seem. Besides dollars, there are demand deposits, savings accounts, money market funds, and other stores of value that are highly liquid means of payment and which we might want to include in our definition of money. This helps explain why the Federal Reserve tracks three definitions of money, whose differences we'll discuss in Chapter 14.

THE IMPORTANCE OF BELIEFS AND INSTITUTIONS TO THE DEFINITION OF MONEY

The intrinsic value of money is less than its value when used in exchange. For example, the intrinsic value of the colored piece of paper called a dollar bill is close to zero, since it can't be used for much besides lighting a fire or making confetti. The reason a dollar bill is worth more than its intrinsic value is that the holder of a dollar believes it's a store of value—something she'll be able to swap for goods and services of real value.

To maintain the *real value of money*, measured by the ratio of the money supply to the price level (i.e., the amount of goods that can be purchased with the money supply), it is critical that this belief be commonly held. To see this, suppose that most people suddenly came to doubt that they would be able to swap U.S. currency for real commodities. How would they react? Most likely they would refuse to accept payment in dollars. This would lead other individuals to question whether they too would be able to swap dollars for real commodities. If enough people came to believe that U.S. currency was worthless, the commonly held belief would turn into a self-fulfilling prophecy: no one would agree to accept the currency because no one would want to end up stuck with useless pieces of paper and metal that could not be swapped for goods or services. Money would become a hot potato (something no one wants to touch), and the price level, the amount of money one would need to purchase a market basket of goods, would be infinite.

What could trigger such a radical change in beliefs? One possibility is a suspicion that the government is printing, or is about to print, huge quantities of money which will dramatically raise the price level and lower the real value of money. Unrestrained printing of money is well within the realm of historical experience. After World War I the governments of Germany, Hungary, Austria, and Poland each began printing enormous quantities of money to pay their bills. More recent examples include Israel, Argentina, and Bolivia in the mid-1980s, and Russia and Brazil in the early 1990s. In each case the result of extraordinary growth in the money supply was **hyperinflation**, in which prices rise at incredible rates.

Hyperinflation *An extremely high rate of inflation*

During Germany's hyperinflation, from 1921 through 1923, prices increased by a factor of 30 billion! Prices increased so fast that workers were paid in wheelbarrows full of currency, which they pushed straight to the store because prices were literally rising by the minute. If they waited too long to spend their money, an entire wheelbarrowfull would be worthless. Eventually, the German public resorted to barter exchange with its attendant transactions costs. They also started using foreign currencies, in a practice called *currency substitution.* The German hyperinflation ended when a new government was formed, a new currency was issued and, most important, growth in the supply of money was tightly controlled. The new currency was accepted because Germans believed it would have value and because they had faith that the new institutional arrangements would limit its supply.

Case Study: Different Monies in U.S. History[2]

One way to appreciate the importance of beliefs and institutions is to consider the different types of money that have been used throughout United States' history. At the beginning of this history—during the American Revolution—the Continental Congress printed *Continentals* to help finance the war. The Continentals were an example of *fiat money*—something declared to be money by the government but which has no intrinsic value. Because it did not offer to redeem Continentals for gold or anything else of value, the Congress was free to print as many of them as it wanted. In fact, it printed so many that prices of commodities in terms of Continentals skyrocketed. By the end of the Revolution the real

2. For an excellent survey and analysis of U.S. monetary history see Milton Friedman and Anna Schwartz, *A Monetary History of the United States, 1867–1960* (Princeton, NJ: Princeton University Press, 1963).

ATTORNEY AT LAW
"I PAID MY GARAGE WITH THIS CHECK, THEY ENDORSED IT OVER TO THE ELECTRICIAN, HE PAID THE HARDWARE STORE WITH IT, AND THEY HAVE PAID THEIR BILL TO ME WITH IT."

Source: ©1994 by Sidney Harris.

value of a Continental—the amount of goods and services it could purchase—was essentially zero.[3]

By 1788, when the Constitution was ratified, two other types of money had also appeared on the scene, *bills of exchange* and *bank notes*. Bills of exchange were IOUs written by prominent individuals thought to be able to repay their debts. For example, Paul Revere might pay for a horse by handing over an IOU. The horse seller might pay for an addition to his barn by endorsing Paul Revere's IOU over to a carpenter. The carpenter might further endorse the IOU to a woodsman in exchange for a large delivery of wood. In this way, the bill of exchange circulated as paper money. Bills of exchange were used for large transactions, rather than everyday purchases.

Bank notes were pieces of paper redeemable for gold at the bank that issued them. The First Bank of the United States, which was established in 1790 but abolished in 1811, was a quasi-governmental agency that made loans to the private sector in the form of its bank notes. Borrowers could use notes of the First

3. Had the public suspected the extent to which the real value of this currency would decline, it would have been much less willing to accept it in the first place. But because the public initially *believed* the Continentals would retain their real value, it did accept them and, consequently, ended up at the end of the Revolution stuck with a large quantity of worthless paper.

Bank in making purchases because other individuals believed the notes could be readily redeemed for gold and so were willing to accept them. The First Bank did not, however, have a monopoly on issuing bank notes. During this period, state-chartered private banks also issued notes.

All the bank notes were claimed to be redeemable in gold, but the public's confidence in the redeemability of a given note varied depending on the financial condition of the bank that issued it. When the public became sufficiently concerned about a bank's ability to redeem its notes, a **bank run**—a demand that the bank hand over gold in exchange for the notes—would ensue. These runs forced many banks with insufficient gold reserves to close.

Bank runs
Situations in which many depositors attempt simultaneously to withdraw funds from their accounts

During the Civil War, the North and the South maintained separate currencies. The Confederate dollar was freely accepted in the South at the beginning of the war when Southerners were confident of victory, but was worthless by war's end. The North's currency was called the "greenback" because it was green on one side. Although the federal government promised to redeem greenbacks in gold, it waited until 1879 to do so. Hence, the period between the end of the Civil War and 1879 was very much like modern times. There was a paper currency, issued by the federal government, that was not convertible into gold. But unlike today, gold and silver coins as well as gold and silver certificates—pieces of paper guaranteeing payment in gold and silver—also circulated as money. So too did national bank notes—bank notes issued by federally chartered national banks during and after the Civil War.

In 1914 the Federal Reserve System was established with a mandate to establish a uniform national currency. In the years since, the Fed has been essentially the sole supplier of U.S. paper currency in the form of Federal Reserve Notes—the one-dollar, five-dollar, and higher denomination bills we use every day.[4] Notwithstanding its interest in a uniform currency, the Federal government permitted the use of gold coins through 1934, the year it effectively abandoned the gold standard.[5]

To summarize, U.S. history has seen a great range of different types of money—Continentals, bills of exchange, bank notes, gold and silver coins, gold and silver certificates, Confederate dollars, greenbanks, national bank notes, and modern-day Federal Reserve notes and coinage. The advent and demise of these different forms of money reflect changes in institutional arrangements and changing beliefs about the real value of these monies. They also reflect changes in the U.S. government's proclivity to print money and use it to purchase real goods and services from the private sector.

Case Study: California's 1992 Warrants

A recent example of the creation of a new form of money was the state of California's decision in 1992 to issue IOUs, called warrants, to pay its bills. The setting for this extreme measure was a severe state budget crisis brought about by

4. The U.S. Treasury issued a limited number of gold and silver certificates through the mid-1960s. Incidentally, the U.S. Treasury, rather than the Fed, is responsible for issuing coins.
5. We'll discuss the gold standard in Chapter 13.

unexpectedly large disaster relief payments and the loss of revenues due to the recession that began in 1990. California's governor, Pete Wilson, sought to meet this problem by reducing the state's spending on a variety of programs, including education. But the California legislature balked. In July 1992 the state ran out of money, and the legislature refused to authorize more borrowing. So the governor resorted to printing warrants to pay the state's bills. State workers received warrants rather than their usual paychecks. Warrants were also sent to many other state creditors.

The warrants were a promise on the part of the state government to pay specific amounts of money, in dollars, at an unspecified future date. The state also promised to pay a 5 percent annual interest rate calculated from the date of issue of the warrants to the date of redemption. As with Paul Revere's bills of exchange, warrants could be used in purchasing goods and services. That's because banks in California were willing to swap dollars for warrants. They believed (in the end, correctly) that the state would eventually redeem its warrants in dollars and that holding warrants was as good as holding short-term state bonds.[6]

THE CLASSICAL VIEW OF MONEY

Now that we've learned about the properties of money and taken a brief tour of U.S. monetary history, let's begin to think about the way money affects the economy. A good starting place is the classical view of money. As mentioned, the classical economists argued that money is neutral: changes in its supply have no influence on GDP or other real variables. They reasoned that the amounts of goods and services produced by the economy should not depend on the amount of money in circulation but rather on the economy's productive capacity and that the price level will adjust to changes in the supply of money. Thus, if there is an increase in the amount of money in the economy, there will be "more money chasing the same amount of real goods and services" and prices of goods and services will simply be bid up. Conversely, if the money supply decreases, there will be less money chasing those goods and services, and prices will be bid down. According to this view, the **real stock of money**—the amount of money divided by the price level—is independent of the nominal money supply.[7]

Real stock of money
The nominal amount of money in circulation divided by the price level

Figure 8-2 shows that the real money stock has fluctuated considerably since 1959. It rose by 12 percent between 1960 and 1970, fell by 7 percent between 1970 and 1980, and rose by 60 percent between 1980 and 1993. Do these fluctuations in the real stock of money disprove the proposition that money is neutral? Not necessarily. The classical economists didn't deny that the real money supply could vary, they simply ruled out the possibility that such changes

6. This belief wasn't absolute. Even bankers who felt sure they would be able to redeem their warrants weren't sure when. Indeed, after about one month of redeeming warrants for dollars at full face value, banks began redeeming them only at a discount.

7. Note that the real stock of money measures the amount of real goods and services that could be purchased with the entire money supply.

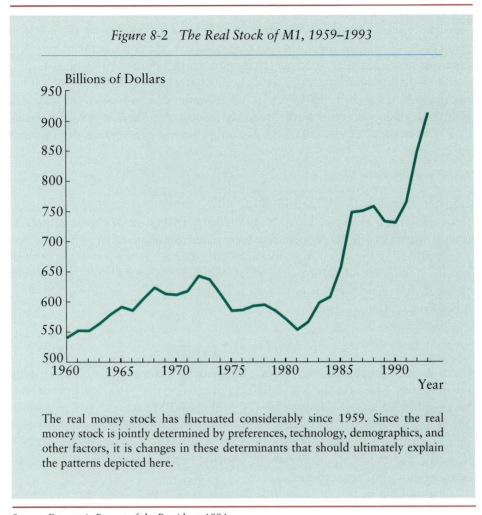

Figure 8-2 The Real Stock of M1, 1959–1993

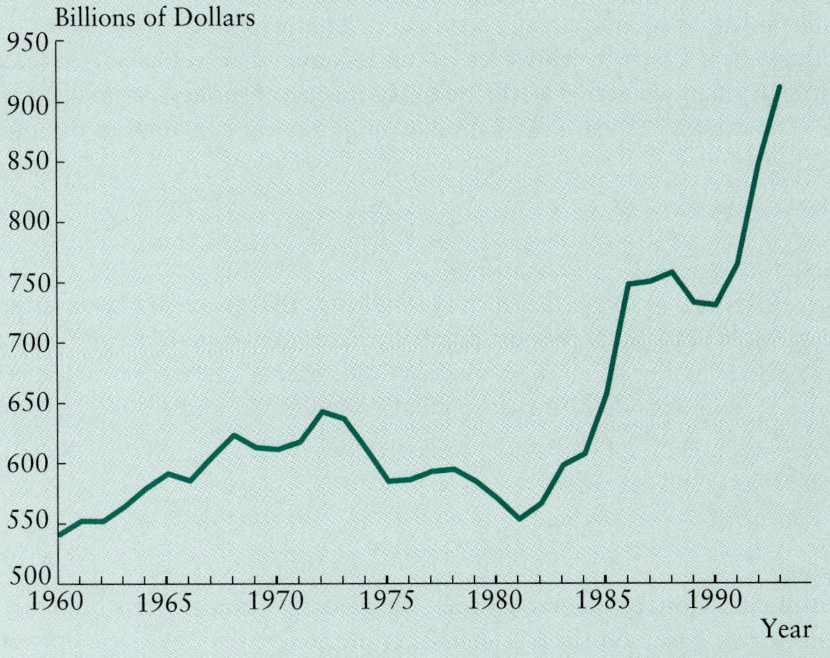

The real money stock has fluctuated considerably since 1959. Since the real money stock is jointly determined by preferences, technology, demographics, and other factors, it is changes in these determinants that should ultimately explain the patterns depicted here.

Source: *Economic Report of the President*, 1994

depended on the nominal quantity of money in circulation. As we'll see, the real quantity of money, like other real variables in the economy, is jointly determined by consumer preferences, technology, demographics, etc. As these factors change through time, we expect all real variables, including the real quantity of money, to change.

The Quantity Equation and Velocity

The classical view that money is neutral can be understood in terms of the **quantity equation**, which connects the level of nominal GDP, denoted by PY (the price level, P, multiplied by real GDP) to the product of the money supply, M, and the **velocity of money**, v. We can write the quantity equation as

$$Mv = PY$$

Quantity equation *Nominal GDP, the price level (P) multiplied by real output (Y), is equal to the nominal money supply (M) multiplied by velocity (v): Mv = PY*

Velocity of money *The ratio of nominal GDP to the nominal money supply*

If we rearrange this equation so that velocity is by itself on the left-hand side, we see that velocity equals the the flow of nominal GDP divided by the stock of money; i.e., $v = PY/M$. Thus, velocity measures how many times the money supply turns over each year in helping to determine the nominal value of GDP.[8]

The quantity equation really just defines what we call velocity. By itself it has no theoretical content. However, *if* we assume that velocity is a constant $\bar{v}$ through time, we arrive at the **quantity theory of money**, which is a special case of the classical view. With this assumption we can rewrite the quantity equation as

Quantity theory of money
The proposition that the velocity of money is fixed, so that changes in the money supply have proportionate effects on nominal income

$$PY = \bar{v}M$$

Since the term $\bar{v}$ is fixed, this formula indicates that increases in the supply of money, M, lead to equal proportionate increases in nominal GDP, PY. If we further assume, as the classical economists did, that Y, as well as all other real variables, is independent of the nominal variables (M and P), we arrive at the classical view that increases in M lead to equal proportionate increases in P; in other words, money is neutral.

Is Velocity Constant?

Unfortunately for the quantity theory, the velocity of money has been anything but constant. Based on the M1 definition of money, the 1993 velocity was 5.6 because 1993 nominal GDP was \$6.374 trillion and M1 was \$1.131 trillion. In 1960 nominal GDP was \$513 billion and M1 was \$141 billion, so velocity that year was only 3.6. Figure 8-3 plots the velocity of M1 between 1960 and 1993. It shows the general rise over time in velocity, but also that velocity fluctuates considerably from year to year.

The increase in velocity over this 33-year period was partly due to technological improvements in the way money is used to conduct transactions. The invention of automatic teller machines (ATMS) is a good example. ATMS reduce the amount of cash individuals need to have on hand to make their purchases; they can quickly obtain additional cash at the nearest machine. Because of ATMS a given amount of cash can circulate more quickly (not spend so much time sitting idly in peoples' pockets) and support a larger nominal value of transactions.

A second reason that velocity rose is the development of substitutes for M1 in making transactions. An example here is credit cards.[9] Since 1980 credit card use has more than quadrupled. Obviously, the more transactions that are made without cash or personal checks, the greater the total volume of transactions that can be supported by a given amount of M1, and the greater the measured velocity of M1.

8. We use the word "helping" here, because a given form of money is not used in all transactions counted in nominal GDP and because many transactions, such as the sale of existing assets, are not included in GDP.

9. One might argue that credit cards are not money because outstanding credit card balances must, eventually, be paid for by cash or check. Regardless of how one classifies credit card lines of credit, there is little question that credit cards reduce the use of money in transactions.

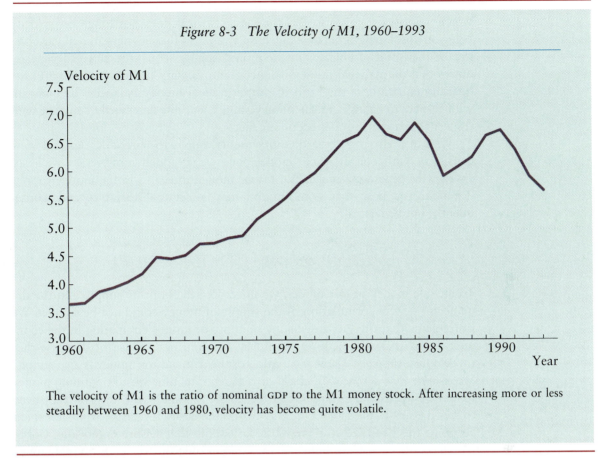

Figure 8-3 The Velocity of M1, 1960–1993

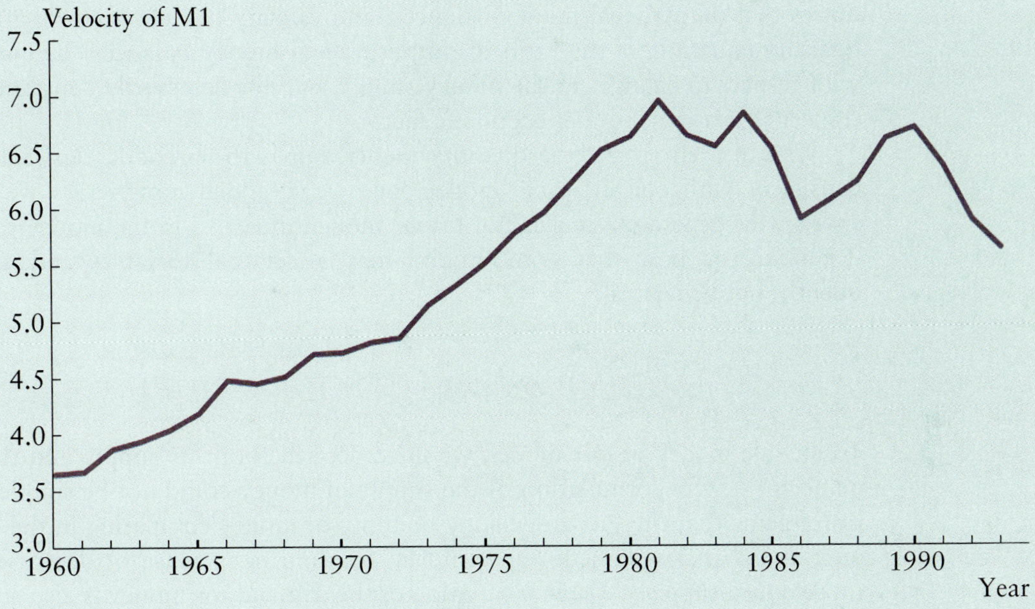

The velocity of M1 is the ratio of nominal GDP to the M1 money stock. After increasing more or less steadily between 1960 and 1980, velocity has become quite volatile.

Source: *Economic Report of the President*, 1994

A third reason why velocity has risen has to do with higher nominal interest rates that have led Americans to economize on their cash balances.[10] When individuals or firms hold money in cash or non-interest- or low-interest-paying checking accounts, they are sacrificing interest income. Rather than hold their money in this form, they could use the funds to purchase interest-bearing assets. As we'll describe shortly, higher interest rates lead people to lower their demand for real money balances (M/P). What does this have to do with velocity? Well, note that given the level of output, velocity is inversely related to real money balances. So, if the public lowers its demand for real money balances because the interest rate has risen and if output is not thereby altered (or not altered very much), velocity will have to increase to make the smaller amount of real money balances circulate more rapidly in supporting an unchanged level of real output.[11]

10. The classic articles on this topic are William Baumol's "The Transactions Demand for Cash: An Inventory Theoretic Approach," *Quarterly Journal of Economics* (November 1952) and James Tobin, "The Interest Elasticity of the Transactions Demand for Cash," *Review of Economics and Statistics* (August 1956).

11. Indeed, the increase since 1960 in M1 velocity has coincided with a secular increase in nominal interest rates. In the 1960s short-term nominal interest rates ranged from 3 to 7 percent. In the 1970s they ranged from 4 to 10 percent. Since 1980 they've ranged from 4 to 14 percent.

As Figure 8-3 makes clear, the data rule out the simple quantity theory in which velocity is constant. But the classical view does not hinge on velocity being an absolutely rigid constant. It only requires that changes in real variables not be the result of changes in the money supply. Thus, the classical view requires that output, real money balances, and velocity (which, according to the quantity equation, is the ratio of output to real money balances) be constant with respect to changes in the money supply, but not necessarily constant with respect to changes in other economic factors.

We can easily reject the quantity theory, but is the broader, classical view consistent with our life-cycle model once we've added money? As we'll see shortly, the general answer is no. In our model, increases in the money supply, depending on how they come about, may affect real variables and, consequently, not be neutral.

ADDING MONEY TO OUR MODEL[12]

To include money in our model, we must describe both its supply and the demand for it. Our formulation of the supply of money could not be simpler. We just assume that there is an existing quantity of money circulating in the economy and that government has complete freedom to increase or decrease that total money supply.[13] Our formulation of the demand for money is also simple. We assume that people care about how much time they spend obtaining money to make purchases. The larger their real money balances, the less time they need to spend going to the bank. One way to add the desire for leisure (time not spent going to the bank) to our model is to assume that leisure enters our Cobb-Douglas utility function. But since the amount of leisure depends on real money balances, we can replace leisure in the Cobb-Douglas function by its dependence on real money balances. Before doing so, let's consider how the demand for money fits into individuals' lifetime budget constraints and influences their real asset accumulation.

The Lifetime Budget Constraint with Money

To keep things simple, we'll temporarily ignore fiscal policy. We'll also retain Chapter 7's assumption that individuals consume only when old. But, although each individual abstains from consumption when young, she doesn't save and invest all her wages in capital. Instead she holds some aside in the form of money. When old, she uses this money, along with the principal and interest on her capital assets, to pay for her old-age consumption.

The following equation restates these points algebraically. It indicates that an individual who is young at time t allocates her real wages, w_t, to two things:

12. In adding money to our stylized two-period life-cycle model, we don't pretend to be modeling the precise role that money plays in facilitating economic exchange. In entertaining all the details of such a model, we could easily miss the broader points we hope to convey.
13. Chapter 14 discusses the institutional mechanisms by which the U.S. government changes the money supply.

real assets, a_{t+1}, and real money balances, m_{t+1}/P_t, where m_{t+1} is the nominal money balances (e.g., the number of dollars) she will take into old age, and P_t is the price level at time t.[14]

$$a_{t+1} + \frac{m_{t+1}}{P_t} = w_t$$

When the individual reaches old age her consumption, c_{ot+1}, is financed by her real assets, the interest on those assets, and her real money balances, which are her nominal money holdings, m_{t+1}, divided by the price level at time $t + 1$, P_{t+1}. Thus,

$$c_{ot+1} = a_{t+1}(1 + r_{t+1}) + \frac{m_{t+1}}{P_{t+1}}$$

In a moment we'll substitute a_{t+1} out of these two equations to form the individual's lifetime budget constraint. Before we do, let's develop some intuition about this constraint. First, suppose there is neither inflation nor **deflation** (a decline over time in prices), so $P_{t+1} = P_t$ and $m_{t+1}/P_t = m_{t+1}/P_{t+1}$. Now consider the first equation. It tells us that, given the individual's wage, there is a one-for-one tradeoff between bringing real assets and bringing real money balances into old age. For every additional unit of real money balances brought into old age, the individual will bring one unit less of real assets. But, according to the second equation, bringing a unit more of real money balances and a unit less of real assets into old age means a reduction in old age consumption by r_{t+1}. This reflects the fact that real assets pay interest, whereas money balances do not. So, the higher the interest rate, the higher the cost, in forgone consumption, of holding money balances. Stated differently, this thought experiment tells us that the opportunity cost of holding money, measured in terms of forgone consumption, involves the interest rate.

Deflation
A decrease in the price level over time

Next, let's consider how an increase in P_{t+1} affects the individual's consumption when old, holding all other variables (including P_t) fixed. According to the last equation, the higher P_{t+1} is (and, therefore, the higher the inflation rate between the two periods), the smaller consumption when old will be. Intuitively, higher inflation dilutes the real value of the individual's money holdings, meaning that she can buy fewer real goods for consumption in old age with her nominal money balances. In this sense, inflation represents a tax on money. So the cost of holding money involves not only the real interest rate, but also the inflation rate. Indeed, the lifetime budget constraint, which we now derive, indicates that the opportunity cost of holding money involves the nominal interest rate, i_{t+1}, which, in turn, depends on both the real interest rate, r_{t+1}, and the inflation rate, π_{t+1}.

14. The reason nominal money balances has a time $t+1$ subscript, rather than a time t subscript, is the same reason that real assets, a, has a time $t+1$ subscript. Both m_{t+1} and a_{t+1} are stocks (in one case, the stock of money, in the other case, the stock of real assets) the individual will have at the beginning of period $t+1$.

The lifetime budget constraint given below results from substituting a_{t+1} out of the last two equations and rearranging terms.

$$\frac{c_{ot+1}}{(1 + r_{t+1})} + \frac{i_{t+1}}{(1 + i_{t+1})} \frac{m_{t+1}}{P_t} = w_t$$

where, as we showed in Chapter 5, $i_{t+1} = r_{t+1} + \pi_{t+1} + r_{t+1}\pi_{t+1}$. Recall that the inflation rate π_{t+1} is just the percentage increase in prices between periods t and $t + 1$: $\pi_{t+1} = (P_{t+1} - P_t)/P_t$. We see that the nominal interest rate equals the real interest rate plus the rate of inflation plus the product of these two rates—the same definition we presented in Chapter 5. There we learned that the nominal interest rate adjusts for the fact that inflation reduces the real value of nominal assets, such as government bonds, whose principal plus interest payments are made in the form of money.

The lifetime budget constraint tells us that the present value of the individual's lifetime income (w_t) equals the sum of the present value of her consumption when old plus the present value of her acquisition of real money balances. Just as $1/(1 + r_{t+1})$ represents the price at time t of consuming when old at time $t + 1$, the term $i_{t+1}/(1 + i_{t+1})$ represents the price at time t of holding real money balances. The numerator in this ratio, i_{t+1}, measures the nominal interest income the individual forgoes as a result of holding \$1 in non-interest-paying money balances. The denominator in the ratio, $(1 + i_{t+1})$, simply discounts, at the nominal interest rate, the nominal interest income sacrificed by holding each dollar.

The Demand for Money

As mentioned, we'll derive our demand for money by assuming that real money balances enter the Cobb-Douglas utility function along with consumption when old (recall, we are leaving out consumption when young to keep things simple). The utility function in this case can be written

$$u_t = [m_{t+1}/P_t]^{\theta} c_{ot+1}^{1-\theta}$$

This looks the same as our previous utility function except that consumption when young is replaced by real money balances, and the parameter α is replaced by θ.

Recall that, in deciding how much to consume when young and old, each individual chooses the combination given by the point where an indifference curve is just tangent to his budget constraint. The same decision process occurs here. Each individual finds the point at which an indifference curve between real money balances and consumption when old is just tangent to the lifetime budget constraint. And just as the choice of (the demand for) consumption when young equaled a fraction (in that case α) of the wage, the demand for real money balances equals a fraction of the wage. We can write the demand for real money balances as

"This year, I'm putting all my money into money."

Drawing by Cline; ©1993 The New Yorker Magazine, Inc.

$$\frac{m_{t+1}}{P_t} = \gamma[i_{t+1}]\, w_t$$

Note that the fraction γ of their wages that young individuals wish to spend on real money balances depends on (is a function of) the nominal interest rate. Indeed, it is easy to show that γ depends negatively on the nominal interest rate.[15] Thus, the higher the nominal interest rate, the smaller the demand for real money balances. Intuitively, a higher nominal interest rate means a higher opportunity cost of holding real money balances, leading to a reduced demand for real balances.

Case Study: Real Money Balances During the German Hyperinflation[16]

If money demand is inversely related to the nominal interest rate, that fact should be evident in the data on countries undergoing hyperinflation. In a period of hyperinflation, nominal interest rates are driven sky-high. The German

15. The precise formula is $\gamma[i_{t+1}] = \theta(1 + i_{t+1})/i_{t+1}$. Inserting this formula into the money demand equation and rearranging the resulting equation leads to the conclusion that individuals' acquisition of real money balances (the price of holding real balances, $i_{t+1}/(1 + i_{t+1})$, multiplied by the quantity of real balances, m_{t+1}/P_t) equal the share θ of their wages.

16. Thomas Sargent's study, "The Ends of Four Big Inflations," in *Inflation—Causes and Effects* (Chicago: University of Chicago Press, 1982) provides an insightful analysis of Germany's hyperinflation.

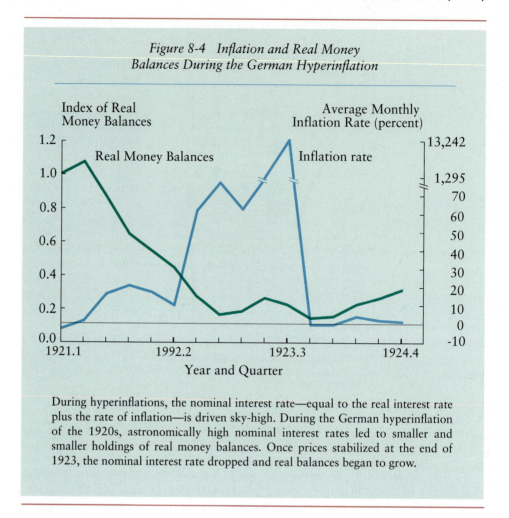

Figure 8-4 Inflation and Real Money Balances During the German Hyperinflation

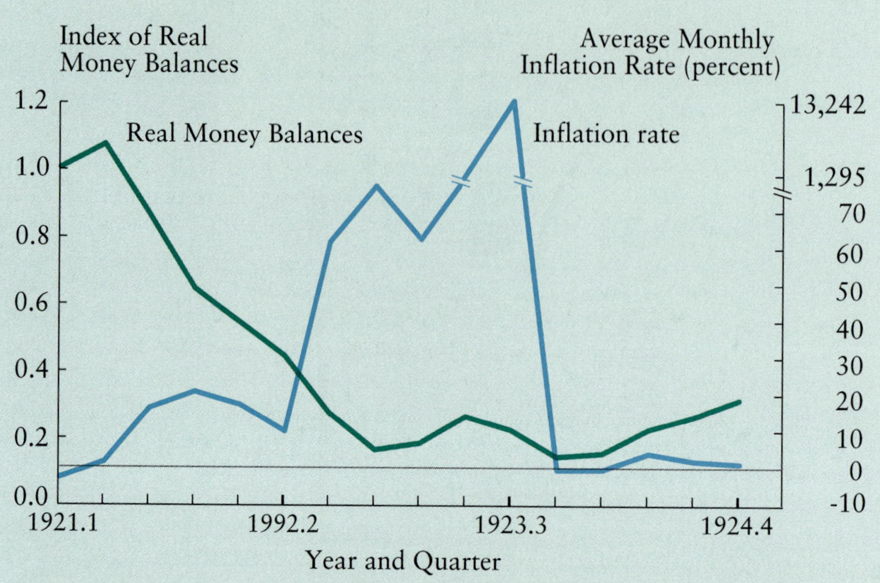

During hyperinflations, the nominal interest rate—equal to the real interest rate plus the rate of inflation—is driven sky-high. During the German hyperinflation of the 1920s, astronomically high nominal interest rates led to smaller and smaller holdings of real money balances. Once prices stabilized at the end of 1923, the nominal interest rate dropped and real balances began to grow.

hyperinflation, which lasted from 1921 to 1923, produced astronomically high inflation rates and nominal interest rates (as our formula for the nominal interest rate suggests). In response to these nominal interest rates, the public went to great lengths to economize on its money holdings. Figure 8-4 shows, on a monthly basis, the German inflation rate and the level of real money balances during the hyperinflation and immediately after prices stabilized at the end of 1923. Note that higher and higher values of the inflation rate (and thus, of the nominal interest rate) between 1921 and 1923 led to smaller and smaller holdings of real balances. However, once prices stabilized, the nominal interest rate dropped precipitously, and real balances began to grow.

Let's also consider the German hyperinflation in terms of the *quantity equation*, $Mv = PY$. Recall that, ignoring changes in output, velocity is inversely related to real money balances; i.e., given Y, the lower M/P is, the higher v is. During the hyperinflation the velocity of money, v, more than quadrupled as Germans played hot potato with their currency, i.e., as they tried to lower their real money balances, M/P.[17] This increase in velocity explains why the price level rose much faster than did the money supply. Prices rose in part because of the increase in the money supply, but they rose even faster because each German mark was circulating at such a rapid rate. The increase in velocity was equivalent, in terms of its impact on prices, to having more German marks in circulation. Similar increases in velocity and declines in real money demand have been observed in every hyperinflation on record.

CAPITAL ACCUMULATION IN THE MONETARY ECONOMY

We turn next to the task of integrating the demand for money into our transition equation for the evolution of the economy's capital-labor ratio. It turns out that our transition equation for the capital-labor ratio is identical to the transition equation of Chapter 7, except that we multiply w_t by the term $(1 - \gamma[i_{t+1}])$.[18] Thus,

$$k_{t+1} = (1 - \gamma[i_{t+1}])A(1 - \beta)k_t^{\beta} - f_t$$

To understand why, recall that the amount of capital per worker at time $t + 1$, k_{t+1}, equals the amount of capital assets per old person at that same time. But the assets of the old at time $t + 1$ are those they acquired when young, at time t. In this case, they equal the real wage each young person earns at time t, w_t, less the amount she holds aside in real money balances, $\gamma[i_{t+1}]w_t$, less the amount she hands over to the government either in net taxes (taxes net of transfers) or purchases of bonds when young, f_t. Hence, $k_{t+1} = (1 - \gamma[i_{t+1}])w_t - f_t$. Our transition equation is derived by replacing the real wage by the formula for the marginal product of labor at time t.

To keep things simple we'll assume for most of what follows that in the money demand formula, the function $\gamma[\ ]$ is a constant equal to $\bar{\gamma}$, regardless of the value of i_{t+1}. That is, we'll consider the simple money demand formula $m_{t+1}/P_t = \bar{\gamma}w_t$. Leaving out the nominal interest rate greatly simplifies our analysis of the transition equation, without materially affecting the conclusions we draw. After presenting the results based on this simplified money demand formula, we'll mention how they would be modified by letting money demand be interest sensitive.

With $\gamma[i_{t+1}]$ set equal to $\bar{\gamma}$, the capital-labor transition equation becomes $k_{t+1} = A(1 - \bar{\gamma})(1 - \beta)k_t^{\beta} - f_t$. Thus, given the value of the capital-labor ratio at some initial time 0 and knowledge of f_0 and subsequent values of f_t, we can use

17. In our model, velocity equals $1/\gamma[i_{t+1}](1-\beta)$. A higher value of i_{t+1} means a lower γ and higher velocity.

18. Here, and throughout the remainder of this book, we assume that a generation's demand for real money balances equals $\gamma[i_{t+1}]$ times the wage it earns when young, rather than $\gamma[i_{t+1}]$ times the present value of the generation's lifetime income. In so doing, we ignore the fact that under certain fiscal policies, the present value of a generation's lifetime income will differ from the wage it earns when young.

the transition equation over and over again to determine the economy's capital-labor ratio at time 1, 2, 3, . . . , ∞—at each date in the future. Armed with this information, we can solve for the time paths of all the other real variables in the economy, including the real wage.

The Determination of the Price Level Through Time

Now that we've seen how the economy's real variables are determined, let's consider how the price level evolves through time. To do so, we need to combine the aggregate demand for money with the aggregate supply of money. We've talked about the demand side—the fact that young people in each period wish to receive some of their real wage in the form of real money balances. Actually, we've also talked about the supply side—the fact that in each period the old people, who hold the money, wish to supply it to the market by spending it to help pay for their old-age consumption. Since we are assuming, for the moment, that the aggregate supply of money in circulation is fixed at $\overline{M}$, this is the total amount of money supplied to the market in each period. In equilibrium, it must also be the amount of money the young collectively end up demanding.

To equate the demand for money by the young to the supply of money by the old, we must write our simplified money demand equation, $m_{t+1}/P_t = \overline{\gamma} w_t$, in terms of the aggregate demand for money at time t, M_{t+1}. But the amount of money demanded by each young person is just the aggregate demand for money divided by N, the number of young people. Thus, we can replace m_{t+1} by M_{t+1}/N in our money demand equation, which leads to $M_{t+1}/P_t = \overline{\gamma} w_t N$. The next and final step is to equate the aggregate demand for money, M_{t+1}, to the aggregate supply of money, $\overline{M}$. Replacing the aggregate demand for money by the aggregate supply in our money demand equation and solving for the price level implies

$$P_t = \frac{\overline{M}}{\overline{\gamma} w_t N}$$

This equation is an equilibrium relationship. It indicates how the price level at time t, P_t, relates to the fixed supply of money, $\overline{M}$, the money demand preference parameter, $\overline{\gamma}$, the real wage, w_t, and the population size, N, of each generation.

Now we can determine the time path of the real wage from the time path of the capital-labor ratio, the calculation of which we discussed above. So, inserting this time path of the real wage into the above equation yields the time path of the price level. At time 0 we can plug w_0 into the above equation together with values of $\overline{\gamma}$, N, and $\overline{M}$ to get P_0. At time 1 we can plug w_1 into the equation together with the same values of $\overline{\gamma}$, N, and $\overline{M}$ to get P_1. And so on, until the economy reaches its steady state.[19] When the economy reaches its steady state, the real wage remains fixed, implying that the price level remains fixed as well.

19. In stating that the economy reaches a steady state, we are considering transitions in which f_t eventually becomes constant.

Hence, we see immediately that when the money supply is fixed, changes in the price level are temporary—eventually, the price level converges to its long-run steady-state value.

The price level equation tells us that there is an inverse relationship between the price level and the real wage. The larger the real wage at a point in time, the lower the price level. Why? Recall that the demand for real balances at time t equals $\bar{\gamma} w_t N$. So the bigger w_t is, the greater the demand for real balances is at time t. But the nominal money supply is fixed at $\bar{M}$, so the only way the real money supply at time t can adjust to satisfy a higher demand is for the price level at time t to fall. Intuitively, then, the bigger w_t is (the real output received by the young), the more real output the young are willing to exchange for the money held by the old. This situation raises the amount of output that is swapped for each unit of money. Equivalently, it lowers the number of units of money that are swapped for each unit of output. But the number of units of money swapped for each unit of output is precisely the price level. So, the real wage and the price level are, indeed, inversely related.

A Numerical Example of a Transition with Money

Let's use the price level equation in conjunction with the capital-labor ratio transition equation to illustrate how the price level adjusts through time to ensure that the real supply of money equals the real demand for money. To do so, let's assume the economy at time 0 has not yet reached its steady state. Specifically, let's suppose that at time 0 the capital-labor ratio is 3. Let's also assume that $\bar{\gamma}$ equals .10, β equals .30, A equals 10, N equals 100, and $\bar{M}$ equals 10,000. Further assume that there is no fiscal policy, so f_t equals 0. Then, as you can readily confirm, the transition equation for the capital-labor ratio is

$$k_{t+1} = 6.30 k_t^{.30}$$

and the equation for the price level is

$$P_t = \frac{1000}{w_t}$$

Table 8-1 presents the values for the capital-labor ratio, the real wage, and the price level for the first seven periods of this economy's transition. It also indicates the steady-state values of these variables. Since the economy's steady-state capital-labor ratio is 13.865 and its time 0 ratio is only 3, the transition path involves an increase over time in the capital-labor ratio. As more capital becomes available per worker, the real wage rises to its steady-state value. The figures in the second column show this: the real wage at time 0 is 9.733; at time 1 it is 13.423; by time 3 it is 15.215; and it eventually reaches 15.405.

The price level is inversely related to the real wage. So the increase in the real wage during the transition implies a decrease in the price level. Had the time 0 capital-labor ratio exceeded the long-run steady-state value, the transition

Table 8-1 An Illustrative Transition Path: The Two-Period Model with Money

Period	k_t	w_t	P_t
0	3.000	9.733	102.746
1	8.759	13.423	74.500
2	12.080	14.782	67.651
3	13.303	15.215	65.722
4	13.694	15.348	65.154
5	13.813	15.388	64.985
6	13.849	15.400	64.934
7	13.860	15.404	64.919
.	.	.	.
.	.	.	.
.	.	.	.
∞	13.865	15.405	64.912

Assumptions: $k_0 = 3$, $\gamma = .10$, $\beta = .30$, $A = 10$, $N = 100$, $\bar{M} = 10{,}000$. Equations underlying the table:

$$k_{t+1} = (1 - \bar{\gamma})w_t$$
$$w_t = A(1 - \beta)k_t^{\beta}$$
$$P_t = \bar{M}/(N\bar{\gamma}w_t)$$

would have involved a falling real wage and a rising price level over time. Hence, we see again that during a transition, the price level can fall or rise even if the money supply is constant.

In the case of the transition shown in Table 8-1, the price level falls by more than one-quarter between period 0 and period 1. Ultimately, it converges to a value 37 percent smaller than it was initially (at time 0). Remember that a period corresponds to roughly 30 years. So the 27 percent decline in the price level between period 0 and period 1 corresponds to roughly a 1 percent annual rate of deflation.

Although we don't mean our example to represent any particular economy at any particular point in time, it is worth noting that a 1 percent annual rate of deflation is well within the historical record of U.S. price changes. Figure 8-5 plots the annual rate of change in the U.S. price level, as measured by the GNP implicit price deflator for the years 1870 through 1993. The U.S. experienced deflation in more than half the years between 1870 and 1899. In this century deflationary episodes were concentrated in the early 1920s and early 1930s. The

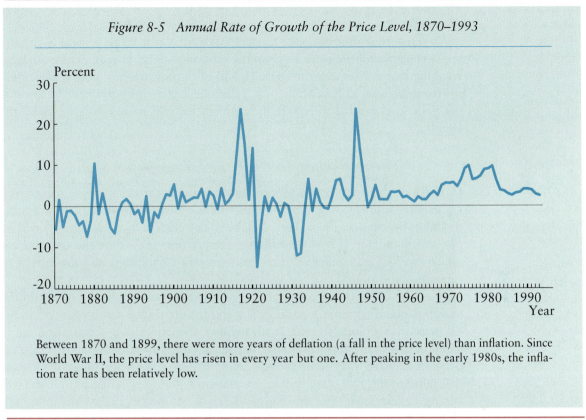

Figure 8-5 Annual Rate of Growth of the Price Level, 1870–1993

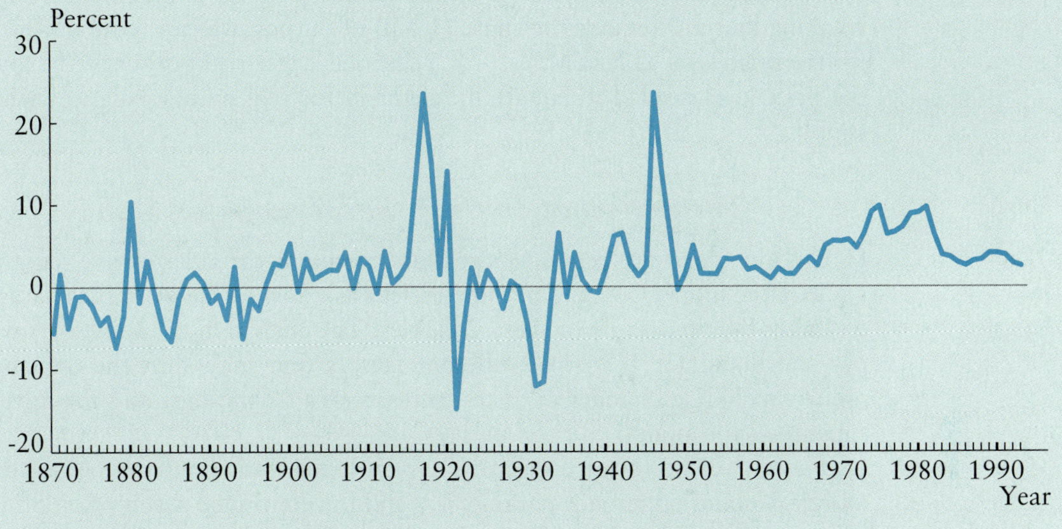

Between 1870 and 1899, there were more years of deflation (a fall in the price level) than inflation. Since World War II, the price level has risen in every year but one. After peaking in the early 1980s, the inflation rate has been relatively low.

Sources: 1870–1939 growth rates from Friedman and Schwartz, *A Monetary History of the United States, 1867–1960* (Princeton, NJ: Princeton University Press, 1963), and 1940–1993 growth rates from *Economic Report of the President*, various issues

largest deflation in a single year occurred in 1921, when prices fell by 15 percent. The largest inflation in a single year occurred in 1946, when World War II price controls were lifted, and prices rose by 24 percent. Since 1983 the U.S. inflation rate has been quite low—running at less than 5 percent per year—after reaching almost 10 percent in the early 1980s.

Case Study: The U.S. Deflation of 1865–1879

The fourteen years between 1865 and 1879 represent the longest sustained deflation in U.S. economic history. During these years wholesale prices, on which there are good data, fell at an average annual rate of over 6 percent. The same item that cost 1 dollar in 1865 cost only 42 cents in 1879. This deflation wasn't caused by a decline in the money stock. On the contrary, the nominal money stock rose by about 15 percent between 1865 and 1879. The cause was the substantial growth over this period in U.S. real GDP, which drove up the demand for money. Between 1865 and 1879 the U.S. population rose by almost one-third and per capita real GDP rose at roughly 4 percent per year. The increase in the nominal supply of money was insufficient to accommodate the increase in demand, so the price level had to fall in order to raise the effective (real) supply of money.

In our formula for the price level, $P_t = \bar{M}/\bar{\gamma}w_tN$, the terms w_t and N capture the dependence of the price level on the economy's level of real income. Indeed, recalling that w_tN equals the share $(1 - \beta)$ of output, we can write our formula for the price level as $P_t = \bar{M}/\bar{\gamma}(1 - \beta)Y_t$. So the larger real output is, the lower is the price level needed to equate the demand for real money balances with the supply.

The Impact of Shifts in the Demand for Money

Having seen how the economy's real and nominal variables evolve for a given value of the money demand parameter, let's ask how a change in that parameter will alter the time paths of these variables. The change in the value of $\bar{\gamma}$ will be our shorthand for a host of different factors that may shift the demand for money, including changes in tastes, transactions technology, and the advent of substitutes for money.

Figure 8-6 shows the economy's capital-labor transition curve based on the money demand preference parameter $\bar{\gamma}$ and the continued assumption of no fiscal policy (so f_t equals zero). It also shows the capital-labor transition curve based on a higher parameter value. A rise in $\bar{\gamma}$ shifts the capital-labor transition curve downward. Whatever the real wage at time t, a higher value of $\bar{\gamma}$ means that more of this real wage will be set aside in real money balances and less will be saved in the form of capital for period $t + 1$. So, whatever the value of k_t is, a higher $\bar{\gamma}$ means a lower capital-labor ratio in the next period (i.e., a lower value of k_{t+1}).

Suppose the economy is initially at its steady state capital-labor ratio, $\bar{k}$, when the change in preferences for money demand occurs. The arrows show the transition path to the lower long-run ratio, $\bar{k}'$. In the diagram let's assume the increase in $\bar{\gamma}$ occurs at time 0. The capital-labor ratio at time 0 is $\bar{k}$, but the capital-labor ratios at times 1, 2, 3, . . . , ∞ are all lower than they would otherwise have been. We can summarize this result by saying that an increase in the demand for money by the young "crowds out" capital accumulation. Intuitively, the more of their wages the young put aside in the form of money, the less they have left over to save, so that capital is "crowded out."[20]

What happens to the price level when $\bar{\gamma}$ increases? Well, according to our formula for the price level, there are two offsetting effects. The higher value of $\bar{\gamma}$ implies a lower path of prices; the lower values of the real wage in periods 1, 2, . . . , ∞, induced by the higher value of $\bar{\gamma}$, imply a higher path of prices. It turns out that so long as the sum of $\bar{\gamma}$ plus β is less than 1, the impact of a higher value of $\bar{\gamma}$ in reducing prices dominates.

In the example of Table 8-1 the steady-state capital-labor ratio is 13.865, and the steady-state price level is 64.912. These results are based on a value of $\bar{\gamma}$ equal to .10. If $\bar{\gamma}$ doubles to .20, the steady-state capital-labor ratio is 11.718,

20. The relationship of money demand to capital accumulation was first stressed by Nobel Laureate James Tobin in "Money and Economic Growth," *Econometrica*, October 1965.

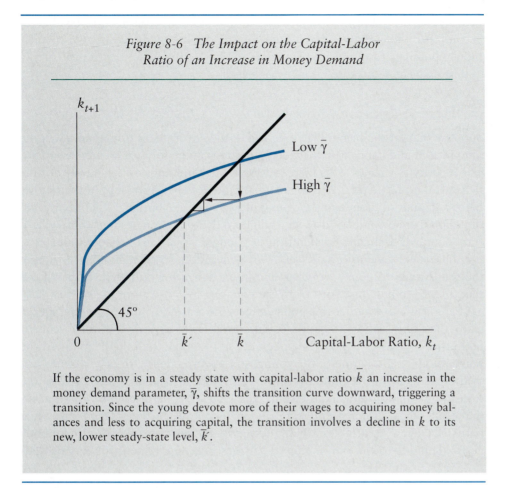

Figure 8-6 The Impact on the Capital-Labor Ratio of an Increase in Money Demand

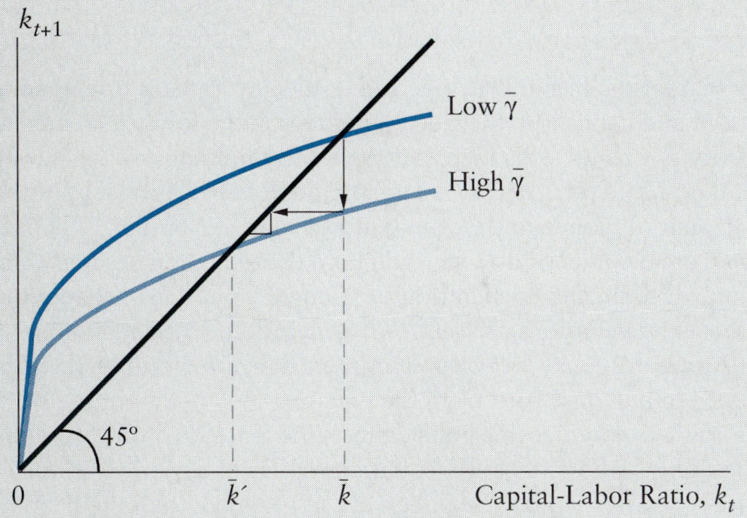

If the economy is in a steady state with capital-labor ratio $\bar{k}$ an increase in the money demand parameter, $\bar{\gamma}$, shifts the transition curve downward, triggering a transition. Since the young devote more of their wages to acquiring money balances and less to acquiring capital, the transition involves a decline in k to its new, lower steady-state level, $\bar{k}'$.

and the steady-state price level is 34.137. Hence, the net impact of this doubling of $\bar{\gamma}$ is to lower the steady-state price level by almost one-half.

WHEN IS MONEY NEUTRAL?

Now that we have a model relating the price level to the money supply, we can use it to examine the neutrality of money—the proposition that a one-time increase in the money supply has no effect on any real variable and simply leads to a proportionate increase in the time path of prices. We'll consider three different ways in which the government might increase the money supply. The first involves printing money to make transfer payments to the elderly. The second involves printing money to finance government consumption (to purchase corn). The third involves printing money to make transfer payments to the young. Only the first of these three policies is neutral, leading to the conclusion that the *manner* in which the money supply is changed determines whether it's neutral.

In considering these cases, it's useful to keep two questions in mind. First, does the way the additional money is injected into the economy affect the saving behavior of the young? If it does, the paths of all real variables will be altered. Second, are the elderly compensated for the decline in the real value of their money holdings resulting from the government's increase in the money supply and its associated increase in the price level?

Case 1: Printing Money to Make Transfers to the Elderly

Suppose that, at the beginning of period 0, the government prints money in the amount ΔM and hands it to the elderly, perhaps in the form of an increase in Social Security payments. This increases the money holdings of the elderly at time 0 from $\overline{M}$ to $\overline{M} + \Delta M$. At the end of period 0 the elderly supply their now-higher amount of money to the young in exchange for output. When the young of period 0 are old in period 1, they will hold the total money supply and will, in turn, supply it to the next generation of young people. This situation holds true for subsequent generations as well; each generation, when it is old, will supply the total stock of money to the young in exchange for output (i.e., they'll use their money to purchase corn from the young).

Let's now ask whether this policy affects the real side of the economy, specifically the capital-labor transition equation, either in period 0 or in subsequent periods. The answer is no. The policy doesn't involve the sale of bonds to the young or any net taxation of the young, so f_t is zero. Hence, the saving behavior of the young at time 0 and in all subsequent periods is unchanged. Because the transition equation remains the same, the policy has no effect on capital accumulation, output, the real interest rate, or the real wage. The fact that the time paths of these real variables are unaffected by the government's printing money and handing it to the old at time 0 satisfies one requirement for money neutrality.

Neutrality also requires the time path of the price level to rise in proportion to the increase in the money supply. This requirement is also satisfied. To see why, note that the formula for the price level is the same as before, except that the money supply from period 0 onward is $\overline{M} + \Delta M$, rather than simply $\overline{M}$. As before, we derive this formula by equating the real supply of money at time t, $(\overline{M} + \Delta M)/P_t$ in this case, to the real demand for money by the young at time t, $\overline{\gamma} w_t N$, and solving for the price level. The modified price level formula is

$$P_t = \frac{\overline{M} + \Delta M}{\overline{\gamma} w_t N}$$

Since the time path of the real wage is not altered by the monetary policy we're considering, our formula indicates that the price level at each point in time will be proportional to the total money supply. Stated differently, the time path of the price level will rise by whatever percentage increase occurs in the money supply.

Finally, let's ask how the elderly at time 0 fare as a result of the money supply policy. In particular, does transferring money to the elderly make them better off? The answer is no. It's true that the elderly at time 0 end up with more money after the transfer, but the resulting increase in the price level dilutes the real value of their initial as well as their additional money. In the end their nominal money holdings are larger, but their real money balances are just the same as in the absence of the government's transfer payment. We can verify this by examining the equation for consumption by an elderly individual at time 0:

$$c_{o0} = a_0(1 + r_0) + \frac{(\overline{M} + \Delta M)/N}{P_0}$$

Clearly, consumption by the elderly at time 0 depends partly on the ratio of nominal money holdings to the price level (the real money balances). But a given percentage increase in the nominal money holdings of each elderly person at time 0, matched by an equal percentage increase in the price level, leaves real money balances of the elderly unchanged. So, consumption by the elderly will be unchanged. In reducing the real value of money, the increase in the price level, in effect, taxes the money holdings of the elderly. This implicit tax exactly offsets the extra money they receive, leaving them in the same real position.

The young are also left in the same real position. They receive the same real wage, and since they initially hold no money balances, the price rise does not affect them. Of course, when they sell their output to the elderly, the young will receive more money. But because of the price increase, the real value of the money received will be the same as in the absence of the government policy.

So, now we've shown that both requirements for the neutrality of money are satisfied. The neutrality with respect to this *particular* type of one-time increase in the money supply does not depend on the specific parameter values we assumed. It follows immediately from the fact that the capital-labor transition equation doesn't depend on the money supply and that the price level rises in proportion to the increase in the money supply.

Case 2: Printing Money to Finance Government Consumption

In our second case, the government prints additional money in the amount ΔM and uses it to purchase output, which it consumes at time 0. In succeeding periods the government prints no additional money and purchases no additional goods and services. The government policy is a one-time event, but the money supply is permanently increased from $\overline{M}$ to $\overline{M} + \Delta M$. As in Case 1, this policy leaves f_t equal to zero and, therefore, has no effect on saving by the young at time 0 or in any subsequent time period. They continue to retain the same portion $\overline{\gamma}$ of their real wages in the form of real money balances and save the rest. Hence, the capital-labor transition equation is not altered by the policy. Since the initial capital-labor ratio, k_0, is unchanged, this transition equation grinds out the same time paths of the capital-labor ratio, output, the real interest rate, and the real wage as in the absence of the government policy. From the perspective of these real variables, the government's printing of money to purchase goods and services at time 0 has no effect.

Turning to the price level, the formula for the price level at time 0 and in all subsequent periods is the same as in Case 1, namely, $P_t = (\overline{M} + \Delta M)/\overline{\gamma} w_t N$. It is the standard price level formula with a total money supply of $\overline{M} + \Delta M$, rather than simply $\overline{M}$. This equation says that the entire time path of the price level rises in proportion to the increase in the money supply—an additional requirement for the neutrality of money.

So far, then, we haven't detected any difference between this policy of spending newly printed money on goods and services and the policy of transferring it to the elderly. But there *is* a difference, and it is precisely with respect to the elderly at time 0. They experience a tax on their nominal money holdings as a result of the increase in the price level at time 0, which is *not* offset by the transfer of money from the government. Indeed, the old at time 0 end up paying entirely for the government spending at time 0 through a decline in their real money balances.

In Case 1 the real money balances of the elderly at time 0 (which they swapped with the young for real output) were $(\overline{M} + \Delta M)/NP_0$. Those balances included the increase in the money supply, ΔM, that had been transferred to them by the government. In Case 2, however, the real money balances of the elderly at time 0 are only $\overline{M}/NP_0$. So the total supply of money swapped by the elderly at time 0 for real goods and services is not the total money supply at time 0, $\overline{M} + \Delta M$, but only the amount $\overline{M}$. The rest of the money supply, ΔM, being supplied to the young (swapped for goods from the young) is supplied directly by the government. In exchange for this ΔM in money, the government is able to obtain real output from the young equal to $\Delta M/P_0$, which is precisely the amount lost by each old person at time 0 multiplied by the number of elderly.

In periods after time 0 the entire money supply will be held by the elderly and their real money balances will equal $(\overline{M} + \Delta M)/NP_t$, as in Case 1. For example, the elderly in period 1 will be the generation that was young at time 0. These are the individuals who acquired the total money supply at the end of period 0; they received $\overline{M}$ from the old and ΔM from the government. So the consumption by the elderly in periods after time 0 will be unaffected by the policy.

To summarize, printing money at time 0 to finance government consumption is *not* neutral because it reduces the welfare of those who are elderly in that period. We also learned that the government was able to get that generation of elderly people to pay for its consumption without explicitly taxing them. The reduction at time 0 in consumption by the elderly precisely equals the increased consumption by the government, so aggregate consumption at time 0 is unaffected. That explains why there is no policy-induced change in aggregate saving at time 0 and therefore no change in the capital-labor transition equation. This is analogous to our result in Chapter 7 that taxing the old to pay for government purchases has no effect on the macroeconomy.

Case 3: Printing Money to Finance Transfers to the Young

In our final case, the government prints ΔM of additional money and uses it to make transfer payments to the young at time 0. These payments might take the form of educational grants, child care tax credits paid to young and middle-aged working parents, or welfare benefits to the young and middle aged. This policy alters the welfare of the initial elderly, as in Case 2, but unlike Case 2, it's not neutral with respect to the path of output and the real money supply. The rise in the price level associated with the increased money supply hurts the elderly at time 0 by diluting the real value of their nominal money holdings of $\overline{M}$. This loss to the elderly means a gain to the young at time 0. Those young people are each handed $\Delta M/N$ in transfer payments, the real value of which ends up equaling $\Delta M/NP_0$ (whatever P_0 turns out to be). But unlike the other two policies, in this case f_0 equals $-\Delta M/NP_0$, so the saving behavior of the young at time 0 *is* altered by the transfer payment. As a consequence, the transition curve is affected and the time path of all real variables is changed.

To be more precise, the policy alters the transition equation at time 1, because it alters f_0 and, thus, the saving by the young at time 0. The equation for the capital-labor ratio at time 1 is

$$k_1 = (1 - \overline{\gamma})A(1 - \beta)k_0^{\beta} + \frac{\Delta M}{NP_0}$$

where we've replaced $-f_0$ with $\Delta M/NP_0$, the real value of the transfer given to the young at time 0. The entire transfer is saved by the young, so it adds to the capital they bring into period 1.

Since the policy is a one-time event and does not directly alter saving behavior after period 0 (f_t is zero after period 0), the form of the transition equation in those later periods is not altered. It remains $k_{t+1} = (1 - \overline{\gamma})A(1- \beta)k_t^{\beta}$. However, because the transition equation for k_1 is altered, the actual value of k_1 that arises is changed by the policy. So after period 1, the time paths of all the economy's real variables will be different from what they would otherwise have been, not because the transition curve is permanently shifted, but because the value of k_1 from which the post-period-1 transition begins is different.

Figure 8-7 shows this. It depicts the transition curve for k_1 as well as the original, no-policy transition curve, which determines the values of the capital-labor ratio after period 1 when no further monetary policy is being conducted. Since ΔM is positive, the transition curve for k_1 lies above the curve that determines the capital-labor ratio in all later periods.

We can use this diagram to trace the impact on the capital-labor ratio of the government's monetary policy. Let's suppose that at time 0 the economy is at the steady-state capital-labor ratio $\overline{k}$ indicated in the diagram, so that $k_0 = \overline{k}$. At time 0, the government prints ΔM of additional money and transfers it to the young. To determine the value of k_1 we need simply to go up to the new transition curve for k_1 and use the 45-degree line to measure k_1 along the horizontal axis. At time 1, the transition curve returns to its original position. Starting with the value of k_1, we use that original transition curve to determine the values of k_2, k_3, and all subsequent capital-labor ratios. Since we are using the no-monetary-policy transition curve from period 2 onward, the economy's capital-labor ratio eventually returns to the steady-state value $\overline{k}$ at which it started. But the monetary policy clearly alters the value of the capital-labor ratio and other

Figure 8-7 The Impact on the Capital-Labor Ratio of Printing Money to Make Transfers to the Young at Time 0

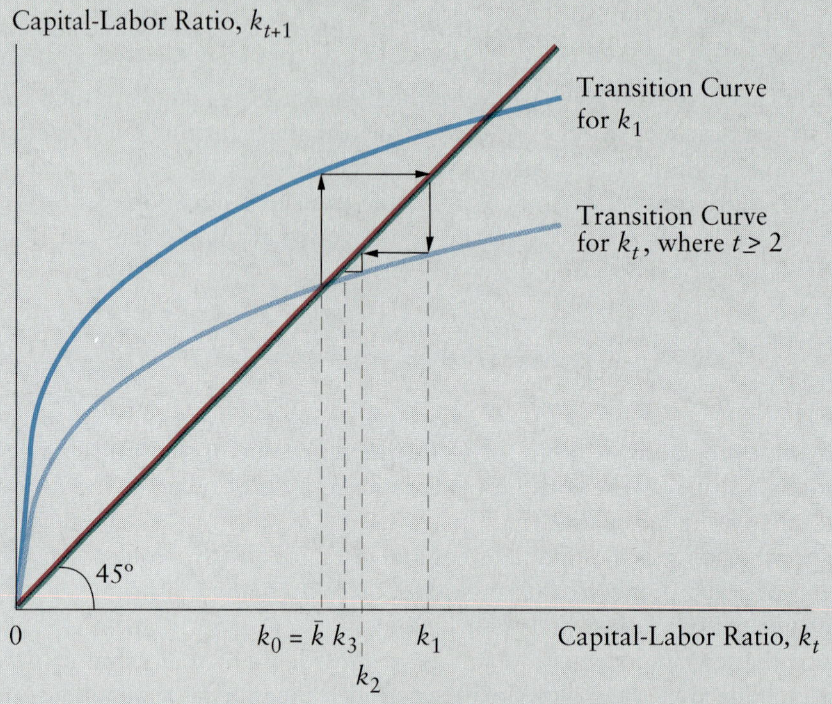

At time 0, with the economy in steady state at capital-labor ratio $k_0 = \bar{k}$, the government prints new money and transfers it to the young. This policy lowers f_0, net payments to government by the young, and shifts the k_1 transition curve upward. Therefore, the capital-labor ratio at time 1, k_1, is determined by the higher transition curve. After time 1, f_t is again zero, so the transition curve returns to its original (lower) position. Subsequent capital-labor ratios are determined along that lower curve as the economy moves back to its original steady state. Because real variables are altered during the transition, this policy is not neutral.

real variables during the transition back to the original steady state. For this reason it is not neutral.

As in both previous cases, the formula for the price level is $P_t = (\overline{M} + \Delta M)/\overline{\gamma} w_t N$. As before, the price level initially increases in proportion to the money stock in period 0, when the wage rate is already determined. But unlike those other two cases, the time path of the wage rate after period 0 (the w_t in the equation) is now altered. As Figure 8-7 implies, the policy produces a temporary rise in the wage rate. As a result, the percentage increase in the price level is smaller than the percentage increase in the money supply until the economy returns to its steady state.

Printing Money to Make Transfers to the Young: A Numerical Example

To see more clearly how increasing the money supply by making transfers to the young differs from increasing it via transfers to the old, let's start in the steady state of the economy of Table 8-1 with a money supply of 10,000. The bottom row in Table 8-1 indicates that the steady-state capital-labor ratio is 13.865, the steady-state wage is 15.405, and the steady-state price level is 64.912. Starting from this steady-state position at time 0, we know that doubling the money supply and giving the additional money to the old at time 0 would simply lead to a doubling of the price level, from 64.912 to 129.824, and otherwise leave the economy unaffected.

If, instead, we double the money supply at time 0 and give the additional money to the young, we get the transition path for prices, the capital-labor ratio, and the real wage shown in Table 8-2. Let's calculate this transition by first noting that the formula for the price level is $P_t = 2000/w_t$. Using $w_0 =$ 15.405, we find that $P_0 = 129.825$. From the formula for k_1, we have $k_1 = .9 \times$ $15.405 + (10{,}000/100)/P_0$, so $k_1 = 14.635$. With this value of k_1, our post-period-1 capital-labor transition equation, $k_{t+1} = .9w_t$, and the fact that $w_t =$ $.70k_t^{.30}$, we can compute all the remaining transition values for the capital-labor ratio and the wage. Based on this time path of the wage, we can use our price level formula to determine the time path of prices.

Table 8-2 indicates that the policy of giving the new money to the young entails a transition path in which the capital-labor ratio rises temporarily above, and the price level falls temporarily below, their steady-state values. In addition to these effects, the young at time 0 are made better off; their lifetime income rises by the amount $(\Delta M/N)/P_0 = .770$. Second, the old at time 0 are made worse off; collectively, they find themselves at the beginning of period 0 with the same amount of nominal money, 10,000, but with a higher price level. They each suffer a decline in the real value of their money balances of .770—precisely the size of the real benefit to the young at time 0. Thus, by printing money and giving it to the young at time 0, the government redistributes real resources from the old to the young. The transfer to the young is paid for, not by the government, but by the implicit tax placed on the nominal money balances of the old.

INFLATION AS THE RESULT OF ONGOING INCREASES IN THE MONEY SUPPLY

In each of the three examples we assumed a one-time increase in the money supply. What happens if, instead, the government continues to engage in one or more of these policies period after period? The answer is inflation. Suppose, for example, the government prints money each period to finance transfers to the old. Then the price level each period will rise by an amount, above and beyond what it would otherwise have risen, equal to the percentage increase in the money supply. Thus, if the government prints 10 percent more money each

Table 8-2 The Impact of a One-Time Transfer to the Young Financed by Printing Money

Period	k_t	w_t	P_t
0	13.865	15.405	129.825
1	14.635	15.657	127.736
2	14.092	15.480	129.194
3	13.932	15.428	129.635
4	13.885	15.412	129.768
5	13.871	15.407	129.808
6	13.867	15.406	129.820
7	13.865	15.406	129.823
.	.	.	.
.	.	.	.
.	.	.	.
∞	13.865	15.405	129.825

Assumptions: $k_0 = 13.865$, $\gamma = .10$, $\beta = .30$, $A = 10$, $N = 100$, $\overline{M} = 10{,}000$, $\Delta M = 10{,}000$.
Equations underlying the table:

$$k_{t+1} = (1-\overline{\gamma})w_t + \Delta M/NP_0 \text{ (holds for } t = 0)$$

$$k_{t+1} = (1-\overline{\gamma})w_t \text{ (holds for } t \text{ greater than or equal to 1)}$$

$$w_t = A(1-\beta)k_t^{\beta} \text{ (holds for all values of } t)$$

$$P_t = (\overline{M} + \Delta M)/(N\overline{\gamma}w_t) \text{ (holds for all values of } t)$$

period to pay for its transfers, the price level will rise by 10 percent more each period than it would otherwise have gone up. In the economy's steady state, prices will continue rising period after period by 10 percent. Given our formulation of the demand for money and the fact that f_t equals zero, this will leave unchanged the capital-labor transition equation, but will hit each successive set of old people with an implicit tax on their real money holdings equal to the concomitant transfers they receive from the government.

In the case of an ongoing policy of paying for government purchases by printing money, each period's inflation rate is also dictated by the growth rate of the money supply in that period. But assuming, as we have, a fixed value of γ, this inflationary finance has no impact on capital accumulation.

Finally, in the case in which the government prints money each period to finance transfers to the young, the capital-labor transition curve will be permanently shifted upward, reflecting the ongoing government redistribution from the old to the young (f_t will be positive each period). The resulting change in the time path of the real wage will influence the rate at which the price level changes through time. In the steady state, however, both the real wage and f_t will be constant, so the inflation rate will not be influenced by feedback effects on the demand for money. Consequently, the steady-state inflation rate will simply equal the growth rate in the money supply.

The Inflation Process Under A More Realistic Formulation of Money Demand

The conclusion that the steady-state inflation rate is determined by the growth rate of the money supply holds equally well if we assume that the function $\gamma[\ ]$ depends on the nominal interest rate, rather than equaling a constant. In this case, the function $\gamma[i_{t+1}]$, rather than the constant $\bar{\gamma}$, enters the time t formula for money demand. With this formulation, the transition path to the steady state as well as the particular steady state toward which the economy moves would both differ. When the nominal interest rate, and thus the inflation rate, influences the demand for real money balances, ongoing inflation will affect real money demand and the capital-labor transition equation. This is true even in Case 1, in which the government prints money each period to transfer to the elderly and f_t equals zero, and Case 2, in which the government prints money each period to finance its purchases. The reason is that now $\gamma[i_{t+1}]$, rather than $\bar{\gamma}$, enters the capital-labor ratio transition equation.

We know that inflation raises nominal interest rates. With money demand based on $\gamma[i_{t+1}]$ and, thus, inversely related to the nominal interest rate, inflation reduces young people's demand for real money balances. Consequently, the young set aside less of their wages in the form of real money balances and invest more of their wages in capital. This shifts the capital-labor transition curve upward, leading to an increase in capital accumulation in Cases 1 and 2. In Case 3, in which the government prints money to make transfers to the young, including the nominal interest rate in the money demand would lead to more of an upward shift in the transition curve than would otherwise occur.

Case Study: What Shares of U.S. and Israeli Government Spending Are Financed by Printing Money?

The money that the government creates directly is called the *monetary base*.[21] The increase in the monetary base divided by the price level is referred to as **seigniorage**. It measures the real resources the government acquires by printing money and using it to make transfer payments or to purchase goods and services.[22] In our model, seigniorage at time t can be written as $\Delta M_t/P_t$, the change in the supply of money between periods t and $t + 1$ divided by the price level. If we divide and then multiply this expression by M_t, we can write seigniorage as

Seigniorage *The real resources the government acquires by printing money*

21. In Chapter 14 we'll discuss the relationship between the monetary base and M1.

22. The word "seigniorage" can be traced to the Middle Ages, when coins were exclusively minted by the sovereign, or seignior, and the difference between the face value of coins and their cost of minting was called seigniorage.

$(\Delta M_t/M_t)(M_t/P_t)$—as the growth rate of the money supply times the level of real money balances. As we just saw, in the steady state the inflation rate equals the growth rate of the money supply. So if we let $\bar{\pi}$ stand for the steady-state inflation rate and $(\bar{M}/\bar{P})$ stand for the steady-state holdings of real money balances, steady-state seigniorage is $\pi(\bar{M}/\bar{P})$. This expression tells us that, in the steady state, the real purchases the government finances by printing money are equivalent to taxing real money balances at the rate of inflation. To understand this, think of $\bar{\pi}$ as a tax rate and $\bar{M}/\bar{P}$ as the tax base.

In the United States, seigniorage has not been a significant source of real resources for the government. Figure 8-8 shows that seigniorage has ranged between 1 and 2 percent of the federal budget for the years 1980–1991. For comparison, the figure also shows the seigniorage-budget ratio for the government of Israel. In the mid-1980s the Israeli government printed significant amounts of money and drove the inflation rate above 300 percent per year. In those years seigniorage represented as much as 12 percent of total Israeli government outlays.

Using Surprise Inflation to Reduce the Real Value of Government Debt

Seigniorage is not the only way governments use monetary policy to acquire real resources. Another way is to use inflation to dilute the real value of their nominal debt. To this point, we have not incorporated nominal government debt into our model with money. But if we had, we would have found that increases in the money supply that increase prices erode not just the real value of money but also the real value of nominal government bonds. As a consequence, the government needs less real revenue to pay the interest and principal on these bonds.

Take the case of Alex, who purchases a 30-year U.S. Treasury bond for $10,000. Suppose the bond promises to pay interest of $1,000 per year for 30 years and then return the $10,000 principal. Both principal and interest are fixed in nominal terms. Now suppose that, immediately after selling this bond, the government doubles the money supply, which leads to a doubling of current and future prices. This is an extreme case, but it clearly illustrates the point. What happens to the real value of Alex's bond? The answer is that it falls by half; the stream of nominal interest and principal payments can now buy only half the amount of real goods and services. Since the real value of government debt falls by half, the real taxes needed to meet these interest and principal payments fall by half as well. The government will experience this reduction in the real value of its outstanding debt in the form of a doubling of its nominal tax revenues as a result of the doubling of all commodity and factor prices. Its nominal revenues will double, but the *nominal* time path of its interest and principal payments will remain unchanged.

This example makes sense, as far as it goes. But it neglects the possibility that the nominal interest and principal payments on the $10,000 bond were bigger to begin with in anticipation of the increase in prices. Indeed, our formula

Figure 8-8 U.S. and Israeli Seigniorage as Shares of Their National Budgets, 1980–1991

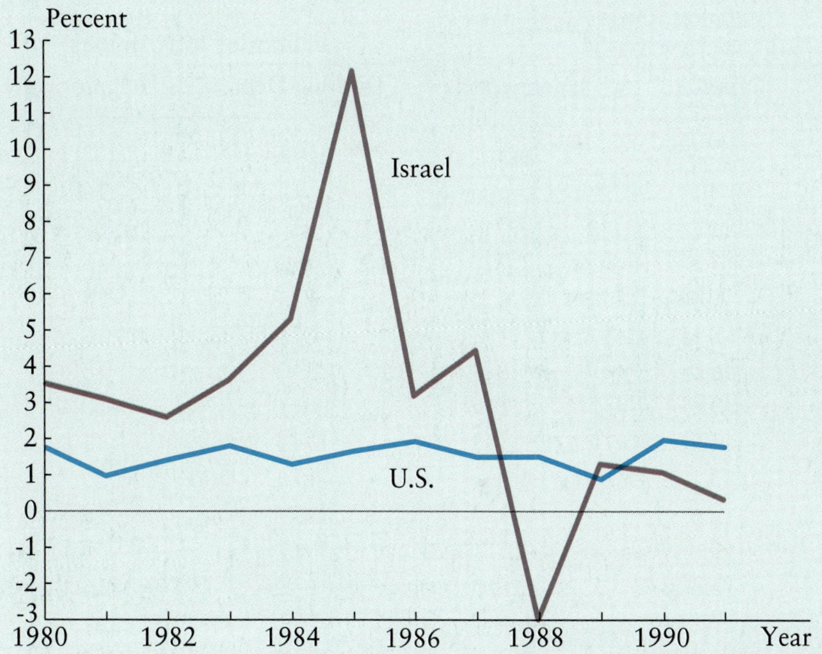

Seigniorage—the change in the monetary base divided by the price level—is the real resources the government acquires by printing new money. This figure shows that seigniorage in the United States has ranged between 1 and 2 percent of the federal budget. In Israel in the mid-1980s, however, seigniorage was a significant source of government revenue. In 1985, for instance, it represented over 12 percent of the Israeli government budget.

for the nominal interest rate tells us that the nominal interest rate will incorporate the anticipated (expected) inflation rate. Stated differently, the nominal interest rate will adjust in response to the expected rate of inflation to make savers indifferent between investing in real capital or in nominal government bonds.

In our model so far we have assumed that whatever inflation is expected actually occurs. But if inflation turns out to be higher (lower) than was expected, the nominal interest rate will undercompensate (overcompensate) government bondholders for the reduction in the real value of their principal and interest receipts. This *unexpected inflation*—the difference between actual and expected inflation —- represents the true degree to which the government acquires real resources by printing money and diluting the real value of its nominal debt.

Table 8-3 Unexpected Inflation and the Dilution of U.S. Government Debt

Year	Inflation Rate (percent per year)			Source of Real Government Resources (billions of 1992 dollars)	
	Actual[a]	Expected[b]	Unexpected	Diluting Debt[c]	Seigniorage[d]
1970	5.7	3.6	2.1	29.2	12.5
1971	4.4	3.8	0.6	8.2	14.2
1972	3.2	3.2	0.0	0.2	20.3
1973	6.2	3.5	2.7	40.1	18.7
1974	11.0	5.4	5.6	77.6	18.4
1975	9.1	7.4	1.7	24.4	16.6
1976	5.8	6.0	−0.2	−3.7	18.8
1977	6.5	5.4	1.1	18.0	20.4
1978	7.6	6.3	1.3	21.6	21.8
1979	11.3	7.1	4.2	68.1	20.7
1980	13.5	9.6	3.9	60.3	18.5
1981	10.3	10.3	0.0	0.2	10.8
1982	6.2	7.2	−1.0	−17.2	16.1
1983	3.2	5.1	−1.9	−36.5	21.6
1984	4.3	5.6	−1.3	−27.1	15.9
1985	3.6	4.8	−1.2	−29.4	21.3
1986	1.9	4.1	−2.2	−60.8	25.8
1987	3.6	3.5	0.1	4.3	20.1
1988	4.1	4.2	−0.1	−1.9	20.2
1989	4.8	5.1	−0.3	−9.1	12.2
1990	5.4	3.9	1.5	51.7	27.4
1991	4.2	3.8	0.4	15.1	24.7
1992	3.0	3.4	−0.4	−15.6	33.5

[a] Percentage change in the consumer price index
[b] This is the Livingston series on expected inflation published by the Federal Reserve Bank of Philadelphia
[c] Gross federal debt multiplied by the rate of unexpected inflation and converted to 1992 dollars using the Consumer Price Index
[d] The change in the monetary base converted to 1992 dollars using the Consumer Price Index

Case Study: How Much Has the U.S. Diluted Its Debt Through Unexpected Inflation?

If we can measure the ex ante ("before the fact") expected rate of inflation and compare it with the ex post ("after the fact") rate, we can estimate the extent of unexpected inflation. One way to do this is simply to ask people in advance what they expect inflation to be. Table 8-3 reports expected inflation rates for the years 1970 to 1992 based on an annual survey of business leaders. It also shows the actual and unexpected rates of inflation over the period. Finally, the table compares the amount of real resources produced by diluting the real value of U.S. government debt through unexpected inflation with the amount of seigniorage, both measured in 1992 dollars.

According to the table, American business leaders have both under- and overpredicted inflation in recent years. The biggest underprediction occurred in 1974 when the expected inflation rate of 5.4 percent fell short of the actual 11.0 percent inflation rate. The biggest overprediction occurred in 1986, when inflation was expected to equal 4.1 percent, but ended up at only 1.9 percent. In years when inflation was underpredicted the government raised real revenues by diluting its debt. But in years when inflation was overpredicted, the government ended up paying (in terms of nominal interest on its bonds) a higher inflation premium than proved, ex post, to have been warranted. In those years, the real value of the debt was raised, rather than lowered, because of unexpected inflation.

The sums involved in altering the real value of government debt can be substantial. Take 1980. In that year unexpected inflation cut real U.S. government debt by $60.3 billion, far exceeding the $17.5 billion raised in real seigniorage. Had this gain to the government been recorded as a source of revenue (it wasn't), it would have essentially eliminated the 1980 federal deficit of $61.3 billion! The federal government's failure to include these real revenue gains and losses in computing the deficit is another reason, in addition to those given in the previous chapter, to question the usefulness of the deficit as a measure of fiscal policy.

Inflation in the Presence of Non-Indexed Government Taxation and Spending

The third way governments use inflation to garner real resources from the private sector is by failing to index their taxes for inflation.[23] A prime example here is progressive income taxation. Most developed countries tax nominal income on a progressive basis, meaning that the higher the nominal income, the higher the marginal tax rate. In causing inflation, governments raise the nominal incomes of individuals and firms and push them into higher tax brackets. As a result, their real taxes rise even if their real incomes remain unchanged.[24]

23. The U.S. government is an exception to this rule. In 1985 the U.S. government indexed the federal personal income tax to inflation.

24. Take the case of a 20 percent tax on income in excess of $20,000. Someone earning $30,000 pays $2,000—20 percent of the $10,000 excess of total income over $20,000. Now suppose inflation doubles all prices and nominal incomes, so that a person who previously earned $30,000 now earns $60,000. The taxes due would now be 20 percent of $60,000 minus $20,000, or $8,000. Even though the person's real income doesn't change, his tax rate doubles from 6.7 percent ($2,000/$30,000) to 13.3 percent ($8,000/$60,000).

A fourth way in which inflation can affect the government's real fiscal position involves the non-indexation of government spending. In the U.S., Social Security benefits are indexed for inflation, but most other transfer payments are not. As the price level rises, the real value of welfare benefits, unemployment insurance, and food stamps falls unless the government explicitly legislates nominal benefit increases. A good example of inflation eroding real transfer payments involves Aid to Families with Dependent Children (AFDC)—the government's principal welfare program. Since 1975 real payments per family receiving AFDC have fallen by over 25 percent.

Chapter Summary

1. This chapter added money to our model. We began by describing the properties of money and one important characteristic of money, its velocity. Next we added the supply of and demand for money to our life-cycle model and used these relationships to derive a formula for the price level. Finally, we used our model to examine the effects of several monetary policies on the economy's nominal and real variables.

2. Money is a highly liquid means of exchange, store of value, and unit of account. What constitutes money in any particular society depends on institutional arrangements, beliefs, and transactions technologies. Historically, money in the U.S. has ranged from Continentals to bills of exchange, to bank notes, to greenbacks, to modern-day Federal Reserve notes.

3. The classical economists argued that money is neutral—that increases in the money supply simply lead to equal proportionate increases in the price level, with no effect on real variables. Their view can be understood using the quantity equation, $Mv = PY$. Assuming that output, Y, is always at its full employment level and that velocity, v, is constant, an increase in the money supply, M, will simply lead to an equal proportionate increase in the price level.

4. In our model money is supplied by the elderly and by the government. It is demanded by the young based on their preferences and their lifetime budget constraints. The demand for money depends positively on the wage rate and negatively on the nominal interest rate, which is the opportunity cost of holding money. A striking illustration of the inverse relationship between the demand for real money balances and the nominal interest rate is provided by the behavior of real money balances during the German hyperinflation.

5. Our model with money reduces to two interrelated equations: the capital-labor ratio transition equation and the price level equation. One lesson from the study of this interrelationship is that transitions involving increases in the economy's real income, captured in our model by the real wage, raise the demand for real money balances. Given a fixed money supply, the increased demand can only be satisfied by a decline in the price level.

6. The model shows that the way the government injects money into the economy determines whether the injection is neutral. If the government increases the money supply by making a one-time transfer to the elderly, monetary policy will be neutral. In this case the value of the transfer to the elderly is offset by their loss in real money balances due to the rise in prices; prices rise in proportion to the increase in the money supply. In contrast, a one-time increase in the money supply that is spent on government consumption is not neutral. Prices rise in proportion to the money supply, and the elderly at the time of the policy change pay for the additional government consumption through a price-induced decline in their real money balances. Finally, a one-time increase in the money supply that is handed to the young as transfer payments stimulates their saving and thereby affects the time path of the capital-labor ratio. Ultimately, the economy ends up at the same steady-state capital-labor ratio to which it was headed, and the price level ends up, in the long run, rising in proportion to the money supply. However, since the economy's real variables are affected during the transition, this policy is not neutral.

7. Ongoing increases in the money supply, regardless of how they are spent, will produce inflation. The long-run inflation rate is determined by the long-run growth rate of the money supply. If the demand for money is sensitive to the nominal interest rate, ongoing increases in the money supply will be non-neutral even if each period's increase in the money supply is spent on transfers to the elderly.

8. Because the impact of money supply increases depends on how the new money is spent, and because increases in the money supply raise prices and implicitly tax existing money holdings and nominal government bonds, monetary policy can be viewed as a form of fiscal policy. The relationship of monetary policy to fiscal policy is even tighter if the tax system and government expenditures are not indexed for inflation.

Key Concepts

Demand deposits
Neutrality of money
Monetary policy
Barter
Liquidity
Hyperinflation
Bank runs
Real stock of money
Quantity equation
Velocity of money
Quantity theory of money
Deflation
Seigniorage

Review Questions

1. What is the *price level*?
2. What is *money*, and what constitutes the *M1* measure of money?
3. What does it mean to say that "money is neutral"?
4. What functions does money perform, and how does the existence of money make economies more efficient?
5. What is *liquidity*?
6. What is the *quantity equation*, and how is it used to derive the *quantity theory of money*?
7. What factors affect the *velocity of money*, and how has the velocity of money in the United States behaved historically?
8. What is the *opportunity cost* of holding money? How is the *lifetime budget constraint* written when individuals hold money?

9. How does the life-cycle model incorporate money into the utility function, and what is the resulting equation for the *demand for real money balances*?
10. How is the *transition equation* written after money is incorporated into the life-cycle model?
11. How is the *price level* determined in the life-cycle model, and what equation describes its time path? How is the price level affected by a change in the wage? by a change in $\overline{\gamma}$?
12. Under what circumstances will money be neutral in the life-cycle model? Under what circumstances will money not be neutral?
13. What is the impact of ongoing increases in money when $\gamma[\ ]$ is constant? when $\gamma[\ ]$ depends on the nominal interest rate?
14. How can money growth and its associated inflation affect the *real fiscal position* of a government?

Numerical Questions

1. Answer each of the following questions based on the data given in the table below.

Year	Real GDP (billions of 1987 dollars)	GDP Deflator (1987 = 100)	M1 (billions of dollars)	M2 (billions of dollars)
1970	2,873.9	35.2	214.5	628.1
1980	3,776.3	71.7	408.8	1,629.5
1990	4,877.5	113.2	826.1	3,339.0

For each year, compute the value of each of the following:

a. The velocity of money using M1. What happens to its value over time?
b. The velocity of money using M2. What happens to its value over time?
c. The real money stock using M1
d. The real money stock using M2

2. Suppose an economy is characterized by the following parameters:

$$\beta = .3,\ A = 5,\ N = 100,\ K_0 = 200,\ \overline{M} = 1000,\ \text{and}\ \overline{\gamma} = .1$$

a. For periods 0 through 5, calculate values of the economy's capital-labor ratio, per capita earnings, and the price level.
b. Compute the steady-state values of the capital-labor ratio, per capita earnings, and the price level.

3. Assume all of the initial values provided in question 2 except the value of $\overline{\gamma}$, which has increased to .3.

a. For periods 0 through 5, calculate values of the economy's capital-labor ratio, per capita earnings, and the price level.
b. Compute the steady-state values of the capital-labor ratio, per capita earnings, and the price level.
c. Use a transition diagram to explain why the values in this question differ from their corresponding values in question 2 (i.e., when $\overline{\gamma} = .1$).

4. a. Based on the parameter values and steady-state values used for question 3, ($\beta = .3$, $A = 5$, $N = 100$, $K_0 = 200$, $\overline{M}=1000$, and $\overline{\gamma} = .3$), compute the steady-state values of each of the following:
   i. Real money holdings per person (m/P)
   ii. The real interest rate (r)
   iii. The nominal interest rate (i)
   iv. Consumption by the old (c_o)
   b. Using the steady-state values calculated above, demonstrate that the intertemporal budget constraint is satisfied.

5. With the economy in the steady state calculated in the previous two questions, the government increases the money supply by 500 and gives it to the young.
   a. For periods 0 through 5, calculate values of the economy's capital-labor ratio, per capita earnings, and the price level.
   b. Compute the steady-state values of the capital-labor ratio, per capita earnings, and the price level.
   c. Compare the resulting steady state to the original steady state. Is the policy neutral? Explain.

Analytical Questions

1. Economist Milton Friedman of the University of Chicago once remarked that "Inflation is always and everywhere a monetary phenomenon." Evaluate Friedman's statement. Is ongoing money growth the only way for ongoing inflation to occur, or are there other economic events that could lead to continual increases in the price level?

2. As part of the economic transformation occurring in the countries of the former Soviet Union and Eastern Europe, the banking systems and banking services of those countries are becoming more sophisticated. Someday, free market reformers in these countries hope to see a proliferation of ATMs, credit cards, and debit card arrangements, among other changes. Discuss the economic effects that such developments might have.

3. Suppose that OPEC suddenly restricts the amount of crude oil that it sells to the United States. Answer the following questions, assuming that γ is constant. (Helpful hint: Think of this as influencing the level of multifactor productivity. Refer to the transition diagram and price level equation when answering.)
   a. What will happen to the price level in the periods after the restriction is imposed?
   b. Will the price level in the new steady state be higher than, lower than, or the same as the price level in the initial steady state?
   c. Will nominal interest rates in the new steady state be higher than, lower than, or the same as in the initial steady state?
   d. Suppose that you are a monetary policy maker and have as your goal price stability. How would you adjust the money supply in light of the restrictions?

4. Suppose that the government has decided to implement a new program whereby transfers are made to the elderly. The government is considering

implementing one of two financing options. In the first, the government taxes the young and gives the proceeds to the elderly. In the second, the government simply prints more money to pay for the transfers. Assume, as we did in this chapter, that young people consume nothing and that γ is constant. If you are an old person when the policy is announced, which plan will you prefer, and why? If you are a young person when the policy is announced, which plan will you prefer, and why?

P A R T   T H R E E

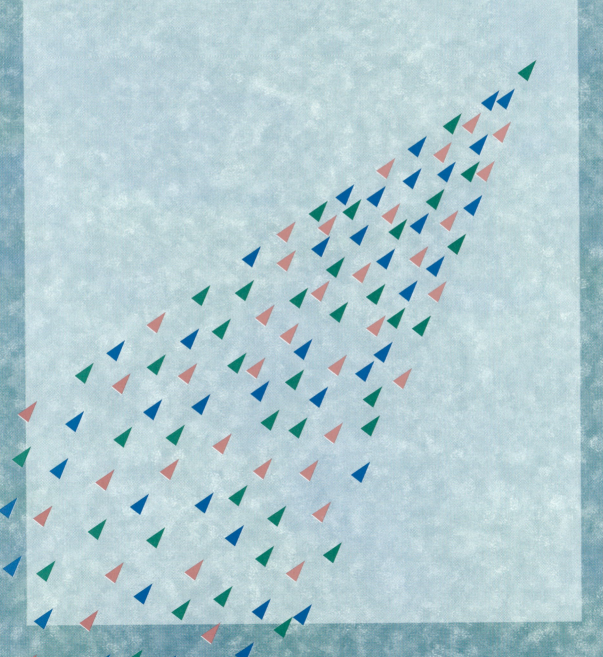

Economic Fluctuations

C H A P T E R 9

Monetary and Fiscal Policy in the Presence of Price and Wage Rigidities

INTRODUCTION

Nominal rigidity
The sluggish adjustment, especially downward adjustment, of a price or nominal wage rate

Keynesian model
A macroeconomic model that emphasizes the role of market imperfections (especially price and wage rigidities) in causing recessions and the role of economic policy in combating recessions

As you've learned, macroeconomics is concerned with the growth and fluctuations of output, employment, prices, and related variables, such as wage rates, interest rates, and the trade balance. Except in Chapter 4, though, we have not focused on short-run business cycle fluctuations. In this and the next three chapters we turn our attention to recessions, their causes, their attendant unemployment, and their alleviation through economic policy.

In previous chapters we've assumed that prices and wages are fully flexible. This chapter abandons that assumption and considers the **nominal rigidities**—the lack of sufficient short-run flexibility in the price level or the nominal wage rate—that form the basis of the **Keynesian model** of business cycle fluctuations. Keynesian theory emphasizes the role of these nominal rigidities in causing recessions and the role of monetary and fiscal policy in combating them.

We begin this chapter by looking at some evidence on wage and price rigidities in the U.S. economy. Next, we introduce nominal rigidities into our life-cycle model and show how they can cause output and employment to fall short of the levels at which the economy's supplies of labor and capital are fully utilized. We use two relationships from Chapter 8—the price level equation (based on the equality of money demand and supply) and the transition equation—to show how monetary and fiscal policy may affect output and employment in the presence of nominal rigidities. Monetary policy works through the price level equation, which relates output and prices to the nominal money stock. Fiscal policy enters through the transition equation, which shows how the next period's capital-labor ratio depends on this period's capital-labor ratio *and* fiscal variables. Depicting these two relationships graphically provides us with a representation, known as the IS-LM diagram, of how the level and composition of output are influenced by monetary and fiscal policy in the short run.

The questions addressed in this chapter include:

- What are wage and price rigidities, and why do they arise?
- How can wage or price rigidities restrict the levels of output and employment?
- In the Keynesian model, how can monetary and fiscal policy be used to raise output and reduce unemployment?
- How do monetary and fiscal policies differ in their effects on the composition of output in the short run and the economy's performance in the long run?
- What factors influence the relative strengths of monetary and fiscal policy in combating recessions? How are these strengths measured?

THE PRICE AND WAGE ADJUSTMENT PROCESS

Through the first part of the book we have viewed prices (whether output prices or wage and interest rates) as mechanisms for clearing markets, with prices adjusting to equate supply and demand. But price adjustment is not always as fluid as this perspective suggests. Prices for commodities or inputs may be *rigid*, changing less often or by smaller amounts than simple economic theory suggests. Such rigidity, more accurately called *price stickiness* (because prices do eventually adjust), is apparent in various commodity and input markets. Let's review the assumption of price adjustment and then consider why prices may not adjust immediately.

Fully Flexible Prices

Many markets encountered in previous chapters *do* follow our flexible-price paradigm closely. For example, the interest rate on U.S. Treasury bills is determined continuously in world financial markets in order to match the supply of and demand for Treasury bills. The prices of gold and wheat fluctuate constantly to clear their respective markets.

Each of these markets satisfies all the requirements for perfect competition: many sellers, many buyers, homogeneous commodities (e.g., one ounce of gold is indistinguishable from any other), and adequate information on the part of buyers and sellers about the current price. In such markets there are strong forces driving prices to adjust. If the price is too low (i.e., the quantity demanded exceeds the quantity supplied), prospective buyers will bid up the price, knowing that for a bit more than the current price they can satisfy their demand. If it is too high (i.e., the quantity supplied exceeds the quantity demanded), suppliers will cut their prices, because accepting a bit less will bring them all the demand they want.

Price and Wage Rigidity

In markets that do not fulfill the requirements for perfect competition, the forces behind price adjustment may be weaker. A seller may be less eager to cut her price if she needs to advertise the price cut extensively to gain customers, or if she expects relatively few customers to shift from other producers. She may also be reluctant to cut her price if doing so may be interpreted as a signal of inferior product quality, or if she is unaware of the prices other producers are charging.

Empirical studies have confirmed that output prices often fail to adjust as quickly as market forces (such as frequent cost increases caused by inflation) would suggest. The studies include investigations of the prices quoted in retail catalogs and prices paid by large companies for manufactured goods.[1]

In labor markets, too, the relationship between suppliers (workers) and demanders (firms) often precludes market-clearing wage adjustment. For example, collective bargaining between labor unions and employers typically determines wages only once every three years. This doesn't mean wages are fixed in nominal terms for a three-year period; what it means is that the pattern of nominal wage growth is predetermined and does not respond to changes in prevailing market conditions during the contract period. For example, a contract might call for annual increases of 4 percent in its second and third years, regardless of ensuing changes in economic conditions, including the inflation rate.

Case Study: U.S. Magazine Prices

One study of price adjustment considered the prices charged for a sample of 38 magazines over the period from 1953 to 1979.[2] Economist Stephen Cecchetti found that magazine prices exhibited substantial stickiness, in that considerable inflation in the general price level—enough to reduce the *real* magazine price (its price relative to the general price level) by as much as one-quarter—typically occurred between any two changes in the price of any particular magazine.

During the low-inflation period of 1953–1965, magazine prices changed on average only once every 7.5 years. As the annual inflation rate rose during the latter portion of the period studied (1965–1979), magazine price changes did

1. See Anil Kashyap, "Sticky Prices: New Evidence from Retail Catalogues," MIT mimeo, 1987; and Dennis Carlton, "The Rigidity of Prices," *American Economic Review* 76 (September 1986): 637–658.
2. Stephen G. Cecchetti, "The Frequency of Price Adjustment: A Study of Newsstand Prices of Magazines, 1953–79," *Journal of Econometrics* 31 (April 1986): 255–274.

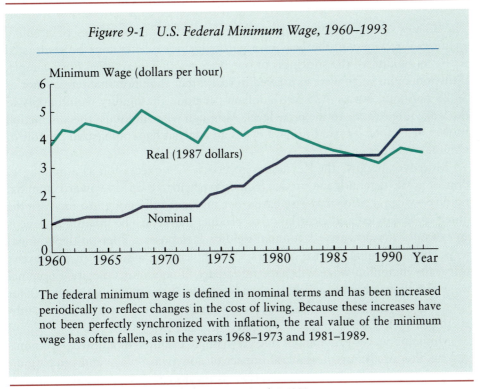

Figure 9-1 U.S. Federal Minimum Wage, 1960–1993

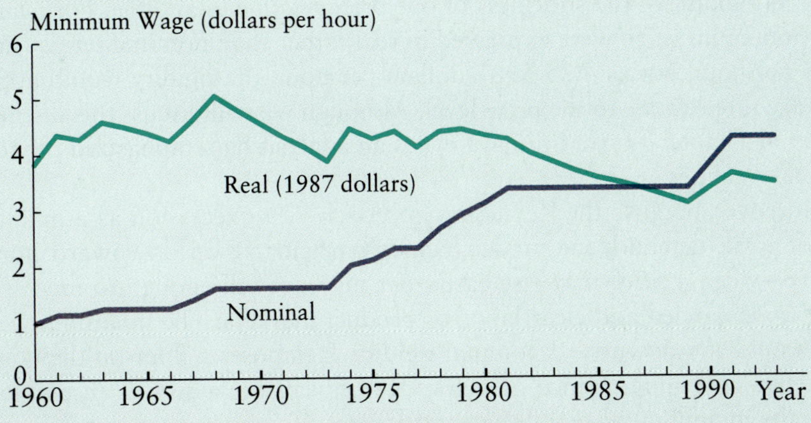

The federal minimum wage is defined in nominal terms and has been increased periodically to reflect changes in the cost of living. Because these increases have not been perfectly synchronized with inflation, the real value of the minimum wage has often fallen, as in the years 1968–1973 and 1981–1989.

Source: U.S. Committee on Ways and Means, "Green Book," 1993

become more frequent: once every 3.25 years. These findings suggest that magazine producers respond to changes in their costs (as represented by the general price level) only after a considerable lag.

Case Study: The U.S. Minimum Wage

Some rigidities are actually introduced by government legislation or regulation. One important example is the minimum wage, a wage rate that the U.S. federal government requires all private sector employers to meet or exceed. As of 1994, the U.S. federal minimum wage was $4.25 per hour.[3] The government has adjusted the minimum wage periodically, with the intention of maintaining the income of minimum-wage workers at some reasonable standard of living. As Figure 9-1 shows, these periodic changes have kept the minimum wage reasonably stable in real terms over the period since 1960. However, like magazine prices, the minimum wage has not changed every year to keep up with increases in the overall cost of living. The minimum wage was not adjusted at all between 1968 and 1973, or from 1981 through 1989, causing its real value to drop during both these periods of sustained inflation.

3. Several states have their own minimum wage laws setting higher levels.

Price Rigidity and the Keynesian Model

Real rigidity *The stickiness, or sluggish adjustment, of one price relative to another, such as the nominal wage relative to the general price level*

These cases of commodity and input price rigidity are examples of *nominal rigidities*—stickiness in the *level* of a particular price. They may be contrasted with **real rigidities**—the stickiness of one price *relative* to another. For example, if the minimum wage were expressed in real rather than nominal terms—not as \$4.25 per hour, but as 4.25 1987 dollars per hour, the rigidity would apply to the wage rate *relative* to the price level. Although we will discuss this distinction further in Chapter 11, traditional Keynesian analysis has emphasized the role of nominal rigidities.

Moreover, because the Keynesian approach views recession as a manifestation of weak demand, the model focuses particularly on downward nominal rigidity—when a price may rise easily but may not fall enough to increase the quantity demanded and clear labor or product markets. The minimum wage is an example of a downward nominal rigidity. It imposes a floor on the nominal wage, but no ceiling. Hence, if market forces call for a rise in an employee's wage, the minimum wage will have no impact. If conditions dictate a nominal wage reduction, though, workers already receiving the minimum wage cannot have their wages reduced. This may benefit some workers, but it may cause others to lose their jobs.

Minimum wages provide but one very simple example of a downward nominal rigidity. Analyzing the general impact of downward wage and price rigidities provides an important introduction to the Keynesian perspective, one on which we will build in subsequent chapters as we compare recent approaches to understanding business cycle fluctuations.

DEVELOPING THE KEYNESIAN APPROACH

As mentioned, Keynesians have traditionally traced recessions and their attendant unemployment to incomplete short-run price or wage adjustment. In the longer run, they assume that prices and wages fully adjust to clear input and product markets. Hence, understanding the Keynesian approach requires us to focus on short-run behavior. In terms of the life-cycle model developed in previous chapters, this means concentrating on the immediate effects of wage and price rigidities in the current period while maintaining the assumption that such rigidities do not apply in subsequent periods as the economy's transition unfolds. Because most of our analysis refers to a single period, time subscripts will generally not be necessary. For simplicity, we will once again use the version of the life-cycle model in which only the older generation consumes. In addition, we'll consider a single, closed economy, leaving to Chapter 13 the extension of the Keynesian approach to the open economy. Our analysis begins with the case in which the price level is rigid. We'll consider nominal wage rigidity later.

Deriving the IS-LM Framework

The Keynesian model can be described with the same two relationships used in Chapter 8 to trace the evolution of the monetary economy. The only difference here will be the assumption that prices do not freely adjust. The first key relationship is the price equation based on the equality of money supply and money demand.

Recall our model of money demand in which the young generation carries a certain fraction, γ, of its wages into old age in the form of money balances. Hence, the amount of money demanded by the younger generation equals γ times the wage rate, w, times the number of young people, N. Setting this total demand for money equal to the real money supply, $\overline{M}/P$, and solving for P yields the expression for the price level, $P = \overline{M}/\gamma N w$. We can use this expression to relate the price level to output by using the fact that the wage, w, equals labor's share of income, $(1 - \beta)$, times output per young person, y:

$$P = \frac{\overline{M}}{\gamma N(1 - \beta)y}$$

The second fundamental equation from Chapter 8 is the transition equation for the economy's capital-labor ratio. We write this transition equation here as a relationship between the next period's capital-labor ratio, k_{+1}, and the current period's output per worker, y, simply by using the production function to replace Ak^{β} by y:

$$k_{+1} = (1 - \gamma)(1 - \beta)y - f$$

This equation also depends on the sum of government debt purchases and net tax payments per young person, f.

Let's recall how we used these two equations in Chapter 8 to trace out the evolution of output, capital, and the price level over time. Starting with the current period's capital-labor ratio, k, we determine the current period's output per young person, y, based on the Cobb-Douglas production function, $y = Ak^{\beta}$. Inserting this value of output in the price level equation gives us a solution for the current period's price level, P. Inserting the solution for y into the transition equation gives us next period's capital-labor ratio, k_{+1}, which then forms the basis for solving for next period's output and price level in the same way.

Now suppose the price level is downwardly rigid, and that the value of the price level obtained in this manner is below the minimum price level, say $\overline{P}$, that can exist in the current period. Then, our solution for P is infeasible. But if we substitute the lowest feasible price level $\overline{P}$ on the left-hand side of the price level equation, something on the right-hand side of the equation must also change in order for the equality to be preserved, i.e., for the real quantities of money demanded and supplied to remain equal. As we'll see shortly, it is output that falls below the level achieved with flexible prices, raising the right-hand side of the equation.

To analyze how price rigidity (and later, wage rigidity) affects output, it will be useful to rewrite our two key equations, rearranging the expressions in three ways. First, we express each in terms of the level of output, Y, rather than output per worker, y, to avoid any ambiguity that might be caused by the fact that, with unemployment, the number of *workers* and the number of young persons need not be the same. Second, because it is now the level of output, rather than the price level, that the price level equation determines, we divide by the fixed price level, $\overline{P}$, and multiply by Y to express the equation in terms of output rather than the price level. Finally, because we'll be interested in the impact of policy on the interest rate as well as output, we combine the transition equation with our expression relating next period's real interest rate to the capital-labor ratio, $r_{+1} = A\beta k_{+1}^{\beta-1}$. The resulting equation based on the equality of money demand and supply, commonly called the **LM curve**, is[4]

LM curve
A curve showing all combinations of current output and next period's interest rate at which the quantity of money demanded equals the money supply

$$Y = \frac{\overline{M}}{\gamma[r_{+1}](1-\beta)\overline{P}}$$

Note that we have written this expression to indicate explicitly how the share of wages allocated to money balances, γ, depends on the next period's real interest rate, r_{+1}. Although much of Chapter 8 focused on the special case in which γ is fixed, we also indicated there that this share normally declines as the opportunity cost of holding money (rather than capital)—the nominal interest rate in the next period, i_{+1}—rises. For simplicity, we will assume in this chapter that the expected inflation rate is zero, so that the nominal interest rate i_{+1} equals the real interest rate r_{+1}.

Our second fundamental equation, relating the next period's interest rate to current output via the transition equation, is called the **IS curve**:[5]

IS curve
A curve showing all combinations of current output and next period's interest rate consistent with the economy's capital-labor ratio transition equation, given a fixed value of the fiscal variable, F

$$r_{+1} = \beta A\left[\frac{(1-\beta)(1-\gamma)Y - F}{N}\right]^{\beta-1}$$

where F equals Nf, total government receipts, and the term in brackets is just k_{+1}.[6]

Let's take a close look at these equations. We'll find that they are not nearly as complicated as they may seem. For example, there are really only two unknown variables in the LM equation. The parameter β is a fixed number. We've assumed that the nominal money supply is fixed at $\overline{M}$ and, of course, that the price level is rigid at $\overline{P}$. So long as that price rigidity remains and the government maintains a fixed money stock, the LM curve is simply a relationship between the level of output, Y, and next period's interest rate, r_{+1}.

4. To remember what this curve represents, note that the L and M stand for *l*iquidity preference (money demand) and *m*oney supply.

5. The I and S stand for the *i*nvestment and *s*aving the young do.

6. As the expression for the IS curve indicates, the capital-labor ratio in the next period equals the capital stock divided by the number of young people, N. This reflects our assumption that there is no unemployment in the next period—that Keynesian rigidities apply only during the current period.

The interest rate actually appears implicitly in a second place in the equation, through its influence on γ. This is a mathematical complication that we can safely ignore for most of our analysis (although it is discussed in this chapter's Appendix). That is, we will treat the fraction $(1-\gamma)(1-\beta)$ in the IS curve expression as a constant.

The IS curve is also a relationship between Y and r_{+1}. A and β are fixed parameters. Each generation's population size, N, is constant. So long as the government fiscal policy maintains F at a given level, the IS curve simply relates Y and r_{+1}.

To summarize, when the price level is fixed because of downward rigidity, each of these equations involves two unknown variables: the level of output, Y, and the next period's interest rate, r_{+1}. Thus, we can use these equations to solve for output and the interest rate. We can also see the channels through which monetary and fiscal policy may be used to influence the values of Y and r_{+1}, to help overcome the impact of the price rigidity on output. Changes in the nominal money supply $\overline{M}$ work through the LM curve, whereas changes in fiscal policy—as represented by government absorption of resources from the young, F—work through the IS curve.

Let's look at each of these curves in a bit more detail before using them to determine output and the interest rate, as well as the impact of monetary and fiscal policy on these two variables.

The LM Curve

The LM curve plots combinations of income, Y, and the real interest rate, r_{+1}, at which money supply equals money demand, given a fixed price level, $\overline{P}$. We can see from the expression for the LM curve that a higher interest rate, and hence a lower value of γ, implies a higher level of output, Y. Figure 9-2 provides a graphical view of this relationship between r_{+1} and Y.

The logic behind the slope of the LM curve is straightforward and relates to the fact that the demand for money increases with income but falls with the interest rate. Suppose we were at a particular point on the curve with the money market in equilibrium. An increase in income would disturb that equilibrium by raising the quantity of money demanded above the fixed real money supply $\overline{M}/\overline{P}$. In order to reestablish equilibrium, γ (the share of income devoted to holding money) must fall, and this requires a rise in the interest rate.

The position of the LM curve depends on the value the government chooses for the nominal money stock, $\overline{M}$. As we'll discuss below, monetary policy operates through shifts in the LM curve. Given the money supply, the slope of the LM curve depends on how sensitive money demand is to the interest rate. If it is very sensitive, i.e, if a small increase in the interest rate causes a large decline in γ, then only a very small increase in the interest rate will be required to keep the quantity of money demanded constant as income rises. Such a curve is shown in Figure 9-3 and is labeled LM^1. On the other hand, if money demand is not very sensitive to the interest rate, then a large change in r_{+1} will be necessary to offset the impact of a given change in Y on the quantity of money demanded. This gives rise to a steep LM curve like the one labeled LM^2 in Figure 9-3. We'll see shortly that the slope of LM—reflecting the interest sensitivity of money demand—plays a crucial role in determining the relative effectiveness of monetary and fiscal policy.

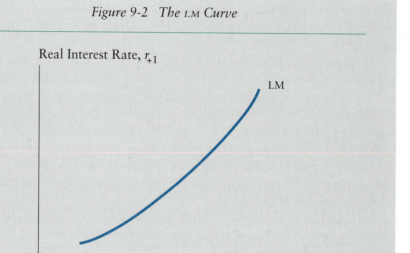

Figure 9-2 The LM Curve

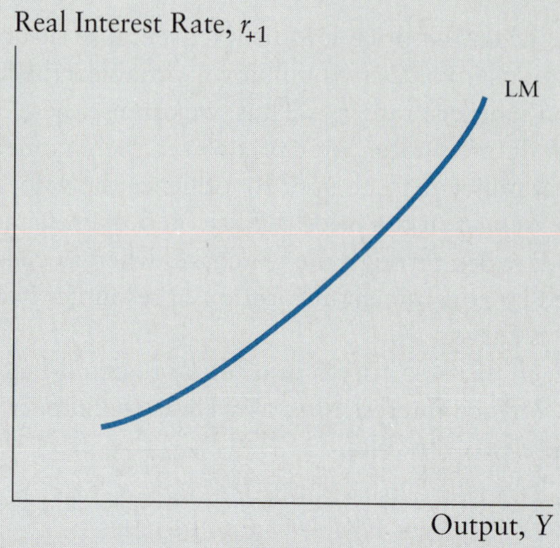

The LM curve plots combinations of income, Y, and the interest rate, r_{+1}, at which money supply equals money demand, given a fixed price level, $\overline{P}$. The curve slopes upward because a higher level of income increases the quantity of money demanded. To reestablish equality with the fixed money supply, there must be an increase in the interest rate, which causes an offsetting decrease in the quantity of money demanded.

The equation for the LM curve, $Y = \overline{M}/(\gamma[r_{+1}](1 - \beta)\overline{P})$, shows that the curve is drawn for given values of the price level, $\overline{P}$ and the nominal money supply, $\overline{M}$. If $\overline{M}$ increases or $\overline{P}$ decreases, the LM curve will shift to the right.

The IS Curve

Given the price level and the money supply, the LM curve provides one relationship between the current level of output and the next period's interest rate. To solve for the precise combination of Y and r_{+1} that will prevail, we must also use our second relationship between Y and r_{+1}, the IS curve.

Our IS curve expression indicates a negative relationship between the current level of output and the next period's interest rate. This relationship is depicted by the curve shown in Figure 9-4. Why should higher current output lead to a lower interest rate in the next period? Here's the logic. The more output produced in this period, the more income each young person will earn. The higher the income of the young, the more capital they purchase and bring into the next period. The more capital is accumulated, the higher the next period's capital-labor ratio will be and the lower the return to capital—the real interest rate—that will be needed to get firms to demand all the capital being supplied. Thus, the higher the output this period, the lower the interest rate next period.

Figure 9-3 Alternative LM *Curves*

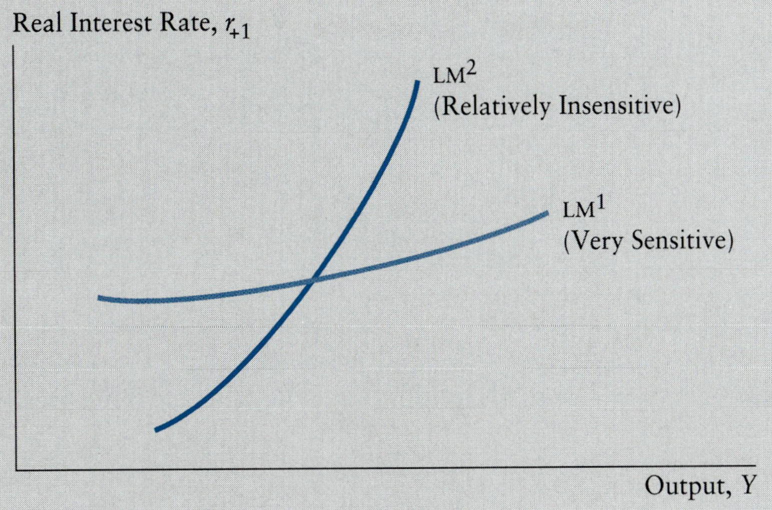

The steepness of the LM curve depends upon the interest sensitivity of money demand, captured by $\gamma[r_{+1}]$. If money demand is very interest-sensitive—so that a small increase in the interest rate causes a large decline in γ—then only a very small increase in the interest rate is needed to keep the quantity of money demanded constant as income rises. In that case, the LM curve will be relatively flat. If money demand is *not* very sensitive to the interest rate, a large change in r_{+1} is needed to offset a given change in Y; the LM curve will be relatively steep.

Note that the position of the IS curve depends on the level of F, the resources the government takes from each young person. We will consider the impact of a change in F below, when discussing fiscal policy.

OUTPUT DETERMINATION WITH RIGID PRICES

For a fixed price level, the IS curve indicates the combinations of the current period's income and the next period's interest rate that are consistent with the transition equation. The LM curve tells us the combinations of the current period's income and the next period's interest rate at which money supply equals money demand. We use these two curves to solve for Y and r_{+1}. The solution is given by their point of intersection, an example of which is given in Figure 9-5, with income Y^0 and interest rate r^0. As this point lies on the LM curve, the demand for money based on the interest rate r^0 and income Y^0 equals the supply of money $\overline{M}/\overline{P}$. Because it also lies on the IS curve, the same interest rate and level of income, r^0 and Y^0, are consistent with the transition equation relating current income and next period's capital stock and interest rate.

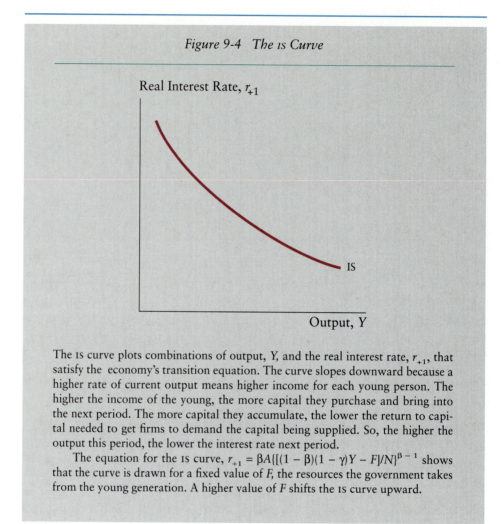

Figure 9-4 The IS Curve

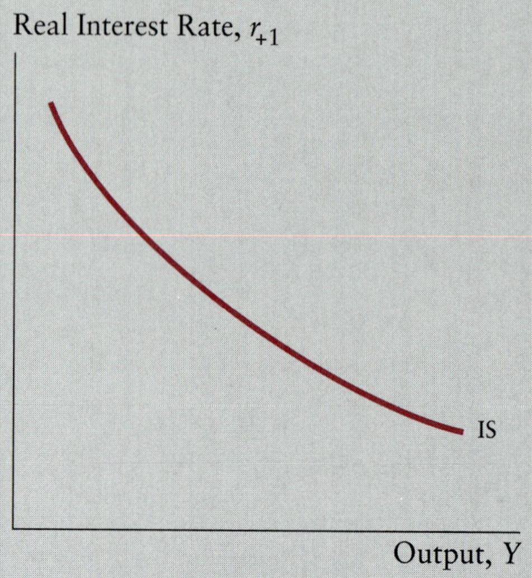

The IS curve plots combinations of output, Y, and the real interest rate, r_{+1}, that satisfy the economy's transition equation. The curve slopes downward because a higher rate of current output means higher income for each young person. The higher the income of the young, the more capital they purchase and bring into the next period. The more capital they accumulate, the lower the return to capital needed to get firms to demand the capital being supplied. So, the higher the output this period, the lower the interest rate next period.

The equation for the IS curve, $r_{+1} = \beta A\{[(1-\beta)(1-\gamma)Y - F]/N\}^{\beta-1}$ shows that the curve is drawn for a fixed value of F, the resources the government takes from the young generation. A higher value of F shifts the IS curve upward.

As we indicated above, when the price level is "too high" (above the one that would prevail under flexible prices), the level of output is "too low." In Figure 9-5, this situation is represented by the fact that Y^0 lies below the value of output determined by the Cobb-Douglas production function with the full utilization of labor and capital, labeled Y^f. We refer to this higher level of output as the economy's **potential**, or **full-employment, output** level.

Potential (full-employment) output *The economy's level of output when all available inputs are fully employed*

Is there a price level for which the IS-LM solution for output equals Y^f? Indeed there is. Note that the position of the LM curve depends on the price level. Suppose the price level were fixed at a value lower than $\bar{P}$. This would mean a larger real stock of money. For any given interest rate and value of γ, the equation for the LM curve indicates that income would be higher. As a result, the LM curve would lie to the right of the original one. Since the position of the LM curve depends on the price level, we can imagine lower and lower values of the price level shifting the LM curve out until, at a price level $\hat{P}$, the IS curve and the

Figure 9-5 Equilibrium with Rigid Prices

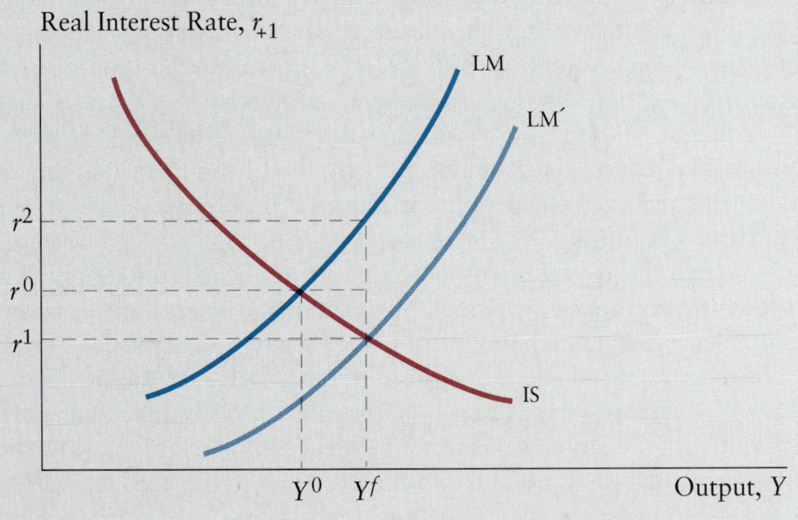

The IS and LM curves represent two relationships between current income and next period's interest rate. The point where the two curves intersect represents the unique combination of Y and r_{+1} that satisfies both relationships. At such an intersection, the money market is in equilibrium (since the point lies on the LM curve) and the transition equation is satisfied (since it lies on the IS curve). Notice that the level of output determined at this intersection (e.g., Y^0) may lie below the full-employment level (Y^f). Because the rigid price level is "too high," the level of output is "too low." If the price level could fall, the LM curve could shift right to intersect the IS curve at full-employment output.

LM curve labeled LM´ in Figure 9-5 intersect at Y^f, with an interest rate r^1. This solution is simply the one we would have obtained had prices been flexible.[7] In other words, we can reinterpret our previous flexible-price analysis in terms of the IS-LM framework. The gap between Y^0 and Y^f results from downward price rigidity.

Aggregate Demand and Unemployment

To see why the output level at which IS and LM intersect lies below the full-employment level Y^f, let's consider what would happen if firms *did* produce Y^f.

7. If—contrary to our assumption—$\hat{P}$ actually exceeded $\bar{P}$, then the downward price rigidity would not be binding. That is, the price level $\hat{P}$ would be feasible, and at this price level the level of output Y^f would be produced. In this case, the LM curve drawn for $P = \bar{P}$ would intersect the IS curve to the right of Y^f at an infeasible level of output. The highest level of output possible would be Y^f, which would be sustained by the price level $\hat{P}$.

At this level of output, the wage income of the young would be $(1-\beta)Y^f$. Of this, they would devote an amount $\gamma(1-\beta)Y^f$ to acquiring money balances, pay F to the government, and use the rest, $(1-\gamma)(1-\beta)Y^f - F$, to purchase capital for use in the next period. The old, meanwhile, would use all of their capital income, βY^f, plus all their money balances, $\overline{M}/\overline{P}$, less their net payments to the government, say F_o, i.e., a total of $\beta Y^f + \overline{M}/\overline{P} - F_o$, to purchase output for consumption. Adding these amounts to government purchases, G, we see that total purchases would equal $Y^f + \overline{M}/\overline{P} - \gamma(1-\beta)Y^f + (G - F - F_o)$. However, the term in brackets equals the amount spent by the government less the amount raised, which equals zero by definition. Thus, total purchases equal $Y^f + \overline{M}/\overline{P} - \gamma(1-\beta)Y^f$.

But note that the last two terms in this expression equal the supply of money less the quantity of money demanded by the young *at the full-employment level of output*. Hence, total purchases will equal Y^f if and only if the demand for and supply of money are equal (i.e, if the difference between the last two terms equals zero) when income is at its full-employment level and the interest rate r_{+1} is consistent with the amount of capital being accumulated by the young at this level of output. But we know $\overline{P}$ is too high for this to happen. As we see from Figure 9-5, the interest rate determined by the IS curve at Y^f, r^1, lies below that on the LM curve, r^2. Thus, if the interest rate is consistent with the amount of capital being accumulated (i.e., if it lies on the IS curve), the demand for money exceeds its supply. This excess demand for money translates into an excess supply of output: purchases will fall short of full-employment production by the extent to which money demand exceeds money supply. Macroeconomists refer to this situation as a lack of *aggregate demand* for output, because total purchases fall short of the level of output at Y^f.

Normally, we would expect producers who are unable to sell all their output to cut their prices. Indeed, a reduction in the price level would raise the level of real money balances and increase purchases. But with rigid prices this can't occur. Being unable to sell all they can produce, firms have little choice but to reduce production to the equilibrium level Y^o.[8]

If firms produce output below their capacity—Y^o rather than Y^f—they will require fewer workers to produce this output. How many workers will they hire? It is not entirely evident, since as output declines, there is not only excess labor but also excess capital available. Perhaps the most straightforward assumption is that firms maintain the same ratio of capital to labor, reducing both employment and the utilization of capital at the same rate.[9] If the number of workers needed to produce the level of output Y^o equals L^o, then we refer to those workers without jobs (equal in number to $N - L^o$) as experiencing *involuntary* (or *Keynesian*) *unemployment*. They would be willing to work at the going wage (and, indeed, at any wage, since labor supply is assumed to be independent of the wage) but are unable to do so. We will discuss the distinction

8. How did the price level get too high in the first place? As we will discuss below, the positions of both IS and LM curves depend on a variety of factors. Hence, a price level might be consistent with full employment when initially established but become too high after a leftward shift in the IS or LM curve and hence in their point of intersection.

9. Recall from Chapter 4 that during recessions, capacity utilization falls along with employment.

between this and other types of unemployment below, when considering the case of wage rigidity.

INFLUENCING OUTPUT: THE ROLE OF MONETARY AND FISCAL POLICY

In the Keynesian model, downward price rigidity may cause output to lie below its full-employment level. How can monetary and fiscal policy be used to address this problem? We'll consider each, in turn.

Monetary Policy

The logic behind monetary policy is straightforward. The lack of aggregate demand comes from too high a price level, making the real money stock, and thus the consumption purchases of the old, too low to sustain the full-employment level of output. But the real money stock equals the ratio of the nominal money stock to the price level. Although the price level cannot fall, the real money stock can still be raised through an increase in the nominal money stock.

How can this be done? As we saw in Chapter 8, the government may increase the nominal money supply in several ways: by making transfers to the old, by making government purchases, and by making transfers to the young. Perhaps the simplest way is the first of these, making transfers to the old in proportion to the money they already hold. This policy is *neutral* in the absence of Keynesian rigidities—we found in Chapter 8 that doubling the money supply would lead to an immediate doubling of the price level, with no change in consumption by the old or saving by the young.

But, in the present context, this same change will not be neutral—it will increase output and employment, by shifting the LM curve to the right. For example, suppose the nominal money supply is increased by ΔM, from $\overline{M}$ to $\overline{M} + \Delta M$. From the expression for the LM curve, we can see that the new value of Y corresponding to any particular value of r_{+1} will be higher, as depicted by the rightward shift from LM to LM′ in Figure 9-6. This makes sense, because the higher real stock of money can meet the increase in money demand that occurs as income rises at a given interest rate. The figure also indicates that the new LM curve intersects the IS curve at a higher level of output, Y^1, and a lower interest rate, r^1, than at the original equilibrium (Y^0, r^0).

To see why equilibrium output increases, let's consider what happens when the old receive a transfer from the government in the form of newly printed money. The old wish to consume all the resources at their disposal. With the additional money, and the same price level, they will have more purchasing power and seek to consume more. In a full-employment situation, as we have already learned, their attempt to increase consumption would simply lead to a commensurate increase in the price level. However, with the price level fixed at $\overline{P}$, the economy has unemployed resources and firms can increase output. Initially, consumption and output will rise by the full increase in the real money stock given to the elderly, $\Delta M/\overline{P}$.

Figure 9-6 Monetary Policy with Rigid Prices

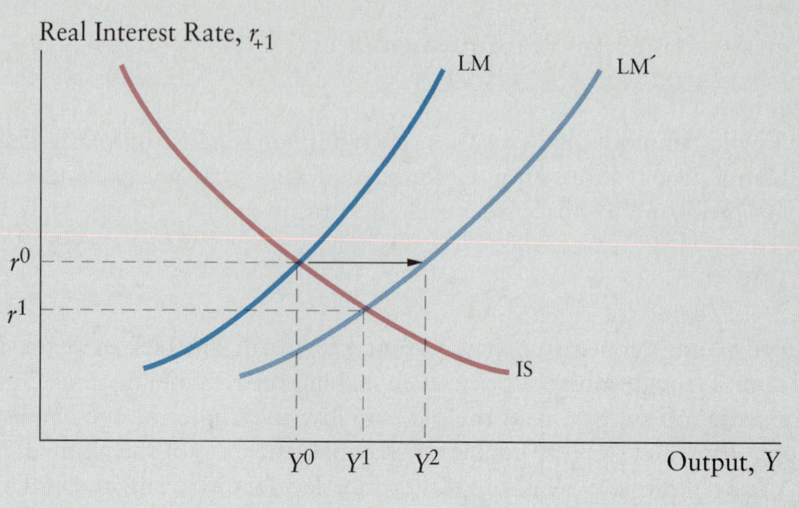

When the price level is downwardly rigid, changes in the nominal money supply are not neutral. An increase in the money supply from M to $M + \Delta M$ shifts the LM curve to the right, leading to an increase in income from Y^0 to Y^1 and a reduction in the interest rate from r^0 to r^1. The initial increase in M raises consumption by the old which, in turn, initiates a chain of further increases in output, consumption, and investment.

Indeed, output will increase by even more than this initial increase in the real money stock. The first-stage increase in output of $\Delta M/\bar{P}$ raises the income of both the young (through higher employment) and the old (more of whose capital comes into use). The increased income of the old raises their consumption and output still further. The increased income of the young raises their acquisition of real assets, which increases investment and output. These increases in output, in turn, contribute to additional increases in the income of the old and the young, and more output increases in the form of consumption and investment. This chain of increases in output that multiplies the initial impact of policy is referred to as a *multiplier* process. We'll discuss multipliers and their relevance more fully below.

How much will output ultimately increase? If the interest rate did not fall, output would increase by $\Delta M/\gamma(1 - \beta)\bar{P}$—the distance of the rightward shift in the LM curve[10]—to Y^2. However, as output and investment increase, so does the capital stock in the following period. This is reflected by the negative slope of the IS curve. Thus, as output increases, the interest rate facing the young must fall. They respond by shifting more of their wages into money and less into the purchase of output for investment. This moderation of the increase in demand

10. We can verify that the curve shifts by this amount by solving the LM curve expression for Y, given r, when the money supply equals M and $M + \Delta M$, respectively.

for investment goods means a smaller increase in output. As a result of the interest sensitivity of money demand, output increases from Y^0 only to Y^1, rather than Y^2.

Fiscal Policy

As we've seen, monetary policy overcomes the lack of aggregate demand resulting from a shortage of real money balances. It does so by increasing the nominal and thus real money balances of the elderly, leading them to increase their consumption purchases. Fiscal policy attacks the problem from a different direction, accomplishing a net increase in output by driving up the interest rate and encouraging a shift out of money and into capital.

In our model, fiscal policy involves changes in the level of government purchases and how the burden of these purchases is distributed among different generations. In Chapter 7 we discussed the impact of fiscal policy on the evolution of future output. In the Keynesian model fiscal policy can also influence the current output level, through its influence on the position of the IS curve. Let's see how, by considering the impact of an increase in government purchases paid for with receipts from the young—through an increase in F, say ΔF, which equals the increase in government purchases, ΔG. The increase in government purchases directly raises aggregate demand by ΔG. But taking ΔF away from the young reduces their aggregate demand, namely, for investment goods. The issue we'll explore is whether the increase in aggregate demand by the government exceeds the reduction in aggregate demand by the young—whether the increased government consumption is associated with a reduction of investment by the young on a dollar-for-dollar basis or on less than a dollar-for-dollar basis. To begin, let's consider how our IS curve is affected by fiscal policy.

Fiscal policy influences the position of the IS curve through the term F on the right-hand side of the expression relating r_{+1} to Y. As the expression indicates, an increase in F increases the value of r_{+1} associated with any given value of Y—representing an upward shift in the IS curve. The logic is that by absorbing more of the income of the young, the government leaves less that can be used to purchase new capital for production in the next period; the less capital, the higher the interest rate. This upward shift of the IS curve is shown in Figure 9-7. It may also be thought of as a rightward shift (higher Y is needed to produce the same level of K_{+1} and r_{+1}). The formula for the IS curve indicates that if F increases by ΔF, then the IS curve shifts to the right by the distance $\Delta F/(1 - \beta)(1 - \gamma)$.[11]

Figure 9-7 also indicates that, given the position of the LM curve, such a shift in the IS curve causes equilibrium output to increase to Y^1 and the interest rate to increase to r^1. Why does output rise? The key is the increase in the interest rate, because it reduces the amount of money demanded by the young and limits crowding out. Indeed, we can confirm that, without a reduction in the quantity of money demanded, the increase in F (with the proceeds spent on government purchases) cannot, *in itself*, induce a change in output or employment. Suppose

11. To see this, note that we can express the IS curve as an expression for Y in terms of r_{+1}, rather than for r_{+1} in terms of Y. From the resulting expression, $Y = [N(r_{+1}/\beta A)^{1/(\beta - 1)} + F]/(1 - \beta)(1 - \gamma)$, we can see that a change in F from F to $F + \Delta F$, holding r_{+1} fixed, changes Y by $\Delta F/(1 - \beta)(1 - \gamma)$.

Figure 9-7 Fiscal Policy with Rigid Prices

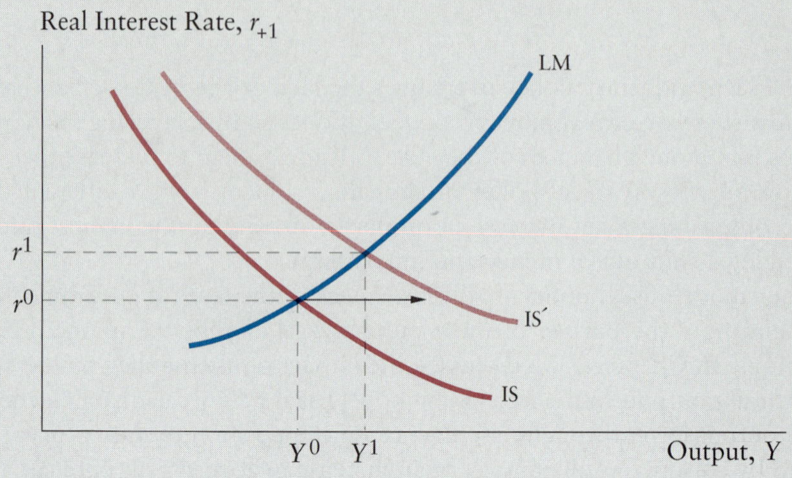

An increase in F, the resources the government takes from the young, leads to an upward shift of the IS curve, resulting in higher output and a higher interest rate. By absorbing more of young people's income, the government leaves less that can be used to purchase capital for production in the next period. That raises the interest rate, reducing the demand for money. To reestablish equilibrium, income must rise so that the quantity of money demanded once again equals the fixed money supply.

that the quantity of money demanded did not change. Then, as a result of the increase in government purchases paid for by the young, the younger generation would simply reduce its own purchases of capital by the additional amount—also ΔG—given to the government. Thus, there would be no increase in aggregate demand and output—the increase in government purchases would come entirely from funds that otherwise would have been used for investment. This displacement process, known as *crowding out*, would be complete.

However, with the demand for money sensitive to the interest rate (and the LM curve positively sloped), this initial crowding out of investment leads to a higher interest rate, a reduction in money demand, and a shift by the young back to investing in capital, limiting the reduction in investment. Though investment still declines, there is incomplete crowding out, and output increases. In other words, the government's increase in aggregate demand is less than fully offset by the decline in aggregate demand by the young. As in the case of monetary policy, this initial increase in output will lead to further increases, as the increased incomes of young and old lead to additional increases in investment and consumption, until the new equilibrium output level, Y^1, is reached.[12]

12. Even though there is additional investment, it never fully reaches its original level. If it did, next period's interest rate would not rise.

Table 9-1 The Impact of Monetary and Fiscal Policy with Rigid Prices: A Summary

Variable	Monetary Policy (increase in M)	Fiscal Policy (increase in F)
Output (Y)	Increases	Increases
Employment (L)	Increases	Increases
Consumption (C)	Increases	Increases
Investment (I)	Increases	Decreases
Interest Rate, next period (r_{+1})	Decreases	Increases

Thus, although the interest sensitivity of money demand works against monetary policy, it makes fiscal policy effective. Fiscal policy works because, as it drives up the interest rate and crowds out investment, the quantity of money demanded also falls. This means that investment purchases by the young fall by less than government spending increases—i.e., total output increases.

Summary

Table 9-1 summarizes the impact of monetary and fiscal policy on important macroeconomic variables. Although the two policies have similar effects on employment, output, and consumption, they have different effects on investment and the interest rate.

Although Table 9-1 focuses on macroeconomic differences in the short run, there are long-run differences as well. In particular, a fiscal policy that reduces investment will reduce the nation's future productive capacity, and hence its future output. A monetary policy that increases investment will have the opposite impact in the future.

MEASURING POLICY EFFECTIVENESS

Our analysis so far has focused on how price rigidity can contribute to Keynesian unemployment and how monetary and fiscal policy can reduce this unemployment and increase output. A way to summarize the strength of a policy is through a **multiplier,** which tells us how much a one-unit change in that policy's instrument (either M or F) changes output.

Multiplier
The ratio of a change in output to the change in the policy variable that causes it

In our model the key to the relative effectiveness of monetary and fiscal policy is the degree to which the demand for money is sensitive to the interest rate. As we noted above, expansionary monetary policy is hindered by the interest sensitivity of money demand, whereas expansionary fiscal policy *depends* on the interest sensitivity of money demand in order for crowding out not to be complete. Intuitively, then, we might expect that as the demand for money becomes

more interest-sensitive, monetary policy will become less effective at increasing output, and fiscal policy more effective.

Monetarism and the Vertical LM Curve

Monetarism
A school of thought that emphasizes the effect of changes in the money supply on economic activity

The degree to which the demand for money is sensitive to the interest rate is an empirical question, about which there is considerable debate. The belief that the demand for money is relatively insensitive to the interest rate is an important component of a school of thought known as **monetarism**. Monetarists believe that changes in the money supply play a central role in determining output. Based on the analysis in Chapter 8, we would expect the quantity of money demanded to decline as the interest rate increased, as households shift more of their wealth out of money and into assets offering the interest rate. Hence, monetarism represents a polar case, in which the response of money demand to changes in the implicit cost of holding money is nonexistent. The assumption that money demand does not respond to the interest rate—that γ equals some constant $\bar{\gamma}$—leads to a vertical LM curve. The relative effects of monetary and fiscal policy under this assumption are exhibited in Figure 9-8. Whereas a rightward shift in the LM curve to LM′ (along the original IS curve) has a significant impact on output, the outward shift in the IS curve to IS′ (along the original LM curve) has none at all.

We have already noted above, in our discussion of how fiscal policy acts to increase output, that interest-insensitive money demand renders fiscal policy completely impotent. As Figure 9-8 shows, an upward shift in the IS curve causes the interest rate to rise from r^0 to r^2, but there is no change in output. Thus, the fiscal policy multiplier—the increase in output for a given change in

Figure 9-8 Monetarism in the IS-LM Framework

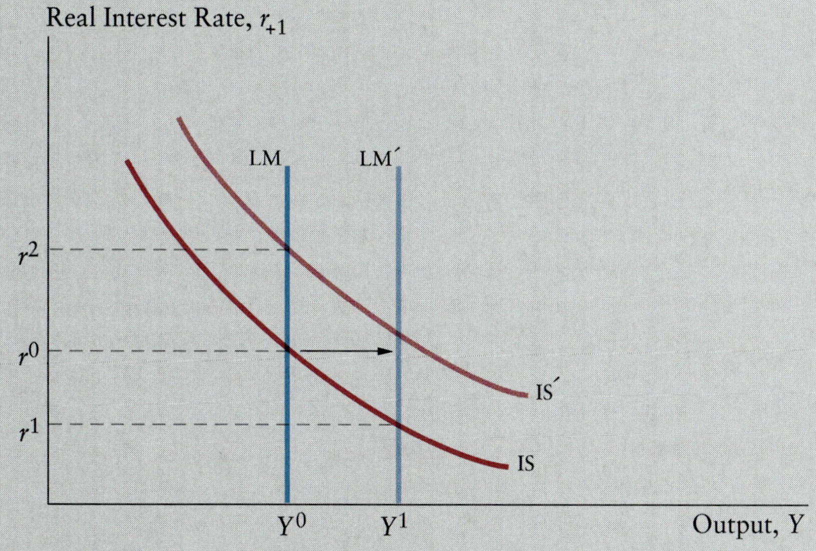

If the demand for money is insensitive to the interest rate, as monetarists believe, then fiscal policy is impotent. With an interest-insensitive money demand, the LM curve is vertical. Fiscal policy, by shifting the IS curve to IS′, succeeds only in raising the interest rate. But since money demand does not respond to the higher rate, income does not need to change to reestablish money market equilibrium.

In the monetarist view, monetary policy is very effective. An increase in the nominal money supply shifts the LM curve to LM′ along a fixed IS curve. The increased money in the hands of the old leads to increased spending, so that output rises from Y^0 to Y^1.

F—is zero. For monetary policy, the ultimate increase in output is nearly as easy to calculate because we need only consider the shift in the LM curve. It does not matter that the interest rate falls as a result of the increase in *M*, because the reduction in the interest rate has no impact on the quantity of money demanded, and hence no effect on output. Thus, output increases by the full extent of the shift in the LM curve, i.e., by the amount $\Delta M/\gamma(1-\beta)\overline{P}$.[13]

13. As discussed above, we can see this increase in output as the sum of output increases arising from an infinite sequence of rounds. In the first round, the consumption spending of the old increases output by $\Delta M/\overline{P}$. In the second round, given the constant income shares of labor and capital, the income of the young increases by their share of the extra output, $(1-\beta)\Delta M/\overline{P}$, and their extra spending on investment (rather than on additional money balances) equals $(1-\gamma)(1-\beta)\Delta M/\overline{P}$. The income of the old in the second round increases by $\beta\Delta M/\overline{P}$, all of which they consume. Hence, additional purchases for investment and consumption in the second round lead to more total output of $(1-\gamma)(1-\beta)\Delta M/\overline{P} + \beta\Delta M/\overline{P}$, or $[1-(1-\gamma)\beta]\Delta M/\overline{P}$. Following this pattern, we'll find the additional increase in output to be $[1-(1-\gamma)\beta]^2\Delta M/\overline{P}$ in the third round, and so on, for a total increase of $\Delta M/\gamma(1-\beta)\overline{P}$.

Figure 9-9 Policy with Interest-Sensitive Money Demand

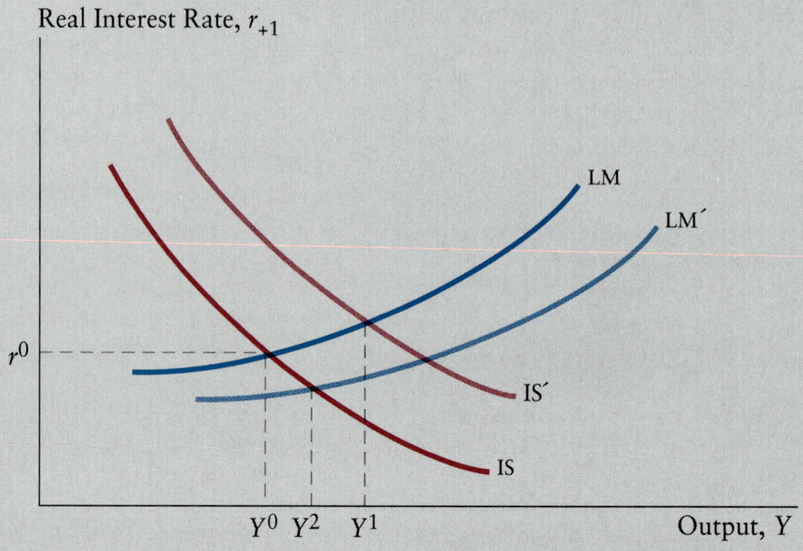

The more interest-sensitive the demand for money, the flatter the LM curve. With a flat LM curve, an upward shift in IS, caused by an increase in F, generates little crowding out to offset the impact of fiscal policy and has little effect on the interest rate. Output increases from Y^0 to Y^1. Monetary policy, by contrast, induces only a very small increase in investment by the young. As investment rises, the interest rate falls, and the young shift away from capital and toward the holding of more money. Output increases only from Y^0 to Y^2.

With a vertical LM curve, the monetary policy multiplier—the increase in output that results if the real money stock is increased by one unit rather than $\Delta M/\overline{P}$ units—is $1/\gamma(1-\beta)$. How large a number is this? Looking once again at the expression for the LM curve, we can see that this multiplier equals $\overline{P}Y/\overline{M}$—which is the velocity of money, v. This makes sense, because if velocity is constant, each additional dollar of money can support v dollars of additional output. As we saw in Chapter 8, velocity is several times larger than 1. For example, in 1993, the velocity of M1 was 5.6.

The Flat LM Curve

If the demand for money is sensitive to the interest rate, then both fiscal and monetary policy will influence output. What happens to the relative multipliers as money demand becomes extremely interest-sensitive? As we saw in Figure 9-3, the more interest-sensitive the demand for money, the flatter the LM curve will be. With extreme interest sensitivity, the LM curve is nearly flat. Figure 9-9 illustrates the effects of fiscal and monetary policy in this case.

As the figure shows, an upward shift in the IS curve caused by an increase in F is very effective in increasing output. Why? Because as crowding out begins to occur, and the interest rate begins to rise, the young, whose money demand is very interest sensitive, hold less money and more capital until most of the crowding out is eliminated. Hence, there is very little crowding out to offset the impact of increased government spending. On the other hand, monetary policy is considerably weakened. An increase in the money supply can induce only a very small increase in investment by the young, because as investment rises and the interest rate falls, the young shift sharply away from capital and toward the holding of more money.[14]

NATIONAL SAVING AND THE PARADOX OF THRIFT

In earlier chapters, we frequently discussed the impact of a change in national saving (which equals output less private and government consumption, $S = Y - C - G$) on the path of output in the future, through changes in investment and capital accumulation. In our IS-LM model, changes in saving may also influence the *current* level of output. In particular, a decline in saving may stimulate output.

We have already seen one example of the stimulative effect of a reduction in national saving, namely, expansionary fiscal policy. The upward shift in the IS curve (in Figure 9-7) is caused by the government's taking resources from savers—the young—and spending them on government purchases. In this policy the initial decline in national saving S (at the level of output Y^0) equals ΔF, the amount taken from the saving of the young and used to increase current government consumption. Ultimately, as output rises, saving and investment by the young rebound so that the net decline in national saving is smaller than the initial one. Still, the policy ends up reducing national saving as it stimulates output.

Note that it is the increase in total consumption (government plus private)—that is, the reduction in national saving—and *not* the increase in government purchases alone, that leads to the increase in output and employment. If the government paid for its purchases in a manner that did not initially (at Y^0) increase total consumption—by levying a tax on the elderly, for example, whose consumption would decline by the same amount as government purchases rose—there would be no change in output. This is quite clear from the expression used to derive the IS curve; it depends only on the resources that are taken from the young, F, and that are therefore not available for saving and investment. Indeed, there is no requirement that government purchases change at all, only that F increase. An increase in taxes on the young to finance transfers to the old (an increase in Social Security benefits, for example) would stimulate consumption by the old and have precisely the same effect on total output as an increase in government spending financed by the young.

14. How strong can fiscal policy be? As we show in this chapter's Appendix, the highest possible multiplier for fiscal policy is $1/(1 - \beta)$. And what of monetary policy? As the Appendix also shows, an increase in the real money stock, M/P, has a minimum multiplier of $1/(1 - \beta)$, which is less than $1/[\gamma(1 - \beta)]$ since the share of wages devoted to holding money, γ, is less than 1.

Figure 9-10 Changes in Saving and Output

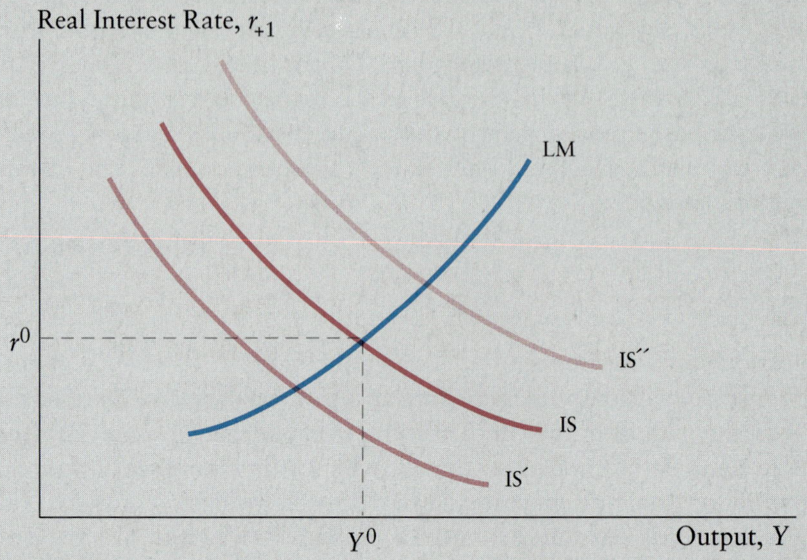

An increase in national saving caused by a decline in consumption shifts the IS curve to the left—from IS to IS′—and leads to a reduction in output. As output declines, some of the initial increase in saving is offset by a reduction in saving induced by the decline in the income of the young. The net increase in saving is smaller than the initial increase in saving. This phenomenon is called the paradox of thrift.

Not all increases in saving are associated with reductions in output. For example, a technology shock, which raises the value of the term A in the production function, leads to a higher value of r_{+1} for each value of Y—an upward shift in the IS curve to IS´´. In this case, the higher interest rate dictated by the new IS curve leads the young to reduce their money holdings and increase their purchases of capital. Saving and investment increase, and so does output.

Just as a reduction in national saving can increase output, an *increase* in national saving can reduce output. This increase in saving could result from a reversal of the fiscal policy just considered or from a change in private saving behavior. In this chapter we have considered a simplified model of household behavior in which individuals do not consume when young. But in our more general model, a decline in the share of resources consumed by the young, α, would have the same impact on the IS curve as a reduction in F, causing the curve to shift downward. It would lead to more saving and investment at any given level of income and hence to a higher capital stock in the next period and a lower interest rate.

As shown in Figure 9-10, an increase in national saving (whether caused by a change in government or private consumption)—which shifts the IS curve from IS to IS′—leads ultimately to a reduction in output. As output declines, the initial increase in saving is partially offset by the reduction in saving and investment by the young caused by the decline in their income. Hence, although saving still increases, it increases by less—perhaps far less—than the initial increase in saving.[15] Thus, in the Keynesian model, an initial attempt to increase saving may not increase saving by very much, whereas it may at the same time reduce output, perhaps by a lot. This phenomenon—attempts to increase saving not succeeding very well—was described by Keynes as the **paradox of thrift**.

Paradox of thrift *Attempts to increase saving may not succeed very well because the initial increase in saving reduces income, which makes the final rise in saving smaller than the initial increase*

Case Study: Financing Social Security During The 1930s

In contrast to recent U.S. concerns about the lack of national saving, the concern of policy makers in the 1930s was *too much* national saving. The difference in these concerns may be traced to different perspectives in the two periods on the nature of output determination. In the period during and immediately after the Depression, nominal rigidities and Keynesian unemployment were a very significant concern. Thus, following the logic just developed, policy makers feared that attempts to increase national saving would reduce output. As memories of the Depression have faded, however, many have come to the view that in the macroeconomy, output is normally close to its full-employment level and nominal rigidities are relatively unimportant. In the case of flexible prices, as we know from earlier chapters, an increase in national saving has no impact on the current level of output but does increase future output through the additional capital it provides.

The concerns of the 1930s are evident in decisions made about how to finance the then-new U.S. Social Security system. As we discussed in Chapter 7, the U.S. Social Security system until very recently operated primarily on a pay-as-you-go basis, paying out in current benefits the funds raised through payroll taxes. When the system was first established, though, this was not the intention of its designers. They foresaw eventually saving a considerable share of the payroll taxes in a trust fund—in our model, paying less of the taxes to the current elderly and saving the rest. In the Keynesian model, what would a change in the use of payroll taxes, from the payment of benefits to the accumulation of capital, do? It would increase national saving at any level of income, raising the next period's capital stock and lowering r_{+1}—that is, it would lower the IS curve.[16] In an economy still not fully recovered from the Great Depression, the fear of such a contractionary policy kept policy makers from accumulating a trust fund and established a policy that lasted for decades.

---

15. We know that saving must increase, since the interest rate falls, and hence the next period's capital stock must be higher, given the production function.

16. As we saw in Chapter 7, when government uses its revenue to purchase capital rather than goods and services for current consumption, this capital is added to that acquired by the private sector to determine the economy's overall level of capital.

Investment Versus Saving, Revisited

Are all increases in national saving associated with reductions in output, according to the Keynesian model? The answer is no. The examples considered above are those in which an increase in national saving, in the form of a decrease in combined household and government consumption, is the initial source of the decline in output. There are other cases in which the Keynesian model predicts that saving increases along with output, but in such cases, the change in saving is a *result* of a change in output.[17]

Let's consider a shift in the IS curve that arises from a technology shock, like that introduced in Chapter 4. Suppose households expect the economy to be more productive in the next period—that is, they expect that the term A in the Cobb-Douglas production function will be higher than at present. This, in turn, leads to a higher value of r_{+1} for each value of Y, meaning that the IS curve shifts upward. (The formula for the IS curve confirms this, indicating that r_{+1} is proportional to A, given Y.) This shift, to the curve labeled IS″ in Figure 9-10, will lead output and saving to increase. Why? Because, at the initial level of output, the higher interest rate dictated by the new IS curve lies above that on the LM curve. This higher interest rate leads to an imbalance in the money market, as the young seek to reduce their holdings of money and increase their purchases of capital. Therefore, investment (and saving) increases, and so does output. However, this initial change in output is due to an increase in investment, not a decrease in private or government consumption.

Thus, although an increase in investment and a decrease in consumption (private or government) both increase national saving, the effects on output are quite different. If the initial change in output is due to a rise in investment, output also rises. If the initial change in output is due to a fall in consumption, output falls. In order to distinguish these two cases, in each of which saving increases, we sometimes refer to the former as a change in investment behavior and the latter as a change in saving behavior. Saving and investment are, of course, equal, but the point is to distinguish changes in saving initiated by changes in investment from those initiated by changes in consumption.

VARIABLE PRICES AND KEYNESIAN UNEMPLOYMENT: WAGE RIGIDITY

Our analysis thus far has assumed downward price-level rigidity. However, the nominal rigidity may take a different form, as a nominal wage rate that cannot, in the short run, be reduced below some level.

As we discussed above, labor contracts often set nominal wages for as many as three years at a time, and the minimum wage is rarely adjusted on an annual basis. Both firms and workers should be interested in the *real* wage (the nominal wage divided by the price level), which measures the cost of labor, holding

17. One case we have already seen in which output and investment—and hence saving—increase together is that of expansionary monetary policy (shifting the LM curve outward). Here, even though national saving ultimately increases, the expansionary process begins with an *increase*—not a decrease—in consumption by the old, who receive the initial transfer of money.

purchasing power constant. However, the nominal wage bargain is struck (or the minimum wage imposed) without knowing for sure what the future price level will be. As a result, variations in the price level can cause the real wage to change and, with it, the level of employment. In this case, the nominal rigidity is in the labor market, rather than in the market for goods and services. Still, Keynesian unemployment may result.

With one adjustment, all of the graphical analysis we have gone through so far applies in the case of rigid nominal wages. This adjustment involves the fact that now, as output changes, the price level changes as well. Because the expression for the LM curve depends on the price level, we must keep track of additional shifts in this curve. We'll begin with a look at the labor market, to see how output and the price level are related.

Wage Rigidity and Unemployment

Recall Chapter 3's analysis of how wages and employment are determined. At any given time, competitive firms demand labor up to the point where the marginal product of labor equals the real wage. This labor demand schedule is labeled D in Figure 9-11, which graphs labor, L, versus the real wage, w.[18] The real wage itself equals the nominal wage, say W, divided by the price level, P. As we have assumed in our basic model that labor supply is fixed (i.e., it doesn't depend on the real wage), the labor supply schedule, labeled S in Figure 9-11, is simply a vertical line at the assumed level of labor supply, say $L = N$. Combining these two curves yields the familiar determination of employment at N and a real wage rate of w^e.

As long as the real wage is w^e, there will be no unemployment. But suppose labor market rigidity prevents the *nominal* wage from falling below a certain value, say $\overline{W}$. Then, since the real wage equals the nominal wage divided by the price level, the smallest real wage that can be paid when the price level is P is $\overline{W}/P$. We can see that this constraint will not allow a real wage as low as w^e unless the price level is at least as high as $\hat{P} = \overline{W}/w^e$.

Figure 9-11 shows the potential impact of nominal wage rigidity on employment. If the price level is P^0 (lower than $\hat{P}$) and the nominal wage is fixed at $\overline{W}$, then the prevailing real wage, $\overline{W}/P^0$, is above w^e. At this higher real wage, firms find it profitable to hire fewer workers—L^0 instead of N. With the supply of workers exceeding the demand, all demand is satisfied and the remaining excess supply of labor goes unused. Firms are still hiring workers to the point where the marginal product of labor equals the real wage, but the labor market does not clear.[19]

18. We saw this curve in a somewhat different form in Figure 3-3, which plotted the real wage offered by firms versus the capital-labor ratio, k. Since the capital stock is given in the current period, increases in k are associated with decreases in employment. Hence, the positive relationship between w and k shown in the earlier figure translates into the negative relationship between w and employment shown here.

19. How does this labor market outcome compare to the outcome in the case of rigid prices? When downward price rigidity causes output to lie below Y^f, say at the level of output that requires L^0 workers, firms simply will not hire additional workers at any wage. Their labor demand curve ceases to apply; i.e., they no longer base hiring decisions on a comparison of the marginal product of labor (indicated by the height of their labor demand curve) and the real wage, because they cannot sell the extra output that additional labor would produce.

Figure 9-11 Nominal Wage Rigidity and Unemployment

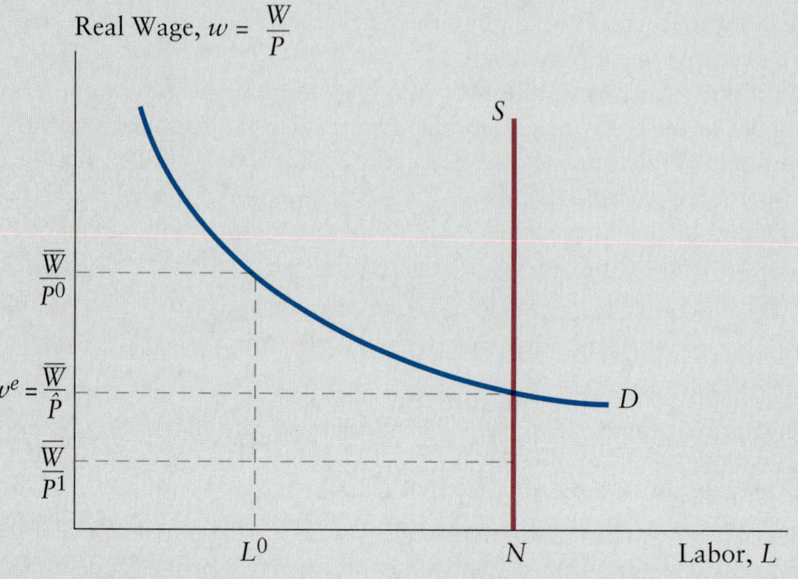

In the absence of wage rigidities, the real wage is determined by the interaction of labor supply (S) and demand (D); N employees are hired at a real wage of w^e. However, if the nominal wage cannot fall below $\overline{W}$, unemployment may result. Unless the price level is at least as high as $\hat{P} = \overline{W}/w^e$, the real wage will be above w^e and employment will be determined along the labor demand schedule. For example, at price level P^0 ($<\hat{P}$), the real wage is above w^e and firms find it profitable to hire only L^0 workers. Unless the price level rises and drives down the real wage, $N - L^0$ workers will suffer involuntary unemployment.

Involuntary unemployment
A situation in which an individual is unable to find work at the going wage

Voluntary unemployment
A situation in which an individual chooses not to accept work at a wage rate being paid to others with comparable skills

The surplus workers, numbering $N - L^0$, suffer from **involuntary unemployment:** they are willing to work at the going wage but are not able to find work. Although we already alluded to this concept, it is worth pausing to discuss more fully what it means. Involuntary unemployment is a very specific concept. It applies only to those who are willing to work at the wage rate actually being paid to others with comparable skills. It does not apply, for example, to the low-skilled individual who is willing to work only for a high wage rate; nor does it apply to the worker in a declining industry who chooses not to work when the industry's lower marginal product of labor dictates paying a reduced wage rate. Each of these workers wishes to be employed *under certain circumstances*, but not at a wage rate *currently* being paid to others with *comparable* skills. If workers can find work at wage rates being paid to others with comparable skills, but choose not to accept such jobs, they are said to experience **voluntary unemployment.**

The distinction between voluntary and involuntary unemployment relates not to the welfare of the unemployed—voluntarily unemployed workers needn't be particularly happy with their circumstances—but to the reasons for their

"I may have something rather outside your field. Would you consider indentured servitude?"

unemployment and, ultimately, to the question of how government should react. As we will see in Chapter 11, the social costs of recession are higher, and the case for government intervention more compelling, if unemployment is involuntary.

Let's return to our discussion of Figure 9-11. If the price level rose high enough, say to P^1, the corresponding real wage compatible with the downwardly rigid nominal wage, $\overline{W}/P^1$, would be below w^e. At this low real wage, labor demand would exceed labor supply. The scarcity of labor would cause the nominal wage to rise to the level w^eP^1, at which point the real wage would equal its market-clearing value, w^e, and employment would equal N. The nominal wage constraint would have no impact, since it prevents the nominal wage from falling below $\overline{W}$ but not from rising above it, and there would be no unemployment.

Thus, in the range of Keynesian unemployment caused by wage rigidity, an increase in the price level will, by lowering the real wage, increase employment and output. How is this relationship affected by the level of the rigid nominal wage? If the nominal wage is fixed at a higher rate, then any given price level will translate into a higher real wage, as well. In this case, each price level will be associated with a lower level of employment and output and a higher level of unemployment.

Monetary and Fiscal Policy in the Rigid-Wage Regime

In the case of price rigidity, price level $\overline{P}$ prevails at any level of output below the full-employment level, Y^f. By contrast, nominal wage rigidity predicts that, as monetary and fiscal policy are used to increase output toward Y^f, the price level will increase, too. The effect will be to dampen the expansionary effects of both types of policies.

To understand why the price level increases, let's consider a particular expansionary policy: a transfer of money to the elderly. As before, a money supply increase raises the elderly's purchasing power and increases their demand for goods and services. Now, though, as they begin spending their money, the excess demand will drive prices up (since only the nominal wage is rigid). As suppliers raise prices, their real labor costs decline, allowing them to hire more workers to meet the extra demand. (In the fixed-price regime, no such price increase was needed, since too-high wages weren't the problem to begin with.) But although output increases, it increases by less than in the case of fixed prices, because the initial increase in consumption, equal to the rise in the real money stock M/P, is reduced in magnitude by the rise in P.

It is clear, then, that the monetary policy multiplier, although still positive, will be smaller than in the case of rigid prices, since some of the stimulus will be absorbed by increases in the price level. The same intuition suggests that fiscal policy will be weakened, too. An increase in output due to a fiscal stimulus will also raise the price level, for the same reason that a money-induced output expansion does. This will reduce the real money stock and have the same impact on output as a direct reduction in the money supply.

The effects of these differences on monetary and fiscal policy multipliers are shown in Figures 9-12 and 9-13, respectively. Figure 9-12 compares the effect of a money supply increase in the rigid-price and rigid-wage regimes. In the former case, the LM curve shifts to LM′. In the latter, the LM curve initially shifts to LM′, but the induced price rise then reduces the real money stock and causes the curve to shift back to LM″. The smaller net shift in the LM curve means that output increases by less and the interest rate decreases by less.

With fiscal policy, an increase in F causes IS to shift to IS′, as illustrated in Figure 9-13. As we've seen, with rigid prices, that is the end of the story. However, in the rigid-wage case, the price-induced shift in the LM curve to LM′ makes fiscal policy less effective at increasing output, as the interest rate increases by more than when the price level is rigid.

In summary, nominal wage rigidity, by permitting some price increase in response to expansionary monetary and fiscal policy, represents a middle ground between the price-rigidity case, in which all expansions of nominal output, PY, go toward real output, and the full-employment case, in which real output cannot increase at all in the short run. In the rigid-wage case, as in the rigid-price case, the relative effectiveness of monetary and fiscal policy will still be partially determined by the slope of the LM curve, which depends on the interest sensitivity of money demand and is not related to the nature of the nominal rigidity.

HOW ACCURATE IS THE SIMPLE KEYNESIAN MODEL? A PREVIEW

The Keynesian model of nominal rigidities offers but one explanation of business cycles. We will discuss others in the next chapter and compare them to the Keynesian model. For now, let's just note and evaluate a couple of the Keynesian model's predictions.

Figure 9-12 Monetary Policy with Rigid Nominal Wages

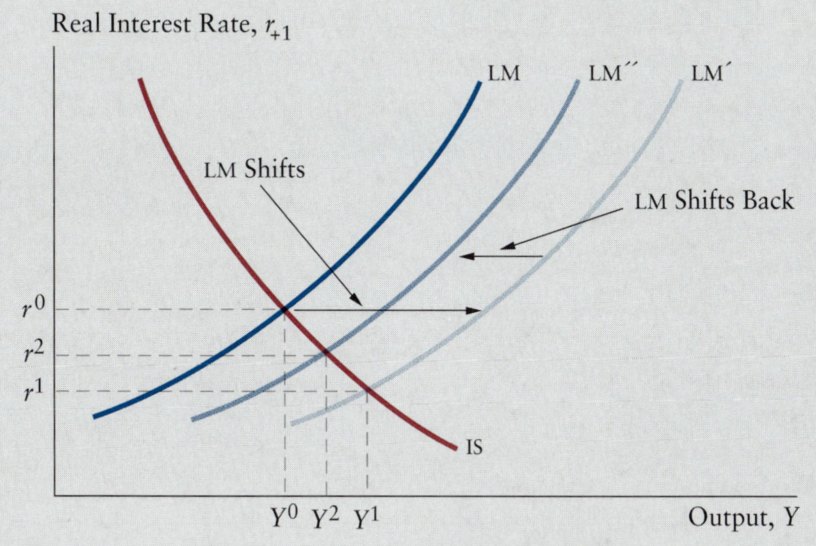

With a rigid price level, an increase in the nominal money supply shifts the LM curve to LM´. Output increases from Y^0 to Y^1 and the interest rate falls (from r^0 to r^1). In a rigid wage regime, the same increase in the nominal money stock leads to the same initial shift of LM to LM´. However, the resulting increase in the price level reduces the real money stock and causes LM to shift back to LM´´. The net result is a smaller increase in output (from Y^0 to Y^2) and a smaller decrease in the interest rate (from r^0 to r^2).

Volatility of Consumption and Investment

In Chapter 4, we observed that investment is much more volatile than consumption over the business cycle. That is, the absolute value of the percentage change in investment is higher than that of consumption, whether income is growing or falling. To put it another way, the ratio of investment to consumption is lower during recessions than during booms. We observed in Chapter 4 that this pattern was consistent with the technology-shock-induced economic fluctuations posited by the real business cycle model. However, the predictions of the Keynesian model are also consistent with this empirical regularity.

To see this, note first that as employment and income fall below their full-employment level, with the shares of income going to labor and capital remaining fixed, consumption purchases by the old and investment purchases by the young both decrease. For the young, investment falls because income falls. However, the old finance their consumption not only from interest income but also by selling their assets, whose values are not directly influenced by the fall in output. Hence, although the drop in interest income causes their consumption

Figure 9-13 Fiscal Policy with Rigid Nominal Wages

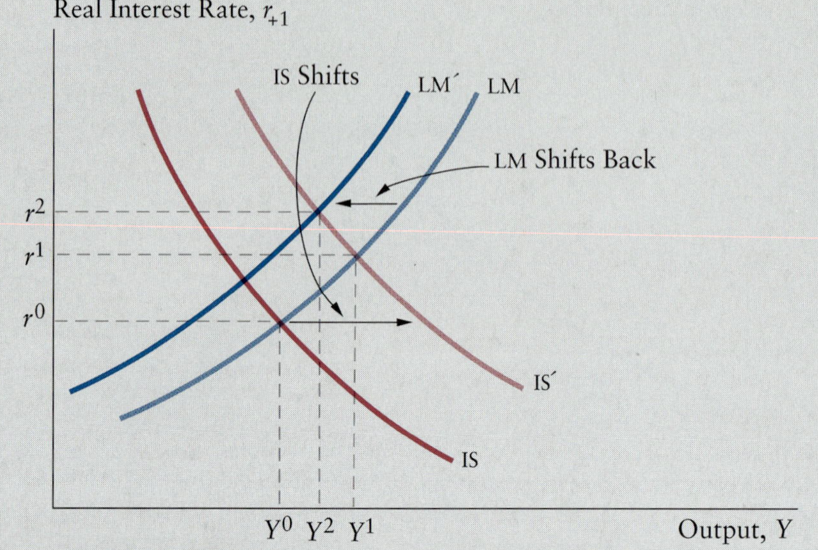

With a rigid price level, an increase in *F* shifts the IS curve to IS´. Output increases from Y^0 to Y^1 and the interest rate increases from r^0 to r^1. In a rigid wage regime, the same increase in F leads to the same shift of IS. In this case, however, as output rises, so does the price level. The resulting decrease in the real money supply shifts the LM curve inward to LM´. The net result is a smaller increase in output (from Y^0 to Y^2) and a larger increase in the interest rate (from r^0 to r^2).

to fall, their overall resources and consumption fall by a smaller proportion than does their income (and aggregate income as well). This illustrates the principle of *consumption smoothing* introduced in Chapter 2: the assets of the old were accumulated in the period prior to the current one in which output is low. Of course, this same reasoning explained the relative smoothness of consumption in response to a technology shock. This prediction of smaller volatility of consumption as output falls is a consequence of the basic life-cycle consumption model and has relatively little to do with the Keynesian explanation of *why* output fluctuates.

The Cyclical Behavior of Real Wages

The nominal-wage-rigidity version of the basic Keynesian model predicts that recession is attributable to firms' inability to lower real wages to their equilibrium level. Given the levels of technology and capital, this suggests that real wages should be countercyclical, moving in the opposite direction from income over the business cycle. In terms of Figure 9-11, increases in the real wage should be associated with lower employment and hence lower output.

There has been considerable debate about whether real wages do behave countercyclically, and some evidence that they do not has been taken to contradict the Keynesian model. However, we should note two caveats. First, the rigid-price version of the Keynesian model gives less than certain predictions about the behavior of real wages during recession. Second, what the rigid-wage model predicts is that real wages are *too high* during recession, but not necessarily higher than during booms. It could be the case that temporary shocks (changes induced by external forces) to technology or the capital stock call for a *lower* real wage at full employment (associated with a downward shift of the labor demand curve), and that recessions occur because the real wage fails to fall enough.

This reasoning illustrates a point on which we will elaborate in the next chapter: the various explanations of recessions are not necessarily inconsistent with one another. For example, a technology shock may lead to a reduction in employment both because labor supply falls as real wages fall (the real business cycle explanation) and because real wages do not fall *enough* to clear the labor market (the Keynesian explanation).

Chapter Summary

1. This chapter has focused on the short run. Using the model developed in previous chapters, we introduced nominal rigidities and considered their impact on output and employment. Nominal rigidities involve the inability of an output or input price to respond immediately to the forces of supply and demand. We considered the impact of downward rigidity of the price level and the nominal wage rate and found that each could contribute to a reduction in output and cause involuntary unemployment, with workers unable to find work at the going wage.
2. Our graphical analysis of the Keynesian model uses two key relationships: the equality of money demand and supply and the transition equation that determines next period's capital stock and rate of interest. These are the same two equations used in Chapter 8 to study the evolution of the economy with flexible prices. With nominal rigidities, they give rise to the LM and IS curves, respectively. The IS and LM curves may be combined to solve for output when output lies below its full-employment level—the level that would be achieved in the absence of such rigidities.
3. According to the Keynesian model, both monetary and fiscal policy may be used to increase output. Increasing the money supply leads to a reduction in the next period's interest rate and an increase in investment. Fiscal policy, on the other hand, works through an increase in the interest rate. The greater government absorption of resources from the young (an increase in F) *crowds out* investment and causes the prospective interest rate to rise. This, in turn, causes the young to shift assets out of money balances and into capital, partially offsetting the decline in investment. Government demand increases by F but investment demand falls by less than F. There is a net increase in aggregate demand and output.

4. Although either monetary or fiscal policy may be used to increase output when nominal rigidities exist, they have opposite effects on the *composition* of output and, according to the transition equation, on the level of capital and hence output in the future. Monetary policy acts to increase next period's capital stock and hence future output, whereas fiscal policy crowds out investment.
5. We measure and describe the impact of monetary and fiscal policy using policy multipliers. These multipliers indicate the increase in output resulting from a unit increase in the real money supply or absorption by the government of a unit of resources from the young. Either type of policy may have an impact on output many times larger than the initial change in the policy variable itself. The relative strengths of monetary and fiscal policy depend on the interest sensitivity of the demand for money; the more sensitive money demand is, the stronger is fiscal policy and the weaker is monetary policy. Both fiscal policy and monetary policy multipliers are smaller in the case of nominal wage (rather than price) rigidity, because as output increases, the price level increases, too.
6. In the presence of nominal rigidities, a decrease in household or government consumption will lead to a reduction in output and moderate the initial increase in national saving itself. This phenomenon is known as the *paradox of thrift*. But increases in national saving are not always associated with decreases in output; saving increases along with output in response to a positive shock to the production function. The paradox of thrift applies only when the initial change in output (and increase in national saving) results from a decline in household or government consumption. A positive productivity shock increases saving initially by increasing investment, not by reducing consumption.
7. The predictions of both the real business cycle model of economic fluctuations discussed in Chapter 4 and the Keynesian model are consistent with the observed relative volatility of consumption and investment over the business cycle. Each model's predictions arise from the *consumption smoothing* of the life-cycle model itself.
8. In the rigid-nominal-wage version of the Keynesian model, unemployment occurs because real wages are too high. Some economists view this as inconsistent with the fact that real wages are not countercyclical—they typically don't rise during recessions. However, the Keynesian theory simply says that real wages are too high. Even if they have not risen, real wages can become too high to sustain full employment if temporary shocks to technology or the capital stock reduce the productivity of labor.

Key Concepts

Nominal rigidity
Keynesian model
Real rigidity
LM curve
IS curve
Potential (full-employment) output
Multiplier
Monetarism
Paradox of thrift
Involuntary unemployment
Voluntary unemployment

Review Questions

1. What is meant by *fully flexible prices?* Provide several examples of markets with fully flexible prices. What properties or conditions in those markets lead to price flexibility?
2. What is meant by *nominal rigidity*? Provide several examples of prices that exhibit nominal rigidity. What conditions lead to such stickiness? Is the stickiness symmetric? Explain.
3. What is meant by *real rigidity?* If the minimum wage were "indexed" to the Consumer Price Index so that it moved equiproportionally in both directions, would this constitute nominal or real wage rigidity? Explain.
4. What have Keynesians traditionally believed about the flexibility of prices and wages in the short run versus the long run? How can this assumption of price adjustment be incorporated into the life-cycle model?
5. Derive the equation for the *LM curve* from the equality of money supply and money demand. What values are constant in the LM equation? What is the nature of the relationship captured by the LM curve?
6. Using the transition equation and the equation for the interest rate in period $t+1$, derive the *IS curve*. What values are constant in the IS equation? What is the nature of the relationship captured by the IS curve?
7. What is *involuntary* (or *Keynesian*) *unemployment*, and how does it arise?
8. What is *monetary policy*, and what effect does it have on the position of the LM curve? What is the *multiplier process*, and how does it arise in response to an increase in the money stock? Why might the ultimate rise in output following a monetary expansion be smaller than the magnitude of the LM curve's shift?
9. What is *fiscal policy*, and what effect does it have on the position of the IS curve? Explain the nature of *crowding out* and how it helps determine the initial and ultimate effects of fiscal policy on both output and investment.
10. In the *short run*, what are the common and differing effects of monetary and fiscal policy? In the *long run*, what differences exist between the use of monetary and fiscal policy? Why?
11. What is *monetarism*, and what belief do monetarists hold regarding the interest sensitivity of money demand? What implications does this view have for the shape of the LM curve? Why?
12. How is the effectiveness of monetary policy related to the interest sensitivity of money demand? Why? How is the effectiveness of fiscal policy related to the interest sensitivity of money demand? Why?
13. What is a policy *multiplier*, and how is it measured? What is the value of the fiscal policy multiplier when the LM curve is vertical? Why?
14. What is the expression for the monetary policy multiplier when the LM curve is vertical? Using the equation for the LM curve, demonstrate that this expression is equal to the velocity of money.
15. What is the *paradox of thrift*, and why is it considered a paradox?
16. Are all increases in national saving associated with reductions in output, according to the Keynesian model? Why or why not?
17. Why does involuntary unemployment arise under *nominal wage rigidity* with price flexibility?

18. Why is the stimulative effect of fiscal and monetary policy on output smaller under nominal wage rigidity with price flexibility than it is under price rigidity? How is this difference shown graphically?

19. Is the observed volatility of investment and smoothing of consumption consistent with the Keynesian model? To what extent do these outcomes depend on the Keynesian assumptions?

Numerical Questions

Use the following initial parameter values for questions 1 through 5. Change the values only when indicated.

Parameter	Value
N	200
A	4
β	0.3
$\overline{P}$	1
$\overline{M}$	297.5
F	0

Also, let the parameter γ be related to the real interest rate, r_{+1}, by the equation $\gamma = 0.727188 - 0.25r_{+1}$.

1. **a.** Calculate the values of r_{+1} that lie along the LM curve and correspond to the given levels of output. Also, calculate the value of γ for each of the computed r_{+1}.

Y	r_{+1}	γ
750		
800		
850		
900		
950		

b. Suppose that the government now decides to increase $\overline{M}$ by 10. Calculate the new level of Y for each of the r_{+1} computed in part a. Has the LM schedule shifted to the right or to the left?

c. Suppose that $\overline{M}$ is back to its initial level, but that money demand becomes more sensitive to interest rate changes. Specifically, assume that the coefficient on r_{+1} in the equation describing γ is −0.5, not −0.25. Calculate the new values of r_{+1} that lie along the LM schedule and correspond to the levels of output given in part a.

Y	r_{+1}
750	
800	
850	
900	
950	

Compare your answers to those calculated in part a. Has the increased interest sensitivity of money demand made the LM schedule steeper or flatter? Explain.

2. a. Using the initial parameter values, calculate the values of r_{+1} that lie along the IS curve and correspond to the given levels of output. In doing so, assume, as is done in the chapter, that γ is *constant*. Use a value of *0.5*.

Y	r_{+1}
750	
800	
850	
900	
950	

b. Suppose that the government decides to increase F from 0 to 10. Calculate the new levels of output that correspond to the values of r_{+1} computed in part a. Has the IS schedule shifted to the right or to the left?

c. Suppose that F once again equals 0, but that the value of γ falls from 0.5 to 0.3. Recalculate the values of r_{+1} for the levels of output given in part a. What does the change in γ do to the position of the IS curve? Give the economic intuition behind the change.

3. Suppose that the initial parameter values hold, but that the Federal Reserve has as its goal to keep the interest rate at 0.908785. That is, the Fed will change the money supply by whatever it takes to keep interest rates constant at 0.908785.

a. What is the equilibrium output level under these circumstances? (Helpful hint: Use the calculations from question 2.)

b. If the government increases F from 0 to 10, by how much will equilibrium output change?

c. When F increases by 10, by how much must $\overline{M}$ change to keep interest rates unchanged?

4. Suppose, as a monetarist would, that the value of γ is constant and equal to 0.5 both for the LM schedule and for the IS schedule. Using the initial values, answer parts a through e.

a. What are the fixed-price equilibrium levels of Y and r_{+1}? (Helpful hint: Use the calculations from questions 1 and 2.)

b. Using the same parameter values, now assume that prices are *flexible*. What are the flexible price equilibrium values of Y and r_{+1}?

c. Based on your answers to parts a and b, is there unemployment? Why?

d. Compute the flexible price equilibrium *price level*. How does this value compare to the initially fixed price level? Is the difference consistent with your answer to part c?

e. Suppose that the government wanted to restore output to its full-employment level using monetary policy. By how much would $\bar{M}$ have to change to accomplish this goal?

5. Suppose that $F = 10$ and that γ is a constant equal to 0.5. Also, assume that the LM curve is flat and described by the equation $r_{+1} = 0.930799$.

a. Using the initial values of the other parameters, calculate the fixed-price equilibrium value of output.

b. How much saving occurs in the fixed-price equilibrium?

c. Suppose that the government wants to increase saving and, to that end, reduces F from 10 to 0. What level of saving would occur after the government's actions? Compare this answer to the one calculated in part b, and explain any difference or similarity.

Analytical Questions

1. Suppose that the economy is characterized by price rigidity and is presently below full employment. In order to raise the level of current output, the government increases its consumption purchases and finances them by taking resources from the young. You are an economist for the Federal Reserve Board, and the Chair asks you to devise a way to exactly offset any crowding out that might result from the fiscal policy. What would you propose, and what would be the ultimate effect of your plan (in conjunction with the fiscal policy) on the interest rate? on the level of output? on the composition of output? Explain.

2. Social upheaval erupts and leads to the theft and burning of large quantities of money. Trace the effects on an economy characterized by price rigidity. In particular, what would happen to the economy's interest rate, the level of current output, and the composition of output? What would be the effect, if any, on the nation's future productive capacity? Explain.

3. The economy is currently below full employment. There is a binding minimum wage rate, though prices are flexible.

a. The Labor Secretary asks Congress to raise the minimum wage rate. What would happen to output, the interest rate, and capital formation?

b. The Labor Secretary loses the battle for an increased minimum wage as a result of successful lobbying efforts by the American Association of Manufacturers, which manages to get Congress to eliminate the minimum wage. What will happen to the nominal wage rate, the real wage rate, current output, and capital formation? Explain how these changes would affect future adjustments in the economy.

APPENDIX

The Flat LM *Curve and the Liquidity Trap*

As we showed graphically in the text, fiscal policy becomes relatively stronger, and monetary policy weaker, as the demand for money becomes more sensitive to the interest rate. Monetary policy is strongest, with a multiplier of $1/\gamma(1-\beta)$, and fiscal policy is ineffective, with a multiplier of 0, when money demand is independent of the interest rate and the LM curve is vertical.

The other extreme occurs when the demand for money is infinitely sensitive to the interest rate. This limiting case is difficult to treat graphically, because as the LM curve becomes horizontal the relationship $\gamma[r_{+1}]$ becomes undefined: any value of γ is consistent with a single value of r_{+1}. However, we can still use the expressions for the IS and LM curves to derive the multipliers for monetary and fiscal policy.

When the LM curve is horizontal, equilibrium in the money market implies that the interest rate r_{+1} cannot change. At any higher interest rate, the demand for money will be zero. For any lower interest rate, the demand for money will be infinite. Since r_{+1} is given, so is the next period's capital stock, K_{+1}. That is, in the expression for next period's capital stock, which formed the basis for the IS curve expression,

$$K_{+1} = (1-\gamma)(1-\beta)Y - F$$

K_{+1} is constant at some value $\hat{K}_{+1}$. If we solve for γ using the LM curve expression, substitute the resulting expression for γ into this equation for K_{+1}, and solve for Y, we obtain

$$Y = \frac{1}{(1-\beta)}\left[\hat{K}_{+1} + F + \frac{\overline{M}}{\overline{P}}\right]$$

from which we can observe that the multiplier of a unit increase in either F or $M/\overline{P}$—the size of the resulting increase in Y—will be $1/(1-\beta)$.

As in the text, we can think of multiplier effects as occurring in stages. Consider, for example, a change in F. Suppose the government purchases 1 dollar of goods, financing the purchase by taxing the young. This increases F by 1 dollar. Output also increases by 1 dollar, because G rises by 1 and, because $\hat{K}_{+1}$ is not

Table 9.2 Multipliers for Monetary and Fiscal Policy (For Different Assumptions About the Interest Sensitivity of Money Demand)

	Insensitive	**Extremely Sensitive**
Monetary Policy	$\frac{1}{\gamma(1-\beta)}$	$\frac{1}{(1-\beta)}$
Fiscal Policy	0	$\frac{1}{(1-\beta)}$

Notes: β is the share of income going to capital (i.e., to the elderly). γ is the share of labor income used to acquire money balances.

affected, there is no crowding out of investment. This increase in output increases income by a dollar. Of this additional output, $(1 - \beta)$ dollars go to labor and β dollars go to capital. The young workers consume none of their additional income, but the old consume all of theirs, increasing consumption and output by an additional β dollars. This, in turn increases income by β, income of the old by β^2, and consumption by another β^2. As this continues, the sum $1 + \beta + \beta^2 + \ldots$ approaches $1/(1 - \beta)$—the multiplier times the original increase in F.

In this case, an increase in the real money stock has the same multiplier effect as an increase in F. The associated transfer to the old increases their consumption by the same amount. This increase in output of 1 increases consumption by β, which increases output by β more, and consumption by β^2 more, and so on. In this extreme case, an increase in the money supply does not increase investment at all. Normally, individuals would hold additional money balances only if interest rates fell, and this, in turn, would be associated with more capital accumulation. However, when money demand is very sensitive to the interest rate, the young are willing to hold more money balances even with essentially no change in the interest rate—an outcome described by Keynes as a *liquidity trap,* because the monetary stimulus is "trapped" by the young in the form of additional money holdings. The only increase in output resulting from a monetary stimulus comes from additional consumption by the elderly.[20]

For the general case, then, the fiscal policy multiplier lies between 0 and $1/(1 - \beta)$; the monetary policy multiplier lies between $1/(1 - \beta)$ and $1/\gamma(1 - \beta)$. The range of fiscal and monetary policy multipliers is summarized in Table 9-2.

20. Some analyses of monetary policy in the presence of a liquidity trap find no effect on output at all. The difference results from the way in which the money supply increase is assumed to occur. If the increased money supply were given to the young rather than the old, the resources of the old would not increase, and neither would their consumption.

C H A P T E R 10

Understanding Recessions

INTRODUCTION

What causes recessions, and how they can be avoided? These are two of the most important, but least settled, questions in macroeconomics. As you'll learn in this chapter, economists have strikingly different theories of recessions and expansions, none of which fits all the facts about the economy's performance over the business cycle. But each provides important insights into the different forces that may precipitate periodic booms and busts.

Actually, we've already mentioned two quite different explanations of recessions: one offered by traditional Keynesians and the other by real business cycle theorists. Recall that traditional Keynesians blame nominal price and wage rigidities for the economy's failure to achieve full employment. They argue that, given these rigidities, there is often too little *aggregate demand*—the total demand for output by the private and government sectors—to sustain full employment. Real business cycle theorists, in contrast, believe economic fluctuations reflect real, rather than nominal, factors. They trace recessions and expansions to changes in the economy's productive capacity, so-called *technology shocks*.

In the pages that follow we'll expand our discussion of traditional Keynesian and real business cycle models. But we'll also examine several other prominent theories of recessions. One is the so-called *misperception theory.* This theory argues that households and firms think rationally about the state of the economy (form what economists call *rational expectations*), but they are forced to make economic decisions with less-than-perfect information about various shocks, policy and otherwise, that impinge upon the economy. As we'll see, and as the so-called rational expectations economists showed, this imperfect information about the state of the economy can lead to fluctuations in output that would not otherwise occur.

Another explanation of recessions is the *sectoral shift model.* Proponents of this model point to shifts in the *composition* of the goods and services produced by different sectors of the economy as leading to temporary declines in output and increases in unemployment for the following simple reason: it takes time for workers laid off from contracting industries to find jobs in expanding industries.

The misperception, real business cycle, and sectoral shift explanations are distinct, but they share the assumption that prices and wages are fully flexible. In that respect they differ from both the traditional Keynesian model as well as more recent models of nominal rigidities proposed by the *New Keynesians.* New Keynesians go beyond traditional Keynesians in seeking to understand the sources of price and wage rigidity. As we'll discuss, New Keynesians have focused on three sources of rigidity: long-term nominal wage and price contracts, simple inertia, and monopolistic price setting by firms with market power. Each of these types of price or wage rigidity, either on its own or in conjunction with inappropriate government policy, can cause, or at least contribute to, recession.

The New Keynesians have also developed an explanation of recession—*coordination failure*—that doesn't hinge on nominal rigidities but does represent another way that markets may perform badly. Their coordination models stress that the economy is more than the sum of its parts and that it needs synchronized (coordinated) action by individual households and firms to sustain a high level of output and employment. In considering coordination failures, we'll see that the potential for such failures is closely connected with the state of business and consumer confidence—what Keynes called *animal spirits.*

The *political business cycle theory* is the last explanation of economic up- and downturns we'll entertain. According to this theory, politicians use monetary and fiscal policies to overexpand the economy prior to an election and then are forced to reverse these policies after the election.

We'll begin our discussion of the causes of recessions and expansions by looking at the U.S. *Phillips curve* for the period 1950–1969. The Phillips curve, named after British economist A. W. Phillips, plots the annual inflation rate against the annual unemployment rate.[1] During the period 1950–1969 there was an inverse relationship between the two rates. As we'll point out, this

1. Professor Phillips studied the relationship between the growth rate of nominal wages and the rate of unemployment in the United Kingdom between 1861 and 1957. Since the growth rate of nominal wages closely tracks the inflation rate, economists have substituted the inflation rate for the growth rate of nominal wages.

inverse relationship is a prediction of the traditional Keynesian model presented in the last chapter. But this inverse statistical relationship between U.S. inflation and unemployment evaporated after 1969, when the Phillips curve appeared to start shifting. The empirical instability of the Phillips curve provides a natural entree into the critique of the traditional Keynesian model by rational expectations economists, their proffered alternative, the misperception theory, and their advocacy of grounding macroeconomics more closely in microeconomics.

Micro-based models of macro phenomena with well-functioning markets are called neoclassical models. The misperception, real business cycle, and sectoral shift models are each neoclassical models, and we'll discuss the latter two once we've examined the misperception theory.[2] Finally, we'll turn to the New Keynesian explanations of recessions as well as the theory of political business cycles. As we'll see, the New Keynesian models share with neoclassical models the attempt to provide a microeconomic basis for macroeconomic outcomes. To keep the theories straight, we will summarize, in Table 10-4, each theory's explanation of recessions as well as its policy implications.

The following are some of the questions we'll address in this chapter:

- What are the principal theories of recessions?
- Are the different theories mutually compatible?
- Are recessions necessarily a sign of market failure?
- What are the policy implications of the different theories?
- What evidence is there for and against particular theories of recessions?

THE 1950–1969 PHILLIPS CURVE AND THE KEYNESIAN MODEL

The relationship between inflation and unemployment in the United States has framed much of the postwar debate about alternative theories of recession. Accordingly, it's a good starting point for discussing these theories.

Figure 10-1 plots U.S. inflation and unemployment rates for the period 1950–1969. Note that most data points in the figure satisfy the following property: when the inflation rate is low, the unemployment rate is high, and when the inflation rate is high, the unemployment rate is low. We can summarize this generally inverse relationship between the inflation and unemployment rates by adding a simple curve—the **Phillips curve**—that lies closest to the data points in the diagram.

Phillips curve *A curve fit to observed combinations of the inflation and the unemployment rates*

The negative slope of the Phillips curve during the 1950s and 1960s suggested the possibility of an inflation-unemployment policy trade-off through which the government could permanently lower unemployment by raising the inflation rate. Such a trade-off is predicted by the Keynesian model with rigid nominal wages presented in the last chapter.

2. In the misperception model markets function as well as possible given the assumed limitations on the transmission of information.

Figure 10-1 The U.S. Phillips Curve, 1950–1969

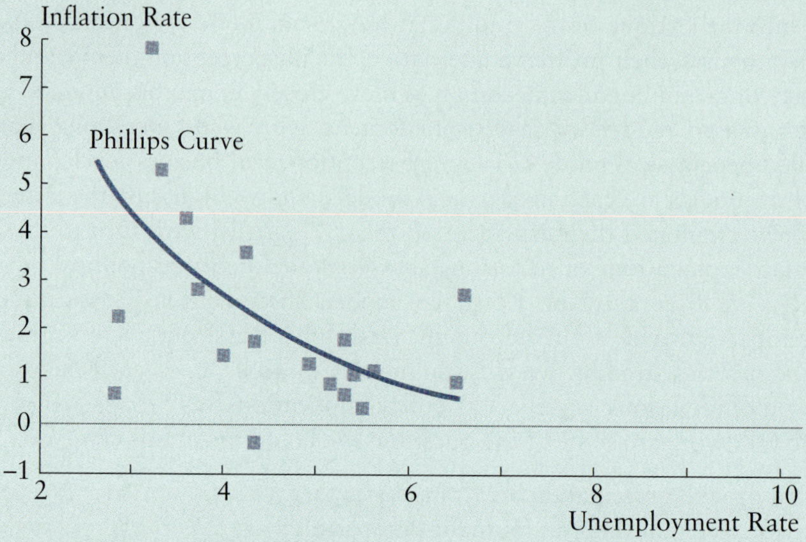

This figure plots combinations of U.S. inflation and unemployment rates for the period 1950–1969. On the average, when the inflation rate was high, the unemployment rate was low, and vice versa. This generally inverse relationship is summarized by the downwardly sloping Phillips curve. Originally, it was interpreted as representing a stable trade-off between inflation and unemployment.

To see why, let's assume that a rigid nominal wage is the reason the LM and IS curves of Figure 10-2 intersect at less than the full-employment level of output. In this case both an expansionary monetary policy, which shifts the LM curve rightward, and an expansionary fiscal policy, which shifts the IS curve upward, will lead to a higher level of prices. As we know, and as Figure 10-2 illustrates for the case of expansionary monetary policy, this increase in prices leads to a secondary leftward shift of the LM curve. But the net impact of either expansionary monetary or fiscal policy is more output and a higher price level. The two go hand-in-hand, because firms will hire more workers and produce more output only if the real wage falls. But with the nominal wage fixed, the only way the real wage can fall is if the price level rises.

Thus, our rigid nominal wage model predicts that a higher price level in the current period, say time t, will be associated with lower unemployment. But a higher price level at time t also means a higher inflation rate between time $t-1$ and time t. Recall that the inflation rate at time t, π_t, is defined as $(P_t - P_{t-1})/P_{t-1}$;

Figure 10-2 Output Determination in the Keynesian Model

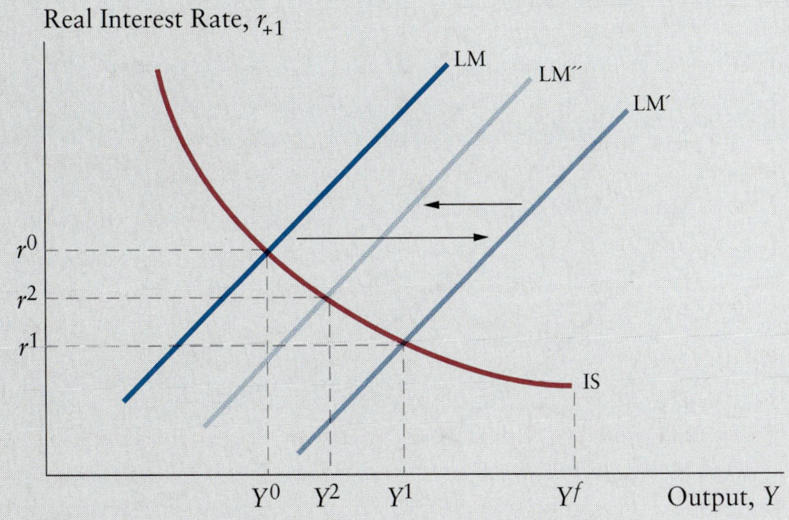

The Keynesian model with rigid nominal wages predicts a trade-off between inflation and unemployment. If the IS and LM curves intersect to determine a less than full-employment level of output, Y^0, an expansionary monetary policy may be employed. An increase in the nominal money stock shifts LM to LM′, but the resulting higher price level drives down the real money supply and shifts LM back to LM″. The net impact is a higher level of output (which lowers the unemployment rate) and a higher price level (which, given the previous price level, implies a higher inflation rate). This is just the inverse relationship between inflation and unemployment represented in the Phillips curve.

so, given the historically determined value of P_{t-1}, π_t will be larger, the larger P_t is. Thus, our model also predicts what the inflation-employment data for the period 1950–1969 seems to indicate: a negative relationship between the inflation rate and the level of unemployment *given the level of the nominal wage at time t.*

THE SHIFTING INFLATION-UNEMPLOYMENT TRADE-OFF

As the previous sentence emphasizes, the relationship between the inflation and unemployment rates depends on the prevailing nominal wage. The reason is that the position of the LM curve depends on the price level, which, as we'll now explain, depends on the level of the nominal wage. Higher levels of the nominal wage lead to higher prices (and, given the previous price level, higher inflation), which shift the LM curve leftward, reducing output and employment.

Figure 10-3 The Phillips Curve's Dependence on the Level of Nominal Wage Demands

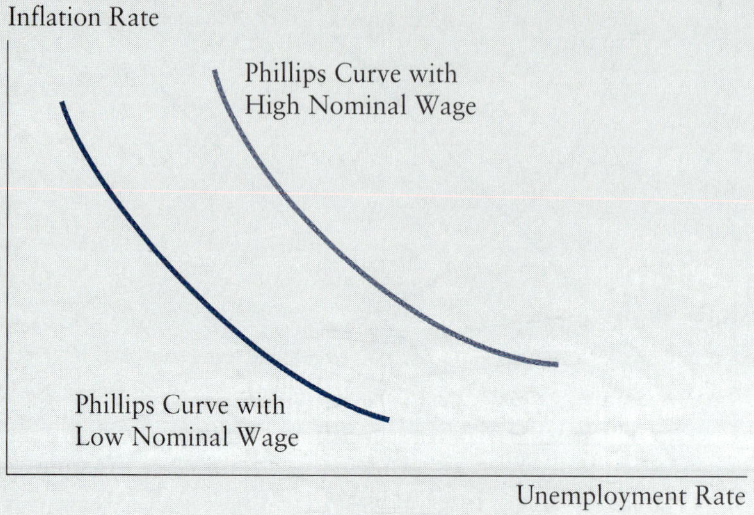

The position of the Phillips curve depends on the level at which the nominal wage is set. The Phillips curve based on a low nominal wage lies to the left of the curve based on a high nominal wage.

To understand this, note that an increase in the nominal wage, with no change in the price level, means an increase in the real wage firms must pay and, consequently, a reduction in the number of workers they employ. This reduction in employment translates into a reduction in the level of output supplied. The resulting excess demand for output causes the price level to rise, shifting the LM curve to the left.

This rise in the nominal wage has implications for the Phillips curve. A higher nominal wage spells a higher real wage, more unemployment, a higher price level and, given the price level in the previous period, a higher inflation rate. So if we plot the inflation and unemployment rates at time t, the data point based on a low nominal wage will lie northeast of the data point based on a high nominal wage. Figure 10-3 summarizes this point—that the position of the Phillips curve depends on the level at which the nominal wage is set. It shows that the Phillips curve based on a low nominal wage lies to the left of the curve based on a high nominal wage.

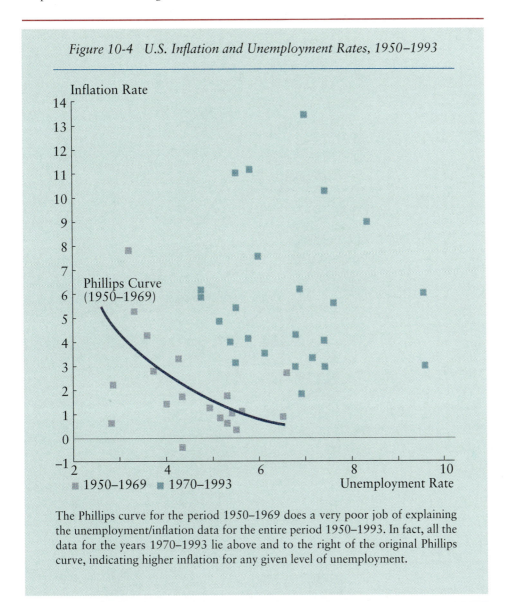

Figure 10-4 U.S. Inflation and Unemployment Rates, 1950–1993

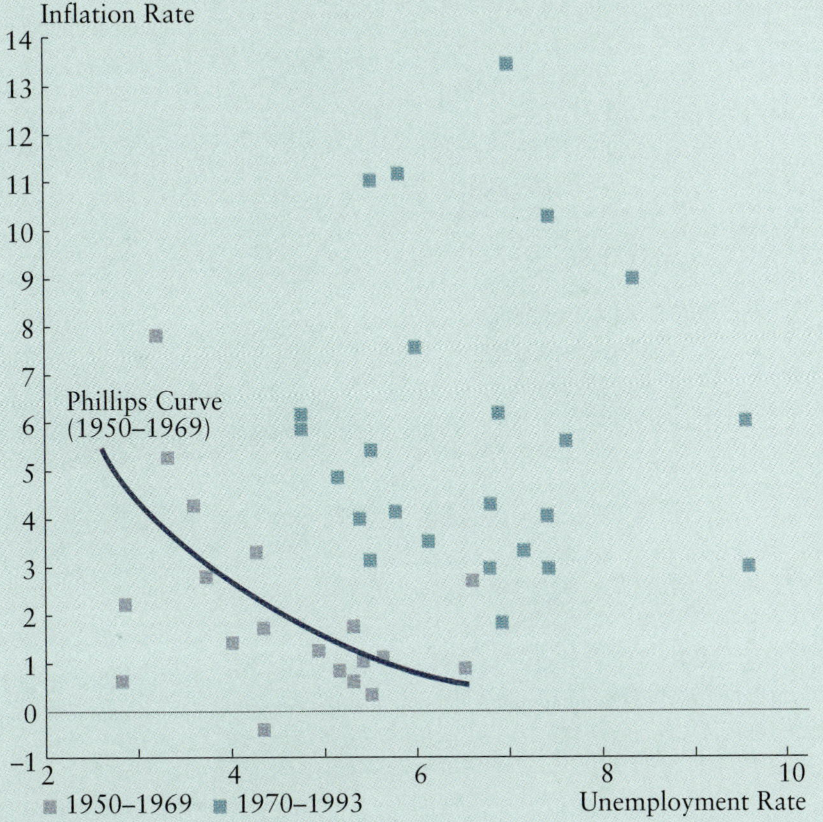

The Phillips curve for the period 1950–1969 does a very poor job of explaining the unemployment/inflation data for the entire period 1950–1993. In fact, all the data for the years 1970–1993 lie above and to the right of the original Phillips curve, indicating higher inflation for any given level of unemployment.

Case Study: The Shifting U.S. Phillips Curve

The dependence of the Phillips curve on the level of nominal wage demands became apparent to economists in the late 1960s and early 1970s as they continued to collect data on inflation and unemployment rates. The new data undermined the idea of a stable empirical relationship between the rates of inflation and unemployment. Figure 10-4 makes this clear. It plots inflation and unemployment rates for the period 1950–1993 as well as the Phillips curve of Figure 10-1 for the period 1950–1969. Note how poorly the Phillips curve for the earlier period fits the data over the entire period.

Figure 10-5 The Shifting U.S. Phillips Curve, 1950–1993

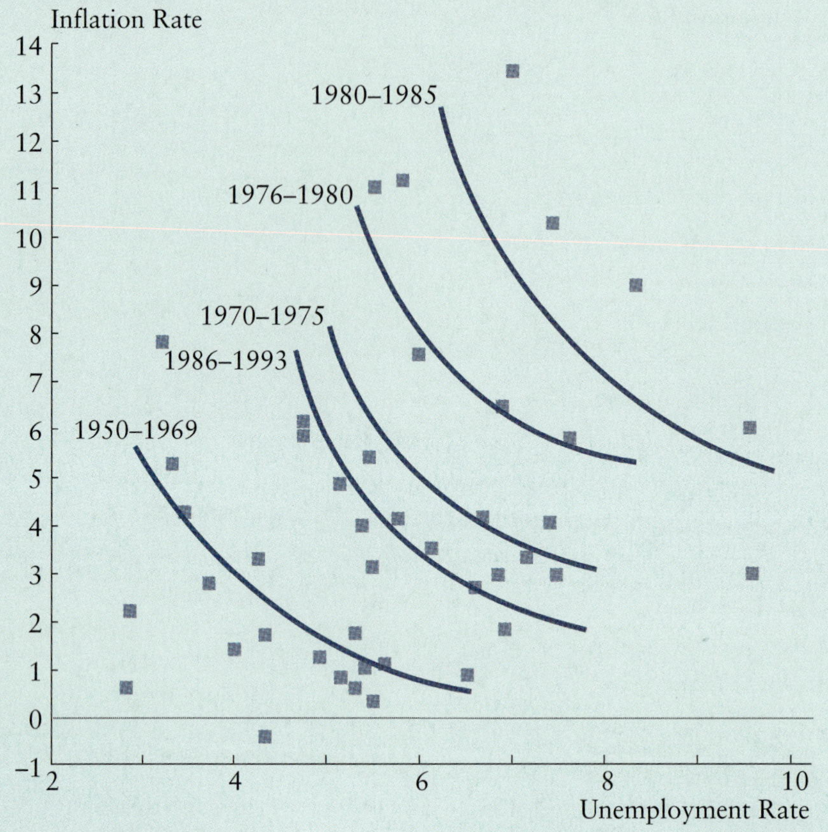

If we fit Phillips curves to data for the periods 1970–1975, 1976–1980, 1981–1985, and 1986–1993, we see that the curve has shifted considerably over time. During 1950–1969, for example, a 6 percent unemployment rate was associated with an inflation rate of about 1 percent. During the period 1976–1980, by contrast, the same unemployment rate was associated with an 8 percent inflation rate!

Figure 10-5 reproduces the 1950–1969 Phillips curve, but it also fits Phillips curves to the inflation and unemployment data for the four other periods 1970–1975, 1976–1980, 1980–1985, and 1986–1993. Note the clear shifts in the Phillips curve across the different periods. For example, during the period 1950–1969, a 6 percent unemployment rate would have been associated with an inflation rate of about 1 percent, whereas in the period 1976–1980, a 6 percent unemployment rate was associated with an inflation rate of roughly 8 percent.

Figure 10-6 A Shifting Phillips Curve Nullifies the Inflation-Unemployment Policy Trade-Off

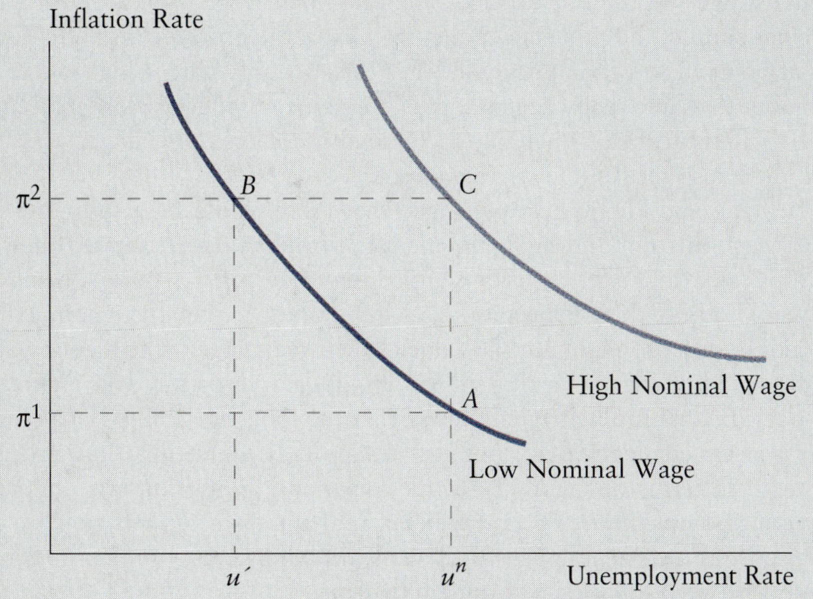

According to Friedman and Phelps, the position of the Phillips curve depends on the level of nominal wages, which ultimately depends on the *expected* inflation rate. Their natural rate hypothesis undermined the notion of a stable unemployment/inflation trade-off. The government may try to use monetary policy to move up the Phillips curve from point *A* to point *B*, thus lowering the unemployment rate. Workers, however, will realize that the higher money supply means a higher price level and a lower real wage. To compensate, they demand a higher nominal wage. This shifts the Phillips curve upward to the one labeled "High Nominal Wage." As a result, the unemployment rate stays at u^n, but the inflation rate rises to π^2.

THE NATURAL RATE HYPOTHESIS

The earliest explanations of a shifting Phillips curve were provided by Nobel Laureate Milton Friedman and Edmund Phelps of Columbia University. They noted that the position of the Phillips curve depends on the level of nominal wages, and stressed the point that nominal wages are set in light of the *expected* inflation rate.

Figure 10-6 shows the Friedman-Phelps argument. Suppose that the government thinks it is facing the Phillips curve labeled "low nominal wage" and announces that it is going to use, say, monetary policy and move the economy from point *A* to point *B*, lowering the unemployment rate from u^n to u'. But also suppose that workers realize that the policy will result in a higher inflation rate. In response to the anticipated inflation, workers demand a higher nominal wage to compensate them fully for the increase in prices, i.e., to preserve their real wage. This shifts the Phillips curve in Figure 10-6 from the one labeled "low nominal wage" to the one labeled "high nominal wage." Because the Phillips curve has shifted, the monetary policy will leave the economy at point *C* rather than at point *B*, i.e., the policy will leave the economy with a higher rate of inflation but the same real wage and, thus, the same number of workers that firms will be willing to hire. Unchanged employment means unchanged unemployment, u^n. It also means unchanged output.

Friedman and Phelps acknowledged that there would be a short-run trade-off between inflation and unemployment if workers underestimated the rate at which prices would rise. But they claimed that, over time, workers, being rational, would adjust their expectations of inflation and alter their nominal wage demands in order to maintain the value of their real wage.[4] The higher wage demands would produce the shift in the Phillips curve pictured in Figure 10-6. Thus, Friedman and Phelps maintained that the long-run Phillips curve was actually vertical, indicating no long-run trade-off between inflation and unemployment. In terms of Figure 10-6, the long-run Phillips curve is obtained by connecting points like *A* and *C* at which actual and expected inflation are equal. This produces a vertical line at u^n. A vertical Phillips curve implies no long-run trade-off between inflation and unemployment.

We can also understand the Friedman-Phelps argument in terms of the IS-LM diagram. Their argument is that any policy-induced initial rightward shift of the LM curve or outward shift of the IS curve leading to a higher price level would ultimately lead workers to demand a higher nominal wage. In demanding a higher nominal wage to offset fully any policy-induced price rise, workers would end up shifting the LM curve leftward by enough to offset fully any policy-induced initial rightward shifts of the LM curve or upward shifts of the IS curve.[3] So output ends up unchanged. This is what we'd expect, given that output depends on employment, that employment depends on the real wage employers must pay, and that the real wage ends up unchanged.

Natural rate of unemployment
The unemployment rate that occurs when expected inflation equals actual inflation

Friedman and Phelps referred to the level of unemployment at which the economy would end up once workers correctly anticipated inflation as the **natural rate of unemployment**. In our model, if the real wage the workers ultimately demand corresponds to the real wage required to sustain full employment, the natural rate of unemployment equals zero. Alternatively, if the real wage demanded by workers is higher than the full-employment real wage, the natural rate is positive.

A natural rate of unemployment of zero is possible in our model, but is it feasible in the real world? The answer is no. In the real world, achieving an un-

3. As described above, an increase in the nominal wage is associated with an increase in the price level, which shifts the LM curve leftward.

"Which came first, the wage boost or the price hike?"

From *The Wall Street Journal*, by permission of Cartoon Features Syndicate.

employment rate that is literally zero is impossible because (1) there are always unemployed workers searching for new jobs as well as new workers searching for their first jobs and (2) searching for a job takes time. Economists use the term **frictional unemployment** to refer to the amount of unemployment arising purely as a result of job changes and first-time job acquisitions. In the real world, then, the natural rate of unemployment reflects frictional unemployment plus the unemployment that arises if the real wage is set above its market-clearing level. It also incorporates voluntary unemployment.[4]

Frictional unemployment *Unemployment arising solely as a result of job changes or first-time job acquisitions*

The Phillips Curve and the Traditional Keynesian Model: A Summary

To summarize, the traditional Keynesian model with wage rigidity explains recession as the result of a real wage that is too high. If workers are setting their nominal rather than their real wages, then government monetary or fiscal policy can be used to raise the price level, lower the real wage, and achieve full

4. In the U.S., individuals are classified as unemployed as long as they are searching for employment. Such individuals may claim to be searching for employment even though they would only work at a wage above the level available to them in the market.

employment. Friedman and Phelps challenged the traditional Keynesian conclusion. They pointed out that rational workers care about their real wages, not just their nominal wages, and would raise their nominal wage demands in response to anticipated price increases. As a result, they argued, monetary or fiscal policies would *not*, in the long run, be effective in lowering the real wage and unemployment. Rather, such policies would simply leave the economy with a higher rate of inflation.

THE SHORT-RUN TRADE-OFF VIEW MEETS THE RATIONAL EXPECTATIONS REVOLUTION

By the early 1970s most economists had acknowledged that there was no long-run inflation-unemployment trade-off. But some still argued that there was a short-run trade-off. "True," they said, "workers might eventually adjust their nominal wage demands in light of inflation, but in the short run, the government need only produce more inflation than workers expect in order to lower the real wage." In effect, these economists argued that the government could, at least in the short run, shift the LM or IS curves without causing an offsetting shift in the LM curve, and thereby lower unemployment.

In arguing that the government could temporarily fool workers into accepting lower real wages, these economists assumed that people form their expectations of future inflation based on simple extrapolations of past inflation without regard to the likely policy of the government. The **rational expectations** revolution of the mid-1970s, led by University of Chicago economists Robert Lucas and Thomas Sargent, questioned this view.

Rational expectation
A forecast of an economic variable based on the rational processing of all available information

Lucas and Sargent argued two things: first, that theories of the macro economy should be derived from the microeconomic behavior of individual households and firms, and second, that the rationality assumption, applied routinely in microeconomics to explain the utility maximization of households and the profit maximization of firms, also applies to the formation of expectations.

Rational workers, Lucas and Sargent pointed out, would not form their expectation of future inflation based simply on some arbitrary extrapolation of past inflation. Rather, they would consider all features of the economy that influence the future inflation rate, including the government's likely monetary and fiscal policy decisions. Thus, Lucas and Sargent questioned the ability of the government to systematically fool workers. In effect, they argued that "if the government is planning to fool the workers, the workers will realize what the government is up to and will set their nominal wages in anticipation of the government's attempt to fool them."

In denying that the government could fool workers into accepting a lower real wage, Lucas and Sargent weren't claiming that workers had perfect knowledge of the government's actions, or that workers couldn't be surprised by those actions. What they were saying is that workers would not *systematically* be surprised by government policy, since the workers would think through what surprises the government was trying to cook up.

Lucas and Sargent also didn't deny the empirical evidence supporting at least a short-run Phillips curve. Rather, they argued that the empirical short-run Phillips curve could be explained as the outcome of shocks to the economy, including policy shocks, that were unanticipated not only by workers and the public generally but also by policy makers. On the other hand, any policy change that was planned, and thus anticipated by policy makers, would be taken into account by workers in setting their nominal wage demands. Therefore, only those policy shocks that were unanticipated by policy makers would move the economy away from its natural unemployment rate.

There are many reasons why policy makers as well as the general public may be unable to forecast future policy decisions perfectly. First, policies are generally not made by a single individual, and predicting the outcome of group decisions is not always easy. Second, most policies require time to be approved and implemented, and the amount of time required for approval and implementation is not necessarily known in advance. Third, the potency of a particular policy may vary over time in ways that policy makers cannot perfectly predict. Fourth, particular policy decisions may depend on contemporaneous economic events that are not fully predictable.

THE MISPERCEPTION THEORY

The rational expectations economists developed their **misperception models** to spell out precisely how unexpected policy shocks would affect the economy. In these models they departed from traditional Keynesians in three respects. First, they emphasized the role of expectations and assumed that firms and households form their expectations in a rational manner. Second, they assumed that nominal prices and wages were fully flexible. Third, they stressed that either firms or households or both may have less-than-perfect information about the economy, including the government's monetary and fiscal policies.

Misperception theory
A macroeconomic model in which workers or employers misperceive the state of the economy and, as a consequence, increase or decrease their labor supply or demand

The models they produced, based on these assumptions, show how the mistakes that firms or households make in predicting the true state of the economy, including economic policy, can lead to observed increases (decreases) in inflation that are associated with decreases (increases) in unemployment. To get a sense of these models, let's take the example of a group of workers trying to decide how much to work. Assume they know the nominal wage they can earn, but not the precise value of the general price level. This means, of course, that they also don't know the precise value of their real wage.

Because they lack full information, those workers have an inference problem. Suppose they are offered a high nominal wage. What are they to make of it? The high nominal wage might reflect an unobserved increase in the money supply that has raised all prices as well as nominal wages. In this case the high nominal wage might not reflect a high real wage; indeed, depending on the size of the increase in the price level, the high nominal wage might really correspond to a low real wage. On the other hand, the high nominal wage being offered might reflect an increased demand for their services. In this case, the higher nominal wage would represent a higher real wage; i.e., the rise in their nominal wage would not be associated with a rise in the general price level.

The strategy that workers will follow in this situation is to supply more labor when their nominal wage is high, but not as much as they would supply if they knew for sure that the price level hadn't risen. Conversely, when their nominal wage is low, workers will supply less labor, but not as little as they would supply if they knew for sure that the price level hadn't fallen.

The outcome of this strategy is that the economy will exhibit a short-run Phillips curve. To see this, consider what happens if there is an unexpected increase in the money supply. This will drive up nominal prices and wages (both of which are flexible in the misperception model). More workers will choose to work, and those who choose to work will work for more hours. Why? Because, in the short run, they observe the nominal wage but not the price level and are thus mistakenly led to believe that their real wage has risen. Note that the data of the economy will record both a higher value of inflation and a decrease in unemployment—we'll have a movement along a short-run Phillips curve.

Now the government, observing this short-run inflation and unemployment relationship, might be tempted to try to exploit it by *systematically* increasing the money supply over time. But such a policy would only lead to an upward shift in the short-run Phillips curve. The reason is that workers, being rational, will adjust upward their expectations of how much the government is systematically increasing the money supply each period.

Illustrating a Misperception Model with a Labor Supply and Demand Diagram

Figure 10-7 illustrates many of these points using a modified version of the labor supply and demand diagram introduced in Chapter 9. There are two modifications to the diagram. First, we graph the nominal wage, W, rather than the real wage, W/P, on the vertical axis. And second, we assume that the supply of labor depends, in a positive way, on the level of the real wage workers believe they are receiving.[5]

In the diagram, $D(W/P)$ stands for the demand for labor, which depends on the real wage firms believe they are paying, and $S(W/P)$ stands for the supply of labor, which depends on the real wage workers believe they are receiving. Suppose the price level has been at P^0 for a long time. Then, in the initial equilibrium at point A, the nominal wage is W^0, and both the actual and perceived price levels equal P^0. So firms and workers correctly perceive that they are paying and receiving a real wage of W^0/P^0. As indicated, the initial equilibrium level of employment is L^0.

Now consider an unexpected increase in the money supply that raises the price level from P^0 to P^1. If firms correctly perceive this increase in the price level, their labor demand curve shifts outward to $D(W/P^1)$. That's because a

5. In the Appendix to Chapter 2 we showed how the supply of labor depends on the current real wage, given the value of the future real wage.

Figure 10-7 The Misperception Theory's Explanation of Employment Increases in Response to a Monetary Expansion

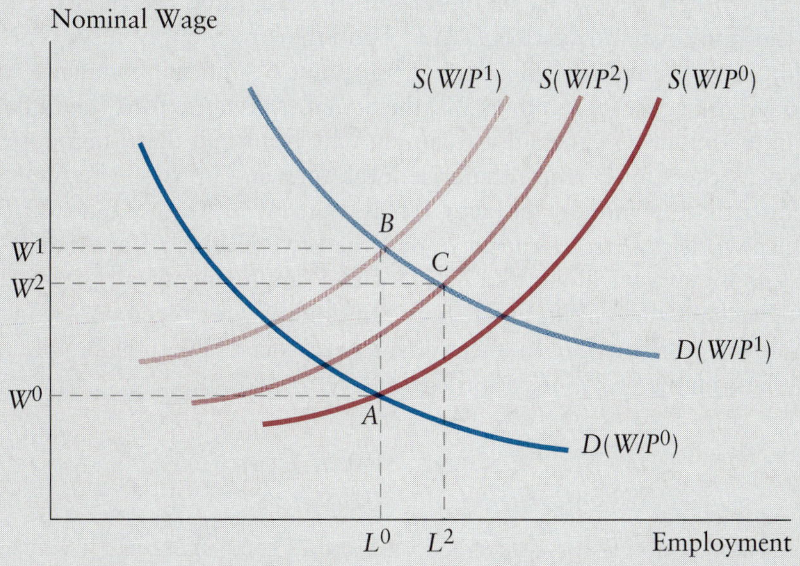

At point A the nominal wage is W^0 and employment is L^0. In addition, the actual and perceived price level equals P^0. Firms and workers correctly perceive that they are paying and receiving a real wage of W^0/P^0. If an unexpected increase in the money supply raises the price level to P^1 and firms realize this, labor demand shifts to $D(W/P^1)$. If workers misperceive the extent of the price increase and believe it is only P^2 (a smaller value than P^1), the labor supply curve shifts to $S(W/P^2)$ and employment increases from L^0 to L^2. Once workers correctly perceive the price level, their labor supply shifts to $S(W/P^1)$ and employment returns to L^0.

given value of the nominal wage now corresponds to a lower real wage, and firms demand more labor, the lower the real wage. If the workers also correctly perceive the price increase, their labor supply curve will shift to $S(W/P^1)$. The reason in this case is that a given nominal wage now corresponds to a lower real wage, and workers supply less labor, the lower the real wage.

To understand the new equilibrium at point B, consider a value, W^1, of the nominal wage that keeps the real wage W^1/P^1 equal to its initial value W^0/P^0. At this value of the nominal wage, the amount of labor demanded and the amount supplied both equal L^0. This observation is confirmed by the original demand and supply curves evaluated at the same real wage, namely W^0/P^0. Hence, as diagrammed, the new demand and supply curves both go through, and, therefore, intersect at, the point (W^1, L^0). We conclude then that if both firms and workers correctly perceive the percentage increase in the price level, the nominal wage will rise by the same percentage, leaving employment unchanged at L^0.

Next suppose that firms correctly perceive that the price level has risen to P^1, but that workers believe it has only risen to P^2, a value less than P^1.[6] In this case, the labor demand curve is $D(W/P^1)$ and the labor supply curve is $S(W/P^2)$. Equilibrium employment will rise to L^2 at point C, and the nominal wage will rise to W^2. Since W^2 is less than W^1, the actual real wage, W^2/P^1, will be lower than in the initial equilibrium, explaining why firms end up hiring more labor. Because workers misperceive the price level, they end up supplying more labor (L^2 rather than L^0) at a lower (actual) real wage (W^2/P^1 rather than W^1/P^1).

Once workers correctly perceive that the price level is P^1 and not P^2, their labor supply curve will shift to $S(W/P^1)$ and employment will return to L^0.[7] Hence, we have the makings of a short-run Phillips curve—temporary increases in employment (reductions in unemployment) associated with higher prices (and inflation given the previous period's price level).

Case Study: International Comparisons of the Inflation-Unemployment Trade-Off

If the misperception theory is correct, we would expect short-run Phillips curves to be steeper in countries with sizable variation in their rates of monetary growth and, thus, their inflation rates. Now the steeper the short-run Phillips curve, the less sensitive unemployment will be to a given change in the inflation rate. So in countries with considerable variation in inflation, changes in nominal variables, such as nominal wages, are more likely to reflect changes in the underlying price level than changes in relative demands and supplies for the services of particular workers or the products of particular firms. Hence, in such countries a given change in nominal variables arising from a given change in inflation is less likely to be misconstrued as a change in real prices or wages and, therefore, is less likely to lower unemployment.

Robert Lucas examined this proposition using data on 18 countries for the years 1952–1967.[8] Lucas studied output, rather than unemployment, and he found striking evidence that the short-run output-inflation trade-off depended on the degree of a country's inflation variability. Compare, for example, Lucas' findings for the U.S. and Argentina. Of the 18 countries in his sample, the U.S. exhibited the least variability in inflation and Argentina the most. Argentina's inflation rate between 1952 and 1967 was 285 times more variable than was the U.S. inflation rate. As Lucas predicted, the response of real output to a given

6. Laurence M. Weiss presents such a model, in which workers and firms have asymmetric information about the state of monetary policy, in "The Role for Active Monetary Policy in a Rational Expectations Model," *Journal of Political Economy* 88, no. 2 (April 1980): 221–233.

7. In terms of our IS-LM diagram we'd have a temporary shift rightward of the LM curve, followed by a shift back leftward to its original position once workers correctly perceive what has happened to the money supply and appropriately evaluate the real wage associated with any particular nominal wage.

8. See Robert E. Lucas, Jr. "Some International Evidence on Output-Inflation Tradeoffs," *American Economic Review* 63 (June 1973): 326–334.

percentage increase in the money supply (as represented by nominal income) was much larger in the U.S. than in Argentina. Indeed, the output response in the U.S. was nine times larger than in Argentina.

Critiquing the Misperception Theory

The misperception theory was in vogue for a good part of the 1970s. However, by the end of that decade many economists began to ask how much of the blame for recessions and credit for expansions could really be attributed to mistaken beliefs about the state of the economy, including the state of economic policy. Critics of the theory pointed out how easily firms and workers could educate themselves about economic conditions and government policies by listening to the business news on radio and television, reading the financial pages of newspapers, or checking government reports. The availability of information about the general price level—which plays a central role in many misperception models—is a case in point. In the U.S., the Bureau of Labor Statistics issues monthly values of consumer and producer price indices.[9]

The misperception theorists' response to this critique is that their models, particularly those featuring imperfect information about the price level, are simply heuristic devices. They refer to a broad array of information about the state of the economy about which individual households and firms have little precise knowledge. True, they'd say, there are a lot of data available on the economy, but these data tend to be highly aggregated, are often reported with a considerable lag, and are frequently revised. Furthermore, firms and households make a host of long-term investments, ranging from building new factories to relocating to take new jobs, based on their forecasts of economic conditions many years in the future. No economic reports available at the time these investment decisions are made will tell them precisely what the future will bring. Although rational firms and households will form their best estimates of the future economic conditions, they aren't clairvoyant. Hence, the possibility exists that large segments of the economy will over- or underexpand as a result of misperceiving, if not the current state of the economy, then at least its future state. To the extent that labor supply is variable, this over- or underexpansion will cause employment fluctuations.

THE REAL BUSINESS CYCLE THEORY

Whether the criticisms of the misperception theory and the traditional Keynesian model were fully justified is an open question. In any case, by the early 1980s Edward Prescott of the University of Minnesota, Finn Kydland of Carnegie-Mellon University, and other prominent economists had begun to forge a new approach to understanding business cycles: the real business cycle theory that we introduced in Chapter 4. The models developed by real business

9. Indeed, these values can be obtained any time, day or night, simply by calling the BLS price index hotline.

cycle theorists to study the effects of shocks are essentially elaborate versions of our life-cycle model with flexible prices and wages and variable labor supply.

The central question posed by the real business cycle theory is, how much of the economy's fluctuations can be explained simply by *shocks* arising in a neoclassical model with neither price rigidities nor imperfect information? The shocks envisaged by the theory include changes in firms' production technologies, changes in households' preferences about when and what to consume, and changes in government policy. They also include exogenous changes in the economy's capital stock, labor force, and natural resources resulting from wars, natural catastrophes, pestilence, etc. Finally, they include changes in international conditions that alter the terms at which the domestic economy can trade its output for foreign output. Good examples of such changes in *the terms of trade* are increases in oil prices that have occurred periodically as a result of Middle East wars and other disturbances and the cartelization of the oil market by OPEC, the Organization of Petroleum Exporting Countries.

Most real business cycle research has focused on supply-side shocks, primarily shocks to the economy's production function. In our model the production function is $Y_t = A_t K_t^{\beta} L_t^{(1-\beta)}$. Recall that in Chapter 4 we illustrated a particular type of supply-side shock when we considered the dynamic effects of a temporary increase in the technology coefficient, A_t. We saw that even a technological improvement that lasts only one period can affect the course of the economy over many periods because it alters the time path of saving and capital accumulation.

Illustrating a Real Business Cycle

To further illustrate the effects of supply-side shocks, including their potential to produce output cycles, let's consider how our simple two-period life-cycle model reacts to a recurring pattern of low, medium, and high values of the technology coefficient, A. In this exercise we'll use the Chapter 3 version of our model, which has no money and no fiscal policy, but does include consumption when young and when old. For the exercise we'll assume that β (capital's income share) equals .3 and that α (the share of wages spent on consumption when young) equals .5. Our simulation will begin at time 0 when A equals 9. At time 1, A will equal 10, and at time 2, it will equal 11. Then the cycle of values will commence again, with A equaling 9 at time 3, and so on.

Given these assumptions, our capital-labor transition equation is $k_{t+1} = A_t(1 - \alpha)(1 - \beta)k_t^{\beta}$, or, after inserting the assumed values of α and β, $k_{t+1} = .35\, A_t k_t^{.3}$. Table 10-1 traces the time paths of the economy's capital-labor ratio, output, the real wage, the real interest rate, aggregate saving, and aggregate consumption. In the table we assume that the capital-labor ratio at time 0 equals 5.987, which is the steady-state capital-labor ratio that would prevail if A_t remained constant at 10.

The table shows how fluctuations in the level of technology produce a cycle in each of the economy's macro variables. In the long run the cycle is regular since, eventually, each variable repeats itself every three years. For example, in

Table 10-1 Illustrating a Business Cycle in the Two-Period Life-Cycle Economy

Period	A_t	k_t	Y_t	w_t	r_t	S_t	C_t
0	9	5.987	1540	10.8	.771	–60	1599
1	10	5.389	1657	11.6	.923	41	1616
2	11	5.801	1864	13.0	.964	72	1792
3	9	6.524	1580	11.1	.726	–99	1679
4	10	5.529	1670	11.7	.906	32	1639
5	11	5.846	1868	13.1	.959	69	1799
6	9	6.539	1581	11.1	.725	–101	1681
7	10	5.533	1671	11.7	.906	31	1639
8	11	5.847	1868	13.1	.959	69	1799
9	9	6.539	1581	11.1	.725	–101	1681
10	10	5.533	1671	11.7	.906	31	1639
11	11	5.847	1868	13.1	.959	69	1799
12	9	6.540	1581	11.1	.725	–101	1681

Assumptions: $k_0 = 5.987$; $\alpha = .5$; $\beta = .3$; $N = 100$; $k_{t+1} = A_t(1 - \alpha)(1 - \beta)k_t^{\beta}$

the long run, the economy's output cycles from 1581, to 1671, to 1868, and then back to 1581, etc. The average of 1581, 1671, and 1868 is 1707, so we can say that, in the long run, the economy fluctuates around a stable value of output equal to 1707.

The induced cycle in saving is particularly noteworthy. During periods when technology is at its lowest value, the economy dissaves. For example, in the long run, when A_t equals 9, the level of this dissaving is –101, which is –7.4 percent of output. In contrast, when technology is at its intermediate and high values, the economy saves. The long-run positive saving is 31 when A_t equals 10 and 69 when A_t equals 11. These values are, respectively, 1.8 percent and 3.7 percent of the contemporaneous long-run levels of output.

The pattern of disinvesting (since saving equals investment) when times are bad and investing when times are good makes the capital-labor ratio lower in good times but higher in bad times than would otherwise be the case. These changes in the capital-labor ratio over the model's business cycle dampen somewhat the impact on output of the changes in technology. For example, in the long run, each time A_t falls from 11 to 9—an 18 percent decline—output falls from 1868 to 1581, which is only a 15 percent decline. In addition to dampening output fluctuations, the volatile pattern of saving serves to stabilize consumption. There is a 9 percent difference between the largest and smallest levels of aggregate consumption over the cycle (1639 and 1799, respectively), compared to the 15 percent difference in the largest and smallest values of output.

Generating Different Business Cycles by Varying the Assumed Path of A_t

A perfectly regular business cycle, like the long-run cycle of Table 10-1, is not something we observe in the data.[10] But if we make alternative assumptions about the way A_t varies through time, we can produce virtually any time path of output we want. For example, we could add some random variation to the cycle in A_t. This would produce nonregular business cycles. In addition, we could add to this random cycle in A_t an underlying time trend, so that A_t would cycle around a trend rather than around some stable value. If we were to assume a large enough trend relative to the amplitude of the cycle in A_t, we could ensure that the value of A_t would never fall below A_{t-1}; i.e., that the change in technology between $t - 1$ and t was never negative. Why might we want to rule out an absolute decline in the level of technology? Well, if we view the technology coefficient A_t as reflecting the state of knowledge, we may not want to assume that knowledge can disappear.

How Do Real Business Cycle Models Explain Unemployment?

Intertemporal substitution
The propensity to supply more labor during periods when the real wage is relatively high and less during periods when the real wage is relatively low

Real business cycle models explain unemployment as the *voluntary* decision of workers to reduce their labor supply in response to temporary declines in their real wage. In the simple model used to produce Table 10-1 we omitted leisure from the Cobb-Douglas utility function and simply assumed that young people work full-time regardless of the wage they receive. But, as shown in the Appendix to Chapter 2, it is easy to add leisure when young, as well as leisure when old, to the utility function. If we do, the amount that each person works when young and when old will depend on the real wage when young and the real wage when old. In particular, the higher the ratio of the real wage when young to the real wage when old, the higher will be the ratio of labor supplied when young to labor supplied when old. This propensity to supply more labor during periods when the real wage is relatively high—called **intertemporal substitution**—is how real business cycle theorists explain unemployment during recessions. Their argument is simply that during recessions real wages are depressed because of adverse productivity shocks, and workers respond to these temporary reductions in their real wages by reducing their labor supply. Unemployment then arises from the voluntary choice of the unemployed not to work. Given this, there is no need for government policy intervention.

10. In addition to assuming a cyclical pattern in A_t, we are free to assume that the variations over time in A_t do not conform to any cyclical pattern. For example, we could assume that A_t obeys a *random walk*. As we discussed in Chapter 4, the current value of a variable obeying a random walk differs from its most recent past value by a random error. With A_t obeying a random walk, our two-period model would exhibit irregular fluctuations. Furthermore, these fluctuations would not, in the long run, be centered around any stable value or even any stable trend.

Table 10-2 Comparing the Predictions of the Kydland-Prescott Real Business Cycle Model with the U.S. Data[a]

	Standard Deviation		Correlation of Real GNP	
	Of Actual Data	Of Predicted Data	With Actual Data	With Predicted Data
Real GNP	1.8	1.8	1.0	1.0
Consumption	NA	.5	NA	0.8
Services	.6	NA	0.7	NA
Nondurables	1.2	NA	0.8	NA
Investment	5.3	5.5	0.9	0.9
Inventories	1.7	2.2	0.5	0.6
Total Hours Worked	1.7	1.2	0.8	0.9
Productivity (GNP per hour)	1.0	0.7	0.3	0.9

[a]All variables are measured as percentage deviations from trend.
NA: Not Available

Source: Edward C. Prescott, "Theory Ahead of Business Cycle Measurement," *Quarterly Review,* Federal Reserve Bank of Minneapolis (Fall 1986): 9–33.

How Well Do Real Business Cycle Models Explain the Business Cycle?

Real business cycle economists test their models by assuming the values of particular parameters and specifying the way they believe real shocks evolve. (In the context of our model, this means assuming values of α and β and a process for how A_t changes through time.) They then simulate their models and compare the simulated data with actual data. Table 10-2 shows how the predictions of the Kydland-Prescott real business cycle model compare with actual data on the U.S. economy. The table shows the actual variability, over time, of real GNP and five other macro variables, as well as the actual correlation, over time, of real GNP with these other variables.[11] It also shows the variability of these variables

11. Variability is measured here by the standard deviation of the variable in question. A standard deviation is a measure of how much a variable (e.g., the annual growth of GNP) varies, on average, from its mean value (e.g., the average annual growth rate of GNP). The correlation coefficients in Table 10-2 measure the extent to which two variables vary over time in the same manner. Correlation coefficients range from −1 to +1, −1 meaning that when one variable rises by a given percentage, the other always falls by the same percentage, and +1 meaning that if one variable rises by a given percentage, the other does as well. A correlation coefficient of zero means that the two variables are unrelated.

as well as their correlation with real GNP as predicted by the Kydland-Prescott model. Note that the predictions accord fairly well with the actual data.

Critiquing the Real Business Cycle Model

Notwithstanding these and similar findings, the theory of real business cycles can be criticized on several grounds. First, since it is hard to measure certain types of real shocks (such as the annual rate of technological advance in computer software), it is hard to know when, or indeed, if, they are occurring. Second, since many real shocks are not readily observable, one can "explain" any change in output as the result of some unobserved real shock. Third, it is hard to believe that the massive and sustained unemployment during the Great Depression and during similar sharp downturns in the economy can really be explained as a voluntary decision by workers to take more leisure in anticipation of working harder as soon as things turned around. Fourth, the labor supply of individual workers does not appear to be sufficiently responsive to intertemporal wage differences—differences in wages across time—to explain the bulk of variation in the use of labor over the business cycle.[12] Fifth, if shocks are technological in nature, they are likely both to be industry-specific and to average out in the aggregate economy.

Real business cycle theorists have responses to each of these criticisms. First, they point out that some real shocks, such as those due to natural disasters and changes in the international terms of trade, are observable. Second, even if it is hard to measure the precise state of technology, we certainly know that technological breakthroughs occur and that many are very important; so there *are* shocks to technology, even if we can't measure precisely their size and frequency. Third, although one could "explain" all macroeconomic fluctuations by assuming enough shocks of the right form, the question is whether one can explain a good deal of the variation over time in macro variables based on a limited and plausible set of shocks. Fourth, much of the blame for the Great Depression may be placed on the banking panics of the early 1930s, the attendant failure of large numbers of banks, the collapse of credit, and the subsequent closing of many businesses.[13] This episode could well be viewed as a type of aggregate productivity shock leading to very low real wages. Fifth, the reason that workers don't alter their hours of work in response to changes in their real wages as much as the simple real business cycle models predict is that their employers find it more profitable to require each worker to work full-time.[14] In this case, firms will lay off workers in downturns rather than permit those they don't lay off to work less than full-time. These layoffs explain the unemployment we see

12. See, for example, Joseph G. Altonji, "Intertemporal Substitution in Labor Supply: Evidence From Micro Data," *Journal of Political Economy* 94, Part 2 (June 1986): 176–215.
13. We discuss banking panics in Chapter 14 and constraints on the availability of credit in Chapter 15.
14. This requirement reflects the fixed costs involved in searching for and hiring workers. For example, a firm that hires one worker to work 40 hours a week rather than two workers to work 20 hours a week each only has to incur the search costs (advertising, interviewing, etc.) required to find one worker. In addition, if the firm provides fringe benefits independent of the hours the employee works, such as health insurance coverage, hiring one worker, rather than two, means these fringe benefits cost half as much.

in recessions. Sixth, although there are undoubtedly industry-specific shocks, they may be correlated and, thereby, produce an aggregate shock. For example, it is hard to think of an industry that did not experience a positive technology shock as the result of postwar improvements in computer chips.

Case Study: Oil Price Shocks and Recessions

Oil and oil-based products represent our major sources of energy. They enter as direct or indirect inputs into the production of virtually every good and service. Accordingly, we expect the performance of the economy to be particularly sensitive to changes in the price of oil. Real business cycle theorists point to periodic sharp increases in the price of oil as a clear-cut example of supply-side shocks.

Since crude oil is an internationally traded good, its price depends on domestic and foreign supplies and demands. When foreign demand rises or foreign supply declines, the price of crude oil rises both at home and abroad. This reflects the *law of one price,* which we'll discuss in Chapter 13. Such price increases represent an external real shock to the domestic economy.

The postwar period has witnessed several quite significant oil price shocks. Figure 10-8 graphs the quarterly percentage change in the real price of crude petroleum for the period from 1947 to 1991.[15] The shading of the figure indicates the nine recessions the U.S. has experienced since 1947. As the figure shows, four of these recessions either have been directly preceded by or occurred at the same time as abrupt increases of 10 percent or more in the real price of oil. Another four recessions have coincided with or followed shortly after price increases ranging from 4 to 7 percent.

The fact that eight of the last nine U.S. recessions have been associated with oil price rises suggests more than just coincidence. From the perspective of our simple real business cycle model, an oil price rise can be viewed as a reduction in A_t. The reason is that A_t captures everything, apart from capital and labor, that determines the production of output. Thus, A_t includes raw material inputs, such as oil. The higher the price of oil, the less oil will be used in production and, so, the lower will be the value of A_t.[16]

Although there is no disputing the fact that sudden rises in oil prices represent real shocks to the economy, we can question the degree to which the recessions associated with these shocks have reflected the factors stressed by real business cycle theorists versus those stressed by Keynesians. Real business cycle proponents would argue as follows: "The temporary decline in the real wage

15. The percentage change in the real price of crude petroleum is measured as the percentage change in the nominal price of crude oil minus the percentage change in the producer price index.

16. To see this, let's amend our Cobb-Douglas production function to include oil as an input. Our amended function is $Y_t = HK_t^{\theta}L_t^{\varepsilon}O_t^{(1-\theta-\varepsilon)}$, where H is the level of technology, θ and ε are production function coefficients, and O_t stands for the amount of oil used in production at time t. Firms will buy oil in each period t up to the point that its marginal product equals its price, P_t^o. Since the marginal product of oil at time t can be written as $(1-\theta-\varepsilon)Y_t/O_t$, we have $P_t^o = (1-\theta-\varepsilon)Y_t/O_t$. Eliminating O_t from this equation and the formula for the production function gives the production function we've used throughout the book, $Y_t = A_tK_t^{\beta}L_t^{(1-\beta)}$, but where $\beta = \theta/(\theta+\varepsilon)$ and $A_t = [H^{1/(\theta+\varepsilon)}]\,[(1-\theta-\varepsilon)/P_t^o]^{(1-\theta-\varepsilon)/(\theta+\varepsilon)}$. Thus, as claimed, A_t is smaller, the higher P_t^o is.

Figure 10-8 Oil Price Shocks and Recessions, 1947–1991

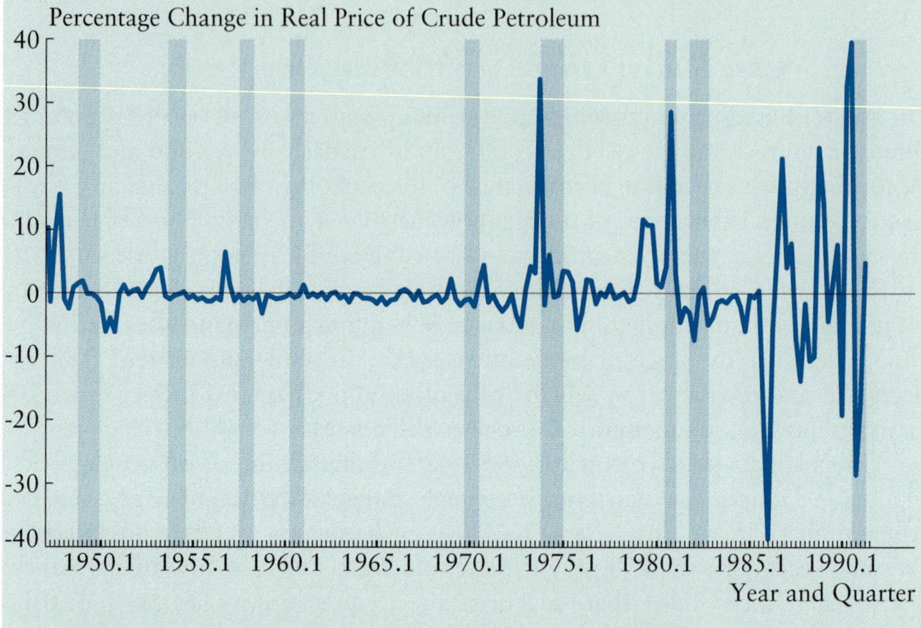

This figure plots quarterly percentage changes in the real price of crude petroleum for the years 1947–1991, with recession periods shaded. Eight of the nine recessions were immediately preceded by, or coincident with, abrupt increases in oil prices. According to real business cycle theorists, these price increases are tantamount to reductions in the technology parameter, *A*. Reductions in *A* lower the marginal product of labor and, consequently, the real wage firms are willing to pay. A lower real wage means workers supply less labor. Hence, output and employment fall. Keynesians argue that employment falls because nominal wage stickiness keeps real wages from falling enough to maintain full employment.

Source: U.S. Department of Commerce

associated with these shocks prompted workers to reduce their labor supply. This labor supply reduction, together with the shock itself, explains the decline in output."

For their part, Keynesians would argue: "The oil price increase meant that nominal wages had to fall to produce the required fall in real wages. Given nominal wage stickiness, this could not be achieved in the short term. As a consequence, firms were forced to lay off enough workers to restore equality between the marginal product of labor and the temporarily rigid real wage."

Who is right? The answer appears to be both. Undoubtedly, some workers responded to the decline in their real wages by reducing their labor supply, and others undoubtedly failed to accept cuts in their nominal wages and found themselves laid off. What remains unclear is precisely what share of the unemployment induced by oil price shocks is attributable to each of these two models or, for that matter, to other models such as the sectoral shift model we'll now review.

THE SECTORAL SHIFT MODEL

Sectoral shift theory *A theory that traces business cycles to shifts of employment and output among industries*

Advocates of the **sectoral shift model** also lay claim to the evidence connecting oil price shocks to recessions.[17] Their model attributes recessions to shocks that favor specific industries but hurt others. These shocks require workers to relocate across industries. The process of relocation temporarily raises unemployment and lowers output. The reason is that many of the workers laid off from contracting industries spend time unemployed until they find jobs in expanding industries. Thus, according to sectoral shift theorists, the degree of frictional unemployment in the economy is not fixed. Instead, they claim, variations in the degree of frictional unemployment explain much of the fluctuation in aggregate unemployment.

Sectoral shifts can result from changes either in the pattern of demand for different products or in the relative costs of producing different products. An oil price shock is an example of the latter. Since certain goods and services are more energy-intensive (use relatively more energy in production) than others, an oil price shock will raise the costs of, and reduce the demands for, energy-intensive goods relative to other products.

Take, for example, the U.S. recession that began in November 1973 and ended in March 1975. As Figure 10-8 shows, this recession coincided with a more than 30 percent increase in the real price of crude oil—the result of OPEC's decision to curtail oil production and, thereby, raise the price of oil following the 1973 Yom Kippur War. During this recession the share of U.S. employment in energy-intensive durable manufacturing fell by over 9 percent, whereas in other industries, such as retail trade and services, total employment (as well as the share of employment) actually rose.

Another example of a U.S. recession that may have been caused by sectoral shifts is the February 1945 – October 1946 contraction that occurred as World War II ended. In the aftermath of the war the U.S. economy faced the task of shifting quickly from producing war materials to producing consumer goods. Between 1945 and 1946 defense expenditures fell by a whopping 78 percent! The U.S. economy also had to contend with large numbers of troops returning home from military service. Between 1945 and 1946 over nine million military personnel (equal in size to almost 17 percent of the labor force) left active duty. If we view the military as an industry, the dramatic decline in the demand for troops, like the dramatic decline in the demand for war materials, represents a shift in the industrial pattern of demand and, consequently, production.

17. A seminal empirical study supporting the sectoral shift model is David M. Lilien's "Sectoral Shifts and Cyclical Unemployment," *Journal of Political Economy* 90, no. 4 (August 1982): 777–793.

Rob Rogers reprinted by permission of UFS, Inc.

Critiquing the Sectoral Shift Model

Critics of the sectoral shift model admit that exogenous shifts in the industrial pattern of costs and demand may be important in raising frictional unemployment in isolated instances, such as in the aftermath of World War II. But they contend that much of the inter-industry shifts in employment may reflect a response to, rather than the cause of, recessions. Recessions, they argue, lower incomes and reduce the demand for income-sensitive goods, such as vacation travel, relative to the demand for income-insensitive goods, such as haircuts and doctors' visits. In addition, they point out that if recessions simply reflected shifts in the composition of demand we would expect to find that periods of high unemployment—periods when contracting industries are laying off workers—are also periods in which expanding industries are trying to hire workers. Thus, a high unemployment rate should be coincident with a high **job vacancy rate**—the fraction of jobs in the economy that employers are trying to fill.[18] But the evidence on unemployment and job vacancies is just the opposite. When the unemployment rate is high, the job vacancy rate is low.

Job vacancy rate
The fraction of available jobs currently unfilled

In response, sectoral shift theorists argue that it is hard to think of a cause of recession that hits all industries uniformly. For example, even if wages or prices are sticky, they are not likely to be equally sticky in all industries. Hence, drawing a clear distinction between recessions due to aggregate shocks (nominal or real) and those due to inter-industry variations in shocks (nominal or real) may

18. The job vacancy rate is calculated based on job vacancies listed in help-wanted ads.

be impossible. Moreover, the sectoral shift proponents concede that some unemployment results from purely aggregate shocks; indeed, they view the inverse relationship between unemployment and job vacancies as reflecting this aggregate shock component of the business cycle. But they point out that the unemployment-job vacancy relationship has not been stable over time and contend that changes in this relationship reflect sectoral shifts. Finally, they point out that job mobility rises during recessions.

Policies to Deal with Sectoral Shifts

Assuming the sectoral shift model is at least partly correct, what remedies for recession does it suggest? One possibility is a policy that helps workers in declining sectors find jobs in expanding sectors. For the government, the practical problem in providing such assistance is knowing ahead of time which sectors are starting to decline and which are starting to expand. If it takes too long to help workers relocate, the recession will already have taken place.

Even if the government can intervene quickly, there is the question of whether it should. After all, expanding sectors are free to place ads in local and national newspapers and engage in other types of advertising and recruiting activities in searching for new workers. And displaced workers are free to advertise their availability. If there is no obvious failure in the market for finding workers, should the government intervene? Maybe not. However, as we'll discuss below when we consider theories of coordination failures, this type of market, in which parties search for each other, does suffer from a particular type of failure. Each party has an incentive to let the other party do all, or most, of the searching.

NEW KEYNESIAN MODELS OF RECESSION[19]

Their differences notwithstanding, the misperception, real business cycle, and sectoral shift theories each connect macroeconomic outcomes to microeconomic behavior. As these theories were being developed, the desirability of grounding macroeconomics in microeconomics also became apparent to another set of economists—the New Keynesians—many of whom felt that nominal rigidities were at the core of macroeconomic fluctuations. Consequently, they set about developing macro models based on microeconomic explanations of such rigidities. We now discuss several of these **New Keynesian models.**

New Keynesian models *Macroeconomic models that seek to provide microeconomic explanations of wage and price rigidities and other sources of market failure*

Long-Term Nominal Wage and Price Contracts

One of the microeconomic facts about the real world is that certain nominal wages and prices are set for extended periods of time by explicit contract. Examples include formal (written) long-term nominal wage contracts negotiated

19. For an excellent collection of the leading articles on New Keynesian economics see N. Gregory Mankiw and David Romer, eds., *New Keynesian Economics* (Cambridge, MA: MIT Press, 1991).

between labor unions and employers and formal long-term contracts that specify the nominal prices producers of final products will pay their suppliers of intermediate products and raw materials. In addition, there are *implicit* wage or price contracts that reflect an informal understanding between the parties concerned about how nominal wages or prices will evolve during a given time period.

In establishing contracts, workers and firms limit the amount of time they spend negotiating with one another. Without these formal or informal understandings, negotiating would be never-ending and very costly. Imagine, if you will, workers negotiating with their employers over each hour's pay. Besides limiting the costs of negotiating, long-term contracts provide mechanisms for the contracting parties to pool their risks.[20] Take the case of a firm that agrees to give its workers a 5 percent pay raise for each of the next three years. In making this agreement the firm is assuring each worker that she'll receive a 5 percent raise regardless of whether the firm makes large or small profits during the three-year period.

An important feature of wage and price contracts is that they are not all negotiated simultaneously and don't all last for the same length of time. Instead, contracts are **staggered** so that, at any point in time, some are being renegotiated and others are not. Consequently, at any point in time, a fraction of the economy's wages and prices are fixed in nominal terms.

Staggered contracts *Contracts with different expiration dates that set the wage rates at various firms*

The New Keynesians have modeled the effects of monetary policy shocks in settings of staggered nominal wage or price contracts.[21] In so doing, they assume that workers and firms think rationally about the future when they negotiate their contracts. Thinking rationally about the future includes thinking about how the government's monetary policy will affect the future course of inflation and, thus, the real value of the nominal wages and prices being set in the contract.

The New Keynesians made several points with their staggered contracts models. First, they showed that increases in the money supply that were unanticipated at the time the contracts were made would temporarily raise output and lower unemployment (i.e., produce a short-run Phillips curve). Second, they showed that increases in the money supply that were anticipated at the time the contracts were made would have no impact on output or employment because workers and firms would form their contracts in anticipation of the money supply increases.[22] And third, they showed that increases in the money supply that

20. If workers could switch from one job to another without cost and receive the prevailing market wage, there would be no risk to the worker associated with his employer's fortunes. But when job-mobility costs are significant, workers and firms face interrelated risks. Firms and workers in this setting will find it advantageous to pool (share) these risks. If, as is typically assumed, firms are more willing to bear risk than workers, the outcome of this risk pooling will be an implicit or explicit contract under which the firm provides the worker some insurance against adverse outcomes befalling the firm.

21. The seminal articles in this literature are Stanley Fischer's "Long-Term Contracts, Rational Expectations, and the Optimal Money Supply Rule," *Journal of Political Economy* 85, no. 1 (February 1977): 191–206 and John B. Taylor's "Aggregate Dynamics and Staggered Contracts," *Journal of Political Economy* 88, no. 1 (February 1980): 1–23.

22. With respect to the first two points, the staggered contract models produce the same general implications as the misperception theory but rely on temporary nominal wage and price rigidities rather than on misperceptions about the course of monetary policy.

occur while a contract is in force have real effects even though they are fully recognized and, thus, anticipated. These effects die out gradually as contracts expire, rather than instantaneously, as in the misperception model. This third point suggested that the distinction between anticipated and unanticipated policies needs to be drawn very precisely, if it is to have any meaning.

Other Explanations of Nominal Rigidities

A different group of New Keynesians has sought to explain price and wage stickiness as the consequence of either inertia, imperfect competition, or firms' and workers' efforts to avoid the costs of changing nominal prices and wages. Inertia refers simply to an irrational failure to make price and wage adjustments. Imperfect competition refers to the hesitancy of firms with market power to (1) raise their nominal prices for fear that their competition won't follow, leaving them with greatly reduced demand for their products or (2) lower their nominal prices for fear of setting off a price war. The third explanation of price and wage stickiness—the costs of adjusting nominal prices and wages—is referred to by the shorthand term, **menu costs**. The term derives from the frequently used example of restaurants, which have to pay the cost of printing new menus each time they change their nominal prices. Menu costs are generally thought to be small, but still large enough to deter firms and workers from adjusting their prices and wages in response to small changes in the level of aggregate demand.

Menu costs
The typically small costs incurred by firms in changing the prices they charge

Regardless of the reasons that firms and workers fail to fully adjust their nominal prices and wages, the consequences for the firms and workers may be minor. Imperfectly competitive firms know that if they set their price a bit too high (relative to the profit-maximizing price), they won't lose all their market. If they set their price a bit too low, they won't lose all their profits. Similarly, groups of workers that have market power in bargaining with their employers (trade unions, for example) realize that if they set their wage a bit too high, they will not all be fired, and that if they set it a bit too low, they will still want to keep working with the firm.

For any particular firm or set of workers, the consequences of failing to adjust nominal prices or wages may be small. However, if enough firms and workers fail to adjust, the consequences for the aggregate economy will not necessarily be small. To see this, consider again the LM equation under the simplifying assumption that γ is fixed at $\bar{\gamma}$: $M/P = \bar{\gamma}(1 - \beta)Y$. Now suppose that the money supply, M, is decreased by a small amount, say 1 percent, but firms fail to lower their prices by 1 percent, as they would if they were maximizing their real profits and faced no menu costs. As argued, in the case of monopolistic competition, the loss to individual firms of not adjusting their prices could well be quite small—much less than 1 percent. What will happen to collective output in this case? According to the LM equation, output will fall by a full 1 percent—a nontrivial decrease.

The inertia and menu costs models, like many of the others we've discussed, generate a short-run Phillips curve, but they also suggest that anticipated monetary policy will alter output and employment. For example, in the case of inertia, firms and workers may know that the government is raising the money supply, but they will still fail to adjust their nominal prices and wages—at least in the short run.

Case Study: Do Anticipated or Unanticipated Money Shocks Affect U.S. Output?

In a famous article published in 1978, Harvard's Robert Barro tested whether deviations of U.S. output growth from its underlying time trend are caused by (1) all changes in the money supply, anticipated or not, as suggested by the traditional Keynesian model, New Keynesian models of menu costs and inertial price and wage setting, and New Keynesian contract models (in the case of anticipations formed within the contract period) or (2) only unanticipated changes in the money supply, as suggested by the misperception model, the New Keynesian price and wage contracts models (in the case of anticipations as of the time of contracting), and other models featuring rational expectations.[23] Barro used a statistical technique to decompose the annual change in the money supply (measured as M1) into two components: the anticipated change in the money supply and the unanticipated change. He then determined which of the two components was causing output to vary from its trend value. Barro's results indicated that only unanticipated changes in the money supply affected output.

Figure 10-9 presents some of the data Barro used in his study. The figure shows three time series for the years 1946–1976: the deviation of output growth from its time trend (output shocks), the unanticipated percentage change in the money supply (unexpected money shocks), and the anticipated percentage change in the money supply (expected money shocks). Note the fairly close relationship between output growth and unexpected money shocks. In contrast, there is little relationship between output growth and expected money shocks.

Although Barro's findings are striking, they are not definitive. Critics point out that there is nothing sacrosanct about the way he divided money supply changes into anticipated and unanticipated components. Different decompositions, they demonstrate, produce somewhat different results about the relative importance of anticipated and unanticipated money shocks. In addition, they point out that even if one accepts Barro's decomposition, the observed correlation between output shocks and unexpected money supply shocks may reflect a reverse causation, in which unexpected output shocks lead the government to alter the money supply in ways that had not been anticipated. Finally, they note that Barro effectively groups all anticipated changes in the money supply together without regard to whether they occurred before or after prevailing nominal wage and price contracts were made. In so doing, they argue, Barro may have biased his test against a finding that anticipated money supply changes matter.

---

23. Robert J. Barro, "Unanticipated Money, Output, and the Price Level in the United States," *Journal of Political Economy* 86, no. 4 (August 1978).

Figure 10-9 Output Shocks and Anticipated and Unanticipated Changes in the Money Supply

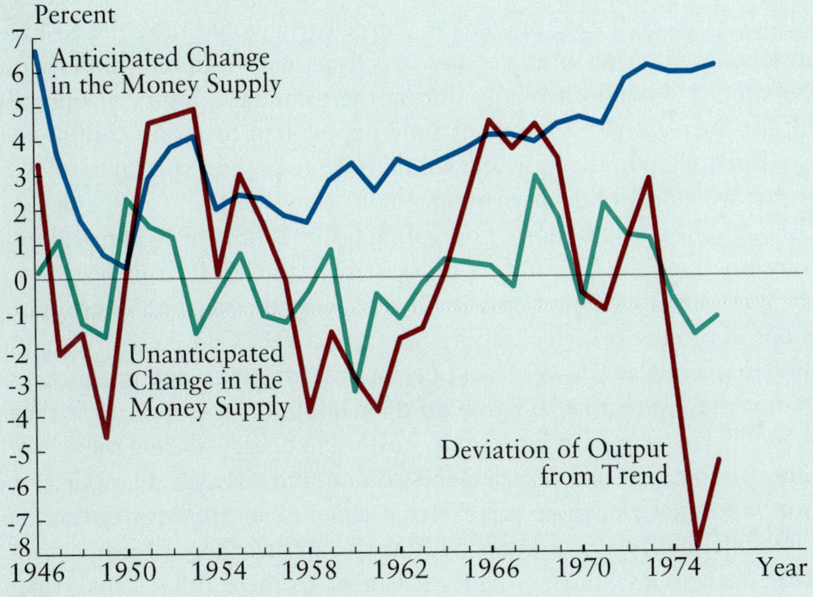

Robert Barro decomposed annual money supply changes into anticipated and unanticipated components to test whether either component caused output to deviate from its trend value. He found a fairly close relationship between output growth and unexpected money shocks but little relationship between output growth and expected money shocks. He interpreted these findings as evidence in favor of the misperception model, New Keynesian wage and price contract models, and other frameworks featuring rational expectations.

Source: Barro, R. J., "Unanticipated Money Output, and the Price Level in the United States," *Journal of Political Economy* 86, no. 4 (August 1978)

Coordination Failures

As already mentioned, the New Keynesians have raised other concerns about the functioning of markets besides the potential for nominal rigidities. One of these concerns falls under the heading of **coordination failures:** the failure of individuals or firms to coordinate their activities in ways that would be mutually beneficial.

Coordination failure
The failure of economic agents to coordinate their activities in ways that would be mutually beneficial

This definition is somewhat abstract, so let's consider a specific example that helps convey the issues arising in models of coordination. The illustration involves the potential failure of firms, which we'll assume produce different goods and services, to coordinate their operating hours. The failure to coordinate operating hours has no direct connection to recessions. But it serves as a parable for the coordination failures that may induce or prolong a recession.

Suppose each firm were to choose its hours of operation with no regard to the operating hours of other firms. The result would be some firms operating from, say, 9 A.M. to 5 P.M., some operating from 11 A.M. to 7 P.M., others operating from 1 P.M. to 9 P.M., and so on. This clearly would raise the cost to firms of transacting with one another; any two firms with different hours would be able to contact one another only during their common hours of operation. It would also increase the amount of time people had to spend shopping; those who routinely shop in the morning would have to make a special trip to shop in stores that were only open after noon.

Although the coordination of operating hours is obviously highly important, it is not something the free market necessarily produces. If firms were operating at very different hours, they might all recognize the need to coordinate their hours but not know on which hours to synchronize. Consequently, they might continue to operate at a lower level of economic efficiency and produce less output than if they were able to agree on their hours of operation or if they were compelled by law or were persuaded by custom to operate during the same hours.

Multiple equilibria *Multiple positions at which the economy can be in equilibrium*

This example contains two elements common to virtually all models of coordination failures. First, there are external benefits, or *spillover effects*. Specifically, imagine that one firm alters its hours to match those of other firms. The firm that changes its hours provides a benefit to these other firms, since they now can contact this firm more easily and their customers can now shop during the same hours at a larger number of firms. Second, there are **multiple equilibria**. Specifically, we can have an equilibrium with no coordination of operating hours. Alternatively, we can have an equilibrium with perfect coordination, indeed a different equilibrium for each potential common choice of operating hours. There will also be equilibria in between the extremes of no coordination and perfect coordination. For example, a third of all firms might coordinate on one set of hours, another third might coordinate on another set of hours, and a third set might coordinate on a third set of hours.

COORDINATION FAILURES AND RECESSIONS. To see how coordination failures might induce or prolong recessions, suppose each individual firm benefits from the level of economic activity of other firms and that each firm produces more if all other firms are producing more as well. One example is suggested by the work of Peter Diamond, the MIT economist who wrote the seminal article on coordination failures in 1982.[24] Diamond's example involves the search costs incurred by firms that are trying to sell products to or buy products from other firms. The more effort the selling firm puts out searching for a buying firm, the less time the buying firm will have to spend searching for the selling firm and vice versa.

If each firm's search effort is positively related to the level of its production, then it will be mutually beneficial for all firms to agree to search more (and thus produce higher levels of output). But if each firm believes other firms are search-

24. Peter Diamond, "Aggregate Demand Management in Search Equilibrium," *Journal of Political Economy* 90 (1982): 881–894.

ing (and producing) at low levels, it will not have sufficient incentive to search, on its own, at a higher level. As a result the economy may end up at an equilibrium with a low level of production, rather than a high one. Moving the economy from such a low output equilibrium to a high output equilibrium may not be easy, since it requires changing business people's beliefs about the state of economy.

ILLUSTRATING COORDINATION FAILURES WITH OUR MODEL. In our simple two-period life-cycle model we have not encountered any problems of multiple equilibria. But if we make different assumptions about households' saving behavior and firms' production functions, we can produce more than one transition path for the capital-labor ratio—more than one dynamic equilibrium.

Figure 10-10 shows two alternative transition paths for the capital-labor ratio resulting from two alternative k_{t+1} curves. These two curves could arise if there were two different transition equations relating k_{t+1} to k_t.[25] The two equations might reflect two possible values of the technology coefficient A that could prevail at time t—one high and one low. The high value of A might arise from coordinated actions by firms (e.g., searching harder for each other or setting the same hours); the low value could reflect a failure to coordinate actions. The decision by firms to coordinate at time t would depend on their beliefs about what actions other firms will take. If each firm believed the other firms were searching hard, it too would search hard, making A high. If each firm believed the other firms were not searching hard, it would not search hard, making A small.

Note that starting at time 0 with a capital-labor ratio of k_0, the economy can either move along the lower capital-labor ratio (and lower output) transition path or move along the higher capital-labor ratio (and higher output) transition path. If it takes the low path, the economy ends up with a steady-state capital-labor ratio of $\bar{k}^l$; if it takes the high path, it ends up with a steady-state capital-labor ratio of $\bar{k}^h$. Alternatively, it could oscillate between the two paths over time in response to changes in firms' beliefs about whether other firms are coordinating their behavior (e.g., searching hard for each other or setting the same hours). If beliefs continue to change through time, the economy will never converge to a steady state but rather will fluctuate between high and low levels of output. It will experience recessions and expansions.

Case Study: Consumer and Business Confidence and the Business Cycle

The potential for coordination failures may explain why there is so much interest in indexes of consumer and business confidence. Figure 10-11 shows how one index of consumer confidence has varied since 1960 during periods of booms and busts. The figure shows that consumer confidence is procyclical; it is low during recessions and high during booms. In addition, as mentioned in

25. Alternatively, the two paths might reflect a single transition equation that features two solution values for k_{t+1} for each value of k_t. Such multiple solutions don't arise in the version of the two-period life-cycle model presented in this text, but could arise in other versions.

Figure 10-10 Illustrating Multiple Equilibria in the Two-Period Model

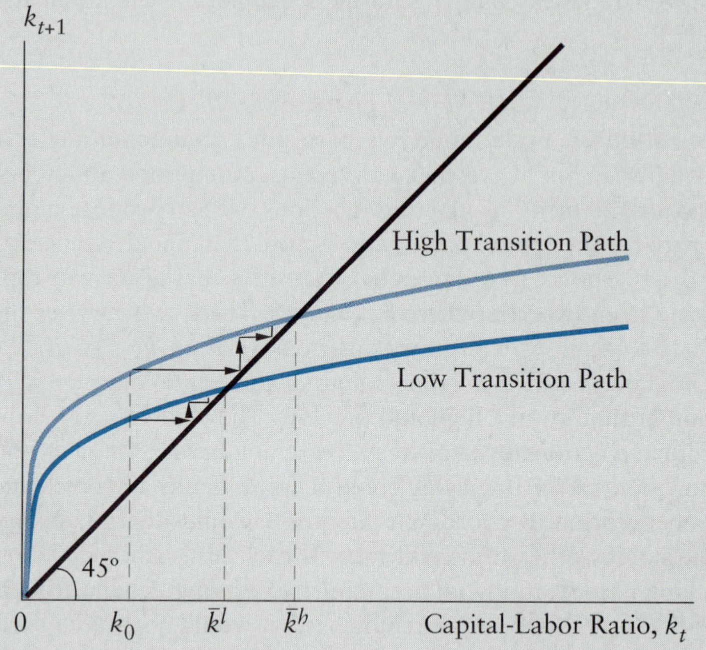

With coordination failures, there may be more than one possible transition path for the capital-labor ratio, and more than one steady state toward which the economy can converge. For example, a high degree of coordination among firms might imply a high value of the technology parameter, A, and a high transition curve. Poor coordination would mean a low A and a low transition curve. If so, then starting at k_0, the economy might move along the lower path and end up at $\bar{k}^l$ or along the higher path and end up at $\bar{k}^h$.

Chapter 4, consumer confidence is a leading indicator. Recall that a leading indicator is a variable that turns down before the economy contracts and turns up before the economy starts to recover.

Figure 10-11 shows that consumer confidence (technically called consumer sentiment) was falling several quarters before the start of each recession between 1960 and 1992. The figure also shows that confidence turned up prior to the ends of recessions that began in 1960, 1980, 1981, and 1990. In the case of the recessions that began in 1969 and 1973, consumer confidence turned up just as the recessions ended. Even these two cases support the view that consumer confidence causes, rather than responds to, economic events. Recessions end when the economy begins to rebound from zero or negative growth, not when it has actually fully recovered in terms of achieving its natural rate of unemploy-

Figure 10-11 Index of Consumer Confidence, 1960–1992

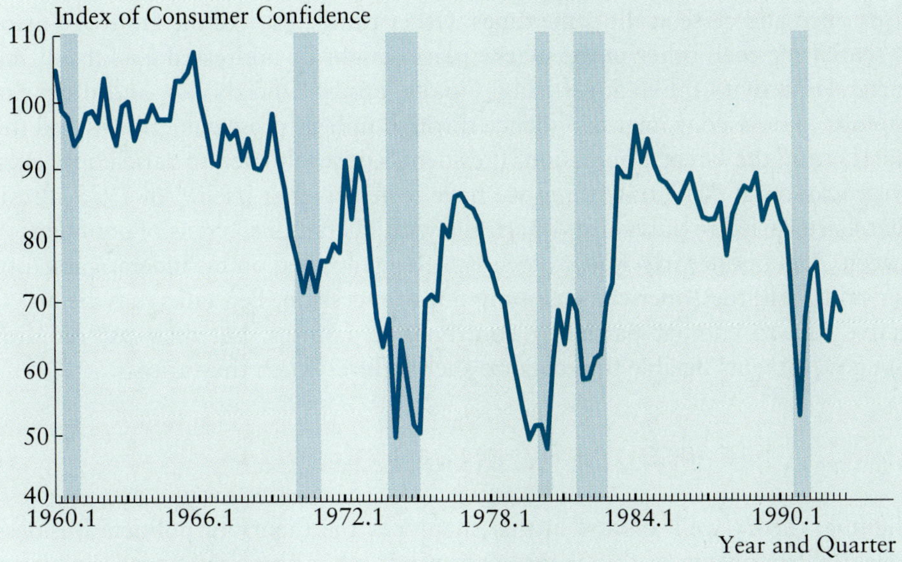

Some models of coordination failure suggest that consumer confidence is critical in moving the economy from a low output equilibrium to a high output equilibrium. If so, an index of consumer confidence should be a leading indicator of output. This figure plots such an index for the years 1960–1992, with recessions shaded. In fact, confidence turned up before or at the ends of all six recessions.

Source: University of Michigan, Survey Research Center

ment. If consumer confidence were determined simply by immediate circumstances, we wouldn't expect a recovery of consumer confidence, coming out of a recession, until the economy actually neared its cyclical peak. So the recovery of confidence at the troughs of recessions means that consumers are really looking beyond the immediate state of the economy in forming their expectations and, presumably, their economic plans for the future.

If, as suggested by certain models of coordination failures, consumer confidence is critical to moving the economy from a low output and employment equilibrium to a high output and employment equilibrium, we would expect the level of consumer confidence to be a leading indicator for the following reason. In these models changes in beliefs about the state of the economy provide the signal to firms that it is advantageous to contract their production (in the case of a reduction in confidence) or to expand their production (in the case of an increase in confidence). Hence, changes in beliefs (consumer confidence) will precede changes in the economy.

POLICY RESPONSES TO COORDINATION FAILURES. What can governments do to prevent coordination failures? Certain coordination problems may be relatively easy to fix. Take the case of firms choosing different operating hours. The government can resolve this problem simply by mandating that all firms open and close at the same times. Other problems, like the failure of firms to search for each other in the marketplace, might be addressed by subsidizing particular activities, like advertising. Finally, public officials can, and often do, attempt to raise consumer confidence through upbeat press conferences and the like. During the Great Depression, President Roosevelt tried to raise confidence by proclaiming, "The only thing we have to fear is fear itself." In 1979, President Carter tried to galvanize Americans with his famous "crisis of confidence" speech. And in the early 1980s, President Reagan relied on his indefatigable optimism to talk the American economy out of recession. Pep talks may be an effective tool to combat particular coordination failures, but their use requires that governments be able to recognize such failures when they arise.

POLITICAL BUSINESS CYCLES

Political business cycle theory
The view that business fluctuations are caused by politicians trying to stimulate the economy prior to elections and contract the economy afterward

The final theory we'll discuss in this chapter is the theory **of political business cycles.**[26] Proponents of this theory argue that when the public votes, it places great weight—potentially, undue weight—on the current state of the economy. Consequently, politicians will take actions to increase output and employment prior to elections and then undo these actions after the election, creating a business cycle. Political business cycles can be understood in terms of either the traditional Keynesian model or the real business cycle model. In the traditional Keynesian model, politicians, prior to elections, can be viewed as using monetary policy to shift the LM curve rightward or using fiscal policy to shift the IS curve outward. Once the election is over, the reversal of these policies (perhaps to curb inflation or lower interest rates) will cause the curves to shift back. In the process output and employment will first expand and then contract.

In the real business cycle model, politicians can use temporary tax cuts to stimulate additional labor supply before an election and then raise tax rates once the election is over. As discussed, the labor supplied by a young generation relative to the labor supplied by the same generation when it is old one period later depends on the ratio of wages that can be earned in the two periods. Although we have not discussed labor income taxes, adding such taxes to the model with variable labor supply would lead to the result that the ratio of labor supplied when young to labor supplied when old depends on the ratio of the *after-tax* wages in the two periods. Hence, if politicians reduce labor income taxes in time t and raise them in time $t + 1$, this will raise the ratio of after-tax

26. One of the first studies of the political business cycle was by William Nordhaus, "The Political Business Cycle," *Review of Economic Studies* 42 (1975): 169–190. More recent studies include those by Alberto Alesina, "Macroeconomics and Politics," NBER *Macroeconomics Annual 3* (1988): 13–52 and Torsten Persson and Guido Tabelini, *Macroeconomic Policy, Credibility, and Politics* (Cambridge, MA: MIT Press, 1990).

wages when young to after-tax wages when old, inducing the young at time t to work more in time t and less in time $t + 1$. If the election is held at time t, there will be more employment and more output to which the politicians can point in claiming that their governance is good for the economy.

What can be done to prevent politicians from manipulating the economy? A possibility is to insulate fiscal and monetary authorities from the political process to the extent possible. One way to do this is to give these authorities long-term contracts, so their own positions are not threatened by actions that displease the incumbents. As we'll discuss in Chapter 14, the U.S. monetary authority—the Board of Governors of the Federal Reserve System—is structured in just this manner, as are the central banks of Germany, Switzerland, and many other countries. On the fiscal side, the Japanese Ministry of Finance represents one of the few cases in which the top fiscal authorities, through long-term tenure in their jobs, are relatively free of political pressure.

Case Study: U.S. Presidential Elections and the State of the Economy

Historically, the state of the U.S. economy has been a remarkably good predictor of the outcome of presidential elections. This suggests that the public bases its votes on prevailing economic conditions and explains why so many incumbent U.S. presidents try so hard to expand the economy in the year they come up for reelection.

Ray Fair, a Yale University economist, has developed a simple statistical model for predicting winners in U.S. presidential elections based on two measures of the state of the economy: the annual inflation rate and the growth rate in the two quarters before the election. According to the model, the lower the inflation rate and the higher the growth rate, the lower the chances of a challenger's unseating the incumbent president.

Since Fair's model had accurately predicted the outcome of 16 of the previous 20 elections, there was considerable interest in the fall of 1992 in its predictions of the prospects of the Democratic challenger, Bill Clinton, winning the 1992 presidential election. Table 10-3 shows these predictions. It indicates the Democratic candidate's predicted share of the popular vote in a two-way race, given different rates of inflation and growth. The table shows a strong dependence of the predicted vote share on the state of the economy. For example, with an inflation rate of 7 percent and a growth rate of −4 percent (the case of a severe downturn), the Democratic candidate was predicted to receive just over half of the popular vote. In contrast, with the pre-election inflation rate at 3 percent and the pre-election growth rate at 2 percent—the actual circumstances prevailing prior to the election in 1992—the Democratic candidate was predicted to receive only 42.6 percent of the vote.

In fact, then-Governor Clinton did receive just about this share of the popular vote. But he won the election nevertheless. The reason he won, despite his low vote share, was the presence of the third-party candidate, Ross Perot. Perot's participation in the race wasn't taken into account in Fair's model, which predicts only the outcomes of two-way races. Though Fair's model didn't capture everything going on in 1992, it nonetheless shows the tendency for the state

Table 10-3 The State of the Economy and the Democratic Candidate's Predicted Share of the Popular Vote in the 1992 Presidential Election

	Inflation Rate							
Growth Rate	0	1	2	3	4	5	6	7
−6	50.0	50.3	50.6	51.0	51.3	51.6	51.9	52.2
−5	49.0	49.3	49.6	49.9	50.2	50.5	50.9	51.2
−4	47.9	48.3	48.6	48.9	49.2	49.5	49.8	50.1
−3	46.9	47.2	47.5	47.8	48.2	48.5	48.8	49.1
−2	45.9	46.2	46.5	46.8	47.1	47.4	47.7	48.1
−1	44.8	45.1	45.4	45.8	46.1	46.4	46.7	47.0
0	43.8	44.1	44.4	44.7	45.0	45.4	45.7	46.0
1	42.7	43.1	43.4	43.7	44.0	44.3	44.6	44.9
2	41.7	42.0	42.3	42.6	43.0	43.3	43.6	43.9
3	40.7	41.0	41.3	41.6	41.9	42.2	42.5	42.9
4	39.6	39.9	40.2	40.6	40.9	41.2	41.5	41.8
5	38.6	38.9	39.2	39.5	39.8	40.2	40.5	40.8
6	37.5	37.9	38.2	38.5	38.8	39.1	39.4	39.7

Source: "By the Numbers, It's Bush," *The Washington Post*, April 14, 1992.

of the U.S. economy to have a great influence on the outcome of presidential elections.

WHAT CAUSES RECESSIONS? A BOTTOM LINE

We've now discussed seven different explanations of recessions: the traditional Keynesian theory, the misperception theory, the real business cycle theory, the sectoral shift theory, New Keynesian theories of nominal price and wage rigidities, New Keynesian models of coordination failures, and models of the political business cycle. Table 10-4 summarizes the seven explanations of recessions as well as their policy prescriptions.

Former President Harry Truman would have seen this large number of explanations as an embarrassment of riches. Truman used to say that he was looking for a one-handed economist, because his economic advisors were always saying "on the one hand this and on the other hand that." Macroeconomists would certainly love to discover the single explanation of, and cure for, recessions. Indeed, the search for *the* explanation has motivated much macroeconomic research, past and present. But why should recessions have a single cause? And why should the set of causes be the same for each recession? There is certainly no theoretical requirement that this be the case.

Table 10-4 Alternative Explanations of Recessions and Their Policy Implications

Theory	Cause of Recession	Policy Implications
Traditional Keynesian Model	Nominal wage or price rigidities prevent economy from equilibrating at full employment.	Monetary or fiscal policy can be used to expand output.
Misperception Theory	Workers (firms) misconstrue decreases in their nominal wages (prices) arising from unexpected decreases in the money supply as reductions in their real wages (prices); they reduce their supply of (demand for) labor; output falls.	Workers and firms have rational expectations, so only unexpected changes in the money supply have real effects.
Real Business Cycle Theory	Workers voluntarily work less during periods when their real wages are low. Temporarily low real wages reflect negative technology shocks.	Since unemployment is voluntary, there is no economic rationale for policy intervention.
Sectoral Shift Model	Shocks to particular sectors of the economy lead to time-consuming reallocation of inputs across sectors; this reallocation temporarily lowers output.	Government assistance in helping labor and capital relocate may mitigate output loss.
New Keynesian Theories of Wage and Price Rigidities	Explicit or implicit long-term contracts, inertia, imperfect competition, or menu costs explain nominal wage and price rigidities that prevent economy from reaching full employment.	Depending on the source of the nominal rigidity, expected as well as unexpected increases in the money supply can raise output.
New Keynesian Models of Coordination Failures	Failure of firms to coordinate actions (e.g., searching for one another or setting the same operating hours) leads to low output equilibrium.	Government pep talks may help the private sector choose high output equilibrium.
Political Business Cycles	Incumbent politicians expand economy prior to elections; once they are reelected, they contract the economy.	Monetary and fiscal policies are used for short-term political expediency. Independence of fiscal and monetary authorities from politicians can help.

Instead of all recessions having the same origin, it seems more likely that there are multiple and varied causes of recessions. The seven general theories discussed here have all probably played major and minor roles in the long history of U.S. and foreign business cycles. Once we accept this view, we can better understand why none of the different theories of recessions has been able to fit all the facts. Unfortunately, this view leaves economists with the very difficult task of sorting out the precise importance of particular theories in particular recessions.

Chapter Summary

1. This chapter has described a range of possible explanations of economic fluctuations. The discussion has been framed, to a large extent, in terms of the Phillips curve—the presumed inverse relationship between inflation and unemployment. During the 1950s and 1960s this relationship seemed fairly stable, and it provided empirical support for the traditional Keynesian model, which stressed the potential for monetary and fiscal policies to raise output and lower unemployment when either nominal wages or prices are sticky.

2. The post-1969 data on inflation and unemployment deviate systematically from the Phillips curve drawn to fit the 1950–1969 data. Milton Friedman and Edmund Phelps explained this outcome in terms of the adjustment of expectations by those setting prices and wages. They argued as follows: over time, nominal wages and prices are set in light of the expected rate of inflation. As a result, the Phillips curve shifts over time, with each new short-run curve depending on the current state of expectations about inflation. In the long run, the Phillips curve is vertical; i.e., there is no long-run trade-off between inflation and unemployment.

3. Friedman's and Phelps's work left open the possibility of a short-run inflation-unemployment trade-off in which the government could try to fool the public by producing more inflation than expected. The rational expectations revolution, led by Robert E. Lucas, Jr. and Thomas Sargent, denied even this means of using monetary policy to lower unemployment. Lucas and Sargent pointed out that a rational public would see through the government's attempts to fool them and would adjust its expectations about inflation accordingly. As a result, anticipated money injections would have no impact on the level of unemployment.

4. The rational expectations school also questioned the traditional Keynesian assumption of nominal rigidities as the underlying factor keeping the economy from attaining full employment. Rather than assume markets were somewhat dysfunctional, rational expectations economists developed the misperception theory, which assumed flexible nominal wages and prices but stressed the lack of complete information on the part of economic agents about the state of the economy, particularly monetary policy and the price level. Their misperception models predicted that only unanticipated injections of money would raise output and lower unemployment. Such unanticipated monetary policy would be unexpected both by the public and by the policy makers themselves.

5. Real business cycle theorists developed other flexible wage and price models in which supply-side shocks, such as oil price increases, altered the productive capacity and output of the economy. These economists explained employment fluctuations in terms of workers' labor supply decisions. During periods of low productivity, wages would be low and workers would choose to take more leisure and, therefore, work less. The opposite would be true during periods of high productivity and high wages.

6. The aggregate supply-side shocks stressed by the real business cycle models raised the question of whether shocks to particular sectors of the economy might not also be important. The sectoral shift model explains unemployment in terms of the search/relocation time required for workers laid off from sectors experiencing negative shocks to find jobs in sectors experiencing positive shocks.

7. The neoclassical misperception, real business cycle, and sectoral shift models did not convince a number of economists who continued to question the assumption of flexible prices and wages. A group of these New Keynesian economists developed microeconomic explanations for nominal rigidities. These explanations include formal as well as informal nominal wage and price contracts, inertia, small costs of altering prices and wages (menu costs), and imperfect competition. According to certain versions of these models, both expected as well as unexpected monetary policy may affect the economy.

8. A different set of New Keynesians began to question the performance of markets along other dimensions, particularly the ability of individual households and firms to coordinate their economic actions when such coordination would be mutually beneficial. Despite the collective benefits, individual economic agents may not have sufficient private incentive to produce at the socially desirable level of output. In addition to externalities, coordination failure models feature multiple equilibria: multiple time paths along which the economy might move. Recessions, according to these models, can be viewed as the economy moving from a good to a bad equilibrium in which economic agents fail to coordinate their actions.

9. The political business cycle model argues that politicians will use monetary and fiscal policies to stimulate the economy prior to elections. In terms of the traditional Keynesian model with nominal rigidities and nonrational expectations, a politician might argue for printing more money prior to an election but reducing the growth in money after the election to limit the attendant increase in inflation. In terms of the real business cycle model, the method by which politicians can spur the economy is by announcing short-term tax cuts. These tax cuts will lead workers to work more while the tax rate is low, knowing that once the tax rate is raised, they'll work less.

10. Each theory discussed in this chapter provides some insight into the potential causes of recessions and expansions. Although there is evidence in support of each, none fits all the facts perfectly. Economists have tended to look for *the* definitive model of the business cycle—but there may not be one. Instead, each of the different explanations may play a part in some, if not all, economic fluctuations.

Key Concepts

Phillips curve
Natural rate of unemployment
Frictional unemployment
Rational expectations
Misperception theory
Intertemporal substitution
Sectoral shift model
Job vacancy rate
New Keynesian models
Staggered contracts
Menu costs
Coordination failure
Multiple equilibria
Political business cycle theory

Review Questions

1. What empirical relationship does the *Phillips curve* describe? How is the Phillips curve affected by changes in the nominal wage? How has the Phillips curve actually changed over the last 40 years?

2. How is the Phillips curve explained by the *traditional Keynesian model*? According to this model, what can government policy do to reduce unemployment during recessions?

3. What is the *natural rate of unemployment*? Is a natural rate of unemployment of zero a realistic possibility?

4. How are *rational expectations* about inflation formed? How do rational expectations affect the government's ability to change the unemployment rate? How can a Phillips curve arise if expectations about inflation are formed rationally?

5. What is the *misperceptions theory* of the Phillips curve? According to this theory, what can government policy do to reduce unemployment during recessions?

6. What criticisms have been raised against the misperceptions model? How have proponents of the model answered these criticisms?

7. How does the *real business cycle theory* explain recessions? What kinds of economic shocks are encompassed by the theory? How does the real business cycle theory explain unemployment? According to this theory, what can government policy do to reduce unemployment during recessions?

8. What criticisms have been raised against the real business cycle model? How have proponents of the model answered these criticisms?

9. How does the *sectoral shift model* explain recessions? What events can initiate sectoral shifts? According to this model, what can government policy do to reduce unemployment during recessions?

10. What criticisms have been raised against the sectoral shift model? How have proponents of the model answered these criticisms?

11. Describe the ways in which *New Keynesians* have modeled nominal wage and price rigidity.

12. Describe empirical evidence that has examined whether *anticipated* monetary policy changes affect output.

13. What are *coordination failures,* and what two elements are common to almost all models of coordination failure? How do models of coordination failure explain business cycles? According to these models, what can government policy do to reduce unemployment during recessions?

14. How does the theory of *political business cycles* explain the economy's cyclical fluctuations? How might this theory operate in the context of a traditional Keynesian model? in the context of the real business cycle model?

Numerical Questions

1. Assume that the economy is characterized by the two-period life-cycle model as presented in Chapter 4, in which the young save a portion of their income, α, but not all of it. In particular, assume the following parameter values: $\alpha = .5$, $\beta = .3$, $N = 200$, and $K_0 = 462.4$.

- **a.** Assuming that $A_t = 5$ for all t, what are the steady-state values of the capital-labor ratio (k), individual earnings (w), the interest rate (r), aggregate output (Y), and aggregate consumption (C)?
- **b.** Instead of the single value of A_t, assume that $A_0 = 4$, $A_1 = 5$, and $A_2 = 6$, and that the pattern repeats beginning in period 3 (and again in periods 6, 9, etc). As in Table 10-1, compute the value of the following for 12 periods after the initial period: the capital-labor ratio (k_t), individual earnings (w_t), the interest rate (r_t), aggregate output (Y_t), aggregate saving (S_t), and aggregate consumption (C_t).

2. Based on the model specified in question 1, answer the following questions regarding economic fluctuations resulting from technology shocks.

- **a.** In the long run, what is the percentage drop in A_t from its maximum value to its minimum value? What is the corresponding drop in output in the long run as A_t drops? Compare the time pattern of changes in the capital-labor ratio over the cycle, and explain why it can be said that these changes in the capital-labor ratio over the model's business cycle dampen somewhat the impact of the changes in technology on output.
- **b.** Compare percentage changes in aggregate output and aggregate consumption, and comment on the following statement: "In addition to dampening output fluctuations, the volatile pattern of saving serves to stabilize consumption." Is consumption more or less volatile than output? Is this view consistent with the Chapter 4 discussion of consumption smoothing?

3. Suppose the Phillips curve is given by the equation $u = 6 - .5(\pi - \pi^e)$, where u is the rate of unemployment, π is the rate of inflation, and π^e is the expected rate of inflation.

- **a.** Assume that the expected rate of inflation is 3 percent. Calculate the rate of unemployment for values of inflation between 0 and 17 percent.
- **b.** What is the value of the natural rate of unemployment?
- **c.** Assume that the expected rate of inflation rises to 7 percent. Recalculate the unemployment rate associated with inflation rates ranging from 0 to 17 percent.
- **d.** With the unemployment rate on the horizontal axis, plot values of actual inflation associated with unemployment rates ranging from 1 to 7.5 (by half points). What has happened to the Phillips curve with changed inflationary expectations?

Analytical Questions

1. Suppose that the government substantially reduces military spending.
   a. Analyze the likely effects of the spending cut on output, employment, and unemployment using (1) the traditional Keynesian model; (2) the sectoral shift model; and (3) the real business cycle model.
   b. How could you use your answers to part a to assess the empirical validity of the alternative theories?
2. In some New Keynesian models, the frequency with which firms change prices depends explicitly on the inflation rate. Would you expect a direct relationship between the level of inflation and the frequency of price change or an inverse relationship, and why?
3. Suppose that past and current monetary growth has led to persistent inflation. Policy makers suddenly announce that money growth will be reversed so that prices will return to their levels of three years ago. Once that goal is achieved, money will then grow at a rate consistent with price stability. Does the misperception model offer a clear prediction about the impact of this policy change on the level of output? If it does, on what does the predicted impact depend?

CHAPTER 11

The Nature and Costs of Unemployment

INTRODUCTION

To the ordinary citizen the unemployment rate is the most familiar and understandable measure of macroeconomic performance. From 1950 through 1993 the unemployment rate for the civilian adult (over age 16) population averaged 7.5 percent at recession *troughs*, but just 4.9 percent at expansion *peaks*.[1] These average values are superimposed on the graph of aggregate unemployment since 1950 that is presented in Figure 11-1.

Reducing unemployment is a key objective of *countercyclical* monetary and fiscal policy. However, as Chapter 10 explained, not all fluctuations in output and employment are as easily attacked with monetary and fiscal policy as those envisaged by the simple Keynesian model developed in Chapter 9. As we will we learn below, the social *benefits* of combating unemployment depend in part on whether unemployment is involuntary or voluntary. Hence, the effectiveness and value of countercyclical policy depend largely on the causes of unemployment.

1. Recall from Chapter 4 that troughs and peaks are the *turning points* of business cycles at which the economy begins to improve and decline, respectively.

Figure 11-1 U.S. Unemployment Rates Since 1950

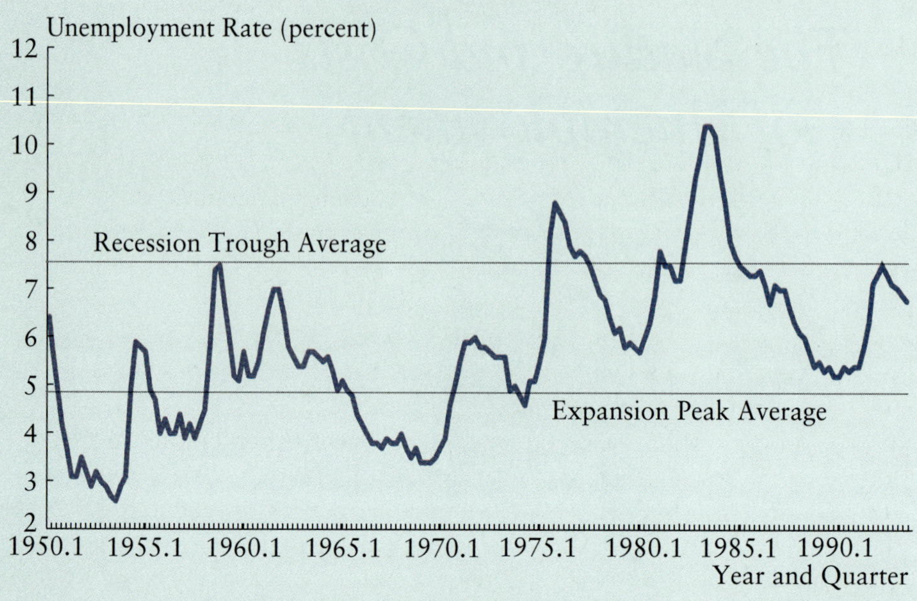

The U.S. unemployment rate has ranged from under 3 percent to over 10 percent since 1950. The typical rise from expansion peak to recession trough is 2.6 percent.

Source: *Economic Report of the President*, 1994

We can learn a considerable amount about the causes of unemployment by studying the *nature* of unemployment spells—how they begin, who experiences them, and how long they last.

This chapter studies the nature and costs of unemployment. Although theories normally simplify matters by attempting to explain "the" unemployment rate, you will see that the rate of unemployment differs markedly among groups in the population and that a considerable share of unemployment is experienced by a relatively small fraction of the labor force. Indeed, there is no "typical" unemployed worker, nor is there even an exact definition of what it means to be unemployed.

Among the questions we address in this chapter are:

- How does the rate of unemployment vary by age, sex, and race?
- How is the burden of higher unemployment distributed across different demographic groups?
- What is *Okun's Law*, and how does it help in measuring the costs of recession?
- What determines the *natural rate* of unemployment?

- What is the relationship between unemployment and the general process of *labor turnover*—the shifts of workers into and out of jobs?
- What is the *duration* of a typical unemployment spell?
- How do government unemployment compensation programs insure workers against the costs of being unemployed, and how do these programs influence the unemployment rate?

As you will see, unemployment is one of the side effects of the complex process of job creation and job destruction that is characteristic of any dynamic market economy. Some unemployment is inevitable, even in booming economies. But there is wide variation in the severity of unemployment over time and across demographic groups. Understanding the reasons for these differences can help guide us toward appropriate policies to reduce unemployment.

To learn about the nature of unemployment, we will begin with a discussion of *labor force dynamics*, the movements of individuals into and out of jobs and the labor force. We will see how these dynamics vary over the business cycle and how well they square with different theories of unemployment. After looking at the aggregate behavior of unemployment, we will turn our attention to the pattern of unemployment across different demographic groups. This detailed analysis will provide further insight into the nature of the unemployment process as well as the distribution of the costs of unemployment. We'll discuss how the government uses *unemployment insurance* to alleviate the burdens of the unemployed and how this program may affect the level of unemployment. Our ultimate goal is to evaluate the costs of unemployment and how government policy might reduce them.

LABOR FORCE DYNAMICS

As we discussed in Chapter 4, the official U.S. unemployment statistics are compiled through a household survey, which classifies individuals into three employment categories. The first two categories of workers, *employed* and *unemployed*, comprise the labor force. At the end of 1993, there were 128.9 million people in the U.S. civilian labor force, of whom 120.7 million were employed and 8.2 million were unemployed. The remaining 65.6 million members of the U.S. civilian adult population were not in the labor force. Among individuals who are not employed, the distinction between being unemployed and not being in the labor force rests primarily on whether individuals are seeking work or are prepared to work.

In some cases, as with full-time students or persons who are seriously ill, the classification "not in the labor force" is straightforward. However, there are many instances in which it is more difficult to distinguish whether an individual is unemployed or truly out of the labor force. We can see this by looking at the behavior over time of the *labor force participation rate*: the fraction of the overall population that is in the labor force.

Figure 11-2 superimposes the labor force participation rate of the civilian adult population on the unemployment rate. The figure clearly shows that the

Figure 11-2 Unemployment and Labor Force Participation Rates Since 1950

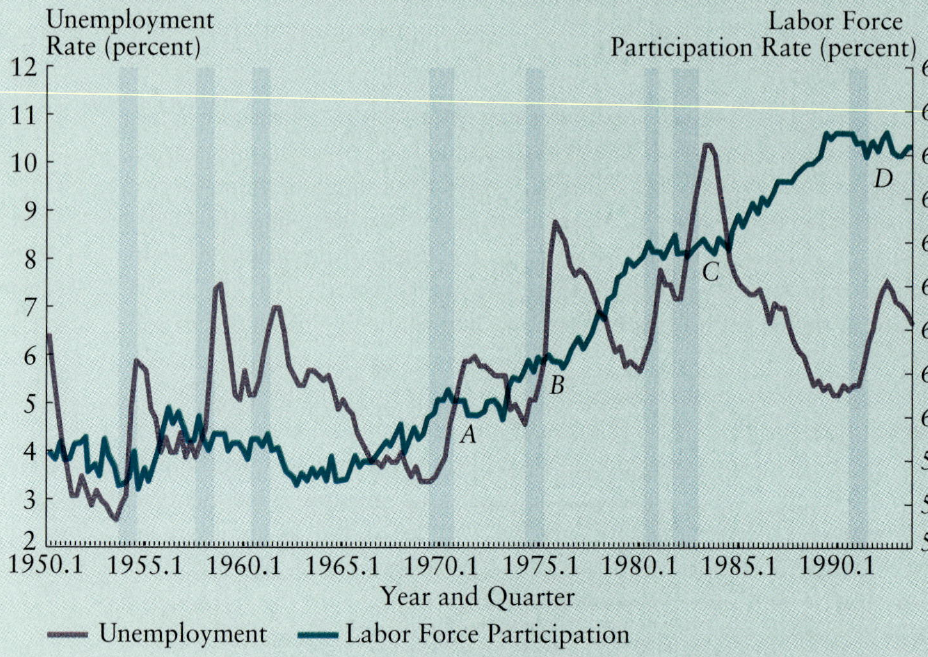

The labor force participation rate measures the fraction of the adult population that is in the labor force. Since the mid-1960s, the participation rate has increased from about 59 percent to about 66 percent today. Despite its upward trend, the participation rate also varies cyclically, often dropping as the unemployment rate increases. This is evident near the troughs of the two recessions of the 1970s (points *A* and *B*), the deep recession of 1981–1982 (point C), and the recession of 1990–1991 (point D).

Source: *Economic Report of the President*, 1994

labor force participation rate has increased since the mid-1960s, from about 59 percent then to around 66 percent today. As we will see below, this increase is due primarily to the increasing participation of women in the labor market and has occurred in spite of the declining rate of male labor force participation that we noted in Chapter 2.

If we look more closely at behavior around recessions (the shaded areas in the figure), we can also see cyclical movements in the labor force participation rate. Indeed, despite its upward trend, the labor force participation rate has often dropped temporarily when the unemployment rate has risen. This pattern is particularly noticeable during the most recent recession (point *D* in the figure) but can also be observed just after the troughs of the two recessions at the beginning and middle of the 1970s (points *A* and *B*) and again near the trough of the deep recession of 1981–1982 (point *C*). This negative correlation between the unemployment rate and the labor force participation rate suggests that, for some individuals, being "out of the labor force" may not be all that different from being unemployed and that it may be impossible to distinguish fully between the two categories.

Net Versus Gross Changes in Work Status

The swings over time in the labor force participation and unemployment rates shown in Figure 11-2 represent *net* changes in employment status, i.e., the net change in the fraction of the labor force that is unemployed and the net change in the fraction of the overall population participating in the labor market. As net measures, they mask the even larger *gross flows* into and out of the labor market and into and out of jobs. Even when there is little or no change in the unemployment rate, many workers lose their jobs, and many others find work. The distinction between gross and net labor force flows is illustrated in Figure 11-3.

It is useful to think of three pools of individuals at any point in time associated with each of the three possible labor force categories, or states: *employed*, *unemployed*, and *not in the labor force*. From period to period (in the case of labor force statistics, we typically measure changes from month to month), each pool's size changes as a result of *net inflows*: the number of individuals entering the state (*inflows*) less the number leaving it (*outflows*). If inflows exceed outflows, net inflows are positive and the category's population increases. If outflows exceed inflows, net inflows are negative and the category's population decreases.

These flows are called labor force *transitions*. Transitions into employment are also called *accessions;* transitions out of employment are called *separations*. As Figure 11-3 indicates, accessions are divided into **new hires** and **rehires** which, as the names indicate, refer respectively to workers hired by a firm for the first time and those recalled to the firm's employ after being out of work. Such recalled workers are returning from **layoffs**, one of the forms of separation. Layoffs are involuntary separations. As you might guess, the other category of separations, **quits**, includes workers who voluntarily leave a firm's employment. As Figure 11-3 shows, individuals who quit or are laid off can become unemployed or leave the labor force, and those who are hired can come either from being unemployed or from being out of the labor force. There are also transitions between the two states of *non*employment—unemployed and not in the labor force—as some individuals without jobs begin looking for work while others stop doing so.

New hires
Workers hired by a firm for the first time

Rehires
Workers recalled to employment by a firm after being out of work

Layoffs
Involuntary separations from (transitions out of) employment

Quits
Voluntary separations from (transitions out of) employment

In any given month, employment grows to the extent that accessions exceed separations. However, even when there is little *net* employment growth—when accessions and separations roughly offset each other—there is considerable labor force mobility; that is, both accessions and separations are large relative to the number of employed individuals. For example, between January 1968 and May 1986, the level of employment increased by an average of .5 percent per month. This net monthly increase in employment resulted from an average of

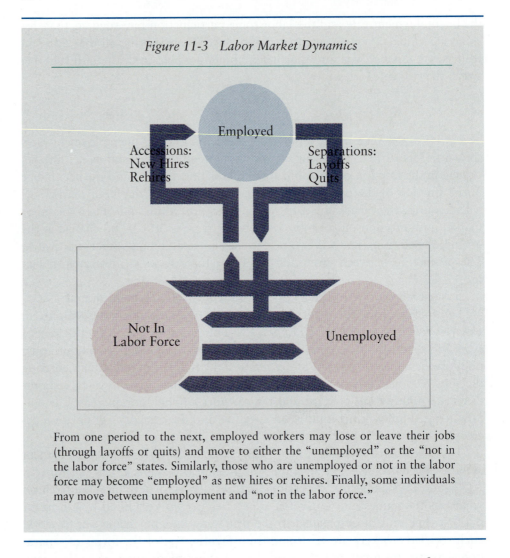

Figure 11-3 Labor Market Dynamics

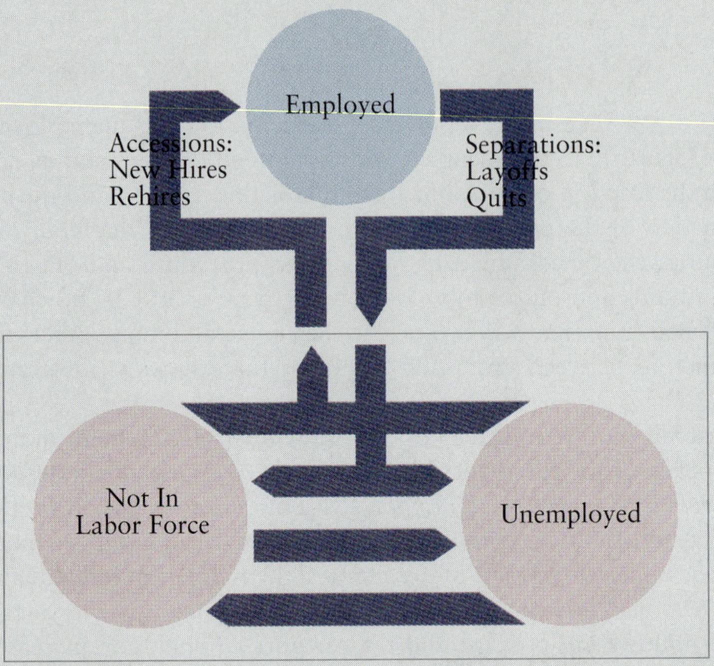

From one period to the next, employed workers may lose or leave their jobs (through layoffs or quits) and move to either the "unemployed" or the "not in the labor force" states. Similarly, those who are unemployed or not in the labor force may become "employed" as new hires or rehires. Finally, some individuals may move between unemployment and "not in the labor force."

3.4 accessions and 2.9 separations per hundred people employed.[2] That is, nearly three in every hundred workers were laid off or quit in the average month during the period, and a slightly larger number was hired.

Both net and gross labor force transitions are important. The net flows indicate the direction of movement of the economy as a whole, and the gross flows indicate how much mobility there is in the labor force—how likely an individual is to move from one labor force classification to another.

Case Study: Small Business—The "Engine" of Job Creation?

Perhaps the best illustration of the distinction between gross and net labor force flows comes from contrasting the economist's and politician's views of the employment process.

2. These statistics are based on Figure 1 of Olivier Jean Blanchard and Peter Diamond, "The Cyclical Behavior of the Gross Flows of U.S. Workers," *Brookings Papers on Economic Activity* 2 (1990): 85–143.

Economists may speak in terms of GDP growth and unemployment rates, whereas politicians are more likely to cast the macroeconomic challenge as one of "job creation," as in "adopting this policy will add 5000 jobs to the local economy" or "my opponent's position on this issue cost the national economy two million jobs." Where do such numbers come from? Estimates of job gains may come from the number of jobs added by the opening of a new factory; those for job losses may reflect the number of workers in a plant or industry that has closed. Frequently, references to job creation are in connection with small business, e.g., "the majority of all new jobs in the U.S. are created by small business."

Is small business that important to the U.S. economy? First of all, it depends on what is meant by "small." As we noted in Chapter 3, most *businesses* employ fewer than 20 workers, but relatively few *workers* are employed by such businesses. In 1986, for example, only 19.8 percent of all nonfarm, nongovernment workers were employed by firms with fewer than 20 employees. However, if "small" is defined more broadly, to encompass firms with no more than 500 workers, then a majority—50.1 percent—of employment is accounted for by small business.[3]

Whatever the definition of small and the associated employment percentage, if employment in large and small firms grew at the same rate, then this percentage would also indicate the share of job growth accounted for by small business. That is, firms with fewer than 20 workers would account for about one-fifth of all job growth, and firms with fewer than 500 workers would account for about half of all job growth. But if we look only at *gross* job creation—i.e., accessions but not separations or, perhaps, only those firms that add employees but not those that shrink or go bankrupt—then small business accounts for a much greater share of the *gross* job creation, because it also leads the way in job destruction. Smaller firms create a disproportionate share of all new jobs, not because they grow faster, but because they have more *labor turnover.* For example, one study documenting the decline of employment in manufacturing during the period 1972–1986 found that the average net annual decline in employment was 2.3 percent among firms with fewer than 100 workers and 1.9 percent among firms with over 1000 workers.[4] That is, the small firms shrank faster than the large firms, on average.[5] However, among only those firms whose employment *increased*, the average annual rate of job growth was 14.0 percent for firms with under 100 workers, and just 6.0 percent among firms with over 1000 employees. Thus, there was pretty impressive growth for small business—among those firms that grew!

3. *The State of Small Business: A Report of the President* (Washington, D.C.: U. S. Government Printing Office, 1990), Table A.20.
4. Steven J. Davis and John Haltiwanger, "Gross Job Creation, Gross Job Destruction, and Employment Reallocation," *Quarterly Journal of Economics* (August 1992): 819–863.
5. The fact that both large and small firms shrank reflects the general shift in employment away from manufacturing during this period, a trend we mentioned in Chapter 1.

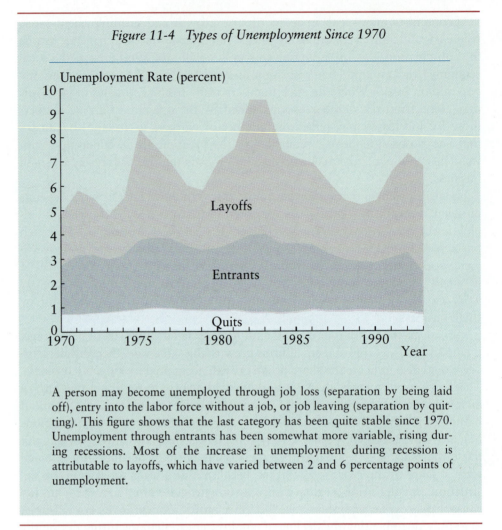

Figure 11-4 Types of Unemployment Since 1970

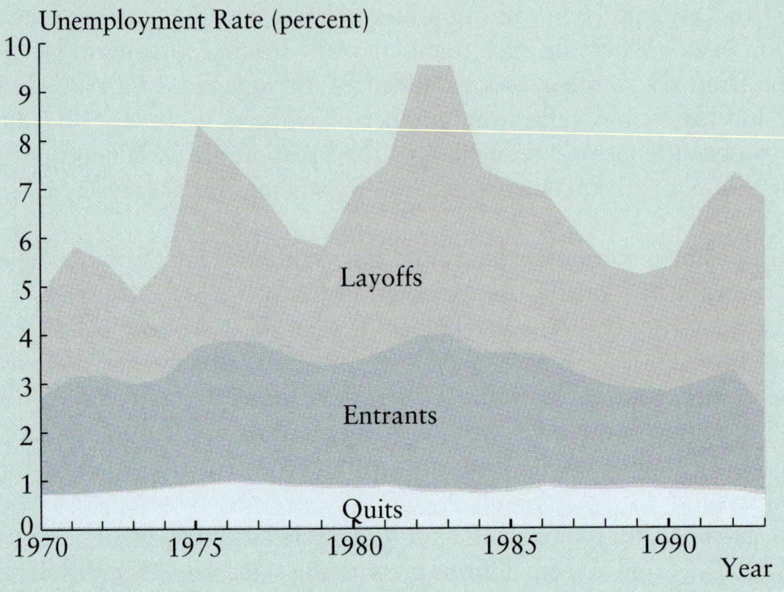

A person may become unemployed through job loss (separation by being laid off), entry into the labor force without a job, or job leaving (separation by quitting). This figure shows that the last category has been quite stable since 1970. Unemployment through entrants has been somewhat more variable, rising during recessions. Most of the increase in unemployment during recession is attributable to layoffs, which have varied between 2 and 6 percentage points of unemployment.

Source: *Economic Report of the President,* 1994

The Nature of Unemployment: Source and Duration

We have seen that unemployment arises as the result of flows from other labor force states (employed or not in the labor force) and that there are considerable flows into and out of the state of unemployment each month. We can learn more about the unemployment experience by considering its source—how each spell of unemployment arises—and how long it lasts—its duration.

There are three possible initial reasons for unemployment: job loss (being laid off[6]), job leaving (quitting), and entry into the labor force without a job. Figure 11-4 shows the composition of unemployment by initial cause for the period since 1970. The figure shows quite clearly that layoff unemployment is the major source of volatility of unemployment, rising sharply when the unemploy-

6. Although we usually use the terms "job loss" and "layoff" interchangeably, the term layoff technically applies only to cases (such as plant closings and bankruptcies) in which the job loss is "without prejudice." It does not formally apply to those relatively few cases of job loss in which an employee is fired "with cause," i.e., for stealing or some other offense.

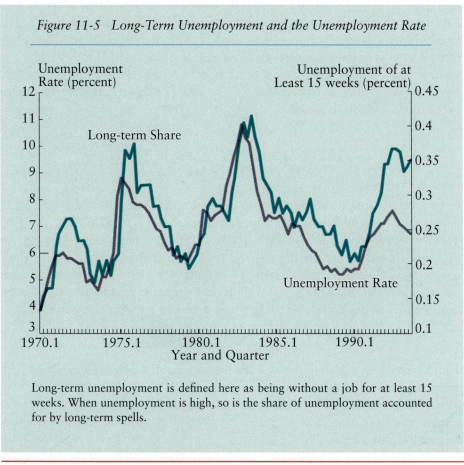

Figure 11-5 Long-Term Unemployment and the Unemployment Rate

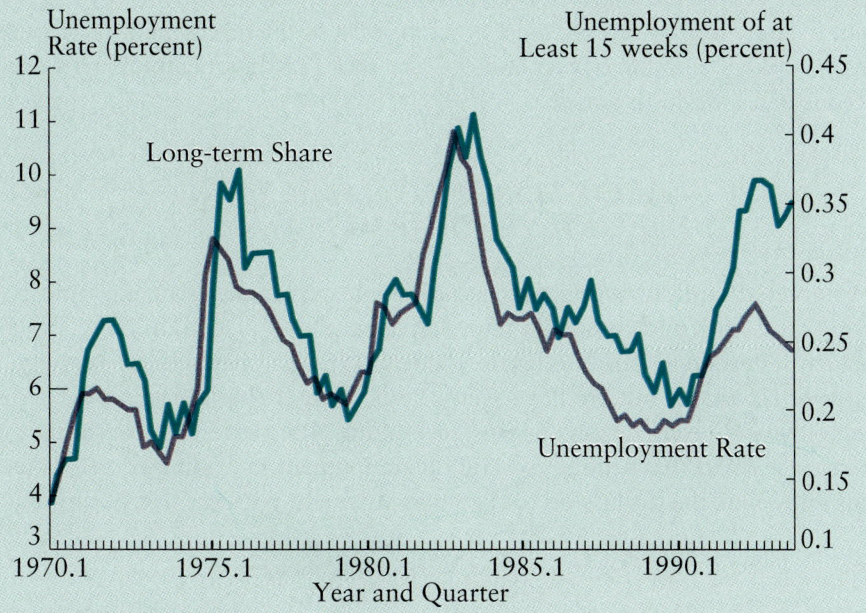

Long-term unemployment is defined here as being without a job for at least 15 weeks. When unemployment is high, so is the share of unemployment accounted for by long-term spells.

Source: *Economic Report of the President*, 1994

ment rate rises. The unemployment rate attributable to quits has been quite stable over time at less than 1 percent. Unemployment due to labor force entry, accounting typically for about 2 percentage points of unemployment, is somewhat more variable over the cycle—it does rise a bit during recession.[7] However, most of the increase in unemployment in recessions is attributable to layoffs, which have accounted for as little as 2 percentage points of unemployment at expansion peaks and over 6 percentage points at recession troughs.

There is also a shift in the duration of unemployment during recessions. Overall, the average amount of time (typically measured in weeks) that a typical unemployed worker has already been unemployed—the length to date of his or her unemployment spell—increases. For example, average duration was 12.0 weeks in July, 1990, the month of the most recent expansion peak, but the average rose to 13.5 weeks by April 1991. A convenient way of illustrating this increased duration is by the change in the share of unemployment accounted for by individuals suffering from long-term unemployment. Figure 11-5 plots the

7. Unemployment attributable to labor force entry rises slightly in recession not because more people enter the labor force, but because those who do enter remain unemployed for a longer period of time—reflecting the association between the duration and level of unemployment that we are about to consider.

aggregate unemployment rate against the fraction of unemployed workers who have been unemployed for at least 15 weeks—the long-term unemployed. The figure shows a strong correspondence between the two series. When unemployment is high, so is the share of unemployment that is accounted for by long-term spells. Thus, during recessions, a greater share of unemployment is accounted for by workers who have been laid off, and more of the unemployment experienced is of a long-term nature.

LABOR FORCE DYNAMICS AND THEORIES OF UNEMPLOYMENT

In Chapters 9 and 10 we introduced different explanations of unemployment during recessions and discussed the relative emphasis placed on these explanations by alternative business cycle models. Our emphasis there was on the causes of recession, but we have seen in this chapter that there is considerable unemployment even during booms, averaging 4.9 percent at business cycle peaks since 1950. We need to explain unemployment in booms as well as recessions and relate the discussion to the unemployment patterns just observed.

Involuntary Unemployment

The Keynesian model emphasizes the importance of *involuntary* unemployment, when an individual is willing to work but unable to find a job at the going wage. The rise in layoffs as a cause of unemployment during recession seems to support the Keynesian view—we do not normally think of layoffs as voluntary acts on the part of workers.

But our story is incomplete. Layoffs account for a significant share of unemployment, even during good times. Can there be involuntary unemployment when the rate of employment is high? There can be if nominal rigidities are not fully overcome, even during expansions of aggregate demand (outward shifts of the IS or LM curve). As we discussed in Chapter 10, if the rigid nominal wage rises with the price level to maintain a *real* wage—if the rigidity is with respect to the *real* wage rate—then increases in the price level may fail to clear the labor market and eliminate all involuntary unemployment. No matter how high the price level goes, the nominal wage may keep pace, in which case firms will not find it profitable to hire all available workers.

Insider-outsider theory *An explanation of labor market behavior that posits that insiders (individuals already employed) negotiate higher real wages for themselves at the expense of outsiders*

MODELS OF REAL WAGE RIGIDITY. Who imposes this wage rigidity? Except with respect to low-skill jobs, for which the government sets the minimum wage, the traditional explanation has involved labor unions and collective bargaining. Recently, economists have sought to explain precisely how this process works. Their research argues that workers already employed by firms attain a special status, either through formal union representation or because they have acquired valuable skills and familiarity with the company's operations, that allows them to bargain with management for wages above the market-clearing level, at the expense of other potential workers who remain unemployed. According to this **insider-outsider theory**, such workers—the "insiders"—care about preserving their own jobs and income and not about the prospects of the unemployed—the "outsiders."[8] Also, although a firm could attempt to increase its profits by lowering its wage offer and hiring from the pool of unemployed workers, the expense of screening and training these new workers might well exceed the direct reduction in wage costs.

An alternative theory places the responsibility for persistent involuntary unemployment on firms rather than on workers. According to this approach, called the **efficiency wage theory**, firms choose to set their wage rate above the level needed to attract new workers, as a way of ensuring good performance even when such performance is difficult to monitor.[9]

Efficiency wage theory
The idea that keeping wages high makes workers perform better for fear of losing their jobs

To understand the efficiency wage theory, let's consider an example. Suppose that labor supply is fixed and that the labor market would clear (supply would equal demand) at a wage rate of 8 dollars per hour. Consider the employment policy of a firm that hires workers to manufacture hand grenades for use on testing ranges. Once hired, each worker can choose whether to work carefully or not, but his decision cannot be observed by the firm. If the worker does exercise care, the hand grenades he produces will always work as designed. If the worker is careless, the grenades he produces will occasionally malfunction, injuring or killing those responsible for testing them. When such malfunctions occur, the worker who produced the defective grenade is immediately fired.

Even though the firm could hire workers for 8 dollars an hour, it might find it desirable to pay more, to give workers a stronger incentive not to be fired. Workers hired at 8 dollars an hour would see little point in being careful—if fired, they could quickly find work elsewhere at the same wage rate of 8 dollars an hour in a full-employment economy. By contrast, workers receiving, say, 12 dollars an hour would have something to lose if they were fired, even if they could find another job right away at 8 dollars an hour. We refer to the higher wage in this example as an efficiency wage, because the firm chooses it in order to elicit more efficient (in this case, more careful) effort from employees whose behavior the firm cannot monitor directly.

Paying efficiency wages may be in a firm's own interest, but if it is used economy-wide, the practice will produce involuntary unemployment. If other employers also choose to offer a wage that exceeds 8 dollars an hour, there will be too few jobs to go around, since the quantity of labor demanded exhausts the available labor supply only at a wage as low as 8 dollars per hour. This involuntary unemployment reinforces the efficiency wages by giving employed workers an additional reason to avoid being fired: the possibility of not being able to find another job at all. Hence, to lessen "shirking" on the job, employers end up relying on a combination of higher wages and the prospect of unemployment. As

8. See Assar Lindbeck and Dennis J. Snower, *The Insider-Outsider Theory of Employment and Unemployment* (Cambridge, MA: MIT Press, 1989).
9. See Carl Shapiro and Joseph E. Stiglitz, "Involuntary Unemployment as a Worker Discipline Device," *American Economic Review* (1984): 433–444; Joseph E. Stiglitz, "Theories of Wage Rigidities," in *Keynes' Economic Legacy: Contemporary Economic Theories*, ed. J. Butkiewicz et al. (New York: Praeger, 1986), 153–206; and Lawrence F. Katz, "Efficiency Wage Theories: A Partial Evaluation," in NBER *Macroeconomics Annual 1986*, ed. S. Fischer (Cambridge, MA: MIT Press, 1986), 235–276.

Figure 11-6 Efficiency Wages and Unemployment

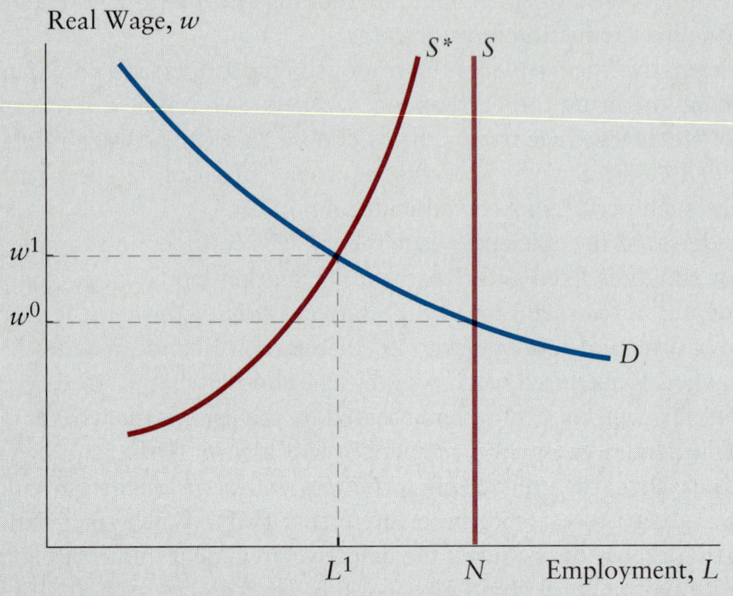

An efficiency wage is a wage set above the rate needed to attract new workers (w^0) as a way of ensuring good performance. The curve labeled S^* is called a no-shirking constraint. At each wage rate, it indicates the level of employment needed to provide workers with an incentive not to shirk. The intersection of S^* with the labor demand curve, D, determines a wage (w^1) that leaves just enough workers unemployed to satisfy the no-shirking constraint. Involuntary unemployment of $N - L^1$ results.

unemployment becomes a more likely consequence of being fired (i.e., as the unemployment rate rises), firms can reduce the wages they pay and still elicit efficient labor effort.

This trade-off is represented in Figure 11-6 by the curve labeled S^*, which is referred to as a "no-shirking constraint."[10] At each wage, it indicates the level of employment (and unemployment) needed to provide workers with a strong enough incentive not to shirk; the higher the wage, the lower the level of unemployment that is necessary. The intersection of the no-shirking constraint and the labor demand curve, D, is the equilibrium point at which the labor demanded at the going wage leaves just enough workers unemployed to satisfy the no-shirking constraint at that wage. In Figure 11-6 this intersection occurs at a real wage w^1 and a level of unemployment ($N - L^1$).

10. This diagram is presented in Bruce C. Greenwald and Joseph E. Stiglitz, "Financial Market Imperfections and Business Cycles," *Quarterly Journal of Economics* (February 1993): 77–114.

The insider-outsider and efficiency wage theories differ in their explanations for involuntary unemployment, but both theories emphasize that it is not exclusively a temporary, recession-related phenomenon.

Case Study: Wages in the Fast-Food Industry

Economists have identified many cases in which individual companies appeared to pay efficiency wages as a way of guaranteeing worker loyalty and effort. Perhaps the most celebrated is Henry Ford's decision early in this century to offer workers 5 dollars a day, far more than the going wage at the time.[11] More recent evidence comes from the fast-food industry.

The individual outlets of fast-food companies (such as McDonald's or Kentucky Fried Chicken) may be owned directly by the parent company or by a local individual who obtains a franchise from the company. In the latter case, the parent company exerts control over production methods and policies as a way of ensuring that all the company's outlets, whether franchised or company-owned, meet certain standards of uniformity from the customer's perspective. However, wage rates vary from location to location according to labor market conditions.

In addition, the wage rates paid by individual outlets vary systematically according to the form of ownership. One study by Alan Krueger of Princeton University found that higher-level employees earned 9 percent more, and full-time crew workers 2 percent more, at company-owned outlets.[12] Why? According to the theory, firms pay efficiency wages when it is difficult for the owner to monitor the effort of workers. It is much harder for the distant owner of a company-owned outlet to check on the quality of workers' effort than it is for the local owner of a franchise. The higher wages act as a substitute for the monitoring that local ownership makes possible.

Voluntary Unemployment

In contrast to the Keynesian view, the real business cycle model attributes recessions to technology shocks, which lower real wages. As a consequence of the drop in real wages, some workers temporarily choose *voluntary* unemployment—they decline work at the lower real wage. We can easily extend this explanation of unemployment to booms as well. There will always be some individuals who are able to work but not willing to accept jobs at the wage rates commensurate with their skills.

How much unemployment is voluntary? A good place to start is the share of the unemployed who are job leavers. Unlike being laid off, quitting is a voluntary act. We might exclude labor force entrants from consideration on the ground that someone not wishing to work would not enter the labor force.

11. Daniel Raff and Lawrence Summers, "Did Henry Ford Pay Efficiency Wages?" *Journal of Labor Economics* (1987).
12. Alan B. Krueger, "Ownership, Agency, and Wages: An Examination of Franchising in the Fast Food Industry," *Quarterly Journal of Economics* (February 1991): 75–101.

Viewing unemployment by those who quit as a proxy for voluntary unemployment suggests that voluntary unemployment may account for a certain share of unemployment in general, but little of the rise in unemployment during recessions; recall Figure 11-4. However, this conclusion needs to be regarded with some caution. Although it may be correct to count job leavers as voluntarily unemployed, some workers who were laid off or who entered the labor force without a job may also belong in that category. For example, a laid-off worker may already, during her current unemployment spell, have rejected other jobs at the going wage.

In summary, quits may be associated with voluntary unemployment, but they needn't account for *all* voluntary unemployment. Therefore, the relative stability of quits over the business cycle does not necessarily *prove* that voluntary unemployment is equally stable.

Misperception Unemployment

The misperception theory of unemployment was introduced in Chapter 10 to explain increases in unemployment during recessions. It is not really aimed at explaining why there is considerable unemployment even in good times. This theory says that workers may temporarily reject work if they believe that the *nominal* wage rate they are being offered corresponds to a lower *real* wage than it actually does—i.e., if they think the price level is higher than it actually is.

We distinguish this type of unemployment from the previous two because it doesn't fit neatly into the voluntary/involuntary categorization. It is voluntary in that workers choose not to work. Yet it also satisfies the definition of involuntary unemployment: workers without jobs would accept work at the nominal wage offered if they knew how high the real wage actually was.

How important is the misperception theory in explaining recessions? Because it presumes that workers voluntarily leave their jobs in search of better wages, it seems contradicted by the relative stability of quits over the business cycle. As we just discussed in relation to the real business cycle theory, though, there may be additional voluntary unemployment in the layoff category. For example, a worker offered a wage cut by an employer might refuse to accept it and prompt a layoff, thinking that the going wage in other jobs is higher than it actually is. However, in this case there is an additional piece of damaging evidence. The notion of workers being "fooled" clearly relates to the short run, until they acquire the correct information on prices. If recessions were caused by lots of workers quitting or accepting layoff because they temporarily thought their wages were too low, we would expect an increase in the share of unemployment accounted for by short-term unemployment—just the opposite of what we actually observe.

Frictional Unemployment

Chapter 10 introduced yet another kind of unemployment: the *frictional* unemployment that occurs as a result of the continual movement of individuals among jobs as the composition of production shifts among industries and regions, as individuals seek better compensation and working conditions, and as older workers retire and younger ones take their places. Also called *search* unemployment, frictional unemployment occurs as workers acquire information about alternative jobs and take the actions necessary (such as moving) to become employed or reemployed.

Like the unemployment envisaged by the misperception theory, frictional unemployment occurs in part because workers do not have perfect information about alternative jobs and wages. However, there is no presumption in this case of wholesale misinformation on the part of workers. The misperception theory was developed to explain unemployment fluctuations, but the concept of frictional unemployment has been viewed as an explanation of why there is always some measured unemployment. Frictional unemployment could arise initially through a layoff, a quit, or labor force entry and, given the dynamic nature of the U.S. economy, there is little doubt that significant frictional unemployment exists.[13]

Like the unemployment envisioned by the misperception theory, frictional unemployment typically could be expected to be of relatively short duration, as individuals move from one job to another or find work after entering the labor force. Hence, it seems at first glance that frictional unemployment, though perhaps always present and significant, does not explain the rise of unemployment during recessions, when the duration of unemployment rises.

However, this conclusion ignores the fact that the degree of labor market stability changes over time. When there is a considerable shift in activity among productive sectors or regions, we expect more workers to experience frictional unemployment. But such major sectoral shifts might also take longer to occur, causing the typical unemployment spell of the frictionally unemployed worker to lengthen. This is the "sectoral shock" model we discussed in Chapter 10—a model that, particularly for the 1970s, successfully explains cyclical swings in unemployment as resulting from sectoral shifts in industry, measured by the variation in job creation (increases in employment) and job destruction (decreases in employment) across different industries.

Summary

In recessions, the fraction of unemployment accounted for by layoffs and long spells of unemployment increases. This is consistent with the Keynesian view, but not necessarily inconsistent with theories of voluntary and frictional unemployment. On the other hand, although frictional unemployment is a standard explanation for the presence of unemployment even in booms, recent extensions of Keynesian theory explain how wage rigidities and involuntary unemployment may also persist even in good times. Hence, unemployment, in good times and bad, seems to have not one, but a variety of explanations. We can learn more about the "anatomy" of unemployment by considering how the unemployment experience differs across groups in the population.

13. For example, Davis and Haltiwanger, *op. cit.*, in their study of manufacturing firms between 1972 and 1986, found that in the average year, growing firms increased their workforce by an average of 9.2 percent whereas shrinking firms reduced their workforce by an average of 11.3 percent.

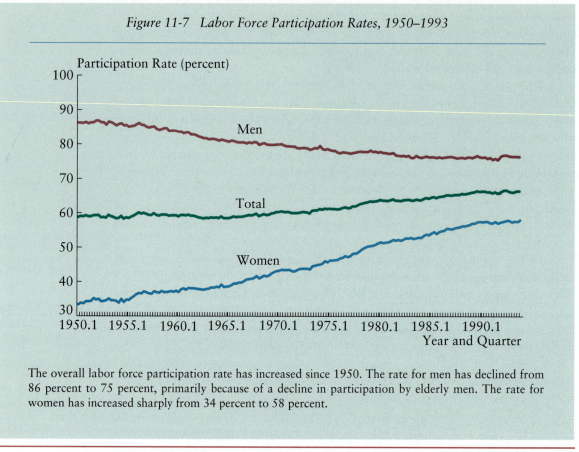

Figure 11-7 Labor Force Participation Rates, 1950–1993

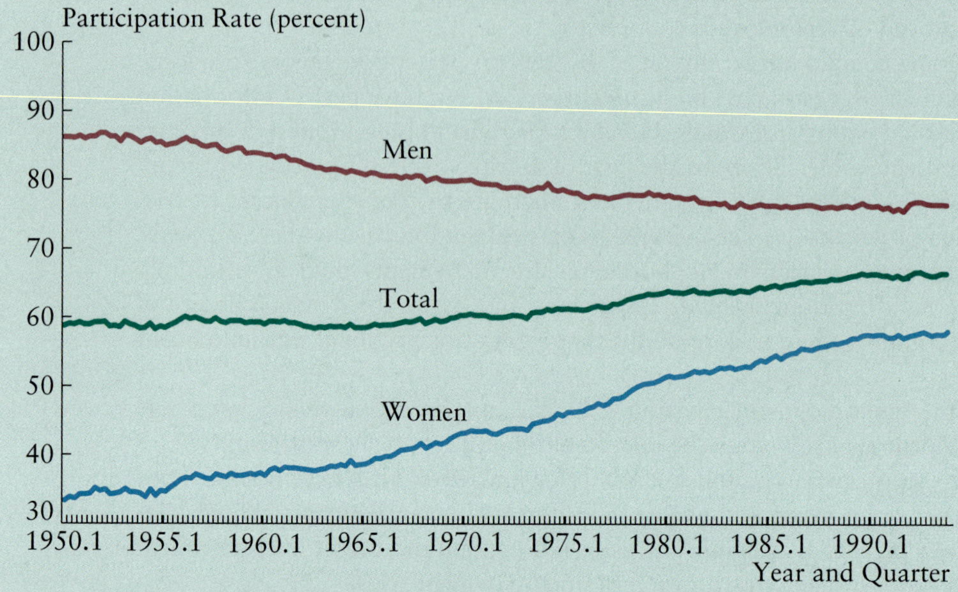

The overall labor force participation rate has increased since 1950. The rate for men has declined from 86 percent to 75 percent, primarily because of a decline in participation by elderly men. The rate for women has increased sharply from 34 percent to 58 percent.

Source: *Economic Report of the President*, 1994

UNEMPLOYMENT: A DISAGGREGATE VIEW

Looking at unemployment among particular groups in the population can help us uncover patterns not observable in the aggregate. It also tells us who suffers the most unemployment, both in recessions and expansions. We'll begin by looking at the differences in labor force participation and unemployment according to sex and then consider differences by age, race, and duration of unemployment spell.

Employment and Unemployment Patterns by Sex

As noted, the aggregate U.S. labor force participation rate has increased during the past few decades. Figure 11-7 indicates the source of this labor force growth. It graphs separately the labor force participation rates of men and women since 1950, along with the aggregate rate discussed earlier.

The figure shows that, among men, the labor force participation rate has declined, from 86 percent in 1950 to 75 percent in 1993. This decline is due primarily to the decline in participation among the elderly. By contrast, the labor force participation rate among women has risen sharply over the same period,

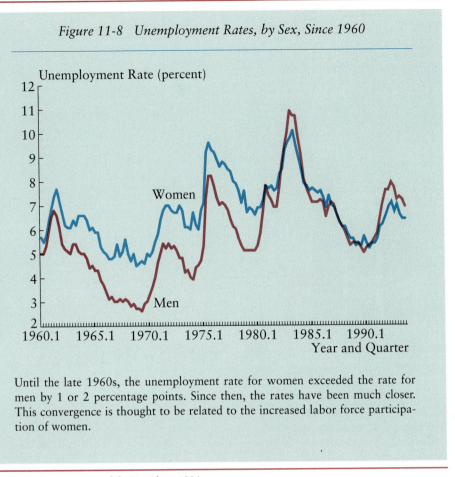

Figure 11-8 Unemployment Rates, by Sex, Since 1960

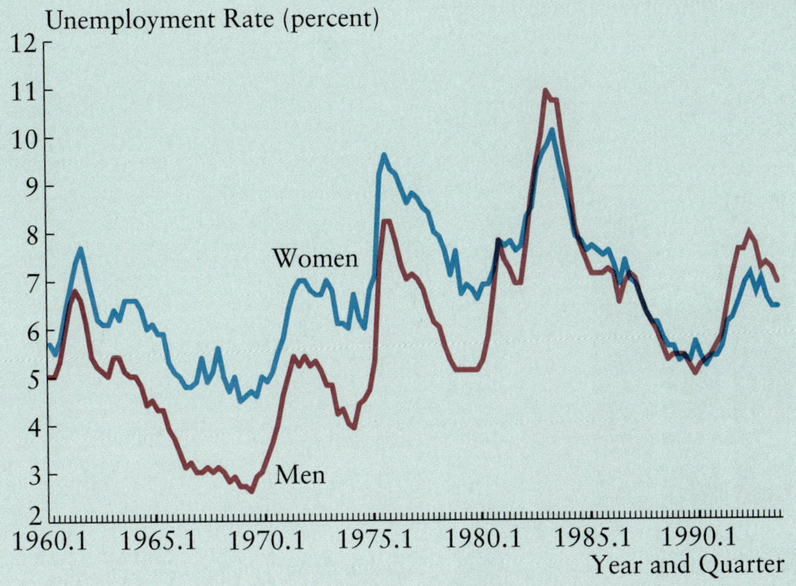

Until the late 1960s, the unemployment rate for women exceeded the rate for men by 1 or 2 percentage points. Since then, the rates have been much closer. This convergence is thought to be related to the increased labor force participation of women.

Source: *Economic Report of the President*, 1994

from 34 percent to 58 percent. Thus, the difference in participation rates between men and women has dropped from 52 percentage points in 1950 to 17 percentage points in 1993.

The growing importance of women in the U.S. work force has been accompanied by a change in their unemployment experience. Figure 11-8 graphs the unemployment rates for men and women for the period since 1960. As the figure shows, the unemployment rate for women exceeded that for men until the 1980s, typically by 1 or 2 percentage points. Since 1980, the unemployment rates among men and women have been much closer to one another.

What explains this phenomenon? It is generally thought to be related to the increasing labor force participation of women. As the typical woman's labor force experience has shifted over time from occasional work to career employment, there has been a reduction in the frictional unemployment normally associated with the job search of labor force entrants. Put simply, as women's labor force participation patterns have become more like men's, so has their unemployment experience.

Although the unemployment rates of women and men are now relatively similar in a typical year, an important difference remains and is discernible in

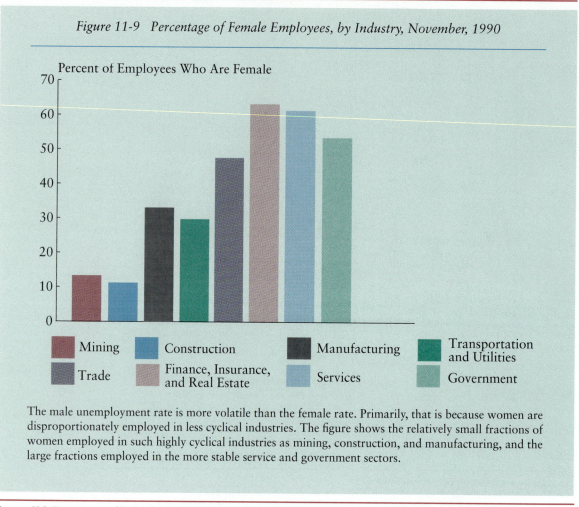

Figure 11-9 Percentage of Female Employees, by Industry, November, 1990

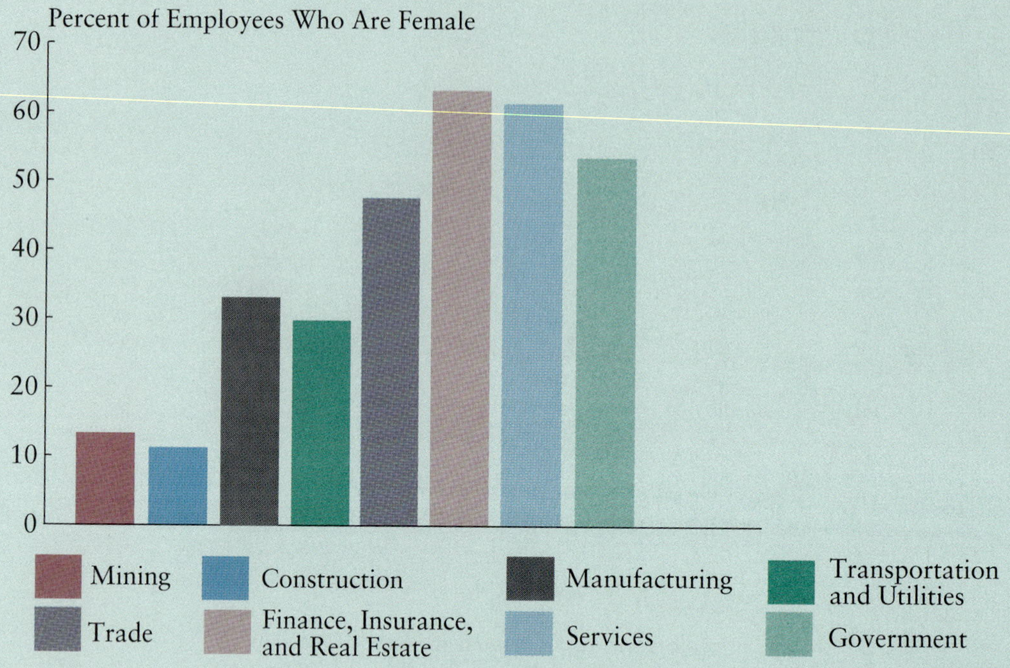

The male unemployment rate is more volatile than the female rate. Primarily, that is because women are disproportionately employed in less cyclical industries. The figure shows the relatively small fractions of women employed in such highly cyclical industries as mining, construction, and manufacturing, and the large fractions employed in the more stable service and government sectors.

Source: U.S. Department of Labor, Bureau of Labor Statistics, *Employment, Hours, and Earnings in the United States, 1909–90*, vol. 2

Figure 11-8. Note that the men's unemployment rate actually has risen above that for women in each of the past two recessions (with unemployment peaks in 1982 and 1991), falling below in between. In other words, the male unemployment rate has been more volatile. The reason is primarily that women are disproportionately employed in less cyclical industries. We saw in Chapter 4 that heavy industries such as manufacturing, mining, and construction have much more volatile swings in output than trade and services, in part because investment is so much more volatile than consumption over the cycle. There is similar volatility in these industries' employment levels. As Figure 11-9 shows, women account for a relatively small share of the employment in the more cyclical industries—around 10 percent in mining and construction and 30 percent in manufacturing, as compared to nearly 50 percent in wholesale and retail trade and over 60 percent in services.

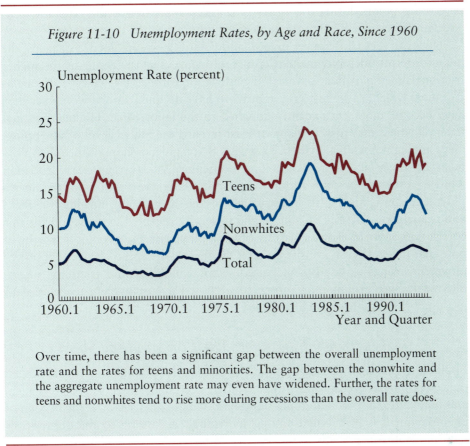

Figure 11-10 Unemployment Rates, by Age and Race, Since 1960

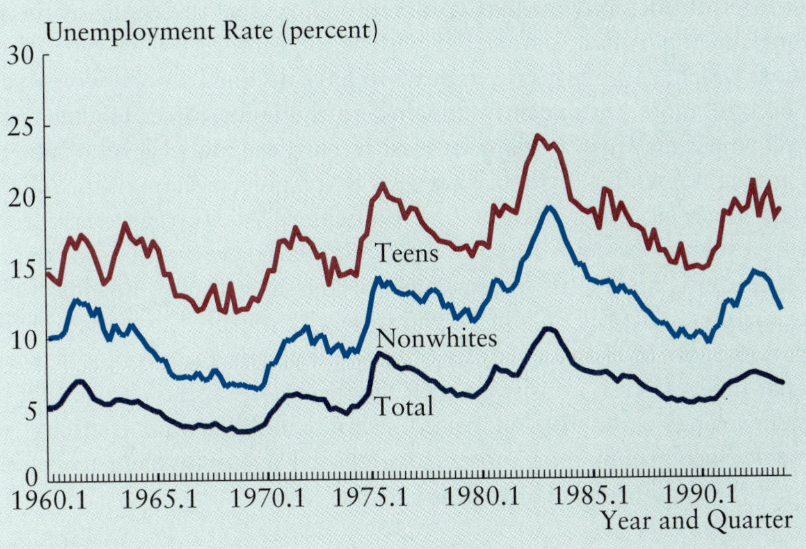

Over time, there has been a significant gap between the overall unemployment rate and the rates for teens and minorities. The gap between the nonwhite and the aggregate unemployment rate may even have widened. Further, the rates for teens and nonwhites tend to rise more during recessions than the overall rate does.

Source: *Economic Report of the President*, 1994

Unemployment Distinctions by Age and Race

Although male-female differences in the unemployment rate have lessened, there remain significant differences according to age and race. Figure 11-10 plots the unemployment rates for teenagers (ages 16–19) and for nonwhites along with the overall unemployment rate for the period since 1960. Each group had significantly higher unemployment rates over the entire period than did the population as a whole. Indeed, individuals falling into both categories—nonwhite teenagers—have experienced truly staggering rates of unemployment. In 1993, for example, nonwhite teenagers had unemployment rates of 40.1 percent (males) and 37.5 percent (females).

Unlike Figure 11-8, Figure 11-10 shows little change in relative unemployment experience. If there is any trend at all, it has been toward a larger gap between nonwhite and aggregate unemployment rates, from around 3 percentage points in the late 1960s to around 5 percentage points in the 1980s. However, it is difficult to draw firm conclusions about trends, as the three series have also differed in terms of business cycle volatility. The rates of unemployment among teens and nonwhites, which are higher to begin with, also tend to rise more during recessions. For example, the aggregate unemployment rate rose by about 3 percentage points during the 1981–1982 recession, whereas the rates for teens and nonwhites rose by about 5 percentage points.

How can these differences in level and volatility be explained? For teens, the higher level of unemployment is commonly viewed as the result of the higher frictional unemployment associated with labor force entry—a type of unemployment which, as we just saw, appears to have declined among women as they have become more permanently attached to the labor force. Higher frictional unemployment may also explain, at least in part, the higher level of unemployment among nonwhites. Evidence suggests that a greater share of the unemployment of lower-income workers—and nonwhites, on average, earn less than whites—results from industrial mobility.[14] Similarly, the volatility of the unemployment rate is higher for lower-wage workers as a group, not just for teens and nonwhites. There is no simple and generally accepted explanation for this correlation of the level and volatility of unemployment. However, it is worthy of note that this pattern is consistent with the theory, discussed above, that unemployment swings arise from increased sectoral mobility and frictional unemployment, since groups more prone to frictional unemployment to begin with presumably would be more affected by its increase.

Spells of Unemployment: The Long and the Short

Looking at different demographic categories in the population, we have seen that unemployment disproportionately affects certain groups, such as teenagers and nonwhites, in both good times and bad. We can also ask how the burden of unemployment is distributed among individuals according to the duration of their unemployment spells.

At any particular time, the unemployed population consists of workers undergoing unemployment spells of different lengths. Some will soon find work (or leave the labor force); others may remain unemployed for a considerable period of time. Any particular rate of unemployment could result from a variety of different combinations of short-term and long-term unemployment. For example, if the unemployment rate stays at 5 percent throughout a year, this could reflect, say, a different 5 percent of the labor force being unemployed each week (i.e., all unemployment spells are of one week's length) or the same 5 percent of the labor force being unemployed for the entire year (all unemployment spells are at least 52 weeks long). These two extreme cases, although they produce the same aggregate unemployment rate, reflect very different patterns of unemployment—from mild and widespread to serious and very concentrated.

Which of these extremes is more accurate? We saw in Figure 11-5 that the answer varies over the business cycle—the share of long-term unemployment in the total increases during recessions. However, even in booms, long-term unemployment is considerable. During the expansion years 1987–1989, for example,

14. See Chinhui Juhn, Kevin M. Murphy, and Robert H. Topel, "Why Has the Natural Rate of Unemployment Increased over Time?" *Brookings Papers on Economic Activity* 2 (1991): 75–126. This paper is also the source for the figures on duration of unemployment spells presented in the next section.

one-tenth of all unemployment in each year resulted from unemployment spells that lasted for the entire year, and nearly half occurred in spells of more than half of the year. On the other hand, over one-fifth of all unemployment came in spells of 13 weeks or less. Hence, there is considerable long-term unemployment but a lot of short-term unemployment as well—there is no "typical" unemployment spell.

THE PRIVATE AND SOCIAL COSTS OF UNEMPLOYMENT

The previous section examined the *distribution* of unemployment—how much of it is experienced by individuals according to sex, age, race, and duration of unemployment. We saw that unemployment is much more prevalent among teenagers and nonwhites and that a considerable fraction of it occurs during long unemployment spells.

A concentration of unemployment is disturbing in itself, for it suggests that the burden is not being shared equally. But this conclusion is premature and requires consideration of two additional factors. First, what are the costs to the individual (and society, as well) of unemployment? We generally think of unemployment as an unfortunate and undesirable experience, but quantifying its costs is important. Second, to what extent does the government's social insurance "safety net" (mentioned briefly in Chapter 7 and discussed again in Chapter 15) cushion unemployment's blows? If social insurance succeeds at its task, then the uneven initial distribution of unemployment's costs can be spread over the wider population.

Unemployment and Welfare

When considering the costs of unemployment, it is useful to distinguish between the costs to the unemployed individual (the *private* costs of unemployment) and those to society as a whole (the *social* costs). Let's start with a case in which these costs are the same.

We might argue that the cost of unemployment to an individual who does not work equals the wages that he loses during the unemployment spell, whereas the cost to society as a whole is the output that the worker does not produce during the same period. How would these costs compare? We know that in competitive markets, a worker's wage rate equals his marginal product—how much additional output his labor produces. Hence, the worker's lost wages would equal society's lost output in this case, and private and social costs of unemployment would be the same. In this example, the private and social measure of loss would be the reduction in output—in GDP—resulting from the worker's lack of employment.

But do lost wages and output provide an accurate measure of the loss to the unemployed individual and society? They could overstate *or* understate the true costs, depending on the reasons for unemployment and the impact of unemployment on the unemployed individual.

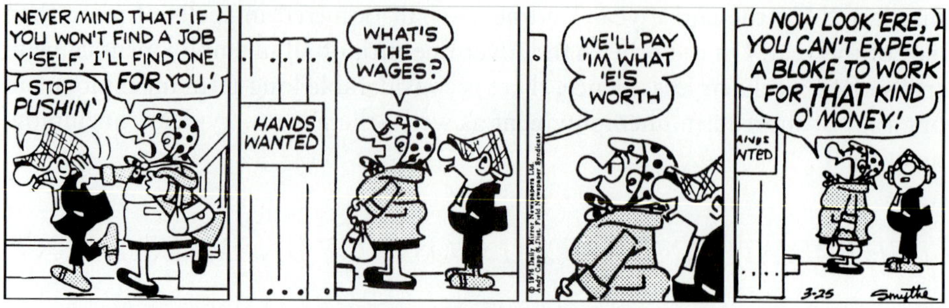

DOES REDUCED OUTPUT OVERSTATE THE COSTS OF UNEMPLOYMENT?

Why does unemployment arise? We have seen that unemployment can be described as *voluntary, involuntary,* or *frictional,* depending on the reason for the unemployment. The most straightforward argument that lost output overstates the cost of unemployment arises in the case of voluntary unemployment. This argument is illustrated in Figure 11-11.

By definition, an individual is voluntarily unemployed if he *chooses* not to work at the going wage for his level of skill and experience. In the figure, there are N potential workers but an upward-sloping labor supply curve, S, indicating that the number of workers accepting employment depends on the real wage, w. In equilibrium, only L^0 workers are willing to work at the going real wage, w^0. The remaining $N - L^0$ individuals are voluntarily unemployed.

By choosing not to work, an individual forgoes the wages he would have earned. But economists would say that he must gain at least as much by not working—he can't be worse off, or else he wouldn't have opted for unemployment. What form does this gain take? The simplest answer is the value of increased leisure time—the time made available by not being at work. By leisure we don't simply mean sitting around watching television, but the whole range of activities one engages in when not at work, such as repairing one's house or helping to care for other family members. An individual might save more money performing these activities himself, rather than working at a low-wage job and hiring someone else to perform the services. We call such activities **home production.**

Home production
Goods and services that an individual produces for himself, rather than purchasing them in a market

In Chapter 5, you learned that GDP is not a perfect measure of national output, and the exclusion of leisure is one reason why. Even though GDP falls as the result of voluntary unemployment, the concomitant increase in leisure could well exceed the loss in *measured* GDP. That is, the costs to the worker of voluntary unemployment could well be *negative* with the increased value of leisure exceeding the lost wages. In terms of Figure 11-11, increasing employment from L^0 to N would increase output by the blue area under the demand curve. This is because the demand curve's height measures the marginal product of each additional worker's labor. In effect, the blue area is the sum of the marginal products of each of the $N - L^0$ workers. However, the lost value of these added workers' leisure would equal the area under the supply curve between L^0 and N, because the supply curve measures the value that each of these additional workers places

Figure 11-11 The Cost of Voluntary Unemployment

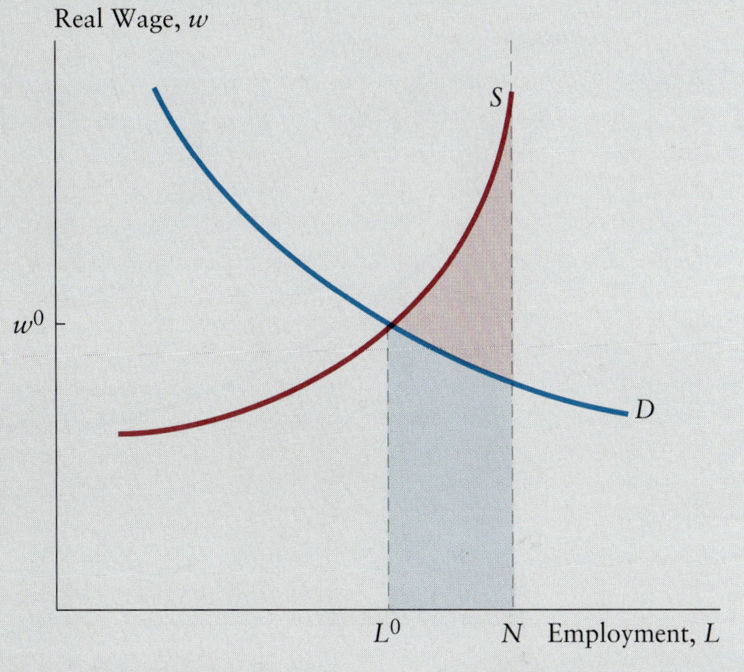

In equilibrium, the level of employment is determined at the intersection of the labor supply and demand curves—at L^0. $N - L^0$ individuals are voluntarily unemployed. Each of these individuals forgoes the wages he could have earned but gains the value of increased leisure time. Increasing employment to N would increase output by the blue area under the demand curve—the sum of the marginal products of each of the $N - L^0$ individuals. However, the lost value of their leisure would equal the area under the labor supply curve between L^0 and N—the sum of the values each worker places on his time. On balance, the lost value of leisure would exceed the increased value of output by the burgundy area.

on her time. On balance, as employment increases from L^0 to N, the lost value of leisure exceeds the increased value of output by the burgundy area in the figure.

Although the costs of voluntary unemployment may be nonexistent or negative, involuntary unemployment presents the other extreme. An involuntarily unemployed person might be willing to work for much less than the going wage and still be unable to find work. Such a person might gain little from being unemployed—it is not an outcome he has chosen. Still, even an involuntarily unemployed worker may place some value on increased leisure time. This situation is shown in Figure 11-12. Here, the labor supply and labor demand curves intersect at a real wage w^0 and a level of employment L^0. However, because the market exhibits a downwardly rigid wage, the real wage is fixed at w^1. As a result,

Figure 11-12 The Cost of Involuntary Unemployment

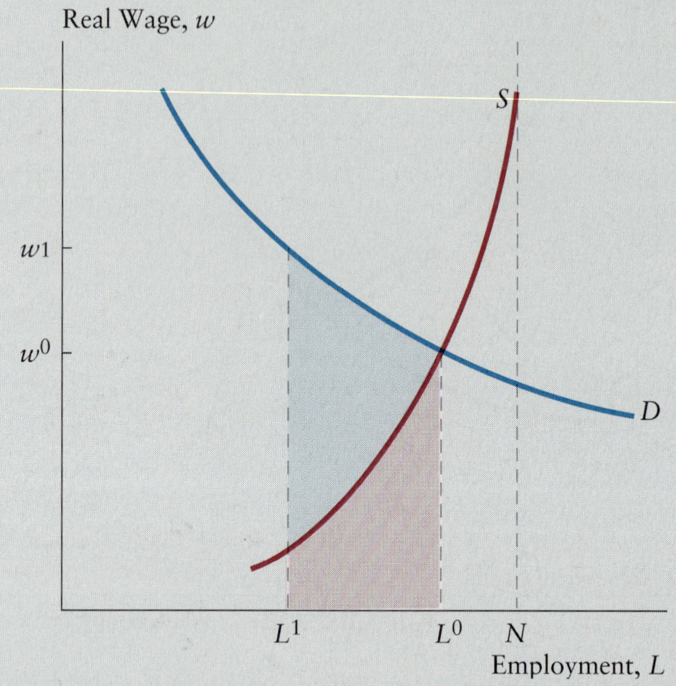

The equilibrium wage rate is w^0 and equilibrium employment is L^0. However, because of downward rigidity, the real wage is fixed at w^1. Involuntary unemployment of $L^0 - L^1$ results. The output loss is the area under the demand curve between L^0 and L^1—the sum of the blue and burgundy areas. The unemployed individuals do place some value on the leisure they gain, equal to the burgundy area under the labor supply curve between L^0 and L^1. The net loss to society equals the blue area, which is less than the value of the lost output.

the market produces involuntary unemployment of $L^0 - L^1$. The output lost as a result equals the value firms would have placed on these workers' production, equal to the area under the demand curve between L^0 and L^1—the sum of the blue and burgundy areas in the figure. However, these unemployed workers do place *some* value on the leisure they gain, equal to the area under the labor supply curve between L^0 and L^1—the burgundy area. Hence, the net loss to society, although positive, equals the blue area—less than the full value of lost output.

Thus, because it fails to account for the increased value of leisure and home production that unemployment permits, the direct loss in measured GDP overstates unemployment's cost to the worker and society, respectively. The magnitude of this overstatement depends on the share of unemployment that is voluntary and the extent to which even involuntarily unemployed workers value the free time that accompanies unemployment.

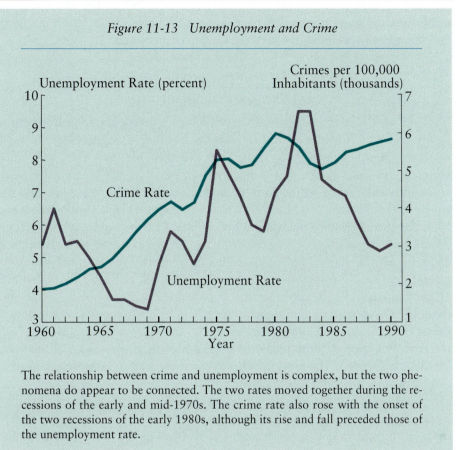

Figure 11-13 Unemployment and Crime

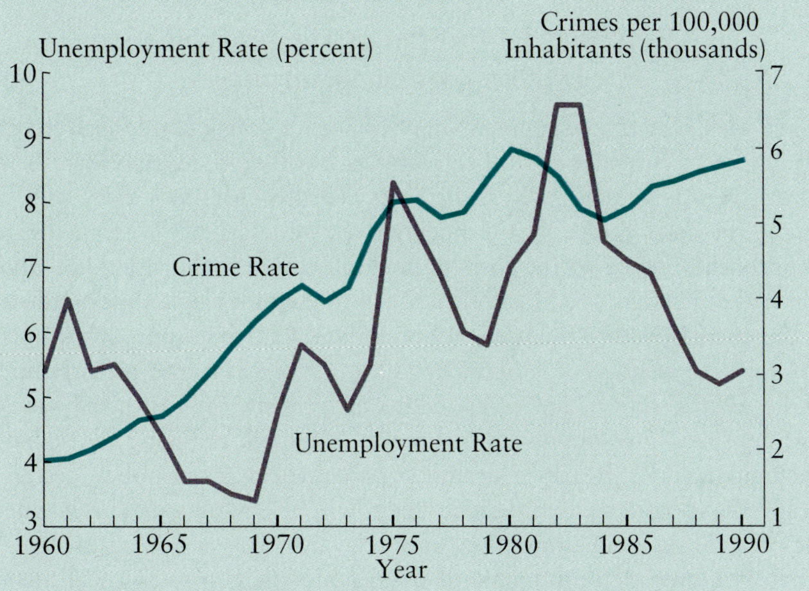

The relationship between crime and unemployment is complex, but the two phenomena do appear to be connected. The two rates moved together during the recessions of the early and mid-1970s. The crime rate also rose with the onset of the two recessions of the early 1980s, although its rise and fall preceded those of the unemployment rate.

Source: *Sourcebook of Criminal Justice Statistics*, 1991

DOES REDUCED OUTPUT UNDERSTATE THE COSTS OF UNEMPLOYMENT?
It is easy to see that individuals might value a short period away from work, but not all unemployment is brief or conveniently timed. For some unemployed workers, enforced, full-time leisure probably has little attraction. Heightened family problems and alcoholism are frequently cited as side effects that detract from the value of this "leisure." Also on the list is crime, committed not only out of despair but also as an alternative means of generating income when the legal labor market fails to deliver. Clearly, the social costs of certain crimes are far greater than the value of the output the criminal might have produced if working legally.

The relationship between crime and unemployment is a complex one. Estimating this relationship empirically is made more difficult by the fact that many crimes go unreported. Still, the two phenomena do appear to be connected. Figure 11-13 plots the U.S. unemployment and crime rates for the period 1960–1990. Although the generally upward movement of the crime rate masks the relationship somewhat, we can see quite clearly that the two rates moved together during the recessions in the early and mid-1970s. The crime rate rose again with the onset of the two recessions of the early 1980s, although its rise and fall actually preceded those of the unemployment rate.

Spreading the Burden of Unemployment: Unemployment Insurance

We have seen that unemployment may impose a considerable cost on the affected worker, a cost that could be greater or less than the wages lost during the worker's unemployment spell. These costs are also costs to society as a whole. How can the costs borne by the unemployed be lessened? We can distinguish two approaches: reducing the costs of unemployment to the individual and society, or, without actually reducing the costs of unemployment, shifting these costs from the unemployed to the general population. The first approach involves reducing the rate of unemployment, by fighting recessions and attempting to reduce the *natural rate* of unemployment that prevails even in good times. The second approach involves social insurance. Although reducing the social costs of unemployment is clearly a desirable objective, realistic policy design must recognize that not all costly unemployment will be eliminated. This is where the "safety net" of social insurance becomes relevant.

There are several components of fiscal policy that provide social insurance for the unemployed. The most important program used to offset the risks of unemployment is *unemployment insurance (UI)*[15]. Unemployment insurance, also called unemployment compensation, does not eliminate the costs of unemployment—it does not address society's loss of output—but it does partially shift the costs of unemployment from unemployed workers to the more general population, who pay the taxes needed to finance the payments to the unemployed.

A worker who becomes unemployed in the U.S. receives benefits based on her prior earnings. The exact rules and benefit levels vary by state, with some federal direction and control. A measure of the generosity of benefits is the *wage replacement rate,* the ratio of weekly benefits to the weekly wages lost by the unemployed workers. In 1991, this rate was about .36, meaning that just over a third of lost wages were replaced by benefits.[16]

Individuals can normally receive benefits for as long as they remain unemployed (i.e., until they find a job or leave the labor force), up to a maximum of 26 weeks. During and after recessions, the 26-week limit is typically extended by federal legislation. For example, in 1992 the unemployed could qualify for as many as 33 additional weeks of unemployment compensation after the initial 26-week period ended. Still, some workers remain unemployed even after 26 (or 59) weeks and exhaust their benefits. Workers who have exhausted their bene-

15. Other components of fiscal policy based on income rather than employment status also provide social insurance to the unemployed. These include programs aimed at low-income individuals and families, such as *food stamps* and *Aid to Families with Dependent Children (AFDC)*. Indirectly, the income tax also provides insurance, because the reduction in income arising from unemployment reduces the affected individual's income tax liability as well.

16. U.S. Committee on Ways and Means, *Overview of Entitlement Programs: 1992 Green Book* (Washington, D.C.: U.S. Government Printing Office, May 15, 1992), Table 23.

fits receive no payments, nor do labor force entrants who did not have a job before their unemployment spell began. Further, there are some specific occupations (such as in agriculture) that are not covered by the unemployment insurance system. Because of benefit exhaustion and lack of coverage or qualification, many unemployed workers do not receive unemployment compensation. In an average week in 1991, for example, 8.4 million U.S. workers were classified as unemployed, but of these only 3.4 million received unemployment insurance benefits.

How successful are unemployment insurance and other social insurance programs in spreading the burden of unemployment more evenly across the population? Although such programs clearly act in the right direction, there still remains a considerable disparity in how different families fare during recession. Because they are more susceptible to elevated unemployment when the general unemployment rate rises, members of lower-income groups have their income fall proportionately more during recessions, even when unemployment compensation and low-income social insurance transfer programs are taken into account.[17]

Case Study: Does Unemployment Insurance Cause Unemployment?

Unemployment insurance spreads the costs of unemployment more evenly across the population, because taxpayers in general pay for the benefits received by the unemployed. However, because the unemployment itself remains, UI does not reduce the costs of unemployment to society as a whole. Indeed, both theory and evidence suggest that unemployment insurance itself may actually *contribute* to causing some of the unemployment it is aimed at cushioning. If unemployment is made less costly to those it directly affects, their incentive to avoid being unemployed is reduced. This reduced incentive may contribute to unemployment in two ways, by making unemployment spells more likely to occur and to last longer, once they occur.

UI may increase the likelihood of unemployment by lessening workers' initial aversion to being employed in highly cyclical industries or in jobs with an elevated prospect of future unemployment. Because they know that the safety net is there, workers may be willing to take greater risks, choosing jobs with higher wages but less certain prospects than they otherwise would. Ultimately, more unemployment will result, in the aggregate.

In addition, UI may increase the duration of unemployment spells by making workers who are already unemployed less willing to accept a new job—more likely to impose higher standards in their job search. The reason is straightforward: they will lose their benefits upon accepting a new job, unless those benefits were about to lapse anyway. Corroborating this theory is a study by Lawrence Katz of Harvard University and Bruce Meyer of Northwestern

17. See Rebecca M. Blank, "Disaggregating the Effect of the Business Cycle on the Distribution of Income," *Economica* (1989): 141–163.

University.[18] Examining the pattern of U.S. unemployment spells, they found that workers receiving unemployment compensation were much more likely to become reemployed around the time of benefit exhaustion, but that no such pattern existed for workers not eligible to receive benefits in the first place. They estimated that a one-week increase in the maximum duration of benefits would increase the average duration of unemployment spells of UI recipients by .16 to .20 week.

THE BENEFITS OF REDUCING UNEMPLOYMENT: OKUN'S LAW AND THE NATURAL RATE

So far, we have emphasized the distinction between the private costs (borne by the worker) and the social costs of unemployment and the distinction between these social costs and a simple measure commonly used to approximate them, the wages and output lost as a direct result of the affected worker's unemployment. However, there are additional factors that make unemployment more costly to society, and reducing it more beneficial, than our previous analysis indicates. First, reductions in unemployment are typically accompanied by other changes in the economy that also lead to increased output. Second, reducing the current rate of unemployment may actually contribute to a subsequent reduction in the natural rate of unemployment, helping to make lower unemployment more sustainable. We will consider each of these factors in turn.

Okun's Law

As we discussed above, when a worker is unemployed, measured output is reduced by the amount the worker would have produced. In a competitive economy, this lost output equals the worker's labor income. If employment goes down by, say, 1 percent, we should expect labor income also to decline by about 1 percent. If labor income declines by 1 percent, total income, GDP, should decline by a smaller percentage, since only one component of income—labor income, but not capital income—is declining. In terms of the Cobb-Douglas production function, labor's share of gross output is $(1 - \beta)$—about .70 of GDP in the U.S. If labor income—about 70 percent of all GDP—declines by 1 percent, overall GDP should decline by about .7 percent.

We may also express this relationship of output to employment in terms of the unemployment rate, since a 1 percent decrease in employment is roughly equivalent to a 1 percentage point increase in the unemployment rate. That is, if the rate of unemployment goes up by 1 percentage point from, say, 5 percent to 6 percent, this represents a decrease in employment from 95 percent to 94 percent of the labor force—roughly a 1 percent reduction in employment. Hence, we should expect an increase in the unemployment rate of 1 percentage point to reduce output by about .7 percent.

18. Lawrence F. Katz and Bruce D. Meyer, "The Impact of the Potential Duration of Unemployment Benefits on the Duration of Unemployment," *Journal of Public Economics* 41 (April 1990): 45–72.

Figure 11-14 GDP *Growth and the Unemployment Rate, 1960–1992*

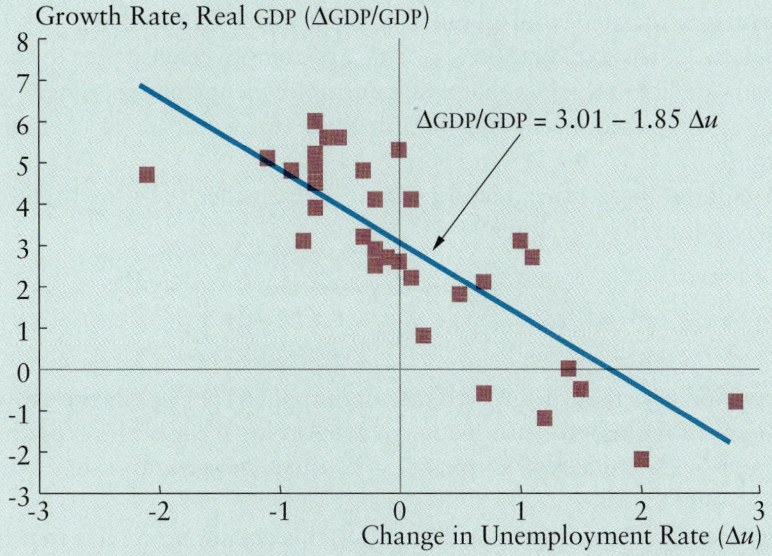

Between 1960 and 1992, there was a negative relationship between annual changes in the GDP growth rate and annual changes in the unemployment rate. Each percentage point increase in the unemployment rate was associated with a 1.85 percentage point decline in the growth rate of real GDP.

Source: *Economic Report of the President,* 1993

How does this conclusion square with the facts? Not very well. Figure 11-14 plots annual changes in the rate of unemployment against the annual rate of GDP growth in the U.S. for each year during the period 1960–1992. As we would anticipate, there is a negative relationship between the two series, with increases in unemployment being associated with lower growth in GDP. However, compared to our theoretical predictions, the implied effect of unemployment on growth is too powerful. Although each percentage point increase in the unemployment rate should be associated with about .7 percent lower GDP growth, the relationship that best fits the data, represented by the straight line in Figure 11-4,[19] indicates a decline in GDP growth nearly *three times* as large: each percentage point increase in the unemployment rate is associated with a nearly 2 percent (almost 3 times .7) decline in the growth of output.

19. This line is derived from the data in the figure using a common technique called *ordinary least squares regression,* which chooses the straight line that minimizes the sum of squared vertical differences between the line and each observation.

This important observation, that output is much more sensitive to the unemployment rate than basic theory would suggest, was first formalized by Arthur Okun, head of the President's Council of Economic Advisers during the late 1960s. The empirical relationship that each percentage point of reduced unemployment is associated with about 2 percent faster GDP growth is known as **Okun's Law.**[20] The explanation for GDP's apparent oversensitivity to the unemployment rate lies in the fact that when unemployment changes, other economic changes also typically occur that reinforce the direct impact of unemployment on output.

Okun's Law
An empirical relationship between reductions in the unemployment rate and increases in the GPD growth rate

To see how these other factors enter, let's consider the growth accounting framework derived in Chapter 1:

$$\frac{\Delta Y}{Y} = \frac{\Delta A}{A} + \beta\frac{\Delta K}{K} + (1 - \beta)\frac{\Delta L}{L}$$

This equation says that the growth rate of output ($\Delta Y/Y$) equals the growth rate of the level of multifactor productivity ($\Delta A/A$) plus β times the growth rate of the capital stock input ($\Delta K/K$) plus (1 – β) times the growth rate of the labor input ($\Delta L/L$).

Consistent with our previous discussion, this equation predicts that for each 1 percent increase in the growth rate of labor input, output will grow by (1 – β) percent more. But we can also see from this relationship that two other factors, capital stock growth and technological progress, also affect the growth rate of output. As we documented in Chapter 1, productivity growth, $\Delta A/A$, also tends to be procyclical. In Chapter 4 we noted that this phenomenon might be attributed to **labor hoarding** during recessions—firms' maintaining excess labor to avoid the hiring and retraining costs associated with new employees. With more labor than necessary to produce the level of output actually produced, the measured level of productivity, based on a comparison of outputs and inputs, falls. Thus, when employment grows rapidly, labor hoarding is reduced and the measured level of technology tends to grow, too, reinforcing the impact of the growth of labor input on the growth of output.

Labor hoarding
A situation in which a firm maintains excess labor in order to avoid hiring and retraining costs

The procyclicality of multifactor productivity helps explain Okun's Law, but it is important to recognize that factors other than a decline in the unemployment rate can increase labor input. Let's consider the ways in which labor input may grow.

Although we have not always emphasized the distinction between labor input and employment, an accurate measure of labor input, L, takes account not only of the number of workers employed, say E, but also of the number of

20. The expression for Okun's Law is $(\text{GDP}_t - \text{GDP}_{t-1})/\text{GDP}_{t-1} = a - b(u_t - u_{t-1})$, where GDP_t is real GDP in year t and u_t is the corresponding unemployment rate. In Figure 11-14, a is estimated to be 3.01 and b is 1.85, indicating that real GDP would grow by about 3 percent annually with no change in the unemployment rate. (Put another way, a real GDP growth rate of more than 3 percent would be required for the unemployment rate to decline.) Actually, when Okun first introduced his "law," the coefficient b was closer to 3 than 2. Nevertheless, his original reasoning concerning why the coefficient exceeds its theoretically predicted value still applies.

Okun's Law is sometimes expressed in a slightly different way, as a relationship between two gaps: the percentage gap between GDP_t and a hypothetical construct known as *potential* GDP and the gap between the unemployment rate u_t and the natural rate of unemployment. The distinction between this and the form used here is not empirically significant.

hours each worker is employed, say H. The resulting measure is the number of worker-hours, $L = E \times H$. Using the definition of the unemployment rate as the fraction of the labor force, LF, that is *not* employed, we may write this expression for the labor input as

$$L = H \times \text{LF} \times (1 - u)$$

which, in terms of growth rates, may approximately be expressed as[21]

$$\frac{\Delta L}{L} = \frac{\Delta H}{H} + \frac{\Delta \text{LF}}{\text{LF}} - \Delta u$$

where $\Delta L/L$, $\Delta H/H$, and $\Delta\text{LF}/\text{LF}$ are the growth rates of the labor input, hours per worker, and the labor force, and Δu is the change in the unemployment rate from the previous period, $\Delta u_t = u_t - u_{t-1}$. This expression says that, holding the growth rates of the labor force and hours per worker fixed, a 1 percentage point decrease in the unemployment rate will increase the growth rate of labor input by 1 percent. This was what our initial calculation assumed. However, as the unemployment rate falls, the other terms on the right-hand side of this expression typically rise.

We saw in Chapter 4 that hours per worker are procyclical, increasing during expansions and decreasing during recessions. This may be viewed as another manifestation of labor hoarding, with firms choosing to spread the lower work load during recessions more thinly among existing workers instead of reducing the level of employment. In the present chapter, we have learned that labor force participation itself is also procyclical, that the labor force participation rate rises as the unemployment rate falls. This relationship between nonparticipation and unemployment highlights the lack of a clear distinction between these two labor force states for some workers. For example, individuals who see that the unemployment rate is high may simply not look for a job or may give up looking; they are said to be **discouraged workers**. When the unemployment rate falls, some of these workers typically reenter the labor force.

Discouraged workers *Individuals who have dropped out of the labor force because of lack of success in finding jobs*

With both the labor force and hours per worker tending to increase as the unemployment rate declines, a 1 percentage point decline in the unemployment rate is normally associated with a growth rate of labor input in excess of 1 percent, leading to an increase in output growth of more than $(1 - \beta)$ percent. Adding to this the increase in productivity growth that also normally occurs yields the output increase of between 2 and 3 percent predicted by Okun's Law.

What does Okun's Law imply about the social benefits of reducing unemployment? It suggests they are larger than would be implied simply by looking at the change in the unemployment rate, because there are many types of **disguised unemployment** that also decrease when the measured unemployment rate declines. This disguised unemployment occurs in the form of underemployment

Disguised unemployment *Unmeasured unemployment that takes the form of underemployment or reduced participation in the labor force*

21. We use two approximations here. First (as in Chapter 1), we assume that the growth rate of any product $a \times b$ equals the growth rate of a plus the growth rate of b; second, we assume that the growth rate of $(1 - u_t)$, equal to $[(1 - u_t) - (1 - u_{t-1})]/(1 - u_{t-1})$, is close to $\Delta u_t = u_t - u_{t-1}$ when u_{t-1} is small compared to 1.

of employed workers (having them work fewer hours or do less productive work) and understatement of the true number of individuals who are unemployed (through reduced labor force participation).

Determining the Natural Rate of Unemployment

Despite the potential benefits of reduced unemployment, policies aimed at lowering the unemployment rate face a barrier in the form of the natural rate of unemployment. In this and the previous chapter, we have developed different explanations of why the unemployment rate stays well above zero, even in booms. Countercyclical monetary and fiscal policy *may* succeed in hastening recovery from recessions, but what of the considerable unemployment that remains? Is there a role for policy in determining the natural rate of unemployment itself, or is fighting unemployment primarily an activity for recessionary times? To address these questions, we must know more about the natural rate itself and its historical behavior.

There is, of course, no exact measure of "the" natural rate of unemployment. Unlike the actual unemployment rate, the natural rate is a theoretical construct—the lowest rate of unemployment that the economy can sustain indefinitely, at a stable rate of inflation. However, if we assume that the economy rarely reduces the level of unemployment below its natural rate, we can estimate the natural rate by looking at the rate of unemployment at the height of expansions. Doing so suggests that the natural rate of unemployment in the U.S. may have increased over time, at least until the late 1980s. As Figure 11-1 showed, the unemployment rate fell as low as 2.5 percent in the 1950s. For several months in the late 1960s, the rate dipped to 3.4 percent. By the early 1970s, economists viewed 4 percent as a reasonable estimate of the natural rate of unemployment, suggesting that the rates below 4 percent during the late 60s were not sustainable without the increasing inflation. But the unemployment rate has exceeded 4 percent since then, and indeed, has exceeded 5 percent since December 1973. Economists now generally place the natural rate somewhere between 5.5 and 6 percent.

If, as it appears, the natural rate of unemployment has risen, then what is the reason? There are several potential answers. Some have argued the importance of demographic shifts, with traditionally high unemployment groups achieving greater representation in the labor force. However, the most significant demographic shift, the increased participation of women, can no longer explain a higher natural rate, given the evidence in Figure 11-8 regarding the similarity of men's and women's unemployment rates since 1980. More general calculations of the increase in the natural rate attributable to demographics have found no appreciable effect. Other explanations involve a general increase in frictional unemployment due to sectoral shifts and an increase in voluntary unemployment due to the stagnant real wages of the 70s and 80s that were documented in Chapter 1's discussion of the productivity slowdown. Each of these explanations finds some support in the data. Neither suggests an obvious role for expansionary monetary or fiscal policy in reducing the natural rate of unemployment.

However, there are other explanations of the natural rate's evolution that provide a clearer role for policy. For example, the insider-outsider theory of involuntary unemployment discussed above posits that real wage rigidities are imposed by "insiders" at the highest levels consistent with the maintenance of their own employment. The population of involuntarily unemployed "outsiders" help account for the natural rate of unemployment, but government might be able to change the size of this population. A policy of increasing aggregate demand (shifting LM to the right or IS upward), thereby increasing the price level, might force down the real wage. The fall in the real wage would induce firms to hire some of the outsiders. After a period of employment, such workers might attain the status of insiders and help keep the real wage down to ensure their own continued employment. This reasoning suggests that the natural rate of unemployment in part may be determined by the *actual* level of unemployment, i.e., that any particular level of unemployment may itself be self-sustaining—an outcome called **hysteresis.**[22]

Hysteresis *Changes in the natural rate of unemployment in response to changes in the actual unemployment rate*

There are other reasons why the natural rate might be affected by policy. For example, there is some evidence that early employment experience affects the future employability of teenagers. Without sufficient work experience when young, they may fail to gain the skills needed for successful job performance and experience unemployment more frequently when older.[23] Hence, if individuals come of age during a period of very low unemployment, when they are more likely to be employed, they will also experience less unemployment in the future, causing the future natural rate to be lower. In addition, increased employment today, by increasing investment by the young (as discussed in Chapter 9), increases the capital stock in future periods. More capital means a higher capital-labor ratio and higher real wages, which would likely reduce the voluntary component of the natural rate.

If the natural rate of unemployment itself can be affected by general economic conditions and the actual unemployment rates that prevail, then policies to reduce the measured unemployment rate take on added value. Beyond reducing the temporary gap between the actual unemployment rate and the natural rate, they might contribute to a more permanent lowering of unemployment through a reduction in the natural rate.

Case Study: Unemployment in the U.S. and the U.K

We may summarize the previous discussion by saying that there are two reasons why the unemployment rate changes over time: cyclical movements around the natural rate of unemployment and changes in the natural rate of unemployment itself. The policy question with which we have been struggling is whether changes in the natural rate depend on cyclical unemployment swings or are independent of them. If the natural rate moves independently, it may also be less

22. See Olivier J. Blanchard and Lawrence H. Summers, "Hysteresis and the European Unemployment Problem," in NBER *Macroeconomics Annual 1986,* ed. Stanley Fischer (Cambridge, MA: MIT Press, 1986), 15–78.

23. See, for example, David Ellwood, "Teenage Unemployment: Permanent Scars or Temporary Blemishes?" in *The Youth Labor Market Problem: Its Nature, Causes and Consequences,* eds. Richard Freeman and David Wise (Chicago: University of Chicago Press, 1982).

easily influenced by government policy. But the importance of this question depends on the extent to which observed swings in unemployment are accounted for by shifts in the natural rate.

Since the natural rate is never observed, we cannot know for sure how much it moves from year to year. Marking the unemployment rate at successive business cycle peaks is helpful, but in some expansions the economy may never quite attain the natural rate. And what about the periods of high unemployment between expansion peaks? Are these entirely cyclical, or do they partially reflect shifts in the natural rate, which may be of a more permanent nature?

Distinguishing between cyclical swings in unemployment around the natural rate and movement of the natural rate itself is not easy. Indeed, we have encountered this problem before, in a related context. In Chapter 4, we compared two theories, that fluctuations in real GDP are largely cyclical and that GDP fluctuations are really driven by more permanent shifts that may sometimes appear to be cyclical. We concluded there that observed output fluctuations may be consistent with either theory. The same argument applies to unemployment rate movements that accompany changes in GDP. An illustration of this ambiguity is provided by Figure 11-15, which compares the unemployment rates of the United States and the United Kingdom.

As the figure shows, the U.K. has seen its unemployment rate rise even more rapidly than that of the U.S. during the past two decades. Until 1974, the U.K unemployment rate hovered in the range of 2 percent. After rising to 5 percent in the late 1970s, the U.K. unemployment rate jumped to the neighborhood of 12 percent in the 1980s and stayed well above the U.S. unemployment rate for a period of several years. It was during this period that many economists concluded that the natural rate of unemployment in the U.K. (and Europe more generally) had risen, and sought to explain why. However, by 1990, the U.K. unemployment rate had fallen sharply, back roughly to the level of the U.S. Did the 1980s witness an increase in the U.K. natural rate of unemployment or simply a very serious and prolonged recession? This remains an open question.

SUMMING UP: UNEMPLOYMENT AND WHAT TO DO ABOUT IT

Now that we have considered the theories of unemployment and the evidence regarding each theory, let's bring together what we've learned and restate the policy implications. Table 11-1 presents a brief summary of the major theories we've discussed in this chapter. In each case, the table notes the explanation for unemployment, evidence that supports the theory, the social costs of unemployment, and the appropriate policy responses. The middle column of the table relates to cyclical unemployment—the rise in unemployment during recession. The third column relates to the unemployment experienced even during periods of economic expansion.

As the table indicates, the only clear case for monetary and fiscal policy intervention occurs when unemployment is involuntary. Even in this case, though,

Figure 11-15 Unemployment in the United States and the United Kingdom

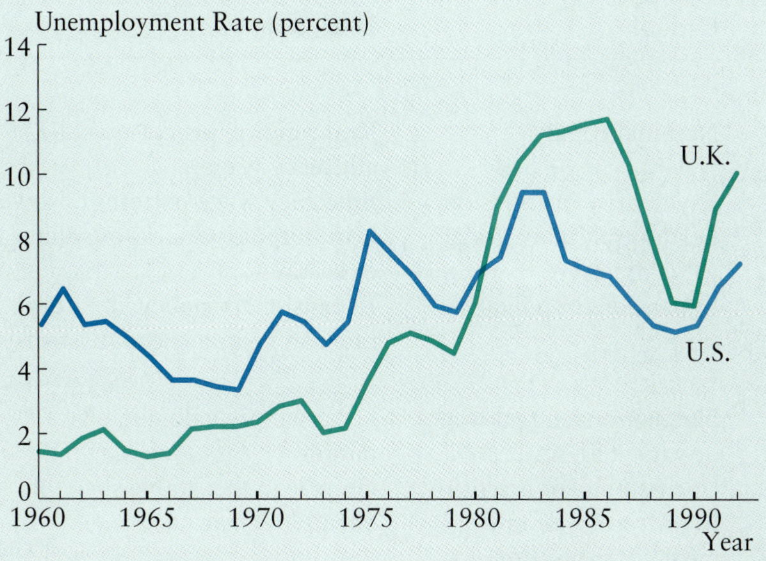

Distinguishing between cyclical swings in the unemployment rate around the natural rate and the movement of the natural rate itself is not easy. In the past several decades, the unemployment rate in the U.K. has risen even more rapidly than the U.S. rate. However, by 1990, the U.K. had fallen back to rough equality with the U.S. rate. Did the 1980s witness an increase in the U.K. natural rate or simply a very serious and prolonged recession there?

Source: OECD *Economic Outlook,* June 1993

there are further issues to consider before taking action. We discuss these issues in the next chapter.

Chapter Summary

1. The U.S. labor market is very dynamic, with sizable *gross flows* among the three labor market states—*employed*, *unemployed*, and *not in the labor force*—determining the status of individuals. The *unemployment rate*—the fraction of the labor force that is unemployed—follows the business cycle very closely and typically ranges between 5 and 10 percent.

2. Unemployment may arise for many initial reasons, including job loss (*lay-offs*), leaving a job (*quits*), and entry into the labor force without a job (*entrants*). It may be of either long or short *duration*—in the late 1980s, one-fifth of all unemployment occurred in spells of less than three months (13 weeks), but nearly half occurred in spells of at least six months.

Table 11-1 Theories of Unemployment: Causes, Evidence, Costs, and Policy Responses

Type of Unemployment	Cyclical	Long-Term
Involuntary		
Cause	Nominal Rigidity	Real rigidity (insider-outsider, efficiency wage)
Evidence	Layoffs rise in recession	Efficiency wage patterns observed
Costs	Lost output in excess of value of leisure	Lost output in excess of value of leisure
Policy	Expansionary policy	Expansionary policy, if natural rate can be influenced (hysteresis)
Voluntary		
Cause	Fluctuations in real wages or value of leisure	Leisure more valuable than output
Evidence	Unemployment is sensitive to the receipt of unemployment compensation	Quits lead to a stable share of unemployment
Costs	None (negative, since being unemployed is a voluntary decision)	None (negative, since being unemployed is a voluntary decision)
Policy	None	None
Frictional		
Cause	Sectoral shifts	Job search and labor turnover
Evidence	Unemployment rate higher during periods of greater industrial transition	Much unemployment comes in short spells
Costs	None (part of normal labor market process)	None (part of normal labor market process)
Policy	None	None

3. Unemployment may be described as *voluntary*, *involuntary*, or *frictional*, although it is difficult to determine the precise importance of each of these causes in explaining either the *natural rate of unemployment*—the economy's lowest sustainable rate of unemployment—or the rise in unemployment that occurs during recessions. Although frictional unemployment might be thought of as a constant factor in labor market dynamics, increased *sectoral shifts* appear to help explain the rise in unemployment observed in some recessions. Conversely, involuntary unemployment, often thought of as primarily a feature of recession, may be present even in better times if labor market imperfections take the form of *real wage rigidities*, as predicted by the *insider-outsider* and *efficiency wage* theories.

4. The nature of unemployment also differs between booms and recessions. The rate of unemployment attributable to quits generally accounts for about 1 percentage point of unemployment in good times and bad, and labor force entry accounts for perhaps another 2 percentage points, but the bulk of the cyclical variation in unemployment comes from layoffs. Although they account for as little as 2 percentage points of unemployment in booms, layoffs lead to as much as 6 percentage points of unemployment during recessions. Unemployment duration varies over the business cycle, too, with the share of unemployment accounted for by long spells closely following the rate of unemployment.

5. Another dimension of the heterogeneity of unemployment is the varied experience of different demographic groups. Although women no longer typically experience higher unemployment rates than men, reflecting the growing similarity of men's and women's roles in the labor force, teens and nonwhites still are much more likely than others to be unemployed and to suffer from additional unemployment in recessions. Although these elevated and volatile unemployment rates may be explained in part by differences in job skills and industries, such explanations do not lessen the seriousness of the unemployment problem.

6. The burden of unemployment may be measured in two ways: the *social* burden, the loss to society as a whole, and the *private* burden, the loss to the unemployed worker herself. Lost output and wages may represent only an initial estimate of the respective burdens. Some factors (such as increased leisure) reduce both social and private costs; other factors (such as increased crime) increase them. Government policy to reduce the unemployment rate seeks to reduce both private and social costs; social insurance seeks to spread the social costs of unemployment more evenly across the population, away from the unemployed. The major social insurance program aimed at unemployment, *unemployment insurance,* does help cushion the shock of unemployment but may also encourage the unemployed to remain so.

7. Programs to reduce the social costs of unemployment depend on lowering the rate of unemployment. *Okun's Law* indicates the output gains associated with reductions in the unemployment rate. Such gains may be quite large, because reductions in the unemployment rate are accompanied by increased hours per worker, labor force participation, and productivity—all signs that as measured unemployment declines, so does *disguised unemployment.* Some view reducing unemployment as a problem of recessionary times, but it may also be possible to reduce the *natural rate of unemployment* itself. Some theories of *hysteresis* view the natural rate of unemployment as being determined in part by actual rates of unemployment, but because the natural rate itself cannot be observed, such theories are hard to confirm.

Key Concepts

New hires
Rehires
Layoffs
Quits
Insider-outsider theory
Efficiency wage theory
Home production
Okun's Law
Labor hoarding
Discouraged workers
Disguised unemployment
Hysteresis

Review Questions

1. What is meant by *labor force dynamics,* and what are the three labor market states a person can be in?
2. What is the *labor force participation rate*? What is a *discouraged worker,* and in what way does the existence of discouraged workers explain the cyclical pattern of the labor force participation rate?
3. What terms describe *transitions* into employment and transitions out of employment? Identify the two categories into which each of these types of transitions can be divided.
4. In general terms, what are *gross flows* and *net flows*? Explain the labor force dynamics that are operating when net flows to employment are negative.
5. Explain the following statement: "The net flows indicate the direction of movement of the economy as a whole, whereas the gross flows indicate how much mobility there is in the labor force."
6. "Small business is the 'engine' of job creation." Use your knowledge of both net and gross flows to comment on the validity of this statement.
7. What are the three initial reasons for unemployment? Which is the major source of the volatility of unemployment? Which of the reasons is most consistent with the Keynesian view?
8. How is the *duration* of unemployment typically measured, and how does the duration of unemployment change during recessions? How is *long-term* unemployment generally defined?
9. What is *insider-outsider theory,* and how does it contribute to an explanation of unemployment?
10. What is *efficiency wage theory,* and how does it contribute to an explanation of unemployment?
11. What type of employment separation is consistent with the notion of *voluntary unemployment* and how does this vary over recessions and booms?
12. What is the nature of *frictional unemployment,* and what happens to frictional unemployment during recessions? What would the sectoral shift model predict about the variation of frictional employment during recessions? Why?
13. Since 1950, what has happened to the labor force participation rates of women and men? How have their relative unemployment rates changed over the same period of time? What demographic groups have experienced both higher levels and more volatile swings in unemployment?
14. What are the *private costs* and the *social costs* of unemployment? In what ways does reduced output overstate and understate the costs of unemployment? Why is the cost of voluntary unemployment said to be zero or negative?
15. What mechanism is used to spread the burden of unemployment? Does this mechanism eliminate the costs of unemployment?
16. What is *Okun's Law*? What insights about the nature of this relationship are gained by using the growth accounting framework?
17. What is the *natural rate of unemployment* and, approximately, what is its current value? What has happened to its estimated value over time? Why?
18. What is meant by *hysteresis*? What implications does this theory have for policy?

Numerical Questions

1. Answer parts a through d using the information in the table below.

Year	New Hires	Layoffs	Quits	Rehires	Net Entrants to Labor Force
1	100	80	12	8	20
2	95	85	11	6	25
3	90	90	9	3	30
4	98	85	10	5	35

   a. Calculate the gross accessions in each of the four years.
   b. Calculate the gross separations in each of the four years.
   c. Calculate the change in employment in each of the four years.
   d. Calculate the change in unemployment in each of the four years.

2. Suppose that there are 50 people in the labor force and that 13 people experience a spell of unemployment during a particular year. Twelve of the 13 without jobs are unemployed for only one month during the year, but each is unemployed in a different month—the first in January, the second in February, etc. The thirteenth jobless person is unemployed for all 12 months of the year. Finally, suppose that the government measures unemployment monthly.
   a. What is the unemployment rate in each month during the year?
   b. What fraction of unemployment in a given month is made up of short-term unemployment? of long-term unemployment? Compare your answers to the proportion of people unemployed for one month versus one year during the year as a whole. Explain any difference.
   c. Suppose that the people who experience unemployment during the year are cloned, so that there are now two of each for a total of 26. What effect does the increase in the number of unemployed people have on the unemployment rate in each month?
   d. Suppose that the initial situation once again holds. Now assume that each person who was unemployed for one month instead is unemployed for two months at a time—the first person in December and January, the second in January and February, etc. What effect does the increased duration of unemployment have on the unemployment rate each month?

3. Using Okun's Law, as illustrated in Figure 11-14, complete the following table.

Change in Unemployment Rate	Percentage Change in Real GDP
.05	
−.02	
−.01	
.03	

Analytical Questions

1. According to the "shirking" model of the efficiency wage theory, employers pay a wage above the market-clearing level as a deterrent to shirking.
   - **a.** Does the possibility of losing an above-market wage itself actually lead workers to shirk less?
   - **b.** Can you think of other financial incentives that employers might use to reduce shirking that would not push wages above the market-clearing level and, hence, would not cause involuntary unemployment?
2. Empirical evidence discussed in the chapter suggests that the unemployment insurance program actually leads to more unemployment. Is the additional unemployment necessarily bad? Is there a sense in which any resulting unemployment might actually help the economy over the long run?
3. How would the following events affect Okun's Law?
   - **a.** A decrease in productivity growth
   - **b.** Faster growth of the labor force
   - **c.** A greater tendency of workers to leave the labor force during recessions and reenter during expansions
   - **d.** Hours per worker cease to be procyclical
   - **e.** A rise in β in the Cobb-Douglas production function

C H A P T E R 1 2

Countercyclical Policy

INTRODUCTION

As you've learned, the *costs* of recession and our ability to influence them depend on the *causes* of recession. According to the real business cycle theory, recessions result from productivity disturbances and are accompanied by a rise in voluntary unemployment, the social costs of which are minimal. Under the sectoral shift hypothesis, recessions reflect shifts of demand among industries that increase frictional unemployment. Such unemployment imposes costs on the workers who experience it, costs that can be shared by the general population through unemployment compensation and other forms of social insurance. But there are no clear *macroeconomic* policy responses to lessen these costs in the aggregate. Like productivity disturbances, sectoral shifts reflect changes in economic conditions, rather than market failures.

In fact, it is the nominal rigidities posited by Keynesian theory, and the associated involuntary unemployment, that provide the clearest argument for macroeconomic intervention. Because any particular recession may partly reflect Keynesian factors, intervention may be warranted even if the rise in unemployment is partly voluntary or frictional.

This chapter is about the practice, effects, and problems of such macroeconomic intervention, also called *stabilization policy.* Although Chapter 9 provided a simple theory of stabilization policy, we'll see here that translating theory into practice offers many challenges. First, the social gains from reducing unemployment must be weighed against the costs of extra inflation that may be induced by particular countercyclical policies. Second, policy makers must correctly assess what causes recession in order to choose the correct policy response. Third, even if policy makers choose the right policy, they may introduce it at the wrong time.

This chapter presents several case studies to show how macroeconomic policy actually works. These examples raise doubts about the efficacy of using monetary and fiscal policy to stabilize the economy. They also raise the possibility that forgoing attempts at stabilization by adopting policy rules may be superior to using discretion in the choice of policy.

Here is a sample of the questions we'll address:

- How do the costs of inflation compare to the costs of unemployment?
- What are the difficulties in measuring the fundamental nature—the stance—of monetary or fiscal policy?
- Has active monetary and fiscal policy stabilized the U.S. economy?
- How long are the lags in implementing monetary and fiscal policy, and why do they arise?
- How can a lack of credibility compromise the effectiveness of government policy? What is dynamic inconsistency?
- How does uncertainty about the economy influence the proper use of monetary or fiscal policy?
- What are incomes policies, and how can they augment, or substitute for, monetary and fiscal policy?

There are three basic parts to this chapter. To provide a sense of the potential gains from using monetary and fiscal policy to fight recession, we'll begin by comparing the costs of inflation and unemployment. Next, we'll consider the origins of activist monetary and fiscal policy during the major economic event of this century: the Great Depression of the 1930s. Then, we'll consider how policy has evolved since the Depression and the lessons that have been learned from the postwar struggles with inflation, oil shocks, and the shifting Phillips curve. The chapter concludes with an overall assessment of the success of policy in improving macroeconomic performance during the postwar period.

ASSESSING THE COSTS AND BENEFITS OF INTERVENTION

The Keynesian model of nominal rigidities tells us that the economy's output may lie below its full-employment level and that a monetary or fiscal stimulus can alleviate the problem. When the nominal rigidity takes the form of rigid nominal wages, growth in output will be accompanied by a more rapid rise in prices than would otherwise have occurred. This positive association between output and inflation translates into a negative association between unemployment and inflation—the Phillips curve relationship introduced in Chapter 10. The association between the two suggests that we must weigh the benefits of reduced unemployment against the costs of increased inflation.

But the real trade-off between output and inflation is not clear, because the Phillips curve has not been stable over time. In the Friedman-Phelps analysis, the economy ultimately returns to a natural rate of unemployment, which suggests only a temporary trade-off of higher inflation for lower unemployment. Eventually nominal wages will catch up with the faster growth of prices, driving real wages back up and eliminating any policy-induced gains in employment. In other words, temporary reductions in unemployment come at the expense of permanently higher inflation. The misperceptions theory is even more discouraging, arguing that reductions in unemployment will be temporary and can arise only if the inflation results from unpredictable policy actions. On the other hand, some more recent Keynesian theories—such as the insider-outsider theory—suggest that the natural rate of unemployment can itself be influenced by policy. If this is so, the trade-off between inflation and unemployment may be permanent, with higher inflation in the short run reducing the natural rate of unemployment that the economy sustains in the longer run.

Thus, different theories predict different trade-offs between policy-induced inflation and unemployment. A sustained increase in the inflation rate may bring about a permanent reduction in the unemployment rate, a temporary one, or none at all, depending on which model best fits the facts. Clearly, a policy that increases the inflation rate is easier to justify in the first case than in the last, but policy makers are often hard-pressed to distinguish among the cases because of confusing evidence and, alas, conflicting assessments by economists.

The Costs of Inflation

What are the costs of higher inflation? To begin, it's important to distinguish between *anticipated* and *unanticipated* inflation. When the inflation rate is higher than anticipated, significant sums can be redistributed from creditors to debtors, including the government.[1] This occurs because the observed real interest rate equals the nominal interest rate less the actual inflation rate. As you've learned, when the inflation rate is higher than expected, the nominal interest rate agreed to in advance ends up being too low to deliver the real interest rate initially anticipated. Hence, lenders may receive a low or even negative real return. The same logic applies to other nominal contracts, such as private pensions, that are not indexed to the price level. A sudden burst of inflation drives the real value of such pensions below what was anticipated, making recipients worse off and pension providers better off.

Although these redistributions caused by unanticipated inflation are significant, they do not represent net costs to society as a whole, because the winners' gains roughly balance the losers' losses. Moreover, in the long run, a steady

1. When the inflation rate is lower than anticipated, the transfers go in the opposite direction. As Table 8-3 revealed, significant over- and underpredictions are common.

inflation rate will become the anticipated rate. Hence, when we consider the costs of a permanent increase in the rate of inflation, we should be concerned primarily with the costs of anticipated inflation.

The Costs of Anticipated Inflation

As we discussed in Chapter 8, the government raises revenue—called seigniorage—by printing money. The effect is the same as if a tax were collected directly from households and institutions; their available resources are reduced because the associated increase in prices reduces the real value of their money holdings. Thus, seigniorage is often referred to as the "inflation tax."

Given the moderate rates of U.S. inflation in recent years, seigniorage has been very modest—only 1 to 2 percent of the U.S. federal budget. Moreover, the cost of seigniorage to society as a whole is much smaller than the total seigniorage collected. Why? Because the government uses its seigniorage to benefit society by purchasing goods and services, making transfer payments, or reducing other taxes. Economists argue that the net social costs of seigniorage arise only from the distortions associated with its accompanying inflation. *Shoeleather costs* are one example: In holding less money at any given time to avoid the inflation tax, households and firms must visit their banks more often (and wear out their shoes) to obtain the funds needed to conduct transactions. Menu costs are another example: As prices rise more rapidly, restaurants and other businesses must change their menus and price lists more often.

How costly are these distortions? Typically, the distortions associated with collecting taxes, which economists call the *excess burden* of taxation, produce social losses equivalent to a small fraction of the tax revenue. But even if the excess burden from seigniorage is as big as the additional seigniorage itself, that is not very big. At the end of 1993, the U.S. monetary base was about $400 billion. An extra 1 percent tax on this base, associated with a 1 percentage point increase in the inflation rate, would produce $4 billion of revenue annually—about 1⁄16 percent of GDP. It is doubtful that the associated excess burden would be any higher than this amount.[2]

Whatever the precise excess burden from seigniorage, the potential loss of perhaps a few billion dollars a year from an extra percentage point of inflation seems very small compared to the associated gains from reducing unemployment. According to Okun's Law, GDP will be roughly 2.5 percent larger—about $160 billion—for each percentage point reduction in the unemployment rate. Based on the short-run Phillips curves presented in Chapter 10, a 1 percentage point increase in the inflation rate produces—at least temporarily—about a ½ percentage point drop in the unemployment rate, which translates into an output gain of about $80 billion.

---

2. Indeed, since virtually all taxes produce excess burdens, the net excess burden of additional seigniorage may actually be negative. The reason is that printing money to pay the government's bills permits reduction of other taxes and the excess burden from collecting them. As a consequence, some seigniorage may actually be beneficial. See Edmund S. Phelps, "Inflation in the Theory of Public Finance," *Swedish Journal of Economics* 75(1973): 67–82, and N. Gregory Mankiw, "The Optimal Collection of Seigniorage," *Journal of Monetary Economics* 20 (September 1987): 327–341.

What Is the Right Comparison?

The benefits of trading off higher inflation for lower unemployment may seem compelling, but there are several complicating factors. The gains from reducing unemployment may be overstated and the costs of inflation understated. In addition, the gains may be temporary and the costs permanent.

As we discussed in Chapter 11, the social loss from unemployment will be overstated by the associated reduction in measured GDP when unemployment is voluntary and, potentially, even when it is involuntary. This is because GDP fails to account for home production and leisure, which are reduced when market employment increases. Also, there may be costs of increased inflation that exceed small shoeleather and menu costs. There is some evidence that higher inflation is associated with more *uncertainty* about the rate of inflation, making risk-averse households worse off.[3] Inflation also interacts with various tax provisions, further distorting the behavior of households and businesses. For example, the government permits firms to deduct depreciation from income in calculating their income tax liabilities. But these deductions are based on the prices originally paid for capital goods which, with ongoing inflation, may be quite low compared to current prices. As a result, inflation reduces the real value of depreciation deductions and increases the income taxes that firms must pay. This discourages them from investing in capital goods that depreciate rapidly.[4]

More important than these refinements is the question of how permanent the changes in inflation and unemployment are. As the natural rate theory suggests, the output gain may be temporary but the inflation increase permanent. An output gain of $80 billion seems large relative to a cost of, say, $4 billion, but a one-time gain of $80 billion is not so large when compared to the total cost of $4 billion a year forever, perhaps growing over time with the size of the economy. Indeed, the present discounted value of the small but permanent costs of higher inflation may outweigh the large but temporary benefits of reduced unemployment.[5]

Summary

The net benefits of reducing unemployment depend largely on how long the reduction lasts. According to the natural rate theory, deviations from the natural rate of unemployment are temporary. Hence, policies to decrease unemployment have a temporary impact on unemployment and output—*unless they alter the natural rate itself*—but a permanent impact on inflation. The benefits of

3. Laurence Ball and Stephen G. Cecchetti, in their article "Inflation and Uncertainty at Short and Long Horizons," *Brookings Papers on Economic Activity* 1 (1990): 215–254, provide supporting evidence and discussion of this hypothesis.

4. See Alan J. Auerbach, "Inflation and the Choice of Asset Life," *Journal of Political Economy* 87 (June 1979): 621–638.

5. For example, if the annual loss from inflation started at $4 billion and grew annually at 1 percent per year, the present value of current and future losses, discounted at an interest rate of 5 percent, would be $100 billion. For an elaboration of this point see Martin Feldstein, "The Welfare Cost of Permanent Inflation and Optimal Short-Run Economic Policy," *Journal of Political Economy* 87 (August 1979): 749–768.

unemployment-reducing stabilization policy are enhanced if the natural rate itself can be influenced by policy, or if the "temporary" deviations of unemployment from its natural rate persist for a long time. At the other extreme, if predictable policy changes have no impact on unemployment, even in the short run (as the misperceptions theory suggests), then the benefits of inflationary policy are nil.

Now that we've considered the costs and benefits of reducing unemployment, let's look at the actual stabilization policies aimed at achieving this goal. We'll begin by considering policy during the Depression.

MONETARY AND FISCAL POLICY DURING THE GREAT DEPRESSION

It is generally agreed that countercyclical stabilization policy began during the Great Depression of the 1930s, with its birth formally marked by the publication of John Maynard Keynes' *The General Theory of Employment, Interest and Money* in 1936. In his classic work, Keynes argued that government intervention, particularly through expansionary fiscal policy, would help restore full employment.

By the standard of recent U.S. business cycles, the depth and length of the Depression were staggering. At the Depression's 1933 trough, the unemployment rate reached 25 percent, compared to less than 8 percent at the trough of the recession of the early 1990s. Figure 12-1, which graphs real GDP from 1929 to 1941, shows that output declined for the four years from 1929 to 1933. By comparison, as you learned in Chapter 4, postwar recessions have lasted an average of less than 11 months. During this prolonged decline, real output fell by 30 percent. And despite the resumption of economic growth in 1933, it took another *six years*—and the recovery from *another* downturn, the 1937–1938 recession—for the U.S. economy simply to regain its 1929 output level. Put another way, an entire decade of economic growth was lost.

It is easy to understand why the Depression led Keynes and others to advocate government intervention. But ideas are not actions. Although the *idea* of countercyclical policy may have originated during the Depression, there is debate about the extent to which it was practiced and how effective it was. In fact, it is still not clear whether the primary economic stimulus came through fiscal policy, as has generally been supposed, or through monetary policy.

The U.S. economic experience during the Depression provides a useful introduction to the practice of monetary and fiscal policy. It illustrates many still-relevant problems, notably the difficulties of determining and implementing the right policies at the right time and of measuring the effectiveness of those policies actually introduced. Indeed, some economists think that monetary policy actually caused the Great Depression.

Case Study: Monetary Policy and the Onset of the Depression

In their classic treatise on U.S. monetary history, Milton Friedman and Anna Schwartz showed that declines in the U.S. money stock in the early 1930s

Figure 12-1 Real GDP During the Depression

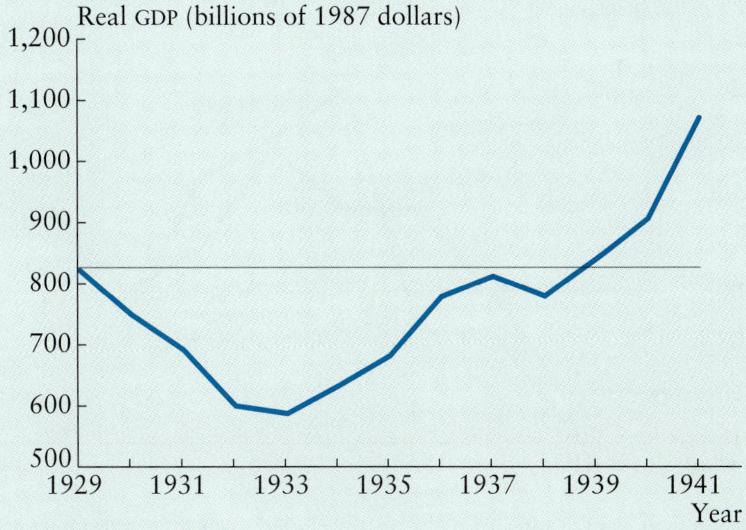

The depth and length of the Great Depression were staggering. Output declined for the four years between 1929 and 1933. By comparison, postwar recessions have lasted an average of 11 months. During the prolonged decline of the Great Depression, real output fell by 30 percent. It took another six years—and the recovery from another downturn—for the U.S. economy to regain its 1929 output level.

Source: *National Income and Product Accounts*

closely paralleled the declines in output.[6] They went further by arguing that the money supply changes were largely responsible for the declines in output. The Friedman-Schwartz argument can be understood by looking at Figure 12-2, which plots the annual growth rates of real GDP and the nominal money stock, M1, during the 1930s, with the growth rate of the money stock lagged one year.[7] The figure shows a clear relationship between money growth and real output changes. In particular, money supply growth was negative throughout the early 1930s as real output fell.

Did monetary policy cause the Depression? Figure 12-2 seems to support this hypothesis. But there is more to the story. Consider the IS and LM curves in Figure 12-3. Recall that each curve relates the interest rate to output, based on a fundamental economic relationship. The IS curve is derived from the transition equation that relates capital accumulation to income. Its negative slope reflects

6. Milton Friedman and Anna Jacobson Schwartz, *A Monetary History of the United States, 1867–1960* (Princeton, NJ: Princeton University Press, 1963), Chapter 7.

7. That is, the growth rate of output for, say, 1932 is the rate of growth from 1931 to 1932, but the growth rate of the money stock shown for 1932 is for the period 1930 to 1931. The logic of the lag is that one would not expect output changes induced by changes in the money supply to occur instantaneously. We discuss the length of such lags in more detail later in the chapter.

Figure 12-2 Growth Rates of Real GDP *and M1*

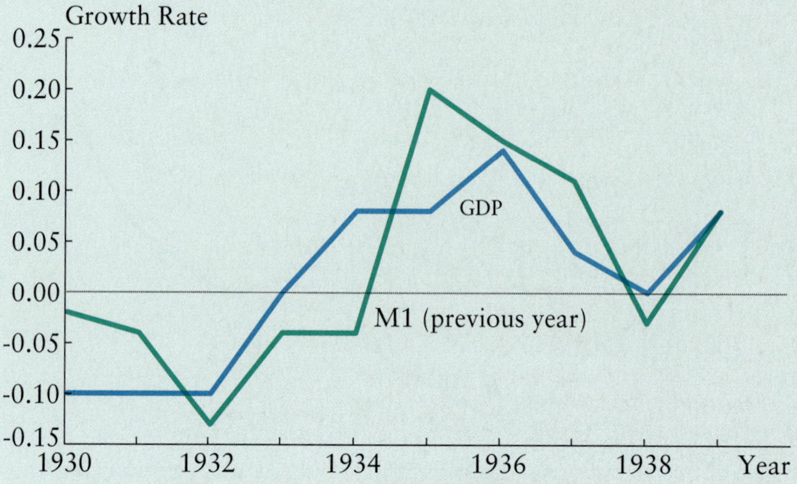

When annual growth rates of real GDP are plotted against growth rates of the money stock lagged one year, there is a clear relationship between the two variables. In particular, money supply growth was negative throughout the early 1930s as real output fell.

Source: GDP: *National Income and Product Accounts*; M1: Friedman and Schwartz, *A Monetary History of the United States*

the fact that higher income means more saving, more capital, and hence lower interest rates. The LM curve is derived from the condition that money demand equals money supply. Its slope is positive, reflecting the fact that a higher level of income, which raises the demand for money, requires an offsetting higher interest rate to reduce the demand for money and reestablish equilibrium with an unchanged money supply. Given the price level, each LM curve is drawn for a fixed value of the nominal money supply, M, and each IS curve is drawn for a particular value of F, the level of resources government takes from the young.

Within this framework, the Friedman-Schwartz argument is that a drop in the money supply affects output through a leftward shift in the LM curve, to the curve labeled LM′ in the diagram. As the equilibrium moves from point A to point B, output falls from Y^0 to Y^1 and the real interest rate rises from r^0 to r^1. In addition, real money balances, M/P, fall. In fact, the initial stages of the Great Depression witnessed all three of these things: a decline in output, a rise in real interest rates, and a decline in real money balances. But the decline in output relative to that of real money balances turned out to be greater than a leftward shift in the LM curve would, by itself, suggest.

To see this, let's write the formula for the LM curve as $(M/P)/Y = \gamma[r_{+1}](1 - \beta)$. As the interest rate rises and discourages the holding of money, γ falls. Therefore, so does $(M/P)/Y$. Put another way, the velocity of money, $v = PY/M$, rises

Figure 12-3 The Causes of Declining Output

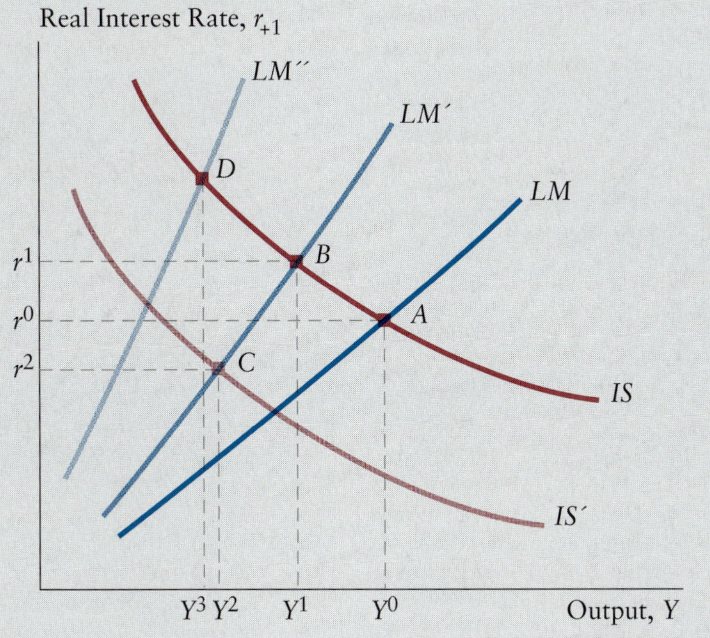

In the IS-LM framework, the Friedman-Schwartz story is that a drop in the money supply affects output through a leftward shift of the LM curve to LM′. The model predicts that as equilibrium moves from point *A* to point *B*, output falls from Y^0 to Y^1 and the interest rate rises from r^0 to r^1. In addition, real money balances fall. In the initial stages of the Depression, all three of these events occurred. However, the decline in output relative to the decline in real balances turned out to be greater than this story suggests.

when the interest rate rises. But, as Figure 12-4 shows, velocity didn't rise during the early 1930s—it fell! This casts doubt on the notion that a decline in the money supply, by itself, caused the Depression.

Are there other explanations for the decline in output in the early 1930s that are consistent with a decline in velocity? One such explanation involves a downward shift in the IS curve arising from a sudden drop in consumer spending. In this story, the decline in spending was caused by a loss of confidence after Black Tuesday, October 29, 1929—the day the stock market crashed.[8] As we showed in Chapter 9, a drop in the share of income consumed by the young—an increase in their propensity to save—increases next period's capital stock and reduces the prospective interest rate for any given level of output. In other words,

8. See Peter Temin, *Did Monetary Forces Cause the Great Depression?* (New York: W. W. Norton & Company, 1976).

Figure 12-4 Velocity and Real Output, 1929–1939

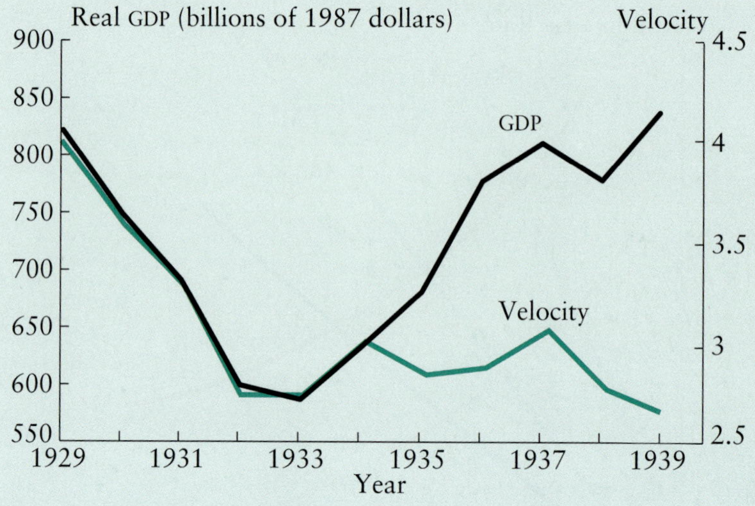

In the IS-LM model, a leftward shift of LM caused by a reduction in the money supply should cause the velocity of money to rise as the interest rate rises. However, velocity actually fell during the early 1930s, casting doubt on the notion that a decline in the money supply alone caused the Depression. Further shifts in IS and LM suggested by other theories can help explain what happened.

Source: *National Income and Product Accounts*; Friedman and Schwartz, *A Monetary History of the United States*

it shifts the IS curve downward, lowering output and the interest rate. Given the value of M/P, a lower value of Y means lower velocity.

For a large enough shift in the IS curve, the interest rate may have fallen even as the LM curve also shifted to the left, as shown by the intersection of the IS′ and LM′ curves at point C in Figure 12-3. This decline in the interest rate would be consistent with an increase in γ and the observed drop in velocity.

This reduced-consumption story seems plausible, because it explains how velocity could have fallen in the face of a contracting money supply. But it encounters a problem in suggesting that the *decline* in velocity should have been caused by a *decline* in the interest rate. As mentioned, real interest rates rose in the early 1930s. In fact, they were quite high relative to their levels in the years just before and after.[9]

How could the real interest rate have risen at the same time velocity, $1/\gamma[r_{+1}](1-\beta)$, fell? Equivalently, how could γ have risen at the same time that the real interest rate rose? Clearly, γ must have risen in response to some other

9. For estimates of real interest rates during this period, see Christina Romer, "What Ended the Great Depression?" NBER Working Paper #3829 (September 1991): Figure 8.

factor, despite the rise in real interest rates. Such a shift is referred to as an increase in *liquidity preference*—people decided to hold more money at any given interest rate. One explanation for an increase in liquidity preference is that there was an increase in the perceived riskiness of other assets, such as stocks and bonds.[10]

In terms of our model, an increase in liquidity preference is represented by an increase in the value of γ corresponding to any given value of r_{+1}, making money demand, $\gamma[r_{+1}](1 - \beta)Y$, higher for any given interest rate and income level and leading to an excess demand for money. With the money supply fixed, equilibrium in the money market can be reestablished only through a fall in income—which means a leftward shift in the LM curve, as shown by the further shift from LM′ to LM″ in Figure 12-3. The intersection of this new LM curve and the original IS curve occurs at point *D*. As the figure shows, this additional shift is consistent with a higher interest rate. Moreover, the further decline in output from Y^1 to Y^3 translates into a decline in velocity, since the money supply does not change as output falls. A large enough rise in liquidity preference could thus have outweighed the positive impact on velocity of the declining money supply, causing a net decline in velocity as output fell and interest rates rose. As we'll discuss in Chapter 14, this explanation may be related to the problems of the banking sector during the Depression.[11]

Once the Depression began, another factor came into play that may also have caused a contractionary shift in the LM curve: deflation. Between 1929 and 1933, the price level *fell* at a 6 percent annual rate. So far, we've made the simplifying assumption in our short-run analysis that the expected inflation rate is zero, and hence the nominal and real interest rates are the same. However, it is unlikely that expectations about the inflation rate remained fixed after the Depression began and individuals saw the severe deflation that was occurring. It can be shown that expected deflation shifts the LM curve to the left.[12]

In summary, the Depression occurred against the backdrop of a declining money supply, but contractionary monetary policy per se cannot explain the concomitant decline in velocity. A loss of confidence, manifested through an increased desire to save, probably helped precipitate the Depression, but does not explain the simultaneous decline in velocity and rise in real interest rates. The decline in velocity appears to reflect a rise in liquidity preference as well as the expectation of inflation. But the relative importance of these factors remains unresolved, notwithstanding more than 50 years of debate.

10. See James Tobin, "Liquidity Preference as Behavior Towards Risk," *Review of Economic Studies* 25 (February 1958): 65–86.

11. See Ben S. Bernanke, "Nonmonetary Effects of the Financial Crisis in the Propagation of the Great Depression," *American Economic Review* 73 (June 1983): 257–276.

12. To understand this, recall that the demand for money is sensitive to the *nominal* interest rate, which equals the real interest rate plus the expected inflation rate. Expected deflation lowers the nominal interest rate below the prospective real interest rate, r_{+1}. This relatively low nominal rate, in turn, increases the demand for money, given any real interest rate and level of income. As in the case of an increase in liquidity preference, the LM curve shifts leftward, reducing output, raising the real interest rate, and also lowering velocity.

Case Study: The Slow Recovery and the Role of Policy

The U.S. economy began to recover in 1933. The NBER places the business cycle trough in March of that year—the same month in which Franklin Roosevelt's inauguration heralded the arrival of the "New Deal" and a commitment to greater government involvement in the economy. But, as indicated above, the recovery took a long time. The 1929 level of real output was reached again only in 1939 and single-digit unemployment rates did not reappear until 1941, at the beginning of World War II.

One reason the recovery took so long is simply that the initial decline in output was so great. Indeed, as Figure 12-1 shows, real output grew very rapidly during the mid-1930s, but from very low levels. Fiscal policy may be another reason for the slow recovery. Indeed, it may have helped cause the 1930s' second serious recession, in 1937–1938.

How active was fiscal policy during the New Deal? Answering this question requires a measure of fiscal policy. According to the Keynesian approach, fiscal policy stimulates output by reducing saving. An increase in F, the resources of the young that are borrowed or taxed, reduces the amount of capital accumulation, raising the prospective interest rate for any given level of output—shifting the IS curve upward—and thereby raising the equilibrium level of output.

Unfortunately, we do not have a direct measure of F for the Depression period. Instead, we have the traditional measure of fiscal stimulus, the federal government's budget deficit. For some policy changes, an increase in F would be related to an increase in the deficit, but for others it would not. For example, a debt-financed increase in government purchases or transfer payments would increase both F and the deficit, whereas paying for such purchases with taxes on the young would increase F but not the deficit. Thus, although increased budget deficits *may* signify expansionary fiscal policy, not all expansionary fiscal policies are associated with increases in the budget deficit.[13]

Figure 12-5 presents the federal budget deficit for the years 1929–1939 measured in 1947 dollars. Subject to the caveat just discussed, the trend does suggest some fiscal expansion in the mid-1930s, as the deficit rose from around \$3 billion in 1933 to between \$5 and \$6 billion during the years 1934–1936. But there is a fundamental problem in interpreting this trend as evidence of intentional fiscal expansion: the deficit itself depends on the level of economic activity, even without a change in policy.

As we saw in Figure 7-2, government receipts and expenditures tend to vary with the business cycle. Some transfer payments automatically rise when unemployment rises and income falls. Most sources of tax revenue, such as the individual and corporate income taxes, automatically shrink as output declines.

13. This ambiguity has been recognized for a long time. Recall that we refer to the size of the output increase associated with any expansionary policy as the policy's *multiplier.* The notion that certain fiscal policies could be expansionary without increasing the deficit was already well understood in the 1940s, when economists conceived of a *balanced budget multiplier.* See, for example, Paul Samuelson, "The Simple Mathematics of Income Determination," in *Income, Employment and Public Policy* (New York: Norton, 1948), 133–155.

Figure 12-5 Fiscal Policy During the Depression

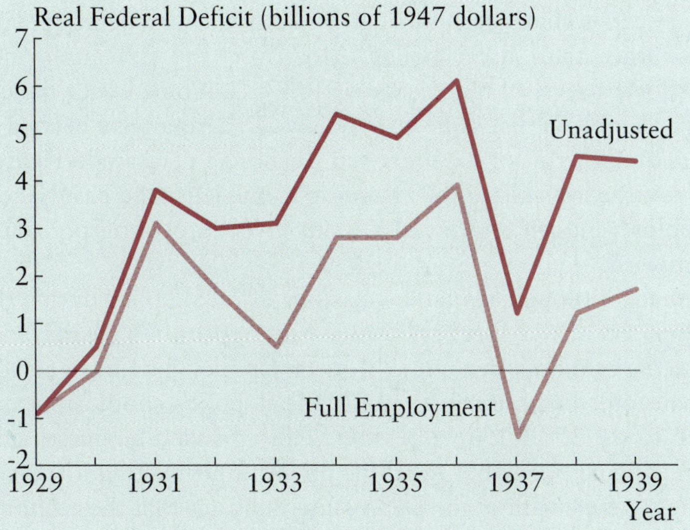

One measure of fiscal stimulus is the federal government's budget deficit. The trend in this variable suggests some expansion during the mid-1930s. But the deficit itself depends on the level of economic activity. A better measure is the full-employment budget deficit, an estimate of what the deficit would be at full employment. Based on this measure, fiscal policy does not appear to have been very expansionary between 1933 and 1936.

Source: Brown, "Fiscal Policy in the 'Thirties: A Reappraisal"

Thus, even without a change in spending programs or tax schedules, the deficit will naturally increase during a recession. To the extent that such changes help keep consumption from falling, they reduce the severity of the recession. For this reason, they are referred to as **automatic stabilizers**. Automatic stabilizers help reduce the economy's volatility, but their presence makes it difficult to identify actual changes in fiscal policy.

Automatic stabilizers
Changes in tax revenues and transfer payments that are automatically triggered by changes in national income and that tend to smooth fluctuations in disposable income over the business cycle

To identify fiscal policy changes in the presence of automatic stabilizers, we can ask what the budget deficit *would* be if the economy were at its full-employment level of output. With output hypothetically held fixed, the deficit can change only if there is an explicit change in government policy, not through the work of automatic stabilizers. This construct, called the **full-employment deficit,** is useful in assessing fiscal policy during the Depression. Indeed, it was actually introduced for this very purpose, and is shown for the period by the burgundy line in Figure 12-5.[14]

Full-employment deficit
An estimate of what the government's budget deficit would be if the economy were at the full-employment level of output

14. See E. Cary Brown, "Fiscal Policy in the 'Thirties: A Reappraisal," *American Economic Review* 46 (December 1956): 857–879.

Based on this measure, fiscal policy does not appear to have been particularly expansionary during FDR's first term, from 1933 through 1936. The full-employment deficit did not surpass its 1931 level until 1936, and even then it did so only by a small amount. If active policy helped speed the 1933–1937 recovery, it appears to have been through expansionary monetary policy (see Figure 12-2) rather than fiscal policy. Moreover, the full-employment deficit reached its lowest level of the decade in 1937. Combined with the contraction of the money supply in that same year, policy can certainly be blamed for the ensuing recession. In terms of the short-run Keynesian diagram in Figure 12-3, the monetary contraction shifted the LM curve to the left, whereas the reduction in the full-employment deficit reduced *F* at any given level of output, shifting the IS curve downward.

In summary, although available measures of fiscal policy during the Depression are imperfect, *active* fiscal policy does not appear to have played an important role in the economic recovery. Monetary policy may have aided the post-1933 expansion, but monetary and fiscal policy both appear to have contributed to the 1937–1938 recession. This episode illuminates not only the problem of gauging policy but the difficulty of implementing it successfully. On the other hand, the length of the Depression indicates that the economy will not always revert quickly on its own to the natural rate of unemployment. Hence, although it is difficult to practice, countercyclical policy may offer a significant payoff if successful.

THE CHALLENGE OF ACTIVIST POLICY

Our study of the Depression suggests that the active use of monetary and fiscal policy is hindered by several difficulties. It is useful to consider these difficulties in further detail. In this section we'll see that most policies take effect with a time lag, are often based on imperfect information about the state of the economy, and may lack credibility in the eyes of the public.

Policy lag
The time that passes between the need for a policy and when it takes effect; the sum of the inside and outside lags

Inside lag
The time that passes between the need for a policy and the actual introduction of such a policy

Outside lag
The time that passes between the introduction of a policy and when it takes effect

Policy Lags

It took at least four years of sharply falling real output—from 1929 to 1933—need for fiscal expansion acknowledged. This episode may exaggerate typical response lags, but such **policy lags** are inherent in the conduct of stabilization policy. There are two types of lags between the date at which a policy *should* take effect and the date at which it *does* take effect. The **inside lag** lasts from the point at which the need for a policy shift arises to the time the policy is finally introduced. One factor contributing to the inside lag is that certain data on economic conditions (such as the level of GDP) become available only after a delay of months and often undergo important revisions thereafter. The **outside lag** extends from when the policies are introduced to when they take effect. Unless economic conditions can be fully anticipated, both lags are inevitable.

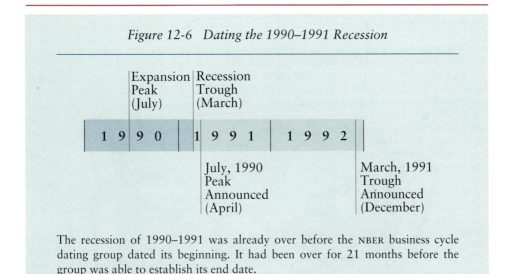

Figure 12-6 Dating the 1990–1991 Recession

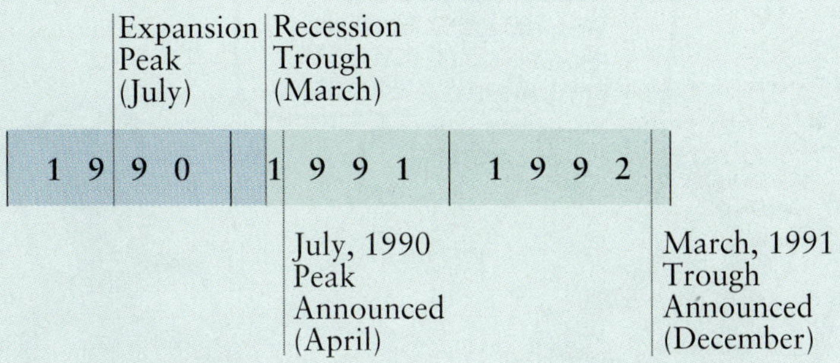

The recession of 1990–1991 was already over before the NBER business cycle dating group dated its beginning. It had been over for 21 months before the group was able to establish its end date.

Case Study: The 1992 Presidential Election and the Recession

Inside lags can affect election outcomes as well as economic policy. As we saw in Chapter 10, voting in U.S. presidential elections depends quite strongly on recent economic performance. But how accurately can recent performance be measured?

The most important issue of the 1992 U.S. presidential campaign was the recession that began in July of 1990 and seemed to many voters to have become permanent. At the end of October 1992—just a week before the election—the first, preliminary figures on third-quarter (July through September) economic growth became available. The estimated third-quarter growth rate of real GNP—equivalent to 2.7 percent on an annual basis—was used by then-President Bush to support his claim that the economy had finally begun to grow strongly. Apparently the voters didn't believe him because he was badly beaten in the 1992 election. But President Bush had been right. Indeed, an important revision in the third-quarter growth estimate came out a month after the election. It showed an even *higher* growth rate of GNP in the third quarter—3.9 percent on an annual basis!

The NBER's business cycle dating group[15] didn't make President Bush any happier when it announced in December that the recession had ended—in March, 1991. Since the NBER had officially recognized the recession's July, 1990 beginning only in April, 1991, this dating of the recession trough meant that the recession had actually ended a month *before* its beginning had been acknowledged. The time line in Figure 12-6 illustrates these delays in the dating of the 1990–1991 recession.

---

15. The dating of business cycles by the NBER was discussed in Chapter 4.

©1992 Luckovich; ATLANTA CONSTITUTION

The moral of this story is that it may take a long time—perhaps longer than a recession itself lasts—for economists as well as voters to make an accurate assessment of the economy's economic performance.

Lags and the Determination of Policy

Even after information becomes available, it takes time to enact a policy. Here, monetary policy has a clear advantage. As we'll discuss in the Chapter 14, the Fed can alter monetary policy almost instantaneously. In contrast, changes in fiscal policy (other than automatic stabilizers) require formulation, congressional action, and presidential signature—a process that can take several months or more. Finally, once these inside lags have been overcome, the outside lags take effect. Whatever their multipliers, changes in monetary or fiscal variables do not have an instantaneous impact on the economy. This is evident in Figure 12-2, where we observed that movements in GDP seemed to follow the previous year's money supply changes.

What causes outside lags? Let's go back to the policy multipliers introduced in Chapter 9. We saw there that the multiplier for any monetary or fiscal policy could be thought of as occurring in a series of successive changes. For example, in our basic two-period life-cycle model with rigid prices and involuntary unemployment, a dollar increase in the money supply, given to the old, would initially increase the elderly's consumption, and hence output, by a dollar. This dollar increase in output (and income) would go to suppliers of labor (the young) and capital (the old), leading to increased investment and consumption and hence another round of increased output and income, and so on. As we saw in our original discussion, similar patterns apply to fiscal policy changes. We did not discuss how long each of these "rounds" takes, but, in all, it may well take as long as one to two years for most of the multiplier impact to be realized.[16]

How do policy lags affect countercyclical policy *design*? Recall, once again, that the average length of postwar recessions has been less than 11 months. Therefore, the economy can be well into a recession even before its existence is recognized and well *out* of the recession before policies can be enacted and have an impact. As a result, the scope for countercyclical policy is greatly reduced, *even if* such policy, instituted at the right time (which might well be before the recession actually began), would be desirable and effective.

Imperfect Information

Closely related to the problem of lags is the problem of information about the state of the economy. Even after information becomes available, it may not be enough for the policy maker to know the right response. Part of the problem here relates to the magnitude and lags of policy multipliers. Not knowing the effect or timing of a policy clearly hinders policy activism.[17] But the uncertainty also relates to the current state of affairs—for example, there may be uncertainty as to why interest rates or inflation might have risen. Along with lags, this uncertainty can hamper policy design.

Case Study: "Whip Inflation Now" and the Oil Shock

This case study illustrates how supply shocks can cause both inflation and Keynesian unemployment and how failure to understand this led to proposals for contractionary fiscal policy during a severe recession.

The 1973–1975 recession was one of the most serious the U.S. economy has experienced since the 1930s. It lasted 16 months and raised the unemployment rate to 9 percent. As we saw in Chapter 10, many postwar business cycle fluctuations have been associated with disturbances in the oil market. This recession was a classic example. It began shortly after the oil price rose sharply due to the 1973 Arab oil embargo. The oil price rise contributed to **stagflation**, the combination of high inflation and poor economic growth. Figure 12-7 shows the quarterly growth rates of real GDP and the GDP deflator for the period 1973–1975. The GDP growth rate was most negative in the first quarter of 1975—the quarter during which prices rose fastest.

Stagflation
A recession accompanied by high inflation

Stagflation was something of a mystery at the time, because the prevailing assumption was that increased inflation should be associated with *faster* growth, as represented by a short-run Phillips curve trade-off. Such a short-run

16. See, for example, the discussion in Otto Eckstein, *The DRI Model of the U.S. Economy* (New York: McGraw-Hill, 1983), which provides estimates of multipliers for various monetary and fiscal policies based on a large-scale macroeconomics model.
17. An early and succinct statement of this point was made by William Brainard, "Uncertainty and the Effectiveness of Policy," *American Economic Review* 57 (May 1967): 411–425.

Figure 12-7 Stagflation: 1973–1975

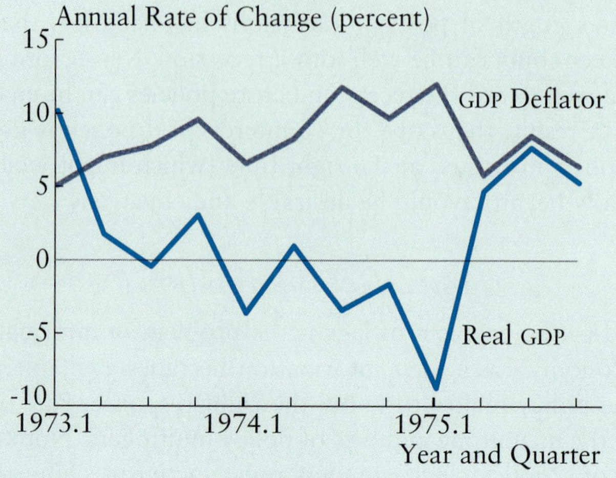

The 1973–1975 recession was the most serious since the 1930s. It lasted 16 months and raised the unemployment rate to 9 percent. Unlike many earlier recessions, it featured stagflation: a combination of high inflation and poor economic growth.

Source: *National Income and Product Accounts*

trade-off can be realized through a monetary or fiscal expansion in our short-run Keynesian model. Either type of expansionary policy will increase both output and prices if nominal wages are rigid.

The key to understanding stagflation is to remember that, just as in the market for a single commodity, higher prices can be caused not only by higher demand but also by lower supply. As we discussed in Chapter 10, an oil shock that increases the cost of imported materials is equivalent to a decline in the productivity term A in our production function. This decline will generally cause a reduction in output and an increase in the general price level (not just the price of oil).

To see this, first suppose there is no change in employment. Then, with the same amount of capital and labor, the reduction in A will cause output to fall. With lower output comes a reduction in the demand for money. Given a fixed nominal money supply, equilibrium in the money market requires either that the interest rate fall to increase money demand or that the price level rise to reduce the real money supply. However, as output decreases, saving and capital accumulation decrease too. These decreases raise the prospective interest rate and lower money demand still further. Thus, to reestablish money market equilibrium, the price level—and the inflation rate as well—must be higher than they would have been without the oil shock. We can understand why prices rise by imagining what happens when the old attempt to spend their assets, including money, and find fewer goods available. A decline in the level of output will cause an excess demand for goods and drive up the price level.

In addition to the direct reduction in output from lower productivity, there may be an additional reduction caused by a decline in employment. The reduction in productivity also reduces the marginal product of labor—and hence the real wage rate that firms can pay for a given level of employment. Under the real business cycle view, as discussed in Chapter 10, this reduction in the real wage would lead to increased voluntary unemployment. Under the Keynesian view, with rigid nominal wages, the impact on employment is not quite as clear. The possibilities are illustrated in Figure 12-8, which depicts the labor market determination of wages and employment in the Keynesian rigid-wage model, first introduced in Figure 9-11. In this variant of the model, the price level itself is not rigid, but nominal wages cannot fall. Recall that the height of the demand curve indicates the marginal product of labor at that level of employment, and hence the highest real wage that firms can pay that number of workers. The productivity shock reduces the marginal product of labor at any level of employment and hence lowers the labor demand curve, from D to D'.

At the original price level, say P^1, and the fixed nominal wage rate $\hat{W}$, the amount of employment would decline from L^1 to L^3, as shown in the figure. Why? Having to pay the same real wage in the face of reduced productivity, firms can hire fewer workers. However, because (as we already have determined) the price level rises, the reduction in employment will be not be as great. It is even possible that employment would increase, as shown at L^2. However, with prices rising, workers might seek to raise the nominal wage to keep pace, in which case employment would stay at L^3. In short, employment could fall to L^3, rise, say to L^2, or end up somewhere in between.

In any case, there actually was a sharp increase in unemployment—whether voluntary or involuntary—after the oil shock, from under 5 percent to as high as 9 percent of the labor force. According to the official dating, the recession began in November, 1973. Figure 12-7 shows that real GDP growth was negative in all but the second quarter of 1974 (when it was barely positive) and very negative—at an annual rate of –8.7 percent—in the first quarter of 1975.

How did President Ford deal with the 1973–1975 recession upon taking office in August, 1974? Initially, he sought to introduce *contractionary* fiscal policy, specifically through reduced government purchases, to fight inflation.[18] Using the slogan "Whip Inflation Now" and passing out buttons with the acronym "WIN" in observation of the goal, he stated that "Inflation is domestic enemy number one."[19] This might have been reasonable had the increased

18. In terms of our short-run Keynesian diagram, this amounted to a downward shift in the IS curve. The oil shock itself would already have shifted the LM curve to the left (can you explain why?), so the proposed fiscal policy move would have accentuated the output reduction.

19. For a lucid account of policy during this period, see Alan S. Blinder, *Economic Policy and the Great Stagflation* (New York: Academic Press, 1979).

Figure 12-8 Productivity Shocks and Keynesian Unemployment

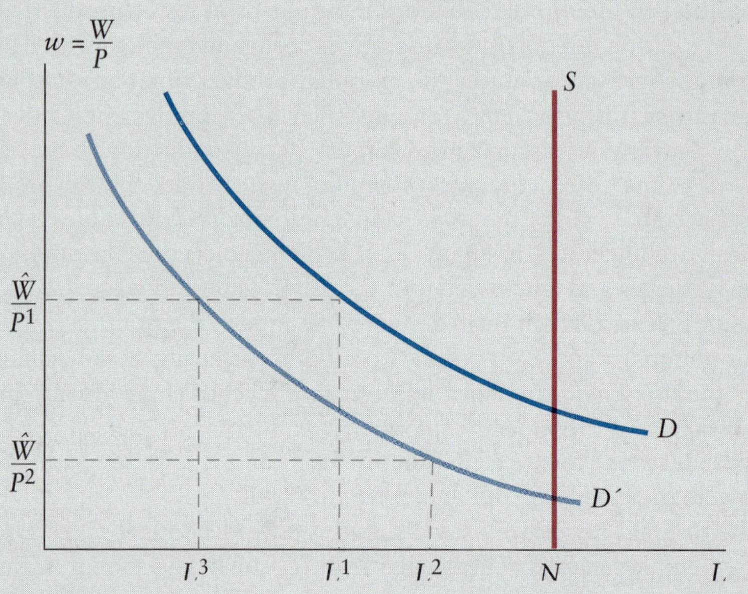

In the Keynesian rigid-wage model, the price level is flexible, but nominal wages cannot fall. The height of the labor demand curve indicates the marginal product of labor at each level of employment and the highest real wage firms can pay for that number of workers. A productivity shock that reduces the marginal product of labor lowers the demand curve from D to D'. At the original price level, P^1, and with a fixed nominal wage, $\hat{W}$, employment would decline from L^1 to L^3. However, because the price level rises, the reduction will not be that great. Employment might even rise, to L^2.

inflation not been due to a supply shock. And, to be fair, there was no *strong* evidence of recession when Ford took his anti-inflation stance. Though GDP growth had been poor, as of August the unemployment rate had risen only slightly (to 5.5 percent)—consistent with the fact that the unemployment rate tends to lag the business cycle.[20] Thus, a combination of uncertainty and lags contributed to policy mistakes. By January, the president had abandoned his WIN campaign and reversed course on fiscal policy. His proposed expansionary fiscal measures were instituted in the spring of 1975—just as the recession ended.

20. Indeed, the unemployment rate actually peaked in May 1975, two months *after* the recession ended.

Rational Expectations and the Lucas Critique

The preceding section emphasized that imperfect information about the state of the economy can frustrate policy makers. As we indicated at the beginning of that discussion, imperfect information about the potential impact of policies—about the lags and magnitudes of policy multipliers—also represents a hindrance. It is often difficult to gauge a policy's impact because so many unstable and unobservable factors can influence outcomes. One example is consumer confidence. A fiscal policy aimed at stimulating consumption purchases, such as transfers to the elderly financed by taxes on the young, might fail if those receiving the transfers were so worried about economic conditions that they saved the funds received.[21]

Consumer confidence represents households' *expectations* about the strength of the economy. Other expectations are also important. As we saw in Chapter 10, the shifting Phillips curve may be explained in terms of changing expectations. In the context of the natural rate view of unemployment, the higher workers' expectations of inflation, the higher their nominal wage demands, and the higher the inflation rate needed to achieve any particular level of employment. Hence, in order to determine the rate of growth of the money supply—and the associated inflation rate—needed to achieve a particular unemployment rate, policy makers must know what inflation rate is expected. The higher the expected inflation rate, the higher the required rate of money growth. Using a Phillips curve estimated from an earlier period of, say, low rates of expected inflation will cause policy makers to underpredict the level of inflation needed to achieve any particular level of employment.

Basing policy on a relationship like the Phillips curve, without accounting for the impact of expectations, may lead to serious policy errors. This argument was forcefully enunciated by Robert Lucas in the 1970s and is now known as the **Lucas critique.**[22] In fact, the Lucas critique goes further, arguing that the policy itself will influence future expectations. Thus, policy makers need to consider not only the current state of expectations but also how their policies may influence these expectations. We encountered the argument that policy influences expectations in the context of the misperceptions theory. That theory, you will recall, argues that the Phillips curve shifts in response to predictable changes in the money growth rate, eliminating the trade-off between inflation and unemployment.

Lucas critique *The idea that policy analysis is mistaken if it does not take into account the way the policy affects expectations and, consequently, economic actions*

In other settings, this influence of policy on expectations may actually cause policy to destabilize the economy. One example that we'll discuss in greater detail in Chapter 16 is the *investment tax credit,* a tax subsidy that, through the years, has occasionally been provided to businesses for purchasing new machinery and equipment. The credit typically has been introduced or increased during recessions in order to encourage more investment. Although this may seem like a reasonable anti-recession policy, it may lead investors during subsequent

21. Although the elderly consume all their resources in our model, we can imagine a more realistic model in which even the elderly would need to save for consumption in their remaining years.

22. See Robert E. Lucas, "Econometric Policy Evaluation: A Critique," in *The Phillips Curve and Labor Markets*, ed. K. Brunner and A. Meltzer (Amsterdam: North-Holland, 1976): 19–46.

recessions to *defer* investment—thereby worsening the recessions—until the credit is put in place or increased.

Expectations can have a pervasive impact on economic behavior. Yet, it is hard to measure them and to determine precisely how they depend on policy actions. This poses serious problems for policy designers.

Dynamic Inconsistency

The Lucas critique emphasizes that economic relationships depend on households' and firms' expectations about future economic conditions, including future policy actions. Sometimes, the government may be hindered in achieving its goals because of the nature of the policy individuals *expect* it to enact. For example, if workers expect the government to pursue a policy of very rapid money growth, they may demand high nominal wages—shifting the Phillips curve up. Once they have done so, the government faces an unpleasant choice, as shown in Figure 12-9. If it pursues the policy workers expect, it may achieve the natural rate of unemployment, but at a high inflation rate—point *A* in the diagram. If it seeks to maintain a low inflation rate by keeping money growth unexpectedly slow, it risks an elevated unemployment rate, as shown by point *B*.

The solution to this problem seems obvious: announce in advance a policy of slow money growth and low inflation, so that this policy is fully expected, and then follow such a policy, landing the economy at the desirable point, C. But suppose that the government actually prefers point *D*, with its even lower unemployment rate achieved at a somewhat higher rate of inflation, to point C. Then, having promised low inflation and convinced the workers of it, the government would have every incentive to renege on its promise, letting money and prices grow more rapidly, temporarily forcing real wages down, and attaining the lower rate of unemployment at point *D* on the lower Phillips curve. However, if the government has this incentive to renege, its promise of low inflation will not be credible in the first place. As a result, high inflation will be expected, and the government faces its unpleasant trade-off. Even though point C is preferable to point *A*, the government must settle for point *A* if it is to achieve full employment.

Dynamic inconsistency *The problem that arises in any situation in which government has an incentive to revise an announced policy after the public has reacted to it*

This example illustrates the problem of **dynamic inconsistency**, also called *time inconsistency*.[23] A policy is time-inconsistent if the government will wish to revise it once time has passed and actions (in this case, the setting of nominal wages) have been taken by the public. The policy of low money growth is time-inconsistent because, once low nominal wage agreements have been established, the government has the incentive to increase money growth above the promised rate. In other words, the government has the incentive to promise low inflation but not deliver.

The problem of dynamic inconsistency leads to a counterintuitive result: things being made worse by the availability of options. If the government had

23. This example is due to Robert Barro and David Gordon. Early work on dynamic inconsistency includes that by Finn Kydland, Edward Prescott, and Guillermo Calvo.

Figure 12-9 The Problem of Dynamic Inconsistency

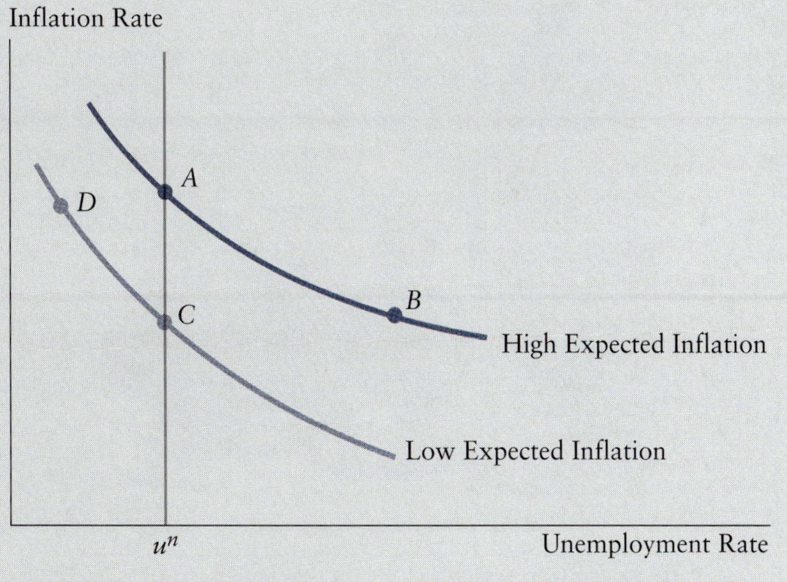

If workers expect rapid money growth, they may demand high nominal wages, shifting the Phillips curve upward. Once they have done so, government faces an unpleasant choice. It can pursue the expected policy and achieve the natural rate, but at a high inflation rate (point *A*). If it attempts to maintain a low inflation rate by keeping money growth unexpectedly low, it risks an elevated unemployment rate, at *B*.

Why isn't the promise of low inflation credible? If government actually prefers point *D* to point *C*, it might promise low inflation, then renege. However, if government has this incentive to renege, its promise of low inflation will not be credible in the first place.

no volition regarding monetary policy—if, once announced, the money growth rate *could not* be changed—then the lower inflation rate at point C in Figure 12-9 could be achieved. This suggests one possible solution to the problem: the government could give up the opportunity to change policy. But, for this approach—called a **precommitment strategy**—to work, the government must *really* give up the option of changing policy, not just say that it is doing so.

Precommitment strategy *Government's deliberate choice to give up the opportunity to change its economic policy*

There are many real-world examples of precommitment strategies involving monetary and fiscal policy. Perhaps the most common is the establishment of an independent central bank to control the money supply, with leaders who believe in maintaining price stability. In the U.S., for example, the Federal Reserve sets monetary policy and often follows a path less expansionary than that desired by the president and Congress. More generally, the adoption of simple money supply rules that are easy to adhere to, easy to monitor, and thus, perhaps, more

"All right, I lied to you. All governments lie!"

Drawing by Dana Fradon: © 1993 The New Yorker Magazine, Inc.

difficult to break—just letting the money supply grow by 3 percent per year, for example—may serve the same purpose.

Along with the inability to time countercyclical policy changes correctly, the problem of dynamic inconsistency represents a second reason to eschew activist policy, favoring an approach of "rules" over one of "discretion." But forsaking activist policy presents costs as well, for it means giving up the opportunity to alter policy even when the benefits may be very clear, as in an unusually serious depression. The government may wish to take steps to strengthen its commitment to maintain a policy while stopping short of surrendering its options entirely.[24]

ADDITIONAL TOOLS TO FIGHT INFLATION: WAGE AND PRICE CONTROLS AND INCOMES POLICIES

As our discussion has indicated, the government's ability to control inflation depends not only on its pursuit of a low-inflation policy but on its ability to get

24. Perhaps the best example of how a precommitment device can backfire comes from the movie world. In the cold-war-era movie *Dr. Strangelove*, the Russians set up not an independent monetary authority but an independent "Doomsday machine" that would automatically destroy the world if U.S. planes attacked. This machine made credible the Russian threat of retaliation (or it *would have*, had its existence been made public), but it did not improve social welfare when U.S. planes attacked. (Ironically, evidence surfaced in 1993 that Russia actually *had* developed such a Doomsday machine during the 1970s—as in the movie, without warning the U.S.)

This example helps illustrate why precommitment to rules should not be absolute; why it is better to have Fed Chairman Alan Greenspan—a committed inflation-fighter, but still a human—controlling the money supply than to have a machine to do so.

firms and workers to adopt wage-setting behavior consistent with this policy. Given the time inconsistency problem, it may be very difficult to bring inflation expectations down, even if the government really does intend to follow a low inflation program. With a citizenry skeptical of government promises, such a policy may have to be practiced for a considerable period before nominal wage growth moderates. In terms of Figure 12-9, the economy may need to spend a long time at point *B* before lower inflation expectations and nominal wage settlements shift the Phillips curve down and make point *C* feasible. This is the nature of the inflation-unemployment trade-off described by the natural rate theory.

To those frustrated by a government's inability to alter expectations, another route suggests itself: induce firms and workers to behave as if they expect low inflation (even though they don't) by making it costly to raise wages and prices. This can be accomplished either by making such increases illegal or by imposing financial penalties on firms that do not play along. The first of these approaches is known as *wage and price controls*. Policies that use the second approach are called **incomes policies**; a common type of incomes policy that uses tax penalties as an enforcement mechanism is called a **tax-based incomes policy** (TIP).[25]

Incomes policy
Government policy designed to control inflation by penalizing firms that raise prices or wages

Tax-based incomes policy (TIP)
The use of tax penalties to enforce government wage and price targets

Combined with an underlying monetary and fiscal policy consistent with a lower inflation rate, temporary controls and incomes policies appear to offer an improved short-run trade-off between inflation and unemployment. The combined approach is depicted in Figure 12-10, in the context of the natural rate theory. First, let's review what would happen under a conventional anti-inflation policy.

Suppose the economy is initially at the natural rate of unemployment, u^n, with an inflation rate of 7 percent and a rate of money growth of 7 percent, and that the government wishes to slow inflation to 3 percent. To do so, it reduces the growth rate of the money supply to 3 percent. If nominal wage growth dropped to 3 percent immediately, the economy could move directly from point *A* to point *C*, with real wages and the real money stock unaffected. But if inflation expectations—and nominal wage growth—remain at 7 percent, this outcome is not possible.

With price inflation of 3 percent and wage growth of 7 percent, real wages will rise, reducing employment. Without a change in inflation expectations, the short-run Phillips curve through point *A* governs the inflation-unemployment trade-off, causing the economy to move initially toward point *B* instead of point *C*. Eventually, a period of 3 percent inflation at point *B* might bring expected inflation down to 3 percent, reducing nominal wage growth and permitting a move back to full employment at point *C*, at the lower rate of inflation. But suppose that upon changing its monetary policy, the government immediately instituted a policy that prevented nominal wages from growing faster than 3 percent annually. Then, with a 3 percent rate of money growth and price inflation, real wages would remain constant, and point *C* would be reached immediately.

25. For a description of such policies, see Laurence S. Seidman, "Tax-Based Incomes Policies," *Brookings Papers on Economic Activity* 9 (Fall 1978): 301–348.

Figure 12-10 Improving the Trade-Off

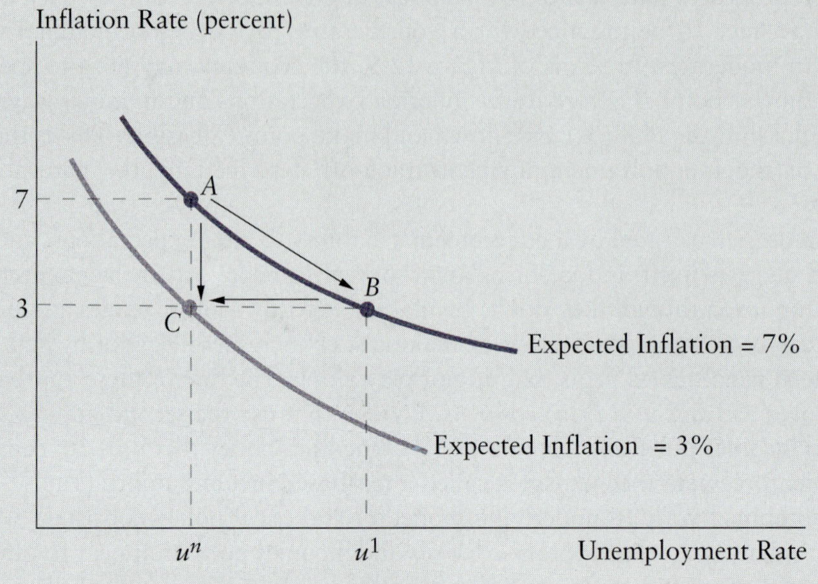

If government is unable to alter expectations, it may use wage and price controls to induce firms and workers to behave *as if* they expected low inflation. Suppose the economy is initially at the natural rate, u^n, with a 7 percent inflation rate. If government slows inflation to 3 percent, but the public continues to expect 7 percent inflation, unemployment will increase to point *B* in the short run. However, with a government policy that prevented nominal wages from rising faster than 3 percent annually, real wages would remain constant and point *C* could be attained immediately.

Eventually, everyone would come to expect the 3 percent inflation rate, the short-run Phillips curve would pass through point *C*, and this point could be maintained without controls.

Controlling the growth of wages and prices in so direct a manner seems simple and straightforward, but the simplicity is deceptive. Except in wartime, U.S. governments have been loath to disturb so fundamentally the market process of wage and price determination. There are two sets of problems with wage and price controls. First, by interfering with the free market, they prevent the natural changes in *relative* wages and prices that normally occur in a dynamic economy, leading to shortages and surpluses.[26] Second, they can be effective only when combined with an underlying monetary and fiscal policy consistent with the rate

26. This problem plagues not just attempts at general price controls but also controls imposed on specific markets. In the U.S., ceilings on mortgage interest rates, apartment rents, and gasoline prices aimed at preventing these prices from rising have typically led to shortages and queues.

of inflation imposed—as clarified in the preceding example. They may be useful as an interim measure to help bring expectations into line with policy, but they don't change the long-run trade-off between inflation and unemployment.

Consider what would happen if, for example, the government imposed wage and price growth of 3 percent *without* slowing the rate of money growth. The real money supply, M/P, would grow, increasing the demand for consumption. But with no change in real wages, employment would stay constant, and so would output. As a result, there would be overall shortages of goods and services—a condition known as *repressed inflation*. Lifting controls under such circumstances would simply cause a sudden rise in prices, back to their uncontrolled level.

Case Study: Nixon's Wage-Price Freeze

On August 15, 1971, President Nixon went on television and made the startling announcement that he was freezing essentially all wages and prices in the economy at their current levels for a period of 90 days, with a period of controlled growth to follow. He soon established a Cost of Living Council to oversee wage and price growth during this period, which began in November 1971. Through a variety of phases, this episode of wage and price controls lasted until spring 1974, by which time the OPEC oil shock had occurred, complicating the process of controlling prices directly.

What did the Nixon policy accomplish? It brought down the inflation rate temporarily, which is hardly surprising given that direct controls were placed on price increases. But it also ushered in a brief period of extremely rapid growth. From the last quarter of 1971 through the first quarter of 1973, the unemployment rate fell from 6 percent to 5 percent, and real GDP grew at an average annual rate of 7.4 percent—a growth rate not sustained for any period of comparable length since. Thereafter, though, as controls were lifted, inflation rose even as growth slowed. Disentangling the effects of the Nixon controls from those of the OPEC shock that occurred in late 1973 is difficult, but economists have generally concluded that the underlying monetary policy followed during the early 70s was far too expansionary to be consistent with the controls—and that, as the result of repressed inflation, prices rose more rapidly once controls were lifted, undoing whatever temporary gains had been achieved.[27]

WHAT HAS POLICY ACHIEVED?

Notwithstanding all the problems that activist policy faces, no postwar U.S. recession has been remotely as serious as the Depression. In fact, recessions have been much shorter since World War II than in the period before the Depression. On the basis of this evidence, activist policy appears to have been a success.

But the importance of these changes in the nature of economic fluctuations is subject to question. As we discussed in a case study in Chapter 4, some econo-

---

27. See Blinder, *Economic Policy and the Great Stagflation*, Chapter 6.

mists attribute the apparently smoother behavior of real GNP and the unemployment rate during the postwar period simply to improved data quality. That is, the sharp up-and-down swings of the pre-Depression era reflect poor measurement rather than the absence of countercyclical policy. Improved measurement cannot make the Depression disappear. However, comparing the postwar and pre-Depression periods does suggest that activist macroeconomic policies have failed to make the economy significantly more stable. This has contributed to the skepticism of many macroeconomists about the ability of countercyclical policy to stabilize the economy.

Chapter Summary

1. In considering whether to use monetary and fiscal policy to influence macroeconomic conditions, the government must compare costs and benefits. Although reduced unemployment and increased growth are the major benefits of stabilization policy, increased inflation is the major cost. Given the inflation-unemployment trade-off suggested by short-run Phillips curves and the unemployment-output relationship given by Okun's Law, the gains from reducing unemployment appear to swamp the costs of increasing inflation.

2. However, according to the natural rate view of unemployment, the short-run Phillips curve is unstable, so unemployment gains will be temporary (unless the natural rate itself is affected) but inflation will be permanently higher. Under the misperceptions theory, the higher inflation caused by expansionary policy occurs without even a temporary reduction in unemployment, eliminating the short-run trade-off entirely. The attractiveness of activist policy thus depends very much on how long, and by how much, unemployment can be reduced.

3. Countercyclical policy began in the U.S. during the Great Depression, spurred by Keynes' *General Theory* and the severity of economic circumstances. The Depression's length and depth suggest that there was considerable scope for activist policy. But even during that period there were signs of the problems that activist policy has encountered in the years since. Contractionary monetary policy may well have deepened and lengthened the Depression in the early 1930s, and both monetary and fiscal policy appear to have contributed to the 1937–1938 recession that further delayed the end of the Depression.

4. Fighting recessions requires deft timing. The average postwar recession has lasted just 11 months. Given the policy lags associated with receiving information, acting on it (inside lags), and waiting for policies to have an impact once introduced (outside lags), it is nearly impossible to use policy to fight a recession before the recession is over. The problem is particularly acute for fiscal policy, given the time it takes for fiscal initiatives to be enacted. An exception is the automatic stabilizers, such as reductions in income tax collections and increases in some transfer payments, that take effect without any change in policy.

5. In addition to lags, imperfect information confounds policy makers, who may be unsure of the causes of economic conditions—for example, whether inflation is due to a supply shock—and the timing and size of policy multipliers. One source of instability is the expectations of households and firms. Failing to account for the importance of such expectations and their dependence on policy—the problem targeted by the Lucas critique—can lead policy astray.

6. Activism can itself contribute to a lack of credibility that further hampers policy from achieving its objectives. Given the problem of dynamic inconsistency, it is sometimes desirable for policy makers to accept obstacles to the practice of activist policy and adhere more closely to simple rules.
7. Given the time-inconsistency problem, wage and price controls and incomes policies may ease the transition to a lower inflation rate by bringing expectations into line with policy. However, such intervention in wage- and price-setting distorts relative prices and can only work if the underlying monetary and fiscal policy is consistent with the inflation rate imposed. Attempting to use controls or incomes policies to lower inflation without reducing the underlying determinants of inflation, in particular the growth rate of the money supply, leads to repressed inflation.

Key Concepts

Automatic stabilizers
Full-employment deficit
Policy lags
Inside lags
Outside lags
Stagflation
Lucas critique
Dynamic inconsistency
Precommitment strategy
Incomes policy
Tax-based incomes policy (TIP)

Review Questions

1. The text states that when comparing the costs of higher inflation with the benefits of lower unemployment, the question of how permanent the changes are is probably more important than refinements to the measured annual costs of inflation and unemployment. Explain this statement.
2. What was the path of output during the 1930s?
3. What evidence exists that changes in the money supply contributed to the Great Depression? Are changes in the money supply the only driving forces in the Great Depression? Identify alternative possible causes of the Great Depression.
4. Why is it difficult to measure the *stance of fiscal policy*? What measure has been constructed to overcome the problem?
5. What types of *lags* are involved in the policy process?
6. What sorts of *uncertainties* do policy makers face?
7. What is the *Lucas critique*?
8. What is a *dynamically inconsistent* policy? How can a *precommitment strategy* help overcome the problem of dynamic inconsistency?
9. What are *wage and price controls*? What problems can wage and price controls cause?
10. What are *incomes policies*? How can these policies be used to improve the inflation-unemployment trade-off faced by policy makers?

Analytical Questions

1. In their original article on dynamic inconsistency, Finn Kydland and Edward Prescott discuss government patent policy. The government's goal is to encourage innovation and to make innovations available to a wide array of firms. To accomplish this goal, the government grants patents on innovations, which

guarantee that all proceeds from the innovation accrue to the inventing firm for some period of time. Kydland and Prescott claim that such a policy is dynamically inconsistent. In what sense is the policy dynamically inconsistent? How might the problems associated with this policy's dynamic inconsistency be mitigated?

2. "The introduction of wage and price controls is likely to give rise to a black market for various goods and services." Explain.

3. Suppose that someone claimed that a recently observed increase in real output was due to an increase in the money supply. What kinds of data patterns would you look for to corroborate or disprove the claim?

4. Suppose that you are a policy maker trying to decide whether it makes sense to stimulate the economy. You know that stimulation is a two-edged sword: the policy action will bring lower unemployment but higher inflation. How would the following developments affect your decision? Would each development make you more or less likely to pursue macro stimulation?

- **a.** The current and expected future real interest rate rises.
- **b.** You place greater weight on the welfare of future generations than you used to.
- **c.** As a result of the proliferation of automatic teller machines and point-of-sale arrangements, the need to carry cash drops markedly.

P A R T   F O U R

Enriching the Model

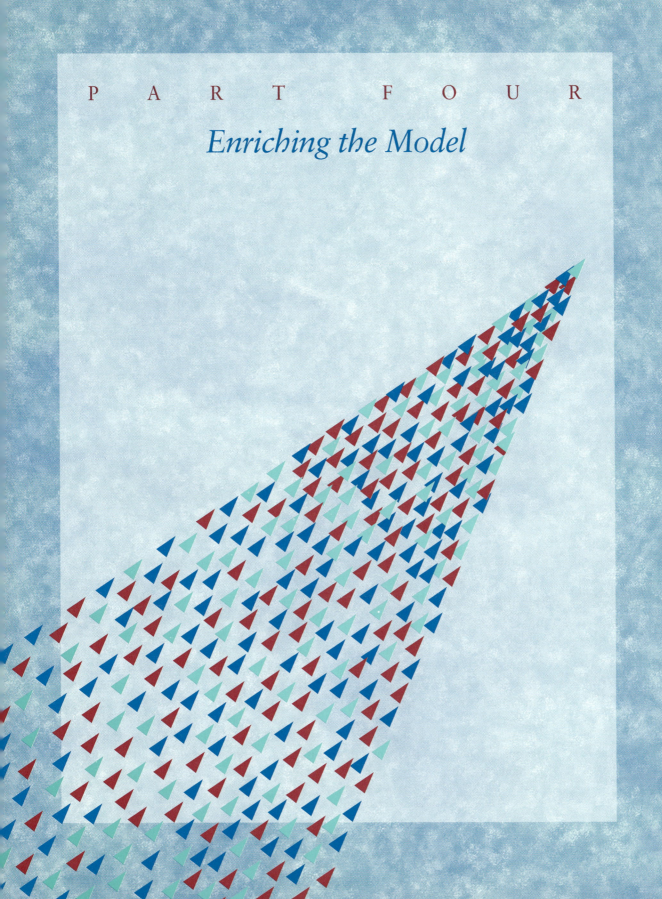

C H A P T E R 1 3

Money, Exchange Rates, and Policy in the Open Economy

INTRODUCTION

Exchange rate
The rate at which one country's currency is traded for another's

In this chapter we consider how nominal variables are determined in the international economy. We are particularly interested in the **exchange rate**: the rate at which one country's money is traded for another. We also discuss the impact and interaction of monetary, fiscal, and exchange rate policies in the open economy.[1] Our strategy is to expand our closed economy model with money by introducing a second country, with its own money supply and money demand. This two-country model exhibits the same kind of real-side behavior as our two-country model without money (presented in Chapter 6), including the possibility of investment by one country in the other. But now that we are considering a model with money, the purchase of foreign goods or assets by domestic residents requires obtaining foreign money. In demanding foreign money, domestic residents will offer their own money in exchange, thus producing a foreign exchange market.

1. This discussion will complement Chapter 7's analysis of fiscal policy in the open economy.

In studying the foreign exchange market we'll see how it relates to the rest of the economy. We'll also consider the scope and limitation of government intervention in this market through its exchange rate policy. The chapter first develops our open economy model under the assumption of fully flexible prices and wages and then considers the possibility that domestic prices or wages are rigid.

Here is a sample of the questions we'll address:

- How do flexible and fixed exchange rate regimes differ?
- What is the U.S. postwar experience with exchange rate regimes?
- How does the law of one price connect prices of traded goods via the exchange rate?
- What is the difference between nominal and real exchange rates?
- How are exchange rate and monetary policies related?
- Under what circumstances will monetary policy in one country affect nominal variables in another?
- How does an economy's openness alter the relative efficacy of monetary and fiscal policies in the presence of nominal rigidities?
- How do nominal rigidities affect the choice of exchange rate regimes?

UNDERSTANDING EXCHANGE RATES

An exchange rate tells us how many units of one type of money are needed to obtain a unit of another type. Exchange rates are generally quoted as the number of units of foreign currency per unit of domestic currency. For example, Americans quote the exchange rate between, say, French francs and U.S. dollars as francs per dollar, whereas the French quote it as dollars per franc. The franc-dollar exchange rate on July 28th, 1992 illustrates these two ways of quoting the same exchange rate. Americans that day quoted the rate as 5.001, or 5.001 francs per dollar; the French quoted the rate as .200, or 20 cents per franc. (Notice that one rate is the reciprocal of the other.) Regardless of how the rate is quoted, on July 28th, 1992 it took about five francs to acquire one dollar or, equivalently, it took about 20 cents to acquire one franc.

Foreign exchange markets are global markets. Accordingly, they operate around the clock. Exchange rates set in these markets are continually changing in response to changes in the supplies of and demands for different countries' monies. Increases in exchange rates are called **appreciations**; decreases are called **depreciations**. Thus, if the franc-dollar exchange rate, as quoted by Americans, rises from 5 to, say, 10, we say that the dollar has appreciated relative to the franc because it takes more francs (10 rather than 5) to purchase one dollar. Alternatively, we say that the franc has depreciated relative to the dollar since it takes fewer dollars, .10, rather than .20, to buy a franc.

Exchange rates can be either **flexible** or **fixed**. Flexible exchange rates, which are also called *floating* rates, are determined by the exchange market, free of government intervention. Fixed exchange rates are exchange rates whose values

Appreciation *An increase in a country's exchange rate due to an increase in demand for that country's currency or a decrease in its supply*

Depreciation *A decrease in a country's exchange rate due to a decrease in demand for the country's currency or an increase in its supply*

Flexible exchange rate *An exchange rate determined by the forces of supply and demand without government intervention*

Fixed exchange rate *An exchange rate determined by government intervention in the foreign exchange market or by government decree*

are fixed by the government at particular levels. When a government raises its fixed exchange rate to a higher value (meaning more foreign currency per unit of domestic currency), we call this a *revaluation*; when it lowers its fixed rate (meaning less foreign currency per unit of domestic currency), we call this a *devaluation.*

Governments can fix their exchange rates in different ways. One way is to buy or sell their own currency in the foreign exchange market, thereby ensuring that demand and supply for their currency equilibrates at the exchange rate they want to set. Another way is to legally forbid their citizens from exchanging domestic for foreign currency at other than the officially designated rate. As with any form of government price fixing, if the exchange rate is not set at the market-determined equilibrium value, supply will not equal demand at the official rate. Consequently, there will be an excess supply of the money that is overvalued, at the official exchange rate, and an excess demand for the money that is undervalued, at the official rate.

Governments with legally determined, rather than market-determined, exchange rates deal with this disequilibrium by restricting the amount of foreign currency they allow their citizens to purchase with domestic currency. This gives rise to illegal *black markets* in foreign exchange in which the public swaps its domestic currency for foreign currency at a rate foreigners find more attractive than the official rate. Officially determined exchange rates and black markets operating side by side are a common feature of many developing economies.

Case Study: Postwar U.S. Exchange Rate Regimes

The U.S. has had considerable experience with both fixed and flexible exchange rate regimes. In the postwar period the U.S. government maintained fixed exchange rates with France, Germany, Great Britain, and most other Western European countries until the early 1970s. This system of fixed rates required government intervention in the foreign exchange market and, as we'll see, close international coordination of monetary policy. But this coordination broke down, in large part because the U.S. wanted to expand its money supply more rapidly than did the other countries. As a result, the fixed rate regime gave way to a flexible rate regime, in which the U.S. dollar floats (fluctuates freely) vis-à-vis the currencies of Western Europe as well as most other countries, including Japan.

When the U.S. moved to flexible rates with its Western European trading partners, these countries, with the temporary exception of Great Britain, chose to maintain fixed exchange rates with one another in what is called the *European Exchange Rate Mechanism* (the ERM). Figure 13-1 illustrates this point. It tracks the franc-dollar, the mark-dollar, and the mark-franc exchange rates over the period 1951–1993. Note that the mark-dollar exchange rate was fixed at around 4 marks per dollar between 1951 and 1970. The franc-dollar exchange was fixed at 3.5 francs per dollar from 1951 through 1956. Between 1957 and 1958 the franc was devalued to 4.9 francs per dollar. This franc-dollar exchange rate prevailed until 1969, when the French and U.S. governments stopped

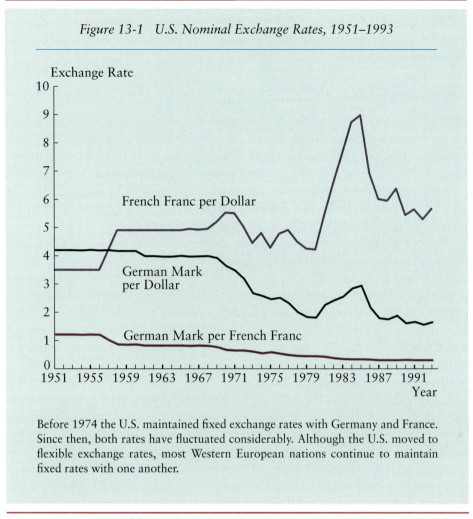

Figure 13-1 U.S. Nominal Exchange Rates, 1951–1993

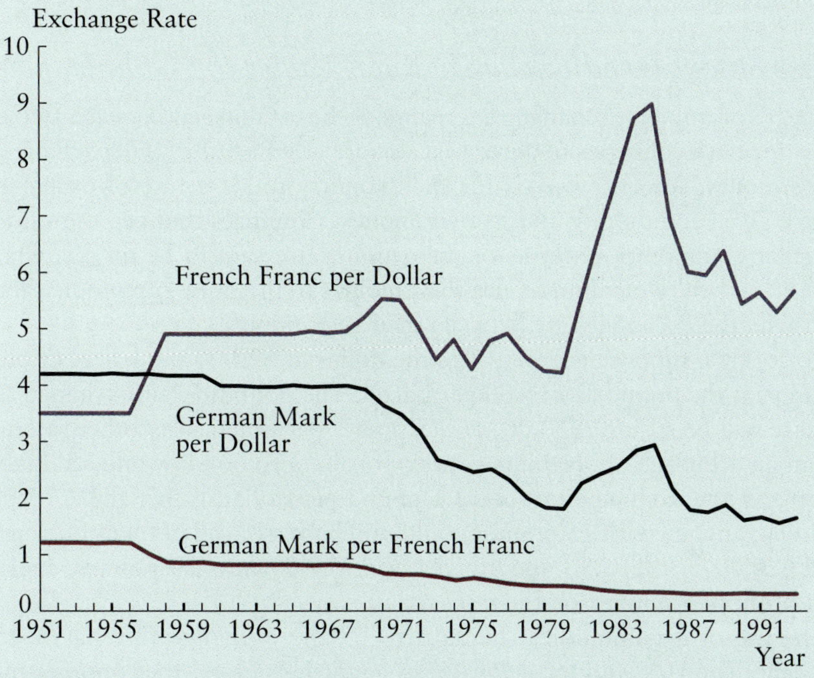

Before 1974 the U.S. maintained fixed exchange rates with Germany and France. Since then, both rates have fluctuated considerably. Although the U.S. moved to flexible exchange rates, most Western European nations continue to maintain fixed rates with one another.

Source: *Economic Report of the President,* 1994

pegging, or fixing, the franc-dollar exchange rate, leaving the franc to float against the dollar.

Since 1970 the mark-dollar and franc-dollar exchange rates have fluctuated considerably. For example, in 1975 the U.S.-French exchange rate stood at only 4.3 francs per dollar. A decade later the franc stood at 8.9 francs per dollar. Between 1970 and 1992 the fluctuations in the franc-dollar exchange rate mirrored those in the mark-dollar exchange rate because of the fact that the French and Germans were pegging the franc-mark rate.

As Figure 13-1 indicates, apart from an occasional discrete devaluation of the franc vis-à-vis the mark, the French and German exchange authorities were very successful between 1951 and 1992 in stabilizing the franc-mark exchange rate. However, things changed in 1993. In the summer of that year several European currencies, including the French franc and the Italian lira, were devalued against the German mark. This marked the end of the old ERM. In its place a new ERM was erected, which permitted currencies to float by as much as 15 percent on either side of specified central rates before governments would intervene to stabilize their values. We'll explain why the old ERM unraveled later in this chapter.

Case Study: Fixed Exchange Rates Under the Gold Standard

One way for a fixed exchange rate regime to be established between two countries is for both countries to agree to a set rate at which they will exchange each other's money. Another way is for each country to set a rate of exchange between a given commodity and its own money. Countries that peg the value of a particular commodity in terms of their money are said to be on a *commodity standard*. When two countries peg their monies to the same commodity, they indirectly fix the exchange rate between their two monies.

To see this, suppose the U.S. pegs the dollar at \$20.00 per barrel of oil, and Britain pegs the pound at £15.00 per barrel. The pound-dollar exchange rate in this case will be £15.00/\$20.00, or .75 pound per dollar. Any other rate would present an arbitrage opportunity—an opportunity to buy low and sell high. For example, if the exchange rate were 1 pound per dollar, rather than .75 pound per dollar, anyone with 15 pounds could purchase a barrel of oil in England, sell it for \$20.00 in the U.S., and convert the \$20.00 into 20 pounds, making a quick profit of 5 pounds on the transaction.

The use of a commodity standard to fix the exchange rate has historical precedent. The U.S. and most European countries pegged their monies to gold throughout most of the last century and a good part of this century. Whenever the exchange rate between two countries on the **gold standard** moved even slightly away from the rate determined by comparing their prices of gold, arbitrageurs responded by purchasing gold in one country and shipping it for sale to the other. The gold standard, together with rough seas, explains why there are so many boats laden with gold lying at the bottom of the Atlantic Ocean.

Gold standard *An arrangement in which the currencies of most countries are convertible into gold at a fixed rate*

THE LAW OF ONE PRICE AND THE DISTINCTION BETWEEN NOMINAL AND REAL EXCHANGE RATES

Law of one price *The proposition that identical goods should have the same real cost everywhere they are traded*

The **law of one price** is the proposition that, ignoring shipping costs, commodity taxes, and tariffs, traded goods should cost the same in all locations, be those locations within a particular country or in different countries. The law of one price is dictated by competition. If the same commodity can be purchased at location A for less than at location B, purchasers will seek to buy the commodity at A, rather than B. This will drive up the price at location A and drive down the price at location B until, in equilibrium, the two prices are identical.

In the international context the law of one price dictates that, apart from shipping fees, commodity taxes, and tariffs, traded goods should cost the same whether they are purchased at home or abroad. Thus, if a bushel of wheat costs \$3 in the U.S., it should only take \$3 worth of francs to buy a bushel of wheat in

France. If the price of a bushel of wheat in France is 15 francs, an American wheat dealer should be able to swap her \$3 for just enough French francs—15—to purchase the wheat in France; i.e., the exchange rate should be 5 francs per dollar. If the exchange rate were not equal to 5 francs per dollar, it would be cheaper to buy wheat in one country than in the other. Such a disequilibrium could be corrected by changes in the dollar price of U.S. wheat, changes in the franc price of French wheat, or a realignment (an increase or a decrease) of the franc-dollar exchange rate.

Case Study: Purchasing Power Parity and International Big Mac Prices

Another way to describe the law of one price in the international context is to say that a given amount of money, say dollars, should have the same power to purchase traded goods (again ignoring shipping fees, commodity taxes, and tariffs) whether those traded goods are purchased at home or abroad. This is why economists refer to the law of one price in the international context as **purchasing power parity**. For some internationally traded goods, such as oil, which are exchanged in well-developed international markets, purchasing power parity can readily be verified by checking that the price paid by one country for oil delivered to its ports is the same as that paid by other countries, after converting the foreign payment into domestic currency and adjusting for differences in shipping costs.

Purchasing power parity
The proposition that a unit of a country's currency should be able to purchase the same quantity of goods and services at home or, after being converted into foreign currency, abroad

For other goods, determining whether purchasing power parity holds, or indeed, should hold, is not so easy. Take McDonald's Big Mac hamburger. McDonald's sells Big Macs around the world. Many ingredients used to produce Big Macs are imported and, for that reason, we might think the price of Big Macs would be the same throughout the world after converting local prices into dollars via the exchange rate. On the other hand, some of the inputs used in producing Big Macs, such as the electricity used to light the store, are nontraded. Since the dollar price of such nontraded inputs will not necessarily be the same internationally, there is no reason to believe purchasing power parity will hold with respect to Big Macs. Even if all inputs into Big Macs were imported, it would still be a challenge to test for purchasing power parity based on Big Macs because of the need to adjust for shipping costs and tax differences across countries.

We shouldn't, on a priori grounds, expect purchasing power parity to hold perfectly with respect to the Big Mac. Still, it's interesting to know the extent to which it fails. Table 13-1 tells us. It presents the dollar prices of Big Macs in 24 different countries plus the U.S. as of April 9, 1994. The table also reports the local currency price of the Big Macs as well as the exchange rates used to convert these prices into dollars. On April 9, 1994 the dollar price of a Big Mac in the U.S. was \$2.30. But around the world the price ranged from \$3.96 in Switzerland to \$1.03 in China—a huge range. The lowest price—that prevailing in China—reflects the relatively low cost of labor there. For Mexico, Chile, and

Table 13.1 The Dollar Price of Big Macs Around the World on April 13, 1994

Country	Currency	Exchange Rate[a]	Big Mac Price In Local Currency	Big Mac Price In Dollars[b]
Switzerland	Franc	1.44	5.70	3.96
Japan	Yen	104	391.00	3.77
Argentina	Peso	1.00	3.60	3.60
Sweden	Kroner	7.97	25.50	3.20
France	Franc	5.83	18.50	3.17
Belgium	Franc	35.2	109.00	3.10
Italy	Lira	1641	4550.00	2.77
Germany	Mark	1.71	4.60	2.69
Britain	Pound	1.46	1.81	2.65
Portugal	Escudo	174	440.00	2.53
Spain	Peseta	138	345.00	2.50
Mexico	Peso	3.36	8.10	2.41
Taiwan	Dollar	26.4	62.00	2.35
UNITED STATES	DOLLAR	1.00	2.30	2.30
Chile	Peso	414	948.00	2.28
Canada	Dollar	1.39	2.86	2.06
Thailand	Baht	25.3	48.00	1.90
Singapore	Dollar	1.57	2.98	1.90
Australia	Dollar	1.42	2.45	1.72
Russia	Rouble	1775	2900.00	1.66
Hungary	Forint	103	169.00	1.66
Brazil	Cruzeiro	949	1500.00	1.58
Hong Kong	Dollar	7.73	9.20	1.19
China	Yuan	8.7	9.00	1.03

[a]Foreign currency per U.S. dollar on April 9, 1994
[b]Calculated as local currency price divided by the exchange rate

Source: *The Economist*, April 9, 1994, p. 88.

Taiwan, the dollar prices of Big Macs are almost identical to the price in the U.S. Hence, we can say that, measured in Big Macs, the purchasing power of a dollar was quite similar at that time in Mexico, Chile, Taiwan, and the U.S.

Real Versus Nominal Exchange Rates

As we've seen, by using the exchange rate to express the foreign price of a specific good or service in units of domestic currency, we can compare the foreign price of that good with the domestic price. For example, we can form the ratio of the dollar price of Big Macs in the U.S. to that in Russia on April 9, 1994 and find that it equals 1.39, indicating that Big Macs cost 39 percent more in the U.S. on that day than they did in Russia. What if we now form such a relative price ratio, not for a particular good or service, but for a representative basket of goods and services produced in the home and foreign countries? If we do this, we arrive at what economists call the **real exchange rate**. The real exchange rate is also known as *the terms of trade*; it is the relative cost of purchasing domestic versus foreign goods and services.

Real exchange rate *The ratio of the price of a fixed basket of goods and services in the domestic economy to the price, in domestic currency, of the same basket in a foreign country*

If we let e_t^R stand for the real exchange rate at time t and e_t stand for the actual or, as economists call it, the **nominal exchange rate**, we can write the real exchange rate as

Nominal exchange rate *The number of units of a foreign country's currency that can be purchased with one unit of the home country's currency*

$$e_t^R = \frac{\text{Domestic price level in domestic currency}}{\text{Foreign price level in domestic currency}} = \frac{P_t}{[P_t^*/e_t]}$$

where P_t stands for the domestic price level and P_t^* stands for the foreign price level, both at time t. (As in Chapter 6, we'll refer to foreign country variables with the superscript *.) Thus, if the U.S. is the home country, the domestic price level is the amount of dollars needed to purchase a specific basket of goods in the U.S. If Spain is the foreign country, the foreign price level is the amount of Spanish pesetas it would take to purchase this same basket of goods in Spain. By dividing the Spanish price level by the nominal exchange rate, we express, in dollars, the cost of purchasing the basket of goods in Spain. This dollar cost of the basket in Spain is then divided into the dollar cost of the basket in the U.S. to arrive at the real exchange rate.

There is no requirement that increases in the nominal exchange rate be associated with increases in the real exchange rate. To see this, first write the real exchange rate as the product of the nominal exchange rate and the ratio of the domestic to the foreign price levels: $e_t^R = e_t(P_t/P_t^*)$. Now observe that if increases in e_t are associated with equal proportionate decreases in P_t/P_t^*, e_t^R will be unchanged.

Also note that if purchasing power parity held for all goods and services in the basket, then the dollar cost of the basket in Spain would equal the dollar cost of the basket in the U.S., and the real exchange rate would equal 1 and be constant over time. Purchasing power parity appears to hold reasonably well for many traded goods (e.g., oil and wheat), but it does not hold very well (nor should we necessarily expect it to hold very well) for nontraded goods. In

Figure 13-2 Indices of U.S. Monthly Nominal and Real Exchange Rates with Japan, January 1973–August 1992

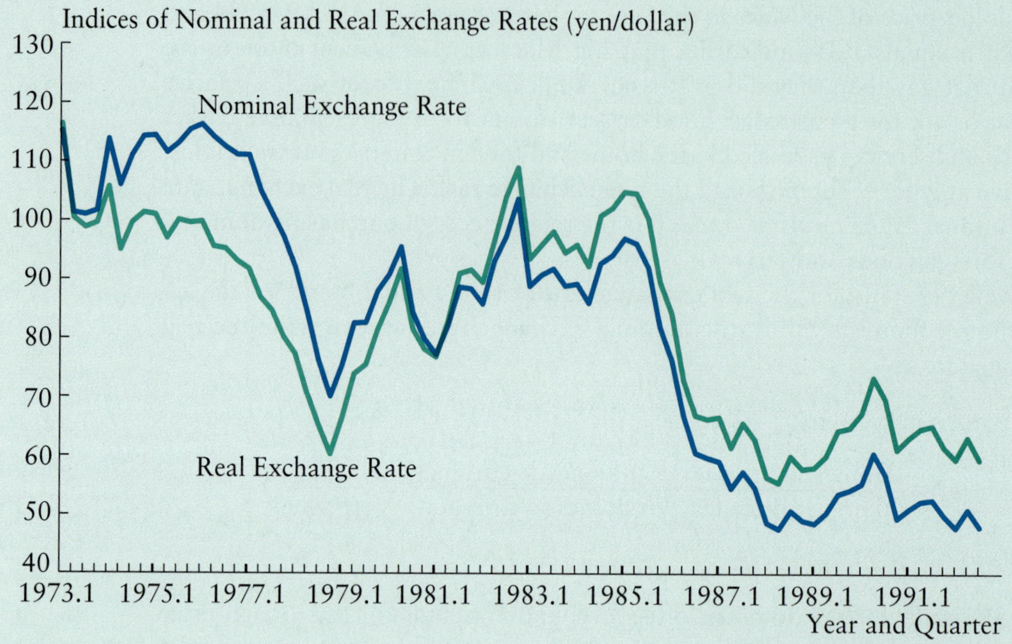

Short-run fluctuations in the nominal exchange rate are associated with similar fluctuations in the real exchange rate. The longer-run movements of the two rates are quite different. This is apparent in the growing gap between the nominal and real exchange rate lines between March 1973 and March 1975.

countries like the U.S. in which nontraded goods constitute a large share of GDP, there is no reason to expect the real exchange rate to remain constant through time.

Figure 13-2 shows changes over time in indices of the Japanese yen–U.S. dollar real and nominal exchange rates. Both indices have base values of 100 for March 1973. Note that the short-run fluctuations in the nominal exchange rate produce similar short-run fluctuations in the real exchange rate. But the longer-run movements of the two curves are quite different. Consider, for example, the period March 1973 through March 1975. Over this two-year period the real yen-dollar exchange rate depreciated by 3 percent, whereas the nominal exchange rate appreciated by 10 percent. In Figure 13-2, this is apparent in the growing gap between the nominal and real exchange rate lines. The explanation for this difference in the movements of the real and nominal exchange rates is that the ratio of the Japanese price level to the U.S. price level rose by about 13 percent over the period.

ADDING ANOTHER COUNTRY TO OUR MODEL WITH MONEY

In this section we first discuss the nominal side of our two-country international economy, including the determination of the nominal exchange rate. We then examine the real side of the economy. Finally, we combine these analyses and describe how to solve for all the real and nominal variables in the economy. We'll assume that prices and wages are fully flexible until we reach the last part of this chapter, which considers nominal rigidities. We'll see there how such rigidities alter our conclusions about fiscal, monetary, and exchange rate policies in the open economy.

Relating the Nominal Exchange Rate to the Foreign and Domestic Price Levels

In adding another country to our model of Chapter 8, which includes money, we'll keep things simple by assuming that each country produces the same good and that there are no shipping fees, commodity taxes, tariffs, or other costs involved in one country's sale of this good to the other. Given these assumptions and a competitive international market for the single good, the law of one price dictates that the foreign price of the good, expressed in terms of domestic currency, is the same as the domestic price. Another way to say this is that the real exchange rate—the ratio of the price of the domestic good relative to the price of the foreign good measured in domestic currency—equals 1 in our model.

What does a real exchange rate equal to 1 mean for the relationship between the nominal exchange rate and the price levels of the two countries? The answer can be seen by setting the real exchange rate, e_t^R, equal to 1 in the expression $e_t^R = e_t(P_t/P_t^*)$. Doing so and rearranging terms produces the following simple formula:

$$e_t = \frac{P_t^*}{P_t}$$

According to this formula the nominal exchange rate is just the ratio of the foreign price level to the domestic price level. If the foreign currency is, say, francs, and the domestic currency is dollars, this formula indicates that the nominal exchange rate equals the number of francs per unit of the good divided by the number of dollars per unit. Canceling the "per unit of the good" from the numerator and denominator of this verbal equation leaves the exchange rate equaling what it is supposed to equal, namely, the number of francs per dollar.

Since the nominal exchange rate equals the ratio of the foreign to the domestic price level, an increase in this ratio will lead to an appreciation, and a decrease to a depreciation, of the nominal exchange rate. Thus, if the foreign price level rises more rapidly than the domestic price level, the ratio of the foreign to the domestic price level will rise and the nominal exchange rate will appreciate. Alternatively, if the foreign price level rises less rapidly than the domestic price level, the foreign to domestic price ratio will fall, and the exchange rate will depreciate. A third possibility is that foreign and domestic prices change at the same rate, i.e., that the inflation rates at home and abroad are equal. In this case the foreign to domestic price ratio will not change and neither will the exchange rate. We can summarize the relationship between the nominal exchange rate and the foreign and domestic inflation rates with the following equation which can be derived, as an approximation, from the above equation.

$$\frac{e_{t+1} - e_t}{e_t} = \pi^*_{t+1} - \pi_{t+1}$$

where π^*_t and π_t are the foreign and domestic inflation rates, respectively. In words, this equation says that, over a given period of time, the percentage increase in the nominal exchange rate equals the contemporaneous difference between the foreign and domestic inflation rates.

Figure 13-3 examines how well this equation explains post-1975 movements of three U.S. exchange rates: the U.S. dollar–German mark rate, the U.S. dollar–Japanese yen rate, and the U.S. dollar–British pound rate. It plots, for each year, the annual percentage changes in these three exchange rates (the left-hand side of the above equation) minus the difference between each foreign country's inflation rate and the U.S. inflation rate (the right-hand side of the equation). If the equation held perfectly, all the points on these three plots would equal zero and would fall on the horizontal line emanating from point 0 on the vertical axis. The three plots clearly differ from zero in most years, but each of the plots straddles the horizontal line marked 0. Hence, the data show that the above relationship appears to hold over long periods of time.

Relating the Exchange Rate to the Money Supplies of Each Country

As we showed in Chapter 8, equating the supply of and demand for money produced an equation relating the price level to the money supply. For the home country this equation is $P_t = M_t/\gamma w_t N$, where M_t stands for the money supply at time t, γ is the money demand preference parameter (which depends, in general, on the nominal interest rate), w_t is the domestic wage, and N is the population size of each cohort in the home country. An equivalent expression relates the price level in the foreign country to the foreign country's money supply, namely, $P^*_t = M^*_t/\gamma^* w^*_t N^*$.

To keep things simple we'll assume, for the moment, that γ and γ^* are both constants and equal to each other. We also know from Chapter 6 that international capital mobility leads to the same capital-labor ratio in each country, and thus the same real wages. Hence, w_t equals w^*_t. If we now form the ratio P^*_t/P_t, we see that all the terms except the two countries' money supplies and their population sizes cancel, so we are left with the expression

$$\frac{P^*_t}{P_t} = \frac{M^*_t/N^*}{M_t/N}$$

Figure 13-3 Percentage Change in U.S. Exchange Rates Less Difference Between Foreign and U.S. Inflation Rates

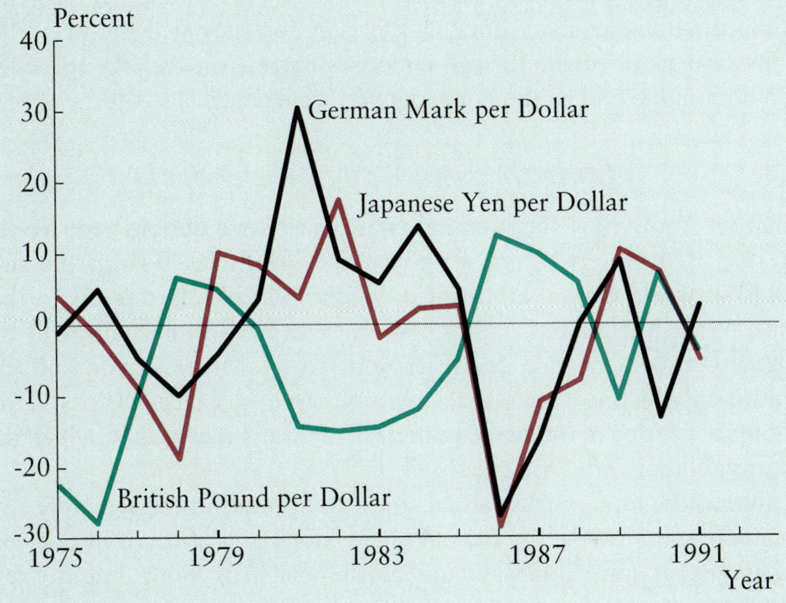

In principle, the percentage increase in the nominal exchange rate over a given period of time should equal the contemporaneous difference between the foreign and domestic inflation rates. Evidence suggests that this relationship does hold over long periods. Although the three plots differ from 0 in most years, each plot straddles the horizontal line at zero.

Source: OECD and *Economic Report of the President,* 1993

The intuition behind this relationship is straightforward. The money demands of young people in the two countries are identical, so differences between the two countries with respect to their price levels can only arise because of differences in the supply of money per young person (or per capita, since multiplying both N^* and N by 2 leaves the equation unchanged). As the formula indicates, if the money supply per young person is twice as large in the foreign country as it is in the home country, the foreign price level will be double the domestic price level.

We've now made two points with our model. First, the exchange rate equals the foreign-domestic price ratio ($e_t = P_t^*/P_t$). Second, the foreign-domestic price ratio equals the foreign-domestic ratio of money supply per young person [$P_t^*/P_t = (M_t^*/N^*)/(M_t/N)$]. Eliminating the foreign-domestic price ratio from these two expressions produces a relationship between the nominal exchange rate and the money supplies of the two countries:

$$e_t = \frac{M_t^*/N^*}{M_t/N}$$

This formula says that the exchange rate equals the ratio of the foreign money supply per young person to the domestic money supply per young person. It tells us that if the foreign money supply increases (decreases) relative to the domestic money supply, the exchange rate will appreciate (depreciate). Intuitively, if the foreign country increases its stock of money per young person relatively more than the home country does, the foreign currency will become relatively abundant, and more of the foreign country's currency will have to be surrendered to obtain one unit of the home country's currency.

Adding the Real Side to the Model

Now that we know how the nominal exchange rate is determined, we turn to the real side of our international economy. Specifically, we'll study the determination of the world capital-labor ratio, where "world" here refers to the two countries. As we learned in Chapter 6, because capital is internationally mobile it will flow between the two countries until the real interest rate and capital-labor ratio, on which it depends, are the same in both places. The equalization of capital-labor ratios in the two countries also means that wages, which depend on the capital-labor ratio, are equalized.

Recall that the total world capital stock at a point in time is simply the sum of the capital assets owned by the elderly at home and abroad. In this chapter, we'll assume that individuals do not consume when young but do demand money. Consequently, the amount of assets the domestic young of time t bring into their old age (time $t + 1$) is $N[(1 - \gamma)w_t - f]$, where f continues to refer to payments by each young person to the government for taxes or the purchase of government bonds. The corresponding formula for the assets of young people in the foreign country is $N^*[(1 - \gamma^*)w_t - f^*]$.

Forming the ratio of total world assets to the total world labor force $(N + N^*)$ and using the fact that the wage equals the marginal product of labor, we can write the transition equation for the world's capital-labor ratio as

$$k_{t+1} = A(1 - \bar{\gamma})\,(1 - \beta)k_t^{\beta} - \bar{f}$$

where

$$\bar{\gamma} = \frac{N\gamma + N^*\gamma^*}{N + N^*} \quad \text{and} \quad \bar{f} = \frac{Nf + N^*f^*}{N + N^*}$$

The terms $\bar{\gamma}$ and $\bar{f}$ stand, respectively, for population-weighted averages of the home and foreign money demand preference parameters and payments collected by the government from the young. This transition formula for the world's capital-labor ratio is exactly the same as in Chapter 6 except for the inclusion of the fiscal policy variable $\bar{f}$ and the fact that $\bar{\alpha}$ is replaced by $\bar{\gamma}$.

In Chapter 7 we described how fiscal policy affects a country's ownership of capital and its net foreign investment. The above equation tells us that a country's fiscal policy also influences total world ownership of capital, i.e., that it influences worldwide capital accumulation. Note that a country's fiscal policy influences the world's capital-labor ratio and, thus, its own capital-labor ratio (since they are the same) only to the extent that it alters $\bar{f}$, the worldwide average stance of fiscal policy. If the home country is very small relative to the foreign country (e.g., Bermuda versus the U.S.), N will be very small relative to N^*, so that an increase in f will have a trivial effect on $\bar{f}$. Thus, we conclude that the fiscal policy of a small open economy will be ineffective in altering either its capital-labor ratio, its real wage, or its real interest rate.

Determining All Real and Nominal Variables in Our International Economy

It's now straightforward to solve for all the real and nominal variables in our international economy from some point, say time 0, onward. The procedure for calculating real variables is essentially the same as that used in Chapter 6 once we take into account domestic and foreign fiscal policy.

First, given the world capital-labor ratio prevailing at time 0 and the measure of worldwide fiscal policy given by $\bar{f}$, we determine the world capital-labor ratio at all future dates using our transition equation. But this also tells us the time paths of the real wage and real interest rate (recall that they are the same at home and abroad), since the time paths of these variables depend on the time path of the world capital-labor ratio. We also determine the total capital stock in each county at any point in time by multiplying its labor force by the world capital-labor ratio. Finally, we enter each country's total capital stock and labor force at any point in time into its Cobb-Douglas production function to determine its output.

Now that we know how to calculate real variables in the economy, let's turn to the nominal variables. Their calculation is also straightforward. First of all, the nominal exchange rate is determined by the ratio of the two countries' money supplies per young person, which, for the moment, we assume are fixed. Given these money supplies, we can solve for the nominal exchange rate. Secondly, given each country's money supply, we can solve for each country's price level at each point in time using the formulas for the domestic and foreign price levels.

MANAGING THE EXCHANGE RATE

Our formula linking the exchange rate to the ratio of money supplies per young person, $e_t = (M_t^*/N^*)/(M_t/N)$, tells us two important things about the relationship between exchange rate and monetary policies. First, it tells us that these policies are not independent. A country can control either its money supply or its exchange rate, but not both. If a country unilaterally changes its monetary policy, this will change its exchange rate. Alternatively, if a country unilaterally tries to fix its exchange rate at a value different from the ratio of the two money supplies, its own money supply will have to adjust to bring the ratio of the two money supplies per worker in line with the level fixed for the exchange rate.

Second, the formula tells us that countries share the same exchange rate and, thus, must coordinate their exchange rate policies. Suppose, for example, the home country wants the exchange rate to appreciate. It can try to produce an appreciation by decreasing its money supply. But if the foreign country wants to keep the exchange rate unchanged, it can follow suit by decreasing, by an equal percentage, its own money supply. The net result will be the same ratio of the two countries' money supplies and the same exchange rate.

Distinguishing Flexible and Fixed Exchange Rate Regimes

Our formula connecting the nominal exchange rate to the ratio of money supplies can also help us think about the difference between flexible and fixed exchange rates. In a flexible exchange rate regime, the governments set their money supplies and let their exchange rates freely adjust according to the resulting ratio of the two money supplies. In a fixed exchange rate regime, one of the two countries, with the acquiescence of the other, sets the exchange rate and permits its money supply to adjust to the level required to satisfy our formula. Thus, in a flexible exchange rate regime the government maintains direct control of its money supply and loses direct control of its exchange rate, whereas the opposite occurs in a fixed exchange rate regime.

Although the variable under direct government control differs in the two regimes, the equation relating the nominal exchange rate to the ratio of money supplies holds in both regimes. Hence, one might ask whether it really matters if a country chooses a flexible or fixed exchange rate regime? The answer is that, assuming freely flexible prices and wages, it may not matter. According to our model, *if* countries with flexible exchange rates can freely adjust their money supplies, they can do so to produce the same real economic outcomes as would arise under a fixed exchange rate regime. Conversely, *if* countries with fixed exchange rates can freely change the value at which their exchange rate is fixed, they can replicate any real outcomes that would arise in a flexible exchange rate regime.

Illustrating Monetary Policy in a Flexible Exchange Rate Regime

To demonstrate the potential equivalence of flexible and fixed exchange rate regimes, we'll now show how a simple monetary policy can be conducted equally well in a flexible or a fixed exchange rate regime. Under this policy the home country prints 10 percent more money each period to finance transfer payments to its elderly. To keep matters simple, we'll assume the foreign country keeps its money supply fixed. Recall that we considered this policy in Chapter 8 for a closed economy. We pointed out in that chapter that this policy raises the price level by 10 percent each period but has no real effects.[2] Each period the elderly end up paying for the transfers they receive through an implicit tax, namely, the decline in the real value of their money balances resulting from the induced price rise.

In our open economy the same situation holds. The home country's printing of money to make transfers to its elderly leaves them with more nominal money

2. We are referring here to our simple formulation of money demand, in which the nominal interest rate is not an argument.

holdings but the same real money balances after taking account of the induced increase in prices. As in the closed economy case, the policy has no impact on the saving of the domestic young. Nor does it alter the saving of the foreign young. Hence, it leaves unchanged the total capital accumulation of the young each period and, thus, the world's capital-labor transition equation. In sum, as in the closed economy model, this monetary policy in the open economy is neutral. It raises domestic prices each period but leaves the real side of the domestic and the foreign economies the same.

The policy does, however, alter the nominal exchange rate. Each period the relative value of the home country's money—the exchange rate—depreciates by 10 percent. We can see this either by considering the formula $e_t = (M^*_t/N^*)/(M_t/N)$ and noting that under the policy we're considering the ratio of the foreign to the domestic money supply per young worker falls by 10 percent each period. Alternatively, we can refer to our formula that relates the percentage change in the exchange rate (from one period to the next) to the difference between the foreign and domestic inflation rates. In this case, the difference between these inflation rates is minus 10 percent, meaning that the nominal exchange rate falls by 10 percent each period.

As an example, take the case in which $N = N^*$ and suppose that the foreign and domestic money supplies are both 100 at time 0. In this case the exchange rate will equal 1.000. At that point, the domestic government begins to raise its money supply each period by 10 percent. In period 1 the domestic money supply will be set at 110.0. In period 2 it will be 121.0. In period 3 it will be 133.1, and so forth. What will be the values of the exchange rate in these periods? The answer, found by forming the ratio of the money supplies, is .909 in period 1, .826 in period 2, .751 in period 3, and so forth, with the exchange rate falling by 10 percent each period.

What happens to the foreign price level as a result of the domestic country's monetary policy? Nothing! The nominal exchange rate fully adjusts to insulate the foreign country from the domestic country's change in its money supply. As a result, this policy produces no changes in any domestic real variables, no changes in any variables (except the nominal exchange rate) in the foreign country, but a 10 percent depreciation of the domestic currency each period as well as a 10 percent domestic inflation.

Illustrating Exchange Rate Policy in a Fixed Exchange Rate Regime

The monetary policy just described can also be conducted in a fixed exchange rate regime. Intuitively, since $e_t = (M^*_t/N^*)/(M_t/N)$, the government can set the value of e_t and let M_t adjust to that value (i.e., set its money supply indirectly), rather than setting the value of M_t directly and letting e_t adjust (as in the case of a flexible exchange rate regime). In a fixed exchange rate regime, governments set their exchange rates by intervening in the foreign exchange market by either selling or buying their own currency. In conducting the above-described policy, the domestic government needs to intervene in the foreign exchange market to produce a lower exchange rate each period. In terms of our numerical example, the domestic government needs to fix its exchange rate at .909 in period 1, at .826 in period 2, at .751 in period 3, etc.—the same values to which the exchange rate equilibrates in the flexible exchange regime.

Let's call the domestic money dollars and the foreign money francs, and let's continue to assume that the foreign government keeps its money supply fixed. To produce a 10 percent depreciation of the dollar each period, the domestic government must print additional dollars each period and sell these dollars for francs on the foreign exchange market. This raises the total supply of dollars being offered in exchange for francs and leads to an increase in the number of dollars needed to purchase one franc, i.e., it leads to a depreciation of the dollar. For example, to set the exchange rate in period 1 at .909, the domestic government needs to print dollars and spend them—on francs in the foreign exchange market—until the market exchange rate settles at .909 franc per dollar or, equivalently, 1.1 dollars per franc. The fact that the government continues to print and sell dollars until its targeted exchange rate is met is why we say that the change in the domestic money supply under this policy is endogenous.

To complete our analysis of this exchange rate intervention we need to clarify what the domestic government does with the francs it purchases on the foreign exchange market. One possibility, the one we'll consider here, is to give them to the domestic elderly as a transfer payment.[3] Of course, the domestic elderly are interested in getting dollars to spend on their final period consumption. Accordingly, they will turn around and exchange these francs for dollars on the foreign exchange market.

The net result of these transactions is that the domestic elderly will purchase back from the foreign exchange market the dollars just sold there by their government. In other words, rather than hand over directly to its domestic elderly the additional dollars it prints, as occurs in the flexible exchange rate scenario, the domestic government does so indirectly by (1) printing dollars, (2) trading these dollars for francs on the exchange market, (3) giving those francs to its elderly, and (4) letting its elderly purchase the dollars just printed by the government. In both the flexible and the fixed exchange rate regimes, the result is the same: the domestic elderly end up with 10 percent more dollars but are no better off because of the induced 10 percent rise in the domestic price level. In addition, the nominal exchange rate depreciates by 10 percent.

Do Flexible and Fixed Exchange Rate Regimes Really Differ?

We've just shown that, absent price or wage rigidities, a particular type of monetary policy can be conducted equally well in both flexible and fixed exchange rate regimes. This is not an isolated example. On the contrary, absent nominal rigidities, any monetary (or, for that matter, fiscal) policy conducted in a flexible exchange regime can also be conducted in a fixed exchange regime and vice versa *if* there are no restrictions in the flexible exchange regime on the govern-

3. It may seem strange to think of the domestic government making transfer payments to its elderly residents in foreign currency. This won't happen if the domestic government purchases foreign assets with the francs, sells the foreign assets for dollars, and transfers these dollars to its elderly.

ment's management of its money supply and *if* there are no restrictions in the fixed exchange regime on the government's management of its exchange rate. These are two big ifs. Under flexible exchange rate regimes, the government may have less latitude to adjust its money supply than is needed to keep its exchange rate either fixed or on a specifically targeted path. Similarly, under fixed exchange rates, a country may have less latitude to adjust its exchange rate than is needed to keep its money supply either fixed or changing in a desired manner.

In switching from one regime to another, governments often take political positions that restrict their repeating the policies they conducted in the former regime. Thus, in our example of a flexible exchange rate regime with an ongoing 10 percent inflation, the price stabilization might come about after the government switches to a fixed exchange rate regime and publicly announces that it will keep the exchange rate perfectly fixed. As we know from our formula relating the exchange rate to the ratio of foreign to domestic price levels, if the foreign price level is fixed and the exchange rate is fixed, the domestic price level will be fixed as well.

Of course, such price stabilization policy could also be conducted in a flexible exchange rate regime by having the government adjust its money supply to keep the price level fixed. But it may be easier for the government to convince the public that it is actively trying to stabilize prices if it fixes the exchange rate than if it announces it is using monetary policy to stabilize prices. In the former case, the government can point to a concrete achievement of its policy, namely, a fixed exchange rate. In contrast, if the government says it is choosing a path of money supply to stabilize prices, the public has to decide whether the changes in the money supply chosen by the government are really those needed to keep prices from rising. Recall that the price level formula contains money demand factors (γ, w_t, and N) as well as the money supply (M_t). If the public isn't sure how these money demand factors are changing through time, it won't know for sure whether the government is really choosing the money supply appropriate to eliminate inflation. Of course, the public can observe inflation directly, but inflation is usually reported with a time lag. In addition, the government can always claim that it missed its inflation target because of unexpected changes in the demand for money.

Case Study: Stabilizing the Argentine Peso

Argentina's economic history redounds with episodes of high inflation followed by short-lived attempts to control the growth of its money supply. One such episode occurred in 1979 when the Argentine inflation rate was running at 150 percent per year. The Argentine Finance Minister, Martinez de Hoz, announced that the government would manage the dollar-peso exchange rate so that its value would depreciate over time according to a set schedule laid out in a "tablita." In terms of our formula, $e_t = (M_t^*/N^*)/(M_t/N)$, the tablita's requirement that e_t fall more slowly than in the past meant that M_t would rise at a slower rate than previously. The tablita policy was reasonably successful, at least in terms of controlling inflation. By the end of 1980 the Argentine inflation rate was running at well below 100 percent per year.

SOME ARGUMENTS FOR AND AGAINST FLEXIBLE AND FIXED EXCHANGE RATE REGIMES

The above discussion suggests that the choice between fixed and flexible exchange rate regimes may have more to do with the issue of political commitment (keeping politicians time consistent) than with any meaningful economic distinctions. But there are additional arguments for and against the two regimes. In the following sections we point out that transactions costs make fixed exchange rates relatively more attractive, whereas the loss of independence in conducting monetary policy, the need for coordination between monetary and exchange authorities, and the possibility of running out of international reserves make flexible exchange rates relatively more attractive. Once we've discussed these issues, we'll add nominal rigidities to our model and show how they alter the comparison of exchange rate regimes.

Transactions Costs and Flexible Exchange Rates

Flexible exchange rates raise the costs of transacting in foreign currencies. With constantly fluctuating rates, international traders must continually check the values of these rates to assess the profitability of their international transactions. The burden of keeping abreast of the latest values of exchange rates and the paperwork involved in exchanging currencies is particularly great in the case of international transactions involving a large number of countries. Thinking about trade among the 50 states of the U.S. can help illuminate this point. The 50 states can be viewed as participating in a fixed exchange rate regime. The only difference between this fixed exchange rate regime and the one between, say, the U.S. and Western Europe in the 1950s and 1960s is that each of the 50 states uses the same form of money: dollars.

Imagine the cost of conducting trade within the U.S. if each state had its own money whose relative values fluctuated continually. A supermarket in Boston considering purchasing apples from Washington state, California, New York, or Ohio would have to ascertain the value of each of these states' exchange rates with Massachusetts in order to convert each of the four local apple prices into amounts of Massachusetts money.[4] Extrapolating this example to the myriad interstate transactions conducted in the U.S., you quickly get a sense of the additional transactions costs arising from flexible exchange rates.

Independence in the Operation of Monetary Policy

One argument against fixed rates is the potential loss in flexibility in conducting monetary policy. We say "potential" because, as we showed above, if a country has enough leeway in setting its exchange rate, it can adjust that rate over time to produce the same changes in its money supply that would occur under fixed

4. Note that if the law of one price always operated perfectly, the supermarket would know that all four apple prices would be the same, measured in Massachusetts currency. In the real world, however, there may be temporary deviations in the law of one price even in case of traded goods.

rates. But in actual practice, nations adopting fixed rate regimes have been quite reluctant to alter their exchange rates.

Figure 13-1 makes this clear. It shows that during the 1950s and 1960s, when the German mark and French franc were pegged to (fixed relative to) the dollar, there was very little movement in either the mark-dollar or franc-dollar exchange rates except for a few occasions when either the mark or the franc was revalued against the dollar. In adhering for long periods of time to an essentially rigid exchange rate with the dollar, Germany and France, in effect, agreed to follow the course of monetary policy being conducted by the U.S. These countries' willingness to adopt the same monetary policy as the U.S. lasted until the early 1970s when the U.S. began increasing its money supply at a faster rate. At this point Germany and France realized (1) that to maintain the same exchange rate with the U.S., they would also have to increase the growth rate of their money supplies and (2) that this would spell higher inflation for them, just as it spelled higher inflation for the U.S. Neither Germany nor France was willing to tolerate higher inflation, so they elected to steer their own course of monetary policy within the ERM and let their exchange rates float against the dollar.

In opting to run independent monetary policies, Germany and France not only were able to choose their own inflation rates but also were able to decide for themselves how much real resources (via seigniorage and the like) they wanted to extract from the private sector through monetary policy. They were also able to use monetary policy to offset recessions caused or exacerbated by Keynesian short-run nominal rigidities.

The original ERM, which lasted from 1974 through 1993, allowed Germany and France to conduct monetary policy independent of the U.S., but it did not permit Germany and France to conduct monetary policy independent of each other. In the summer of 1993 France's desire to conduct a more expansionary monetary policy than that being pursued by Germany led to the devaluation of the franc relative to the mark and to a new, much looser ERM.

The Need for Intergovernment Coordination in Fixed Rate Regimes

Another concern in running a fixed rate regime is that it requires coordinating the actions of those government officials in charge of the money supply and those directed to regulate the exchange rate. In the U.S., the Department of the Treasury has one set of officials, referred to as the foreign exchange desk, charged with managing U.S. foreign exchange rates.[5] The Federal Reserve has a separate set of officials, referred to as the open market desk, charged with controlling the U.S. money supply.[6] Quite often the steps taken by the foreign exchange desk are offset, or **sterilized**, by the open market desk and vice versa.

Sterilization of exchange rate intervention *Central banks' practice of reversing the exchange market transactions of the exchange authorities*

5. Actually, the Federal Reserve plays a role, albeit a secondary one, in determining the actions taken by the foreign exchange desk.
6. Chapter 14 discusses in detail the Fed's open market desk and its procedures for increasing the money supply by printing money to buy U.S. Treasury bonds and for decreasing the money supply by absorbing money by selling Treasury bonds.

International reserves
A government's holdings of assets denominated in foreign currencies

Here's an example of such sterilization. Suppose the Treasury's foreign exchange desk wishes to lower the value of the dollar vis-à-vis the German mark and attempts to do so by creating dollars and selling them for marks.[7] Let's suppose that the foreign exchange desk, rather than holding the marks (or, as in our discussion above, transferring them to the elderly), spends them on a German bond. If no further actions are taken by the Fed, this policy will increase the U.S. money supply, leave the German money supply unchanged, and leave the Fed holding a German government bond as part of its **international reserves**—its holdings of assets denominated in foreign currencies. But now suppose the Fed's open market desk is under orders to keep the U.S. money supply fixed. What will it do? It will turn around and sell enough U.S. Treasury bonds to the public in exchange for dollars to sop up all the extra dollars supplied by the foreign exchange desk. The net impact of these transactions is (1) no change in either the U.S. or German money supplies and (2) no change in the U.S. government's net wealth position. True, the U.S. government (including the Fed) ends up holding an additional asset, namely, a German government bond, but it also has an additional outstanding liability, namely, the additional Treasury bonds it sold to the public. At the prevailing exchange rate, the additional liability has the same value as the German bond. In sum, unless the exchange rate and monetary authorities coordinate their actions, attempts to fix the exchange rate may not succeed.

Maintaining a Fixed Exchange Rate with Limited International Reserves

Yet another concern with fixed exchange rates is that the exchange rate authorities may not have sufficient resources with which to intervene on the foreign exchange market and fix the exchange rate at the level they desire. Suppose, for example, the Irish government wants to revalue its currency, the punt, vis-à-vis the dollar. To do so, it needs to sell dollars and buy punts. But where will it get the dollars that it needs to sell in exchange for punts? The first possible source is its international reserves—its holdings of foreign financial assets (e.g., U.S. Treasury bonds). It will sell these assets for dollars and use the dollars to purchase punts. By selling reserves for dollars, the exchange authorities reduce the number of dollars in circulation, but in selling these dollars for punts, they restore the dollars back into circulation. The net result of these transactions is equivalent to directly selling foreign reserves for punts. This approach reduces the supply of punts held by the public, raises the ratio of the U.S. to Irish money supplies and, as our formula for the exchange rate indicates, raises the value of the punt vis-à-vis the dollar.

Now what happens if the Irish exchange authorities run out of foreign reserves before they have moved the exchange rate to the degree they intended? Well, with the agreement of the rest of the government, they could sell other

7. The Treasury has an automatic line of credit with the Federal Reserve that permits it to get the Fed to create the dollars it wants to sell on the foreign exchange market.

types of government assets for punts (or, if you like, for dollars and then spend the dollars on punts). If there are no other government assets available to sell, the exchange authorities could tax the public and purchase assets with the tax proceeds. But the rest of the government may balk at this proposition, putting an end to the attempt to fix the exchange rate at the desired level. This potential for the government to give up trying to peg the exchange rate at a particular value (to, so to speak, punt) does not arise in our model because the model does not consider the specific institutional framework of the government.

To be evenhanded in evaluating the two exchange regimes, we need to point out that in a flexible exchange rate regime the Irish government may encounter the same sort of difficulty in reducing its money supply. In a flexible regime, the counterpart of the above policy is for the Irish government to reduce the money supply by increasing taxes on the elderly. As we showed in Chapter 8, this policy doesn't affect the welfare of the Irish elderly because what they lose in taxes, they gain in an increase in the real value of their remaining money balances associated with the decline in the price level. This point notwithstanding, the political fallout from raising taxes may preclude conducting such a monetary policy.

Speculation Against Fixed Exchange Rate Regimes

One of the concerns about fixed exchange rates is that they are subject to speculative attacks. In a typical attack speculators come to believe the government will not be able to maintain the current rate and will have to devalue. In terms of the above example, speculators might come to believe that, once the Irish government's foreign reserves are exhausted, it will simply devalue the punt. If the punt is currently pegged at .7 punt per dollar but is expected to be devalued in the near future to, say, .8 punt per dollar, a speculator can expect to make, in short order, a .1 punt profit on each dollar she buys from the government. Each dollar obtained by selling .7 punt prior to the devaluation can be exchanged for .8 punt after the devaluation. Notice that anyone holding punts prior to the devaluation can speculate against the punt by selling them for dollars. Hence, if enough people come to expect a devaluation, the Irish government will find itself forced to purchase huge quantities of punts or devalue.

THE OPEN ECONOMY MODEL WITH NOMINAL RIGIDITIES

Our strategy for adding nominal rigidities to our open economy model is simply to modify our IS-LM framework to take into account the economy's openness.[8] Once we've done this we'll be in a position to consider how nominal rigidities influence the choice of exchange regimes. In what follows we drop time subscripts to keep things simple.

8. Adapting the closed economy IS-LM model to the open economy produces the Mundell-Fleming model, originally developed by Robert Mundell of Columbia University and Marcus Fleming of the International Monetary Fund.

The IS Curve in the Open Economy

The key modification to our IS-LM framework concerns the IS curve, which relates a country's interest rate next period to its income and fiscal policy this period. The logic of the IS curve for a closed economy is simple: a country's income and fiscal policy in this period affect the young people's saving in this period and, thus, its capital stock next period, on which next period's interest rate depends.

In an open economy, however, the interest rate is no longer determined by the saving of the domestic young, but rather by the saving of the young at home and abroad, i.e., by worldwide capital accumulation. Consequently, a country's own income and fiscal policies this period influence the interest rate next period only to the extent that they alter world saving and, thus, next period's world capital stock.

The following equation relating the world's capital stock next period to this period's domestic and foreign income and fiscal policies makes this clear.

$$K^{w}_{+1} = (1 - \gamma)Y + (1 - \gamma^{*})Y^{*} - (F + F^{*})$$

If we add to this formula the fact that $r_{+1} = A[K^{w}_{+1}/(N + N^{*})]^{\beta-1}$, we have everything we need to form the open economy IS curve. That is, since domestic income, Y, affects the world capital stock, K^{w}_{+1}, and the world capital stock determines the interest rate, r_{+1}, we have a relationship between domestic income and the interest rate.[9]

How does the open economy IS curve compare with the closed economy curve in which Y^{*} and F^{*} are set equal to zero? As shown in Figure 13-4, it's flatter. To understand why, consider point *A*, which lies on both the closed and open economy IS curves. Now consider the change in domestic income needed to lower the interest rate from r^{0} to r^{1}. In the closed economy case, income must rise from Y^{0} to Y^{1}, as depicted by the movement from point *A* to point *B*. In the open economy case, this same increase in domestic income would produce the same absolute increase in capital next period, but a smaller increase in next period's world capital-labor ratio, since we divide the world capital stock by $N + N^{*}$, rather than just N. Consequently, an increase in domestic income of only $Y^{1} - Y^{0}$ would not suffice to lower the interest rate (which depends on the world capital-labor ratio) from r^{0} to r^{1}. Rather, a bigger increase, namely, $Y^{2} - Y^{0}$, is needed. Thus, the open economy IS curve runs through points *A* and *C*.

Note that the smaller an economy is relative to the world economy, the flatter will be its IS curve. It's also true that the smaller the size of the economy, the less effective will be its fiscal policy as a tool for combating nominal rigidities. In terms of the IS curve, this means that the upward shift of the IS curve will be smaller, the smaller the size of the economy.

For a small open economy—one too small to materially affect the world's capital stock or its overall fiscal policy—the IS curve will be a horizontal line

9. In our analysis of the open economy IS curve we take the foreign income level, Y^{*}, and fiscal policy, F^{*}, as given.

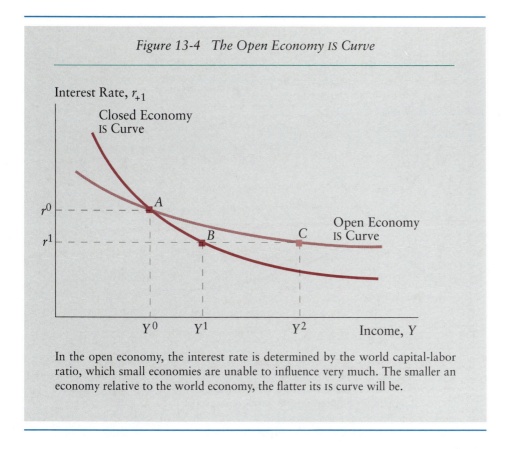

Figure 13-4 The Open Economy IS Curve

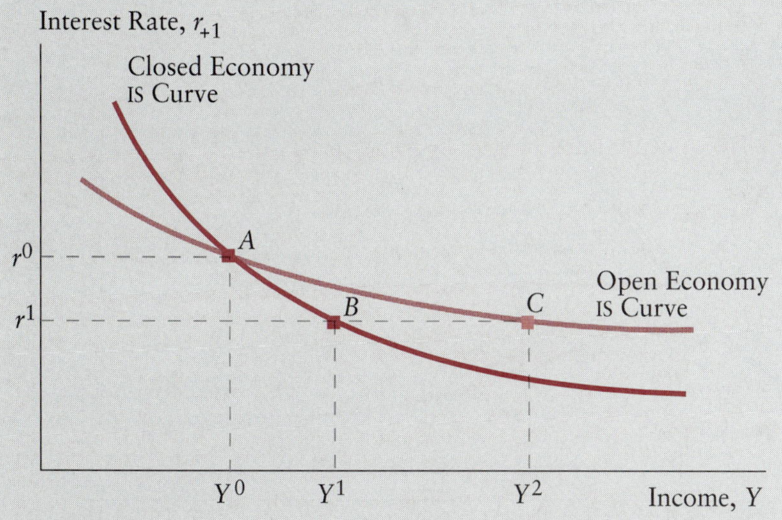

In the open economy, the interest rate is determined by the world capital-labor ratio, which small economies are unable to influence very much. The smaller an economy relative to the world economy, the flatter its IS curve will be.

whose height is set by next period's exogenous interest rate and whose position doesn't change in response to changes in its fiscal policy. Since it no longer shifts the IS curve, fiscal policy in a small open economy is completely impotent as a means of overcoming short-run nominal rigidities.

On the other hand, we have seen that compared to a downward-sloping IS curve, a flat IS curve makes monetary policy more effective. Figure 13-5 shows that a given rightward shift of the LM curve will produce a bigger increase in output and employment if the IS curve IS flat than if it slopes downward. The reason is that with a downward-sloping IS curve, the interest rate would fall. That would raise the demand for money and would mean that income need not rise by as much (as with a flat IS curve) to reestablish money market equilibrium with the larger money supply.

To summarize, we've shown that although small open economies facing nominal rigidities can't rely on fiscal policy, they can expect their monetary policy to be more effective than that of a large open economy, since their IS curve is flat. But, as we've discussed, the choice of exchange regime affects the ability to conduct independent monetary policy. Let's examine this choice for a small open economy facing nominal wage rigidity. After doing so, we'll turn to the case of a small open economy facing price rigidity.

Figure 13-5 Why Monetary Policy Is More Effective in an Open Economy

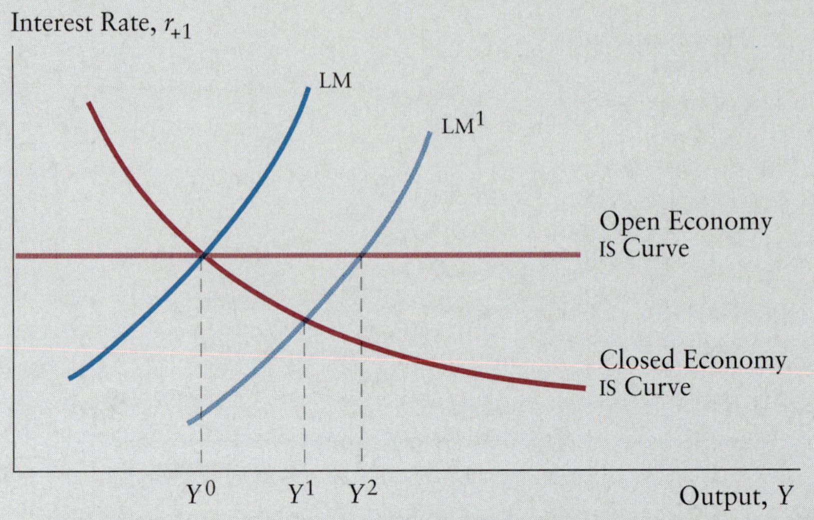

For a small open economy, the IS curve is effectively horizontal and of fixed height. This makes fiscal policy completely ineffective as a way of overcoming short-run nominal rigidities. On the other hand, a flat IS curve makes monetary policy more effective. For a given shift in LM, there is a larger increase in output than with a downward-sloping IS curve.

Monetary Policy and Exchange Regimes in the Small Open Economy with Rigid Nominal Wages

While thinking about monetary policy and exchange regimes in the context of rigid nominal wages, we need to bear in mind three points about the price level. First, firms will only increase their employment and output if the real wage they face falls, i.e., if the price level rises (given that the nominal wage is fixed). Second, since the price level enters the LM curve, an increase in M will produce an initial rightward shift of the LM curve as well as a partially offsetting leftward shift in the LM curve, because it will raise the price level. Third, the law of one price dictates that $eP = P^*$. So, any changes in P must be consistent with this relationship.[10]

Now, let's turn to the case of a flexible exchange rate. In this case, our analysis of the operation of monetary policy is identical to that in Chapter 9, except that the IS curve is now a flat line. A rise in the money supply shifts the LM curve rightward, but causes the price level to rise (and the real wage to fall), producing

10. In what follows, we take P^* as given.

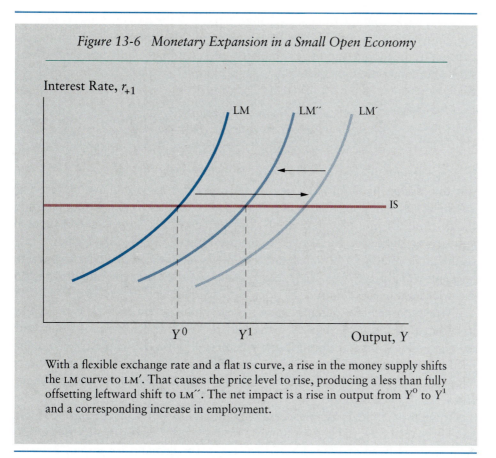

Figure 13-6 Monetary Expansion in a Small Open Economy

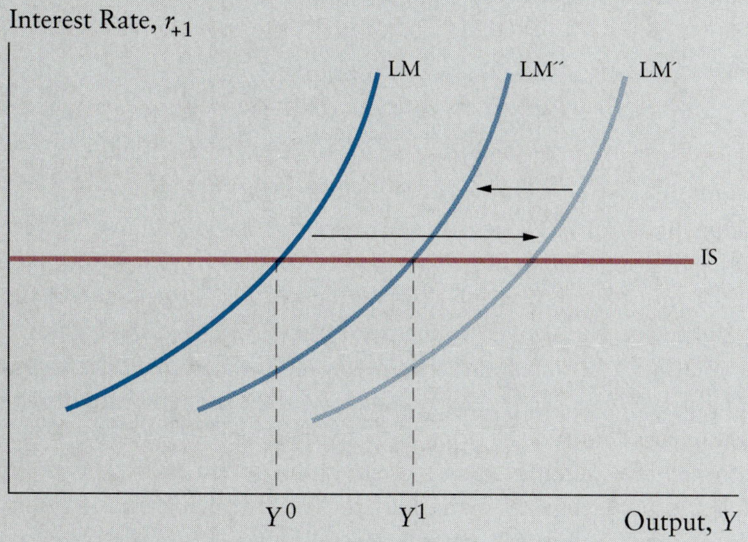

With a flexible exchange rate and a flat IS curve, a rise in the money supply shifts the LM curve to LM′. That causes the price level to rise, producing a less than fully offsetting leftward shift to LM″. The net impact is a rise in output from Y^0 to Y^1 and a corresponding increase in employment.

a less than fully offsetting leftward shift in the LM curve. As shown in Figure 13-6, the net impact of the monetary expansion is a rise in output and employment. With a flexible exchange rate, any change in P leads to a change in e to satisfy $eP = P^*$. So the law of one price places no restriction on the movement of the price level.

Next consider our small open economy with rigid nominal wages but an exchange rate fixed at $\bar{e}$. In this case the law of one price fixes the price level P at the value $P^*/\bar{e}$. Since both the price level and the nominal wage are fixed, the real wage is fixed as well, meaning that employment and output will also be fixed. Hence, in a small open economy with a fixed exchange rate, neither fiscal nor monetary policy will be able to raise output and employment.

Let's examine this conclusion in terms of our IS-LM diagram. Suppose the government tries to expand the money supply to raise employment and output. In Figure 13-6, which assumed a flexible exchange rate, we saw that this policy would be effective in shifting the LM curve rightward. With a fixed exchange rate, however, the LM curve ends up where it started; i.e., there is no net shift in the curve. The reason is that with a fixed exchange rate, the government loses control of the money supply. As it tries to expand the money supply, it finds that its exchange rate is depreciating. In order to keep this from happening, it has to purchase back from the foreign exchange market all the money it injects into the economy. Hence, the initial rightward shift of the LM curve arising from the expansion of the money supply is completely reversed by the leftward shift arising from the contraction in the money supply needed to maintain the fixed exchange rate.

An Argument for Fixed Exchange Rates: Mitigating Output Fluctuations

If, as we've said, monetary policy can only work if the exchange rate is flexible, can any case be made for fixed rates in the context of rigid nominal wages? The answer is yes. Suppose that liquidity preference, which in our model refers to the demand for money function, $\gamma[\ ]$, is highly volatile, shifting the LM curve leftward or rightward for a given monetary policy. In a flexible exchange rate regime, this volatility translates into a highly volatile output level. It also translates into a highly volatile exchange rate, because the exchange rate depends on the price level ($e = P^*/P$), and the price level depends on the level of γ.

Now with flexible exchange rates the government can use monetary policy to offset those output declines emanating from sporadic leftward shifts in the LM curve. But what if it doesn't—perhaps because of a delay in recognizing the need for intervention? Then, as shown in Figure 13-7, when the LM curve shifts leftward, there will be less output and employment than under a fixed exchange rate.

To see why a fixed exchange rate regime stabilizes output, recall that with a fixed exchange rate, the money supply automatically adjusts to keep the domestic price level fixed at $P^*/\bar{e}$. So an increase in the demand for money brought about by an increase in the value of γ at each interest rate, which shifts the LM curve leftward, will induce a fall in the price level. Other things equal, this fall in the price level means an exchange rate appreciation as well as a higher real wage. To keep this from happening, the exchange authorities end up selling more of the home country's money in the foreign exchange market, thereby raising the money supply and shifting the LM curve rightward. The rightward shift will fully offset the initial leftward shift, leaving the economy at the same level of output and employment.[11] The reason is that with the exchange rate fixed, P will remain fixed at $P^*/\bar{e}$, so the real wage will remain at its initial value.

We conclude that a fixed exchange regime will stabilize the economy in response to shocks to its money demand. If the economy is initially at full employment, using a fixed exchange rate to make sure it stays there seems like a good idea. On the other hand, if the economy is not initially at full employment, the government will have to abandon its fixed exchange rate if it wants to use monetary policy to expand output and employment.

11. Note that depending on precisely how the $\gamma[\ ]$ function changes, the slope of the LM curve may change, although it will still end up intersecting the horizontal IS curve at the initial level of output.

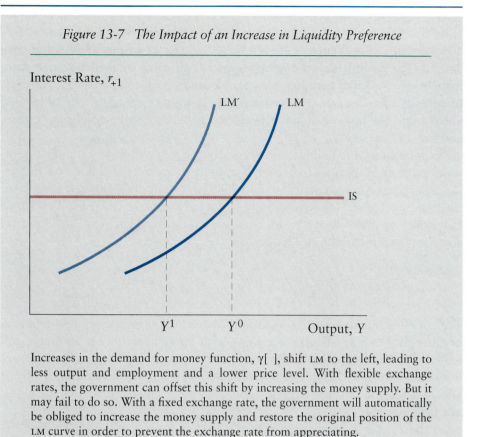

Figure 13-7 The Impact of an Increase in Liquidity Preference

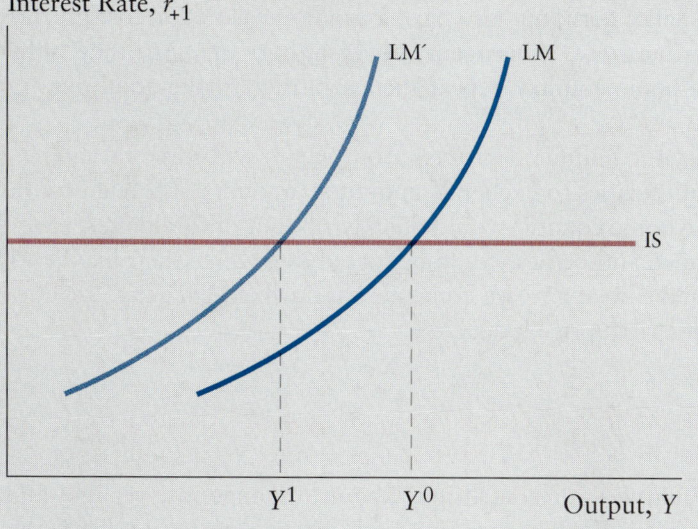

Increases in the demand for money function, γ[ ], shift LM to the left, leading to less output and employment and a lower price level. With flexible exchange rates, the government can offset this shift by increasing the money supply. But it may fail to do so. With a fixed exchange rate, the government will automatically be obliged to increase the money supply and restore the original position of the LM curve in order to prevent the exchange rate from appreciating.

Monetary Policy and Exchange Regimes with Rigid Prices

Having considered monetary policy and exchange rate regimes for the case of nominal wage rigidity, let's turn to the case of price rigidity. With a flexible exchange rate, the level of e will adjust to ensure that $e\overline{P} = P^*$, where $\overline{P}$ refers to the rigid price level. If the IS-LM curves intersect below the full-employment level of output, an expansion of the money supply, which shifts the LM curve rightward, will raise output. Unlike the case of a rigid nominal wage, there is no secondary shift in the LM curve, because the price level cannot rise. Since the price level doesn't rise, there is no depreciation of the exchange rate.

Next let's consider a fixed exchange rate in the presence of price rigidity. A quick glance at the law of one price, $e\overline{P} = P^*$, tells us that unless the government sets e equal to $P^*/\overline{P}$, this condition will be violated, leaving an opportunity for arbitrage. For example, suppose the government chooses a value of $\overline{e}$ such that $\overline{e}\,\overline{P}$ exceeds P^*. Economists refer to such a situation as one in which the home country's nominal as well as real exchange rates (recall that $e^R = eP/P^*$) are *overvalued*; i.e., they are higher than can be reconciled by the law of one price.[12] This situation permits arbitrageurs to sell a bushel of corn at home for $\bar{P}$, take the proceeds to the domestic exchange authorities and demand $\bar{e}\bar{P}$ in foreign currency in exchange, and then use P^* of the $\bar{e}\bar{P}$ to buy a bushel of corn abroad. The result is that the arbitrageurs end up with what they started with, namely, one bushel of corn, but also have a profit, measured in foreign currency, of $\bar{e}\bar{P} - P^*$. Furthermore, arbitrageurs could import the corn they purchased abroad into the home country, repeat their arbitrage, make additional profits, and begin again.

In their quest for unlimited profits, arbitrageurs will force the home country's exchange authorities to exchange unlimited amounts of foreign for domestic currency. The home country would quickly run out of foreign reserves. Eventually the exchange authorities would be forced to devalue their fixed exchange rate policy to make $\bar{P}e = P^*$. We conclude that a fixed exchange regime is incompatible with a rigid price level.

Policy in the Small Open Economy Model with Nominal Rigidities: A Summary

Table 13-2 summarizes our conclusions about exchange rate regimes and economic policy in a small open economy with nominal rigidities. The table will remind you that with flexible exchange rates, monetary policy will be effective in raising output and employment regardless of the type of nominal rigidity. It also reminds you that price rigidity and a fixed exchange rate regime are mutually incompatible.

A fixed exchange rate regime is compatible with nominal wage rigidity. But such a regime rules out using activist monetary policy to overcome this rigidity. The fixed exchange regime not only prevents shifts in the LM curve originating with changes in the money supply, it also prevents shifts originating with shocks to money demand. Thus, the fixed exchange regime provides an automatic stabilizer against shocks to money demand.

Case Study: The Debate over a Single European Currency[13]

A quick review of the European debate over the adoption of a single currency is a good way to conclude this chapter. The debate brings together many of the points we've made. The proposed currency is called the ECU, which stands for European Currency Unit. Adoption of the ECU must be approved by all countries in the European Economic Community. If the ECU is adopted it will become the common currency throughout Europe. In this case, European monetary policy will be conducted by a European Central Bank with the seigniorage raised by this bank distributed back to the member countries.

12. Similarly, an *undervalued exchange rate* refers to nominal and, thus, real exchange rates that are lower than can be explained by the law of one price.

13. A good reference on this topic is Barry Eichengreen, "European Monetary Unification," *Journal of Economic Literature* xxxi (September 1993): 1321–1357.

Table 13-2 Monetary Policy and Exchange Regimes in a Small Open Economy with Nominal Rigidities

	Rigid Nominal Wages	**Rigid Prices**
Flexible Exchange Rate	Monetary expansion raises Y and P and lowers e.	Monetary expansion raises Y, but leaves P and e unchanged.
Fixed Exchange Rate	Money supply is endogenous; it can't be used to shift LM. But the endogenous response of money supply insulates economy from shocks to money demand (keeps LM curve from shifting).	Fixed exchange rate regime is infeasible. An overvalued rate must be devalued; an undervalued rate must be revalued.

Part of the impetus for a single European currency is political, reflecting the belief that a single currency and monetary policy will contribute to the goal of a "United States of Europe"—a single European nation with a single set of domestic and foreign policies. Apart from political motivations, there are economic arguments for a single currency, chief among which are first, the reduction in transactions costs of inter-European commerce associated with trading in so many different currencies, and second, eliminating the economic fallout from currency instability (modeled in this chapter as arising from fluctuations in the money demand function). The chief economic argument against a single currency is that member countries will lose an important policy instrument, namely, their own monetary policies, used to combat recessions and to finance government programs.

Chapter Summary

1. This chapter adds a second country to our life-cycle model with money. The result is an open economy model with an important new variable, namely, the nominal exchange rate. The nominal exchange rate indicates how many units of foreign money will be received in exchange for one unit of domestic money.

2. Nominal exchange rates determined by private market forces are described as floating, or flexible, exchange rates. Nominal exchange rates that either are legally imposed by governments or reflect government intervention in the foreign exchange market are called fixed exchange rates.

3. A fixed exchange rate that is set by law gives rise to a black market if it differs from the rate at which supply and demand for a country's money are equal. In most of today's fixed exchange rate regimes governments directly exchange their money for that of other countries in the foreign exchange market. In the last century and part of this century, countries established fixed exchange rates by fixing the amount of their monies that would be exchanged for a particular commodity, namely, gold.

4. Regardless of how the nominal exchange rate is determined, it can be used to compare the prices of goods and services in one country with those in another, where the foreign and domestic prices are both measured in the same currency. If we form such a relative price ratio for a comprehensive basket of goods and services, the result is the real exchange rate. If all goods were traded and there were no shipping costs, commodity taxes, or tariffs—the world of our model—the real exchange rate would be unity. This is a reflection of the law of one price, which states that the price of a good or service cannot be higher at one location than at another.

5. Because the real exchange rate in our model is unity, the nominal exchange rate equals the ratio of the foreign to the domestic price level. Consequently, changes over time in the nominal exchange rate reflect differences in countries' inflation rates. Since the ratio of the foreign to the domestic price level depends on the ratio of the foreign to the domestic money supply, exchange rate policies and monetary policies are linked. Specifically, a country can set either its money supply or its exchange rate, but not both. In flexible exchange rate regimes, countries set their money supplies and allow their nominal exchange rates to equilibrate endogenously. In fixed exchange rate regimes, countries set their nominal exchange rates and let their money supplies adjust to whatever level is needed to sustain the rate being fixed.

6. Even though the same monetary policy can, in principal, be run in either regime, the switch from one monetary policy to another may, for political and credibility reasons, be associated with a change in exchange rate regimes. Indeed, switching from flexible to fixed exchange rates is a common feature of price stabilization policies. By rigidly controlling their exchange rates, governments indirectly slow the growth rate of their money supplies and, thereby, lower the rate of inflation.

7. Besides helping some countries control their inflation rates, fixed exchange rates can reduce the information and other costs associated with transacting in multiple currencies whose relative values are continually changing. Against the advantages of fixed exchange rates must be piled several disadvantages. First, since countries share their exchange rates, they need, in fixed rate regimes, to coordinate their exchange rate policies. Second, this coordination may entail one country's effectively adopting the monetary policy of the other, thus forgoing the option of independently altering its money supply. Third, managing a fixed rate regime also requires coordination between the government's exchange rate and monetary authorities. Without such coordination, monetary authorities may sterilize (undo) the changes in the money supply made by the exchange rate authorities. A fourth concern is the potential problem of running out of international reserves amidst a speculative attack on the exchange rate.

8. The final part of this chapter added nominal rigidities to our two-country model. The resulting open economy IS-LM model differs from the closed economy model because the IS curve is flatter. Indeed, in the case of a small open economy, the IS curve is a horizontal line, which is unaffected by domestic fiscal policy. This impotence of fiscal policy in a small open economy leaves monetary policy as the means by which such an economy can combat nominal rigidities. A horizontal IS curve also makes monetary policy more effective.

9. In the case of nominal wage rigidity, monetary expansion will expand output and employment, assuming the exchange rate is flexible. If it is fixed, the exchange authorities will end up purchasing back on the foreign exchange market all the additional money that has been created. The net impact will be no expansion in the money supply and no change in output. This automatic stabilization of the level of output that occurs in a fixed exchange regime is an attractive way to deal with output volatility brought about by sporadic shifts in the money demand function.

10. If the exchange rate is flexible, expansionary monetary policy will be effective in dealing with the output and employment implications of a rigid price level. On the other hand, a fixed exchange rate is incompatible with a rigid price level.

Key Concepts

Exchange rate
Appreciation
Depreciation
Flexible exchange rates
Fixed exchange rates
Gold standard
Law of one price
Purchasing power parity
Real exchange rate
Nominal exchange rate
Sterilization of exchange rate intervention
International reserves

Review Questions

1. What is an *exchange rate*? How is it measured? Compare the exchange rate between the U.S. and France as viewed by each country.

2. What is meant by the *appreciation* and *depreciation* of a country's currency?

3. How are exchange rates determined under a *flexible exchange rate system*? How are they determined under a *fixed exchange rate system*?

4. What is meant by the terms *devaluation* and *revaluation*? How do these adjustments occur?

5. In what ways can a government fix its exchange rate? What is an *overvalued* and an *undervalued* currency?

6. What is a *commodity standard,* and what is the effect of two countries' adopting the same standard? What commodity has been used in this way?

7. Explain the concept of *arbitrage* and its relevance to the *law of one price.* What factors must be considered in determining whether an arbitrage opportunity exists or whether the law of one price holds? What is *purchasing power parity*?

8. Distinguish between the *nominal exchange rate* and the *real exchange rate*. What is meant by the *terms of trade*?

9. What assumptions are made in introducing a second country into the life-cycle model? What do they imply about the real and nominal exchange rates?

10. Assuming constant and equal money demand parameters as well as factor price equalization, what determines the nominal exchange rate between two countries in the life-cycle model? What happens to the domestic exchange rate if the domestic money supply rises faster than that of the other country?

11. "The fiscal policy of a small open economy will be ineffective in altering either its capital-labor ratio, its real wage, or its real interest rate." Explain.

12. Why is it said that a country can control either its money supply or its exchange rate, but not both?

13. Under a flexible exchange rate system with no nominal rigidities, what are the real and nominal effects of a rise in the domestic money supply? What are the effects on the foreign price and the exchange rate?

14. In the context of foreign exchange, what is meant by *intervention*?

15. What are the arguments raised in support of and against fixed and flexible exchange rate systems?

16. How does the open economy IS curve differ from that derived in the closed economy model? Why? What are the implications for the effectiveness of fiscal and monetary policy in a small economy that faces nominal rigidities?

17. "With a fixed exchange rate, neither fiscal nor monetary policy will be able to raise a small open economy's output and employment." Explain.

18. Under a flexible exchange rate system, how does the effectiveness of monetary policy on output depend on the nature of the nominal rigidity? What are the implications for the exchange rate?

19. Why is a fixed exchange rate system said to be incompatible with price rigidity?

Numerical Questions

1. Below are the price levels for three countries: A, B, and C.

Year	P_t^A	P_t^B	P_t^C
1990	100.0	100.0	100.0
1991	103.0	110.0	101.0
1992	106.1	121.0	116.2
1993	109.3	133.1	124.3

a. For country A, compute the nominal exchange rate over the years 1990 through 1993 consistent with purchasing power parity with each of the other two countries (e_t^{AB} and e_t^{AC}). Do the same for country B (e_t^{BA} and e_t^{BC}) and country C (e_t^{CA} and e_t^{CB}). Altogether, you will have computed six exchange rate series. Which pairs of the series are reciprocals?

b. Do country A's two exchange rates behave similarly over time? Explain the time path of each series. Do the same for countries B and C.

2. Below is a table containing information on consumer prices in the U.S. and Japan as well as the U.S. nominal exchange rate with Japan.

	Consumer Prices (1982–1984 = 100)		
Year	U.S.	Japan	e_t (Yen/$)
1987	113.6	104.9	144.60
1988	118.3	105.7	128.17
1989	124.0	108.0	138.07
1990	130.7	111.4	145.00
1991	136.2	115.0	134.59

a. For each year, compute for the U.S. the value of its real exchange rate with Japan. Do these figures demonstrate purchasing power parity?

b. Are these figures consistent with the statement made in the text regarding the short-run relationship between nominal and real exchange rates? Explain.

3. Below is a table containing money supply figures for Lower and Upper Slobovia. Their respective labor force sizes are 10 and 100.

	Money Supply	
Year	Lower Slobovia	Upper Slobovia
1990	200	1000
1991	300	1500
1992	375	1650
1993	375	1980

a. You live in Upper Slobovia. For each year, compute your country's nominal exchange rate with Lower Slobovia.

b. Explain the time path of the exchange rate series in terms of relative growth rates of the money supply.

Analytical Questions

1. For each of the following events, identify whether an appreciation, a depreciation, a revaluation, or a devaluation has occurred.

a. What has happened to the yen if the yen-dollar exchange rate changes from 105 to 120?

b. What has happened to the deutsche mark if the German government changes the fixed franc-deutsche mark exchange rate from 3.5 to 3.8?

c. What has happened to the U.S. dollar if the U.S. government intervenes to push the Canadian dollar–U.S. dollar exchange rate from 1.3 to 1.4?
d. What has happened to the dollar if the pound-dollar exchange rate changes from 0.5 to 0.7?
e. What has happened to the lira if the Italian government changes the fixed lira-deutsche mark exchange rate from 980 to 1000?

2. Suppose that there are two countries, Big and Bigger, that each produce a set of freely traded goods. The cost of the set of goods in Big is $150 bigbucks, and the cost of the set of goods in Bigger is $100 biggerbucks. The bigbuck-biggerbuck exchange rate, which is set by the governments in a fixed exchange rate regime, currently is 1.5.
a. Calculate the bigbuck-biggerbuck purchasing power parity exchange rate and compare it to the prevailing exchange rate. Is an exchange rate, realignment needed?
b. Suppose that a technological innovation in Big causes the price of goods to fall to $125. Recalculate the purchasing power parity exchange rate, and compare it to that found in part a. Explain any difference.
c. Compare the prevailing exchange rate to the new purchasing power parity exchange rate. Is the bigbuck appropriately valued, overvalued, or undervalued?
d. Suppose that you are a foreign currency trader. Given your assessment in part c, is the time right for a speculative attack on the bigbuck? If so, how would you proceed?

3. Suppose that there are two countries, Ipso and Facto, that are identical in every way. Capital is completely mobile between the two countries, but labor is completely immobile. The currency unit in Ipso is the spam, and the currency unit in Facto is the velveeta. The money supply in each country is fixed, and money demand in each country is insensitive to changes in the interest rate. Suddenly, a technological change occurs in Ipso, but not in Facto.
a. What happens to the capital-labor ratio in Ipso compared to that in Facto? Why?
b. What happens to the nominal spam-velveeta exchange rate? Why?
c. Suppose that capital is immobile but labor is mobile when the technological change occurs. Are your conclusions about the effect on the nominal exchange rate the same as or different from those in part b? Why?

4. The chapter ended by reviewing briefly the debate over a single European currency. Critics of the plan have argued that such a system at best will work only under limited circumstances. At worst, the system will destabilize foreign exchange markets and eventually self-destruct. Evaluate these claims, identifying economic conditions for which the system is well-suited and those for which the system is ill-suited. Also, comment on the effects of the system on foreign exchange markets.

CHAPTER 14

The Banking System, the Federal Reserve, and the Money Supply

INTRODUCTION

This chapter describes how the banking system operates and how central banks control their countries' money supplies. In the United States the central bank is the **Federal Reserve System**—the Fed. We discussed the Fed briefly in Chapter 8 and we'll examine it here in some detail. We begin by pointing out that a bank is a type of *financial intermediary*—a business that helps households and firms conduct financial transactions with one another, including borrowing and investing. We then enumerate the different types of financial intermediaries and indicate, in general terms, how they fit into our model.

Federal Reserve System
The central bank and monetary authority of the United States; known as "the Fed"

With this background, we will study banks as a special type of financial intermediary—one that offers households and firms a highly liquid way of investing, or at least temporarily parking their funds. Remember that the word "demand" in demand deposits (checking accounts) reflects the fact that funds deposited in a bank can be accessed at a moment's notice simply by writing a check. The liquidity of demand deposits as well as their other money-like properties has led to their inclusion, along with currency, traveler's checks, and other

M1
A measure of the money supply consisting of currency and coin held by the nonbank public, checkable deposits, and traveler's checks

Monetary aggregates
Measures of the economy's money supply

Reserve requirements
The legally required minimum level of reserves a bank must maintain, as a fraction of its deposits

checkable deposits, in **M1**, the principal definition of money. Demand deposits as well as the other components of M1 are also included in the government's broader definitions of money, M2 and M3. These three definitions of money are referred to as the government's **monetary aggregates**.

Another feature that makes banks such special financial intermediaries is their ability to increase the total volume of demand deposits and thus expand the M1, M2, and M3 money supplies. Banks do this by lending to borrowers a portion of the funds that have been deposited with them. A good part of these re-lent funds ends up back in banks as additional demand deposits. As we'll see, the extent of this deposit expansion by the banks depends on the fraction of their deposits they do not lend out, but rather hold as *reserves* against the possibility that the funds deposited with them will be withdrawn.

The Federal Reserve's **reserve requirements** specify the minimum fractions of their deposits that banks must hold as reserves. Through these requirements the Federal Reserve influences the extent to which initial deposits in the banking system are expanded (or multiplied) through bank lending in determining total deposits. Since demand deposits constitute a large part of M1 (over 50 percent in 1993) as well as the other monetary aggregates, the Federal Reserve's reserve requirements influence the size of these aggregates.

The Federal Reserve has another, more direct, method of controlling the monetary supply. It determines the basic amount of money the government injects into the economy—*the monetary base*. We'll see that each one-dollar increase in the monetary base can lead to more than a one-dollar increase in M1 depending on how much of that dollar increase is held in currency and how much is deposited in banks and other depository institutions, setting off the deposit-expansion process just mentioned.

The ratio of M1 to the monetary base is called the *M1 money multiplier*. It indicates by how much M1 rises as a result of each one-dollar increase in the monetary base. After discussing the private banking system, we will take a close look at the determinants of the M1 money multiplier. Next we'll consider the two basic methods the Federal Reserve uses to increase the monetary base: *open market operations* and *discount window lending*. We'll also discuss how the Fed's reserve requirements influence the sizes of money multipliers.

Although it directly controls the monetary base, the Federal Reserve has only indirect control of the money multipliers and, therefore, only indirect control of the monetary aggregates. This raises the question of how well the Federal Reserve can exercise that control, the next subject considered in this chapter. Specifically, we'll examine the divergent paths taken by different monetary aggregates in the postwar period. We'll also consider how much of the variability in the monetary aggregates is due to variability in money multipliers. Finally, we'll consider the Federal Reserve's failure to control M1 during the Great Depression.

Beyond the question of how well the government can control the monetary aggregates is the question of whether it should try to control them. Nobel Laureate Milton Friedman and other economists believe the government should target the growth of a particular monetary aggregate. Other economists believe the

Fed should adjust the monetary aggregates to target the level of interest rates. We'll consider this debate as well as the episode in the late 1970s in which the Federal Reserve sought to target the growth of M1. Finally, we'll consider the possibility that the money supply is endogenous—that the government's control of the money supply is a response to, rather than a cause of, changes in the economy.

The next-to-last section of this chapter is also concerned with monetary control. It discusses banking panics—episodes that have severely tested the Fed's ability to control M1 and other broad monetary aggregates. It also considers the role of *deposit insurance* in preventing bank panics. This section provides the occasion to review the near-collapse of the U.S. banking system during the Great Depression as well as the savings and loan crisis of the 1980s.

The final section will, as always, sum up what we've discussed, including the answers to the following questions:

- What are financial intermediaries?
- How do banks affect the money supply?
- What factors determine the size of the money multiplier?
- How does the Federal Reserve attempt to control the money supply?
- How effective are the Federal Reserve's efforts to control different monetary aggregates?
- What causes bank panics, and what can the government do to prevent them?
- What problems are caused by government policies designed to eliminate banking panics?

UNDERSTANDING FINANCIAL INTERMEDIARIES

Financial intermediaries match suppliers of funds with demanders of funds, but in an indirect way. Take, for example, a bank that makes a loan to a local business. The funds the bank uses to make the business loan are, in part, those supplied to it by its depositors. The bank acts as a go-between in helping its depositors lend money to that firm. A second example is an investment bank that helps a start-up company sell shares of stock to the public. By selling stock, the company seeks to obtain (demands) the funds needed to finance its business operations. In buying the stock the public is supplying the funds to meet this demand. By bringing the seller and purchasers of the stock together, the investment bank is intermediating between the two.

Financial intermediary *An institution that serves as a go-between, accepting funds from savers and lending those funds to consumers and investors*

Matching suppliers of funds with demanders is just one service financial intermediaries provide. They also help reduce the transactions costs of buying or selling financial assets. A mutual fund can combine the savings of a large number of small investors and make bulk purchases of a diversified set of financial securities. A savings and loan association (S&L) can combine small deposits of individual savers to provide mortgages to home buyers who might otherwise need to spend a great deal of time borrowing small sums of money from a large number of friends, relatives, and other acquaintances.

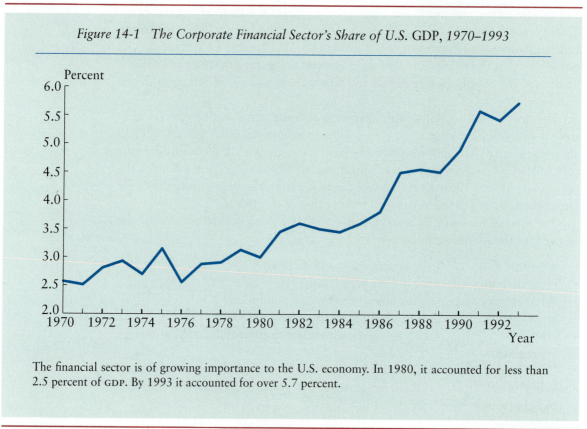

Figure 14-1 The Corporate Financial Sector's Share of U.S. GDP, *1970–1993*

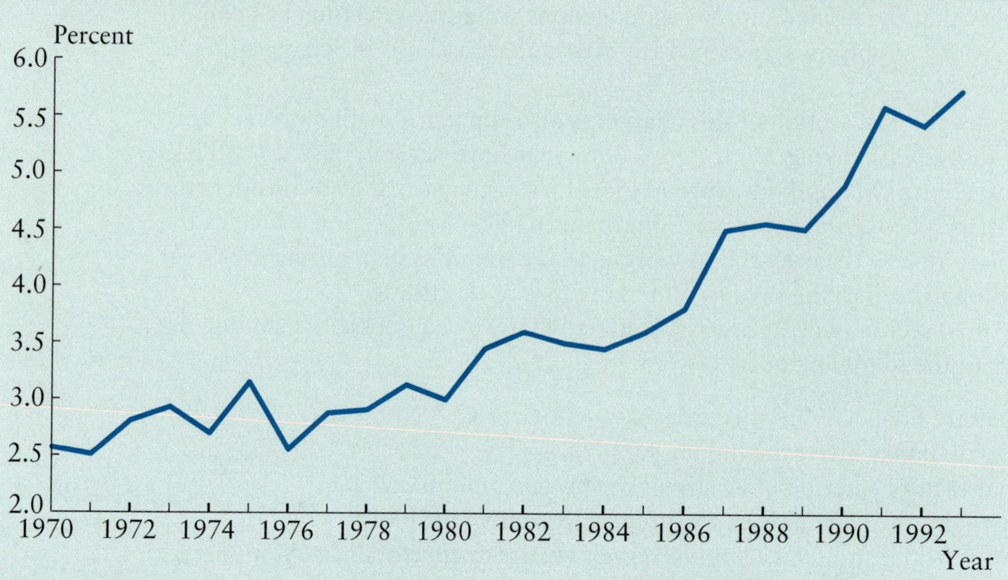

The financial sector is of growing importance to the U.S. economy. In 1980, it accounted for less than 2.5 percent of GDP. By 1993 it accounted for over 5.7 percent.

Source: *Survey of Current Business*, 1970–1994

A third service provided by financial intermediaries is the efficient acquisition and provision of information. Consider a stock broker who invests time and money to learn the value of a particular company. The broker can share this information at no additional cost to all his clients, advising them in the process whether to buy or sell the company's stock. The alternative—having each of the broker's clients collect this same information—would result in much higher information costs.

Advanced economies like the United States have a broad array of financial intermediaries, including commercial banks, investment banks, savings and loan associations, credit agencies, credit unions, finance companies, mutual funds, pension funds, money market mutual funds, insurance brokers, real estate brokers, stock brokers, and bond traders. These businesses help households and firms obtain loans and other types of financing, invest their savings, economize on their cash balances, diversify the risk of their investments, and acquire insurance.

Figure 14-1 depicts the share of total U.S. GDP generated by the financial services sector in the years 1970 through 1993. It shows that the financial services sector is of growing importance to the U.S. economy. In 1980 this sector accounted for less than 2.5 percent of U.S. GDP. By 1993 it accounted for over 5.7 percent.

Financial Intermediaries and Our Model

In our model so far we've ignored financial intermediation. In effect, we've assumed that each generation can invest its savings with the model's firms and incur no costs in doing so. This assumption ignores the transactions costs involved in making investments, imperfect information about the ability of different firms to make profitable investments, and uncertainty surrounding the profitability of a firm's investments. Adding these factors to our model would produce a demand by each generation for the services of financial intermediaries to reduce transactions costs, obtain information, and diversify investment risk. *Risk diversification* refers to the simple idea that you shouldn't put all your investment eggs in the same basket.

The Balance Sheets of Financial Intermediaries

We can summarize the activities of a financial intermediary in terms of a *balance sheet* that lists its assets and debts. The IOUs received by an intermediary in exchange for loans it makes or the financial assets it purchases enter its balance sheets as assets. They indicate amounts owed to the financial intermediary by borrowers or by firms in which the intermediary has invested. The IOUs issued by the financial intermediary in exchange for the funds placed with it enter the intermediary's balance sheets as liabilities.

Every financial intermediary needs an initial sum of money to begin operation. This *owners' equity* is provided by the owners of the intermediary and some of it is used to purchase the office space, computers, and furniture needed to get the operation going. The rest is kept in the form of money for use in initiating lending. Owners' equity counts as another liability, since it is ultimately owed to the owners of the intermediary. On the other hand, the office buildings and other physical capital, as well as any financial assets acquired, are counted as assets. The amount of liabilities of a financial intermediary always equals the amount of its assets. That's because every dollar received by an intermediary is counted as a liability and every dollar lent or otherwise invested by an intermediary is counted as an asset.

Case Study: The Balance Sheets of U.S. Financial Intermediaries

Table 14-1 presents the 1993 balance sheet for all U.S. private financial institutions taken together. Note first that the assets controlled by these intermediaries totaled over $16 trillion. To put this figure in perspective, total 1993 assets of households and nonfinancial businesses were $38.5 trillion. Hence, in 1993 over two-fifths of all U.S. private sector assets were controlled by financial intermediaries.

Of about $16 trillion in financial intermediary assets, $3.1 trillion was invested in corporate equities (corporate stocks), $7.9 trillion was invested in bonds and other nonmortgage credit market instruments, and $2.2 trillion was invested in mortgages. Hence, we can conclude that about two-thirds of U.S. financial intermediation involved helping the private sector acquire stocks and bonds, and about one-seventh involved helping it obtain real estate mortgages.

Table 14-1 1993 Balance Sheet: U.S. Private Financial Institutions (billions of dollars)

Assets

Type	Amount
Tangible Assets	589.0
Demand Deposits and Currency	91.2
Savings and Time Deposits	283.5
Money Market Fund Shares	77.3
Federal Funds and Repurchase Agreements	130.3
Foreign Deposits	10.1
Corporate Equities	3,116.8
Bonds and other Credit Market Instruments	7,866.3
Mortgages	2,200.3
Other Financial Assets	1,675.8
Total Assets	**16,040.4**

Liabilities

Type	Amount
Demand Deposits	902.8
Savings and Time Deposits	2,593.0
Money Market Fund Shares	559.1
Federal Funds and Repurchase Agreements	457.9
Life Insurance Reserves	477.5
Pension Fund Reserves	4,444.8
Mutual Fund Shares	1,426.8
Credit Market Instruments	1,309.1
Other Liabilities	2,613.4
Owners' Equity	1,256.0
Total Liabilities	**16,040.4**

Source: The Federal Reserve *Flow of Funds*

Next consider the 1993 liabilities of financial intermediaries. The largest components here were savings and time deposits, totaling $2.6 trillion, and pension funds, totaling $4.4 trillion. Owners' equity totaled $1.3 trillion.

Liabilities of Financial Intermediaries and U.S. Monetary Aggregates

Demand deposits are the most liquid liabilities of financial intermediaries. But they are not the only liabilities included in some definitions of money. Savings accounts, time deposits, and money market mutual fund shares are reasonably liquid and, consequently, are counted in the broader definitions of money called **M2** and **M3**.[1] M2 primarily adds savings accounts, small time deposits, and money market mutual funds to M1.[2] M3 primarily adds large time deposits to M2.[3] Figure 14-2 shows the relative sizes of M1, M2, and M3 in 1993, as well as their components. In that year, M1 was less than one-third the size of M2 and less than one-fourth the size of M3.

M2
A monetary aggregate consisting of M1 plus savings deposits, small time deposits, and money market mutual funds balances

M3
A monetary aggregate consisting of M2 plus large time deposits and negotiable certificates of deposit

In contrast to the liabilities entering M1, M2, and M3, other liabilities of financial intermediaries are fairly illiquid and do not qualify for inclusion even in M3, the most broadly defined monetary aggregate. Take, as an example, pension fund reserves. Households that place their savings in pension funds may be permitted to withdraw the funds and use them to make purchases. But withdrawing these funds is not an instantaneous proposition. It requires contacting the pension fund and requesting disbursement of the desired sum. In addition, the receipt of the requested sum may take some time. Thus, although pension fund reserves can be liquidated, they are not easily liquidated, and thus are not considered a form of money.

BANKS AS SPECIAL FINANCIAL INTERMEDIARIES

In most of this chapter, we will study those functions of financial intermediaries that involve creation of checkable deposits. To keep our terminology simple, we refer to these intermediaries as "banks." But our definition really includes any institution that accepts deposits and allows its depositors to write checks on those balances. Commercial banks, savings and loans, mutual savings banks, and credit unions all qualify under this definition. Their demand deposits and other checkable deposits are counted as part of the M1 money supply, and each of these financial intermediaries is capable of "creating money."

Banks as Repositories of Money and Issuers of Liquid Liabilities

Banks provide the standard services of financial intermediaries, including matching suppliers and demanders of funds, reducing the transactions costs of

1. Checks can be written on a money market mutual fund, but they typically must exceed a certain minimum amount.
2. M2 also includes saving certificates, overnight repurchase agreements (essentially, interest-bearing checking accounts of businesses), and Eurodollar deposits (dollar deposits in European banks).
3. M3 also includes term repurchase agreements, term Eurodollar deposits, and money market mutual fund shares owned by institutions.

Figure 14-2 Size and Composition of U.S. Monetary Aggregates, 1993

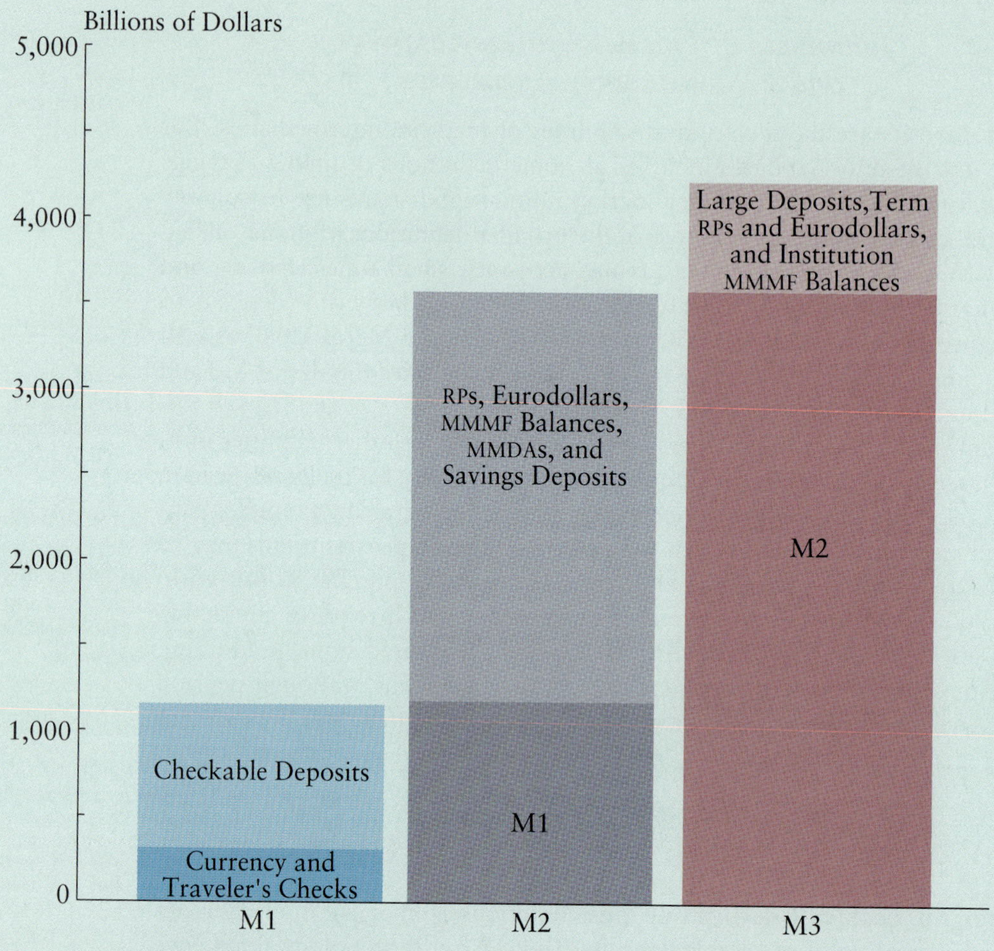

In 1993, M1 was less than one-third the size of M2 and about one-fourth the size of M3.

Source: *Economic Report of the President*, 1994

investing and borrowing, and acquiring information about the profitability of particular investments. But banks also play a special role as depositories for the money held by individuals and firms. Indeed, the earliest banks were temporary repositories used by people worried about having their money stolen.

Negotiable checks, which are IOUs of banks that can be exchanged for goods and services, trace their origins to the Middle Ages. It was awkward for depositors to withdraw their money each time they wanted to make a purchase. So, banks permitted depositors to use a written claim on money they held in the bank. This precursor to the modern-day bank check could then be presented by the recipient to the bank in exchange for the indicated sum of money. Negotiable checks, then and now, reduce the necessity for frequent trips to the bank and also reduce the likelihood of having money stolen while shopping.

Bank Reserves and the Expansion of Demand Deposits

The earliest banks simply stored all of their depositors' money for as long as those depositors desired. But it didn't take long for astute bank managers to notice that they were continuously holding large amounts of money in their vaults. Not all depositors withdrew their money at the same time. Also, as ongoing businesses, banks were constantly receiving new deposits of money that offset any old deposits that were withdrawn. The banks soon realized they could lend or invest at least some of the monies deposited with them and still be able to cover periodic withdrawals by their depositors.

Funds that banks keep in reserve to cover withdrawals are called **bank reserves.** These reserves play a key role in determining the expansion of demand deposits and the money supply. To see this, let's take the case of the hypothetical First National Bank of Lake Wobegon, Minnesota. First National is established by a group of investors who contribute $1,000 of owners' equity to set up the bank. In its first act of business First National Bank lends the $1,000 to Dewey, Cheatham, and Howe, a local law firm. The loan is an asset of the bank. At this stage of First National's financial dealings its balance sheet looks like this:

Bank reserves *Funds held in reserve by banks against the possibility that deposits will be withdrawn*

First National Bank Balance Sheet

Assets		Liabilities	
Type	**Amount**	**Type**	**Amount**
Loans	1,000	Owners' Equity	1,000
Total Assets	1,000	Total Liabilities	1,000

In the balance sheet we call the $1,000 of owners' equity a liability of the bank, since it represents a claim by the owners on the bank's assets.

Now suppose Dewey, Cheatham, and Howe decides to hold the $1,000 it borrows in the form of a checking account balance at First National Bank. Also suppose the bank adds these funds to its reserves, which previously were zero. In this case the bank's balance sheet becomes:

First National Bank Balance Sheet

Assets		Liabilities	
Type	**Amount**	**Type**	**Amount**
Reserves	1,000	Deposits	1,000
Loans	1,000	Owners' Equity	1,000
Total Assets	2,000	Total Liabilities	2,000

Although owner's equity isn't changed by Dewey, Cheatham, and Howe's decision to keep its money in First National Bank, both the bank's liabilities and its assets rise by $1,000. The $1,000 increase in liabilities reflects the $1,000 checking account balance of Dewey, Cheatham, and Howe, and the $1,000 increase in assets reflects the bank's increased reserves. Since checking account balances are part of M1, this transaction has increased the economy's money supply by $1,000.

Excess reserves *Reserves held by depository institutions over and above the legally required minimum level*

So far the initial $1,000 placed in First National Bank by its founders has led to the creation of an equal amount of demand deposits. But what if the bank is required to hold, say, only 20 percent of the funds deposited with it as reserves? In that case, it will find itself holding $800 in **excess reserves**—reserves in excess of those required to cover the risk of a withdrawal of deposits. Realizing it has $800 in excess reserves, First National Bank lends $800 to Specific Motors Corporation, which also deposits the funds back in First National Bank. Now the balance sheet is:

First National Bank Balance Sheet

Assets		Liabilities	
Type	**Amount**	**Type**	**Amount**
Reserves	1,000	Deposits	1,800
Loans	1,800	Owners' Equity	1,000
Total Assets	2,800	Total Liabilities	2,800

We can see that the $1,000 originally put in the bank has supported the creation of $1,800 in demand deposits, which are part of M1. The $1,000 of reserves is now made up of $360 (20 percent of $1,800) in required reserves and $640 of excess reserves. Because the bank still has excess reserves, it can make additional loans and create additional demand deposits. If this process continues, with First National Bank always lending out its excess reserves, where will it end up? The answer is given in the following balance sheet:

First National Bank Balance Sheet

Assets		Liabilities	
Type	**Amount**	**Type**	**Amount**
Reserves	1,000	Deposits	5,000
Loans	5,000	Owners' Equity	1,000
Total Assets	6,000	Total Liabilities	6,000

According to this balance sheet, the original $1,000 contributed to the bank has led to the creation of $5,000 worth of demand deposits. At this point, First National's $1,000 of reserves equals its required reserves, namely, 20 percent of its $5,000 demand deposits. Its excess reserves are zero, so we say the bank is "loaned up." Thus, the process of deposit creation continues until the reserves on the volume of demand deposits created just equal the amount of money injected into the bank, namely, $1,000.

In this example, we assumed that any funds lent by First National Bank were always deposited right back into that bank. So, the amount of demand deposits created by the banking system as a whole are the same as the amount created by this individual bank, namely, $5,000. More realistically, suppose the funds lent by First National Bank are deposited in other banks that also keep 20 percent of their deposits as reserves and lend out all their excess reserves. It turns out that the result is the same. The $1,000 initially injected into the banking system will lead to creation of $5,000 of demand deposits (which, again, are M1 money). It really makes no difference in which bank the deposits are held. All that matters is the total amount of demand deposits created. These transactions illustrate the so-called money multiplier, whose formula we'll now derive.

THE MONEY MULTIPLIER AND THE MONETARY BASE

As just shown, the banking system multiplies the amount of money put into banks through the process of deposit creation. Suppose for a moment that there were no currency. In that case, all money injected into the economy by the government—which we call the **monetary base**—would be deposited in banks and end up being held as reserves against deposits created by the banking system. The M1 money supply would include only demand deposits, and we would have the following formula relating M1 to the monetary base, MB:

Monetary base
The sum of bank reserves and currency held by the public

$$M1 = \frac{1}{rd} MB$$

In this equation rd stands for the *reserve-deposit ratio*—the amount of reserves per dollar of demand deposits. If we multiply both sides of the equation by rd, we find that all of the monetary base ends up being held as reserves against the demand deposits (equal here to M1) created by the banking system. In this case, in which all of the monetary base is deposited in banks, the **M1 money multiplier** is 1/rd. It indicates by how much the monetary base is expanded, through the process of deposit creation, to determine total demand deposits and, thus, M1. For example, if rd equals .2, indicating that banks keep reserves equal to 20 percent of their deposits, the money multiplier equals 1/.2, or 5, and M1 equals five times the monetary base.

M1 money multiplier
The ratio of the M1 monetary aggregate to the monetary base

In reality, of course, not all of the monetary base is held as reserves against demand deposits. Some is held by the public as cash (currency), and some is held as reserves against time and other types of deposits. Obviously, the monetary base must be held somewhere. So, if it's not being held by individuals and firms as cash, then it must be sitting as reserves in commercial banks, in savings and loans, or in other depository institutions. Thus, we can write

$$\text{Monetary Base} = \text{Currency} + \text{Reserves}$$

In November 1993, the U.S. monetary base was $386 billion, of which $321 billion was held as currency and the rest as reserves.

Since the U.S. monetary base is not all held as bank reserves, we have to modify our formula relating M1 to the monetary base. Let's start by noting that M1 equals currency plus demand deposits and letting cd stand for the public's desired ratio of currency to demand deposits.[4] Then,

$$\text{M1} = \text{Currency} + \text{Demand Deposits} = (\text{cd} + 1) \times \text{Demand Deposits}$$

Now the monetary base, MB, equals currency plus bank reserves. But bank reserves equal rd times demand deposits. Hence,

$$\text{MB} = \text{Currency} + \text{Reserves} = (\text{cd} + \text{rd}) \times \text{Demand Deposits}$$

Dividing the equation for M1 by the equation for MB, we have

$$\text{The M1 money multiplier} = \frac{\text{M1}}{\text{MB}} = \frac{\text{cd} + 1}{\text{cd} + \text{rd}}$$

We see that the M1 money multiplier depends on two things: the public's desired ratio of currency to demand deposits, cd, and the reserve-deposit ratio, rd.

How big is the M1 money multiplier? Well, in December 1993, cd equaled .41 and rd equaled .07, so the multiplier was 2.9. Figure 14-3 shows that there has been a decline in the M1 money multiplier since 1959. In 1959 the multiplier stood at 3.4—17 percent larger than its value in 1993. The decline in the money multiplier reflects a rise in cd from .26 to .41 that offset a decline in rd from .11 to .07.

To this point, we have focused on the M1 money multiplier, but the analogous money multipliers for the M2 and M3 monetary aggregates have also changed over time. As we'll see, the variability of all three money multipliers has affected the Fed's ability to control the growth of the money supply, however defined. But before we discuss how well the Federal Reserve has been able to control these aggregates, let's review the origins and functions of the Federal Reserve and its monetary control mechanisms.

THE FEDERAL RESERVE AND THE CONDUCT OF MONETARY POLICY

The Federal Reserve System was established in 1913 in the aftermath of the banking panic of 1907. It replaced the National Banking System—a set of federally chartered national banks created during the Civil War. The National Banking System did provide the country with a fairly uniform currency.[5]

4. In this formula, demand deposits include all noncurrency components of M1.

5. It did so by taxing the notes of state-chartered banks, thereby forcing these banks out of the note-issuing business. The notes of the national banks were completely safe because they were 100 percent backed by federal government bonds, the prices of which were guaranteed by the U.S. Treasury.

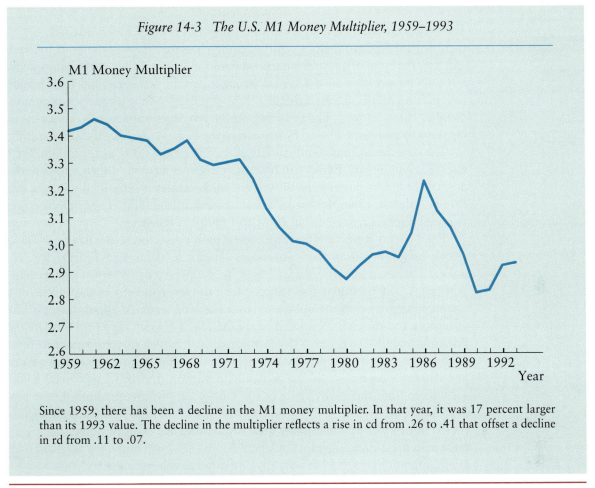

Figure 14-3 The U.S. M1 Money Multiplier, 1959–1993

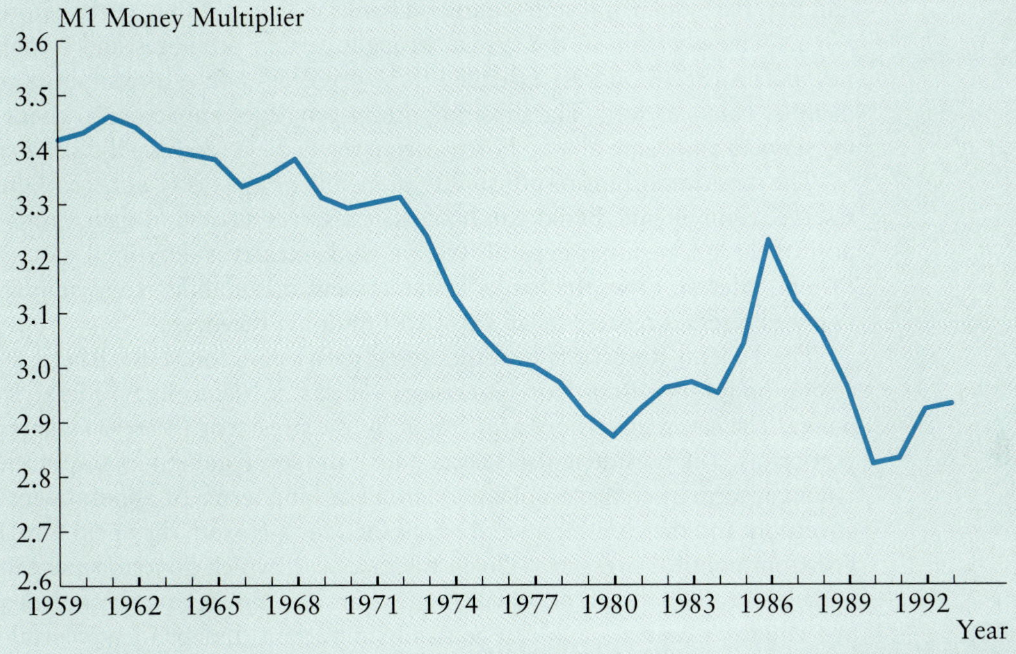

Since 1959, there has been a decline in the M1 money multiplier. In that year, it was 17 percent larger than its 1993 value. The decline in the multiplier reflects a rise in cd from .26 to .41 that offset a decline in rd from .11 to .07.

Source: *Economic Report of the President*, 1994

However, it had no governing body to direct member banks to adjust the money supply to prevailing economic conditions, including periodic banking panics and seasonal fluctuations in the demand for money.

The Federal Reserve's main purpose was "to furnish an elastic currency" in order to "safeguard the country from the possible results of financial panic or stringency" and to ensure that "there will be no ... wide fluctuations of interest rates from season to season."[6] Its secondary purposes were to provide a clearing house for checks, to maintain the country's position in the international gold standard, and to reduce interregional interest rate differentials. Since its founding, the functions of the Federal Reserve have been expanded. They now include regulating the banking system and intervening in the foreign exchange market.

6. The first quote is taken from the Federal Reserve charter. The latter two quotes are from Parker H. Willis, *The Federal Reserve: A Study of the Banking System of the United States* (New York: Doubleday, Page and Co., 1915).

The Structure and Governance of the Federal Reserve System

The Federal Reserve System includes 12 regional Federal Reserve banks, one in each Federal Reserve district.[7] All federally chartered banks belong to the Federal Reserve System and state-chartered banks may join if they wish. Before 1980 a bank's membership in the system brought certain privileges and responsibilities, but in 1980 Congress extended these privileges and responsibilities to nonmember banks as well. The most important privileges are access to check-clearing services and being able to borrow from the Fed—a topic we'll discuss shortly.

The most important responsibility of member banks is to adhere to the Fed's reserve requirements. Banks can hold their reserves as cash in their vaults or deposit them in a regional Federal Reserve bank. Reserves deposited with the Fed earn no interest. From the banks' point of view, this inability to earn interest on required reserves represents an extra cost of doing business.[8]

The Federal Reserve is headquartered in Washington, D.C. There, its governing body—the *Board of Governors*—meets to determine Federal Reserve policy. The seven governors are chosen by the president to serve staggered 14-year terms. The president also selects one of the seven governors to preside for a four-year term as chairman of the Board. The long terms of appointment of the governors and the chairman were established for a reason: they help insulate the Fed from political pressures. Given the ease with which governments can print money and the political goodwill money can buy, preserving the independence of a country's central bank can be vitally important. Independent central banks are able to limit the growth rate of the money supply, thereby limiting the rate of inflation and avoiding the problem of time-inconsistent monetary policy discussed in Chapter 12.[9] Germany and Switzerland are cases in point. Their central banks are among the most independent in the world and have presided over lower inflation rates than in virtually any other developed country.

The Federal Reserve's Mechanisms of Monetary Control

Open market operation
The purchase or sale of government securities by the Federal Reserve in order to change the money supply

The Fed employs three methods to control the money supply: engaging in open market operations (which we mentioned briefly in Chapter 8), making loans to banks through its discount window, and setting reserve requirements. In an **open market operation** the Fed increases the monetary base by printing money and using it to purchase U.S. Treasury bonds held by the public.[10] This base

7. The Federal Reserve banks are located in New York, Boston, Philadelphia, Richmond, Atlanta, St. Louis, Cleveland, Chicago, Kansas City, Dallas, Minneapolis, and San Francisco.
8. Not surprisingly, prior to 1980 many banks turned down membership with the Fed in order to avoid the Fed's implicit tax on their reserves. Indeed, in the years leading up to 1980, when interest rates were exceptionally high, ever larger numbers of banks began declining Fed membership. Fearing that the Fed was losing too much of its control of the banking system and the money supply, Congress passed the Depository Institutions Deregulatory and Monetary Control Act in 1980. This law forced all banks to belong, in fact if not in form, to the Fed.
9. See Alberto Alesina and Lawrence H. Summers, "Central Bank Independence and Macroeconomic Performance: Some Comparative Evidence," Harvard University, mimeo, 1990.
10. The term "printing money" is used here to refer to the Fed's creation of money, rather than the actual printing of currency. When the Fed makes a purchase it simply writes a check on itself. The bank that ultimately receives the check will present it to the Fed and be credited with an increase in its reserve account. In other words, the Fed ultimately makes its purchases by creating what is essentially a larger checking account for the bank that demands payment of the Fed's check. Currency is actually printed by the Bureau of Engraving and Printing, a part of the U.S. Treasury.

money finds its way into banks and triggers the deposit expansion process. **Discount window lending** also increases the monetary base. In this case the Fed prints money to make loans to individual banks. Since M1 and the other money aggregates are related, via their money multipliers, to the monetary base, increases in the monetary base produced by open market operations or discount window lending increase the size of monetary aggregates. In contrast, changing reserve requirements leaves the monetary base unaffected, but alters the size of monetary aggregates by influencing the reserve-deposit ratios entering the money multipliers. Let's consider each of the three money control mechanisms in turn.

Discount window lending
Loans made by the Fed to banks, thereby increasing the monetary base

Open Market Operations

Every month or two, the Fed's Board of Governors meets with the president of the Federal Reserve Bank of New York and a rotating set of four of the presidents of the other regional Federal Reserve banks. This larger assembly, called the *Federal Open Market Committee* (FOMC), issues directives to the bond-trading desk of the Federal Reserve Bank of New York concerning the type and quantity of open market operations it should engage in. If the FOMC wants to increase the money supply via an open market operation, it will direct the desk to buy Treasury bonds on the bond market. In purchasing the bonds, the desk gives the bond seller, say Salomon Brothers, a check written on the Federal Reserve. Salomon Brothers deposits the check in its bank, which, in turn, presents it to the Federal Reserve for payment. The Federal Reserve makes payment by crediting Salomon's bank with additional bank reserves equal to the amount of the check. As a result of this transaction the Fed ends up holding additional Treasury bonds and Salomon ends up with a larger demand deposit. Salomon's bank, assuming it was fully loaned up prior to the transaction, finds itself holding excess reserves. This triggers the process of deposit creation described above.

The opposite set of transactions arise if the FOMC orders the trading desk to sell Treasury bonds. In this case the trading desk will hand over Treasury bonds in exchange for a check from Salomon Brothers. The Fed will then clear the check with Salomon's bank by reducing that bank's reserves in the amount of the check. If Salomon's bank was fully loaned up, it will find itself with insufficient reserves and begin reducing its loans. This leads to a contraction of demand deposits that is just the opposite of the expansion of demand deposits described earlier.

Using Open Market Operations to Finance Government Expenditures

Although the route is somewhat circuitous, the open market operations just described play a critical role in the government's printing of money, some of which may be used to finance its expenditures. We first discussed monetary finance of government expenditures in Chapter 8, where we assumed that the governmental authority that purchases goods and services and makes transfer payments is also authorized to print the money needed to cover such expenditures. In reality,

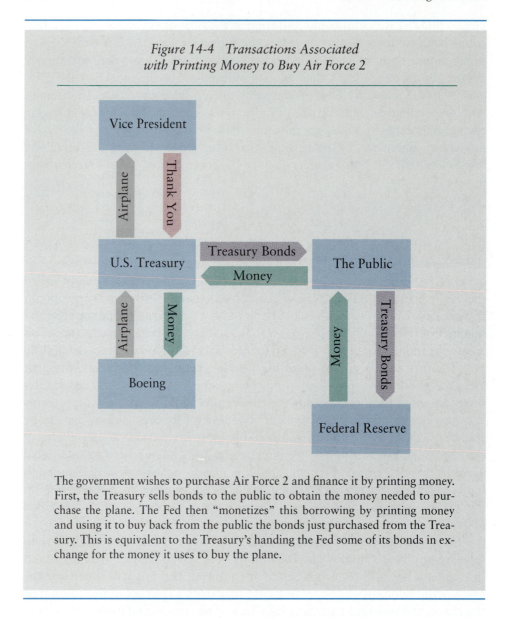

Figure 14-4 Transactions Associated with Printing Money to Buy Air Force 2

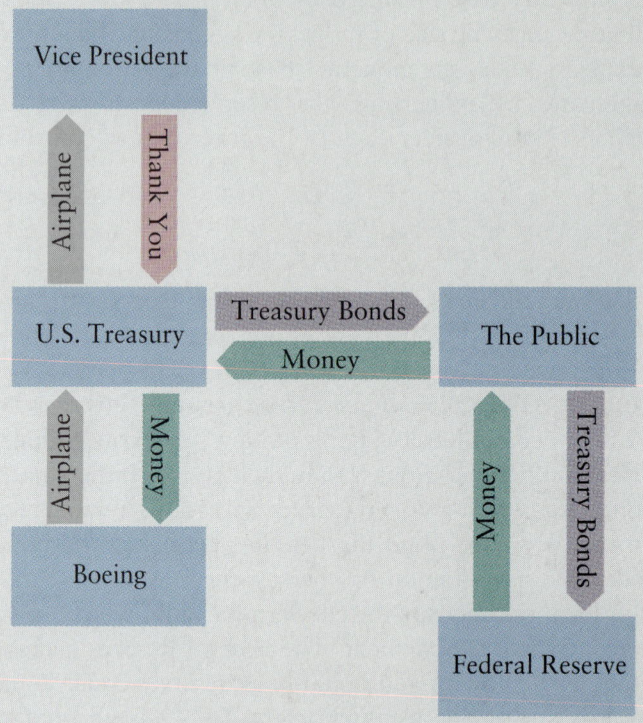

The government wishes to purchase Air Force 2 and finance it by printing money. First, the Treasury sells bonds to the public to obtain the money needed to purchase the plane. The Fed then "monetizes" this borrowing by printing money and using it to buy back from the public the bonds just purchased from the Treasury. This is equivalent to the Treasury's handing the Fed some of its bonds in exchange for the money it uses to buy the plane.

two different agencies, the Treasury and the Federal Reserve, must act jointly in order for a government expenditure to be financed by money creation.

To see how this works, suppose the government wants to purchase a new airplane (Air Force 2) from the Boeing Company for the Vice President and finance it by printing money. The transactions, diagrammed in Figure 14-4, proceed as follows. First, the Treasury sells bonds to the public to obtain the money to purchase the plane. Second, the Federal Reserve "monetizes" this government borrowing by printing money and using it to buy back from the public the bonds just purchased from the Treasury. The results of these transactions are that the Vice President ends up with a new plane paid for by freshly printed money! The Treasury and the Federal Reserve go through the act of selling bonds to and buying bonds from the public. But in the end, the Treasury is really just handing the Federal Reserve some of its bonds in exchange for money, which it then uses to buy the plane.[11]

Lending Through the Discount Window

As we've just seen, open market operations involve the Fed's exchanging money for a financial security, namely, a U.S. Treasury bond. The Fed's lending through its discount window involves quite similar transactions. As before, the Fed swaps money for a financial security; in this case, the security is an IOU from a bank. Banks that borrow through the discount window receive their borrowed funds in the form of increases in their reserve accounts at the Fed.

Why do banks occasionally need to borrow funds? Usually, it is because they find themselves with too few reserves to meet their reserve requirements. To see how this may happen, consider again the balance sheet of First National Bank when it is fully loaned up, with $1,000 of reserves, which equal 20 percent of its $5,000 in deposits.

First National Bank Balance Sheet

Assets		Liabilities	
Type	**Amount**	**Type**	**Amount**
Reserves	1,000	Deposits	5,000
Loans	5,000	Owners' Equity	1,000
Total Assets	6,000	Total Liabilities	6,000

Starting from this position, suppose that Dewey, Cheatham, and Howe withdraws its $1,000 deposit by writing a check to make a $1,000 purchase. If First National Bank can't call back or sell off $1,000 of its loans, it will be forced to use its $1,000 of reserves to pay this check. Its balance sheet will then look like this:

First National Bank Balance Sheet

Assets		Liabilities	
Type	**Amount**	**Type**	**Amount**
Reserves	0	Deposits	4,000
Loans	5,000	Owners' Equity	1,000
Total Assets	5,000	Total Liabilities	5,000

The bank now finds itself with zero reserves. Since its deposits equal $4,000 and it needs to keep its reserves equal to 20 percent of its deposits, it needs to come

11. The transaction is completed when the Treasury pays interest and principal to the Federal Reserve on the Treasury bonds held by the Fed. But these receipts are funneled back to the Treasury when the Federal Reserve hands over the profits it earns on its operations.

up with $800 in additional reserves. One possibility is to borrow the $800 either from the Fed or from other banks that may have excess reserves. The market for the interbank borrowing of excess reserves is called the *federal funds market*, and the interest rate charged there is called the **federal funds rate.**

Federal funds rate *The interest rate prevailing in the federal funds market for day-to-day lending and borrowing of reserves among financial institutions*

Once First National Bank borrows the $800, its balance sheet becomes:

First National Bank Balance Sheet

Assets		Liabilities	
Type	Amount	Type	Amount
Reserves	800	Deposits	4,000
Loans	5,000	Borrowings	800
		Owners' Equity	1,000
Total Assets	5,800	Total Liabilities	5,800

The $800 the bank borrows shows up in this balance sheet as an additional liability as well as an additional reserve asset.

The ability to borrow from the Fed is particularly important for banks experiencing unexpectedly large withdrawals of deposits. In such circumstances, banks may find they can't borrow as much as they'd like in the federal funds market, at least not at the going federal funds rate. In this circumstance they may be forced to turn to the Fed, the so-called *lender of last resort*, and borrow funds through the discount window.

There is a key difference between an open market purchase of bonds and providing loans through the discount window. In the former case, the Fed initiates the increase in the monetary base and, thus, the money supply. In the latter case, the borrowing bank initiates the increase. If banks were free to borrow as much and as often as they wished through the discount window, the money supply would be completely dependent on their decisions. But the Fed doesn't allow such unlimited borrowing. On the contrary, it decides how much to lend on a bank-by-bank basis. The more a particular bank borrows, the more likely it is the Fed will prohibit further borrowing. This leads banks to think twice about borrowing from the discount window. They don't want to jeopardize their ability to borrow at future dates when their need may be greater.

The Fed also influences the amount borrowed by adjusting the rate of interest it charges on its loans—the **discount rate.** As Figure 14-5 indicates, since the Federal funds market was established in 1955, the Fed has set the discount rate both above and below the federal funds rate. The lower the Fed sets the discount rate compared to the prevailing federal funds rate, the more it encourages borrowing through its window rather than through the federal funds market. Hence, in setting its discount rate the Fed can indirectly control the expansion of the monetary base arising from borrowing through the discount window.

Discount rate *The interest rate charged by the Federal Reserve on its loans to banks*

Reserve Requirements

According to our formula for the M1 money multiplier, (cd + 1)/(cd + rd), a fall in the reserve requirement, rd, holding base constant, will produce an increase

Figure 14-5 The Federal Reserve Discount Rate and the Federal Funds Rate, 1955–1993

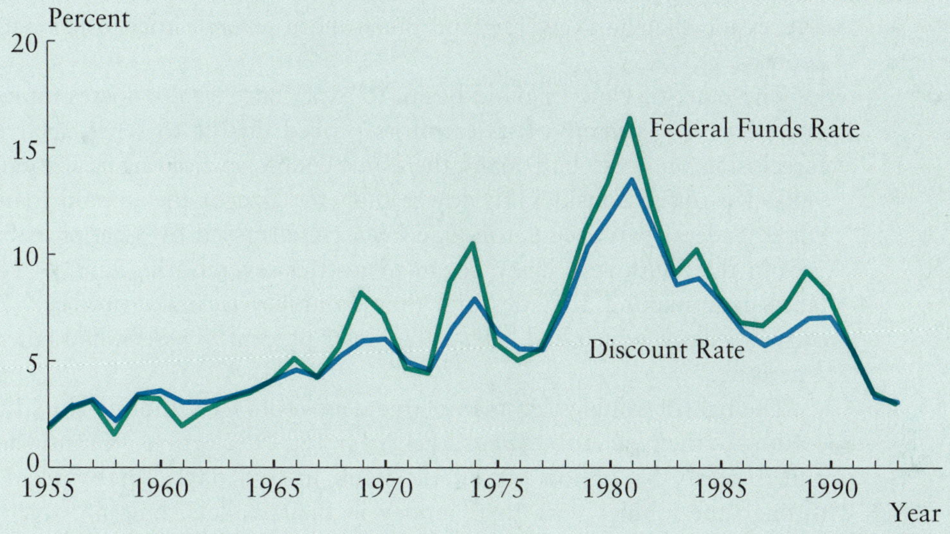

The Fed influences the amount banks borrow by setting the discount rate—the rate it charges on loans. The lower it sets the discount rate relative to the federal funds rate, the more it encourages borrowing through the discount window rather than through the federal funds market. By adjusting the discount rate, the Fed indirectly controls the expansion of the monetary base.

Source: *Economic Report of the President,* 1994

in M1. As previously mentioned, the Federal Reserve determines the minimum amount of reserves banks must hold. Currently the Fed subjects all depository institutions, including commercial banks, savings and loan associations, mutual savings banks, and credit unions, to the same reserve requirements on their checkable deposits. These required reserves equal 3 percent of the depository institution's first $42.2 million of deposits, and 10 percent of its deposits over $42.2 million. Changes in the Fed's reserve requirements are infrequent, but when the requirements do change, they can change significantly. For example, in April 1992 the Fed reduced what was a 12 percent reserve requirement on banks' deposits over $42.2 billion to the present 10 percent figure.

Case Study: The Fed as Lender of Last Resort and the Bank of New England

In the late 1980s the Bank of New England, the second largest bank in New England and the thirty-third largest in the country, became swept up in the New England real estate boom. The bank chose to invest over 40 percent of its assets in loans on commercial real estate, most of which was situated in New England.

The bank experienced phenomenal growth between 1985 and 1988, a period during which its assets doubled. But this growth came to an abrupt halt as the result of two related events. First, New England commercial real estate prices stopped rising and indeed fell by about 25 percent. Second, the nation went into a recession that hit New England much more severely than other parts of the country.

The Bank of New England began to experience sizable losses on its real estate portfolio as many of its creditors proved unable to repay their loans. In foreclosing on these bad loans the bank ended up holding real estate whose value was often considerably lower than the size of the unpaid loan. Meanwhile, Federal bank regulators had been embarrassed by a series of bank failures in the Southwest. They began to restrict severely the Bank of New England's loan-making activities and thus its ability to make profits.[12] By 1990, owners' equity, which had been as high as 5 percent of assets, had fallen to only 1 percent.

The bank's troubles led many large depositors to withdraw their funds. According to the *New York Times*'s February 18, 1992 article, "Frantic depositors pulled nearly $1 billion out of the bank in two days; small savers trouped through the lobbies with their money in their wallets, bulging envelopes and briefcases, and money managers yanked out multimillion-dollar deposits by remote control with computer and telex orders. Some local crooks even tried to get in on the action. The FBI said it foiled a plan by six men to rob an armored car they figured would be loaded with cash for all the withdrawals."

To meet these withdrawals the Bank of New England found itself forced to borrow from the Fed's discount window. In 1990 this borrowing was close to $2 billion—a huge sum, considering that the total increase in the monetary base that year was $24 billion. But in the end, even this huge amount of borrowing failed to buy the Bank of New England enough time to improve its financial condition. In January of 1991 the Federal Deposit Insurance Corporation, a federal agency we'll discuss below that is charged with insuring deposits, took over operation of the bank. Ultimately, this agency arranged for Fleet Financial Group to buy the bank's remaining assets and absorb a portion of its liabilities.

HOW WELL DOES THE FED CONTROL THE MONEY SUPPLY?

In earlier chapters we discussed how changes in the money supply can have important effects on macroeconomic performance. This section examines the Fed's ability to use the instruments just discussed to control the money supply. We begin be asking which of the three monetary aggregates, M1, M2, or M3, the Fed should try to control. As we'll see, the answer is not obvious.

12. The regulators even forced the Bank of New England to write off, as a partial loss, performing loans (loans on which interest was being paid on time) on real estate whose market value had declined. This effectively raised the bank's capital requirement, a banking regulation we'll discuss below.

Figure 14-6 U.S. Monetary Aggregates and the Monetary Base, 1959–1993

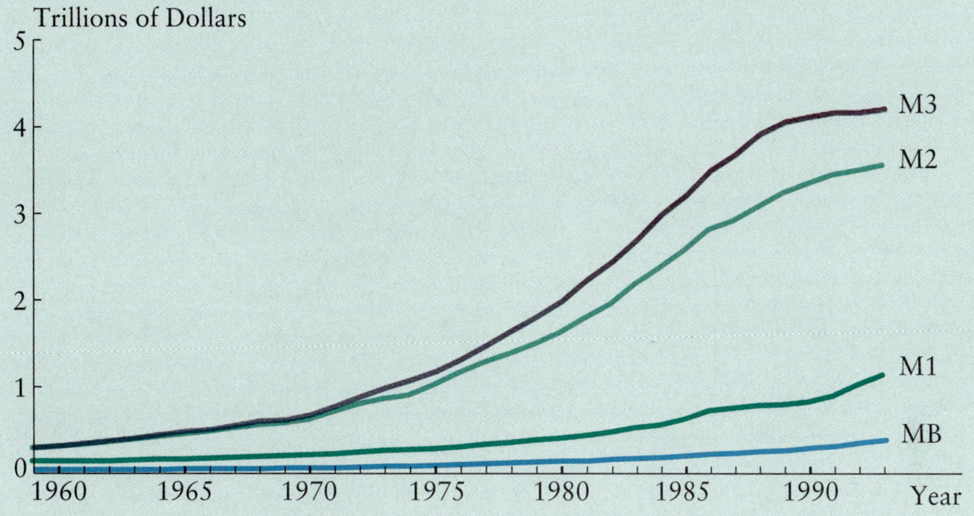

U.S. monetary aggregates have grown at different rates. In 1959 M2 and M3 were both about twice the size of M1. By 1993 M2 was over four times the size of M1, and M3 was over four and one-half times the size of M1.

Source: *Economic Report of the President,* 1994

The Divergent Paths of the Monetary Aggregates

If M1, M2, and M3 always grew at the same rate, the choice among the three aggregates would be unimportant. But Figure 14-6 shows that the three aggregates have grown at quite different rates over time. The figure plots the three aggregates, as well as the monetary base, for the years 1959 through 1993. In 1959, M2 and M3 were both just over twice the size of M1. By 1993, M2 was almost four times, and M3 was over four and one-half times, the size of M1.

Since the three monetary aggregates grow at different rates, it's difficult to assess the stance of monetary policy. Figure 14-7 highlights this point. It compares the annual growth rates of the monetary aggregates over the years 1980 through 1993. Although the three curves follow roughly the same pattern, in any given year the growth rates of the three aggregates can be considerably different.

Take the recession year 1982 as an example. In that year M1 growth accelerated, reaching 8.7 percent, compared with 6.7 percent for 1981. In contrast, growth of both M2 and M3 decelerated. 1982 M2 growth was 8.9 percent, down from 10.0 percent in the previous year; 1982 M3 growth was 9.3 percent, down from 12.4 percent in the previous year. What should we make of these

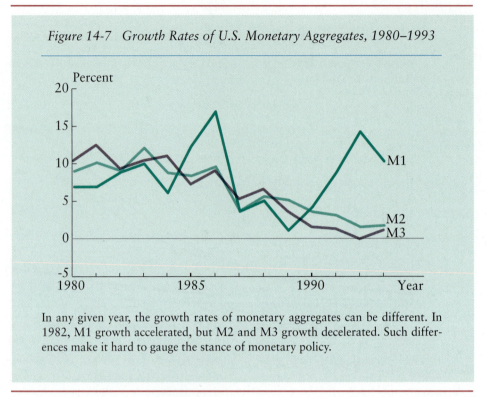

Figure 14-7 Growth Rates of U.S. Monetary Aggregates, 1980–1993

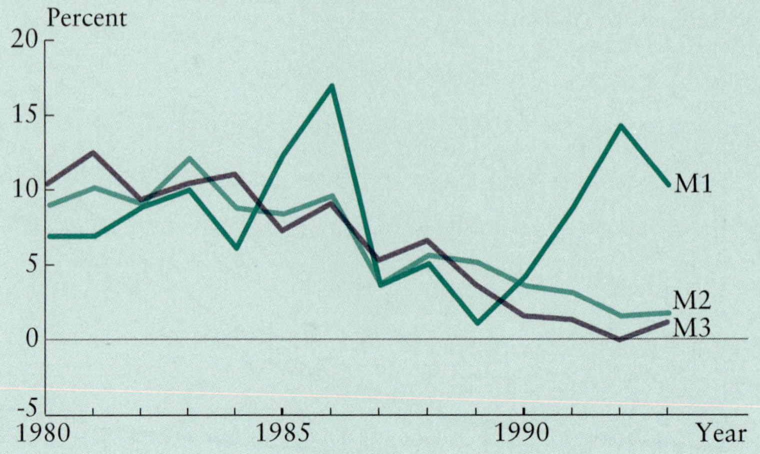

In any given year, the growth rates of monetary aggregates can be different. In 1982, M1 growth accelerated, but M2 and M3 growth decelerated. Such differences make it hard to gauge the stance of monetary policy.

Source: *Economic Report of the President*, 1994

facts? If we take M1 as our definition of the money supply, we have to conclude that during 1982, when the economy was in recession, monetary policy was expansionary. On the other hand, if we take M2 or M3 as our definition, we conclude that monetary policy was contractionary.

One answer to this conundrum, which is less than fully satisfying, is that there is no single best measure of the money supply. Rather, there is a range of items—coins, currency, demand deposits, savings and money market accounts, etc.—all of which have money-like properties and all of which must be considered if we are to gain a complete understanding of the state of monetary affairs. According to this line of argument, the Fed should simultaneously consider each of its different measures of money, with the degree of attention paid to particular measures depending on prevailing economic circumstances. The problem with such ad hoc assessments is that the Fed may end up placing too much emphasis on certain monetary aggregates and not enough on others. Consequently, it may inadvertently pursue expansionary monetary policy by increasing the monetary base, lowering its discount rate, or lowering reserve requirements, when a contractionary policy is called for, or vice versa.

Understanding the Variability of the Monetary Aggregates

Figure 14-6 shows that the monetary aggregates have not maintained a stable relationship over time to the monetary base. Another way to say this is that the money multipliers of the different aggregates have varied through time. We already mentioned that the M1 money multiplier declined from 3.4 in 1959 to 2.9 in 1993. The M2 and M3 money multipliers also changed during this period, but in the other direction: they rose dramatically. In 1959 the M2 and M3 multipliers (the ratios of M2 and M3 to the monetary base) were 6.9 and 7.0, respectively. In 1993 they were 9.2 and 10.9.

How significant are such fluctuations in the money multipliers? The question is important because we've seen that the Fed can control the size of the monetary base directly, but can only influence the size of money multipliers indirectly. The Fed can determine exactly how much it wants to increase the monetary base by deciding how much to spend on the purchase of Treasury bonds and how much to lend through its discount window. In contrast, the elements entering the money multipliers are largely determined by the private sector.

To understand this, recall that the formula for the M1 money multiplier depends on two parameters: the ratio of currency to demand deposits, cd, and the reserve-deposit ratio, rd. The Fed has no direct control over cd. Instead, the public decides how to divide its money between cash and demand deposits. The Fed can set a floor under the reserve-deposit ratio through its reserve requirements. But the banking system is free to set a reserve-deposit ratio above the Fed's reserve requirement by choosing to hold excess reserves. In addition, a large fraction of nonbank checkable deposits entering M1 is not subject to reserve requirements.

Figure 14-8 compares the variability of annual growth rates of M1, M2, and M3 over the years 1950 through 1993 with the variability of growth in the monetary base.[13] It shows that the variability of growth in each of the three monetary aggregates exceeds that of the monetary base by a wide margin. For example, variability of M1 growth is over twice as large as variability in monetary base growth. Clearly, then, a large portion of the changes in the monetary aggregates are due, not to changes in the monetary base, over which the government has direct control, but rather to changes in money multipliers, over which the government has only indirect control.

Case Study: Monetary Control During the Great Depression

In their famous book *A Monetary History of the United States*, economists Milton Friedman and Anna Schwartz laid much of the blame for the severity and length of the Great Depression on the Federal Reserve's monetary policy. As discussed in Chapter 12, there was a significant decline in M1 in the early 1930s and again in 1937. Both declines were followed in quick succession by sharp drops in U.S. output. These comovements of M1 and output during the Great Depression raise two questions. First, did the decline in M1 cause output to decline? Second, did the Fed cause M1 to decline?

We addressed the first question in Chapter 12, where we pointed out that the decline in M1 seems insufficient, by itself, to explain the severity of the drop in

13. The figure's index of variability equals 100 times the variance of the growth rate of MB, M1, M2, or M3 divided by the variance of the growth rate of MB.

Figure 14-8 Variability of Growth Rates of U.S. Monetary Aggregates and the Monetary Base, 1950–1993

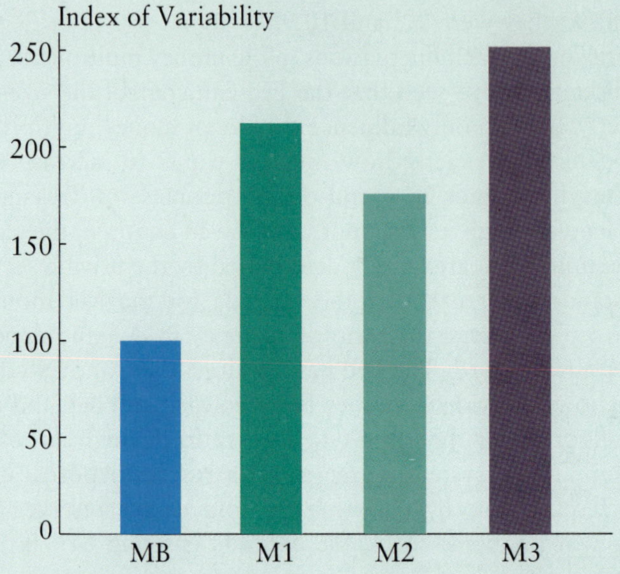

The variability in the growth of the three monetary aggregates has exceeded that of the monetary base by a wide margin. Consequently, many of the changes in the aggregates have been due to changes in the money multipliers rather than to changes in the base.

output. To answer the second question we must recognize that the Fed did not directly attempt to reduce M1. In fact, as shown in Figure 14-9, the Fed increased the monetary base by 18 percent between August 1929 and March 1933—the beginning and the end of the first recession of the Great Depression—and by 8 percent between May 1937 and June 1938—the beginning and the end of the second recession. Despite these increases in the base, M1 declined by 28 percent between August 1929 and March 1933 and 5 percent between May 1937 and June 1938. The reason is that the M1 money multiplier declined dramatically during both these periods. In August 1929 the M1 money multiplier was 2.7. By March 1933 it was 2.3. In May 1937 the multiplier again equaled 2.3, but it fell to 2.0 by June 1938.

Both declines in the M1 multiplier were due to increases in cd, the public's desired ratio of currency to demand deposits, as well as in rd, the fraction of deposits held by the banking system as reserves. The increases in cd and rd reflect a natural reaction to the events of the day. Since one of every three banks failed during the Great Depression, it is not surprising that the public became wary of depositing funds in banks and other depository institutions and shifted toward

Figure 14-9 U.S. Currency Holdings, Monetary Base, and M1, January 1929–December 1933

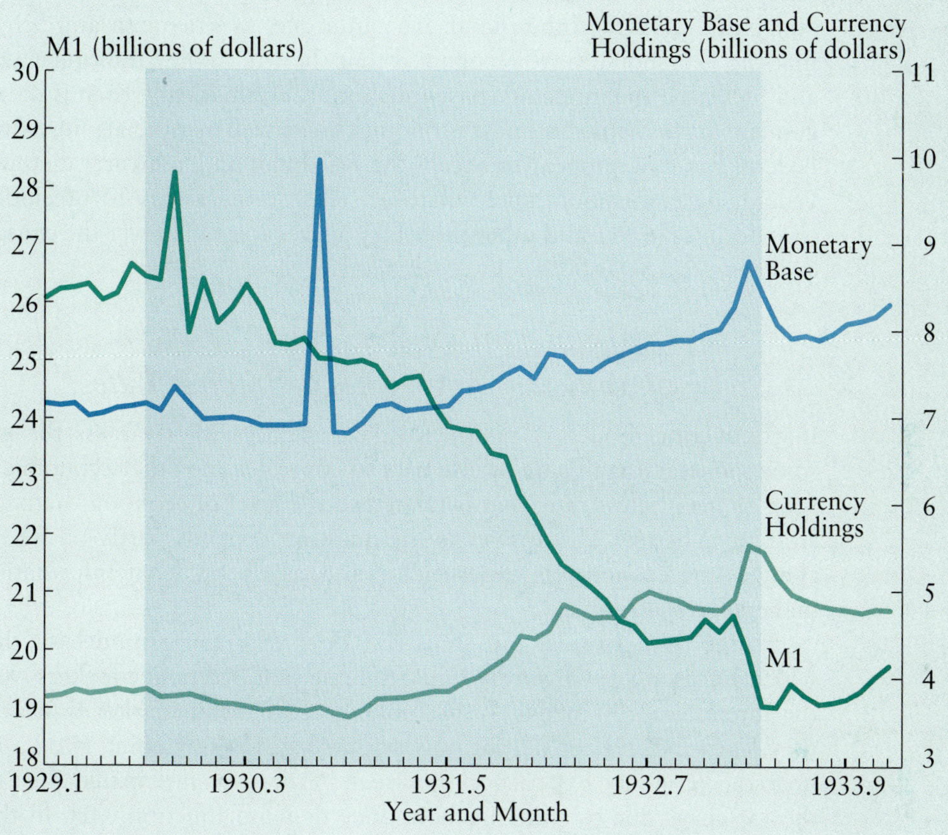

Did the Fed cause M1 to decline during the Great Depression? Not directly, since it increased the monetary base by 18 percent between August 1929 and March 1933. Nevertheless, M1 declined by 28 percent during the period as the money multiplier fell from 2.7 to 2.3. This reflected, in part, a substantial increase in the ratio of currency to demand deposits.

Source: Friedman and Schwartz, *A Monetary History of the United States, 1867–1960*

holding currency. Nor is it surprising that banks became cautious about having too low a level of reserves and took steps to raise their reserve-deposit ratios.[14]

Figure 14-9 also shows what happened to the currency holdings of the public and to M1 during the period 1929—1933. Since the difference between M1 and currency is essentially the amount of demand deposits, the figure also documents a substantial increase in the ratio of currency to demand deposits.

14. In doing so, the banks produced a "credit crunch" with negative implications for the economy, which are spelled out in Chapter 15.

Now that we've considered the evidence in Figure 14-9, should we conclude that Friedman and Schwartz are right or wrong in indicting the Fed for causing the Great Depression? On the one hand, we can say that the Fed did nothing directly to reduce M1 and actually took steps to raise it by increasing the monetary base.[15] On the other hand, we can argue, as Friedman and Schwartz do, that the Fed should have recognized that the M1 money multiplier was falling and increased the monetary base much more dramatically than it did. Both arguments have merit, but most economists—as well as officials now running the Federal Reserve—appear to accept the Friedman and Schwartz dictum that the Federal Reserve should take whatever steps are necessary to preclude precipitous declines in M1 and other monetary aggregates, whatever the causes of such declines.

Should the Fed Target the Growth of Monetary Aggregates or Interest Rates?[16]

In conducting monetary policy, the Fed usually either targets the growth of some monetary aggregate or else tries to control some other economic variable, such as the interest rate, that is related to the level of economic activity. Which strategy is better? The answer to the question depends partly on what sorts of changes the economy is experiencing and partly on what information policy makers have available.

To see this, consider our short-run Keynesian IS-LM model for the case in which prices are downwardly rigid. Assume that Fed policy makers can observe the interest rate immediately by looking at financial market transactions but they learn the level of output only with a lag. Let's examine two cases. In the first, the economy experiences *nominal shocks*—unanticipated fluctuations in the LM curve due to shifts in the money demand function, $\gamma[r]$. In the second case, it experiences *real shocks*—unanticipated fluctuations in the IS curve due, for example, to changes in the consumption propensity of the young, α.[17]

Consider Figure 14-10, in which the IS and LM curves initially intersect at point *A* with output level Y. An unfavorable nominal shock would cause the LM curve to shift leftward to LM'; a favorable shock would move it rightward to LM". In either case, policy makers see the interest rate move away from its original level of r. If the Fed is trying to maintain an interest rate target of r, it would respond to an increase in r by printing more money and to a decrease in r by reducing the money supply. In both cases the effect is to shift the LM curve back to the right, restoring it to its original position. Regardless of the nature of the nominal shock, the Fed's policy maintains the level of output and interest rate that originally prevailed at point *A*.

15. Part of the increase in the monetary base was automatic. At the time, the United States was still on the gold standard, and in the early 1930s it experienced an inflow of gold from abroad which it was obligated to purchase with dollars. Another reason to question the Fed's efforts in the early 1930s in increasing the monetary base is that the Fed kept its discount rate fairly high.

16. A seminal paper on this issue is William Poole's "Optimal Choice of Monetary Policy Instruments in a Simple Stochastic Macro Model," *Quarterly Journal of Economics* 84 (May 1970): 197–216.

17. As indicated in Chapter 12, it's easy to derive the IS curve for the case in which each generation consumes when young as well as when old, i.e., when α is positive.

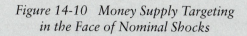

Figure 14-10 Money Supply Targeting in the Face of Nominal Shocks

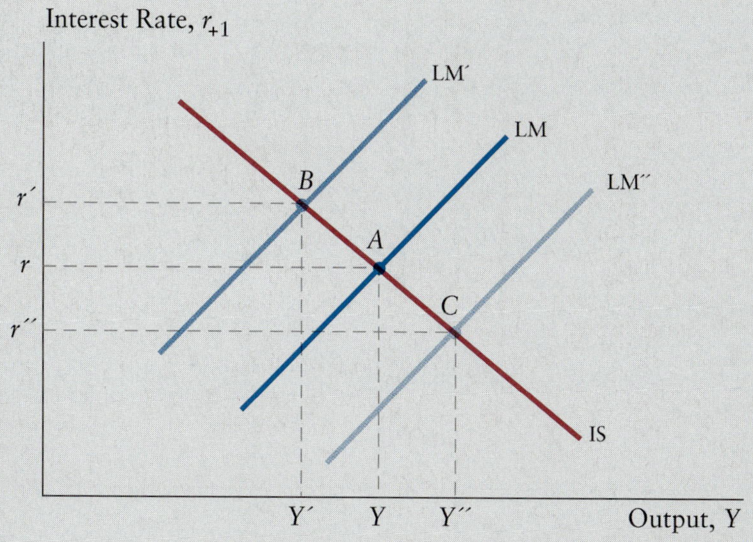

An unfavorable nominal shock shifts the LM curve leftward to LM', whereas a favorable shock shifts it rightward to LM″. In both cases, policy makers see the interest rate move away from its original level. To maintain its interest rate target, the Fed responds to a rise (fall) in the interest rate by increasing (decreasing) the money supply. In so doing, it restores LM to its original position.

What if the Fed were targeting the money supply? That amounts to accepting any shift in the LM curve, since the Fed's only means of moving that curve is to change the money supply. If the LM curve shifts to the left, Fed policy is to leave it there. In effect, it accepts the higher interest rate and lower level of output. If LM shifts rightward, money supply targeting results in a lower interest rate and more output. We can conclude that money supply targeting in the face of nominal shocks leads to fluctuations in interest rates (between r' and r'') and output (between Y' and Y''), whereas interest rate targeting does not.

What if the economy experiences real shocks? This situation is depicted in Figure 14-11. Starting from point *A*, suppose an unfavorable real shock shifts the IS curve inward to IS'. Again, the Fed cannot immediately observe the level of output but does see the interest fall from r to r' (point *B*). If it is pursuing an interest rate target, the Fed will reduce the money supply, thus shifting the LM curve leftward to LM' (point C). This restores the interest rate and, although the Fed doesn't know it, reduces output to Y'. The opposite would be true if a favorable real shock shifted the IS curve outward. Thus, interest rate targeting under real shocks exaggerates fluctuations in output.

Figure 14-11 Interest Rate Targeting in the Face of Real Shocks

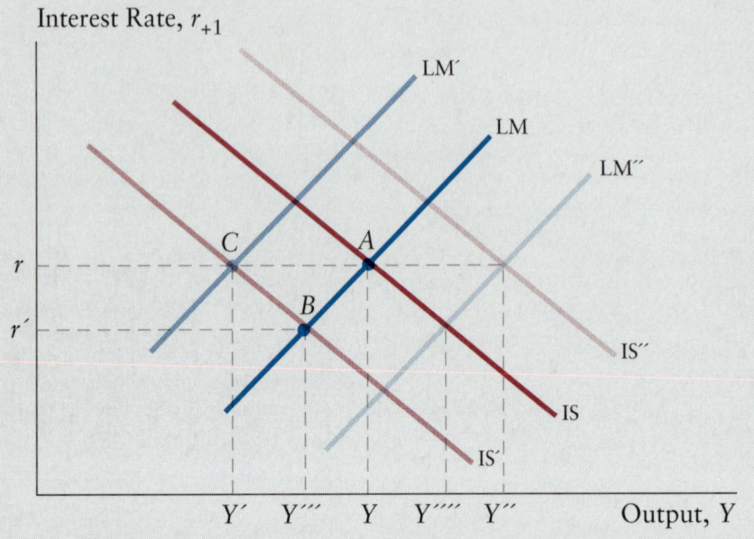

Starting at point *A*, an unfavorable real shock shifts the IS curve inward to IS'. The Fed sees the interest rate fall from *r* to *r*' at point *B*. If it is targeting the interest rate, the Fed reduces the money supply, shifting the LM curve to LM' and producing an equilibrium at point *C*. This restores the interest rate but reduces output to *Y*'. Interest rate targeting amplifies real shocks. If the Fed targets the money supply, it does nothing when IS shifts down.

If the Fed is targeting the money supply, it does nothing. Holding the money supply constant means holding the original LM curve constant. After an unfavorable real shock (downward shift of IS) this means accepting the lower interest rate and, in effect, allowing output to fall. For a favorable shock, it means accepting a higher interest rate and level of output. But note that the fluctuations in output are smaller with a money supply target. With interest rate targeting, output fluctuates between *Y*' and *Y*". With a money supply target, the fluctuations are only from *Y*''' to *Y*''''.

To summarize, in a Keynesian setting in which the interest rate is immediately observable but output is not, targeting the interest rate is appropriate if the economy is experiencing nominal shocks (which shift the LM curve, reflecting changes in money demand). On the other hand, if the economy is experiencing real shocks (which shift the IS curve, reflecting changes in saving and investment), targeting the money supply will dampen the fluctuations in the interest rate and output.

Figure 14-12 Growth Rates of M1 and Real GDP, the Inflation Rate, and the Federal Funds Rate, October 1979–October 1982

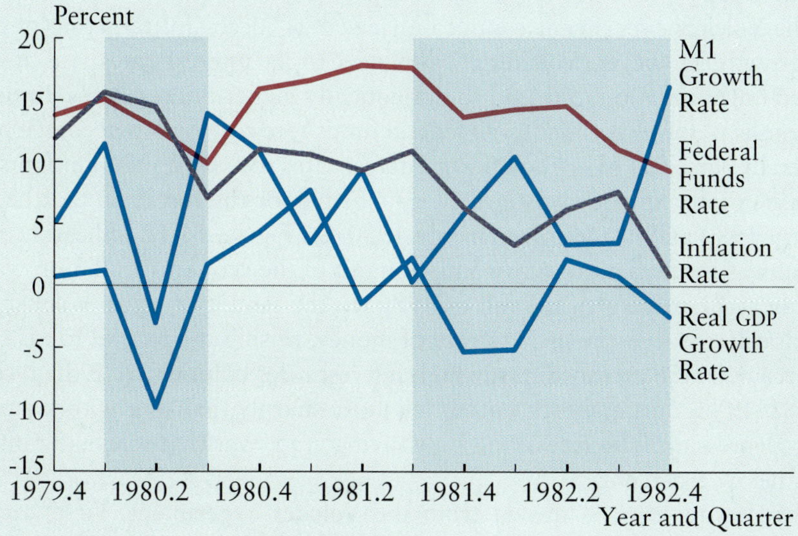

In October 1979, Paul Volcker announced M1 growth rate targets of 4.5–7 percent for 1980, 6–8.5 percent for 1981, and 2.5–5.5 percent for 1982. The evidence shows that the Fed missed each of these targets. In addition, M1 growth varied widely from quarter to quarter.

Source: *Economic Report of the President*, 1981–1983

Case Study: Paul Volcker's Experiment in Money Supply Targeting

In August 1979 Paul Volcker became Federal Reserve Chairman. His mandate was to lower an inflation rate that had reached double digits. In October Volcker announced that the Fed would no longer use its monetary control instruments (open market purchases, discount lending, and reserve requirements) to target the federal funds rate but rather would target much more closely the growth of the monetary aggregates. The Fed even announced a set of target ranges for the annual growth of M1. In 1980, 1981, and 1982, for example, the M1 growth target ranges were set at 4.5–7.0 percent, 6.0–8.5 percent, and 2.5–5.5 percent, respectively.

Figure 14-12 shows the growth rate of M1, the federal funds rate, the inflation rate, and the growth rate of output during the Volcker experiment, between October 1979 and October 1982. The first thing to notice is that the Fed repeatedly missed its M1 growth target over this period. Over the 13 quarters of the period the M1 growth rate, measured at an annual rate, ranged from a low of –3 percent to a high of 16 percent. In addition to permitting M1 growth to vary widely from quarter to quarter, the Fed failed to keep the annual growth of M1 within its target ranges in either 1980, 1981, or 1982. The annual M1 growth rates in those years were 7.5 percent, 5.1 percent, and 8.8 percent, respectively.

The Volcker experiment cannot be viewed as successful targeting of monetary growth. However, Volcker's willingness to let interest rates rise, if necessary, to lower inflation, did lead to dramatically higher interest rates. In the first six months of the experiment, the federal funds rate rose by 5 percentage points, to over 15 percent. Other short-term interest rates rose by similar amounts. This increase in interest rates was largely responsible for the recession that began in January 1980 and lasted through July 1980. As Figure 14-12 indicates, this recession was insufficient to wring inflation out of the economy; inflation was still running at 11 percent in the fall of 1980. In the winter of 1981 Volcker again temporarily reduced the growth rate of money, raising the federal funds rate to 17 percent. These extraordinarily high interest rates culminated in the recession of 1981–1982, during which output fell more sharply than at any time since the Great Depression. The recession's only saving grace was that it brought inflation down below 5 percent.

Two lessons can be drawn from the Volcker experiment. First, targeting money supply growth, come what may, is easier said then done. The Fed could have hit its targeted growth rates of M1 between 1979 and 1982, but chose not to, apparently because it felt the need to respond to events as they unfolded. These events included a larger than expected response of interest rates to the Fed's change in policy, President Carter's credit controls imposed in March 1980, substantial increases in oil prices at the end of 1979 and again in early 1981, and, finally, the period's two recessions. In terms of Figure 14-10, we can think of the first three of these events as producing a leftward shift of the LM curve that raised interest rates and made setting money supply growth targets quite difficult.[18]

The second lesson is that it takes more than words to convince financial markets that inflation is coming down. Recall that the nominal interest rate is the sum of the real interest rate and the expected inflation rate. In declaring war on inflation, Volcker may have hoped that the inflation premium embedded in nominal interest rates would fall, thereby lowering nominal rates. Evidently, that did not occur until the two recessions actually put a damper on price increases.

The Endogeneity of the Money Supply

A final question is whether the Fed actually sets its monetary policies independently or whether it merely accommodates whatever price level the public

18. Volcker's October 1979 announcement produced major concern about a credit crunch. As described in Chapter 15, such concern can be viewed as raising the demand for money and, thus, shifting the LM curve to the left. The imposition of credit controls added to concern about a credit crunch, further shifting the LM curve to the left. Finally, the rise in oil prices in a setting in which other prices were growing at rather inflexible rates meant a higher price level, which also shifted the LM curve to the left.

Figure 14-13 Is Monetary Policy Endogenous?

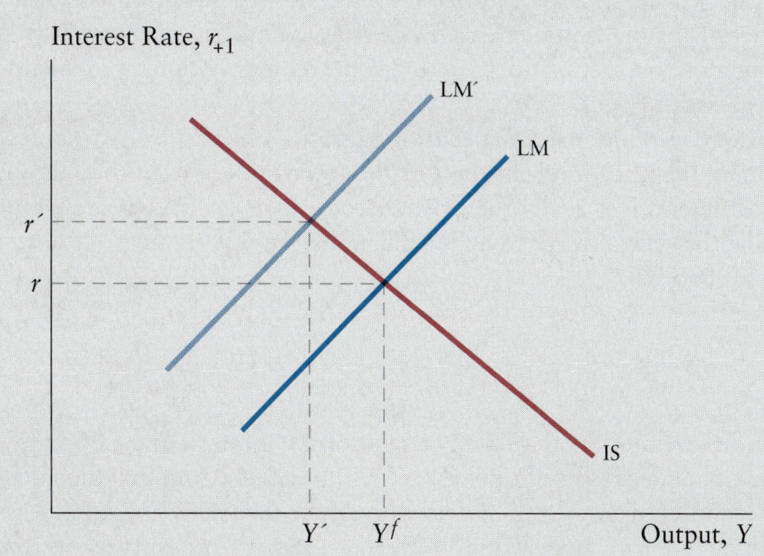

With price level P and money supply M, IS and LM intersect to determine full-employment output, Y^f. If the public comes to believe the price level will be $P' > P$, the LM curve shifts to LM' and the resulting equilibrium output level is $Y' < Y^f$. The Fed can accommodate that higher price level by increasing the money supply, restoring the LM curve to its original position and ensuring full employment, but at the cost of an increase in prices.Or, it can keep the money supply fixed at M and generate unemployment. If the Fed accommodates the higher prices, the private sector is really determining monetary policy by forcing the Fed to adapt to the price level it chooses.

chooses to believe will arise. This possibility of **endogenous monetary policy** can be understood through our IS-LM diagram. Figure 14-13 shows one possible short-run equilibrium in which the IS and LM curves intersect at the full-employment level of output, Y^f. The money supply and price level underlying this LM curve are M and P, respectively. The figure also shows another short-run equilibrium, based on the same value of the money supply, M, but a higher price level, P'. Output in this short-run equilibrium is Y', which is less than the full-employment level.

Endogenous monetary policy
A monetary policy that merely accommodates whatever price level the public believes will arise

Now while the Fed is pursuing its monetary policy, private sector decision makers are formulating their estimates of future inflation rates. Suppose the private sector, for whatever reason, believes the price level will be P' rather than P. Prices are set, wages are negotiated, and the price level ends up at P'. The central bank now faces a dilemma. It can accommodate the higher price level P' by increasing the money supply to M', so that M' exceeds M by the same percentage as P' exceeds P. If it does so, it will restore the LM curve to its initial position and ensure full employment, but at the cost of an increase in prices. Alternatively, it can stick to its guns, keep the money supply fixed at M, and generate unemployment. This unemployment will put downward pressure on prices, leading, over time, to a lower price level, P, and restoring full employment. So the trade-off for the central bank is between maintaining full employment, but accepting a rise in prices, and accepting some temporary unemployment with no long-term rise in prices.

If it does accommodate, the central bank still remains free to claim that it is determining the price level through its monetary policy, even though the reality is quite different. It is really the private sector that determines monetary policy by forcing the central bank to adapt the money supply to the price level the private sector chooses.

BANK RUNS AND DEPOSIT INSURANCE

In choosing to hold less than 100 percent of the money deposited with it in reserve, any bank leaves itself open to the risk of a *bank run*, in which depositors, suddenly and en masse, seek to withdraw their deposits. The bank's assets are the ultimate security underlying its deposits. So it's not surprising that many runs on banks were precipitated by fears that banks were insolvent—that their assets were less than their liabilities (excluding owner's equity). Banks can respond to a run by trying to retrieve the funds they have lent or invested. But liquidating loans and other assets takes time. Depending on the economic circumstances of their creditors, banks may be unable to retrieve all the funds they have lent out or otherwise invested. Finally, banks may be unable to borrow from other banks, financial intermediaries, or the government to stave off a run on their deposits. The simple reason is that these potential lenders cannot be sure that they'll be repaid.

Banks could try to avoid bank runs by holding 100 percent reserves. They could also make their liabilities less liquid by requiring a waiting period before returning their depositors' money. But either option would reduce bank profits. Indeed, the second option—reducing the liquidity of bank liabilities—would eliminate the special service provided by banks, namely, enabling depositors to have ready access to their money by writing negotiable checks.

The difference between the liquidity of banks' liabilities and their assets is illustrated in Table 14-2, which shows the composition of U.S. commercial bank assets and liabilities as of January 1994. A total of 67 percent of commercial bank liabilities listed in the table consisted of demand deposits, savings deposits, and time deposits—all of which can be withdrawn from banks quite quickly. Owners of demand deposits can withdraw their funds at any time from the bank, and owners of saving and time deposits can withdraw their funds over a very short period of time (although early withdrawal may entail a loss of interest). The other liabilities of banks—bank borrowing and owners' equity—are much less liquid.

On the asset side of the commercial banks' balance sheet, the most liquid bank assets are reserves (including banks' vault cash), cash items in process of

Table 14-2 January 26, 1994 Balance Sheet of U.S. Commercial Banks (billions of dollars)

Assets	
Total Assets	**$3,706.9**
Reserves with Federal Reserve	31.6
Cash in vault	34.9
Cash items in process of collection	74.9
Deposits with other banks	30.3
Other cash assets	38.2
Investment Securities	
U.S. government securities	692.9
Other	167.6
Loans	
Commercial and Industrial	587.9
Real estate	922.4
Consumer	392.5
Interbank	151.9
Other loans	268.5
Other Assets	313.5
Liabilities	
Total Liabilities	**$3,706.9**
Checkable deposits	790.1
Nontransaction deposits	
Saving deposits	777.1
Time deposits	927.3
Borrowing	528.5
Other liabilities	377.4
Owners' Equity	306.5

Source: *Federal Reserve Bulletin,* April 1994

collection, deposits with other banks, other cash assets, and investment securities. Together, these assets constitute just 29 percent of total commercial bank assets. Their remaining assets, such as commercial and industrial loans, real estate holdings, and consumer loans, are fairly illiquid.

Thus, we can conclude that the liabilities of U.S. commercial banks are much more more liquid than are their assets. In the absence of deposit insurance, which we discuss below, U.S. commercial banks would be highly vulnerable to bank runs.

Case Study: The Banking Panic of the Great Depression and the Establishment of Deposit Insurance[19]

Of the periodic banking panics experienced throughout U.S. history, the panic of the early 1930s was by far the most severe. From the end of 1930 through March 1933, one of every three U.S. banks failed or was taken over by a competitor. There were actually three separate crises during this period. The first began in October 1930, a year after the stock market crashed. It was touched off by the failure of a relatively small number of banks in the Midwest and South. These failures sent depositors across the country flocking to withdraw their funds. In November 1930, 256 banks failed; another 352 failed in December, including the Bank of the United States, which was the largest commercial bank failure to that point. Even though the Bank of the United States was a private bank, its name led many to mistake it for an official bank, thereby producing even greater concern about the viability of the banking system.

The initial banking panic subsided in January 1931, but a second panic began in March and continued through the end of 1931. It was brought on by the continuing decline in real output at home, news of major bank closings in Europe, and Britain's decision in September of 1931 to abandon the gold standard. In January 1932 the contagion of bank failures again subsided, but in the fall of 1932 as well as the winter of 1933, bank failures in the Midwest and West touched off yet a third round of panic. Almost 2000 banks nationwide were forced to close. As in the previous runs, the public attempted to convert deposits into currency; in the first two months of 1933 alone, currency held by the public rose by 16 percent!

On March 6, 1933 President Franklin D. Roosevelt ordered U.S. banks closed for a week—a suspension of banking operations without precedent in the nation's history. During this "bank holiday," depositors were unable to withdraw their funds. Roosevelt's action put a temporary lid on bank failures, but it didn't bring them to an end. Another 2000 or so banks chose to go out of business rather than reopen after the bank holiday.

Deposit insurance *A government program that insures bank deposits against the possibility of bank failure*

What ultimately eliminated banking panics was the establishment of the Federal Deposit Insurance Corporation (FDIC). Starting on January 1, 1934 the FDIC provided **deposit insurance** to all member banks of the Federal Reserve as well as to nonmember banks that applied for and were approved for this insurance. If an insured bank failed, the FDIC would cover deposits up to $2,500. This amount has been increased over time. Currently, the FDIC insures deposits up to $100,000. In order to cover losses on deposits from troubled banks, the

19. Chapter 7 of Friedman and Schwartz's *A Monetary History of the United States* presents an excellent description of the banking crisis of the early 1930s.

FDIC charges all its enrolled banks insurance premiums that vary with the amount of deposits the bank has at risk.

Deposit insurance was an instant success. By early 1934 most commercial banks, accounting for virtually all bank deposits, had signed up for FDIC insurance. The protection afforded by the government's deposit insurance dramatically reduced runs on banks as well as the number of bank failures. In 1934 there were only 61 bank failures, compared with 4000 in 1933.

Problems Caused by Deposit Insurance and the Need for Bank Regulation

Notwithstanding its success in eliminating bank runs, deposit insurance, like other forms of insurance, produces a problem called *moral hazard*. Moral hazard refers to the tendency of those covered by insurance to take less care to avoid the risk of a loss. For example, insured car owners may be less likely to lock their cars and garage them in safe places; homeowners with fire insurance may be less likely to check their smoke detectors. In the case of deposit insurance, bank managers may take unwarranted risks in investing their institutions' assets. They realize that if their potentially high-stakes gambles pay off, their banks will earn large profits. On the other hand, if the gambles fail, and they end up with too little money to cover their deposits, their depositors will be paid by the FDIC. Investment losses that are passed to the FDIC are ultimately paid for by the general public, either through higher service fees charged by banks to cover their insurance premium payments to the FDIC or in general taxes, when the FDIC's insurance premiums are insufficient to cover its insurance payments.

To prevent the managers of banks and other federally insured depository institutions from gambling at the expense of the general public, the government employs three methods of regulating the investment strategies of these financial intermediaries. The first are laws stipulating the kinds of investments these intermediaries can and cannot make. For example, the Glass-Steagall Act of 1933 prohibits commercial banks from investing in stocks.

The second regulatory device is *capital requirements*, which stipulate that owners' equity must exceed a certain fraction of the bank's total assets. When owners' equity is small, the owners of the bank have little to lose if the bank fails. By specifying minimum levels of owners' equity, the government seeks to ensure that the bank's owners have a personal stake in the outcome of their investments. Currently, capital requirements range from 3 to 6 percent of assets, depending on the bank's financial condition.

A third regulatory mechanism is periodic examination of the investments of banks and other insured depository institutions. Three regulatory bodies oversee the investments of federally chartered banks: the Comptroller of the Currency, the FDIC, and the Federal Reserve. Examiners from these agencies make frequent unscheduled visits to banks in order to check their books, review the quality of their loans, and make sure they are meeting their capital requirements. These federal regulators can raise banks' capital requirements, force banks to sell off assets they view as too risky, and replace bank managers.

Case Study: The S&L Crisis

In 1934 the federal government established the Federal Saving and Loan Insurance Corporation (FSLIC)—to insure the savings accounts and time deposits of savings and loans and mutual savings banks. The federal government also established the Federal Home Loan Bank Board (FHLBB) to regulate the S&LS. The FHLBB had great success until the 1980s when a combination of policy changes, external events, regulatory failures, and moral hazard led to the fiasco known as the S&L crisis.

In 1980 federal legislation deregulated the investments of the S&LS. Previously, S&LS had been forced to invest the funds deposited with them almost exclusively in home mortgages. Now, they were permitted to invest the bulk of their funds in other types of assets, including commercial real estate, consumer loans, and commercial loans. They were even allowed to invest up to 10 percent of their assets in financial securities such as common stock, government and standard corporate bonds, and high-risk corporate bonds. The new legislation raised the size of FSLIC-insured deposits from $40,000 to $100,000 and eliminated a government-imposed ceiling, *Regulation Q*, on the interest rate that banks and S&LS could pay depositors.

With the lifting of Regulation Q, the S&LS were forced to pay the high short-term interest rates prevailing in the early 1980s. At the same time, most of their investments were still tied up in home mortgages, a large portion of which had been issued at low interest rates. The resulting squeeze on profits led many S&L managers to pursue higher yielding, if riskier, investment strategies. Many of these new investments, as well as many of the S&LS' previous investments, proved highly unprofitable, both because of the sharp national recession of 1981–1982 and because of the collapse of real estate prices in Texas and elsewhere.

By the mid-1980s almost half of the S&LS in the country were technically insolvent. Their owners' equity was negative, because their liabilities (apart from owners' equity) exceeded their assets. But the Bush administration and Congress did not wish to admit publicly that FSLIC needed about $25 billion in tax revenues to cover the insured deposits of these insolvent S&LS. So, they put off dealing with the problem. Since the S&L depositors knew that the government stood behind their deposits, they did not make a run on the S&LS. Such a run would have forced the government to confront immediately the full scope of its problem, including the necessity to remove a number of high-rolling managers of technically insolvent S&LS. Some of these managers were extremely shady characters who ultimately landed in jail.

While regulators dallied, the crisis worsened. By 1990 the losses of the S&LS had grown to a staggering $200 billion! Finally, the federal government took action. It eliminated the FHLBB and the FSLIC and set up a new institution, the *Resolution Trust Corporation*, to manage and resolve the outstanding claims of the insolvent S&LS. It also transferred to the FDIC the responsibility for regulating the S&LS and insuring their deposits.

Chapter Summary

1. This chapter discussed the banking system, the Federal Reserve, and money supply determination. It began by describing the role of financial intermediaries in the economy. Financial intermediaries bring together suppliers and demanders of funds, reduce transactions and information acquisition costs, and help savers diversify the risk of their investments.

2. Banks are a special type of financial intermediary that provide suppliers of funds with very liquid demand deposits that can be accessed simply by writing a check. Because demand deposits are so liquid, they are included, along with currency and traveler's checks, in the U.S. government's principal definition of money, M1. The government's other two definitions of money, M2 and M3, incorporate M1, but also include time deposits and other fairly liquid liabilities of financial intermediaries.

3. In lending out a portion of the funds deposited with them, banks are able to multiply the size of their demand deposits. They can do so because funds lent by one bank are generally redeposited in some other bank. The total amount of demand deposits created through the banks' deposit-expansion process depends on the fraction of their deposits that banks hold as reserves.

4. The Federal Reserve also plays a role in determining the size of the money supply. The Fed determines the size of the monetary base—the basic amount of money injected by the government into the economy. A portion of the monetary base is held by the public as currency, but the rest is held as reserves by banks and other depository institutions, providing the basis for the deposit-expansion process.

5. The amount of M1 created for each dollar of monetary base is called the M1 money multiplier. Similar multipliers can be defined for M2 and M3. The size of the M1 money multiplier depends on (1) the public's desired ratio of currency to demand deposits and (2) the reserve-deposit ratio. The Federal Reserve directly influences the reserve-deposit ratio through its reserve requirements, which establish a minimum value for this ratio. Banks are free to hold reserves in excess of the Fed's reserve requirement.

6. Every few months the Federal Open Market Committee decides how much to change the monetary base through open market operations. Open market operations involve the purchase or sale by the Fed of U.S. Treasury bonds. To increase the monetary base, the Fed purchases bonds using newly printed money, thereby injecting money into the economy. If it wants to decrease the base, the Fed sells bonds for money.

7. The Fed may also alter the size of the monetary base by lending through its discount window. Discount window lending is similar to an open market purchase. The Fed prints money to purchase an IOU, but a bank IOU rather than a Treasury bond. The interest rate the Fed charges is called the discount rate. Banks borrow from the Fed and from each other when they need extra money to meet their reserve requirements.

8. The Fed has complete control over changes in the monetary base. But it has only indirect control over the M1, M2, and M3 money multipliers. These multipliers are not stable over time, and their variability accounts for much of the variability of the monetary aggregates. In fact, the three multipliers do not ordi-

narily change at the same rate or even in the same direction. This greatly complicates the Fed's problem of monetary control and raises the question of which monetary aggregate the Fed should target.

9. Even if the Fed knew which aggregate was "the" money supply and even if it could completely control that aggregate, there would remain the question of how to conduct monetary policy. Some economists argue that the Fed should target the money supply; others argue that the Fed should target interest rates. Using our IS-LM framework, we showed that targeting the interest rate is appropriate for an economy experiencing nominal shocks, whereas targeting the money supply is better if the economy is experiencing real shocks.

10. The final topics we considered in the chapter were bank runs and deposit insurance. Congress established deposit insurance in 1933 after repeated bank panics. Deposit insurance has proved quite successful in strengthening public faith in financial institutions. However, deposit insurance has its own problems. Chief among them is the problem of moral hazard: the tendency of bank managers to make excessively risky investments, knowing that much of the risk is covered by deposit insurance. In the U.S., banking legislation, capital requirements, and examinations are used by the government to combat this moral hazard problem. These regulatory mechanisms were less than successful during the S&L crisis of the 1980s.

Key Concepts

Federal Reserve System
M1
Monetary aggregates
Reserve requirements
Financial intermediary
M2
M3
Bank reserves
Excess reserves
Monetary base
M1 multiplier
Open market operation
Discount window lending
Federal funds rate
Discount rate
Endogenous monetary policy
Deposit insurance

Review Questions

1. What are *financial intermediaries,* and what functions do they perform? What special role do banks play? Provide some examples of other financial intermediaries. What fraction of U.S. private sector assets were controlled by financial intermediaries in 1993?

2. With regard to a financial institution's *balance sheet*, which assets are the most liquid? Which liabilities are the most liquid? Under what circumstances would *owners' equity* be negative?

3. Define each of the following concepts and comment on any relationships among them.

a. *Demand deposits*
b. The *reserve-deposit ratio*
c. *Excess reserves*

d. Being *loaned up*
e. The *M1 money multiplier*, assuming all money is deposited in banks in the form of demand deposits and held as reserves (i.e., people hold no currency)

4. What is the *monetary base*? How do the formula for and value of the *M1 money multiplier* change if people choose to hold some fraction of money in the form of currency? Explain intuitively (not just mathematically) why the formula changes.
5. What are the privileges and responsibilities of banks that are part of the *Federal Reserve System*? In what way does depositing reserves at the Fed constitute a cost to participating banks?
6. Describe the institutional characteristics of the Fed's *Board of Governors* and the *Federal Open Market Committee*.
7. What are the three principal tools used by the Fed to control the money supply? What would the Fed do with each of them if it wished to increase the money supply? if it wished to reduce the money supply?
8. What does it mean for government borrowing to be *monetized*? What two agencies are involved? Do they work together to accomplish this task?
9. Why do banks borrow from the *discount window*? Where else do they borrow funds? What are the names of the interest rates paid in each of those markets? What would influence which market a bank would enter for funds? How does such borrowing affect the monetary base? Why?
10. The Fed can directly control the size of the monetary base but can only indirectly influence the size of the money multipliers. Comment, being sure to explain why the Fed has either direct or indirect control over the elements of the money supply.
11. Have the *monetary aggregates* behaved similarly over time? What implications does this behavior have for the conduct and measurement of monetary policy?
12. Explain the dramatic drop in M1 at the outset of the Great Depression. In particular, did the Fed explicitly engage in contractionary policy at that time? According to Friedman and Schwartz, what should the Fed have done at the time?
13. How are *nominal shocks* and *real shocks* characterized in the IS-LM model? Explain the effects of interest rate targeting and money supply targeting under each type of shock. What is the most appropriate target under each of the shocks? Why?
14. Explain the change in targeting (often referred to as a "regime change") that occurred under Fed Chairman Paul Volcker in the period from 1979 to 1982. What were the effects of the change? How accurate was the targeting itself?
15. What is meant by *endogenous monetary policy*? If the public expects a higher price level, what will happen if the Fed chooses not to print more money? What if it does print more money?
16. What is a *bank run*, and how does one typically start? What were the consequences of bank runs in the 1930s? What public policy changes have been made since then to improve the financial stability of banks and savings and loan

institutions? What problems have arisen despite, or even because of, those public policy measures, and how does the government try to cope with them?

Numerical Questions

1. Answer parts a through d using the following parameter values: rd = 0.1 and cd = 0.4.
   a. Calculate the value of the money multiplier.
   b. Suppose that rd rises to 0.2. Assuming the initial value for cd, calculate the new value of the money multiplier. Compare your answer to that obtained in part a. Provide economic intuition for any difference.
   c. Suppose that cd falls to 0.3. Assuming the initial value for rd, calculate the new value of the money multiplier. Compare your answer to that obtained in part a. Provide economic intuition for any difference.
2. Suppose that individuals hold their financial wealth totally as demand deposits and that banks hold as cash reserves 10 percent of any demand deposits. Suppose also that the Fed buys a $100 T-bill from a bank.
   a. Does the open market purchase itself, (i.e., prior to the issuance of bank loans) change the money supply? Why or why not?
   b. What are the values of the first three loans that are made in the money creation process? How much money is created by the first three loans?
   c. How does the monetary base change as a result of the open market purchase? Does the monetary base change further as loans are made?
   d. Suppose that individuals choose to hold as cash 20 percent of any amount loaned to them. How much money is created by the first three loans?
3. Answer parts a through c using the following parameter values: rd = 0.05, cd = 0.3, and the monetary base is $200.
   a. Calculate the values of the money multiplier and M1.
   b. Suppose that cd falls to 0.2. What is the new value of M1? If the Fed desires to change reserve requirements so as to return M1 to its initial value, at what value must it set rd?
   c. Suppose again that cd drops to 0.2. If the Fed desires to change the monetary base so as to return M1 to its initial value, at what value must it set the base?

Analytical Questions

1. Suppose that a bank uses its cash reserves to buy a T-bill from a private securities dealer instead of using the reserves to make loans. Will the impact on the money supply be different than if the bank makes a loan of equal value? Will the impact on the economy differ depending on the bank's use of the funds?
2. The text concluded that the choice between money supply targets and interest rate targets hinged on the *type* of shock that hit the economy. In reality, both nominal and real shocks can occur, sometimes simultaneously. In such an environment, what rule would you, as a monetary policy maker, follow to stabilize

output? (Helpful hint: The rule need not focus on just one type of target or the other.)

3. Reserve requirements are a feature of many economies. Yet their use is often criticized. Some commentators argue that the requirements serve no useful purpose. Others claim that reserve requirements raise costs and put banks at a competitive disadvantage relative to other financial intermediaries.

   a. Demonstrate that reserve requirements cannot by themselves guarantee that banks will have sufficient funds to meet depositor withdrawals. (In doing so, it might help to use balance sheet accounts.)
   b. Explain how reserve requirements raise the costs to banks of acquiring funds from depositors for use in making loans.

4. Insurance companies and commercial banks perform exactly the same function. Only the details of the operations differ. Comment.

CHAPTER 15

Saving Behavior and Credit Markets

INTRODUCTION

In past chapters we showed that saving is the driving force behind capital accumulation, which helps determine the economy's future performance. You also learned from the IS-LM analysis that saving can influence the economy's current performance. Because saving plays such a central role in macroeconomics, it is important to explore its determinants more fully. This chapter does just that. It goes beyond our simple life-cycle model's explanation of saving—saving for retirement—to consider alternative saving motives and behavior. Specifically, we consider *precautionary saving*—saving against unforeseen contingencies—and saving for bequests and other private intergenerational transfers. We'll also consider the desire and ability of certain individuals in society to dissave—to consume more than their current income.

Dissaving often requires borrowing against future income. Since borrowing is facilitated by credit markets, our discussion of dissaving leads us to examine these markets—how they work, how they affect capital accumulation, and why they often break down, especially during economic downturns. We'll see that how well credit markets function depends on two critical factors: the quality of information available to lenders about the likelihood of their being repaid and the legal/institutional arrangements for enforcing repayment. Although the lessons of our analysis apply to virtually all credit markets, the specific market we study here is the market for consumer loans. Chapter 16's discussion of business loans will complement this analysis.

We begin this chapter by cataloging the economic risks households face and by describing how households factor these risks into their saving decisions. Then we extend our two-period model to consider a simple case of income uncertainty. We'll see that the precautionary saving response to this uncertainty depends on whether insurance is available to hedge this risk. If such insurance is not available, precautionary saving will increase the total saving by the young and stimulate aggregate capital accumulation.

Our second topic is saving and bequests. We first show how to adapt our model to account for bequests and other private intergenerational transfers. Next, we describe the importance of private intergenerational transfers to aggregate U.S. wealth accumulation. We then contrast two types of bequest behavior, intended and unintended.

Unintended bequests arise from precautionary saving or, more accurately, from a cautious rate of dissaving by the elderly. Because they realize they may live longer than expected, the elderly are careful about how fast they "eat up" their assets. Such cautious dissaving makes it more likely that the elderly will die before exhausting their wealth and, as a result, will make an unintended bequest.

The economic risks of lifespan uncertainty, as well as the unintended bequests it engenders, can be reduced or eliminated through **annuities**. Annuities are income streams, such as Social Security and private pension benefits, that continue until the recipient dies. Annuity recipients are assured that they'll receive their annuity income no matter how long they live. On the other hand, the recipients understand that their annuity dies when they die, since the annuity cannot be bequeathed. In a case study, we'll see that there has been a dramatic increase in the degree to which the remaining lifetime income of the elderly in the U.S. has been annuitized. This increased annuitization appears to be reducing both unintended bequests and national saving in the United States.

Annuity
An income stream that continues until the recipient dies

Intentional bequests and gifts are funds saved with the express intention of making bequests and other private transfers. We'll consider how economists conceptualize the decision to make intentional bequests and gifts. We'll also show how adding intentional private transfers to our model can alter our conclusions about the effects of government intergenerational policy. Specifically, we'll consider *Ricardian equivalence*. This is the proposition, mentioned in Chapter 7, that private intergenerational transfers may fully offset government intergenerational transfers, thereby nullifying the effects of the government's generational policy.

Our third topic is credit markets, specifically, how they fit into our model and how imperfections in these markets can alter the availability of credit and the level of national saving. We'll see that credit may be restricted because of limits on the enforceability of loan contracts and the amount of information lenders have about borrowers. The credit restrictions, or **credit constraints**,

Credit constraint
A restriction on the availability of credit

caused by imperfect information can be especially severe for particular socioeconomic groups. We discuss this point in a case study on race and mortgage lending in Boston. We also present case studies on credit liberalization and saving in Norway, credit constraints among U.S. households, and the role of credit constraints in determining how quickly consumption and saving respond to changes in taxes and transfer payments.

The following questions are some we'll explore in this chapter:

- What are the different types of economic uncertainties that individuals face and that motivate their saving?
- How does insurance pool economic risks and reduce precautionary saving?
- How do bequests fit into our two-period model?
- How important are private intergenerational transfers to U.S. wealth accumulation?
- How can the importance of Ricardian equivalence be tested?
- How can we add credit markets to our model?
- How do credit markets affect the economy's saving?
- What explains credit market imperfections?

PRECAUTIONARY SAVING

Life is full of economic risks and uncertainties. Most workers don't know whether they'll be employed in future years, let alone precisely what their real wages will be. Retirees don't know what return they'll receive on their savings or whether they'll live long enough to spend the assets that took years to accumulate. The healthy don't know how long they'll remain well, nor what it will cost if they become ill. Parents don't know what it will cost to send their children to college or even if their children will choose to go to college. The list goes on and on.

As overwhelming as these risks and uncertainties may be, households are not likely simply to ignore them when deciding how much to save. Economic theory argues that households will, instead, make their saving decisions by considering each possible future economic circumstance as well as the likelihood of that circumstance's occurring. In evaluating their different possible economic futures, households are likely to exhibit *risk aversion*. That is, they weigh bad outcomes, such as the unexpected loss of $1,000, more heavily than good outcomes, such as the unexpected receipt of $1,000. One way risk-averse households seek to limit their economic setbacks is by increasing their current saving. Such **precautionary saving** (saving induced by uncertainty) provides households with additional assets they can draw upon in the event unpleasant economic conditions materialize.

Precautionary saving
Saving aimed at building up assets to protect against unforeseen contingencies

The Impact of Uncertainty on Saving and Capital Formation: An Example

In Chapter 2, we studied the behavior of Joan. As a typical young person born at time t, Joan's income is w_t in her first period of life. She must decide how

Figure 15-1 Joan's Budget Constraint with Certain Second-Period Income

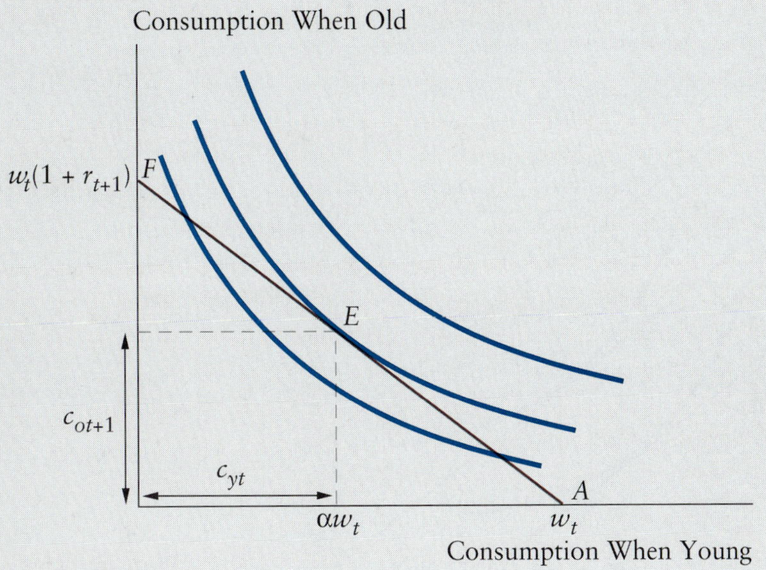

Joan uses her utility function to evaluate each possible consumption combination along budget constraint *FA*. She chooses the one at *E*. She consumes αw_t when young, saves and invests $(1 - \alpha)w_t$ and consumes $(1 - \alpha)w_t\,(1 + r_{t+1})$ when old.

much to consume and how much to save for her old age. Given the opportunity to invest any income she saves at an interest rate of r_{t+1}, Joan faces the budget constraint illustrated in Figure 15-1. Each point along this budget constraint represents an affordable combination of first- and second-period consumption. For example, at point *A* Joan would consume her entire income of w_t when young and nothing when old. At point *F* she would save her entire first-period income, enabling her to consume $w_t(1 + r_{t+1})$ when old. Or Joan may choose any other combination along the constraint that allows her to consume some income when young, save the rest, and consume those savings plus interest when old.

Given this budget constraint, Joan uses her utility function to evaluate each possible consumption combination and then choose the combination that gives her the largest amount of utility, or satisfaction. As we learned in Chapter 2, that best combination is the one on the highest attainable indifference curve. This combination is shown as point *E*, where an indifference curve is just tangent to (just touches) her budget constraint. Joan consumes αw_t when young, saves and invests $(1 - \alpha)w_t$, and consumes $(1 - \alpha)w_t(1 + r_{t+1})$ when old.

Now, let's introduce uncertainty and see how it changes Joan's decision making. We do this by assuming Joan's second-period income is uncertain. Specifically, let's suppose that Joan, at the end of her old age, faces a 50-50 chance of

Figure 15-2 Joan's Precautionary Saving

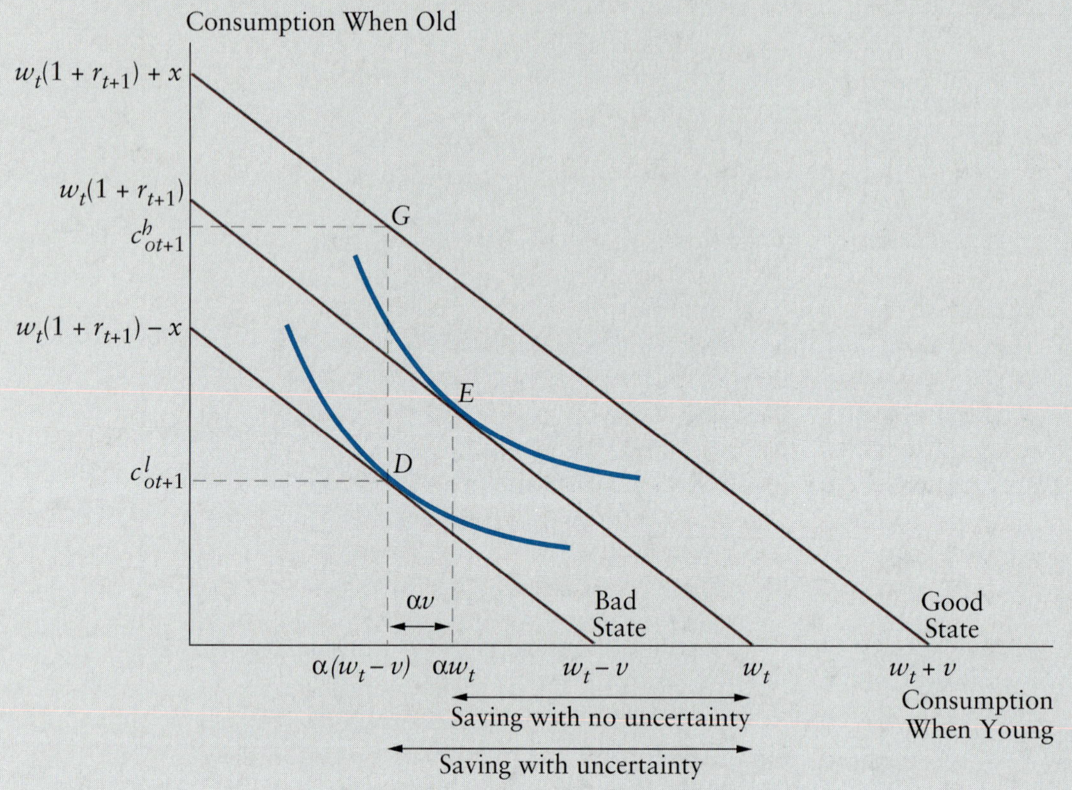

At the end of her old age, Joan faces a 50-50 chance of either receiving or losing an amount of income equal to x, with present value v. The "Good State" budget constraint shows her consumption opportunities if she receives x; the "Bad State" constraint shows what happens if she loses x. If Joan is very risk-averse, she considers only the bad state and chooses point D along the lower constraint. She consumes $\alpha(w_t - v)$ when young and saves $(1 - \alpha)w_t + \alpha v$. The extra, precautionary saving (αv) is her response to this uncertainty.

either receiving or losing an amount of income equal to x. The present value of x is v, i.e., $v = x/(1 + r_{t+1})$. If Joan is lucky, her old-age income and consumption will be higher than they are under certainty; but if she is unlucky, both will be smaller. Figure 15-2 shows how these two outcomes affect Joan's lifetime budget constraint. The constraint labeled "Good State" shows Joan's consumption opportunities if she is lucky and receives an extra x in old age. The one labeled "Bad State" shows her opportunities if she is unlucky and loses x in old age.

Faced with this uncertainty, what will Joan do? Because she's risk-averse, we expect her to be more concerned with the downside risk—the possibility of losing x—than with the upside potential of gaining x. Suppose Joan is so risk-averse that she considers only the worst-case scenario. To be on the safe side, she determines which combination along the bad state budget constraint gives her the most satisfaction. That combination is shown at point D, where an indifference curve is tangent to the low budget constraint.

Joan decides to consume a fraction, α, of $w_t - v$, which is the present value of her lifetime income in the worst-case scenario. Again, v is the present value of the windfall gain or loss at the end of her life. Joan's saving when young will equal her (certain) income when young, w_t, less this amount of consumption; it will equal $(1 - \alpha)w_t + \alpha v$. By comparing points D and E, we can see how uncertainty about her future income leads Joan to save αv more than if x were zero and she were certain what her future income would be. This extra, precautionary saving is Joan's response to uncertainty.[1]

Let's think now about the aggregate effect of precautionary saving. As a result of income uncertainty, Joan (and everyone else in her generation) will save more. This raises capital accumulation. To see this, recall our familiar conclusion that the amount of capital per worker in period $t + 1$ is just the amount of saving per worker in period t. Therefore, the formula for the capital-labor transition equation with income uncertainty is $k_{t+1} = (1 - \alpha)w_t + \alpha v$; in the absence of uncertainty the formula is $k_{t+1} = (1 - \alpha)w_t$.

Figure 15-3 graphs the two capital-labor transition curves. In the absence of uncertainty about second-period income, the economy's capital-labor ratio would converge to $\bar{k}$, determined by the intersection of the lower transition curve with the 45-degree line. With uncertainty, the transition curve will be αv higher and its intersection with the 45-degree line will determine a higher steady-state capital-labor ratio, $\bar{k}'$.

Private Insurance and its Impact on Capital Formation

Although income uncertainty is good for capital formation, it comes at the expense of everyone's worrying about suffering a decline in their living standard in old age. Individuals will naturally try to avoid this risk by purchasing insurance. Insurance provides a mechanism for transferring windfalls from the lucky to the unlucky members of each generation. Since we'll assume the total income received by each generation is certain, i.e., there is no *aggregate uncertainty*, insurance will leave everyone in exactly the same position as if there were no uncertainty. Thus, with insurance everyone ends up on the middle constraint in Figure 15-2.

Here's how the insurance might operate: Joan would purchase a policy that would cost her x in premium payments to be paid at the end of her old age. The

1. Joan's consumption during her old age will be determined by which budget constraint actually materializes. If she is unlucky, her second-period consumption will be c^l_{ot+1}, the value determined by point D along the low budget constraint. However, if she is lucky, her consumption will be c^h_{ot+1}, determined at point G along the high budget constraint.

Figure 15-3 Income Uncertainty and the Capital-Labor Transition Curve

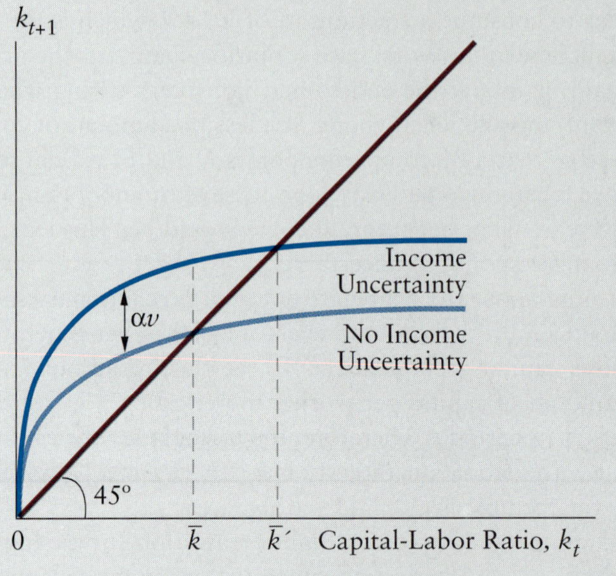

As a result of income uncertainty, each generation will save more than if income were certain. This raises capital accumulation and shifts the transition curve upward. The steady-state capital-labor ratio will be higher—$\bar{k}'$ rather than $\bar{k}$.

policy would promise to pay her nothing if she is lucky but $2x$ if she is unlucky. The following table summarizes how Joan fares (if she is lucky and if she is unlucky), assuming she has purchased the insurance. Note how the insurance fully insulates Joan from the income uncertainty. If she is lucky, her receipt of x at the end of her old age will just cover her premium payment. If she is unlucky, her loss of x plus her premium payment of x will be offset by her insurance payoff of $2x$.

Offsetting Income Uncertainty with Insurance

	Joan Is Lucky	**Joan Is Unlucky**
Second-Period Windfall	x	$-x$
Premium Payment	$-x$	$-x$
Insurance Payoff	0	$2x$
Net Change	0	0

By purchasing the insurance policy Joan ensures herself the middle budget constraint in Figure 15-2. Since Joan is no different from anyone else in her cohort, everyone in her cohort will buy the insurance. As a result the insurance industry will break even. Insurance companies will collect Nx in premium payments from each generation. Half of those individuals will be unlucky, so the companies will pay out $2x$ to each of those $N/2$ members of each generation. Total payouts will equal $2x$ times $N/2$, which equals Nx—precisely the amount the insurance companies receive in premium payments.

This insurance fully offsets the uncertainty about future income. Consequently, there is no need for precautionary saving. With insurance, the relevant capital-labor ratio transition curve is the lower curve in Figure 15-3 that leads to the lower steady-state capital-labor ratio.

We caution that the elimination of uncertainty and its associated precautionary saving through insurance hinges critically on the absence of aggregate uncertainty. To see this, consider what happens if we drop the assumption that there is an equal number of winners and losers in each generation and assume, instead, that *all* the members of each generation either end up winners or losers. In this case, there is no way for the winners to pool their winnings with losers. When one member of a generation wins, everyone else in her generation wins, and when one member loses, everyone else loses. Such aggregate income uncertainty precludes the establishment of a private insurance market.[2] It also leaves the economy operating on a higher capital-labor ratio curve, as in Figure 15-3.

The Government's Provision of Social Insurance

To supplement private insurance, governments maintain an array of **social insurance** programs that mitigate the economic risks we face and, thereby, influence our precautionary saving. Governments may do this out of a paternalistic concern that some individuals will underinsure on their own or because private insurance markets either don't exist or function poorly. Take our original example of uncertain old-age income in which there is no aggregate uncertainty and suppose private insurance companies are unable to verify whether a particular individual is lucky or not. If so, a private insurance market cannot exist because anyone who was insured would have an incentive to lie and claim that she had been unlucky and had lost x.

Social insurance *Government programs designed to partially insulate individuals from economic misfortune*

Fraud is just one of the problems private insurance companies face. Another is *moral hazard*, the propensity of those covered by insurance to take less care to avoid the risks against which they are insured. A third problem is *adverse selection*, the fact that individuals with higher risks of an insurable loss have a greater incentive to purchase insurance than those with lower risks. If high-risk individuals cannot be distinguished from low-risk individuals, insurance companies have to worry about getting saddled with a pool of particularly high-risk policy holders.

These problems confronting private insurers explain why certain forms of insurance (e.g., insuring future labor earnings) are either unavailable or are so expensive that most people remain uninsured. In response to particular

2. Any insurance company that charged x in premium payments to all its policy holders would face the prospect that the bad state might occur, in which case it would have to pay $2x$ to each of these policy holders; i.e., it would go bankrupt in the bad state. Knowing this, individuals would refuse to purchase the insurance even were it offered on the market.

insurance market failures, many governments provide the insurance directly. Governments, through their tax and other records, have certain informational advantages over private insurance companies. In addition, they can force everyone to purchase insurance and so avoid adverse selection. Finally, governments do not necessarily need to break even. They can operate their insurance programs at a loss that ends up being absorbed by taxpayers.

This last point is particularly relevant when we consider the government's response to aggregate uncertainty. Such uncertainty may preclude pooling of risks within a generation, but the government can use its intergenerational tax and transfer policies to pool risks across generations. As an example, consider a government decision to lower taxes during a recession and raise them many years in the future in order to satisfy its intertemporal budget constraint. In taking these steps, the government benefits current generations, who are suffering the effects of the recession, at the expense of future generations. In other words, the government pools risks among current and future generations. Such intergenerational risk-sharing is beyond the scope of private insurance markets because future generations obviously cannot purchase policies being sold in the present.

Types of Government Insurance

Government insurance may be quite extensive. In the United States, the federal government insures workers against unemployment and disability through unemployment compensation and Social Security disability insurance. It insures citizens against falling into poverty through Aid to Families with Dependent Children, food stamps, Medicaid, and other welfare programs. It provides life insurance through Social Security survivor benefits, health insurance to the elderly through Medicare, and life span insurance (which we'll discuss momentarily) through Social Security retirement benefits and other annuities. Even so, providing insurance is not the only function of these social insurance programs. They also serve systematically to transfer funds across and within different generations independent of issues of economic risk. They are components of U.S. intergenerational and intragenerational redistribution policy.

In the postwar era, government transfer programs, including social insurance, have grown at remarkable rates in developed countries. Figure 15-4 provides one measure of this growth. It shows how the ratio of government transfer payments to government purchases changed between 1960 and 1992 in each of the G-5 countries (the United States, the United Kingdom, Germany, Japan, and France). Each of the countries except Germany experienced a rapid growth in the ratio. The German ratio was high in 1960 and remained high thereafter. The U.S. ratio, which was below 0.3 in 1960, exceeded 0.7 by 1992.

Governments have other means of providing insurance and redistributing funds within and across generations. They also use their tax systems. Consider, for example, the *progressive income taxation* that occurs in most countries. A progressive tax places a proportionately larger tax burden on those with larger incomes. As a result, it makes the distribution of after-tax income more equal than the distribution of before-tax income. This redistribution benefits those

Figure 15-4 Government Budgets in G-5 Countries, Transfers Relative to Purchases

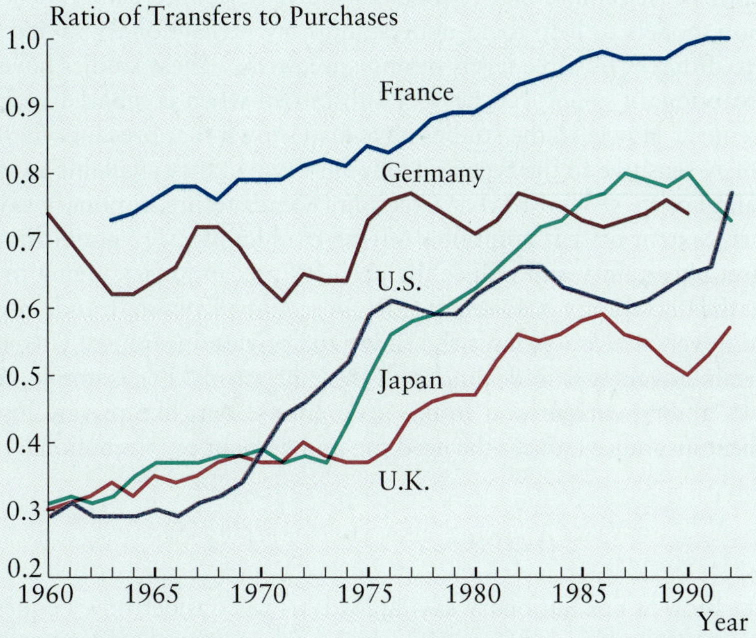

Since 1960, the U.S., the U.K., Japan, and France have each experienced rapid growth in the ratio of government transfers to government purchases. The German ratio was already high in 1960 and has remained so.

with permanently low incomes. It also helps those with temporarily low incomes resulting from loss of a job or ill health. Thus, progressive income taxation plays two roles. First, it systematically redistributes income from the rich to the poor. Second, it helps provide insurance by taking proportionately more from those whose incomes are unexpectedly high and proportionately less from those whose incomes are unexpectedly low.

How Important Is Precautionary Saving?

Measuring precautionary saving is a very difficult task. As we've discussed, the extent of precautionary saving depends on economic risks that are hard to quantify. We've also seen that precautionary saving depends on government and private insurance. In the case of government insurance, discerning precisely the amount of insurance provided by complex tax and transfer provisions is no easy task. For private insurance, we must consider informal insurance arrangements as well as the formal sale of insurance contracts by insurance companies. The reason is that friends and relatives can also provide one another with insurance.

They do so by standing ready to assist each other financially and in other ways in the event of economic reverses. Since the scope of such informal or implicit insurance arrangements is hard to measure, it is difficult to know for sure what uninsured risks any particular saver faces.

In the absence of hard facts, economists have developed elaborate computer simulation models to help them understand how precautionary saving may be related to different possible levels of uninsured risk.[3] These studies have shown that precautionary saving can be very substantial when compared with saving for retirement. However, the studies have also shown that precautionary saving is extremely sensitive to the type and amount of insurance available to savers.

To sum up, we've learned that uncertainty leads to precautionary saving, although the extent of that additional saving is unknown. Private insurance can help offset uncertainty and reduce the need for precautionary saving to the extent that the uncertainty is not aggregate uncertainty. Even so, fraud, moral hazard, and adverse selection limit the scope for private insurance. Governments have certain advantages in dealing with these problems. For example, they can pool risks among current and future generations. But, like private insurance, government insurance reduces the need for, and amount of, precautionary saving.

SAVING AND BEQUESTS

Our discussion of precautionary saving leads us to consider how bequests may influence saving and capital formation. A significant fraction of bequests appear to result from people's dying sooner than they expect, leaving behind assets they had planned to consume. Before considering various kinds of bequests, including those associated with lifespan uncertainty, let's clarify how such intergenerational transfers alter capital accumulation. Let's also consider the importance of private intergenerational transfers for U.S. wealth accumulation.

The Impact of Bequests on Capital Accumulation

Modifying our capital-labor transition equation to incorporate bequests and other intergenerational transfers is very simple. As we've seen throughout this book, the key to determining capital next period is knowing how much the young save this period. Bequests and other transfers made by the elderly can influence the saving of the young who receive these transfers at the end of their youth. It is at this point that the young decide how much to consume and how much to save and invest.

Let d_t stand for the bequests and other transfers received by each young person at time t. Then each young person will have d_t plus her wages, w_t, less her

3. See, for example, Jonathan Skinner, "Risky Income, Life Cycle Consumption, and Precautionary Saving," *Journal of Monetary Economics* 22 (September 1988): 237–255; Ricardo J. Caballero, "Earnings Uncertainty and Aggregate Wealth Accumulation," *American Economic Review* 81(4) (September 1991): 859–871; and R. Glenn Hubbard, Jonathan Skinner, and Stephen P. Zeldes, "The Importance of Precautionary Motives in Explaining Individual and Aggregate Saving," National Bureau of Economic Research Working Paper no. 4516 (November 1993).

Figure 15-5 Bequests and the Capital-Labor Transition Curve

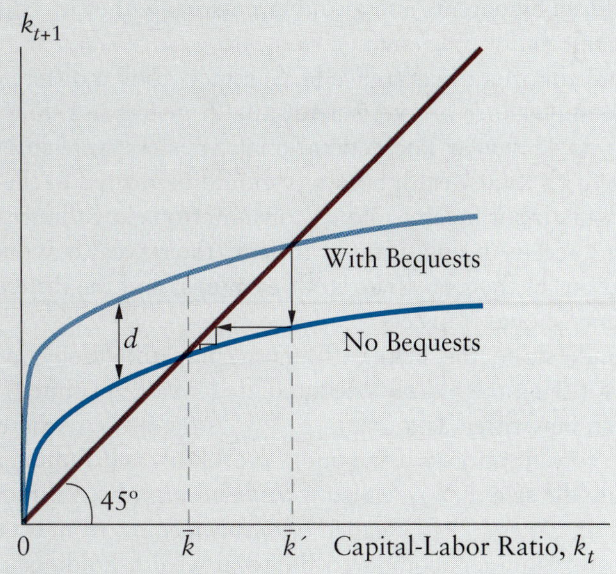

The larger the level of bequests and other transfers each young person receives at time t, the higher the transition curve will be at time $t + 1$. A higher curve means a higher steady-state capital-labor ratio.

payments to the government for taxes and bond purchases, f_t, out of which to save for old age. Let's take the simple case that the young do not consume (α, the propensity to consume when young, is zero). In this case, $k_{t+1} = w_t - f_t + d_t$. Replacing w_t by the formula for the marginal product of labor yields the following version of the transition equation:

$$k_{t+1} = A(1 - \beta)k_t^{\beta} - f_t + d_t$$

Note that the larger d_t is (the amount generation t inherits and the amount generation $t - 1$ bequeaths or gives as gifts), the larger the capital-labor ratio at time $t + 1$ will be. Figure 15-5 shows, for the case in which f_t and d_t are constant, that intergenerational transfers shift the transition curve upward and raise the capital-labor ratio.

Case Study: Private Intergenerational Transfers and U.S. Wealth Accumulation

Are private intergenerational transfers a significant part of total wealth accumulation? Answering this question is harder than it might seem because most intergenerational transfers are not reported. For example, in the United States there is information from estate-tax returns about the bequests made by the super-wealthy, but no systematic information about bequests made by other households.[4] There is also very little information about transfers made to children and grandchildren by parents and grandparents while they are still living. What data are available are of poor quality.

Laurence Kotlikoff and Lawrence H. Summers took a different approach to measuring the importance of intergenerational transfers in U.S. wealth accumulation.[5] They noted that if intergenerational transfers were insignificant, then each living cohort's total wealth holdings should be related to the difference between its after-tax labor income and its consumption expenditures.[6] In contrast, if cohorts had received significant transfers, their wealth would exceed the amount saved out of their post-tax labor earnings, and the difference would be due to intergenerational transfers.

We can understand the Kotlikoff-Summers methodology in terms of our model by considering the elderly's accumulated wealth at time t. Each old person's assets can be written as $a_t = w_{t-1} - c_{yt-1} - f_{t-1} + d_{t-1}$, where we allow the possibility of consumption when young. Kotlikoff and Summers's procedure was to estimate the size of d_{t-1}, called *transfer wealth*, by subtracting the calculated value of $w_{t-1} - c_{yt-1} - f_{t-1}$, called *life-cycle wealth*, from total wealth, a_t.

Kotlikoff and Summers compared the total wealth holdings of each cohort alive in 1974 with its life-cycle wealth. Their calculations required constructing an elaborate historical data set detailing these cohorts' past earnings, consumption, and net taxes. To their surprise, they found that life-cycle wealth represented only about a fifth of total U.S. wealth in 1974, with the other four-fifths traceable to transfer wealth. However, the share of transfer wealth was closer to one-half once they took into account that the past consumption of cohorts alive in 1974 would have been smaller (and their life-cycle wealth larger) in the absence of intergenerational transfers.

Although these findings have not been universally accepted, almost all economists agree that bequests are important enough to U.S. wealth accumulation to merit careful study.[7] Kotlikoff and Summers also pointed out that bequests are not necessarily incompatible with life-cycle saving behavior. That's because funds saved for retirement may be bequeathed by people who die before they have a chance to consume them. Let's now take a close look at how such unintended bequests can arise in our life-cycle model once we augment it to include lifespan uncertainty.

---

4. The federal estate tax is levied only on taxable estates that exceed $600,000.

5. Laurence J. Kotlikoff and Lawrence H. Summers, "The Role of Intergenerational Transfers in Aggregate Capital Formation," *Journal of Political Economy* 89(4) (August 1981): 706–732.

6. After-tax labor income here refers to labor income minus taxes plus transfer payments.

7. Franco Modigliani, who won a Nobel Prize for developing the life-cycle model, is the most prominent critic of the Kotlikoff-Summers analysis. Kotlikoff and Modigliani debate their views about the importance of intergenerational transfers in a symposium in the Spring 1988 issue of *Journal of Economic Perspectives* 2(2). Modigliani's paper (pp. 15–40) is entitled "The Role of Intergenerational Transfers and Life Cycle Saving in the Accumulation of Wealth." Kotlikoff's paper (pp. 41–58) is "Intergenerational Transfers and Savings."

Lifespan Uncertainty, Annuities, and Unintended Bequests

Lifespan uncertainty is a particularly pressing problem for the elderly who face a significant chance of dying each year. Their problem, apart from death itself, is knowing how quickly to spend their accumulated assets. If they spend too fast and live longer than expected, they risk a significant drop in living standards. On the other hand, if they spend too slowly, they risk dying with a lot of unconsumed assets, thereby leaving unintended bequests. This second option, consuming assets at a slow rate, is the safe bet that risk-averse individuals will choose. In so doing they will save more, or at least dissave less. In effect, lifespan uncertainty gives rise to precautionary saving.

Death is unavoidable, but there is a way to hedge the economic risks of not knowing when you will die. The way is to use annuities. For our purposes, an annuity is a financial security that pays a stream of income to its owner as long as the owner lives. To understand how an annuities market works, let's add to our two-period model the assumption that half the members of each generation die before they engage in second-period consumption. Let's further assume that no one knows who will die early.

Now suppose that all members of each generation agree to place all of their saving when young into a collective investment pool. The funds placed in this pool, plus interest income, are to be paid out at the end of the next period to those members of the generation lucky enough to survive. In handing over their saving, members of each generation would be buying an annuity—a claim to income in their old age conditional on their survival.

Establishment of an annuity market allows the survivors to consume all the funds their generation saved when young. Consequently, it eliminates the unintended bequests that generation would otherwise have made. If the annuity market is first established for generation t, then no subsequent generation will receive an inheritance from its parents. By eliminating the need for precautionary saving, the annuity market eliminates a source of wealth accumulation for those later generations. The effect, depicted in Figure 15-5, is a downward shift in the capital-labor transition curve. The transition to the new, lower steady-state capital-labor ratio, $\bar{k}$, is shown by the arrows.

Case Study: The Increasing Annuitization of the Elderly in the United States

In Chapter 2 we pointed out that the U.S. national saving rate has fallen dramatically since the 1950s and 1960s. Part of the explanation for the saving decline may lie in the increased share of the remaining lifetime resources of America's elderly that has been annuitized. Annuitized wealth is nonbequeathable. It is the sum of the elderly's human wealth (the present value of their future labor earnings) plus their pension wealth (the present value of their Social Security and private pension benefits). Nonannuitized wealth is bequeathable and equals the elderly's net wealth (the difference between their financial and real assets and their liabilities).

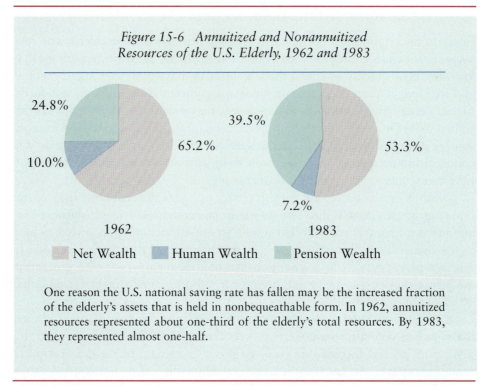

Figure 15-6 Annuitized and Nonannuitized Resources of the U.S. Elderly, 1962 and 1983

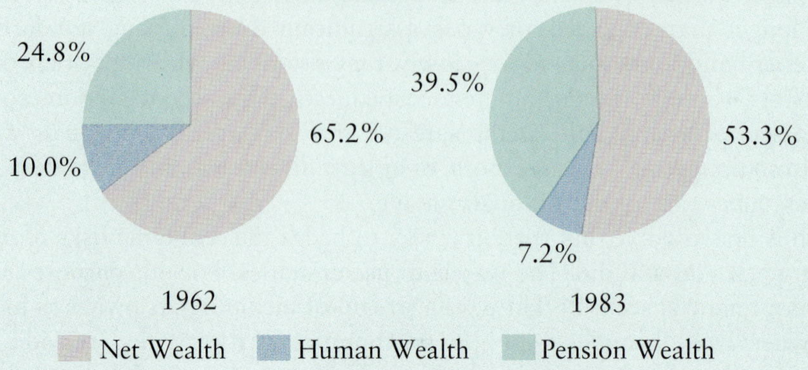

One reason the U.S. national saving rate has fallen may be the increased fraction of the elderly's assets that is held in nonbequeathable form. In 1962, annuitized resources represented about one-third of the elderly's total resources. By 1983, they represented almost one-half.

Source: A. Auerbach, L. Kotlikoff, and D. Weil, "The Increasing Annuitization of the Elderly—Estimates and Implications for Intergenerational Transfers, Inequality, and National Saving," NBER Working Paper No. 4182, 1992; revised April 1993.

This increased annuitization reflects the growth in Social Security and private pension benefits. Social Security benefits currently represent almost 10 percent of U.S. personal income compared with only 4 percent in 1960. In 1960, only about 5.3 percent of the elderly's income came from private pension benefits. Today's figure appears to be over 15 percent.

Figure 15-6, based on a study by the authors of this text and Brown University's David Weil, compares the annuitized share of the elderly's remaining lifetime resources in 1962 and 1983.[8] It shows that annuitized resources represented only about one-third of the elderly's resources in 1962, but almost half in 1983. Since annuitized resources are not bequeathable, this increase in annuitization has implications for the amount of unintended bequests.[9] All told, the increased annuitization appears to be responsible for reducing the annual flow of bequests in the United States by about one-third. Since every dollar not bequeathed by the elderly is a dollar the elderly, as a group, consume, the increased annuitization has also meant more consumption by the elderly and less national saving.

8. See Alan J. Auerbach, Laurence J. Kotlikoff, and David Weil, "The Increasing Annuitization of the Elderly—Estimates and Implications for Intergenerational Transfers, Inequality, and National Saving," National Bureau of Economic Research Working Paper No. 4182, 1992; revised April 1993.

9. This would not be true if elderly households purchased additional life insurance to offset their increased degree of annuitization. But the evidence on life insurance actually goes the other way. Between 1960 and 1990, life insurance declined relative to the size of the elderly's total remaining lifetime resources.

Intergenerational Altruism and Intentional Bequests and Gifts

Unintended bequests represent a substantial portion of total private intergenerational transfers. However, it appears that most bequests and all *intervivos gifts*—gifts made between the living—are intentional. Intervivos gifts take many forms. When parents pay their children's college tuition, give them automobiles, provide them with low-interest loans to buy a house, or give them a share of the family business, they are providing intervivos gifts. Among the very wealthy, large transfers of money or financial securities are common forms of gift giving.

Individuals who purchase life insurance desire to leave a bequest. Those elderly who engage in significant saving also appear to be doing so in order to leave a bequest. For the superwealthy, who would find it almost impossible to consume all their wealth, there is no question that the bulk of the bequests they make are fully anticipated and intended.

How can we add the desire to make intergenerational transfers to our life-cycle model? Gary Becker, Nobel Laureate in Economics and University of Chicago professor, and Robert Barro of Harvard University have provided one answer.[10] Becker and Barro pointed out how parents' altruistic concern for their children may be modeled by assuming that parents obtain utility from the utility attained by their children. In other words, the utility of individuals born at time t, u_t, depends not only on c_{yt} and c_{ot+1}, but also on u_{t+1}, the utility enjoyed by their children. u_{t+1} itself depends on the consumption when young and old enjoyed by children born at time $t + 1$. Therefore, parents care not only about their own consumption when young and old but also about their children's consumption when young and old.

Barro took the analysis one step further. He pointed out that if every generation is intergenerationally altruistic, the children born at time $t + 1$ will care about the utility of *their* children—those born at time $t + 2$. Consequently, the generation born at time t will care not only about its children's consumption but also about its grandchildren's consumption. Continuing with this reasoning, Barro concluded that those born at time t will care about the consumption by *all* their descendants into the infinite future. For this reason, economists refer to the life-cycle utility function, augmented to include altruistic concern for children, as the *infinite horizon utility function*. Maximizing this utility function produces a plan for how much each member of the altruistically linked dynasty will consume when he is alive and how much he will intentionally transfer to his children either as a gift (while he is living) or as a bequest (after his death).

Intergenerational Altruism and Ricardian Equivalence

Becker and Barro pointed out that altruistically linked generations will pool their incomes in deciding how much each of them should consume and, for that matter, how much they collectively should leave to their descendants. Barro showed that this income sharing has strong implications for the effectiveness of government intergenerational redistribution policies.

---

10. See Gary Becker, *A Treatise on the Family* (Cambridge, MA: Harvard University Press, 1981) and Robert Barro, "Are Government Bonds Net Wealth?" *Journal of Political Economy* 82 (November/December 1974): 1095–1117.

To understand Barro's argument, consider the case of Stan and his son Rudi, with whom Stan is altruistically linked. Stan has a higher lifetime income than Rudi does and decides to transfer \$10,000 to Rudi. Now the government comes along, takes \$5,000 from Rudi, and gives it to Stan as part of its policy of taxing the young to make Social Security transfer payments to the old. How will Stan respond? According to Barro, Stan will return the \$5,000 to Rudi as a gift or bequest. Stan will offset the government's intergenerational transfer with his own private intergenerational transfer. In so doing, he will produce **Ricardian equivalence.**[11] David Ricardo was a famous nineteenth century British economist who first raised the possibility that private transfers may nullify the effects of government intergenerational transfers.

Ricardian equivalence *The proposition that private intergenerational transfers neutralize government intergenerational transfers*

Stan realizes that the government's policy has not changed his and Rudi's collective income. Unless he hands back the \$5,000 to Rudi, Stan will not succeed in his utility-maximizing objective of raising Rudi's consumption by a total of \$10,000. Indeed, Ricardian equivalence will hold whether the government redistributes from Rudi to Stan or from Stan to Rudi. To see this, consider Stan's reaction to a government policy that redistributes \$5,000 from himself to Rudi. Stan will reduce his own private transfer from \$10,000 to \$5,000 because he realizes that the government has already transferred \$5,000 of his income to Rudi.

Here is the point of the example: If altruistic linkages across generations are strong enough, they will give rise to private sector transfers that fully offset the government's intergenerational redistribution. This is true for all government intergenerational redistribution policies, including those associated with increases in the government's official debt (which "pay-as-you-go" Social Security transfers are not). It is also true for redistribution across generations that are not alive at the same time. If the government uses its fiscal policies to redistribute \$5,000 to Stan from Rudi's child, Greg, Stan will transfer the \$5,000 to Rudi who will then transfer the funds to Greg.

If Ricardian equivalence holds, then intergenerational redistribution will not alter private sector consumption or national saving. We can see this by using our transition formula for the capital-labor ratio. Take the simple case in which individuals consume only when old. As we mentioned above, the transition equation is then $k_{t+1} = w_t - f_t + d_t$. Now consider a government policy of taxing the young at time t to finance transfer payments to the old at time t. This policy raises f_t. If d_t remains unchanged, k_{t+1} will be reduced. However, Ricardian equivalence predicts that the old at time t, who, after all, are the parents of the young at time t, will simply transfer back to the young the funds the government gives them. The result is an increase in d_t that exactly equals the increase in f_t, leaving k_{t+1} unchanged.

11. The word "equivalence" in Ricardian equivalence reflects the point that in the presence of intergenerational altruism, taxing current generations is equivalent to taxing future generations, because of offsetting private intergenerational transfers.

Case Study: Are U.S. Extended Families Altruistically Linked?

If altruistically linked extended family members really do pool their incomes in deciding how much each should consume, then the amount any particular member consumes will depend on the total income of the extended family, not on that person's share of the total. In our example, this means that Stan's share of his plus Rudi's total consumption should not depend on Stan's share of their total income. Another way to state this is that the ratio of Stan's consumption to Rudi's should not depend on the ratio of Stan's income to Rudi's.

Northwestern University economist Joseph Altonji, Columbia University economist Fumio Hayashi, and Laurence Kotlikoff used U.S. data to study whether the ratio of parents' consumption to that of their adult children depends on the ratio of parents' income to their children's.[12] They found strong evidence that relative incomes do influence the relative consumption levels of extended family members. In fact, their findings suggest that extended family members have essentially no economic interdependence when it comes to deciding how much to consume and save. Thus, although the Barro-Becker altruism model may describe particular extended families, it does not appear to do a good job of explaining how most U.S. extended families behave. Ricardian equivalence does not appear to hold in the United States.[13]

MODELING CREDIT MARKETS

We've seen how uncertainty and bequests can raise a country's saving. Next, let's explore how credit markets can reduce saving by expanding consumption opportunities. We add credit markets to our two-period life-cycle model by assuming that in each generation there are two types of individuals, borrowers, B, and lenders, L. Borrower types wish to borrow from the lender types. To produce this result, we assume B types can work only when old and wish to consume only when young; L types work only when young and wish to consume only when old. These assumptions are summarized in the following table.

	Type L	**Type B**
When Young	Works	Consumes
When Old	Consumes	Works

12. See Joseph G. Altonji, Fumio Hayashi, and Laurence J. Kotlikoff, "Is the Extended Family Altruistically Linked? Direct Tests Using Micro Data," *American Economic Review* 82(5) (December 1992): 1177–1198.

13. The Altonji et al. study is based on household survey data. There is also an extensive literature testing Ricardian equivalence using macro time-series data. The results of this literature are quite mixed. For a recent review, see John J. Seater, "Ricardian Equivalence," *Journal of Economic Literature* 31(1) (March 1993): 142–190.

As the table shows, there is a mismatch between when the B and L types receive their income and when they wish to do their consumption. Let's consider how they can resolve this mismatch.

The Demand for Credit

To consume when young, B types will have to borrow against their old-age labor income. Let's assume that Bs can find lenders willing to make them loans at the prevailing interest rate. In this case, the amount each B borrows when young is the amount she consumes when young. Hence, her assets at time $t + 1$, a_{t+1}, will be negative (she'll be in debt) and will equal minus her consumption when young. Thus,

$$a_{t+1} = -c_{yt}$$

When our type B individual is old she'll use her old-age labor earnings, w_{t+1}, to repay her debt as well as the interest owed on it:

$$w_{t+1} = -a_{t+1}(1 + r_{t+1})$$

Combining these two equations gives us the lifetime budget constraint facing type B individuals, namely,

$$c_{yt} = \frac{w_{t+1}}{1 + r_{t+1}}$$

As always, the budget constraint indicates that the present value of consumption expenditures equals the present value of labor income. Compare this lifetime budget constraint and the one introduced in Chapter 2 (page 51). Note that old-age consumption does not appear on the left-hand side here. Also, the present value of earnings when old, rather than earnings when young, appears on the right-hand side.

Figure 15-7 graphs this budget constraint. The intersection of the constraint with the vertical axis indicates second-period labor earnings. Its intersection with the horizontal axis shows the present value of this income, which also equals consumption when young.

Because each B wants to borrow the present value of her old-age labor earnings, the total demand for loans each period equals this desired amount of borrowing times the number of type Bs. Recall that there are N individuals in each generation. Of these, we'll assume that the fraction m are type Bs and the remainder $(1 - m)$ are type Ls. Thus, the total credit demanded at time t is N times m times $(w_{t+1}/1 + r_{t+1})$.

The Supply of Credit

Who will supply credit (make loans) to young B types at time t? It will not be the elderly of time t. They will all be dead at time $t + 1$ when the young B

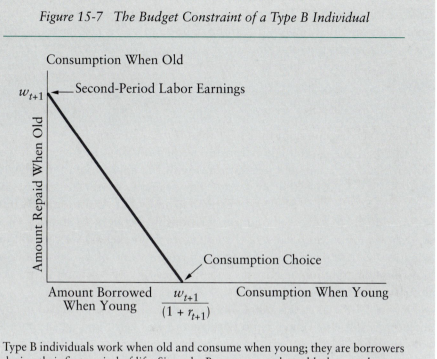

Figure 15-7 The Budget Constraint of a Type B Individual

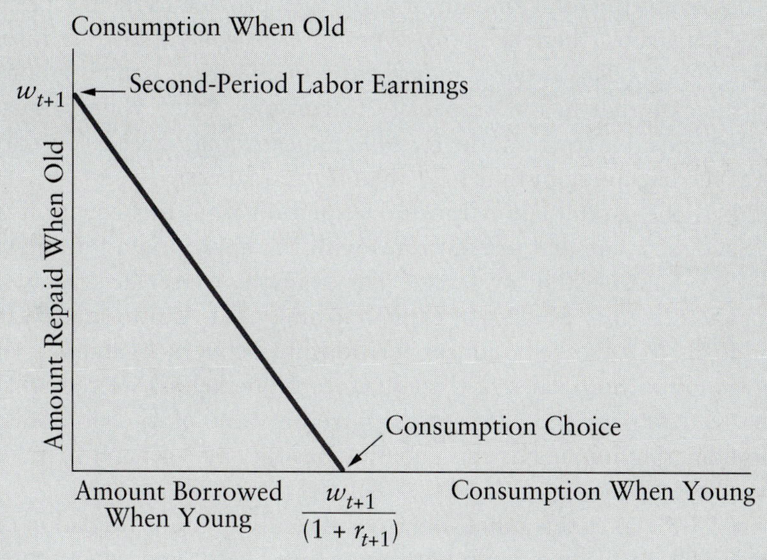

Type B individuals work when old and consume when young; they are borrowers during their first period of life. Since the Bs earn w_{t+1} when old, they can borrow and consume a maximum of $w_{t+1}/(1 + r_{t+1})$ when young.

borrowers are in a position to repay their loans. Therefore, it must be those L types who are young at time *t*. We'll assume for the moment that the Ls are sure that any funds they lend to their B contemporaries will be repaid at the same interest rate available by investing in capital. In that case, the young L types will be indifferent between making loans to Bs and investing in capital.

There are *N* times $(1 - m)$ lenders in each generation, and each saves her entire wages, w_t. Therefore, the total savings of the L types at time *t* is *N* times $(1 - m)$ times w_t. As long as those total savings exceed the amount the B types wish to borrow, the Ls can fully satisfy the demand for credit and still have funds left to invest in capital.

Capital Accumulation in the Presence of Borrowing

As the previous sentence indicates, the amount of capital brought into period $t + 1$ by the generation born in period *t* equals the total savings of the young Ls less the amount of those savings they lend to the young Bs. Hence, our formula for the capital-labor ratio at time $t + 1$ is

$$k_{t+1} = (1 - m)w_t - m\frac{w_{t+1}}{1 + r_{t+1}}$$

To understand this formula better, multiply both sides of this equation by the total work force N.[14] Then the left-hand side of the equation is the absolute amount of capital at time $t + 1$ and the right-hand side is just the total savings of the L types minus the total amount of loans they provide to the B types.

If m equals zero (there are no B types in each generation) the formula reduces to $k_{t+1} = w_t$. This is our standard expression for the capital-labor ratio at $t + 1$ in the case that α, the propensity to consume when young, equals zero. When m is a positive fraction, the formula indicates that there is less capital per worker at the beginning of time $t + 1$ than if m equals zero.

To derive the capital-labor transition equation from this equation we need only replace the wage and interest rates with the appropriate formulas for the marginal products of labor or capital. For example, we replace r_{t+1} by the formula for the marginal product of capital at time $t + 1$. Unfortunately, this substitution leads to a messy nonlinear relationship between k_t and k_{t+1} in which k_{t+1} shows up on both sides of the equation. Nonetheless, we can still use the equation to determine the value of k_{t+1} given a value of k_t.[15] In addition, the transition diagram implied by this equation has the same general shape as in the absence of borrowing.

Figure 15-8 makes this point. It graphs the capital-labor transition equation for both cases: when there is no borrowing (m is zero) and when there is borrowing (when m is greater than zero). Note that the curve with borrowing lies below the one without borrowing. This reflects the fact that as more of the young generation's saving is channeled into lending, that generation invests less in capital. An increase in the proportion of borrowers in a generation (an increase in m) rotates the transition curve downward and leads to a lower steady-state capital-labor ratio.

Credit Market Imperfections

So far, we've assumed that the B types always repay their loans. To see the importance of this assumption, let's now check the other extreme. Suppose the Bs are given loans when young and choose not to work when old. With no wage income, they default on their loans. This could happen if the legal system permitted personal bankruptcy and could not be used to compel the Bs to work in their old age. Under these rather extreme assumptions, the credit market will collapse. The L types, knowing they face default on any loans they make, won't make any. As a result, the B types will face a *credit constraint* (a restriction on credit); they'll be unable to borrow (to obtain credit) and consume when young. Clearly, if there were some way to compel the B types to work when old to repay their borrowing, they would be better off.

This credit market imperfection cannot be cured by raising the interest rate charged on loans. Since they have no intention of repaying, the Bs will agree to

---

14. The work force equals N because at any point in time there are N times m old Bs working alongside of N times $(1 - m)$ young Ls, and $Nm + N(1 - m) = N$.
15. Given the value of k_t, the value of k_{t+1} that satisfies the equation can be found by trying different values of k_{t+1} until we find one that makes the right-hand side of the equation equal to the left-hand side.

Figure 15-8 Borrowing and the Capital-Labor Transition Curve

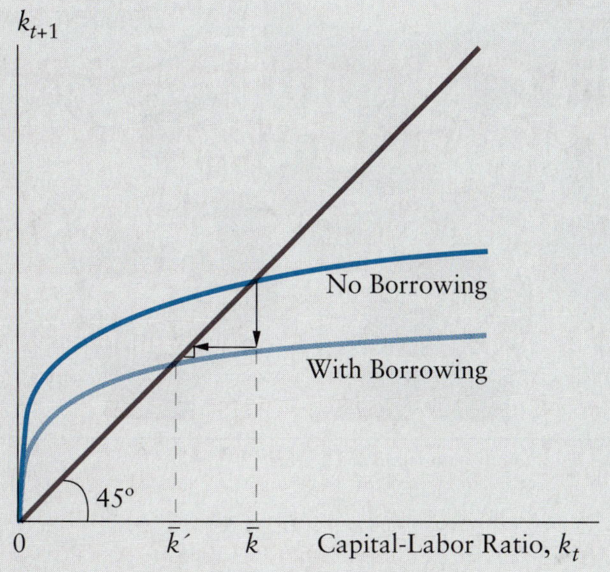

If m is the fraction of borrowers in each generation, then an increase in m raises total borrowing and reduces capital formation. Here, the transition curve marked "No Borrowing" corresponds to $m = 0$. As m increases, less is saved, and the transition curve rotates downward.

any interest rate, no matter how high, and still default in their old age.[16] Regardless of what interest rate lenders charge, the effective interest rate they actually receive is zero once they take default into account.

The inability of some people to borrow at prevailing interest rates is not simply a theoretical possibility. On the contrary, real-world lenders routinely turn down loan applications from borrowers they deem to be poor risks. Even borrowers who are generally viewed as creditworthy may find themselves unable to borrow during economic downturns—when lenders realize the likelihood of loan default has risen.

Why Borrowing Rates May Exceed Lending Rates

If Bs never repay their loans, a complete collapse of the credit market is guaranteed. A more realistic assumption is that some B types are trustworthy and will

16. The potential inability of interest rates to equate the supply of credit to its demand was pointed out in Joseph Stiglitz and Andrew Weiss's seminal article "Credit Rationing in Markets with Imperfect Information," *American Economic Review* 71 (June 1981): 393–410.

Rob Rogers reprinted by permission of UFS, Inc.

repay their loans. Others, who cannot be distinguished in advance, are untrustworthy and will default on their loans. If the proportion of trustworthy borrowers is sufficiently high, lenders may be willing to make loans, but only at an interest rate that factors in the likelihood of default. For example, if the *lending rate*—the real rate of interest lenders can earn by investing in capital or other nonloan assets—is 10 percent and the likely default loss is 5 percent of each dollar loaned out, lenders might charge borrowers 15 percent. They would require 10 percent to cover their opportunity cost (investing in real capital) and an additional 5 percent to cover the risk of default. If lenders pool their loans through financial intermediaries that deal with large numbers of borrowers, each lender can safely expect to lose only 5 percent of his funds through default. Hence, by altering our assumption about the likelihood of default, we can generate an outcome that is also quite commonplace in the real world. Namely, the *borrowing rate* of interest exceeds the lending rate.

Interestingly, the real losers here are the trustworthy borrowers. The bad risks can borrow at 15 percent, default on their loans, and consume for free when young. However, the good risks (who do repay their loans) must pay a higher interest rate on the funds they borrow. Furthermore, since they will be forced to use more of their old-age earnings to repay interest, the amount of principal they can borrow when young is reduced.

Figure 15-9 documents the excess of borrowing rates over lending rates. It compares the mortgage interest rate charged new home buyers, assuming the mortgage is paid off in ten years, with the interest rate on ten-year U.S. Treasury bonds. Note that the mortgage rate has exceeded the Treasury bond rate in all but one of the 21 years considered. Over the entire period, the mortgage

Figure 15-9 U.S. Mortgage and Ten-Year Treasury Bond Rates, 1970–1993

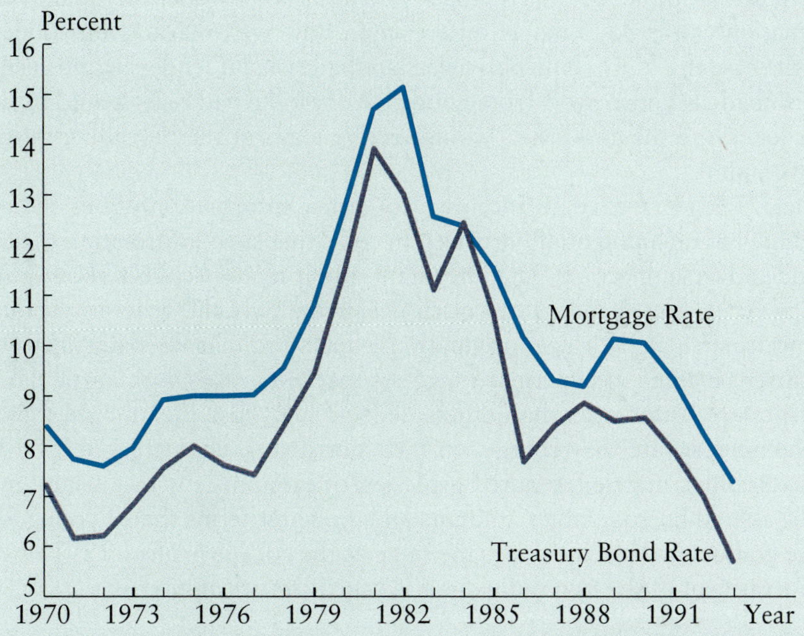

When the proportion of untrustworthy borrowers in the population is sufficiently low, lenders may make loans, but only at an interest rate that factors in the likelihood of default. Between 1970 and 1993, the ten-year mortgage interest rate (a borrowing rate) exceeded the ten-year Treasury bond rate in all but one year.

Source: *Economic Report of the President*, 1994

rate averaged 10.2 percent whereas the Treasury bond rate averaged 9.0 percent.[17]

Other Types of Credit Market Outcomes: Adverse Selection

So far we've considered three different assumptions about the behavior of borrowers. First, all borrowers are good risks and repay their loans. Second, all borrowers are bad risks who default. This second assumption leads to a complete collapse of the credit market. Third, some borrowers, who cannot be identified in advance, are bad risks, leading lenders to charge borrowing rates that

17. Not all of the difference between mortgage and bond interest rates reflects concern about loan default. Part of the differences can be attributed to the transactions costs banks incur in attracting mortgagees, in checking their credit references, and in issuing them the mortgages.

exceed lending rates and reduce the amounts they are willing to lend. Each assumption leads to a different credit market outcome, and each has a different implication for macroeconomic performance.

Upon reflection, it should be clear that the real key to credit market behavior is the information lenders have about potential borrowers. The quality of this information can make a major difference in how well markets function. Consider the case that only some borrowers are bad risks. If lenders could easily distinguish bad-risk borrowers from good-risk ones, the bad risks would be unable to get loans and the good risks would receive loans at the prevailing rate of return to capital.

Clearly, lenders have an incentive to gather information about the creditworthiness of each potential borrower. In collecting such information they try to preclude adverse selection. The information that lenders collect about borrowers is never perfect. Lenders can often determine only the general attributes of borrowers, such as their age, occupation, education, marital status, net wealth, and current income. If experience suggests that borrowers with particular characteristics are better risks than others, lenders may base the amount they lend, and the interest rate they charge, on their borrowers' characteristics.[18] For example, an older, married, tenured professor of economics with a secure income may be able to borrow larger amounts and on better terms than a young, single, college graduate whose income is the same as the college professor's. This differential treatment of the two individuals is called *statistical discrimination.*[19]

Case Study: Race and Mortgage Lending in Boston

In 1992 the Federal Reserve Bank of Boston conducted a study of mortgage lending to determine whether minority mortgage applicants were being discriminated against by Boston financial institutions.[20] The study showed that minority applicants with the same economic and financial characteristics as white applicants were roughly 60 percent more likely to be denied a mortgage.

Two types of discrimination may be at work here, and it is very difficult to distinguish between them. The first is overt racial discrimination, whereby minority applicants are denied mortgages because the lenders are racially biased. Overt racial discrimination not only harms minority mortgage applicants but also penalizes those financial institutions that discriminate. By rejecting perfectly sound mortgage applicants solely on the basis of race, the financial institutions are lowering their profits.

The second type of racial discrimination is the statistical discrimination mentioned above. If certain unmeasurable characteristics, such as poor future income prospects, raise the probability of mortgage default, and if minority

18. In fact, most large commercial banks use statistical *credit scoring models* to help predict the likelihood that a particular borrower, with known characteristics, will repay a loan.

19. For an excellent treatment of this issue see Steven Coate and Glenn C. Loury, "Will Affirmative Action Eliminate Negative Stereotypes?" *American Economic Review* (December 1993).

20. Alicia H. Munnell, Lynn E. Browne, James McEneaney, and Geoffrey M. B. Tootell, "Mortgage Lending in Boston: Interpreting HMDA Data," Federal Reserve Bank of Boston Working Paper No. 92–7 (October 1992).

mortgage applicants are more likely to have such characteristics, financial institutions may use race as an indirect means of screening applicants. Unlike overt racial discrimination, statistical racial discrimination is aimed at raising profitability and for this reason is not easily overcome by market forces.

Credit Constraints and Capital Accumulation

Consider again the polar cases in which the B types are either all good risks who can borrow or all bad risks who cannot. As Figure 15-8 indicates, this difference in the functioning of credit markets influences the position of the economy's capital-labor transition curve and, thus, all the economy's real economic variables at all future dates. The capital-labor transition curve is higher when borrowing is not permitted. Borrowing allows additional consumption by each young generation, leading it to save less. Complete elimination of borrowing is an extreme case, but any restriction on the availability of consumer credit rotates the capital-labor transition curve upward and expands saving. The converse is also true. Any liberalization of credit rotates the curve downward and reduces saving.

Case Study: Credit Liberalization and the Dramatic Decline in Norwegian Saving

So far we've talked only about the market determination of credit conditions. Government policy can also influence credit availability and thus the position of the capital-labor transition curve. The Norwegian government's highly restrictive *interest rate ceilings* and **credit controls** are a case in point.[21] Before 1984, the government's interest rate ceilings limited the rate of return that financial intermediaries could pay to depositors and other suppliers of funds. Naturally, this limited the amount of funds that such suppliers made available to these financial intermediaries. In addition, the government's credit controls directly restricted the amounts financial intermediaries could lend.

Credit controls *Government-imposed limits on the amount of funds that financial intermediaries may lend*

In 1984 the Norwegian government deregulated its financial markets, including its credit markets. The result was a dramatic surge in borrowing by young and middle-aged Norwegians to purchase consumer durables and homes as well as nondurable consumption goods and services. In the housing market, so much pent-up demand was released that urban housing prices rose by almost 80 percent between 1984 and 1987. Since the existing housing stock was owned primarily by older Norwegians, this tremendous windfall gain permitted them to join the country's consumption spending spree.

Not surprisingly, Norwegian saving plunged. In 1984 the Norwegian private saving rate stood at 9.5 percent.[22] By 1986 it was actually negative 1.8 percent! Norway is not an isolated example. Denmark, Sweden, Finland, and Italy also

21. The United States has also periodically used interest rate ceilings and credit controls to try to influence interest rates and the availability of credit.

22. The private savings rate is defined as (1) national saving less the government deficit divided by (2) GDP less net taxes.

deregulated their credit markets in the 1980s and all experienced sharp reductions in their saving rates.[23]

Credit Constraints and the Keynesian Short Run

When there are nominal rigidities, credit market conditions can also influence the position of the IS and LM curves and the economy's short-run levels of output and employment. Let's consider the IS curve first. We derived the IS curve on the assumption that individuals consume only when old. However, it is a minor matter to include the possibility that individuals consume as well as acquire real money balances when young. The more young people consume, the less they save, and the higher will be the position of this modified IS curve. Accordingly, any change in credit market conditions that involves an expansion in consumer credit will shift the IS curve upward. Any change that reduces the availability of consumer credit shifts it downward.

When the economy moves into recession, lenders become more concerned about their borrowers' abilities to repay. The result is a reduction in consumer credit that shifts the IS curve downward. As indicated in Figure 15-10, the induced downward shift exacerbates the reduction in output and employment.

Next consider the LM curve. Recall the function $\gamma[\ ]$ that determines the share of their real wages the young allocate to real money balances. If this function changes, so that the value of $\gamma[\ ]$ is higher for each value of r_{+1}, the LM curve will shift leftward, reducing output and employment. As mentioned in Chapter 12's discussion of the Great Depression, heightened concern about the riskiness of investing, including investing in consumer loans, will make individuals want to hold more real money balances at any given interest rate. This increases the $\gamma[\ ]$ function and shifts the LM curve leftward.

In sum, concern about the creditworthiness of borrowers during recessions can shift the LM curve leftward and the IS curve downward as the young generation's demand for real money balances rises and its ability to dissave and consume falls. During expansions, of course, the LM and IS curves shift in the opposite directions as investor confidence improves and as more credit becomes available. Hence, changes in credit market conditions over the business cycle can magnify business cycle fluctuations.

Case Study: Are U.S. Citizens Credit-Constrained?

The importance we should attach to credit constraints obviously depends on the degree to which the public is constrained. In the United States we need only look at household net wealth—which exceeds $20 trillion—to realize that the household sector as a whole is not credit-constrained. Collectively, U.S. citizens have enough funds to finance their consumption for nearly five years even if their current income were to fall to zero.

---

23. For a discussion of these episodes see Olli-Pekka Lehmussaari, "Deregulation and Consumption: Saving Dynamics in the Nordic Countries," in International Monetary Fund *Staff Papers* 37(1) (March 1990): 71–94; and Luigi Guiso, Tullio Jappelli, and Daniele Terlizzse, "Saving and Capital Market Imperfections: The Italian Experience," *Scandinavian Journal of Economics* 94(2) (1992): 197–213.

Figure 15-10 Shifts in the IS and LM Curves Due to Changes in Credit Conditions

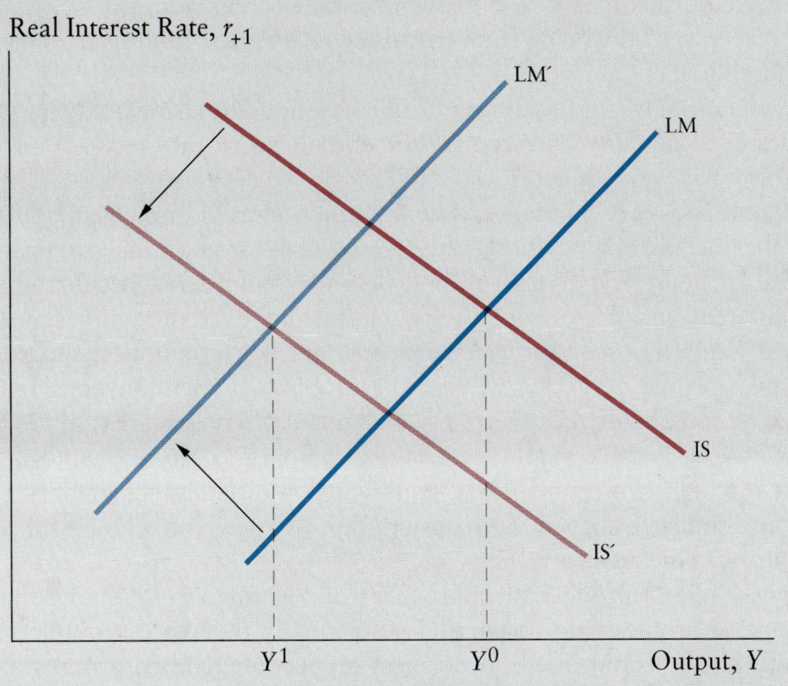

The more young people consume, the less they save and the higher is the position of the IS curve. In a recession, the contraction of consumer credit shifts IS downward and exacerbates the reduction in output and employment. Also, if investing becomes more risky, individuals want to hold more money, so LM shifts leftward.

Although the United States is a wealthy country, not all citizens are wealthy. The distribution of wealth holdings is highly skewed. According to the latest available data, the richest 1 percent of U.S. households own over one-third of all U.S. household net wealth. The poorest 20 percent of households own less than 1 percent of wealth.[24] In addition, much of the wealth that low- and middle-income households own is in the form of housing and cannot be easily liquidated to spend on consumption. Roughly one-quarter of U.S. households appear to have few, if any, liquid financial assets.[25]

24. See Arthur B. Kennickell and R. Louise Woodburn, "Estimation of Household Net Worth Using Model-Based and Design-Based Weights: Evidence from the 1989 Survey of Consumer Finances," mimeo, The Board of Governors of the Federal Reserve System (April 1992).
25. For some evidence on this point see Peter A. Diamond and Jerry A. Hausman, "Individual Retirement and Saving Behavior," *Journal of Public Economics* 23 (February/March 1984): 81–114.

Having few or no liquid assets doesn't necessarily mean that all such households are credit-constrained. Most of them may neither need, nor wish to borrow. Those that do need to borrow may be able to borrow from banks, credit unions, or other formal suppliers of credit. Other sources of credit include using unspent credit card balances, borrowing from existing creditors by paying off bills more slowly, borrowing from friends or relatives, or taking out equity lines of credit on homes.

Low financial wealth holdings of some U.S. households raises the possibility of widespread liquidity constraints, but doesn't prove they exist. As a result, economists have sought other ways to identify credit constraints. Christopher Carroll and Lawrence Summers compared the age profiles of consumption and disposable income of U.S. households, classified according to the occupation of the head of household.[26] Carroll and Summers considered occupations with quite different growth rates of disposable income over the work span. They reasoned that if households *are* credit-constrained, consumption should track disposable income very closely, regardless of the occupation considered. In contrast, if households are not credit-constrained, there is no reason for households whose disposable income is growing rapidly to delay consuming. In the absence of credit constraints, then, households in different occupations should have quite similarly shaped age–consumption profiles, even though their age–disposable income profiles differ.

Figure 15-11, reproduced from the Carroll-Summers study, shows that age-consumption profiles tend to parallel quite closely the age–disposable income profiles. This seems to provide evidence in support of credit constraints. But the fact that consumption tracks disposable income may simply reflect households' uncertainty about what their future earnings will be. When earnings are uncertain we would also expect age–consumption profiles to track age–disposable income profiles as households adjust their consumption spending upward or downward in response to their actual realized incomes.[27]

More sophisticated studies have been designed to test for credit constraints in the context of income uncertainty.[28] These studies suggest that about one in five U.S. households is credit-constrained, but their findings are far from definitive for a variety of reasons. The bottom line is that economists do not yet have a precise understanding of the extent and importance of credit constraints in the U.S.

26. Christopher D. Carroll and Lawrence H. Summers, "Consumption Growth Parallels Income Growth: Some New Evidence," in *National Saving and Economic Performance*, NBER volume, ed. B. Douglas Bernheim and John B. Shoven (Chicago: University of Chicago Press, 1991, 305–348).

27. This point is illustrated in Figure 15-2, which shows that Joan's second-period consumption tracks her second-period income.

28. See, for example, Robert E. Hall, "Stochastic Implications of the Life Cycle–Permanent Income Hypothesis: Theory and Evidence," *Journal of Political Economy* 86 (December 1978): 971–987; Robert E. Hall and Frederic S. Mishkin, "The Sensitivity of Consumption to Transitory Income: Estimates from Panel Data on Households," *Econometrica* 50(2) (1982): 461–481; Fumio Hayashi, "The Effects of Liquidity Constraints on Consumption: A Cross-Sectional Analysis," *Quarterly Journal of Economics* 100 (February 1985): 183–206; and Stephen P. Zeldes, "Consumption and Liquidity Constraints: An Empirical Investigation," *Journal of Political Economy* 97 (1989): 305–346.

Figure 15.11 Age-Consumption and Age-Disposable Income Profiles by Occupation Groups, 1972–1973.

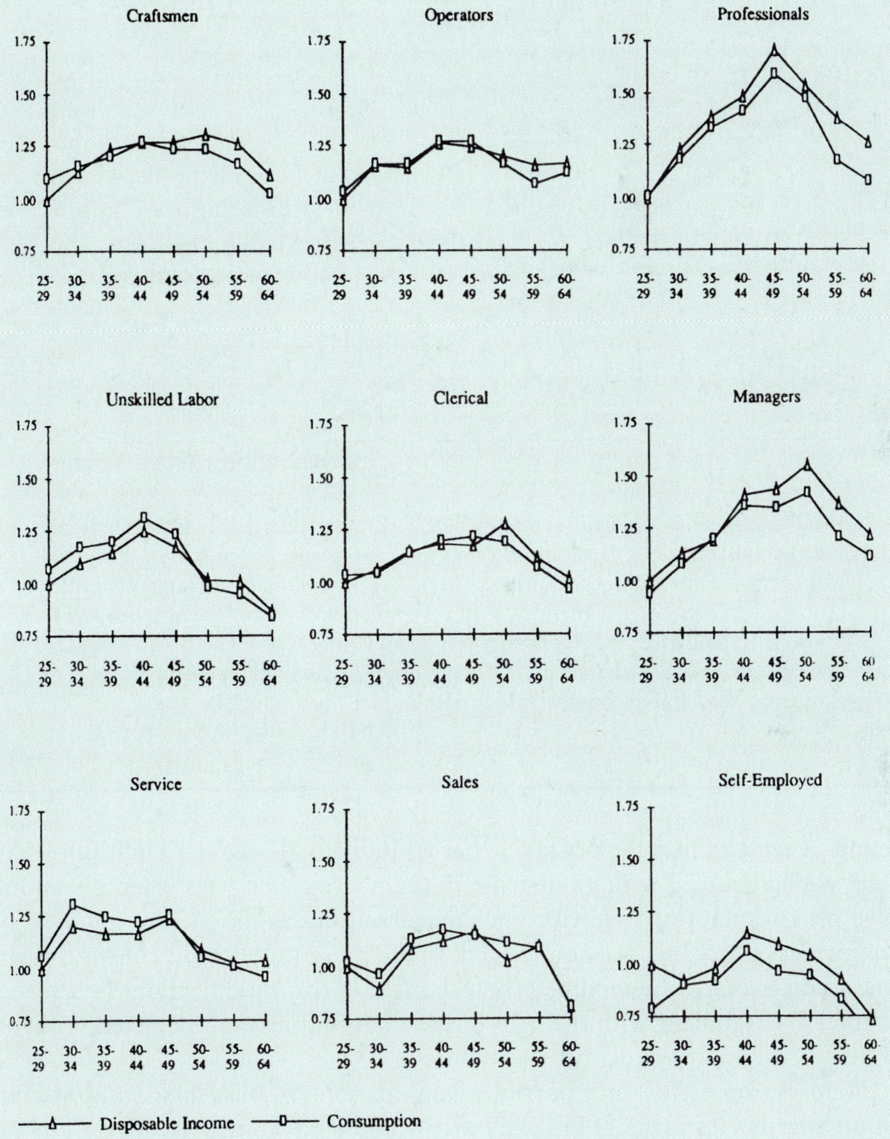

Source: C. D. Carroll, and L. H. Summers, "Consumption Growth Parallels Income Growth: Some New Evidence," in *National Saving and Economic Performance*, ed. B. D. Bernheim and J. B. Shoven (Chicago: University of Chicago Press, 1991, 325).

Credit Constraints, the Timing of Taxation, and Deficit Finance

In Chapter 7 we found that an individual's consumption decisions will be based on the present value of his net tax payments over his lifetime, not on their

Figure 15-12 Bill's Lifetime Budget Constraint

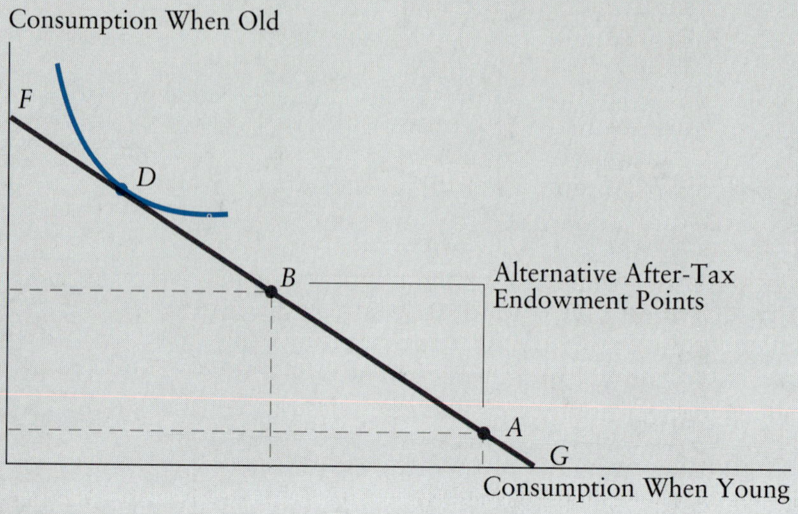

If Bill can borrow and lend at interest rate r_{t+1}, he can reach any point along his budget constraint *FG*. *D* is his utility-maximizing point. *A* and *B* are other combinations of first- and second-period after-tax earnings, both with the same present value. Compared with *A*, *B* features higher taxes when young, but lower taxes when old. At *D*, Bill's consumption when young is less than his after-tax income when young. A change in the timing of his lifetime tax payments from *A* to *B* does not lead him to borrow, but it does reduce the amount he saves.

timing. A reduction in the net taxes that an individual—let's call him Bill—pays when young coupled with an increase in the net taxes he pays when old should leave his consumption behavior unchanged as long as the present value of his lifetime net tax payments is unchanged. In the presence of credit constraints this conclusion needs to be modified. Before making this modification, let's review Chapter 7's argument with the help of the budget constraint depicted in Figure 15-12.

Point *A* represents one possible combination of Bill's first- and second-period after-tax earnings. If Bill can borrow and lend at interest rate r_{t+1}, he can attain any consumption combination along his budget constraint. By lending part of his current after-tax income, he can reach any point between *A* and *F*. By borrowing, he can reach points between *A* and *G*. Point *D* represents Bill's utility-maximizing choice of how much to consume when young and old.

Point *B* represents another possible combination of Bill's first- and second-period after-tax earnings. Since both *A* and *B* lie on the same budget constraint, they reflect the same present value of after-tax lifetime labor earnings.[29] Let's

29. By "after-tax" we mean after tax payments net of transfer payments received.

Figure 15-13 Hillary's Consumption With and Without Credit Constraints

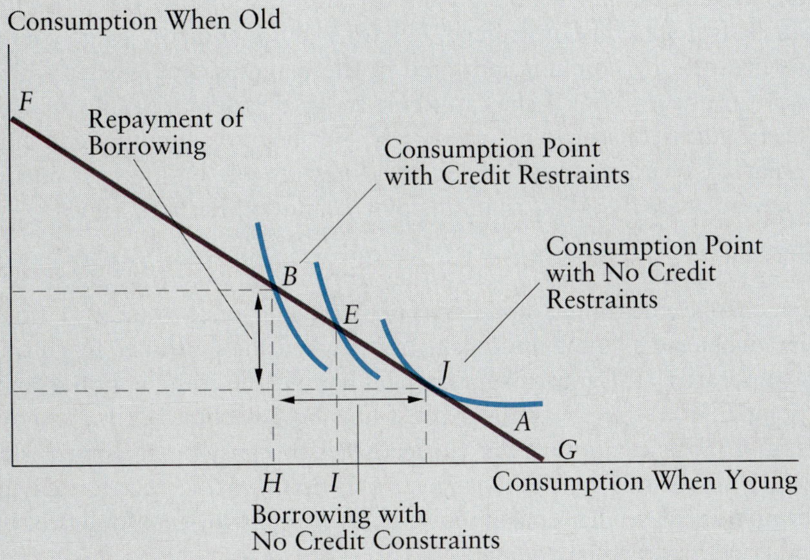

Hillary's budget constraint is identical to Bill's (Figure 15-12), but she chooses point *J*, which lies between *A* and *B*. If the government changes the timing of her lifetime tax payments from *A* to *B* and Hillary is credit-constrained, her budget constraint becomes *FBH*. She then consumes at *B*, rather than *J*, and has lower utility. If the government cuts her taxes when young and raises them when old, her constraint becomes *FEI*, and she consumes at *E*. Her consumption increases by one dollar for each dollar her net taxes when young are reduced.

suppose the different positions of the two points on the budget line reflect differences in the timing of net taxes, not differences in pretax earnings. Compared with *A*, point *B* features higher taxes when young but lower taxes when old. Both points reflect the same present value of net taxes.

Note that point *D* lies to the left of both *A* and *B*, so Bill's desired consumption when young is less than his after-tax income when young. If the government changes the timing of young Bill's lifetime tax payments from point *A* to point *B*, the change does not lead him to borrow, although it does reduce the amount he saves.

Figure 15-13 shows another possibility. It illustrates the budget constraint faced by Hillary, a young person whose first- and second-period after-tax earnings are identical to Bill's at point *A*. Bill and Hillary face the same lifetime pattern of net tax payments. They differ only in their preferences for current versus future consumption. Although Hillary's points *A* and *B* are in the same positions as Bill's were in the previous figure, the utility-maximizing point is not. Hillary has a stronger preference for current consumption, so her consumption combination at point *J* now lies between points *A* and *B*.

Let's suppose that, as it did with Bill, the government changes the timing of Hillary's lifetime tax payments, moving her after-tax endowment point from *A* to *B*. If she is not credit-constrained, Hillary will now borrow when young and repay when old the amounts indicated in the diagram. But what if Hillary *is* credit-constrained? What if she can't borrow at all? Geometrically, that would mean her budget constraint becomes *FBH*. Her best consumption combination is at point *B*, where she reaches her highest attainable indifference curve. She consumes at point *B*, rather than at point *J*, and experiences a lower level of utility.

Let's pursue our analysis a bit further to consider what happens if the government changes the timing of Hillary's tax payments once again. By cutting her net taxes when she's young and raising them when she's old (i.e., by cutting her taxes temporarily), the government changes her income combination from point *B* to point *E*. Her effective budget constraint now becomes *FEI*. As shown in Figure 15-13, this temporary tax cut leads her to consume at point *E*. Rather than being unaffected by this change in the timing of her net tax payments, Hillary now increases her consumption by one dollar for each dollar of reduction in her net taxes when young.

The cases of Bill and Hillary reveal that in the presence of credit constraints, changes in the timing of the government's net taxation can have real effects on aggregate consumption and national saving. In particular, temporary tax cuts can stimulate consumption in the short run. This happens even if the tax cuts are associated with future tax increases that leave the present value of net tax payments of each generation—the generational accounts—unchanged. Such temporary tax cuts would increase the size of the government's budget deficit. Hence, we've shown that deficit finance, even if it is not associated with redistribution across generations, can still stimulate consumption when there are credit constraints. In the context of nominal rigidities, such tax cuts can be used to shift the IS curve upward, expanding output and employment.

Case Study: The Consumption Response to the Timing of Social Security Benefit Payments

David Wilcox, an economist with the Federal Reserve, tested the proposition that household consumption is independent of the timing of the government's net taxation.[30] He noted that Social Security benefit increases are announced at least six months before they are paid. If households are not credit-constrained, they should increase their consumption spending when they receive news of a benefit increase, rather than wait until they actually get the cash. Wilcox

30. David W. Wilcox, "Social Security Benefits: Consumption Expenditure, and the Life Cycle Hypothesis," *Journal of Political Economy* 97(2) (April 1989): 288–304. Although Wilcox's study considered whether the timing of government transfer payments matter, his main objective was to test Ricardian equivalence.

showed this prediction was wrong. Social Security recipients wait until they actually receive their benefit increases before spending them.

Wilcox's study shows that the timing of the government's net taxation matters, but it is not definitive evidence of credit constraints for three reasons. First, most Social Security beneficiaries have sufficient liquid assets to pay for an increase in consumption at the time they first learn about the rise in their future benefits. They simply choose not to do so. Second, some recipients may not know about the pending increase in benefits. Third, recipients spend most of the increase on durables. Since purchasing durables constitutes a form of saving rather than immediate consumption, we can read Wilcox's evidence as indicating that the timing of the government's net taxation has little, if any, effect on the timing of consumption. That is precisely the prediction of the non–credit-constrained life-cycle model.

Chapter Summary

1. In addition to saving for retirement, people save against economic uncertainties and save to make bequests and gifts. This chapter explored these saving motives. It also considered the potential for young people to dissave by borrowing against their future income.
2. Adding uncertain second-period income to our model generates precautionary saving that, in turn, leads to an upward shift in the capital-labor ratio transition curve and more capital accumulation over time. Private insurance may reduce or eliminate the need for precautionary saving and, as a result, shift the capital-labor ratio transition curve downward.
3. Governments also provide insurance and thereby influence the amount of precautionary saving. They do so through their social insurance programs and through progressive taxation.
4. Although no one knows for sure the contribution of precautionary saving to total saving, simulation studies suggest that precautionary saving can be very substantial depending on the type of uncertainty and the availability of insurance.
5. Like precautionary saving, intentional saving for bequests and gifts shifts the capital-labor transition curve upward. This leads to a higher long-run level of capital per worker. The transition curve will also be higher as a result of unintended bequests. Unintended bequests are those left by individuals who die before consuming all the accumulated assets they did not plan to bequeath.
6. Research on U.S. bequests and other private intergenerational transfers suggests that, intended or not, such transfers have played a significant role in explaining total U.S. wealth accumulation. This role appears to be diminishing as more of the resources of the elderly become annuitized.
7. If private intergenerational transfers arise as the result of altruistic links between parents and children, Ricardian equivalence will hold. Ricardian equivalence is the proposition that private intergenerational redistribution will offset government redistribution, dollar for dollar. Particular extended families may exhibit altruistic linkages, but as a group, U.S. citizens apparently do not. Hence, Ricardian equivalence does not appear to hold for the economy as a whole.

8. Borrowing and credit markets arise in our two-period model if, in each generation, there are those who want to borrow and those who want to lend. By making loans to their contemporaries, young lenders reduce the amount of their saving used to invest in capital. This extension of credit shifts the capital-labor transition curve downward and depresses the economy's capital accumulation.
9. The availability of credit hinges on the knowledge lenders have about the creditworthiness of borrowers. It also depends on the legal institutions available to enforce repayment. These factors can influence the spread between borrowing rates and lending rates. In the United States a segment of society appears to be credit-constrained. This is disproportionately the case for minority households and may reflect racial bias or statistical racial discrimination.
10. Governments can influence capital accumulation through the imposition of credit controls and interest rate ceilings. They can also alter the timing of their tax and transfer policies. Such timing changes will alter consumption and saving to the extent that the affected public is credit-constrained. Evidence from Norway's credit market liberalization and the timing of U.S. Social Security benefit payments indicates that governments can use both credit market policies and tax and transfer timing policies to alter their nations' saving.
11. Credit and interest rate liberalizations as well as temporary tax cuts can lead to an expansion of consumption and an outward shift in the IS curve. Such policies can be used during recessions to offset the downward shift of the IS curve and leftward shift of the LM curve that worsening credit conditions during a recession are likely to produce.

Key Concepts

Annuities
Credit constraints
Precautionary saving
Social insurance
Ricardian equivalence
Credit controls

Review Questions

1. What is *risk aversion*? What implications does it have for the amount of saving? What impact does risk aversion have on the transition diagram and the steady-state capital-labor ratio?
2. How can *insurance* affect the amount of *income uncertainty* that individuals face? What implications does the existence of insurance have for saving and the steady-state capital-labor ratio?
3. What factors can limit the provision of private insurance? How can the government's provision of insurance overcome some of the difficulties faced by private insurers? Give some examples of government insurance programs.
4. What effect do *bequests* have on the transition diagram and the steady-state capital-labor ratio?
5. What are *annuities*? How do annuities affect the amount of bequests that are made? What impact do annuities have on the transition diagram and the

steady-state capital-labor ratio? What has happened during the past few decades to the fraction of the elderly's resources that is annuitized?

6. What are *intervivos transfers*? Give some examples. What implications do intervivos transfers have for government intergenerational transfer programs? How important are intervivos transfers in explaining individuals' consumption and saving behavior?

7. How are *borrowing* and *lending* incorporated into the life-cycle model? How is the *lifetime budget constraint* faced by borrowers written? What expression describes the total amount of credit demanded at a point in time? What expression describes the total amount of saving at a point in time? What impact does the existence of borrowing have on the transition diagram and the steady-state capital-labor ratio?

8. What does it mean to say an individual is *credit-constrained*? How can such a situation arise?

9. What are *lending rates*? What are *borrowing rates*? Why might the two differ in magnitude?

10. What is *statistical discrimination*?

11. In the life-cycle model, what impact do *credit constraints* have on the transition diagram and the steady-state capital-labor ratio?

12. How can credit market conditions affect the economy's level of output and employment in the short run?

13. What implications do credit constraints have for the impacts of government-mandated changes in the *timing* of tax payments?

Numerical Questions

1. Consider an economy that is characterized by the following parameters: $A = 4$, $\alpha = .5$, and $\beta = .3$.
   a. What is the steady-state capital-labor ratio and level of individual income?
   b. Beginning with the steady state, assume that all individuals face uncertainty about second-period income. Specifically, individuals face a 50-50 chance of receiving or losing \$1. Trace the value of the capital-labor ratio and the level of individual income for the next three periods, assuming individuals are risk-averse as described in the text.
   c. What effect does precautionary saving have on capital formation and income?
2. Suppose an economy's parameters are as follows: $A = 10$, $\alpha = .4$, and $\beta = .3$.
   a. What is the steady-state capital-labor ratio and level of individual income?
   b. Beginning with the steady state, assume that all individuals in all subsequent periods decide to bequeath \$2 to their offspring. Trace the value of the capital-labor ratio and the level of individual income for the next three periods. What effect do bequests have on capital formation and income?

Analytical Questions

1. Suppose that someone offers you two deals. In the first, you have a 50 percent chance of winning $4 and a 50 percent chance of winning nothing. In the second, you are certain to get $2.
   a. If you are risk-averse, which deal do you prefer?
   b. Assume that the second deal is modified so that you are only sure to receive $1. If you are risk-averse, which deal do you prefer in this case?

2. Suppose that you are in the business of lending money. Careful research has shown that you lose 2 percent of all the money that you lend, although different groups have different default rates. Specifically, you lose 2 percent of the money loaned to people with red hair, 1 percent of the money loaned to people with black hair, and 3 percent of the money loaned to people with blond hair. Because everyone knows the default rates, people with red or blond hair dye their hair black so that they appear to be better risks. Finally, suppose that you loan equal amounts to people of different hair color, and that the risk-free lending rate is 10 percent.
   a. Assume that you are neither risk-averse nor a risk lover. If a person asks you for a loan, what is the minimum interest rate that you will charge? If you are risk-averse, how will your calculation differ?
   b. Suppose that the hair dye factory blows up, making it impossible for people to dye their hair. Once again, assuming that you are neither risk-averse nor a risk lover, what is the minimum interest rate that you will charge people of different hair color? How does risk aversion alter your calculation?

3. Consider four individuals. John, who owns a tailor shop, and his friend Bob, who lives down the hall, work in the current period. They lend their current income and wait until next period to consume. Andy and Ben plan on writing a book and earning money from it next period. They wish to consume in this period but not in the next period. To consume now they must borrow from John and Bob and promise to repay the money with interest next period. Assume that John and Bob each earn $1,000 and that Andy and Ben expect to earn $550 each in the future. Also, assume that the interest rate next period, r_{t+1}, is 10 percent.
   a. How much will Andy and Ben each consume this period?
   b. How much saving will be devoted to capital formation in the current period?
   c. Suppose that unbeknownst to Andy and Ben, John and Bob receive inside information that a book like Andy and Ben's will be published next period and will likely reduce their earnings by half. Consequently, John and Bob will lend only half as much as before. How much are Ben and Andy able to consume in this case?
   d. Under the circumstances described in part c, how much saving will be devoted to capital formation? How does your answer compare to that in part b? Explain any difference.

4. Assume the same initial situation described in question 3. Now suppose that the government levies a current-period tax on Andy and Ben of $100.
   a. What is the value of Andy and Ben's generational account?
   b. In what direction and by how much will Andy and Ben's consumption change as a result of the tax?

c. Suppose that the government decides to levy a tax of $110 on Andy and Ben in the next period rather than $100 in the current period. What impacts does this fiscal policy change have on Andy and Ben's generational accounts and consumption? Explain.

d. Suppose that Andy and Ben are credit-constrained, so that each consumes $200 less than his preferred amount. Under these circumstances, what effects would shifting the tax liability from $100 in the current period to $110 in the following period have on Andy and Ben's generational accounts and consumption? Explain.

5. In the early 1980s, the Federal Reserve imposed limits on the amounts of consumer credit that lenders could provide. Analyze the likely short-run and long-run impacts of this policy on output. When discussing the possible short-run effects, discuss alternative outcomes that could arise depending on whether nominal price rigidity is present.

C H A P T E R 16

Financial Markets and the Investment Decision

INTRODUCTION

Investment is the purchase of capital goods to be used in producing output. In an average year, it accounts for about one-sixth of U.S. GDP. However, macroeconomists spend considerably more than one-sixth of their time analyzing investment behavior, in recognition of investment's central role in both long-run and short-run macroeconomic performance. Through earlier chapters, you have become relatively familiar with the investment process. In this chapter, our goal is to study this process in more detail.

As you learned in Chapter 1, the rate of capital accumulation affects the growth rates of a nation's output and labor productivity. Over shorter periods, as noted in Chapter 4, investment is highly volatile. It often fluctuates more than household consumption, although the latter accounts for about two-thirds of GDP. This volatility does not, in itself, mean that investment behavior causes macroeconomic instability. But we saw in Chapter 9 that disturbances in the investment process itself can magnify or even initiate fluctuations in output. In response, governments rely on monetary and fiscal policy to influence investment.

In this chapter, we will elaborate on investment dynamics and the impact of government policy on the level and composition of the capital stock. Instead of simply viewing investment as the passive consequence of saving, we will recognize the separate role played by firms in determining investment, considering how they choose among different types of capital and how they obtain the funds needed for investment. We will consider why the composition of the capital stock has shifted over time and the macroeconomic implications of the shifts that have occurred. In drawing the distinction between saving and investment behavior, we will examine the ways in which firms obtain their funds from households—how investment is financed—as well as how government policies influence investment behavior through their impact on firm financial decisions.

The full cost of using any particular type of capital may be represented by a single measure, known as the **user cost of capital**. Using this important tool, we will explore how policy has influenced the level and composition of investment in the past, as well as the effects that alternative policies might have in the future. We will also explore how additional factors, such as the technology of investment, investors' expectations, and their access to credit markets, alter the user cost of capital and hence investment itself.

User cost of capital *The total cost to a firm of using a unit of capital for one period*

Among the questions we'll address are:

- How and why has the composition of investment changed over time?
- How do tax policies influence the user cost of capital and investment?
- What special tax policies have encouraged investment in housing?
- How has the financing of U.S. investment changed in recent years?
- How do credit constraints affect the level and stability of investment?
- Why are some types of investment more volatile than others?

Our study of investment behavior begins with a look at changes in the composition of investment during the postwar years.

THE ANATOMY OF POSTWAR U.S. INVESTMENT

Table 16-1 presents a breakdown of private U.S. gross investment in 1993, expressed in real (1987 dollars) terms.[1] That year's gross investment of $820.9 billion accounted for 16.0 percent of real GDP.

Investment includes both *fixed investment* and *inventory investment*. Fixed investment is the purchase of durable goods (those lasting more than a year) that are used to produce output. *Inventory investment* is the purchase of goods that the firm will process or is holding for sale. Think of the assembly line used to manufacture automobiles. Fixed capital (the machines along the line) and labor are used to add value to inventories that enter as raw materials (steel, glass, etc.) and leave as finished goods. The addition of robots and other

1. Recall from Chapter 1 that *gross* investment equals the amount of capital purchased, whereas *net* investment equals the change in the capital stock. Net investment equals gross investment minus the depreciation of existing capital.

Table 16-1 Private Investment in the U.S., 1993 (billions of 1987 dollars)

Gross Private Domestic Investment	820.9	
Inventory Investment	15.4	
Fixed Investment	805.5	
Nonresidential Structures		151.4
Nonresidential Equipment		439.9
Residential Structures		214.2

Source: *Economic Report of the President*, 1994

machines used along the assembly line is counted as fixed investment. Increases in the stock of raw materials held ready for production, the work in process along the assembly line, or finished cars awaiting shipment all represent inventory investment.[2]

Inventories may include durable goods, but the distinction is that the durable goods held in inventory are themselves the subject of the production process. When General Motors adds a finished automobile to a lot awaiting shipment, that constitutes inventory investment. However, if the same car is immediately purchased by a limousine service to be used to provide limousine rides, it is considered as fixed investment. This distinction between inventory and fixed investment may exist even within a single company. For example, a retail electronics store may purchase a personal computer it intends to resell. This is considered inventory investment, because the store's production process *is* the retail distribution of computers. At the same time, the store may purchase a computer for its own use, to manage its accounts and billing. This is considered fixed investment, because this computer is not being marketed by the firm.

Inventory investment is typically a very small component of investment. For example, it equaled just $15.4 billion in real terms in 1993, out of $820.9 billion in total investment. Most private investment is fixed investment, which includes both nonresidential investment (also called *business fixed investment*) and residential investment: construction of houses, apartment buildings, condominiums, etc. In 1993, business fixed investment accounted for nearly three-fourths of all fixed investment. Almost three-fourths of this nonresidential investment was purchases of *producers' durable equipment*—machinery, trucks, tractors, tools, computers, etc.—rather than the construction of factories, office buildings, and other nonresidential structures.

2. As discussed in Chapter 5, inventory accumulation is not always intentional. Firms may plan to accumulate inventories of goods that they wish to sell but may also find themselves in possession of unwanted inventories if current sales fall short of expected sales. The car manufacturer, for example, may find itself with an unexpectedly high inventory of finished cars if demand for its products drops suddenly.

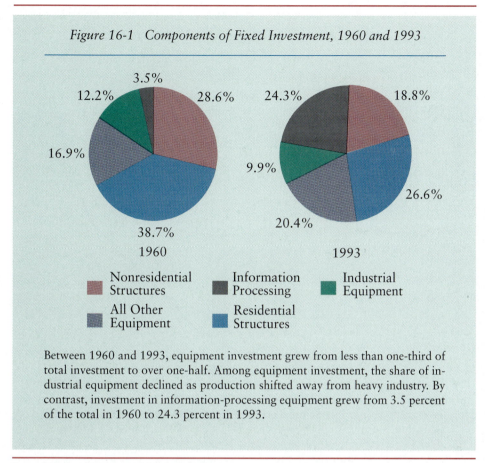

Figure 16-1 Components of Fixed Investment, 1960 and 1993

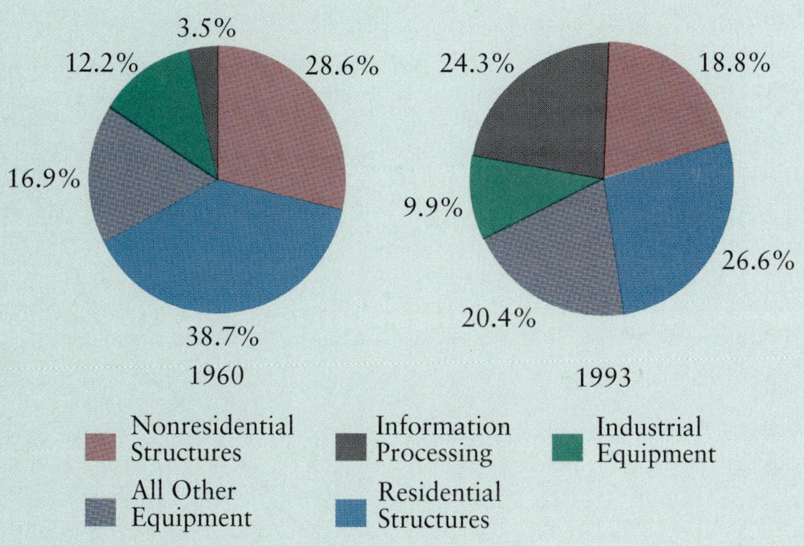

Between 1960 and 1993, equipment investment grew from less than one-third of total investment to over one-half. Among equipment investment, the share of industrial equipment declined as production shifted away from heavy industry. By contrast, investment in information-processing equipment grew from 3.5 percent of the total in 1960 to 24.3 percent in 1993.

Source: *National Income and Product Accounts*

The importance of equipment investment reflects a long-term trend. Figure 16-1 compares the composition of U.S. fixed investment in 1960 and 1993. It divides producers' durable equipment into three subcategories: information-processing equipment, industrial equipment, and all other equipment.

The figure shows that residential construction has fallen as a share of total fixed investment in recent decades. This drop is at least partly attributable to the slowdown in household formation—a prime determinant of new housing construction—that followed the postwar baby boom.[3] The share of investment in nonresidential structures also fell over the period. Together, nonresidential and residential construction fell from over two-thirds of fixed investment in 1960 to less than half in 1993.

The rising importance of equipment investment masks differing trends in its components. For example, investment in industrial equipment declined in

3. See N. Gregory Mankiw and David N. Weil, "The Baby Boom, the Baby Bust, and the Housing Market," *Regional Science and Urban Economics* 19 (May 1989): 235–258.

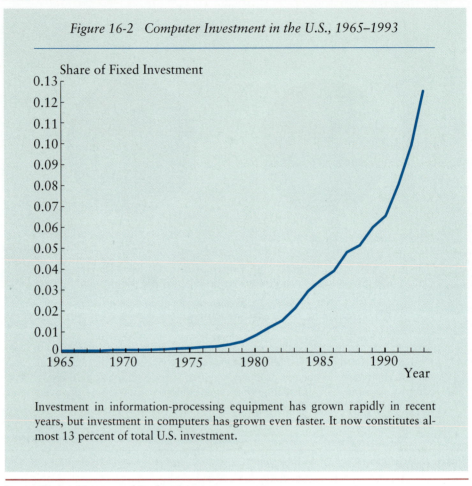

Figure 16-2 Computer Investment in the U.S., 1965–1993

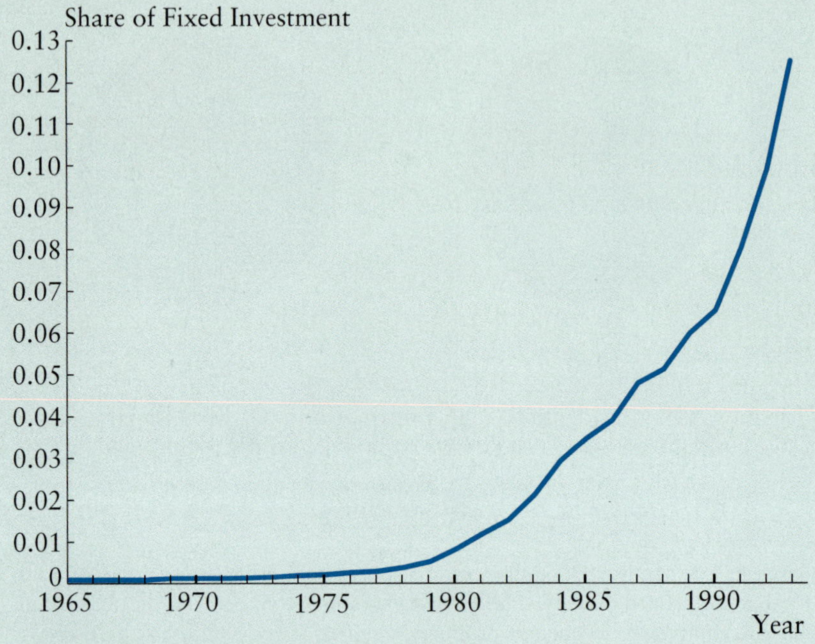

Investment in information-processing equipment has grown rapidly in recent years, but investment in computers has grown even faster. It now constitutes almost 13 percent of total U.S. investment.

Source: *National Income and Product Accounts*

importance, reflecting a shift of production away from heavy industries, like manufacturing, that use such equipment. The most striking change from 1960 to 1993, though, is in the share of investment accounted for by information-processing equipment, including computers. From just 3.5 percent of fixed investment in 1960, investment in information-processing equipment expanded to 24.3 percent of the total by 1993. As Figure 16-2 shows, the share of investment accounted for by computers—essentially zero until the mid-1960s—has grown even more rapidly.

Thus, investment has changed over the past few decades. It is increasingly typified by lawyers buying computers and investment bankers buying mobile telephones and less by steel companies building blast furnaces, automobile companies installing assembly lines, and home builders developing large tracts of "starter" homes for new families. Clearly, this trend is partly attributable to the changing structure of the U.S. economy. But you will see that economic policy has also played an important role. As we'll show, the composition of investment changes over the business cycle as well, because some types of investment are more sensitive to economic conditions than others.

DETERMINING THE INCENTIVE TO INVEST

According to our life-cycle model, the economy's capital stock in a particular period equals the capital brought into old age by that period's older generation. The period's net investment equals the increase in the capital stock over the previous period. At the beginning of their old age, the elderly may invest their capital in their own firms or supply it to other firms that pay the market rental rate for capital, the real interest rate. The real interest rate is determined by the amount of capital (and labor) in the economy as a whole, and each saver/capital supplier receives this rate of return in the following period.

In reality, there are many types of capital, and the acts of saving and investment are directly linked only in certain cases. Typically, most nonresidential investment, and some residential investment as well, is undertaken by businesses. To finance this investment, businesses obtain funds from households with the assistance of financial intermediaries. (Even when saving and investment are directly linked, as in the case of a household's purchase of *owner-occupied housing*, most of the necessary funds typically come from a mortgage lender.) We will discuss below why the method of obtaining funds may matter. Initially, though, we'll continue to assume that, regardless of how a firm obtains funds, it must offer the market rate of return—the interest rate.

The User Cost of Capital

Imagine that a firm is considering the purchase of a unit of capital to use for one period. (As we'll discuss later, the same general approach will apply to multiperiod decisions as well.) For each dollar it obtains from households, directly or through financial intermediaries, it must repay the dollar of principal plus interest in the following period. Part of this repayment will consist of the capital itself or the funds raised by selling the capital to a third party.

How much must the firm earn in order to repay principal plus interest? Let's first review our earlier analysis of this problem, from Chapter 3. With the dollar of capital still in hand one period later, the firm needs to earn the rate of interest, r, on its investment in order to have the $1 + r$ dollars to repay. Hence, the investment's return—its *marginal product*—must be at least as high as the interest rate, r. Firms acquire capital as long as it is profitable to do so. That is, they acquire it to the point where the marginal product of capital, MPK, equals r:

$$\text{MPK} = r$$

In this case, we may think of r as the price that the firm pays in order to use one dollar of capital for one period.

ACCOUNTING FOR DEPRECIATION. As a tangible asset, capital will depreciate in the period between its purchase and its sale one period later. Let's assume it has lost a fraction δ of its value, and is now worth just $(1 - \delta)$ per dollar originally invested. Then, for each dollar of capital originally purchased, the firm will have $(1 - \delta)$ dollars of capital, but must repay a total of $(1 + r)$ dollars.

Hence, the capital itself must yield a return of at least $(r + \delta)$. The firm will invest in capital to the point where its marginal product just equals this value:

$$MPK = r + \delta$$

We call this required return—to which the firm equates its marginal product of capital—the *user cost of capital*, because it indicates the full cost to the firm of using capital in production. In the previous instance, the user cost of capital was simply the interest rate. However, the physical investment's loss of value imposes another cost, depreciation, that must be made up by a higher rate of return.[4]

The basic user cost of capital, $(r + \delta)$, varies considerably among different types of asset. For some assets, depreciation may be a much more significant component of the user cost than the interest rate. Whereas buildings may depreciate only 2 percent per year, computers depreciate much more rapidly, losing perhaps one-third of their value each year.[5]

THE USER COST: A NUMERICAL EXAMPLE. A numerical example will illustrate how to calculate the user cost of capital. Suppose a company is considering whether to purchase a computer for \$2,000. Once it is purchased, the computer will lose 35 percent of its value after one year, at which time the firm must pay the suppliers of funds 6 percent interest, along with principal, or \$2,120. Selling the computer would raise only \$1,300 (.65 times \$2,000), so the firm needs to earn an additional \$820—41 (6 + 35) percent of the initial purchase price—to break even.[6]

THE CORPORATE INCOME TAX, THE USER COST, AND INVESTMENT

We know from earlier chapters that monetary and fiscal policy can affect the interest rate and the amount of capital in the economy. The impact on the interest rate represents one way that government policy influences the user cost of capital, for all types of investment. However, through specific tax provisions, the

4. We have seen the user cost of capital before in a different context. In Chapter 5, we showed that the *imputed rent* on owner-occupied housing, which national income accountants must calculate for inclusion in the national income accounts, equals the housing stock multiplied by $(r + \delta)$. The assumption of that imputation is that each investor in owner-occupied housing earns just enough in the form of implicit housing services to cover the user cost of the investment.

5. The rapid depreciation of computers illustrates an important point stressed in Chapter 5. Economists measure depreciation in terms of an asset's loss in value, not by any physical decay. From the investor's point of view, the user cost of capital of a computer is high because that computer will lose its value rapidly—even if it continues to function perfectly.

6. We can also demonstrate that our analysis carries over to investments lasting more than one period. If the firm earned \$820 but wished to keep the computer for at least one more year, it would need to obtain \$1,300—the funds it would otherwise have raised by selling the computer—to pay off its initial suppliers of funds. Although this would leave the firm with a liability of \$1,300 to the new suppliers of funds, it would still have broken even during the first year—it would end the year with no change in its *net worth* because it would hold an asset (the computer) worth \$1,300 in addition to the \$1,300 liability.

government also influences the *composition* of the capital stock. The impact of such tax provisions can be determined by considering how they affect the user cost of particular types of capital. This section considers the most important of these tax provisions, the corporate income tax.

The Corporate Income Tax

Most U.S. nonresidential investment is undertaken by corporations. This preponderance of corporate investment is illustrated by the relative sizes of the corporate and noncorporate capital stocks. At the end of 1993, for example, there were \$6.7 trillion dollars worth of plant, equipment, and inventories in the U.S., \$4.7 trillion of which were held by nonfinancial corporations. Businesses choose the corporate form of organization for a variety of legal and financial reasons, but being a corporation has tax consequences as well. The income a corporation earns for its owners—its *stockholders*—is subject to the **corporate income tax.**

Corporate income tax
A tax on corporations' profits

The corporate income tax adds a third term to the user cost of capital. For each dollar of interest the corporation pays to its suppliers of funds, it must also remit a certain amount to the government. This tax component, say τ per dollar of capital, increases the user cost to

$$\text{MPK} = r + \delta + \tau$$

The term τ accounts for the share of a firm's earnings after depreciation that must be paid in taxes. Thus, it is proportional to the interest rate, r, and increases with the corporate tax rate.[7]

Let's see how this works, using the numerical example introduced earlier, with a value of τ equal to 3 percent. With a 6 percent interest rate and a 35 percent depreciation rate, it is now no longer sufficient to earn a rate of return of 41 percent on the investment. If the firm did earn 41 percent, it would have to pay some of this to the government in taxes, leaving it with less than it would need to cover interest and depreciation. The user cost formula tells us that to cover these costs and taxes as well, the marginal product of capital would have to be 6 + 35 + 3 = 44 percent.

How does the corporate income tax affect the economy's capital stock? Let's start by assuming that the tax applies to all types of capital, and then ask how our answer is affected by the fact that the corporate tax does not apply to all types of investment.

7. How big will the tax component τ be? To get an idea, suppose that the corporate tax rate equals 35 percent, as it now does for most large corporations. Then, to pay suppliers of funds a dollar of interest, the firm will have to earn enough income so that a dollar remains after 35 percent of the income has been taken by taxes. The total amount needed will be $1/(1 - .35) = 1.54$ dollars, with 35 percent of this, 54 cents, being paid in taxes. In this case, τ is about half as big as r. In general, the ratio of τ to r will be $c/(1 - c)$, where c is the corporate tax rate.

As we will discuss later, the corporation may be able to mitigate the effects of this tax through its financial policies.

Relating Changes in the User Cost to Changes in Investment

We have just observed that for a given interest rate, a rise in the corporate tax raises the user cost of capital. Now let's consider, graphically and algebraically, how this tax affects the economy's capital stock and investment. To do so, we must remind ourselves that the capital stock and the interest rate are jointly determined by the demand for capital by firms and the supply of capital by households, so that the interest rate itself may change in response to the corporate tax.

The demand for capital by firms is governed by the production function and the user cost of capital just derived. For any given interest rate, introducing a corporate tax raises the user cost, thereby requiring a higher marginal product of capital. This leads each firm to demand less capital at any interest rate. The drop in demand for capital for the economy as a whole may be calculated if we equate the marginal product of capital from the Cobb-Douglas production function to the user cost of capital. For period $t + 1$, this yields the expression

$$A(1 - \beta)k_{t+1}^{\beta-1} = r_{t+1} + \delta + \tau$$

which, as we vary r_{t+1}, traces out a demand curve for capital relating the capital-labor ratio to the interest rate. Figure 16-3 shows two such demand curves. The first, labeled D, corresponds to the case where $\tau = 0$. The second, labeled D', corresponds to a positive value of τ. It lies a distance τ below curve D because if r_{t+1} falls by exactly τ as the tax is introduced, the user cost doesn't change and neither does the quantity of capital demanded.

Now let's consider supply conditions. Recall from Chapter 8 how the supply of capital by households is determined when there is no first-period consumption ($\alpha = 0$). In this case, the next period's capital stock (per young person) equals

$$k_{t+1} = (1 - \gamma)(1 - \beta)y_t - f_t$$

where $1 - \beta$ is the share of income going to labor, γ is the share of labor income put into money holdings (rather than capital), and f_t is the sum of taxes paid and government bonds purchased by each young person. In words, the equation says that, per worker, the total amount of capital in the economy equals the amount the young save, net of the amount they choose to hold as money and the amount they give to the government.

This expression gives us a supply curve for k_{t+1}. Unlike the demand curve, the supply curve is not shifted by the imposition of a corporate tax, unless the tax alters the overall level of f_t, the payments to the government by the young.[8]

8. The term f_t would change if, upon receiving corporate tax revenues (from the old), the government reduced taxes on the young. However, the net effect of the corporate tax and the tax reduction would be a change in the generational burden of fiscal policy. It would be this shift in the fiscal burden, and not the introduction of the corporate tax itself, that would lead to the change in supply. By contrast, replacing the corporate tax with another tax collected from the elderly would have no impact on f_t.

Figure 16-3 Capital Stock Determination: The Corporate Tax

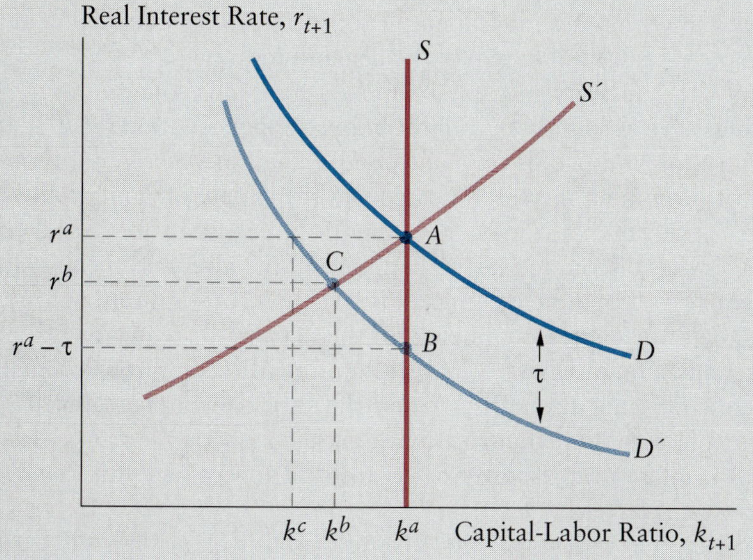

A corporate income tax shifts the demand for capital curve downward from D to D'. If the supply of capital is independent of the interest rate, the tax merely lowers the interest rate from r^a to $r^a - \tau$, with no change in the capital-labor ratio. If the supply of capital does depend on the interest rate, the tax lowers both the interest rate (to r^b) and the capital-labor ratio.

Logically, then, introducing a corporate tax can alter the overall amount of capital only if the quantity supplied depends on the interest rate, as shown by the upward sloping supply curve labeled S' in Figure 16-3. Otherwise, with the vertical supply curve, S, the corporate tax shifts the demand curve downward, reducing the interest rate from r^a at point A to $r^a - \tau$ at point B, but leaving the capital-labor ratio unchanged at k^a.

Could the supply of capital depend upon the interest rate? There are three reasons why it might. First, a reduction in the interest rate will increase γ if the demand for money is interest-sensitive. Second, the level of output may be interest-sensitive if Keynesian nominal rigidities prevail. We can see this using the IS-LM analysis developed in Chapter 9. Recall that the IS curve—which relates the interest rate r_{t+1} to output y_t—is derived by combining the above supply equation relating household saving to income with the previous demand equation relating the interest rate to the marginal product of capital. Our original derivation of the IS curve in Chapter 9 didn't include the corporate tax. Adding it shifts the IS curve downward by an amount τ because, although the marginal product of capital associated with any level of output is the same as before, the interest rate associated with this marginal product of capital is reduced by τ. For a given price level and a nonvertical LM curve, the downward shift in the IS curve causes both the interest rate and output to fall. The increased money demand induced by a lower interest rate cannot be satisfied through a reduction in the price level, so output must fall to reduce the demand for money.

Finally, the quantity of capital supplied may fall along with r_{t+1} if young households save less as a result. In the above supply equation for k_{t+1}, α is fixed at zero—young households consume none of their income. In our more general model with $\alpha > 0$, an increase in α reduces the supply of capital. As we saw in Chapter 7, the value of α may effectively be increased by individual capital income taxes that discourage saving by reducing the after-tax interest rate households receive. A corporate income tax is levied on corporations, not individuals, but has the same depressing impact on the net rate of return to savers. In this case, the reduction in what savers receive comes directly through a reduction in the interest rate, not through taxes on the savers themselves. But it shouldn't matter to a household making its saving decision whether it receives less interest because the interest rate is lower or because the government taxes away some of the interest it receives.

If, in fact, the supply of capital is interest-sensitive, a corporate tax may discourage overall saving. With a positively sloped supply curve, such as S' in Figure 16-3, a tax that shifts the demand curve downward lowers both the interest rate and the quantity of capital per worker, as shown at point C.

The Effects of Sector-Specific Taxation

Let's return to the fact that the corporate tax does not affect all types of investment equally. Nonresidential investment (mostly undertaken by corporations) is generally subject to a tax, whereas residential investment (mostly undertaken by households) is not. Going through our previous analysis, we see that, for a given interest rate, only the corporate cost of capital will rise. This will reduce the quantity of capital demanded by corporations for any given interest rate. Because the demand curve for noncorporate capital is not affected, overall (corporate plus noncorporate) demand also falls at each interest rate. Once again, if the supply of capital is fixed, the interest rate must fall in order to stimulate demand back to its original level. Now, though, as the interest rate falls, the user cost of noncorporate capital will fall. The demand for capital, and hence investment, by the noncorporate sector will rise. Even if the supply curve for capital is not completely vertical, the initial reduction in demand will still lead to some reduction in the interest rate, as shown in Figure 16-3, and hence some increase in the quantity of noncorporate capital demanded.

Thus, the fall in the interest rate will be accompanied by a shift in the *composition* of the capital stock. Whether the overall capital stock declines will depend on whether the supply of capital falls with this decline in the interest rate. But regardless of what happens to the overall capital stock, the corporate tax will cause a change in the capital stock's composition.

In summary, a corporate tax will drive capital out of the corporate sector and into other sectors not subject to that tax. In the process, the interest rate will be depressed. In a sense, then, the burden of the corporate tax is spread to capital suppliers in both the corporate and noncorporate sectors of the economy.[9] By driving down the rate of return savers receive, the tax may also reduce the overall amount of investment. This will happen if individuals are discouraged from saving or from holding their assets in the form of capital by the lower after-tax rate of return, whose impact can be magnified by a reduction in output in the presence of nominal rigidities. The same logic applies to other tax measures that affect the user cost of capital, some of which we now consider.

TAX POLICY AND THE USER COST IN PRACTICE

Often, the government seeks to influence the level and composition of investment by offering **investment incentives**, provisions that reduce a firm's taxes according to the amount of investment it undertakes. One of the most common investment incentives is the **investment tax credit**, which gives each investor a tax rebate equal to some fraction of the cost of newly purchased capital. A 7 percent investment tax credit was first introduced by President Kennedy in 1962. In the decades since, the credit has been temporarily suspended (in 1966), repealed (in 1969), reinstated (in 1971), increased to 10 percent (in 1974), and repealed again (in 1986). In 1993, President Clinton proposed (unsuccessfully) having it reinstated.

Investment incentives
Tax subsidies designed to encourage particular types of investment spending

Investment tax credit
A provision in the tax code that gives an investor a tax rebate equal to some fraction of the cost of newly purchased capital

Accelerated depreciation
A provision in the tax code that increases the present value of deductions for depreciation by allowing firms to take the deductions soon after investment is undertaken

Another investment incentive is **accelerated depreciation** allowances. The corporate income tax permits deductions for depreciation, called depreciation allowances. An accelerated depreciation program increases the deductions investors are permitted to take. The higher the firm's deductions, the lower its taxes.

Investment incentives affect the user cost of capital by reducing the taxes the firm must pay for each unit of capital it buys. This lowers the value of the tax component, τ, in the user cost formula, thereby lowering the user cost itself. Thus, the value of τ depends not only on the corporate tax rate, but also on the generosity of investment incentives. A low value of τ could be consistent with a high corporate tax rate, if investment incentives were generous enough. Indeed, in the early 1980s, the value of τ for corporate investment in equipment was actually *negative*, despite a high corporate tax, because of the combined impact of accelerated depreciation and the investment tax credit.[10]

Most investment qualifying for investment incentives is undertaken by corporations also subject to the corporate income tax. We might ask what purpose

9. This analysis of the *incidence* of the corporate tax was first put forward in a classic article by Arnold C. Harberger, "The Incidence of the Corporation Income Tax," *Journal of Political Economy* 70 (June, 1962): 215–40.

10. See Alan J. Auerbach, "Corporate Taxation in the United States," *Brookings Papers on Economic Activity* 14 (1983): 451–505.

is served by simultaneously having tax provisions that raise and lower the corporate user cost of capital. There are two reasons for having both a corporate income tax and investment incentives.

First, the corporate income tax is levied on the income from all types of corporate capital, whereas investment incentives typically apply only to *some* types of corporate investment. For example, the investment tax credit has typically applied to purchases of machinery and equipment but not inventories or structures.

Second, the generational consequences of the policies differ. A corporate tax introduced in period t immediately lowers the income of the elderly in period t; an investment incentive introduced in period t offers a reduction in taxes only for those undertaking investment—the young in period t and future generations. Used in concert, then, the corporate income tax and the investment tax credit provide a way of increasing taxes on those currently holding assets—in our model, the elderly—without necessarily altering the user cost of capital. Put another way, the government can preserve a tax on asset holders while lowering the user cost of capital if it uses investment incentives rather than reducing the corporate tax rate. This advantage of investment incentives is sometimes expressed in terms of their having a greater "bang for the buck" than cuts in the corporate tax rate—entailing a smaller loss in tax revenue to produce a given reduction in the user cost of capital.[11]

Case Study: The Corporate User Cost of Capital, 1960–1988

Over the years, there have been many changes in the tax treatment of U.S. corporate investment, including the repeated use of the investment tax credit along with accelerated depreciation and variations in the corporate income tax rate. What were the impacts on the user cost of capital? How do changes in the user cost due to these tax factors compare to changes resulting from movements in the real interest rate? Figure 16-4 provides the answer. It divides the user cost of capital for corporate fixed investment into two components: the basic piece, equal to the sum of interest and depreciation rates, $(r + \delta)$, and the tax component, τ, that results from the combination of the corporate tax rate and investment incentives.[12]

The figure shows the effects of some of the tax changes we've mentioned. Introducing the investment tax credit lowered the user cost of capital in the early 1960s and again in the early 1970s; increasing the credit from 7 percent to 10 percent lowered the user cost yet again in the mid-1970s. Removal of the credit helps explain the increase in the tax component of the user cost in the late 1960s

11. This topic is discussed in more detail in our book, *Dynamic Fiscal Policy* (New York: Cambridge University Press, 1987, Chapter 9).

12. See Alan J. Auerbach and Kevin Hassett, "Investment, Tax Policy and the Tax Reform Act of 1986," in *Do Taxes Matter? The Impact of the Tax Reform Act of 1986*, ed. J. Slemrod (Cambridge, MA: MIT Press, 1990, 13–40). The basic user cost $(r + \delta)$ equals the real commercial paper rate (equal to the nominal commercial paper rate less the rate of inflation of the GDP deflator) plus 7 percent, roughly the average rate of depreciation of fixed corporate capital during the period.

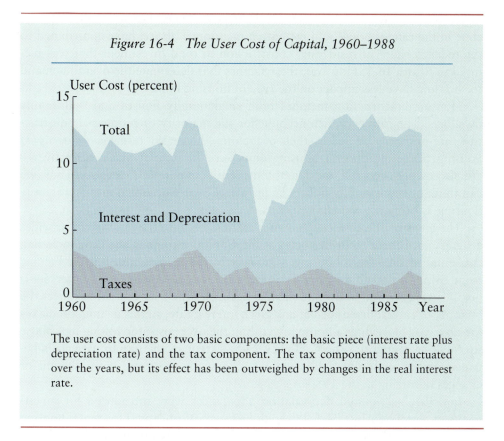

Figure 16-4 The User Cost of Capital, 1960–1988

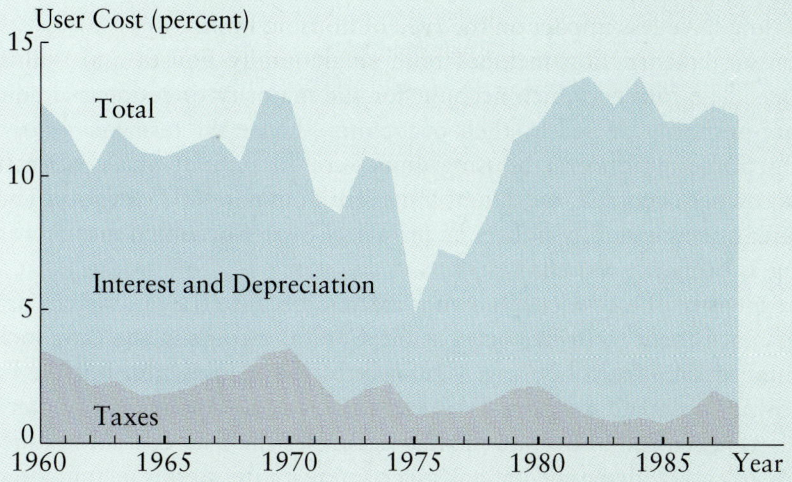

The user cost consists of two basic components: the basic piece (interest rate plus depreciation rate) and the tax component. The tax component has fluctuated over the years, but its effect has been outweighed by changes in the real interest rate.

and again in 1986. The generous accelerated depreciation system introduced in the early 1980s explains the reduction in the tax component during those years. However, although tax factors have changed over the period, they have often been outweighed by changes in the real interest rate. For example, even though the tax burden on corporate investment was reduced in the early 1980s, the user cost rose to its highest levels in decades, because of the very high real interest rates during the period.

In general, the most significant swings in the user cost of capital have been due to changes in interest rates, not corporate tax provisions.[13] However, recall that interest rate changes affect all investment, whereas tax changes often apply only to particular types of investment. The latter may be crucial to determining the composition of the capital stock, if not its level.

Case Study: Housing Investment in the 1980s

How significant have changes in the user cost of capital been in influencing the composition of investment? Changes in the tax treatment of housing in the

13. As discussed above, interest rates may change *because* of changes in corporate tax provisions. However, as Figure 16-4 indicates, interest rate changes have been much larger in magnitude and have not always coincided with tax provision changes.

1980s offer a natural experiment. Over the years, many factors, such as the decline in the rate of household formation mentioned above, have contributed to the reduced share of residential construction in total investment that was pictured in Figure 16-1. However, these factors that determine the overall demand for housing have less impact on the *type* of housing built.

Housing construction includes both single-family houses and multifamily dwellings. The former, which account for the majority of residential construction, are primarily owned by their occupants—hence the term *owner-occupied housing*. Some multifamily housing units—condominiums and cooperatives—are also owner-occupied, but rental units still dominate this category. Thus, we can think of single-family houses as primarily owner-occupied and multifamily housing as primarily rented.

The identity of a residence's owner matters because the tax system provides a significant benefit to owner occupation. Capital income in the U.S., including the rental income from housing, is subject to the income tax, but the income from owner-occupied housing—the *imputed rent* discussed in Chapter 5—is not. As we discussed above, an income tax raises the user cost and reduces the quantity of capital demanded at any given interest rate, so this distinction makes the user cost of owning a house lower than the user cost of investing in a house that will be rented to others. However, the extent of the gap in user costs between owned and rented housing has changed over time, with two major changes occurring in the 1980s.

In 1981, accelerated depreciation allowances were introduced for investments in rental housing. They lowered the user cost of capital for rental housing and made it a relatively more attractive investment than owner-occupied housing, which was unaffected by this provision. In 1986, the accelerated depreciation provisions of 1981 were reversed, and other rules changed as well. All of these changes acted to increase the user cost of capital for rental housing. As Figure 16-5 shows, these two tax changes affected the pattern of housing investment during the 1980s. In the recession year of 1982, investment in single-family housing dropped sharply, whereas newly favored multifamily housing investment declined only slightly. In 1987, on the other hand, despite the generally good economic climate and the increase in single-family housing construction, multifamily housing construction fell. In short, the very different patterns observed in 1982 and 1987 are exactly what the theory of the user cost would predict.

A Note on Expectations

The user cost of capital indicates the rate of return that a firm's new investments must earn to break even, under any single set of tax rules. But matters become more complicated when the tax system changes over time. Anticipated future changes in tax policy can, themselves, influence current investment.

Take the investment tax credit which, as noted above, has been altered several times since it was originally introduced in the U.S. in 1962. Often, changes in the credit were anticipated by investors even though they had not been announced in advance. In some cases, though, the impending changes were even built into law.

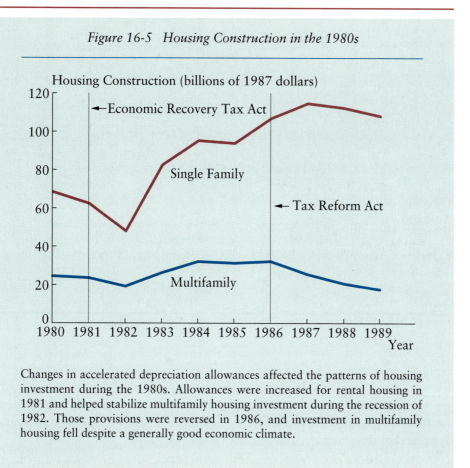

Figure 16-5 Housing Construction in the 1980s

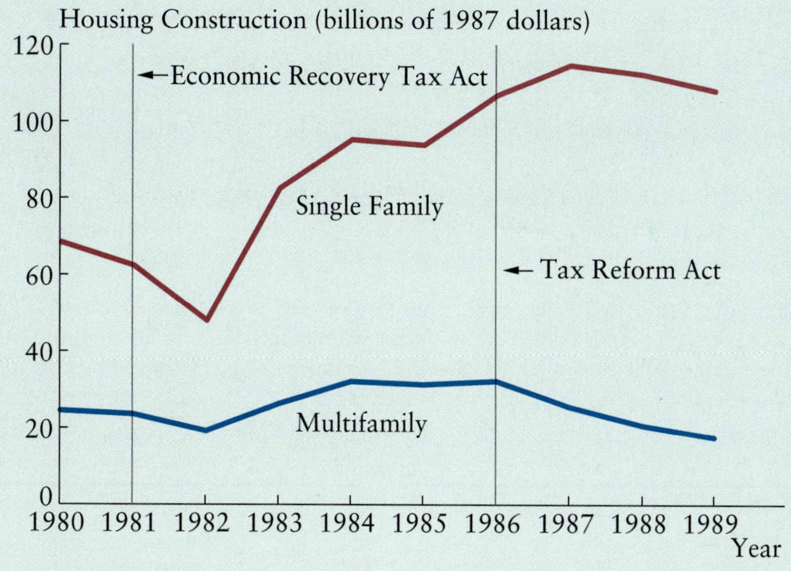

Changes in accelerated depreciation allowances affected the patterns of housing investment during the 1980s. Allowances were increased for rental housing in 1981 and helped stabilize multifamily housing investment during the recession of 1982. Those provisions were reversed in 1986, and investment in multifamily housing fell despite a generally good economic climate.

Source: *National Income and Product Accounts*

How do anticipated changes in the investment tax credit affect investment? An investment tax credit, in itself, reduces the user cost of capital and encourages investment. Knowledge that it will apply only temporarily provides a further spur to investment, as firms try to squeeze investment that they might have undertaken over the succeeding few years into the period when the credit applies. This makes the temporary investment tax credit an even more powerful tool for influencing investment in the short run than a permanent investment tax credit.[14]

A temporary tax credit has its costs, too. Suppose the government alters the investment tax credit frequently. Firms anticipating that the government will introduce or increase the investment tax credit may delay some of their investment in order to have it qualify for the credit. This delay may be particularly severe at

14. Thus, if investment tax credits are usually temporary, they will be associated with larger swings in investment than if they were expected to be of more permanent duration. This illustrates the main point of the *Lucas critique* of stabilization policy that we discussed in Chapter 12: we cannot know how policy will affect behavior unless we know what expectations are and how these expectations are influenced by the policy itself.

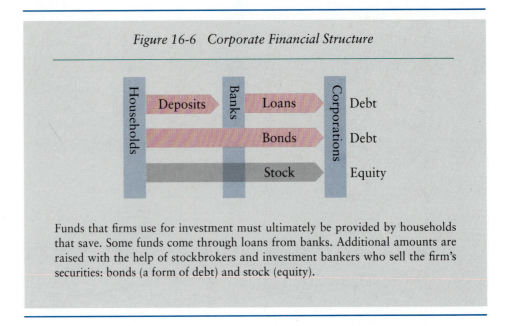

Figure 16-6 Corporate Financial Structure

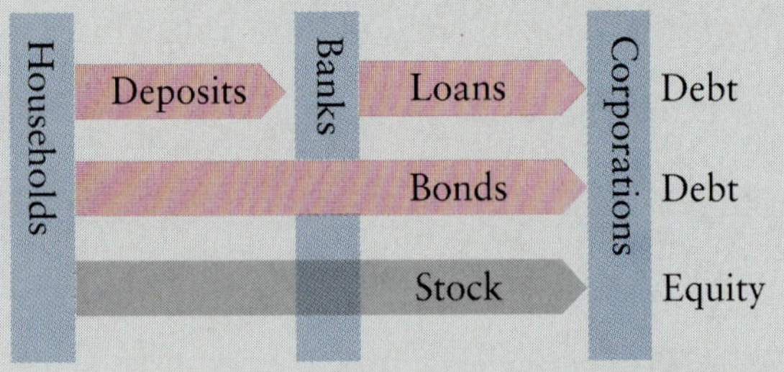

Funds that firms use for investment must ultimately be provided by households that save. Some funds come through loans from banks. Additional amounts are raised with the help of stockbrokers and investment bankers who sell the firm's securities: bonds (a form of debt) and stock (equity).

the onset of recessions, if firms anticipate that the government will introduce the investment tax credit as an antirecession device, as it often has. As a result, the temporary tax credit and other investment incentives may actually contribute to the instability of investment. Evidence for the U.S. over the past few decades suggests that this has indeed been the case.[15]

CORPORATE FINANCIAL POLICY

When a firm determines how much to invest, it must also decide on its *financial policy*—how to obtain the funds to pay for its investment. A firm's financial policy, and the constraints that it faces in setting such policy, may affect its cost of capital and therefore its level of investment.

Ultimately, any funds the firm obtains for investment must be provided by households that save.[16] But, as we learned in Chapter 14, financial intermediaries often play a role in bringing savers and investors together. A small business may be run directly by an individual who both provides the funds for investment and makes investment decisions, but most large businesses—predominantly corporations—obtain their funds from individuals who have very little to do with the actual management of the firm.

Funds may be obtained in a variety of ways, as indicated in Figure 16-6. Some funds come through loans from banks. Additional amounts are raised

15. See Alan J. Auerbach and Kevin Hassett, "Tax Policy and Business Fixed Investment in the United States," *Journal of Public Economics* 47 (April 1992): 141–170.
16. In an open economy, as we learned in Chapter 6, these savings may come from abroad.

with the help of stockbrokers and investment bankers who sell the firm's *securities*—financial assets representing claims on the assets of the business—directly to savers in exchange for the funds. These securities can take the form of *stock*—each share of which represents ownership of a small part of the business—or *bonds*—essentially loans made by the household to the business. A firm's *debt* equals the sum of its bonds and bank loans; its *equity* equals the amount of stock outstanding. An important decision for the firm is determining the composition of its *capital structure*: how much of its investment to finance with debt and how much with equity.

The Debt-Equity Decision

Equity ownership nominally provides a shareholder with voting power over a firm's management decisions. In practice, this power is so dispersed that the typical shareholder is essentially just a supplier of funds like a lender and should expect to receive the same rate of return from the firm whether it comes in the form of interest or dividends.[17] But if the firm must offer the same rate of return to suppliers of equity and debt, it is logical to ask whether it matters how firms obtain their funds. Indeed, one of the classic results in the field of financial economics, known as the **Modigliani-Miller theorem**, says that under certain conditions, the debt-equity choice is irrelevant precisely because neither firms nor those who supply funds care about the label given to the transaction between them.[18] Households or banks should require the same rate of return, regardless of whether the return comes in the form of interest payments or in the form of dividends. Given this requirement, choosing one method of finance instead of another offers firms no advantage or disadvantage in terms of their user cost of capital.

Modigliani-Miller theorem
The proposition that the value of a firm is the same whether it is financed by debt or by equity

The Modigliani-Miller theorem is significant, but the conditions on which it is based are not always satisfied in the real world. In particular, there are tax advantages to using debt finance, and there are reasons why debt finance may be disadvantageous or simply not feasible. As a result, corporate financial structure may have an important impact on the cost of capital and on the investment behavior of individual firms as well as the economy's overall performance.

Debt and Taxes

In our discussion above, we found that a corporate income tax may raise the user cost of capital, because the corporation must pay a tax in addition to the return paid to its shareholders. However, the corporate income tax does not apply to interest payments. That is, interest payments, like allowances for depreciation, are deducted from the income on which the corporation must pay tax.

17. For example, in 1993, an individual who purchased $10,000 worth of stock in the General Motors Corporation would have owned about .00003 percent of the company, hardly enough to assert any influence over the firm's decisions.

18. The theorem takes its name from its two authors, both Nobel Laureates: Franco Modigliani of MIT and Merton Miller of the University of Chicago.

The deductibility of interest reduces the tax component, τ, in the user cost formula presented earlier. In fact, the use of debt finance may entirely neutralize the impact of the corporate tax on the user cost, eliminating the term τ altogether. The logic is that if neither basic component of user cost, interest or depreciation, is subject to tax, then there is no tax collected on the new investment the firm undertakes.[19] We can see this using the numerical example considered earlier, with an interest rate of 6 percent and a rate of depreciation of 35 percent. Without a corporate tax, the firm's new capital must generate a marginal product of 41 percent to cover its user cost. With a corporate tax, a marginal product of 41 percent will still suffice if debt finance is used. Because the firm can deduct both interest and depreciation, it may deduct the full 41 percent return, which will leave no income subject to the corporate tax and hence no tax.

If the user cost of capital is lower for debt-financed investments, why don't corporations rely solely on debt finance? There are several possible reasons. One is that debt finance restricts the firm's flexibility, because by law interest payments are tax-deductible only if they are fixed. Thus, during bad economic times, when its earnings may be low, an equity-financed corporation may reduce the dividend payments it makes. A debt-financed corporation may not do so. If required interest payments cannot be met, the debt-financed corporation may default on its debt and be forced into bankruptcy.

A second reason why firms may not rely on debt finance is that they may be subject to *credit rationing*. As discussed in Chapter 15, financial markets sometimes fail to operate well when information about the borrower is lacking. Many firms seeking to borrow may find lenders unwilling to commit funds to enterprises whose success cannot be guaranteed or willing to do so only at very high interest rates.[20] In this case, firms may face a lower user cost of capital—despite the tax benefits of debt finance—by relying on the funds they already have on hand. Rather than paying their current earnings out to existing shareholders as dividends, firms can use these *retained earnings* to finance new investment. Such a strategy, called **internal finance**, increases the firm's equity.

Internal finance
A firm's strategy of retaining its current earnings to finance new investment

Because of bankruptcy risk, credit rationing, and other factors, firms do rely heavily on equity finance despite the tax advantages of borrowing. However, there are major differences in financial structure across firms and, for the same firm, over the business cycle. In addition, financing patterns have changed over time.

Case Study: Interest Rate Spreads and the Business Cycle

In Chapter 15, we saw that interest rates faced by borrowers generally exceed those promised to lenders, reflecting in part the general uncertainty about borrowers' prospects for repayment. Because lenders cannot perfectly separate bad credit risks from good, they must charge even some creditworthy firms a higher

19. See Joseph E. Stiglitz, "Taxation, Corporate Financial Policy and the Cost of Capital," *Journal of Public Economics* 2 (February 1973): 1–34.

20. Indeed, such firms may not be able to sell new equity shares either, without, in effect, offering a high rate of return by selling their shares at a low price.

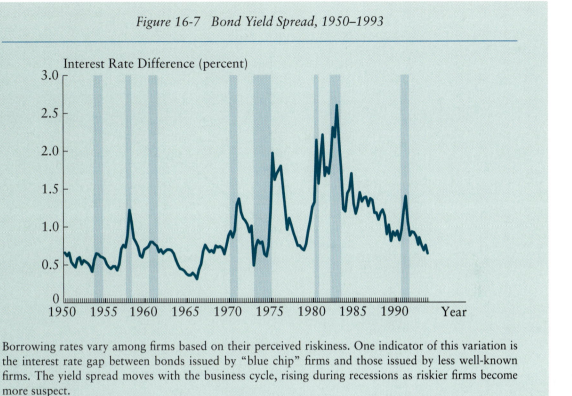

Figure 16-7 Bond Yield Spread, 1950–1993

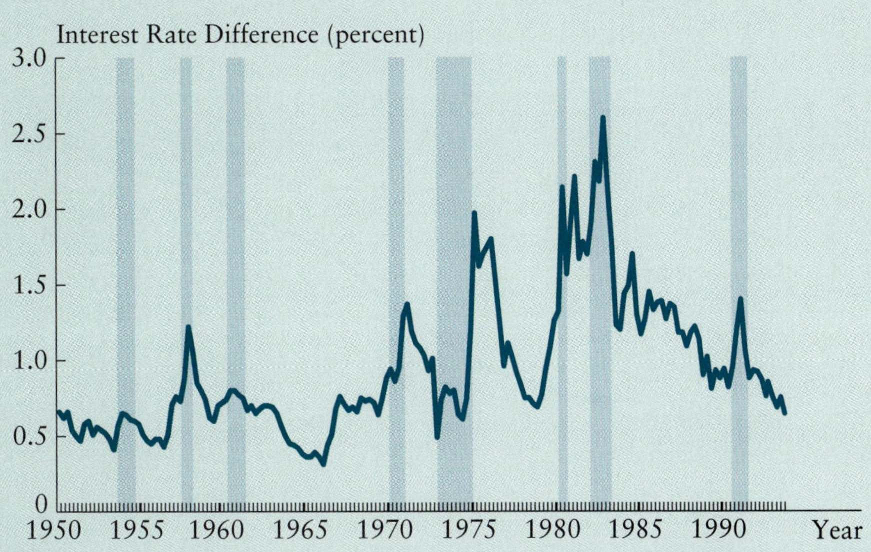

Borrowing rates vary among firms based on their perceived riskiness. One indicator of this variation is the interest rate gap between bonds issued by "blue chip" firms and those issued by less well-known firms. The yield spread moves with the business cycle, rising during recessions as riskier firms become more suspect.

Source: *Economic Report of the President,* 1994

interest rate. The greater the uncertainty, or the lower the average quality of firms, the higher the rate lenders must charge. Based on this logic, we would expect borrowing rates to vary among firms according to their perceived prospects, with firms classified as bad risks, or those whose prospects are unknown, facing higher borrowing rates, even if they are actually creditworthy.

One indicator of this variation in borrowing rates is the interest rate gap between bonds issued by "blue chip" companies and those issued by companies with less well-known prospects. The greater the gap—called the *yield spread*—between these two types of bonds, the less attractive debt finance will be for the riskier enterprises.

Figure 16-7 graphs the yield spread on corporate bonds since 1950. The spread is measured by the difference between the interest rate offered on bonds given an AAA rating (the safest) by Moody's Investors Service and those given a BAA rating (a much lower one). The figure shows quite clearly that yield spreads move with the business cycle, rising during recessions, as the prospects of riskier companies become more suspect. This evidence provides an additional reason why investment is sensitive to business cycle conditions, namely, that the potentially attractive source of debt finance becomes less accessible to riskier companies.

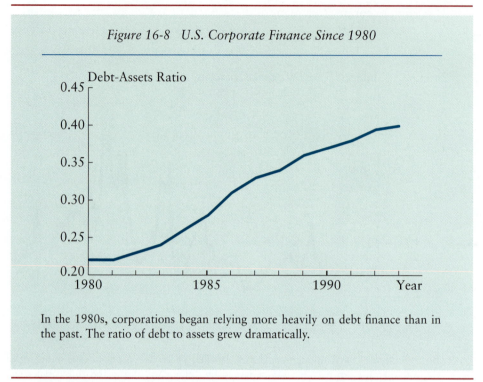

Figure 16-8 U.S. Corporate Finance Since 1980

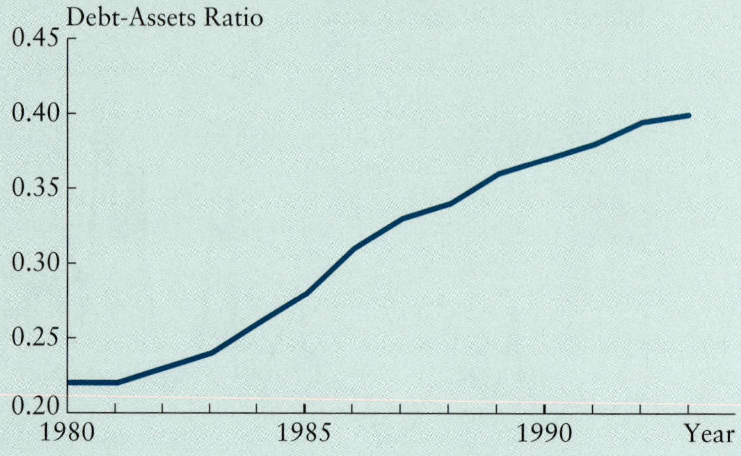

In the 1980s, corporations began relying more heavily on debt finance than in the past. The ratio of debt to assets grew dramatically.

Source: Board of Governors, Federal Reserve System

In addition to its cyclical behavior, the yield spread also exhibits a certain trend, reaching higher levels in the 1980s than before. This relates to another phenomenon, the increased borrowing that occurred during that period.

Case Study: Corporate Borrowing in the 1980s

The corporate income tax and the tax incentive for corporate borrowing have been in existence since 1909. However, in the 1980s, corporations began relying more heavily on debt finance than in the past. Figure 16-8 shows the trend in the ratio of debt to capital (or assets) of the U.S. nonfinancial corporate sector since 1980. In just thirteen years, the ratio rose from 22.3 percent to 39.9 percent. During this period, the aggregate corporate capital stock actually fell in real (1987 dollars) terms by $648.2 billion even as the real debt outstanding rose by $757.0 billion. That is, in the aggregate, none of the debt raised during the period was actually needed to buy new capital. Instead, it simply went to redeem equity from shareholders, as corporations replaced equity with debt. Some of the replacement of debt for equity occurred as companies borrowed to repurchase their own stock. In other cases the equity disappeared through *leveraged buyouts*, transactions in which one company borrowed funds to purchase the equity of another company.

Why did corporate borrowing increase? There are many theories, but it is difficult to find one that is entirely convincing.[21] The tax advantage to borrowing existed before. Had the risks of bankruptcy suddenly fallen, we should have observed a decline in bankruptcies and business failures during this period and a drop in the yield spread between safe and risky firms. However, as we just saw, the yield spread rose in the 1980s. Furthermore, as we observed in Chapter 4, the rate of business failures rose sharply in the 1980s, reaching unprecedented postwar levels even during the long economic expansion that began in late 1982 and carried into 1990. This evidence does not support the hypothesis that reduced risk led to more borrowing, but seems merely to demonstrate that additional borrowing makes firms more likely to fail.

Should the heightened risk of business failure concern us? Some researchers argue that higher levels of corporate debt increase the potential severity of recessions, because small initial reductions in income may set off a wave of business failures and further reductions in output and employment.[22] However, the short and relatively mild recession of 1990–1991 does not seem to have borne out this concern.

Case Study: Credit Constraints in the U.S. and Japan

Even in the 1980s, not all firms participated in the borrowing binge. As we discussed above, credit rationing limits the extent to which some firms can borrow. Such firms must rely on internal funds to finance their investment. This not only increases the share of equity in their financial structure but may also raise the volatility of their investment.

Can credit rationing make a firm's investment more volatile? For the economy as a whole, investment equals saving, which in turn depends on income. As our discussion of the accelerator mechanism in Chapter 4 stressed, the volatility of investment is closely related to the volatility of income. But a credit-constrained firm's investment is determined by its own current earnings, not the economy-wide level of income. Figure 16-9 shows that corporate profits are far more volatile than income, as measured by net domestic product (NDP).

What types of firms are credit-constrained? The answer differs across countries. In the U.S., reliance on internal funds to finance investment is strongly related to a firm's size. Smaller corporations are much more likely than large ones to have their investment determined by the availability of internal funds.[23] That's because smaller firms are often younger firms with less of a track record to show prospective lenders, making it harder for lenders to assess their creditworthiness.

21. For further discussion, see Alan J. Auerbach, "Debt, Equity, and the Taxation of Corporate Cash Flows," in *Debt and Corporate Restructuring*, eds. J. Shoven and J. Waldfogel (Washington, DC: Brookings, 1990) 91–126.
22. See Ben S. Bernanke and John Y. Campbell, "Is There a Corporate Debt Crisis?" *Brookings Papers on Economic Activity* 19 (1988): 83–125.
23. See Steven M. Fazzari, R. Glenn Hubbard, and Bruce C. Petersen, "Financing Constraints and Corporate Investment," *Brookings Papers on Economic Activity* 19 (1988): 141–195.

Figure 16-9 Output Versus Profits, 1960–1992

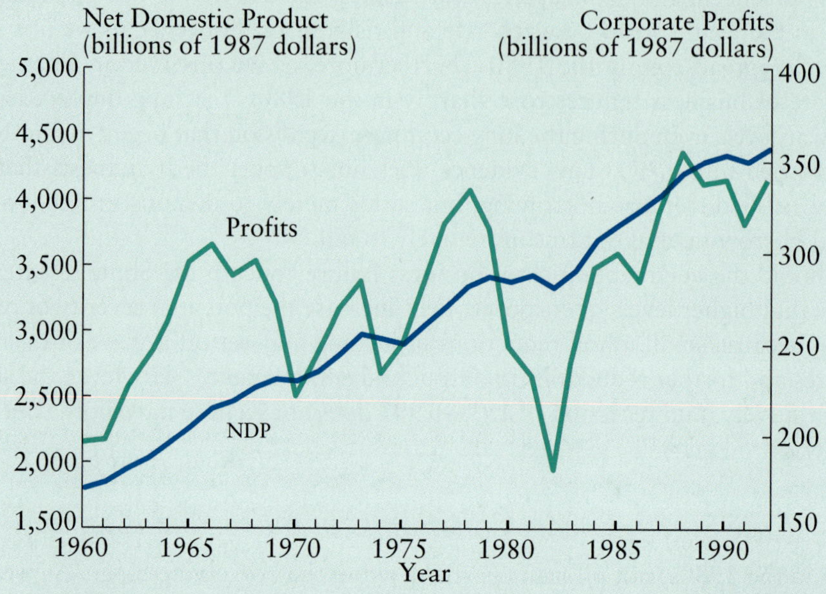

Credit rationing can make investment more volatile since a credit-constrained firm's investment is determined by its own earnings, not by aggregate income. Corporate profits are far more volatile than income, measured by net domestic product.

Source: *National Income and Product Accounts*

In Japan, though, size does not appear to be the most important determinant of whether a firm relies on internal finance. The critical factor there seems to be the lack of affiliation with a *keiretsu*, a group of industrial firms tied together by their relationship to a "main bank." Many firms in Japan, large and small, belong to such groups, centered around some of the world's largest banks.[24] Firms outside the groups must issue corporate debt and rely on various bank lenders for loans, much as U.S. companies do. Within the groups, however, firms obtain a considerable share of their debt through loans from a single bank, and even the smaller firms do not appear to experience credit rationing.

The keiretsu increases credit availability in two ways. First, it encourages the gathering and transmission of information about each member company's management and prospects. Second, it coordinates responses to financial distress. A U.S. bankruptcy might involve a protracted court proceeding pitting several different classes of lenders against one another. A member of a Japanese group, on

24. See Takeo Hoshi, Anil Kashyap, and David Scharfstein, "Corporate Structure, Liquidity, and Investment: Evidence from Japanese Industrial Groups," *Quarterly Journal of Economics* 106 (February 1991): 33–60.

the other hand, has one major lender well-informed about the firm's problems and prospects. This improves the chances of reaching an agreement regarding the changes necessary for renewed success.[25]

These international differences in credit markets have important implications for financial and investment behavior. The prevalence of industrial group membership in Japan, and the associated freedom from credit rationing, helps explain why Japanese firms, on average, have used a higher ratio of debt to equity finance than their U.S. counterparts.[26] Given the tax advantages to borrowing (which are similar in Japan to those in the U.S.), this higher debt-equity ratio may itself have led to a lower Japanese user cost of capital and contributed to Japan's higher rate of investment.

UNDERSTANDING INVESTMENT DYNAMICS

An important characteristic of investment is its volatility. We have already encountered several complementary explanations of why investment is more volatile than output. The accelerator theory shows that investment is related to *changes* in output, which vary more than the level of output itself. Credit rationing may become more severe during recessions. Firms dependent on internal funds will experience large swings in investment simply because of the volatility of corporate profits. In addition, changes in tax policy may actually destabilize investment. These factors explain the volatility of investment, regardless of type. However, other factors explain why certain types of investment are particularly volatile.

Figure 16-10 graphs the three types of nonresidential investment (structures, equipment, and inventories) for the period since 1960. For each type of investment, the graph shows net investment in each year relative to its average annual value since 1960. Values above (below) 1.0 indicate stronger (weaker) than average investment, and those below 0 indicate negative net investment. The extent and frequency of deviations from a ratio of 1.0 measure how volatile investment is.

The figure shows evidence of the impact of particular tax policies on investment. For example, equipment investment jumped from its low point in 1961 once the investment tax credit was introduced the following year. Structures investment reached its highest value in 1981, the year accelerated depreciation was greatly enhanced. However, the figure also exhibits the differing volatility of the types of investment. Inventory investment was negative in four different years (the recession years 1975, 1980, 1982, and 1991) and equaled nearly four

25. Hoshi et al. cite the case of Mazda, the large Japanese automobile manufacturer, which encountered serious financial problems in the 1970s. A member of the Sumitomo group, Mazda emerged from financial trouble under the leadership of one of the Sumitomo bank's managing directors.

26. Albert Ando and Alan J. Auerbach, "The Cost of Capital in the United States and Japan," *Journal of Japanese and International Economies* 2 (1988): 134–158, found that until the U.S. borrowing surge in the 1980s, Japanese debt-asset ratios were roughly double those in the U.S.

Figure 16-10 Investment Volatility by Type, 1960–1992

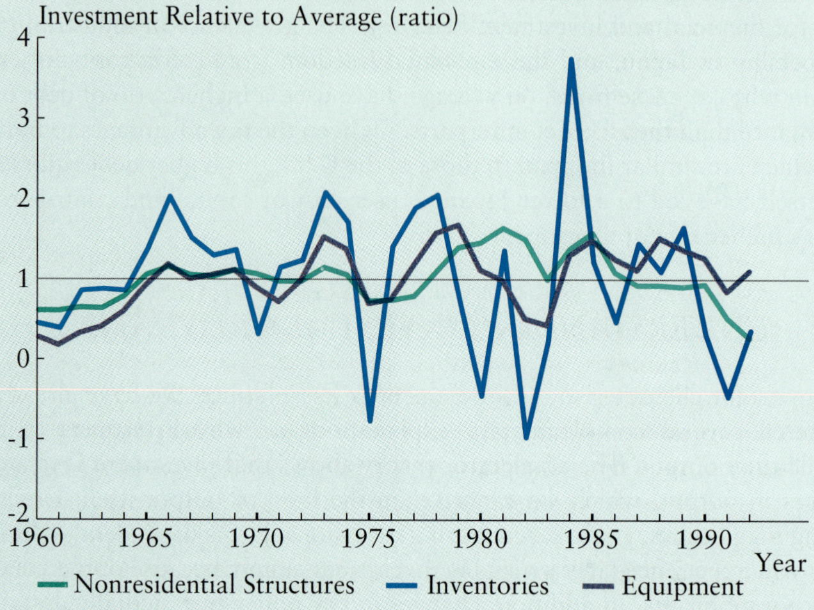

Of the various types of investment, inventory investment is the most volatile and structures investment the least. Fluctuations are also influenced by tax policies. Equipment spending leaped after the investment tax credit was introduced in 1962. Structures investment peaked in 1981 when accelerated depreciation provisions were enhanced.

Source: *National Income and Product Accounts*

times its annual average in the boom year 1984.[27] On the other hand, neither equipment nor structures investment was ever negative, with the range of values for equipment investment (.19 to 1.68) indicating a bit more volatility than that for structures investment (.27 to 1.64).

The volatility of inventory investment means that, despite its small share of investment in a typical year, it accounts for a significant share of the swings in investment over the business cycle. For example, by falling in real terms by $45.5 billion—from +28.1 billion (at annual rates) in the second quarter of 1990 to –$17.4 billion in the first quarter of 1991—inventory investment alone accounted for nearly half the drop in total investment from expansion peak to recession trough.

27. The drops in inventory investment occurred in spite of declining sales which, as indicated above, could lead to unexpectedly high inventory accumulation. Such unplanned increases in inventory investment *are* often observed as recessions begin. However, these accumulations are quickly reversed as firms realize that their sales prospects have dimmed and adjust production accordingly.

The different cyclical behavior of inventories and other types of investment may be explained by technical factors that influence firms' responses to changes in user cost. By its nature, fixed investment in equipment and structures is subject to constraints on how fast and by how much firms can invest in response to changes in the amount of capital they wish to have. Economists characterize these constraints in terms of **irreversibility**—the difficulty in disposing of capital goods once they have been purchased—and **adjustment lags**—the delays firms encounter in altering their investment plans.

Irreversibility
The difficulty of reversing an investment once it has been initiated

Adjustment lag
A delay in the response that brings investment to its desired level

Irreversibility

In our two-period life-cycle model, we may think of the existing capital stock as being consumed by the old at the end of each period, with new capital being accumulated by the young. As these two acts are separate, it is entirely feasible for the young to accumulate less capital than the old generation consumes. In the actual economy, this represents an accurate description of inventory investment. Inventories are continually being turned over, as the existing stock of goods held in inventory is used up and replaced. Even if the number of shirts held in a retailer's inventory is the same at the end of a year as at the beginning, they are not the same shirts. Hence, there is no reason why the business cannot reduce its shirt inventory if it wishes to do so—it simply does not replace every shirt it sells from inventory.

Unlike inventories, fixed capital goods are not used up each year. Under normal circumstances, this distinction is not important. In our model, rather than consuming their capital goods directly, the old could sell their capital to the young, who would purchase less new capital and provide the old with the funds necessary to finance their consumption. But this means the capital stock the young carry into the next period must be at least as large as that being sold by the old. Put another way, *gross* investment—the amount of new capital purchased—cannot be negative. We characterize this restriction by saying that fixed investment is irreversible.

Irreversibility doesn't quite imply that *net* fixed investment must be positive. Recall that net investment equals gross investment less depreciation. If gross investment is small enough, net investment will be negative. In terms of our model, the capital the old wish to sell has depreciated, so the capital stock carried into period $t + 1$, K_{t+1}, must at least equal the capital carried into period t, K_t, less depreciation in period t, D_t. In fact, net fixed investment in the U.S. has been negative at times, during both the Depression as well as in World War II, when government absorption of funds (represented in our model by a high value of F_t) *crowded out* private investment.

How, then, does irreversibility help explain why *net* investment is usually positive? In an economy experiencing shifts in production among several sectors, irreversibility may constrain some sectors without affecting others. Even in a declining economy, some industries' output may rise, and with it their demand for capital. Since each type of gross investment is subject to its own irreversibility constraint, the types of capital in increased demand (say, computers) will experience positive gross investment even as there is zero gross investment in other types of capital (for example, coal furnaces in North Dakota). Thus, gross investment will be positive in the aggregate, even during recessions, making it more likely that net investment will be positive, too.[28]

What types of fixed investment would be most subject to the irreversibility constraint? Aside from those used in declining industries, we normally expect long-lived capital goods, particularly structures, to be most susceptible. Capital goods that depreciate rapidly (like trucks or computers) can experience quite negative *net* investment while gross investment is still positive. This helps explain why net structures investment typically accounts for an increased share of fixed investment during recessions. It also helps us understand why, even during booms in which investment as a whole is strong, certain types of investment may not be.

Case Study: The Empty Office Buildings

Figure 16-10 indicates that investment in nonresidential structures was weak in the boom years of the late 1980s. Rather than looking at conditions that prevailed during this period for an explanation, many economists blame the strong investment in structures that occurred during the early 1980s.

As we discussed above, the Economic Recovery Tax Act of 1981 provided investment incentives in the form of accelerated depreciation. The incentives applied not only to multifamily rental housing, which we have already considered, but also to business fixed investment. In the case of commercial office buildings, the interaction of accelerated depreciation with other tax provisions transformed such investments into *tax shelters*—investments that provided wealthy individuals with large tax deductions against their other income. This possibility for tax shelters sparked a boom in the construction of commercial buildings. But, as Figure 16-11 shows, the building was excessive. The vacancy rate of office space grew throughout the early 1980s, as more and more office space became available.

The Tax Reform Act of 1986 eliminated not only accelerated depreciation but also the other provisions that gave rise to tax-shelter opportunities. This reform raised the user cost of capital for nonresidential structures, making investors less interested in owning such structures. But the scores of modern office buildings that had been accumulated in the early 80s, with the expectation that beneficial tax provisions would be maintained, did not disappear—their construction was irreversible. This excess capacity inhibited additional commercial building as the rest of the economy boomed. Despite several years of reduced construction activity, the vacancy rate in 1989 remained well above its level of the early 1980s. Then it began to rise again, as the recession of 1990–1991 took its toll on the demand for office space.

---

28. We have seen other evidence of the presence of irreversibility. For example, we observed (in Figure 4-6) that capacity utilization in manufacturing is typically well below 100 percent—meaning that some businesses and sectors have too much capital.

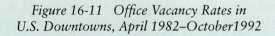

Figure 16-11 Office Vacancy Rates in U.S. Downtowns, April 1982–October1992

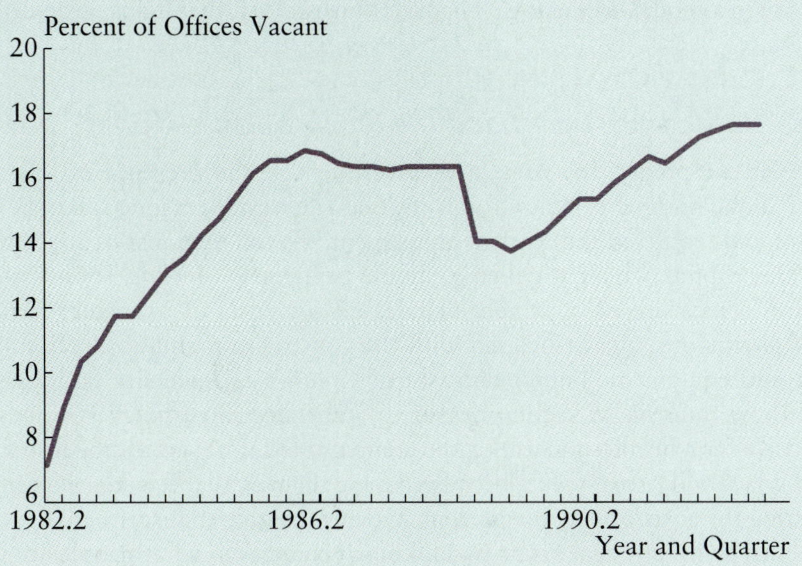

The investment incentives of the early 1980s led to increased commercial construction and a rise in office vacancy rates. This excess capacity remained in place even after the Tax Reform Act of 1986 discouraged holding of such property. Even with a sharp drop in new construction in the late 1980s, vacancy rates remained high and the need for new investment remained low.

Source: Coldwell Banker Commercial

Adjustment Lags

Even when irreversibility is not an issue, firms are still constrained in how fast they can respond to changing investment incentives. It is relatively simple to purchase more computers or stock more shirts in inventory as income rises. However, building an extra factory, office building, or nuclear power plant takes time, generally years, to complete. We refer to the delayed response in bringing investment to its desired level as an adjustment lag.

Adjustment lags exist because it is difficult to make large changes in the capital stock immediately. In economic terms, rapid capital stock adjustment is *costly*. Very rapid adjustment may be possible but too expensive to justify under normal economic circumstances. For example, it might be possible to build a new factory in a year, rather than two, by hiring more construction workers and paying them to work longer hours, but this would increase production costs. Unless having the building completed a year earlier increases the firm's earnings sufficiently, it will not elect the faster, costlier production schedule.

With production lags, firms will not instantaneously equate the marginal product of capital to the user cost of capital. Instead, they will only gradually adjust their capital stock in the direction dictated by the user cost. Adjustment costs make the investment process more complicated to explain, but they also give rise to a model, called the q-theory of investment, that helps us describe this process.

Case Study: Investment and the Stock Market: Tobin's q-theory

Tobin's q-theory *The proposition that the rate of investment depends on the ratio of the market value of capital to its replacement cost*

How can we predict the pattern of investment in the presence of adjustment costs? Nobel Laureate James Tobin of Yale University reasoned that as investment booms confront the costs of adjustment, the full unit cost of acquiring and installing capital, which he called q, should be higher.[29] Testing **Tobin's q-theory** requires a measure of q, which includes all the costs of overtime, retraining, work disruptions, etc. associated with the construction and absorption of new plant and equipment. Fumio Hayashi of Columbia University had an insight about how to arrive at such a measure.[30] Whenever investment becomes more expensive for a firm to undertake, the comparable capital goods the firm already has in place will rise in value, because having them available saves the firm from incurring the costs of new investment. We may be able to discern changes in the value of a firm's physical assets by looking at changes in what people are willing to pay for the firm—its value in the stock market.

Simply put, this interpretation of Tobin's q-theory says that investment booms should be accompanied by rises in the stock market, other things being equal. It also has the important implication that firms, seeking a signal from financial markets regarding how much they should invest, need only look at the performance of their company's stock. If their stock is highly valued, they should increase their investment.

Figure 16-12 puts this theory to the test, plotting real net investment by the U.S. corporate sector[31] (excluding farms and financial businesses) against a measure of Tobin's q: the aggregate stock market value of these corporations, divided by their net assets (assets less liabilities). The figure offers only mixed support for the q-theory. During the periods 1963–1972, 1980–1985, and 1990–1993, the stock market and investment moved together fairly well. However, for reasons still not well understood, the stock market plunged far more in the late 1970s than changes in investment would have indicated; and, during the late 1980s, when investment performance was relatively weak, the stock market boomed.

What can we conclude from this evidence? Perhaps the q-theory does not explain changes in investment behavior. Alternatively, the theory may apply, but stock market value may not be a very accurate measure of the value of the firm's

29. James Tobin, "A General Equilibrium Approach to Monetary Theory," *Journal of Money, Credit, and Banking* 1 (February 1969): 15–29.

30. Fumio Hayashi, "Tobin's Marginal q and Average q: A Neoclassical Interpretation," *Econometrica* 50 (January 1982): 213–224.

31. Not all businesses in the U.S. are organized as corporations, but firms whose shares are traded in the stock market are.

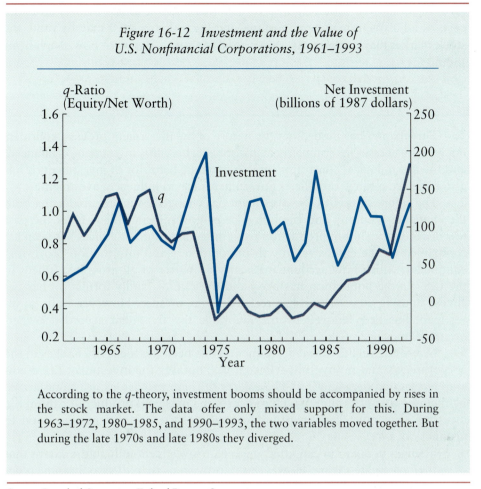

Figure 16-12 Investment and the Value of U.S. Nonfinancial Corporations, 1961–1993

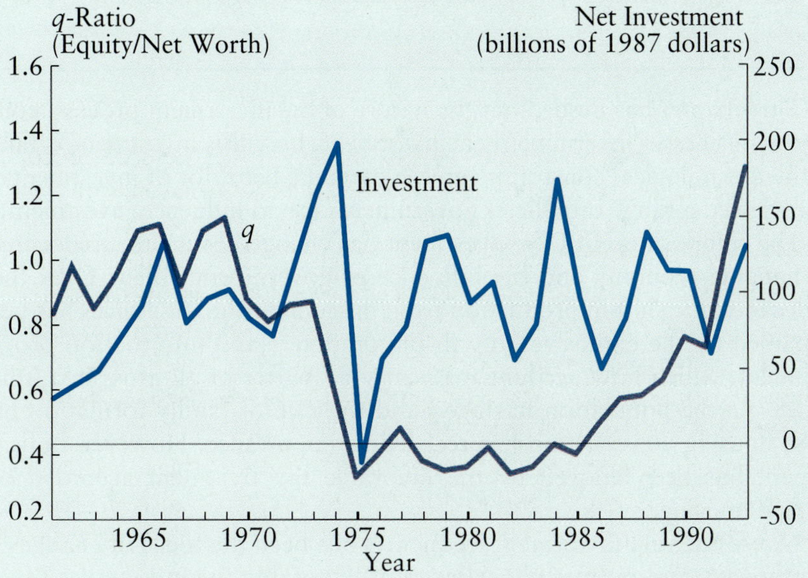

According to the q-theory, investment booms should be accompanied by rises in the stock market. The data offer only mixed support for this. During 1963–1972, 1980–1985, and 1990–1993, the two variables moved together. But during the late 1970s and late 1980s they diverged.

Source: Board of Governors, Federal Reserve System

capital stock. Indeed, the question of whether the stock market tracks the underlying value of corporate assets—whether it reflects "market fundamentals"—is a controversial one in the field of financial economics.

Many economists accept the central hypothesis underlying empirical tests of the q-theory, that the stock market accurately reflects the value of the firm. This **efficient markets hypothesis** says that at any given time, the stock market value of a firm represents the value of that firm's underlying assets, based on all information currently available. But others question whether such a hypothesis is plausible, arguing that daily movements in the stock market are far too large to be justified by changes in the underlying value of corporate assets.[32] Perhaps the best evidence here is the stock market crash of October 1987, when the market lost roughly one-fifth of its value in a single day. Was there an underlying 20 percent reduction in the value of corporate assets that just happened to come to light that day? Few economists think so. Not surprisingly, then, corporate

Efficient markets hypothesis
The proposition that the stock market value of a firm reflects the true value of that firm's underlying assets based on all available information

32. See Robert J. Shiller, "Do Stock Prices Move Too Much to Be Justified by Subsequent Changes in Dividends?" *American Economic Review* 71 (June 1981): 421–436.

investment showed little response to the stock market crash. Hence, although costs of adjustment may be important, and the q-theory itself may be valid, the stock market may not provide a very good indicator of q or of how much firms should invest.

Chapter Summary

1. This chapter has fleshed out the nature of the investment process, considering how businesses determine their investment, how this investment is financed, and the technological constraints on the dynamic behavior of investment. It has also reviewed a range of policies governments use to influence investment.
2. The composition of U.S. investment has changed over time, reflecting both the changing economy and the influence of government policy. Over the past few decades, the shift in production from manufacturing to services has been accompanied by the explosive growth of computers and information processing equipment, which now account for nearly a quarter of all gross investment in the U.S. As the population has aged and the rate of family formation has declined, housing construction has receded in importance. However, housing investment has been buoyed by the favorable tax treatment accorded owner-occupied housing.
3. Nonresidential investment frequently has been the focus of changes in the corporate tax and in investment incentives, notably the investment tax credit and accelerated depreciation. The effects of these provisions are summarized by the user cost of capital, which indicates the marginal product of capital the investing firm must earn in order to cover all the costs of using capital in production.
4. Changes in taxation can affect aggregate investment only to the extent that they alter aggregate saving. However, tax provisions that affect only some types of investment also influence the composition of investment. The frequency with which some tax provisions have been changed highlights the importance of investor expectations and the potential of policy to be destabilizing.
5. Although they are equal in the aggregate, investment and saving are typically distinct acts undertaken by different parties. Directly or through the banking system, households supply funds to the businesses that actually undertake investment. Through its financial policy, each firm makes several decisions regarding how to obtain the funds it needs for investment, including the appropriate mix of debt and equity and the extent to which it will rely on internal finance.
6. Although the Modigliani-Miller theorem cautions that financial policy is relevant only to the extent that there are underlying differences among methods of finance, such differences are indeed present. The corporate tax system provides a tax benefit for the use of debt finance that lowers the user cost of capital for debt-financed investment. This benefit must be weighed against the reduced flexibility that fixed interest payments impose on the firm. The recent increased reliance of U.S. firms on debt finance has raised concerns about such a lack of flexibility and whether it might magnify the severity of recessions.

7. Riskier firms may be credit-constrained, able to borrow only at very high interest rates and thus forced to depend on internal finance. Dependence on internal finance influences not only the level of a firm's investment but also the investment's cyclical volatility.
8. The volatility of investment also depends on technological factors, the irreversibility of fixed investment, and lags in the investment process that help to explain why inventory investment exhibits much wider swings than fixed investment. With these technological constraints on investment, firms cannot follow the simple rule of equating instantaneously the marginal product of capital to its user cost.
9. Tobin's *q*-theory of investment suggests that firms facing adjustment costs can take movements in their stock prices as indicators of how much to invest. This is a useful approach only if a firm's stock price reflects the underlying value of that firm's assets, as dictated by the efficient markets hypothesis—the accuracy of which remains hotly disputed.

Key Concepts

User cost of capital
Corporate income tax
Investment incentives
Investment tax credit
Accelerated depreciation
Modigliani-Miller theorem
Internal finance
Irreversibility
Adjustment lags
Tobin's *q*-theory
Efficient markets hypothesis

Review Questions

1. What is *investment spending*? On average, how much U.S. GDP is devoted to investment goods?
2. What is *fixed investment*, and what subcategories of investment goods does it include? What fraction of fixed investment does each subcategory comprise? What is *inventory investment*, and what are some examples of inventory investment?
3. Describe how the *composition* of fixed investment spending has changed over the past three decades. Identify some possible reasons for these trends.
4. What is the *user cost of capital*? What factors does the basic (before-tax) user cost of capital include? What is the equation for the basic user cost of capital? How does knowledge of the user cost help a firm decide how much capital investment it should undertake?
5. What is the tax base for the *corporate income tax*? How does the existence of the corporate income tax affect the user cost of capital?
6. What does the *demand schedule for capital* indicate, and how is it derived? What slope does the demand schedule have (positive or negative), and why? How does an increase in the rate of depreciation affect the demand schedule?

How is the demand schedule affected by an increase in the tax per dollar of capital?

7. Identify three reasons why the *supply* of capital might depend on the real interest rate.

8. Explain the statement in the text that the burden of the corporate tax is spread to suppliers of capital in both the corporate and noncorporate sectors of the economy.

9. What are government *investment incentives*, and what is their purpose? Give examples of two important investment incentives. What effect do investment incentives have on the cost of capital? Why does it make sense for the government to levy a tax on corporate income and simultaneously offer investment incentives? Have changes in the tax treatment of capital income historically been a predominant influence on the user cost of capital?

10. Describe the possibly different effects that *permanent* versus *temporary* tax changes might have. What problems might arise from the use of a temporary tax change?

11. What is a firm's *financial policy*? Define the terms *securities, bonds, debt*, and *equity* as they relate to a firm's financial policy.

12. What is the *Modigliani-Miller theorem*? What practicalities does the Modigliani-Miller theorem ignore?

13. What is the *yield spread*, and what does it indicate?

14. What types of firms are *credit-constrained* in the United States? What is a Japanese *keiretsu*? How do keiretsus diminish the extent of credit rationing in Japan?

15. What is meant by the *irreversibility* of investment? What types of capital are most subject to irreversibility?

16. What are *adjustment lags*, and why do they arise?

17. What is *Tobin's q*? What does Tobin's *q*-theory imply about investment spending? Is there empirical support for the theory?

Numerical Questions

1. Suppose that a firm owns two types of capital, half of which is durable equipment and half of which is nonresidential structures. The annual depreciation rate for equipment is 20 percent and that for structures is 4 percent. Also, assume that the real interest rate equals 12 percent and that the corporate income tax rate, c, equals 25 percent.

   a. Compute the basic, before-tax, user cost of capital for equipment and for structures.
   b. Compute the average user cost of capital.
   c. Compute the value of τ, the tax per dollar of capital. (Helpful hint: Review footnote 7 in the chapter, which describes how τ depends on the corporate tax rate, c, and the real interest rate, r.)
   d. Compute the full, tax-inclusive, user cost of capital for each type of capital and for the capital stock as a whole.

e. Suppose that Congress enacts a 2 percent investment tax credit for producers' durable equipment. Compute the new user cost of capital for equipment and for structures.

f. Compute the new average user cost of capital (including the effect of the tax credit), assuming that, at the margin, the proportions of each type of capital purchased remain unchanged.

2. Assume the economy is characterized as in the life-cycle model of Chapter 3 (i.e., no fiscal policy term, no international trade, and no money or price level). Specifically, assume that the economy's parameter values are $A = 10$, $\alpha = 0.3$, and $\beta = 0.4$.

a. There is presently no corporate income tax and capital does not depreciate. For values of the real interest rate, r, from 0.1 to 0.9 by increments of 0.1, compute the values of the user cost of capital and the demand for capital.

b. Suppose that a corporate income tax of 20 percent is imposed and that capital depreciates at a rate of 10 percent. For values of the real interest rate, r, from 0.1 to 0.9 by increments of 0.1, compute the values of tax per dollar of capital, τ, the user cost of capital, and the demand for capital.

c. Explain what has happened to the position of the demand curve for capital because of the introduction of the corporate income tax and depreciation.

3. Using the same parameter values as in question 2 ($A = 10$, $\alpha = 0.3$, and $\beta = 0.4$), compute the equilibrium values of the capital-labor ratio, k, and the real interest rate, r, under the following conditions.

a. There is no corporate income tax and no depreciation.

b. The corporate income tax is 20 percent, and the depreciation rate is 10 percent. Is your result consistent with the shift in the demand curve for capital obtained in question 2 above? Explain.

4. Suppose that the saving propensity is now directly related to the interest rate—that is, the consumption propensity α is inversely related to the interest rate. Specifically, assume that the formula for the consumption propensity is $\alpha = 0.5 - 0.14r$.

a. For values of the real interest rate, r, from 0.1 to 0.9 by increments of 0.1, compute the values of the supply of capital. (Helpful hint: Using the transition equation, replace α with the formula given above.)

b. What relationship is there between the real interest rate and the quantity of capital supplied? What is the intuition behind this relationship?

c. Using the demand relationships developed in questions 2 and 3, verify that the equilibrium when there is no corporate income tax and no depreciation happens to be the same as in question 3. That is, verify that the equilibrium interest rate and capital-labor ratio are as before. (Helpful hint: Substitute the old equilibrium interest rate into both the demand schedule and the supply schedule, and verify that the values of k in the two schedules are equal.)

d. Verify that the new equilibrium interest rate is 0.51875 upon introduction of the corporate income tax rate of 0.2 and the depreciation rate of 0.1. What is the equilibrium value of the capital-labor ratio? (See the hint in part c.)

e. How do your results in part d differ from those obtained in question 3b? That is, when the saving propensity is directly related to the interest rate rather than being constant, what effect do changes in taxes or depreciation rates have on the resulting values of r and k? Explain the intuition.

Analytical Questions

1. The chapter discussed the use of the investment tax credit as an investment incentive. Critics of the investment tax credit argue that it is an inefficient incentive, in that the government ends up forgoing a lot of tax revenue per dollar of additional investment undertaken.

a. What aspect(s) of the investment tax credit might result in the shortcoming identified by the critics?

b. An alternative investment tax credit has been proposed, which applies only to a firm's investment spending that exceeds a specified percentage of past years' investment spending. Would this variant of the credit be a more efficient investment incentive?

c. What are some practical shortcomings of the alternative tax credit scheme described in part b?

2. Suppose that a firm can raise funds for investment either by issuing bonds (debt) or by issuing shares of stock (equity). The market interest rate on bonds is r, and the rate on stock is e. The firm faces a depreciation rate of δ per dollar of capital and a tax liability of τ per dollar of capital.

a. Assuming that a firm raises funds only by issuing equity, write the expression describing the firm's user cost of capital.

b. Now assume that the firm raises 40 percent of its funds by issuing debt and 60 percent by issuing equity. Write the expression describing the firm's user cost of capital.

c. Finally, assuming that the firm raises funds as in part b, suppose that Congress allows firms to deduct the interest payment on debt for purposes of computing taxable income. Write the expression describing the firm's user cost of capital.

3. Suppose that Congress is considering two tax incentive proposals. The first would grant a 30 percent investment tax credit on the price of all newly purchased capital. The second would allow firms to deduct from taxable income the annual value of depreciation on a machine, an amount fixed at 20 percent of the machine's purchase price, for each of the next five years. If the risk-free real interest rate is expected to be 5 percent for the next five years and the corporate tax rate is 35 percent, which proposal provides the bigger investment incentive? That is, which proposal reduces the user cost of capital more?

Index

U.S. FINANCIAL MARKET DATA; EXCHANGE RATES

Year	M1	M2	M3	Monetary Base	3-Month U.S. Treasury Bill Rate	10-Year U.S. Bond Rate	Exchange Rate Mark/Dollar	Exchange Rate Yen/Dollar
	(billions of dollars)				*(percent)*			
1959	140.0	297.8	299.8	40,880	3.405	4.33		
1960	140.7	312.3	315.3	40,977	2.928	4.12		
1961	145.2	335.5	341.0	41,853	2.378	3.88		
1962	147.8	362.7	371.4	42,957	2.778	3.95		
1963	153.3	393.2	406.0	45,003	3.157	4.00		
1964	160.3	424.8	442.5	47,161	3.549	4.19		
1965	167.9	459.3	482.2	49,620	3.954	4.28		
1966	172.0	480.0	505.1	51,565	4.881	4.92		
1967	183.3	524.3	557.1	54,579	4.321	5.07		
1968	197.4	566.3	606.2	58,357	5.339	5.65		
1969	203.9	589.5	615.0	61,569	6.677	6.67	3.9251	358.36
1970	214.4	628.0	677.3	65,013	6.458	7.35	3.6465	358.16
1971	228.3	712.6	776.1	69,108	4.438	6.16	3.4830	347.79
1972	249.2	805.1	886.0	75,167	4.071	6.21	3.1886	303.13
1973	262.8	860.9	984.9	81,073	7.041	6.84	2.6715	271.31
1974	274.3	908.4	1070.3	87,535	7.886	7.56	2.5868	291.84
1975	287.5	1023.1	1172.1	93,887	5.838	7.99	2.4614	296.78
1976	306.3	1163.5	1311.6	101,515	4.989	7.61	2.5185	296.45
1977	331.1	1286.4	1472.3	110,323	5.265	7.42	2.3236	268.62
1978	358.2	1388.5	1646.2	120,445	7.221	8.41	2.0097	210.39
1979	382.5	1496.4	1802.6	131,143	10.041	9.44	1.8343	219.02
1980	408.5	1629.2	1986.8	142,004	11.506	11.46	1.8175	226.63
1981	436.3	1792.6	2233.4	149,021	14.029	13.91	2.2632	220.63
1982	474.4	1952.7	2440.6	160,127	10.686	13.00	2.4281	249.06
1983	521.2	2186.5	2693.1	175,467	8.630	11.10	2.5539	237.55
1984	552.4	2376.0	2988.2	187,237	9.580	12.44	2.8455	237.46
1985	620.1	2572.4	3203.6	203,585	7.480	10.62	2.9420	238.47
1986	724.5	2816.1	3491.7	223,667	5.980	7.68	2.1705	168.35
1987	750.0	2917.2	3674.8	239,872	5.820	8.39	1.7981	144.60
1988	787.1	3078.2	3915.4	256,932	6.690	8.85	1.7570	128.17
1989	794.6	3233.3	4056.1	267,734	8.120	8.49	1.8808	138.07
1990	827.2	3345.5	4116.7	293,185	7.510	8.55	1.6166	145.00
1991	899.3	3445.8	4168.1	317,169	5.420	7.86	1.6610	134.59
1992	1026.6	3494.8	4163.4	350,798	3.450	7.01	1.5618	126.78
1993	1131.2	3551.7	4207.7	386,072	3.020	5.87	1.6545	111.08